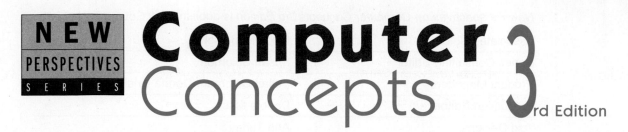

NEW PERSPECTIVES SERIES

Computer Concepts 3rd Edition

COMPREHENSIVE

Includes CD-ROM with Videos, Animations, Labs, and More!

June Jamrich Parsons

Dan Oja

A Susan Solomon Book

COURSE TECHNOLOGY

ONE MAIN STREET, CAMBRIDGE, MA 02142

an International Thomson Publishing company I(T)P®

Cambridge • Albany • Bonn • Boston • Cincinnati • London • Madrid • Melbourne • Mexico City
New York • Paris • San Francisco • Singapore • Tokyo • Toronto • Washington

New Perspectives on Computer Concepts 3rd Edition is published by **Course Technology.**

Associate Publisher	Mac Mendelsohn
Series Consulting Editor	Susan Solomon
Product Managers	Susan Solomon, Donna Gridley
Production Editor	Debbie Masi
Text Designer	Ann Turley
Cover Illustrator	Douglas Goodman
Photo and Video Researcher	Abby Reip
Video Editor	Jeanne Busemeyer, Hyde Park Publishing Services
CD-ROM Development	MediaTechnics Corporation
Animations	Planet Interactive
Composition	GEX, Inc.

© 1998 by Course Technology—ITP®

For more information contact:

Course Technology
One Main Street
Cambridge, MA 02142

ITP Europe
Berkshire House 168-173
High Holborn
London WCIV 7AA
England

Nelson ITP, Australia
102 Dodds Street
South Melbourne, 3205
Victoria, Australia

ITP Nelson Canada
1120 Birchmount Road
Scarborough, Ontario
Canada M1K 5G4

International Thomson Editores
Seneca, 53
Colonia Polanco
11560 Mexico D.F. Mexico

ITP GmbH
Königswinterer Strasse 418
53227 Bonn
Germany

ITP Asia
60 Albert Street, #15-01
Albert Complex
Singapore 189969

ITP Japan
Hirakawacho Kyowa Building, 3F
2-2-1 Hirakawacho
Chiyoda-ku, Tokyo 102
Japan

ISBN 0-7600-5500-9

Printed in the United States of America

3 4 5 6 7 8 9 10 BM 02 01 00 99 98

From the
New Perspectives Series Team

At Course Technology we have one foot in education and the other in technology. We believe that technology is transforming the way people teach and learn, and we are excited about providing instructors and students with materials that use technology to teach about technology.

Our development process is unparalleled in the higher education publishing industry. Every product we create goes through an exacting process of design, development, review, and testing.

Reviewers give us direction and insight that shape our manuscripts and bring them up to the latest standards. Every manuscript is quality tested. Students whose backgrounds match the intended audience work through every page and assignment. Together with academic and our own technical reviewers, these students help us ensure that everything that carries our name is error-free and easy to use.

As the New Perspectives Series team at Course Technology, our goal is to produce the most timely, accurate, creative, and technologically sound product in the entire college publishing industry. We strive for consistent high quality. This takes a lot of communication, coordination, and hard work. But we love what we do. We are determined to be the best. And look how far we've come. Just four short years ago, our team numbered six people! Write to us and let us know what you think. You can also e-mail us at NewPerspectives@course.com.

The New Perspectives Series Team

Joseph J. Adamski	Jessica Evans	William Newman
Judy Adamski	Marilyn Freedman	Dan Oja
Roy Ageloff	Kathy Finnegan	David Paradice
Tim Ashe	Robin Geller	June Parsons
David Auer	Donna Gridley	Harry Phillips
Daphne Barbas	Kate Habib	Sandra Poindexter
Dirk Baldwin	Roger Hayen	Mark Reimold
Rachel Bunin	Charles Hommel	Ann Shaffer
Joan Carey	Cindy Johnson	Karen Shortill
Patrick Carey	Janice Jutras	Susan Solomon
Sharon Caswell	Chris Kelly	Susanne Walker
Barbara Clemens	Mary Kemper	John Zeanchock
Rachel Crapser	Stacy Klein	Beverly Zimmerman
Kim Crowley	Terry Ann Kremer	Scott Zimmerman
Melissa Dezotell	John Leschke	
Michael Ekedahl	Mac Mendelsohn	

NEW PERSPECTIVES SERIES

Preface to Students and Instructors

"I have just two things to say about NP 3rd Edition. First, it's way cool. And second, I wish I'd had a book and CD like this when I took my intro to computers course!"

Jessica Sisak, student tester

Presenting NP3

We are pleased to present the jewel in the crown of the New Perspectives Series—*Computer Concepts 3rd Edition*, as we call it, NP3. It's a book. It's a CD-ROM. It's either or it's both. If you've used a New Perspectives book before, you've come to expect the best in content accuracy, timeliness, and the latest technology to teach technology. And NP3 will not disappoint you. If you've never used a New Perspectives book before, you're in for a treat.

What's the Same?

NP3 is available in three versions: *Brief*–Chapters 1 through 6, *Introductory*–Chapters 1 through 9, and *Comprehensive*–Chapters 1 through 15. The content has been thoroughly updated, including a brand new chapter on software applications (Chapter 3) and new art and photographs. We've retained the hallmark features that contributed to the great success of NP2: the ability to "read the pictures," in other words large, clear illustrations with many helpful, detailed labels; Focus Questions attached to the major headings that are designed to engage, pique interest, and motivate the relevance of the material that follows; and a rich collection of interesting and entertaining Review Questions and Projects, including Internet Assignments.

What's New?

Every book now includes a CD, which contains the *entire* book as well as animations, videos, links to the Web, Labs, and three ways for interactive self-assessment.

Quick Checks

At the end of each section you will find a Quick Check designed to help make sure key concepts have been grasped. Answers to the Quick Checks are at the end of the book, or, if you are using the CD, you can click the "Check Answers" button.

Key Word Practice and Practice Test

Both the Key Word Practice and Practice Test are available if you are using the CD. Both have tracking disk capability for student/instructor feedback, printing capability, and study guide generation to guide the re-study of incorrect answers.

InfoWebs

The InfoWeb icon connects you to Web links, film, video, TV, print, and electronic resources. InfoWebs keep you up-to-date and solve the problem of constantly changing URLs. If you're using the CD and have Internet access, you can click the InfoWeb icon and be linked directly to resources on the Internet using your browser of choice. If you are using the CD and do not have Internet access, you will be linked to the *InfoWeb* section at the end of the chapter. Otherwise refer to the number of the InfoWeb in the *InfoWeb* section at the end of each chapter.

CD Connections

If you are the using the CD-ROM, you'll love clicking these icons. They reveal videos, animations, screen tours, and other treasures to enhance learning and retention of key concepts.

Labs

Concepts come to life with the Labs—27 highly interactive tutorials that combine illustrations, animations, digital images, and simulations. The Labs guide you step-by-step through a topic, present you with Quick Checks, let you explore on your own, test comprehension, and provide printed feedback. Lab icons at the beginning of the chapters and in the text's margins indicate when a topic has a corresponding Lab. Lab Assignments are included at the end of each relevant chapter. If you are using the CD, you can launch a Lab from any Lab icon.

CyberClass

Course Technology is pleased to bring you CyberClass from HyperGraphics Corporation. CyberClass is a totally new Web-based tool for distance and on-campus settings. It is available in three levels:

Level 1
- CyberClass Stories: Stories about real corporations and their use of computers with links to their sites
- Practice Tests: Randomly generated 20 test questions covering the key concepts of each chapter that can be taken repeatedly to test understanding of each chapter's content
- Link to InfoWebs
- Electronic FlashCards: A self study aid for students to test their understanding of key concepts and terminology

Level 2
- All of Level 1 features plus a customizable and secure Web site for instructors to use for their class(es)
- Syllabus Posting
- Assignments Posting
- Submit Assignments: A template designed to efficiently have students submit assignments to the instructor via e-mail
- Hot Links: Links that the instructor can post for students
- Student Bulletin Board
- Send and View Messages: Messaging among class members and instructor
- Class Roster: Can be secured by the instructor. Students can enter their personal data into the roster (including name, phone number, email address, and so on)

- CyberChallenge: An online real-time game testing knowledge of computer concepts
- Instructor-supervised Text Chat: For such things as online real-time office hours, mini-lectures, group work, discussion groups, and so on
- Administration Utilities: Accessible by instructors only, such as editing the roster and editing user information

Level 3
- All of Level 1 and Level 2 features
- Audio Class Conferencing: Servers can run off of instructor's Windows 95 Pentium computer (up to 30 students), the school's network (up to 200 students), or HyperGraphics's servers (upon sign-up with HyperGraphics). Instructor controlled and monitored.
- Synchronous Assessment over the Web: Using Course Technology's Course Test Manager as the backbone

At the CyberClass site—**www.cyber-class.com**—we will be continually updating and improving the site based on student and instructor feedback.

Supplements

Online Companions: Dedicated to Keeping You Up-To-Date at www.course.com As with NP2, we will continue to offer you a dedicated Web site for NP3. Instructors can browse the password-protected Faculty Online Companion to obtain an online Instructor's Manual, Solution Files, Student Files, and more. Students can access this text's Student Online Companion, which contains the InfoWebs, Internet Assignments and other useful materials.

Course Presenter Course Presenter is a lecture presentation tool providing instructors a replacement for overhead transparencies. It includes a predesigned presentation for each chapter of the textbook, including the video clips, animations, and Labs. But instructors can also customize this presentation to their own preferences.

Course Test Manager: Testing and Practice at the Computer or on Paper Course Test Manager is cutting-edge, Windows-based testing software that helps instructors design and administer practice tests and actual examinations. With Test Manager students can randomly generate practice tests that provide immediate on-screen feedback and detailed study guides. Instructors can also use Course Test Manager to produce printed tests. Course Test Manager can automatically grade the tests students take at the computer and can generate statistical information on individual as well as group performance.

Instructor's Manual This all new enhanced Instructor's Manual offers an outline for each chapter; suggestion for instruction on chapter content, including how to effectively use and integrate the InfoWebs, the CD connections, and the Labs; answers to all end of chapter materials; and numerous teaching tips.

Application Software Instruction NP3 is part of the New Perspectives Series, which includes microcomputer applications textbooks. These applications textbooks include Quick Checks, Labs and Lab Assignments, Student and Faculty Online Companions, Course Presenter, Course Test Manager, and more. Or you might try a new alternative, computer-based application software instruction with the e-Course Series. You'll find that either the text-based or the computer-based instructional materials fit perfectly with NP3.

Custom Books   The New Perspectives Series offers instructors two ways to customize a New Perspectives text to fit their courses exactly: CourseKits®, two or more texts packaged together in a box, and Custom Editions™, your choice of books bound together. Custom Editions offer unparalleled flexibility in designing concepts and applications courses. Instructors can build their own book by ordering a combination of titles bound together to cover only the topics they want. Students save because they buy only the materials they need. There is no minimum order, and books are spiral bound. Both CourseKits and Custom Editions offer significant price discounts.

Acknowledgments

This edition was a major undertaking for all the people who worked on it. Everyone made sacrifices, offered their creative talents, stayed on schedule, and was dedicated to making this book and CD the best it could be. The dedication and commitment they exhibited made us proud to be a part of the New Perspectives team. So, our thanks and deep appreciation go to the entire staff at GEX Inc., Planet Interactive, the many student testers and beta testers, Donna Schuch, Jeremy Gaboury, Sue Oja, John Reynolds, John Zeanchock, Ann Turley, Doug Goodman, Susanne Walker, Abby Reip, Jeanne Busemeyer, Joe Myers, Marilyn Freedman, Rachel Crapser, Scott MacDonald, Fatima Nicholls, Mac Mendelsohn, and especially to the triumvirate of Debbie Masi, Donna Gridley, and Susan Solomon.

June Jamrich Parsons
Dan Oja

C O N T E N T S

C h a p t e r   6

The Computer Marketplace 6-1

C h a p t e r   9

Data Security and Control   9-1

C h a p t e r   1 3

Chapter 14

Managing the Data in Files and Databases **14-1**

COURSE LABS

27 Course Labs offer the absolute best when it comes to interactive learning reinforcement. The Labs offer:

- Steps, which guide students step-by-step as they learn/review basic concepts.

- Quick Checks, which appear as students work through the Steps and which draw attention to key points.

- Quick Check Summary Reports, which can be printed as homework and as validation that students have completed the Steps.

- Explore, in which students can experiment, practice skills, and complete the Lab Assignments at the end of each chapter.

Chapter 1

Using a Mouse
This Lab guides students through basic mouse functions and operations, Interactive exercises using dialog boxes allow students to practice mouse skills by creating posters.

Using a Keyboard
Students learn the parts of the keyboard and basic keyboard operations. They practice basic keyboarding with interactive typing exercises, including a self-paced typing tutor that helps improve speed and accuracy.

User Interface
Students are presented with user interfaces on a general/conceptual level, and then have the opportunity to interact with menu driven, prompted dialog, command line, graphical, and combination interfaces.

DOS Command-Line Interface
This Lab presents students with concepts and basic skills associated with the DOS command line, and provides hands-on practice entering commands at a live DOS prompt.

Peripheral Devices
Descriptions, drawings, and animations explain the functions of many popular peripheral devices.

Chapter 2

Computer History Hypermedia
This dynamic Lab has been updated for the 3rd edition and contains descriptions, drawings and photos related to the history and development of computing devices. Students learn to use hypertext links to research historical events and trends.

Multimedia
This Lab shows students what it's like to work with multimedia and see what it might be like to design some aspects of multimedia projects.

Chapter 3

Word Processing
This Lab guides students through essential word processing skills, such as typing and editing text, formatting, saving, and opening a document. They interact with a word processing program, specially designed for this Lab, that offers a hands-on introduction to word processors.

Spreadsheets

Students are introduced to essential spreadsheet skills. A spreadsheet program, specially designed for this Lab, allows students to practice and explore these skills on their own.

Database

After learning essential database concepts, students learn to use query by example to search a visual database for specific records.

Chapter 4

Using Files

Students see what happens on the screen, in RAM, and on the disk when they save, open, revise, and delete files.

Defragmentation and Disk Operation

In this Lab, students interact with simulated disks, files, and FATs to discover how the computer physically stores files. This Lab demonstrates how files become fragmented and how defragmentation utilities work.

Windows Directories, Folders, and Files

Students work with a directory tree to learn basic concepts of directory hierarchies and file types.

DOS Directories and File Management

Students learn the basics of DOS file management, including subdirectories, copying, and moving files.

Chapter 5

Troubleshooting

Students use a simulated computer to step through the boot process. They learn to identify and troubleshoot the most common boot-related problems.

Binary Numbers

This Lab introduces students to binary numbers, demonstrates how data is stored electronically using 1s and 0s, and provides practice converting between binary and decimal.

CPU Simulator

Students use a microprocessor simulation to see what happens in the ALU, control unit, and register during execution of simple assembly language programs. They can run prepared programs or write their own to see how a microprocessor actually works.

Chapter 6

Buying a Computer

Completely updated for this edition, this Lab is ever more helpful to students. An online glossary helps students interpret the technical specifications and advertisements to compare features and make purchase decisions.

Chapter 7

E-mail

Students use a simple e-mail simulation to learn essential e-mail skills including creating, sending, forwarding, replying, printing and saving mail.

Chapter 8

The Internet: World Wide Web
Students interact with a simulated Web browser to explore home pages, URLs, linking, and hypertext. You can assign this Lab even if an Internet connection is not available.

Web Pages & HTML
This Lab is a primer on HTML basics and shows how HTML is used to create pages. Students then see how they can modify these pages and view them in a browser.

Chapter 9

Data Backup
Using a simulated business environment, this Lab teaches basic backup procedures. Students experience data loss, attempt to restore lost data, and learn first-hand the value of regular backup procedures.

Chapter 10

Data Representation
This Lab consists of multiple sections that build upon student's understanding of binary numbers. It demonstrates how 0's and 1's are used to represent all types of data, including text, numbers, graphics and animations. This Lab also explains the concepts of data compression.

Chapter 11

Building a Network
This Lab begins with a basic network consisting of a file server and two workstations. Students, playing the part of the Network Manager, are guided through a hands-on process of adding devices and modifying the network.

Chapter 13

System Testing
Students play the role of a beta tester who must systematically test an information system to determine if it processed data correctly.

Chapter 14

SQL Queries
Students learn how to use relational and logical operators and how to locate specific records or groups of records in a database.

Chapter 15

Visual Programming
Students use a simple visual programming environment to write elementary programs. This Lab introduces programming and event-driven visual programming in a Visual Basic style environment.

Credits

Chapter One: Chapter Opener: Courtesy of Photofest. Figure 1-1: Courtesy of Corbis-Bettmann. Figure 1-3a: Courtesy of Hewlett-Packard. Figure 1-3b: Courtesy of Digital Equipment Corporation. Figure 1-3c: Courtesy of IBM Corporation. Figure 1-3d: Courtesy of US Robotics. Figure 1-3e: Courtesy of Casio. Figure 1-4: Courtesy of IBM Corporation. Figure 1-5: Courtesy of Royal Caribbean Cruises Ltd. Figure 1-6: Courtesy of IBM Corporation. Figure 1-7: Courtesy of American Airlines. Figure 1-8: Courtesy of Cray Research. Figure 1-9: Video courtesy of Synchromic Studios Inc. Figure 1-11a: Courtesy of David Young Wolff/Tony Stone Images. Figure 1-11b: Courtesy of Caere Corporation. Figure 1-11c: Courtesy of 3M Visual Systems Division. Figure 1-11d: Courtesy of Hewlett-Packard Company. Figure 1-11e: Used by permission © Logitech 1997. Figure 1-11f: Courtesy of Dragon Systems. Figure 1-13g: Courtesy of Creative Labs, Inc. Figure 1-13h: Used by permission © Logitech 1997. Figure 1-11i: Courtesy of Hewlett-Packard Company. Figure 1-11j: Courtesy of Epson America, Inc. Figure 1-11k: Courtesy of Epson America, Inc. Figure 1-11l: Courtesy of Hewlett-Packard Company. Figure 1-11m: Courtesy of PictureTel Corporation. Figure 1-11n: ©1997 Wacom Technology Corporation. Figure 1-14: Video courtesy of Microsoft Corporation. Figure 1-23: Screen tour courtesy of Microsoft Corporation, video images from Bergwall Productions. IW1: Courtesy of Photofest. IW2: Courtesy of AP/Wide World Photos. IW3: Courtesy of Microsoft Corporation. IW4: Courtesy of Dragon Systems.

Chapter Two: Chapter Opener: Courtesy of AP/Wide World Photos. Figure 2-2: Courtesy of Shelly R. Harrison. Figure 2-5: Courtesy of Durvin & Co. Photography. Figure 2-17: Courtesy of CompUSA, Inc. Figure 2-18: Courtesy of Shelly R. Harrison. Figure 2-21: Photo provided courtesy of Proxima Corporation. Figure 2-22: Courtesy of SAS Institute. Figure 2-24: Courtesy of ProCD, Inc. Figure 2-26: ©PC-TV. Figure 2-27: Courtesy of Virgin Interactive Entertainment. Figure 2-28: Courtesy of Intuit. Figure 2-29: Courtesy of Joe Baraban/The Stock Market. Figure 2-30: Courtesy of Microsoft Corporation. Figure 2-31: Courtesy of Shelly R. Harrison. Figure 2-33: Courtesy of Microsoft Corporation. Figure 2-35: Courtesy of Creative Labs, Inc. Figure 2-36: Courtesy of Intel Corporation. Figure 2-39: Video images courtesy of Bergwall Productions, screenshots courtesy of Microsoft Corporation. IW1: Courtesy of CompUSA, Inc. IW2: Courtesy of Shelly R. Harrison. IW3: Courtesy of Intuit.

Chapter Three: Chapter Opener: Courtesy of USGS. Figure 3-1: Still shots courtesy of Corbis-Bettman and North Wind Picture Archives, video images from Real to Reel Productions. Figure 3-4: Courtesy of Gamma Liaison. Figure 3-7: Courtesy of Vatican Library. Figure 3-13: Courtesy of National Archives and Records. Figure 3-16: Courtesy of Jacques m. Chenet/Gamma Liaison. Figure 3-18a-b: Courtesy of Smith Corona Corporation. Figure 3-18c: Courtesy of Hewlett-Packard Company. Figure 3-19: Courtesy of Robert Frerck/Odyssey Productions. Figure 3-28: Courtesy of AP/Wide World Photos. Figure 3-30: Courtesy of Rodale Press and Jerry O'Brien. Figure 3-31: ©Jeff Lowenthal/Chicago. Figure 3-39: Courtesy of Stewart Cohen/Tony Stone Images. Figure 3-40: Photo provided courtesy of Proxima Corporation. IW1: Courtesy of North Wind Picture Archives. IW2: Courtesy of Gamma Liaison.

Chapter Four: Chapter Opener: Courtesy of Dilip Mehta/Contact Press Images, Inc. Figure 4-14: Courtesy of IBM Corporation, Research Division, Almaden Research Center. Figure 4-18a-d: Courtesy of Shelly R. Harrison. Figure 4-18e: Courtesy of Iomega. Figure 4-19a: Courtesy of Shelly R. Harrison. Figure 4-19b: Courtesy of Iomega. Figure 4-20: Video courtesy of Western Digital Corporation. Figure 4-26: Courtesy of Iomega. Endnote: Courtesy of IBM Research. IW1: Courtesy of Iomega. IW2: Courtesy of IBM Archives.

Chapter Five: Chapter Opener: Courtesy of James Kaczman. Figure 5-2: Video segments courtesy of Motorola Semiconductor Products Sector, ©1997 SEMATECH, INC., Portions of Silicon Magic used with permission of Semiconductor Equipment and Materials International, ©1991. Figure 5-3a-b: Courtesy of Texas Instruments. Figure 5-3c-d: Courtesy of Intel Corporation. Figure 5-14: Courtesy of Smithsonian Institution. Figure 5-15: Photo courtesy of Intel Corporation, video segments courtesy of Motorola Semiconductor Products Sector, ©1997 SEMATECH, INC., Portions of Silicon Magic used with permission of Semiconductor Equipment and Materials International, ©1991. IW1: Courtesy of Intel Corporation.

USINGCOMPUTERS:
ESSENTIALCONCEPTS

1

In the classic science-fiction film *2001: A Space Odyssey*, astronaut Dave Bowman and four crew members depart on a mission to Jupiter. The mission objective: to discover the source of a mysterious object from space. Midway through the mission, the onboard computer, named HAL, begins to exhibit strange behavior. Dave leaves the spacecraft to make some external repairs. When he is ready to reboard, he speaks to the computer, "Open the pod bay door, HAL." HAL's reply is chilling, "I'm sorry, Dave, I'm afraid I can't do that."

2001
1

This dialog between a human and a computer raises some intriguing questions. How realistic is it? Can humans and computers communicate this fluently? What went wrong with the communication? Why won't the computer let Dave back into the spaceship?

To use a computer effectively, you must communicate tasks to the computer and accurately interpret the information the computer provides to you. The means by which humans and computers communicate is referred to as the user interface, and this is the central theme of Chapter 1.

In this chapter you will learn which computer components are necessary for communication between humans and computers. You will also learn about the user interfaces typically found on today's computer systems and how to respond to what you see on the computer screen. This chapter concludes with a discussion about manuals, reference guides, and tutorials that will help you learn how to interact with a specific computer system or software package.

CHAPTER**PREVIEW**

This chapter is a practical introduction to computers that you can immediately apply in the Lab component of this course: starting a computer, logging into a network, starting programs, and using a variety of user interfaces. When you have completed this chapter you should be able to:

- Define the term "computer"
- Describe the relationship between computer hardware and software
- Identify the parts of a typical microcomputer system
- List the peripheral devices that are typically found on microcomputer systems
- Define the term "user interface"
- Describe how you use interface elements such as prompts, commands, menus, and graphical objects
- Describe the resources you can use to learn how to use computers and software

LABS

Peripheral
Devices

User Interfaces

DOS
Command-Line
User Interface

Using a
Mouse

Using a
Keyboard

A Computers: Mind Tools

Computers have been called "mind tools" because they enhance our ability to perform tasks that require mental activity. Computers are adept at performing activities such as making calculations quickly, sorting large lists, and searching through vast information libraries. Humans can do all these activities, but a computer can often accomplish them much faster and more accurately. Our ability to use a computer complements our mental capabilities and makes us more productive. The key to making effective use of the computer as a tool is to know what a computer does, how it works, and how you can use it. That is the focus of this book.

Von Neumann's Definition

What is a computer? If you look in a dictionary printed before 1940, you might be surprised to find a computer defined as a person who performs calculations! Machines also performed calculations back then, but they were referred to as calculators, not computers. The modern definition and use of the term "computer" emerged in the 1940s when the first electronic computing devices were developed as a response to World War II military needs.

von
Neumann
2

In 1945, a team of engineers began working on a secret military project to construct the Electronic Discrete Variable Automatic Computer, referred to by the acronym EDVAC. At the time, only one other functioning computer had been built in the United States. Plans for the EDVAC were described in a report by the eminent mathematician John von Neumann, pictured in Figure 1-1.

The InfoWeb icon connects you to Web links, film, video, TV, print, and electronic resources. If you're using the CD and have Internet access, click the InfoWeb icon to go directly to resources on the Internet. Otherwise, refer to the InfoWeb section at the end of each chapter.

Figure 1-1

When this photo was published in 1947, the caption read, "Dr. John von Neumann stands in front of a new Electronic 'Brain,' the fastest computing machine for its degree of precision yet made. The machine which can do 2,000 multiplications in one second and add or subtract 100,000 times in the same period was displayed today for the first time at the Institute for Advanced Study. Its fabulous memory can store 1,024 numbers of 12 decimal places each. Dr. von Neumann was one of the designers of the wonder machine."

Von Neumann's report has been described as "the most influential paper in the history of computer science." It was one of the earliest documents to specifically define the components of a computer and describe their functions. In the report, von Neumann used the term "automatic computing system." Today, popular usage has abandoned this cumbersome terminology in favor of the shorter terms "computer" or "computer system." Based on the concepts presented in von Neumann's paper, we can define a **computer** as a device that accepts input, processes data, stores data, and produces output. Let's look more closely at the elements of this definition.

A Computer Accepts Input

What kinds of input can a computer use? Computer **input** is whatever is put into a computer system. "Input" is also used as a verb that means to feed information into a computer. Input can be supplied by a person, by the environment, or by another computer. Some examples of the kinds of input a computer can process are the words and symbols in a document, numbers for a calculation, instructions for completing a process, pictures, audio signals from a microphone, and temperatures from a thermostat.

An **input device** gathers and translates input into a form that the computer can process. As a computer user you will probably use the keyboard as your main input device.

A Computer Processes Data

In what ways can a computer process data? **Data** refers to the symbols that describe people, events, things, and ideas. Computers manipulate data in many ways, and we call this manipulation "processing." Some of the ways a computer can process data include performing calculations, sorting lists of words or numbers, modifying documents and pictures according to user instructions, and drawing graphs. In the context of computers, then, we can define a **process** as a systematic series of actions a computer uses to manipulate data. A computer processes data in a device called the **central processing unit** or **CPU**.

A Computer Stores Data

Why does a computer store data? A computer must store data so it is available for processing. The places a computer puts data are referred to as storage. Most computers have more than one location for storing data. The place where the computer stores data depends on how the data is being used. The computer puts data in one place while it is waiting to be processed and another place when it is not needed for immediate processing. **Memory** is an area that holds data that is waiting to be processed. **Storage** is the area where data can be left on a permanent basis while it is not needed for processing.

A Computer Produces Output

What kinds of output does a computer produce? Computer **output** is the results produced by a computer. "Output" is also used as a verb that means the process of producing output. Some examples of computer output include reports, documents, music, graphs, and pictures. An **output device** displays, prints, or transfers the results of processing from the computer memory.

Study Figure 1-2 to make sure you understand fundamental computer functions and see if you recognize the modern devices that help the computer accomplish each function.

Figure 1-2

Basic computer functions

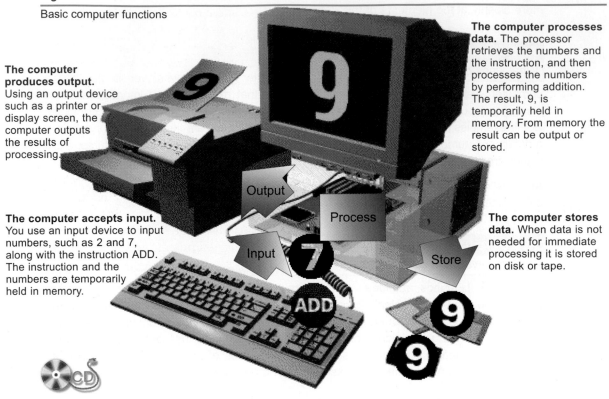

The computer produces output. Using an output device such as a printer or display screen, the computer outputs the results of processing.

The computer processes data. The processor retrieves the numbers and the instruction, and then processes the numbers by performing addition. The result, 9, is temporarily held in memory. From memory the result can be output or stored.

The computer accepts input. You use an input device to input numbers, such as 2 and 7, along with the instruction ADD. The instruction and the numbers are temporarily held in memory.

The computer stores data. When data is not needed for immediate processing it is stored on disk or tape.

Output

Process

Input

Store

ADD

At the end of each section in this book, you will find a "Quick Check" designed so you can make sure you understand what you have read before you continue. The answers to the Quick Checks are at the end of the book, just before the Index.

QuickCheck A

1. The four functions performed by a computer are input, storage, output, and _____.

2. _____ refers to the symbols processed by a computer.

3. A computer processes data in a device called the _____ processing unit.

4. The computer puts data temporarily in _____ while the data is waiting to be processed.

5. When data is not needed for processing, the computer puts it in _____.

ⒷComputer System Basics

A computer system includes a computer, peripheral devices, and software. The electric, electronic, and mechanical devices used for processing data are referred to as **hardware**. In addition to the computer itself, the term "hardware" refers to components called **peripheral devices** that expand the computer's input, output, and storage capabilities. Computer hardware in and of itself does not provide a particularly useful mind tool. To be useful, a computer requires a set of instructions, called **software** or a **computer program**, which tells the computer how to perform a particular task. Computers become even more effective when connected to other computers in a **network** so users can share information.

Software

Why does a computer need software? A computer without software is like a record player without any records; a tape player without any tapes; or a CD-player without any CDs. Without software, a computer is just a useless gadget with a power switch. Fortunately, software is plentiful and available for an astonishing number of tasks. Walk into a large computer store and you will see shelves full of software, including software for producing resumes, software for managing a small business, software to help you study for the Graduate Record Examination, software that teaches you Spanish, software to help you plan your diet, software for composing music, and software that takes you on an adventure through a dangerous labyrinth.

Software sets up a computer to do a particular task then tells the computer how to interact with the user and how to process the user's data. For example, music composition software sets up the computer to show you a musical staff. It tells the computer to let you input notes from your keyboard or synthesizer. Then the software tells the computer how to process this input into electrical signals that will play your music through a speaker.

One of the best things about using computers is browsing through a computer store or a computer software catalog to find just the right software to make your life easier and more interesting.

Categories of Computers

How is using a microcomputer different from using a mainframe? Computers traditionally have been divided into four categories, based on their technology, function, physical size, cost, and performance. These categories, however, evolve with the technology. The lines that divide the different computer categories are fuzzy and tend to shift as more powerful computers become available.

Because the characteristics of each computer category shift and change as technology advances, it is difficult to categorize a particular computer unless you have up-to-date technical expertise. So, if you want to categorize a particular computer, look at the sales literature to find out how the manufacturer classifies it.

InfoWeb

Microcomputers
3

Microcomputers, also known as personal computers, are the computers you typically find in homes and small businesses. A microcomputer usually costs about $2,000, and its processor performs about 200 million operations per second. The microcomputer you use might be a stand-alone unit, or it might be connected to other computers so you can share data and software with other users. However, even when your computer is connected to others, it will generally carry out processing tasks for only one user. Microcomputers come in many shapes and sizes, as you can see in Figure 1-3.

Figure 1-3

Microcomputers

A standard **desktop microcomputer** fits on a desk and runs on power from an electrical wall outlet. The display screen is usually placed on top of the horizontal desktop case.

A microcomputer with a **tower case** contains the same basic components as a standard desktop microcomputer, but the vertically-oriented case is large and allows more room for expansion. The tower unit can be placed on the floor to save desk space.

A **notebook computer** is small and light, giving it the advantage of portability that standard desktop computers do not have. A notebook computer can run on power from an electrical outlet or batteries.

A **personal digital assistant (PDA)**, or **palmtop computer** achieves even more portability than a notebook computer by shrinking or eliminating some standard components, such as the keyboard. On a keyboardless PDA, a touch-sensitive screen accepts characters drawn with your finger. PDAs easily connect to desktop computers to exchange and update information.

Figure 1-4

A typical minicomputer handles processing tasks for multiple users.

Terminals act as each user's main input and output device. The terminal has a keyboard for input and a display screen for output, but it does not process the user's data. Instead, processing requests must be transmitted from the terminal to the minicomputer.

The minicomputer stores data for all the users in one centralized location.

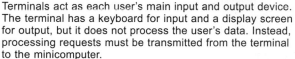

InfoWeb

Minicomputers
4

A **minicomputer** is somewhat larger than a microcomputer and can carry out the processing tasks for many users. If you are using a minicomputer system, you use a terminal to input your processing requests and view the results. A **terminal** is a device with a keyboard and screen used for input and output, but not for processing. Although a terminal resembles a microcomputer because it has a keyboard and screen, a terminal does not have any processing power of its own.

When you input a processing request, your terminal transmits it to the minicomputer. The minicomputer sends back results to your terminal when the processing is complete. The minicomputer system in Figure 1-4 is fairly typical of minicomputers that cost between $20,000 and $250,000.

Minicomputer systems typically help small and medium-sized businesses perform specific tasks such as accounting, payroll, and shipping. For example, the main office of Royal Caribbean Cruises uses a minicomputer to track passenger bookings (Figure 1-5).

Figure 1-5

Stop in at any Caribbean port and you'll see ships emblazoned with the distinctive blue-anchor logo of Royal Caribbean Cruises, Ltd. With a fleet of ten ships and over five million passengers a year, the company uses IBM minicomputers to keep track of passenger bookings and corporate accounting.

InfoWeb

Mainframes
5

Mainframes are large, fast, and fairly expensive computers, generally used by business or government to provide centralized storage, processing, and management for large amounts of data. As with a minicomputer, one mainframe computer carries out processing tasks for multiple users who input processing requests using a terminal. However, a mainframe generally services more users than a minicomputer. To process large amounts of data, mainframes often include more than one processing unit. One of these processing units directs overall operations. A second processing unit handles communication with all the users requesting data. A third processing unit finds the data requested by users.

Mainframes remain the computer of choice in situations where reliability, data security, and centralized control are necessary. The price of a mainframe computer system is typically several hundred thousand dollars. A mainframe computer is housed in a closet-size cabinet, as shown in Figure 1-6 and its peripheral devices are contained in separate cabinets.

Figure 1-6

The closet-sized system unit for the IBM S/390 G4 mainframe computer contains the processing unit, memory, and circuitry to support multiple terminals.

When you use a mainframe, your processing requests are transmitted from your terminal to the computer. At the same time, other users may also transmit requests. The computer processes each request in turn and transmits back the results. Mainframes service user requests quickly. Even though there might be 200 people submitting processing requests, the speed of the computer's response makes it seem as if you are the only user (Figure 1-7).

Figure 1-7

During a recent airline fare war, an American Airlines mainframe handled over 4,000 reservation transactions per second.

Supercomputers
6

Supercomputers are the fastest and most expensive type of computer. The cost of a supercomputer such as the one in Figure 1-8, ranges from $500,000 to $35 million.

Originally designed for "compute-intensive" tasks such as weather prediction, molecular modeling, and code-breaking, supercomputers today have also expanded into business markets where the sheer volume of data would cause lengthy processing delays in a traditional mainframe environment. For example, MCI uses supercomputer technology to manage a huge pool of customer data. Queries that once took over two hours, now take about a minute of supercomputer time.

The speed of a supercomputer can reach one trillion instructions per second, making it possible to perform complex tasks such as modeling the movement of thousands of particles in a tornado or creating realistic animations (Figure 1-9).

Figure 1-8

The Cray T3E supercomputer, configurable with six to 2,048 processors, provides the computing power to tackle the world's most challenging computing problems.

Figure 1-9

To create the animated dinosaur skeleton for the McDonald's commercial that aired during Super Bowl XXX, each frame typically takes one hour of computer time on a very fast microcomputer. With 24 frames per second, it would take 24 hours to complete one second of animation. The animators at Synchromics used the power of the supercomputer at the Maui High Performance Computing Center to reduce the time from 24 hours to 2 hours.

System Components

When I use a computer system, what hardware components will it include? This book focuses on microcomputers because that is the category of computers you are likely to use. Although the focus is on microcomputers, most of the concepts you will learn apply to the other categories of computers as well.

Microcomputer, minicomputer, mainframe, and supercomputer systems include devices to input, output, process, and store data. Study Figure 1-10 to learn about the hardware components you are likely to use on a typical microcomputer system.

Figure 1-10

Microcomputer system components

The **system unit** is the case or box that contains the power supply, storage devices, and the main circuit board with the computer's main processor and memory.

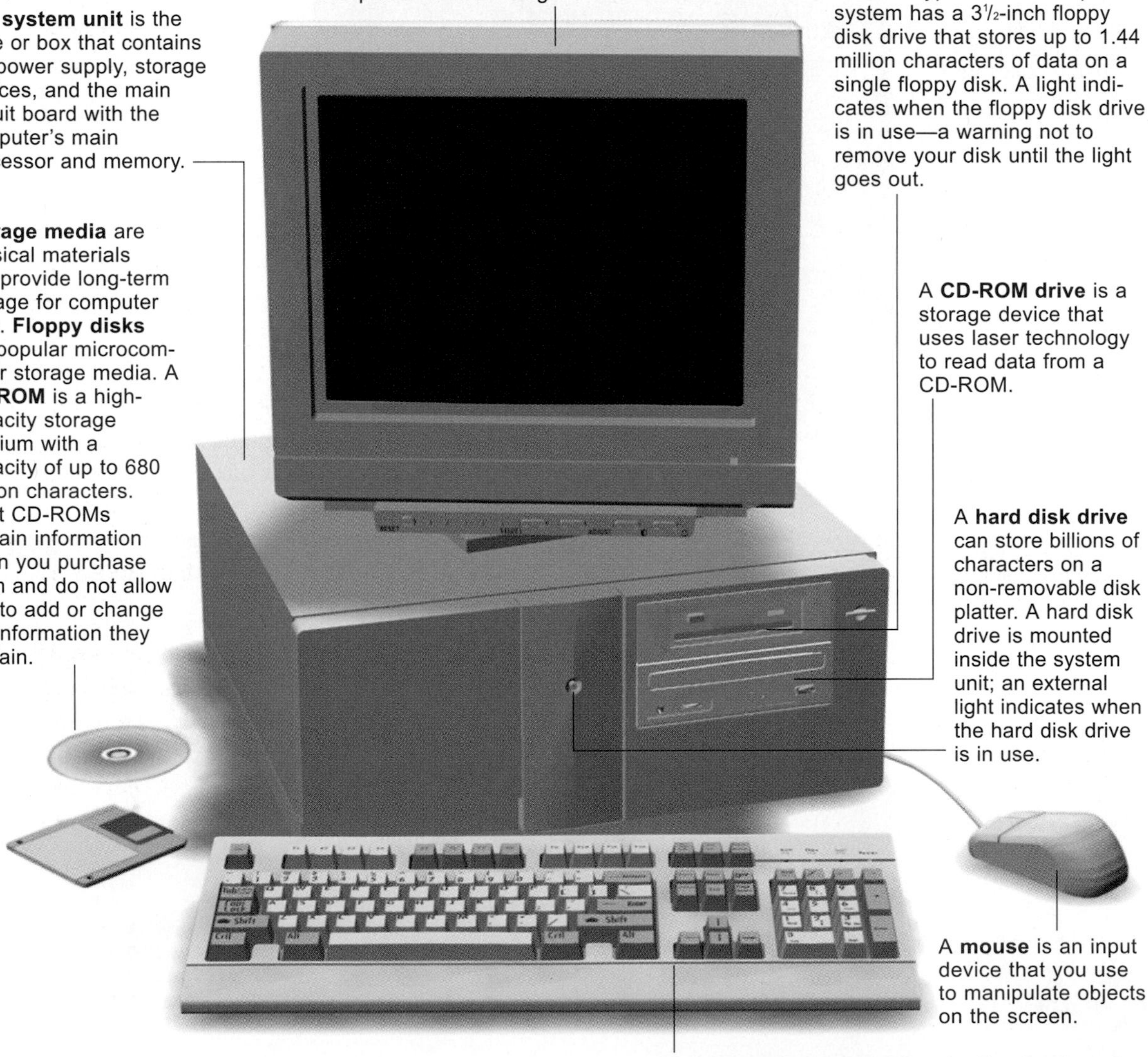

Storage media are physical materials that provide long-term storage for computer data. **Floppy disks** are popular microcomputer storage media. A **CD-ROM** is a high-capacity storage medium with a capacity of up to 680 million characters. Most CD-ROMs contain information when you purchase them and do not allow you to add or change the information they contain.

The primary output device on a microcomputer is the **monitor**; a display device that forms an image by converting electrical signals from the computer into points of colored light on the screen.

A **floppy disk drive** is a storage device that writes data on floppy disks. A typical microcomputer system has a 3½-inch floppy disk drive that stores up to 1.44 million characters of data on a single floppy disk. A light indicates when the floppy disk drive is in use—a warning not to remove your disk until the light goes out.

A **CD-ROM drive** is a storage device that uses laser technology to read data from a CD-ROM.

A **hard disk drive** can store billions of characters on a non-removable disk platter. A hard disk drive is mounted inside the system unit; an external light indicates when the hard disk drive is in use.

A **mouse** is an input device that you use to manipulate objects on the screen.

Most computers are equipped with a **keyboard** as the primary input device. A computer keyboard includes the letter and number keys, as well as several additional keys that control computer-specific tasks.

Microcomputer Compatibility

Can all computers use the same software? Hundreds of companies manufacture microcomputers, but there are only a small number of microcomputer designs or **platforms**. Today there are two major microcomputer platforms, popularly called PCs and Macs. **PCs** are based on the architecture of the first IBM microcomputers. PCs are manufactured by IBM, Compaq, Dell, Gateway, and hundreds of other companies. **Macs** are based on the Macintosh computer, manufactured by Apple Computer, Inc. Because about 80% of the microcomputers in use today are PCs, the examples in this book focus on the PC platform.

Computers that operate in essentially the same way are said to be **compatible**. Two computers are compatible if they can share the same software and use the same peripheral devices.

Not all microcomputers are compatible with each other. PCs and Macs are not regarded as compatible because they cannot use the same hardware devices or use the same programs without hardware or software to translate between them. In the past, sharing data between platforms was often difficult, and sometimes impossible. However, sharing data between these two platforms is inconvenient, but not impossible.

Peripheral Devices

LAB

Perlpheral
Devices

Is it possible to expand or modify a basic computer system? The term **peripheral device** designates equipment that might be added to a computer system to enhance its functionality. For example, a printer is a popular peripheral device used with micro, mini, and mainframe computers. Keyboards, monitors, mice, and disk drives are sometimes classified as peripheral devices, even though they are included with most basic computer systems.

Peripheral devices allow you to expand and modify a basic computer system. For example, you might purchase a computer that includes a mouse, but you might prefer to use a trackball. You might want to expand your computer's capabilities by adding a scanner so you can input photographs. If you're an artist, you might want to add a graphics tablet, so you can sketch pictures using a pencil-like stylus. A peripheral device called a modem connects your computer to the telephone system so you can access information stored on other computers.

Most microcomputer peripheral devices are designed for installation by users without technical expertise. When you buy a peripheral device it usually comes with installation instructions and specially designed software. You should carefully follow the instructions to install the device and its software. Also make sure the computer is turned off before you attempt to connect a peripheral device so you don't damage your computer system. Figure 1-11 on the next page shows some of the peripheral devices that are typically added to microcomputer systems.

Figure 1-11

Peripheral devices

A **bar code reader** gathers input data by reading bar codes from product labels or price tags.

A **dot matrix printer** creates characters and graphics by printing a fine pattern of dots using a 9-pin or 24-pin print mechanism.

An **LCD projection panel** is placed on an overhead projector to produce a large display of the information shown on the computer screen.

A **color ink-jet printer** creates characters and graphics by spraying ink onto paper.

A **sheet scanner** converts a page of text or images into an electronic format that the computer can display, print and store. A hand scanner converts a 4-inch section of a page.

A **plotter** uses pens to draw an image on paper.

A **sound card** can be installed inside a computer system unit to give a computer the capability to accept audio input from a microphone, play sound files stored on disks and CD-ROMs, and produce audio output through speakers or headphones.

A **computer video camera** records an image of the person sitting at a computer or of a small group. Special digitizing hardware and software convert the image into a signal a computer can store and transmit.

A **trackball** is a pointing device that you might use as an alternative to a mouse. You roll the ball to position the pointer on the screen.

A **graphics tablet** accepts input from a pressure-sensitive stylus, converting pen strokes into images on the screen.

A **laser printer** uses the same technology as a photocopier to print professional-quality text and graphics.

Computer Networks

What's different about using a network? A **computer network** is a collection of computers and other devices connected to share data, hardware, and software. Network users can send messages to others on the network and retrieve data from a centralized storage device. Using a computer on a network is not much different from using a stand-alone computer except that you have access to more data, the ability to communicate with others, and you'll have to follow security procedures.

A network must be secured against unauthorized access to protect the data it stores. Most organizations restrict access to the software and data on a network by requiring users to log in with a unique user ID and password.

A **user ID** is a combination of letters and numbers that serve as your "call sign" or "identification." Your user ID is public—it is usually part of the address someone would need to send you messages over the network. You can let people know your user ID, but you should never reveal your password.

A **password** is a special set of symbols known only to you and the person who supervises the network. You should not reveal your password because it would violate your responsibility to help maintain network security. Also, you should understand that if someone logs into a network using your user ID and sends offensive messages or erases important files, it will look as if you did it. Figure 1-12 shows you what to do when a computer asks you to log in.

Figure 1-12

A network log in screen

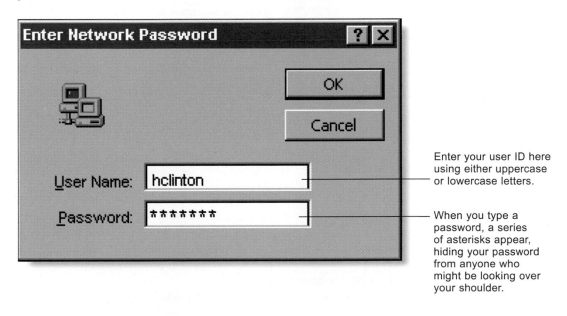

Enter your user ID here using either uppercase or lowercase letters.

When you type a password, a series of asterisks appear, hiding your password from anyone who might be looking over your shoulder.

A network can connect microcomputers, minicomputers, and mainframes. Small networks connect a few computers within a building, whereas larger networks can stretch across the country. The world's largest computer network, the **Internet**, provides connections for millions of computers all over the globe. The Internet provides many information services, but the most popular is the **World Wide Web**, often referred to as the **Web**.

The Web is a sort of "flea market" for information. Computer sites all over the world store data of various sorts, such as weather maps, census data, product information, course syllabi, music, and images. When you connect your computer to the Web, you can access this information. Search engines, like the one shown in Figure 1-13 help you find the information you want from among the millions of sites and the thousands of pages on each site.

Figure 1-13

Lycos is a popular search engine that helps you find information on the Web

To use this search engine, type in the keyword(s) for your search or select a category.

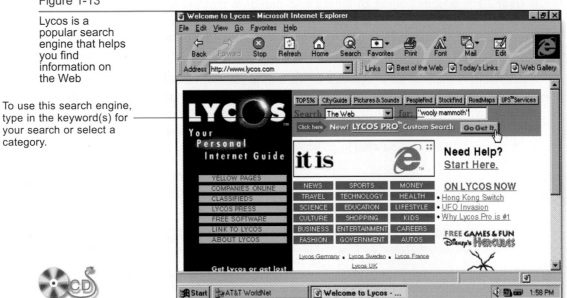

QuickCheck B

1. Most microcomputers are equipped with a(n) _____ as the primary input device and a(n) _____ as the primary output device.

2. A(n) _____ is generally devoted to carrying out the processing tasks of only one user, even when it is connected to other computers.

3. A(n) _____ is a device that resembles a microcomputer but does not have any processing capability.

4. If an organization wants to provide processing for more than 200 users and reliability, security, and centralized control are necessary, a(n) _____ computer would best meet its needs.

5. An IBM computer is _____ with a Compaq computer because it operates in essentially the same way.

6. A computer _____ allows you to send messages to other computer users and access data from a centralized storage device.

C The User Interface

User
Interfaces
7

To effectively use the computer as a mind tool, you must communicate with it; you must tell the computer what tasks to perform, and you must accurately interpret the information the computer provides. The means by which humans and computers communicate is referred to as the **user interface**. Through the user interface, the computer accepts your input and presents you with output. This output provides you with the results of processing, confirms the completion of the processing, or indicates that data was stored.

Ideally, a good user interface makes a computer easy to use, intuitive, and unobtrusive. However, this ideal is not always the reality. Donald Norman, a well-known cognitive scientist, wrote a delightful book called *The Psychology of Everyday Things* in which he says, "Well-designed objects are easy to interpret and understand. They contain visible clues to their operation. Poorly designed objects can be difficult and frustrating to use. They provide no clues—or sometimes false clues. They trap the user and thwart the normal process of interpretation and understanding."

As with many objects in everyday life, some computer user interfaces are not well conceived, and using them is frustrating. User interfaces are still evolving in response to the needs of a rapidly growing community of computer users that includes children, as shown in Figure 1-14.

Figure 1-14

User interfaces are supposed to be intuitive.

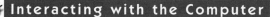

LAB

User
Interfaces

Interacting with the Computer

Is the user interface hardware or software? The user interface is a combination of software and hardware. The software that controls the user interface defines its characteristics. For example, software controls whether you accomplish tasks by manipulating graphical objects or typing commands. The hardware controls the way you physically manipulate the computer to establish communication, for example, whether you use a keyboard or your voice to input commands. After you have a general understanding of user interfaces, you will be able to quickly figure out how to make the computer do what you want it to do.

The software interface elements you'll typically encounter include prompts, wizards, commands, menus, dialog boxes, and graphical objects. The hardware interface elements you'll use include pointing devices, keyboards, and monitors.

Prompts

Why is it sometimes hard to figure out what the computer wants me to do?   A **prompt** is a message displayed by the computer that asks for input from the user. In response to a computer prompt, you enter the requested information or follow the instruction. Some prompts, such as "Enter your name:", are helpful and easy to understand, even for beginners. Other prompts, like A:\>, are less helpful.

A sequence of prompts is sometimes used to develop a user interface called a **prompted dialog**. In a prompted dialog, a conversation of sorts takes place between the computer and user. In the following example of a prompted dialog, the computer's prompts are in uppercase; the user's responses are in bold.

HOW MUCH MONEY IS CURRENTLY IN YOUR ACCOUNT?
1000
HOW MUCH MONEY WILL YOU DEPOSIT EACH MONTH?
100
WHAT IS THE YEARLY INTEREST RATE PERCENT?
6
WHAT IS THE LENGTH OF THE SAVINGS PERIOD IN MONTHS?
36
O.K. AFTER 36 MONTHS YOU WILL HAVE $5149.96 IN YOUR SAVINGS ACCOUNT.

A prompted dialog is rarely found in commercial software packages. There are two reasons why. First, the process of interacting with such a dialog is very linear. You must start at the beginning of the dialog and respond sequentially to each prompt. It is difficult to back up if you make an error.

The second reason that a prompted dialog is difficult to use is due to the ambiguity of human language. If a prompt is not clear and you respond to it with something unexpected, the dialog will not function correctly. In Figure 1-15 you can see an example of this difficulty in the dialog with a computer-based library card catalog system.

Figure 1-15

An unsuccessful dialog

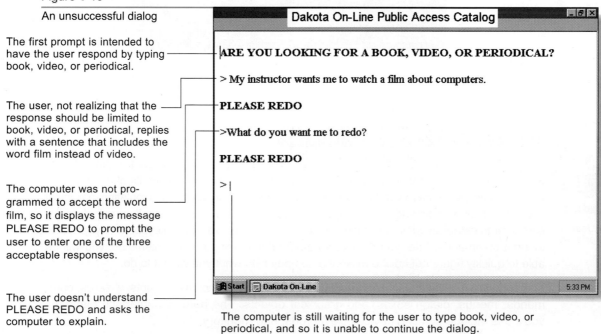

The first prompt is intended to have the user respond by typing book, video, or periodical.

The user, not realizing that the response should be limited to book, video, or periodical, replies with a sentence that includes the word film instead of video.

The computer was not programmed to accept the word film, so it displays the message PLEASE REDO to prompt the user to enter one of the three acceptable responses.

The user doesn't understand PLEASE REDO and asks the computer to explain.

Dakota On-Line Public Access Catalog

ARE YOU LOOKING FOR A BOOK, VIDEO, OR PERIODICAL?

> My instructor wants me to watch a film about computers.

PLEASE REDO

>What do you want me to redo?

PLEASE REDO

> |

Start   Dakota On-Line   5:33 PM

The computer is still waiting for the user to type book, video, or periodical, and so it is unable to continue the dialog.

The difficulty with the dialog in Figure 1-15 was not necessarily the fault of the user. The prompts should have provided more specific instructions, and the computer program should have accepted a wider vocabulary. Unfortunately, if this were the interface on your online library card catalog, you would need to learn how to work within its limitations.

Today's commercial software tends to use "wizards" instead of prompted dialogs. A **wizard** is a sequence of screens that direct you through multi-step software tasks such as creating a graph, a list of business contacts, or a fax cover sheet. Wizards, like the one in Figure 1-16, use graphics to help explain the prompts and allow users to back up and change their responses.

Figure 1-16

Using a wizard

The Business Card Wizard helps you create business cards that you can print on a laser printer.

The wizard prompts you at each step. First, you enter the information you want printed on the card.

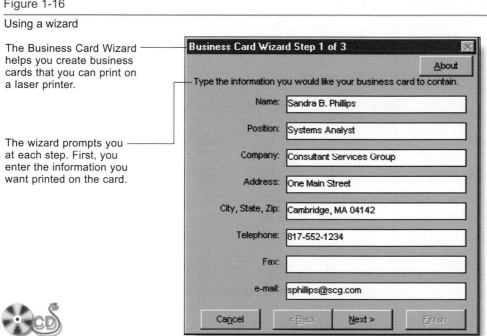

Next you decide what style you'd like for your business card. The wizard lets you move forward, or backward to change your responses until the business card is set up to your satisfaction.

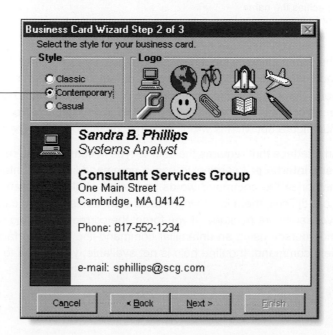

Commands

Is it true that I have to memorize lots of commands to use a computer? A **command** is an instruction you input to tell the computer to carry out a task. When you use older micro-computer interfaces and many mainframe interfaces, you must type commands, then press the Enter key to indicate that the computer should now carry out the command. Each word in a command results in a specific action by the computer. Command words are often English words, such as *print*, *begin*, *save*, and *erase*, but command words can also be more cryptic and might even use special symbols. Some examples of cryptic command words include *ls*, which means list; *cls*, which means clear the screen; and *!*, which means quit. Figure 1-17 shows how you might use a command to find out what is on your disk.

Figure 1-17

Using commands

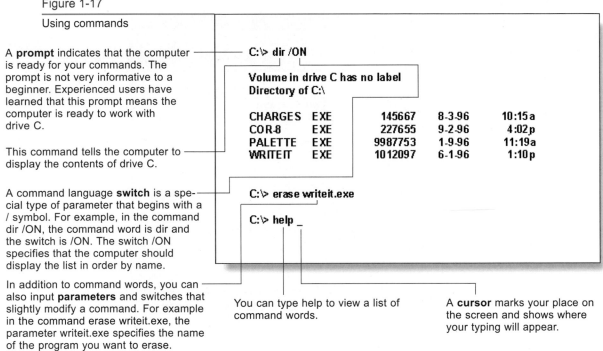

A **prompt** indicates that the computer is ready for your commands. The prompt is not very informative to a beginner. Experienced users have learned that this prompt means the computer is ready to work with drive C.

This command tells the computer to display the contents of drive C.

A command language **switch** is a special type of parameter that begins with a / symbol. For example, in the command dir /ON, the command word is dir and the switch is /ON. The switch /ON specifies that the computer should display the list in order by name.

In addition to command words, you can also input **parameters** and switches that slightly modify a command. For example in the command erase writeit.exe, the parameter writeit.exe specifies the name of the program you want to erase.

You can type help to view a list of command words.

A **cursor** marks your place on the screen and shows where your typing will appear.

The commands you input must conform to a specific syntax. **Syntax** specifies the sequence and punctuation for command words, parameters, and switches. If you misspell a command word, leave out required punctuation, or type the command words out of order, you will get an **error message** or **syntax error**. When you get an error message or syntax error, you must figure out what is wrong with the command and retype it correctly.

An interface that requires the user to type in commands is referred to as a **command-line user interface**. Learning to use a command-line user interface is not easy. You must memorize the command words and know what they mean. To make the situation even more difficult, there is no single set of commands that you can use for every computer and every software package. If you forget the correct command word or punctuation, or if you find yourself using an unfamiliar command-line user interface, you can usually enter the Help command. If online help is not available, you'll need to use a reference manual.

LAB

DOS Command-Line User Interface

Menus and Dialog Boxes

Are menus easier to use than commands? Menus were developed as a response to the difficulties many people experienced trying to remember the command words and syntax for command-line user interfaces. A **menu** displays a list of commands or options. Each line of the menu is referred to as a **menu option** or a **menu item**. Figure 1-18 shows you how to use a menu.

Figure 1-18

Using a menu

Most of today's software includes a **menu bar** with a list of **menu titles** such as File, Edit, and View. Clicking a menu title displays the menu.

A menu shows you a list of **menu options**. You can select an option using the mouse.

Some menu options lead to a **submenu** that gives an additional set of command choices.

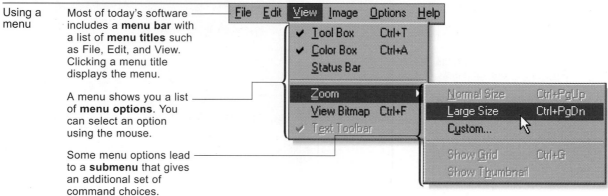

Menus are popular because when you use them, you do not have to remember command words. You just choose the command you want from a list. Also, because all the commands on the list are valid commands, it is not possible to make syntax errors.

You might wonder how a menu can present all the commands you might want to input. Obviously, there are many possibilities for combining command words, so there could be hundreds of menu options. Two methods are generally used to present a reasonably sized list of menu options, submenus, and dialog boxes.

A **submenu** is an additional set of commands that that the computer displays after you make a selection from the main menu. Sometimes a submenu displays another submenu providing even more command choices.

Instead of leading to a submenu, some menu options lead to a dialog box. A **dialog box** displays the options associated with a command. You fill in the dialog box to indicate specifically how you want the command carried out, as shown in Figure 1-19.

Figure 1-19

Using a dialog box

The Print option displays three dots to indicate that this menu leads to a dialog box.

When you select Print, the Print dialog box appears. The dialog box prompts you to enter specifications about how the computer should carry out the print task.

Click this button to display a list of printers you can use.

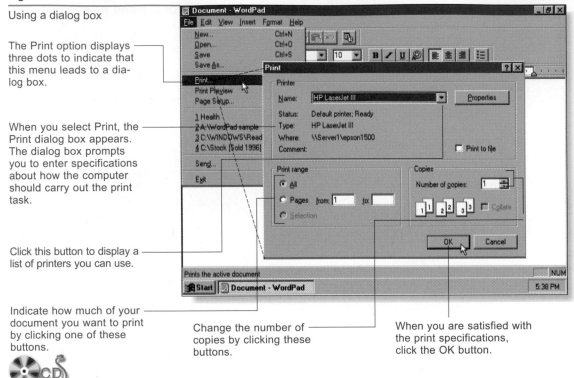

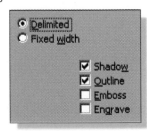

Indicate how much of your document you want to print by clicking one of these buttons.

Change the number of copies by clicking these buttons.

When you are satisfied with the print specifications, click the OK button.

Dialog boxes display controls that you manipulate with the mouse to specify settings and other command parameters. Figure 1-20 explains how to use some of the dialog box controls that you are likely to encounter.

Figure 1-20

Dialog box controls

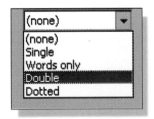

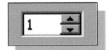

Round **option buttons** allow you to select one of the options. Square **check boxes** allow you to select any or all of the options.

Drop-down lists display a list of options when you click the arrow button.

Spin boxes let you increase or decrease a number by clicking the arrow buttons. You can also type a number in the box.

Graphical Objects

Why are GUIs so popular? A **graphical object** is a small picture on the screen that you can manipulate using a mouse or other input device. Each graphical object represents a computer task, command, or a real-world object. You show the computer what you want it to do by manipulating an object instead of entering commands or selecting menu options. Graphical objects include icons, buttons, tools, and windows, as explained in Figure 1-21.

Figure 1-21

Graphical objects

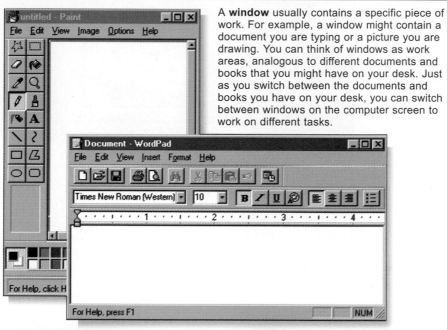

A **window** usually contains a specific piece of work. For example, a window might contain a document you are typing or a picture you are drawing. You can think of windows as work areas, analogous to different documents and books that you might have on your desk. Just as you switch between the documents and books you have on your desk, you can switch between windows on the computer screen to work on different tasks.

An **icon** is a small picture that represents an object. When you select an icon, you indicate to the computer that you want to manipulate the object. A selected object is highlighted. The My Computer icon on the right is selected, so it is highlighted with dark blue.

A **button** helps you make a selection. When you select a button, its appearance changes to indicate that it has been activated. The Paintbrush button is selected and it appears to be pushed in. Buttons are sometimes referred to as **tools**.

An example of manipulating on-screen objects is the way you delete a document using Windows software. The documents you create are represented by icons that look like sheets of paper. A Recycle Bin icon represents the place where you put documents you no longer want. Suppose you used your computer to write a report named "Sport Statistics," but you no longer need the report stored on your computer system. You use the mouse to drag the Sport Statistics icon to the Recycle Bin and erase the report from your computer system, as shown in Figure 1-22.

Figure 1-22

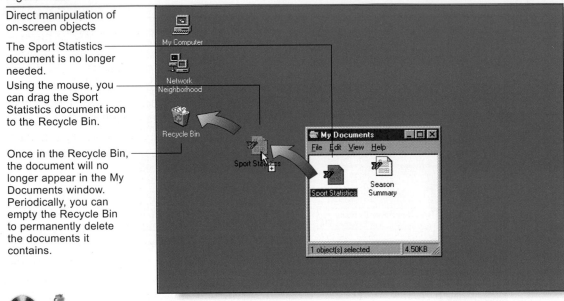

Direct manipulation of on-screen objects

The Sport Statistics document is no longer needed.

Using the mouse, you can drag the Sport Statistics document icon to the Recycle Bin.

Once in the Recycle Bin, the document will no longer appear in the My Documents window. Periodically, you can empty the Recycle Bin to permanently delete the documents it contains.

Graphical objects are a key element of **graphical user interfaces** or GUIs (pronounced "gooies") found on most of today's microcomputers. GUIs are based on the philosophy that people can use computers intuitively—that is, with minimal training—if they can manipulate on-screen objects that represent tasks or commands.

Graphical user interfaces often contain menus and prompts in addition to graphical objects because graphical user interface designers found it difficult to design icons and tools for every possible task.

Most graphical user interfaces are based on a metaphor in which computer components are represented by real-world objects. For example, a user interface with a **desktop metaphor** might represent documents as pages of paper and storage as a filing cabinet. Metaphors are intended to make the tasks you perform with computers more concrete, easier to explore, and more intuitive.

Pointing Devices

LAB

Using a Mouse

Some mice have three buttons, while others have only one or two—why? A **pointing device** such as a mouse, trackball, or lightpen helps you manipulate objects and select menu options. The most popular pointing device is the mouse. The mouse was developed by Douglas Engelbart in the early 1970s to provide an input method more efficient than the keyboard. Englebart's work coincided with efforts to construct graphical user interfaces. The popularity of the mouse and graphical user interfaces grew slowly, until Apple Computer, Inc. produced the Macintosh computer in 1983. Now virtually every computer is equipped with a mouse.

When you move the mouse on your desk, a **pointer**—usually shaped like an arrow— moves on the screen in a way that corresponds to how you move the mouse. You select an object on the screen by pressing the left mouse button a single time. This is referred to as **clicking**. Some operations require you to click the mouse twice in rapid succession. This is referred to as **double-clicking**. You can also use the mouse to **drag** objects from one screen location to another by pointing to the object, holding down the mouse button, and moving the mouse to the new location for the object. When the object is in its new location, you release the mouse button. Figure 1-23 shows you how to hold a mouse and use it to manipulate graphical objects.

Figure 1-23

Using a mouse

A pointer on the screen, usually shaped like an arrow, moves as you move the mouse.

To hold the mouse, rest the palm of your right hand on the mouse so your index finger is positioned over the left mouse button. Lightly grasp the mouse using your thumb and ring finger.

To select an object, use the mouse to position the pointer on the object, then click the left mouse button.

If you move the mouse to the right on your desk, the pointer moves to the right on your screen. When you pull the mouse toward you, the pointer moves toward the bottom of the screen.

The mouse moves the pointer only when the mouse is in contact with a hard surface like a desk. If you pick up the mouse and move it, the pointer will not move. This is handy to know. Suppose you are dragging an object, but your mouse runs into an obstacle on your desk. You can just pick up the mouse, move it to a clear space, and continue dragging.

The mouse you use with a Macintosh computer only has one button. PCs use either a two- or three-button mouse. A two-button mouse allows you to **right-click** an object and provides another way of manipulating it. For example, if clicking the left button selects an object, clicking the right button might bring up a menu of actions you can do with the object. On a three-button mouse you rarely use the third button. Some three-button mice, however, allow you to click the middle button once instead of double-clicking the left mouse button. This feature is useful for people who have trouble double-clicking. It also helps prevent some muscular stress injuries that result from excessive clicking.

Keyboard

Do I need to be a good typist to use a computer? Virtually every computer user interface requires you to use a keyboard. You don't have to be a great typist, but to use a computer effectively you should be familiar with the computer keyboard because it contains special keys to manipulate the user interface. Study Figure 1-24 before you read the rest of this section.

LAB

Using a Keyboard

You use the typing keys to input commands, respond to prompts, and type the text of documents. A cursor or an insertion point indicates where the characters you type will appear. The **cursor** appears on the screen as a flashing underline. The **insertion point** appears on the screen as a flashing vertical bar. You can change the location of the cursor or insertion point using the arrow keys or the mouse.

The **numeric keypad** provides you with a calculator-style input device for numbers and arithmetic symbols. You can type numbers using either the set of number keys at the top of the typing keypad or the keys on the numeric keypad. However, notice that some keys on the numeric keypad contain two symbols. When the Num Lock key is activated, the numeric keypad produces numbers. When the Num Lock key is not activated, the keys on the numeric keypad move the cursor in the direction indicated by the arrows on the keys.

The Num Lock key is an example of something called a toggle key. A **toggle key** switches back and forth between two modes. The Caps Lock key is also a toggle. When you press the Caps Lock key you switch or "toggle" into uppercase mode. When you press the Caps Lock key again you toggle back into lowercase mode.

Now here's an interesting problem that faced the designers for word processors that use command-line interfaces. Suppose someone is typing in the text of a document and wants to issue a command to save the document on a disk. If the user types SAVE, it will just appear as another word in the document. How does the computer know that SAVE is supposed to be a command and not just part of a sentence such as "Save your money." Interface designers solved this problem by introducing function keys, control keys, and Alt keys.

Function keys, like those numbered F1 through F12, are located at the top of your keyboard. They do not exist on the keyboard of a standard typewriter but were added to computer keyboards to initiate commands. For example, with many software packages F1 is the key you press to get help. The problem with function keys is that they are not standardized. In one program, you press F7 to save a document, but in another program, you press F5.

The Alt and Ctrl keys work in conjunction with the letter keys. If you see <Ctrl X>, Ctrl+X, [Ctrl X], Ctrl-X, or Ctrl X on the screen or in an instruction manual, it means to hold down the Ctrl key while you press X. Ctrl+X is a **keyboard shortcut** for clicking the Edit menu, then clicking the Cut option.

Figure 1-24

The computer keyboard

☐ Editing Keypad   ☐ Typing Keypad

☐ Numeric Keypad   ☐ Function Key Array

The **Esc** or "escape" key cancels an operation.

The **Caps Lock** key capitalizes all the letters you type when it is engaged, but does not produce the top symbol on keys that contain two symbols. This key is a **toggle key**, which means that each time you press it, you switch between uppercase and lowercase modes. There is usually an indicator light on the keyboard to show which mode you are in.

The **function keys** execute commands, such as centering a line of text or boldfacing text. The command associated with each function key depends on the software you are using.

Each time you press the **Backspace** key, one character to the left of the cursor is deleted. If you hold down the Backspace key, multiple characters to the left are deleted one by one until you release it.

The function of the **Scroll Lock** key depends on the software you are using. This key is rarely used with today's software.

The **Print Screen** key prints the contents of the screen when you use some software. With other software, the Print Screen key stores a copy of your screen in memory that you can manipulate or print with graphics software.

Indicator lights show you the status of each toggle key: Num Lock, Caps Lock, and Scroll Lock. The Power light indicates whether the computer is on or off.

The **Pause** key stops the current task your computer is performing. You might need to hold down both the Ctrl key and the Pause key to stop the task.

Page Up displays the previous screen of information. **Page Down** displays the next screen of information.

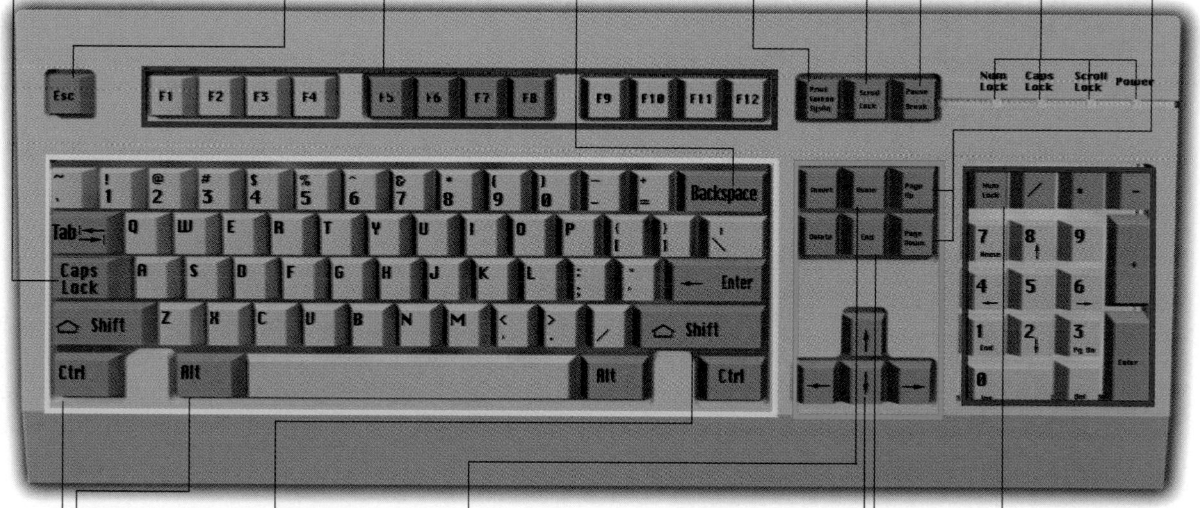

You hold down the **Alt** key while you press another key. The result of Alt key combinations depends on the software you are using.

You hold down the **Ctrl** key while you press another key. The result of Ctrl key combinations depends on the software you are using.

You hold down the **Shift** key while you press another key. The Shift key capitalizes letters and produces the top symbol on keys that contain two symbols.

Home takes you to the beginning of a line or the beginning of a document, depending on the software you are using.

The **arrow keys** move your position on the screen up, down, right, or left.

End takes you to the end of the line or the end of a document, depending on the software you are using.

The **Num Lock** key is a toggle key that switches between number keys and arrow keys on the numeric keypad.

Monitor

How are the monitor and user interface related? A monitor is a required output device for just about every computer user interface. Whereas you manipulate the keyboard and mouse to communicate with the computer, the monitor is what the computer manipulates to communicate with you by displaying results, prompts, menus, and graphical objects. Monitor display technology determines whether the interface designer can include color and graphical objects.

The first microcomputer monitors and the displays on many mainframe terminals still in use today were character-based. A **character-based display** divides the screen into a grid of rectangles, which can each display a single character. The set of characters that the screen can display is not modifiable; therefore, it is not possible to display different sizes or styles of characters. The only graphics possible on character-based displays are those composed of underlines, exclamation points, and other symbols that already exist in the character set. One of the reasons that mainframes rarely support graphical user interfaces is because of the legacy of character-based terminals connected to mainframe systems.

A **graphics display** or **bit-map display** divides the screen into a matrix of small dots called **pixels**. Any characters or graphics the computer displays on the screen must be constructed of dot patterns within the screen matrix. The more dots your screen displays in the matrix, the higher the **resolution**. A high-resolution monitor can produce complex graphical images and text that is easier to read than a low-resolution monitor. Most of the monitors on microcomputers have bit-map display capabilities. This provides the flexibility to display characters in different sizes and styles as well as the graphical objects needed for GUIs. Monochrome or gray-scale monitors display text and graphics in shades of gray. Color monitors allow the interface designer to use the impact of color to create pleasing screen designs and use color as a cue to direct the user's attention to important screen elements.

User Interface Comparison

What's it like using different types of user interfaces? Now that you have learned about user-interface elements, let's see how they work for a typical computer activity. One of the most frequent computer activities is starting a program. Figure 1-25 illustrates the different ways you could start a program—using commands, using graphical objects, and using a menu.

Figure 1-25

Starting programs
with different types
of user interfaces

To start Microsoft Works using the
DOS command-line user interface, you need to know the name
the computer has given the program. In this case the computer
calls Microsoft Works "works". At
the C:> prompt, type **works** then
press the Enter key.

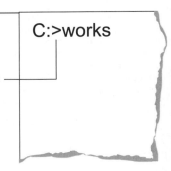

C:>works

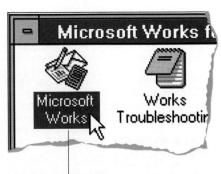

To start Microsoft Works using a graphical
object, you must move the pointer to the
Microsoft Works graphical object and double-
click the left mouse button.

Figure 1-25

Starting programs
with different types
of user interfaces
continued

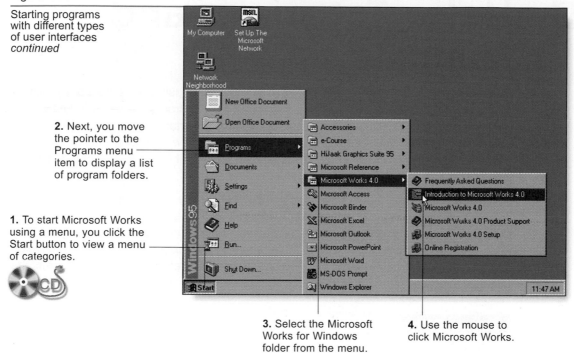

2. Next, you move
the pointer to the
Programs menu
item to display a list
of program folders.

1. To start Microsoft Works
using a menu, you click the
Start button to view a menu
of categories.

3. Select the Microsoft
Works for Windows
folder from the menu.

4. Use the mouse to
click Microsoft Works.

QuickCheck C

1 A(n) _____, such as "Enter your name:", is one way a computer can tell the user what to do.

2 Instead of prompted dialogs, today's software tends to use _____ to direct a user through multi-step software tasks, such as creating a graph or creating a fax cover sheet.

3 When you use a command-line interface, you press _____ when you are done typing a command.

4 If you type a command, but leave out a required space, you have made a(n) _____ error.

5 When you make a menu selection, a(n) _____ or a dialog box might appear to let you enter more details on how you want the computer to do a task.

6 Most _____ are based on a metaphor, such as a desktop metaphor in which documents are represented by folder icons.

7 The flashing underline that marks your place on the screen is called the _____; the flashing vertical bar is called the _____.

8 You can use the _____ key and the Alt key in conjunction with letter keys instead of using the mouse to control menus.

9 _____ are work areas on the screen analogous to different documents and books you might have open on your desk. (Hint: Don't forget to read the figure captions!)

User Focus

D Help, Tutorials, and Manuals

InfoWeb

Computer Terms 8

No class can ever teach you all you need to know about using computers or everything about one software package. You should not feel frustrated if you don't "know" how something on your computer works. One of the most important skills you can develop as a computer user is the ability to figure out how to do new computing tasks. But don't expect to figure things out in a flash of inspiration! You usually have to get some additional information.

You can find information about installing computer hardware and using computer software in books, on your computer screen, on videotapes, and on audio cassettes. We can refer to these books, tapes, and so forth as "resources." To use these resources effectively, you need to know they exist, you need to know where to find them, and you need to develop some strategies for applying the information they contain. Let's take a look at some of the resources you can use to do this.

Online Help

If I'm using a program and I "get stuck," what help can I get from the computer? The term "online" refers to resources that are immediately available on your computer screen. Reference information is frequently available as online help, accessible from a Help menu or by typing HELP at a command-line prompt. Figure 1-26 shows how you access online Help for the Microsoft Office 97 software.

Figure 1-26

Using the Office Assistant to get online help

The Office Assistant provides help in response to questions you type.

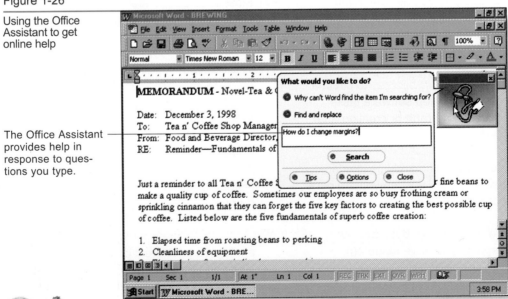

Tutorials

How can I get the most out of a tutorial? A **tutorial** is a guided, step-by-step learning experience. Usually this learning experience teaches you the generic skills you need to use specific hardware or software. For example, suppose you purchase CorelDRAW software, and the first thing you want to draw is your company logo. When you use a tutorial that teaches you how to use CorelDRAW, you learn how to do such things as draw straight lines and wavy lines, use color in the drawing, and change the sizes of the pictures you draw. The tutorial does not teach you exactly how to draw your company logo. To get the most out of a tutorial, therefore, you need to think about how you can generalize the skills you are learning so you can apply them to other tasks.

When you use a tutorial, don't try to cover too much ground at once. Two 60-minute sessions each day are probably sufficient. As you work on a tutorial, take notes on those techniques you expect to apply to your own projects. When you have completed enough of the tutorial to do your own project, put the tutorial aside. You can complete the rest of the tutorial later if you need to learn more. Tutorials come in a variety of forms, as shown in Figure 1-27.

Figure 1-27

Tutorials and reference resources

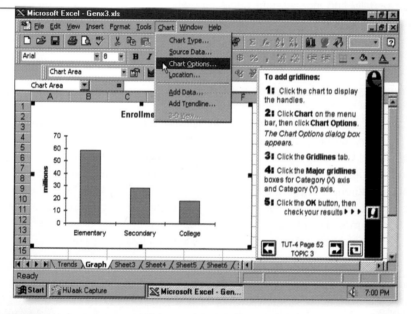

Computer-based tutorials display step-by-step instructions in boxes or windows on the screen. Computer-based tutorials have an advantage over their printed counterparts because they can demonstrate procedures using computer animation.

Audio tutorials on cassette verbally walk you through the steps of the tutorial. An advantage to this type of tutorial is that you do not have to read instructions. However, you must stop the tutorial and rewind, if you do not hear or understand the instructions. You might like audio tutorials if you easily retain information presented in lectures.

Video tutorials on videotape visually illustrate how the software or hardware works. Some video tutorials are designed so that you watch them, take notes, then try the steps on the computer later. Other video tutorials are designed to be used while you are sitting at the computer. As with audio tutorials, you can stop and rewind video tutorials if you miss something.

Printed tutorials are very popular. To use a printed tutorial, you read how to do a step, then you try to do it on the computer.

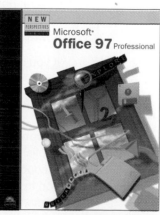

Reference Manuals

When should I use a reference manual instead of a tutorial? **Reference manuals** are usually printed books or online resources that describe each feature of a hardware device or software package. They might also include examples of how to use these features. A reference manual is organized by features, rather than by lesson.

Think of reference manuals as encyclopedias, containing descriptions of all features of the software. Do not assume that you should read a reference manual from cover to cover. Instead, leaf through it to get a quick overview of all the features. A reference manual can be quite long, sometimes thousands of pages.

You should use a reference manual to find out if a feature exists or to find out how to use a feature. When you use a reference manual, first check the index to locate the information you need, then turn to the appropriate section and read it carefully.

Reference manuals are usually included with the hardware or software that you buy. Most often, reference manuals are printed documents, but a recent trend is to provide computer-based reference manuals that you can read on the computer screen. Computer-based reference manuals are extensive and are often distributed on CD-ROMs.

You can usually find independent publishers who produce reference manuals for popular hardware and, particularly, for popular software. You might want to purchase one of these reference manuals if it is easier to understand or better organized than the manual included with the hardware or software you purchased.

Other Sources of Information

InfoWeb

Learning Styles 9

Who needs a manual? Individuals have different learning styles. Whereas some people enjoy discovery learning, others prefer structured lectures or demonstrations. Your learning style is related to the way you'll best learn how to use a computer. If you like reading and easily remember the things you read in books, you will probably like using printed reference manuals and tutorials. If you are a visual learner, you will probably like video tutorials. If you are an adventurous learner, you might enjoy exploring software applications without referring to printed materials or video tutorials. Graphical and menu-driven user interfaces make this sort of exploration possible, as do interfaces that include online help.

Another approach to learning how to use computers is to take a course. Because you're reading this book, you are probably enrolled in an introductory computer course. Courses are available from schools, manufacturers, and private training firms and might last from several hours to several months. Courses about software packages tend to be laboratory-based with an instructor leading you through steps. Some courses might be lecture only, however; you might want to ask about the course format before you register.

If you run into a problem and are pressed for time, ask an expert. You might have a friend who knows a lot about computers, or on the job you might know a computer "guru." These are both good sources of information, as long as you don't overuse them.

You might also seek help from the support line of a software or hardware company. A **support line** is a service offered over the phone by a hardware manufacturer or software publisher to customers who have questions about how to use a software or hardware product. Sometimes these support line calls are toll-free; sometimes they are not. In addition to paying for the phone call, you might also pay a fee for the time it takes the support person to answer your question.

EndNote

Artificial Intelligence (AI) is the ability of a machine to simulate or surpass intelligent human behavior. Science fiction usually depicts computers as intelligent devices. HAL, though dangerous, certainly seemed to think for himself. Can computers have intelligence? This is a debate that has been raging among computer scientists and philosophers for half a decade. In 1950, British mathematician Alan Turing proposed a "test" of machine intelligence. The Turing test, as it is now called, is somewhat like a TV game show. It pits a contestant against two backstage opponents—one a computer and one a human. The contestant asks questions to try to identify the computer. Turing suggested that if the computer could not be identified, then it was acting just as intelligently as the human.

InfoWeb

Artificial
Intelligence
10

In Turing's original test, the questions and responses were typed out because computers could not understand or output speech. Today, it would be difficult to envision an intelligent computer that could not talk. We've all watched the Star Trek crew converse easily with the on-board computer. Most computers today are equipped to record and play sounds—most computers can play your regular music CDs in the CD-ROM drive—but your dialog with the computer remains silent, carried out with a mouse and keyboard. Will future user interfaces be conversational?

For a computer to understand spoken commands, it must be able to interpret human language, a process called **speech recognition**. Developers have run into problems, however, programming computers to understand different voices and different accents—an added complication in the ambiguity of human language. Suppose you tell your computer, "Open the Financial document, highlight the September data, then print it." Do you mean to print the entire document or only the September data?

Researchers are making progress solving speech recognition problems. The next time you encounter an automated telephone operator, for example, you might have the option of speaking instead of pushing the buttons on your phone.

InfoWeb

InfoWeb
Chapter
Links

The InfoWeb is your guide to print, film, television, and electronic resources. Use it to obtain updates on quickly changing technical information and to locate information for research papers. If you're using the New Perspectives CD-ROM, click the InfoWeb icon on the left side of this paragraph to access the online InfoWeb links. Otherwise, use your Web browser and type in the address of the New Perspectives site: www.cciw.com/np3. At the New Perspectives site you'll find up-to-date links to the topics covered in this chapter.

1 **2001: A Space Odyssey**

One of the themes in the 1968 science fiction classic, *2001: A Space Odyssey*, is the relationship between humans and computers. Written by scientist and novelist Arthur C. Clarke, the book *2001: A Space Odyssey* (New York: New American Library, 1968) was the basis for a movie directed by Stanley Kubrick. The film *2001: A Space Odyssey* (MGM, 1968) is thought-provoking, and its special effects are still pretty impressive, even after 30 years. Perhaps Clarke's vision of the future is so powerful because of his strong background

in science and research. Clarke is well known for his theoretical contribution to the invention of the communications satellite. For soundtracks and images from the film, critical commentary, and essays by Arthur C. Clarke, visit the 2001 Internet Resource Archive, at **www.design.no/2001**.

2 **John von Neumann**

Perhaps the greatest mathematician of his time, John von Neumann (1903–1957) had a photographic memory and a superhuman ability to perform mental calculations. Von Neumann's security clearance allowed him access to ENIAC and EDVAC, the first large scale digital computers developed in the United States. Find out more about von Neumann at **ei.cs.vt.edu/~history/VonNeumann.html**. His 1945 paper, "First Draft of a Report on the EDVAC" is reprinted in Nancy Stern's book **From ENIAC to UNIVAC: An Appraisal of the Eckert Mauchly Computers** (Digital Press, 1981).

For information about the exciting early days of computing, visit the Computer Museum's Web-based timeline **www.tcm.org/history/timeline/** and look at the years 1945–1952. If you'd like more information, check your library for the video, **The Machine That Changed the World, Episode 1: Giant Brains** (WGBH Television in cooperation with the British Broadcasting Corp., 1991).

3 **Microcomputers**

In 1977, Digital Equipment Corporation CEO Ken Olsen proclaimed, "There is no reason for any individual to have a computer in their home." It was a statement he would later regret. Microcomputer technology and the vision of pioneers like Apple Computer's Steve Jobs made personal computers a reality. A detailed history of Apple Computers is on the Web at **www.hypermall.com/History**. For more information about the heady days of the microcomputer industry, read the fast-paced book **Accidental Empires: How the Boys of Silicon Valley Make Their Millions, Battle Foreign Competition, and Still Can't Get a Date** by Robert X. Cringely (Published by HarperCollins, 1996).

4 Minicomputers

In 1957 Kenneth Olsen and Harland Anderson formed a company called Digital Equipment Corporation (DEC). Their original objective was to grab a slice of IBM's business market and sell million-dollar mainframes. Financial realities prevailed, however, and a new plan emerged—build a slightly scaled down computer and sell it for $125,000 to scientific and engineering markets. DEC computers proved successful even in other markets and by 1969, the era of miniskirts and miniseries, these computers were universally referred to as "minicomputers."

The book **Computer: A History of the Information Machine** by Campbell-Kelly and Aspray (Basic Books, 1996) contains a good history of minicomputers. On the Web, you can tour Carl Friend's mini-computer museum at **www.ultranet.com/~engelbrt/carl/museum**.

Today's minicomputer vendors include IBM, DEC, and Hewlett Packard. For an update on what's new about minicomputers, visit DEC's Web site at **www.digital.com**.

5 Mainframe Computers

IBM is synonymous with mainframe computers. The company traces its lineage back to the Tabulating Machine Company built around an 1890's card punch device invented by Herman Hollerith. IBM did not dominate the computer market until 1964 when it introduced the IBM System/360 mainframes that were to be the staple of business computing for a quarter of a century. The history of IBM is expertly chronicled in **Building IBM: Shaping an Industry and its Technology** by Emerson W. Pugh (MIT Press, 1995), and the video **The Computer Revolution: Birth of the Computer** (available from Films for the Humanities and Sciences).

IBM is not the only mainframe vendor, but its Web site at **www.ibm.com** is a good place to find information on the latest mainframe technology.

6 Supercomputers

It takes a supercomputer to beat the World's best chess player. In 1997, Gary Kasparov admitted defeat to IBM's Deep Blue supercomputer. IBM has an excellent Web site devoted to the match, at **www.chess.ibm.com**.

In the past three years, supercomputer technology and applications have changed remarkably. Today, supercomputer technology is largely based on "super" versions of the same processors that you find in microcomputers. Although supercomputers have not abandoned their specialized markets, they frequently perform the same tasks as mainframes. Seymour Cray was the well-known pioneer of supercomputer technology. You can read a 1994 interview with Cray from the Smithsonian archives at **www.si.edu/resource/tours/comphist/cray.htm** or an excellent book, **The Supermen: The Story of Seymour Cray and the Technical Wizards Behind the Supercomputer** by Charles J. Murray (John Wiley & Sons, 1997). Cray's company, Cray Research, was purchased by Silicon Graphics in 1996.

The World's Fastest Computers (*Byte*, January 1996) is an excellent article on supercomputers, accessible on the Web at **www.byte.com/art/9601/SEC6/ART1.HTM**. For an update on supercomputer technology, visit the sites of supercomputer vendors using the Web link **www.cs.cmu.edu/~scandal/vendors/htm**.

7 User Interfaces

In the film *2001: A Space Odyssey*, HAL wouldn't open the pod bay door, but users every day run into examples of computers that stubbornly refuse to open a particular file, locate a Web site, or carry out a requested command. Why does this happen? Although hardware and software bugs account for some user frustrations, many problems are due to miscommunication—a breakdown in the human-computer interface. Donald Norman's **Things That Make Us Smart: Defending Human Attributes in the Age of the Computer** (Addison-Wesley,

1994) is a book about how technology should enhance human intelligence, but only if it is user-friendly.

Today's graphical user interfaces have come a long way to making computers usable. Many people believe that GUIs were "invented" at Apple computers, because Apple's Macintosh was the first commercially successful computer with a GUI. However, GUIs evolved from Alan Kay's 1970 vision of the "Dynabook"—a portable, personal computer much like today's notebook computers and PDAs. The Web site **www.acm.org/sigchi/nci-sites/** is a good gateway to links on user interfaces.

8 Computer Terminology

Whether you're learning about computers for the first time or you're a computer pro, an up-to-date computer dictionary is always a handy companion to help you read computer magazines or look at computer ads. **The Computer Desktop Encyclopedia** by Alan Freedman (American Management Association, 1996) is one of the best references available today. You'll find the Web version at **www.techweb.com/encyclopedia/defineterm.cgi**. Another excellent Web-based compendium of computer terms is the *Webopedia* at **www.webopedia.com**. At **wfn-shop.princeton.edu/foldoc/** you can quickly look up any computer term you type at the "ever-expanding dictionary of computing." Users keep this Web dictionary up-to-date by adding new terms.

Check your library for a more in-depth reference, **The Encyclopedia of Computer Science** by Anthony Ralston (Van Nostrand Reinhold, 4th ed. 1997). Microsoft's Multimedia encyclopedia, **Encarta 97** (Microsoft Home, 1997) also provides a good assortment of computer definitions.

9 Learning Styles

What's the best way for you to learn? Do you absorb more information from a lecture than a book? Would you rather watch a demonstration or do it yourself? Educators agree that people learn in different ways, including auditory (hear it), kinesthetic (do it), and visual (see it). Take a quick inventory of your learning style at **www.howtolearn.com/personal.html**. Your personality also seems to affect the way you learn—extroverts succeed in different learning environments than introverts. You can fill out a questionnaire to find out your personality type at **www.keirsey.com**.

10 Artificial Intelligence

In the film *2001: A Space Odyssey*, the computer HAL became operational on January 12, 1997. At the film's 1968 release, computer scientists were not altogether uncomfortable with the prediction that a computer like HAL might be achievable in 30 or so years. The science of artificial intelligence (AI) was in its infancy, but technology and software were developing at a dizzying pace.

The question "Can computers think?" is still under debate. Alan Turing and Marvin Minsky would argue "Yes!" Alan Turing's paper, **Computing Machinery and Intelligence** (*Mind 59*, 1950) got the discussion rolling and describes the famous Turing Test of machine intelligence. For an expanded perspective on the argument, read Minsky's paper, "Why People Think Computers Can't" at **ww.ai.mit.edu/people/minsky/papers/ComputersCantThink.txt**.

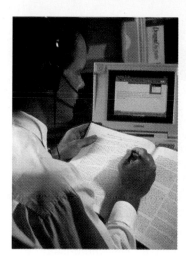

On the computers-can't-think side of the argument are John Searle and Hubert Dreyfus. A "must read" is **What Computers Still Can't Do: A Critique of Artificial Reason** by Hubert L. Dreyfus (MIT Press, 1992). Another classic in this continuing argument is **Minds, Brains, and Programs** by John Searle (Behavioral and Brain Sciences 3, 1980). The fourth episode of **The Machine that Changed the World: The Thinking Machine** sums up the arguments for and against machine intelligence and describes the challenges still in the forefront of artificial intelligence research.

It would be hard nowadays to envision an "intelligent" computer that couldn't understand human speech. So what's the current status of speech recognition and speech synthesis? Check out "An Introduction to Speech Recognition" at **www.speech.be.philips.com/intro.htm** at the Philips Speech Processing Web site.

Review

1 Using your own words, write out the answers to the questions below each heading in the chapter.

2 List each of the boldface terms used in this chapter, then use your own words to write a short definition of each term. If you would like clarification of one or more terms, refer to a computer dictionary or a computer science encyclopedia such as those listed in the InfoWeb section of this chapter. You can also refer to the Glossary/Index at the back of this book.

3 At the top of a sheet of paper write "Definition of the term computer," then make a list of important words, names, and phrases that are related to your list.

4 Use lines to divide a sheet of paper into four equal sections. In the top-left corner write "microcomputer." Write "minicomputer" in the top-right corner, "mainframe" in the bottom-left corner, and "supercomputer" in the bottom right corner. Place words, phrases, and definitions in each section that describe and differentiate each type of computer.

5 Draw a sketch of a microcomputer system, without referring to this book. Then label as many components as you can. When you have finished, look at Figure 1-10 to see if you omitted anything.

6 List as many peripheral devices as you can, without referring to this book. Indicate whether each peripheral is an input device, an output device, or both. When you have finished, refer to Figure 1-11 and review any devices you omitted.

7 Make a list of the user interface elements covered in this chapter. Write at least three terms or phrases associated with each. For example, user interface element: prompt. Associated terms and phrases: (a) prompted dialog, (b) wizards, (c) can be ambiguous or confusing.

8 Make a list of information resources that might help you install hardware and learn to use software. Write a one-sentence description of each resource.

9 Use the New Perspectives CD-ROM to take a practice test or to review the terms presented in this chapter.

Projects

1 **Your Computer** Draw a sketch of a computer system in your computer lab, home, or office and do the following:

a. Title the sketch appropriately, for example, "My Computer at Home."

b. List its brand name and model number, for example, "Dell Dimension."

c. Label the following parts, if applicable:

monitor	screen
keyboard	3½-inch disk drive
5¼-inch disk drive	hard drive light
CD-ROM drive	power switch
power light	system unit
mouse	printer

2 **Getting Started on Your Network** Do this project only if your school has a computer network for student use. If the network requires a user ID and password, get them. Learn how to log in. Write a one- to two-page step-by-step tutorial on how to log into the network. Your tutorial should include the following:

a. A title

b. An introductory paragraph explaining where the network is located, who can access it, and how students can get a user ID and password

c. Numbered steps to log into the network (if your lab policy requires that you turn on the computer each time you log in, you should include instructions for doing this in your tutorial)

d. Numbered steps for logging out of the network

3 **Evaluate a User Interface** Select a computer interface with which you are familiar. For example, you might select your bank's ATM machine or your favorite arcade game. Using the terminology you learned in this chapter, write a complete description of the user interface and its features. Your description might answer questions such as: Does the interface use menus? If so, what type? What hardware elements are required for the user interface? Is the interface intuitive? Does the interface use a metaphor? If so, what? Don't limit yourself to answering just these questions.

4 **Your Library Card Catalog** Find out if your library has a computerized card catalog. If it does, use it to answer the following questions:

a. What is the name of the software your library uses for its computerized card catalog?

b. What type of user interface does it have?

c. Explain the steps you would take to find the call number for the book *War and Peace*.

d. Is the computerized card catalog efficient to use, or do you need to enter a lot of extra information to find a book?

e. What kind of online help is available?

f. Is the computerized card catalog easy to learn and to use?

g. How much had you used the computerized card catalog before this assignment?

5 **Research Tool: The Internet** Do this project only if you have access to the Internet. The Internet is a worldwide computer network that provides access to a wealth of information including a World Wide Web site designed to accompany this textbook. Although the Internet

is the main topic of Chapter 8, using the Internet can come in handy even as you begin using this book. Several of the end-of-chapter projects refer you to information resources on the Internet. If you would like to use the Internet for these projects, this is a good time to get started.

There are several software tools to help you use the Internet, such as Netscape Navigator and Microsoft Internet Explorer. It is not possible to cover these software tools here. Therefore, this is an exploratory project that you can accomplish with the help of your instructor or with a tutorial prepared by your school or Internet service provider. Find out how to use the Internet and then answer the following questions:

a. What is the name of the software tool you use to access the Internet?

b. How do you access the "home page" for your school?

c. Use your Internet software to access the World Wide Web site **http://www.cciw.com/np3**. How can the information at this site help you with the end-of-chapter projects in this textbook?

d. List at least five other locations or "sites" that are available from your home page. How do you get to these other sites?

e. How can you keep track of where you have been on the Internet? (In other words, is there a way to backtrack to sites?)

f. When you are finished browsing on the Internet, how do you quit?

6 **Micros, Minis, Mainframes, and Supercomputers** In this chapter you read about several organizations and the computers they use. Use your library and Internet resources to find case studies that describe how computers are used in specific organizations or businesses and what category of computer (micro, mini, mainframe, or supercomputer) is used. Write a one-paragraph summary of your findings. Remember to include citations for the resources you used.

7 **Reference Manuals** Locate a software reference manual in your computer lab, home, or library; then answer the following questions:

a. What is the title of the reference manual?

b. How many pages does it have?

c. What are the titles of each section of the manual? For example, there might be a "Getting Started" section or an "Installation" section, and so on.

d. Does the reference manual include an index? If so, does it look complete? You should be suspicious of a large reference manual with a short index—it might be difficult to find the information you need.

e. Does the reference manual contain a list of features? If so, is this list arranged alphabetically? If not, how is it arranged?

f. Read a few pages of the reference manual. Write one or two sentences describing what you read. Does the reference manual seem to be well written and easy to follow? Why or why not?

8 **Identify Your Learning Style** In this chapter, you learned that you can take many approaches to learning how to use hardware and software. For this project, think about your own learning style and how it might affect the resources you select for learning about computers and software. Use the resources in InfoWeb #9 to assess your learning style. Write a one-page paper and include the following:

a. Describe the way you like to learn things in general—do you like to read about them, take a class, listen to a cassette, watch a video, think about them, do library research, or take a different approach?

b. If you have access to the Internet, provide the results of your learning style assessments. Do these seem to accurately reflect your learning style?

c. If you had to learn how to use a new software application, which approach would you like best: working through a tutorial, using a reference manual, exploring on your own, taking a class, or asking an expert? Why?

d. How does this relate to the way you like to learn other things?

9  **Practice Tests** Have you mastered the material in this chapter? You can test yourself using the Course Test Manager (CTM). If your instructor has installed the CTM software in your lab and given you a user ID and password, you can take practice tests. To start CTM, use the Course Test Manager icon (Windows 3.1) or the Course Test Manager menu option (Windows 95). When prompted, enter your user ID and password. Click the Practice Test button, then select a chapter. You can take as many tests as you like. CTM selects 20 questions at random from a test bank of thousands of questions.

Take a practice test for Chapter 1 and print your results.

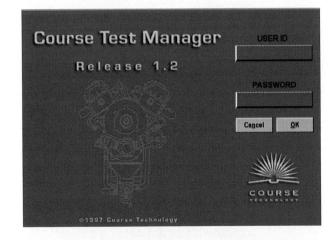

10 **Why Not Just Talk to It?** Computer scientists have discovered that it is quite difficult to develop a "conversational" user interface that you could use to simply "talk" to a computer. One of the stumbling blocks is the ambiguity of human speech. For example, if someone tells you "My friend was looking at a bicycle in the store window, and she wanted it," you assume that "it" refers to the bicycle, not the store window. But English grammar does not make the meaning of "it" explicit, so a computer would have a hard time understanding what you mean. Hubert Dreyfus discusses this problem in the video *The Machine That Changed the World* and in the book entitled *What Computers Still Can't Do*. To pursue this topic, do one or more of the following activities:

a. With a small group of other students, try to think of other examples of ambiguity in human conversation that a computer would probably have difficulty understanding. You can share your list with the rest of the class or turn it in to your instructor.

b. Use the resources from InfoWeb #10 to research this topic so you more fully understand the problem. Write a term paper summarizing your research.

Lab Assignments

The New Perspectives Labs are designed to help you master some of the key computer concepts and skills presented in each chapter of the text. If you are using your school's lab computers, your instructor or technical support person should have installed the Labs software for you. If you want to use the Labs on your home computer, ask your instructor for the appropriate software.

Each Lab has two parts: Steps and Explore. Use Steps first to learn and review concepts. Read the information on each page and do the numbered steps. As you work through the Lab, you will be asked to answer Quick Check questions about what you have learned. At the end of the Lab, you will see a Summary Report of your answers to the Quick Checks. If your instructor wants you to turn in this Summary Report, click the Print button on the Summary Report screen.

When you have completed Steps, you can click the Explore button to complete the Lab Assignments. You can also use Explore to practice the skills you learned and to explore concepts on your own.

If you're viewing this textbook on screen, just click the icon for the Lab you want to use. Otherwise, use the instructions below. Your instructor or technical support person might help you get started.

If you have your own New Perspectives CD-ROM:

1. Insert the NP3 CD and wait a few seconds. If the program doesn't start automatically:

   Windows 95: Click Start, click Run, type d:\start and press Enter.

   Windows 3.1: Click File, click Run, type d:\start and press Enter.

If the New Perspectives software has been installed on a network or local hard disk drive:

1. **Windows 95:** Click Start, point to Programs, point to New Perspectives 3/e, click Textbook 3/e.

   Windows 3.1: Double-click the New Perspectives 3/e group icon, double-click the Textbook 3/e icon.

To select a Lab:

1. From the Computer Concepts menu bar, click Labs, then click the Lab you want to use.

2. Follow the instructions on the screen to enter your name and class section.

3. Read the instructions for using the Lab by clicking the Instructions button.

4. When you are ready to begin the Lab, click the Steps button.

Peripheral Devices

A wide variety of peripheral devices provide expandability for computer systems and provide users with the equipment necessary to accomplish tasks efficiently. In the Peripheral Devices Lab you will use an online product catalog of peripheral devices.

1 Click the Steps button and begin the Steps. Complete the Steps to find out how to use the online product catalog. As you work through the Steps, answer all of the Quick Check questions. When you complete the Steps, you will see a Summary Report of your performance on the Quick Checks. Follow the directions on the screen to print the Summary Report.

2 After you know how to use the product catalog to look up products, features, and prices, use the catalog to do the following:

a. List the characteristics that differentiate printers.

b. List the factors that differentiate monitors.

c. Describe the factors that determine the appropriate type of scanner for a task.

d. List the peripheral devices in the catalog that are specially designed for notebook computers.

3 Suppose that the company that produces the peripheral devices catalog selected your name from its list of customers for a free scanner. You can select any one of the scanners in the catalog. Assume that you own a notebook computer to which you could attach any one of the scanners. Click the Explore button and use the catalog to help you write a one-page paper explaining which scanner you would select, why you would select it, and how you would use it.

4 Suppose you are in charge of a new college computing lab. The lab will include 25 computers that are used by students from all departments at the college. You have a $3,000 budget for printers. Use the product catalog to decide which printers you would purchase for the lab. Write a one-page memo to your boss that justifies your choice.

5 Suppose you own a basic computer system, such as the one in Figure 1-10 of this textbook. You have an idea that you can earn the money for your college tuition by using your computer to help other students produce spiffy reports with color graphs and scanned images. Your parents have agreed to "loan" you $1,000 to get started. Click the Explore button and look through the online peripheral devices catalog. List any of the devices that might help you with this business venture. Write a one-page paper explaining how you would spend your $1,000 to get the equipment you need to start the business.

User Interfaces

You have learned that the hardware and software for a user interface determine how you interact and communicate with the computer. In the User Interfaces Lab, you will try five different user interfaces to accomplish the same task—creating a graph.

1 Click the Steps button to find out how each interface works. As you work through the Steps, answer all of the Quick Check questions. When you complete the Steps, you will see a Summary Report of your performance on the Quick Checks. Follow the directions on the screen to print the Summary Report.

2 In Explore, use each interface to make a 3-D pie graph using data set 1. Title your graphs "Cycle City Sales." Use the percent style to show the percent of each slice of the pie. Print each of the five graphs (one for each interface).

3 In Explore, select one of the user interfaces. Write a step-by-step set of instructions for how to produce a line graph using data set 2. This line graph should show lines and symbols, and have the title "Widget Production."

4 Using the user interface terminology you learned in this Lab and in Chapter 1 of this textbook, write a description of each of the interfaces you used in the Lab. Then, suppose you worked for a software publisher and you were going to create a software package for producing line, bar, column, and pie graphs. Which user interface would you use for the software? Why?

DOS Command-Line User Interface

 The DOS command-line user interface provides a typical example of the advantages and disadvantages of command-line user interfaces. DOS was included with the original IBM PC computers to provide users with a way to accomplish system tasks such as listing, moving, and deleting files on disk. Although today's typical computer user prefers to use a graphical user interface such as Windows, DOS commands still function on most IBM-compatible computers.

1 Click the Steps button to learn how to use the DOS command-line interface. As you work through the Steps, answer all of the Quick Check questions that appear. When you complete the Steps, you will see a Summary Report that summarizes your performance on the Quick Checks. Follow the directions on the screen to print the Summary Report. Remember to use the EXIT command to close the DOS window when you're ready to quit.

2 In Explore, write out your answers to a through d.

a. Explain the different results you get when you use the commands DIR, DIR /p, and DIR /w.

b. What happens if you make a typing error and enter the command DIT instead of DIR? What procedure must you follow to correct your error?

c. Enter the command, DIR /? and explain what happens. Enter the command VER /? and explain what happens. What generalization can you make about the /? command parameter?

d. Enter the command VER /w. Why do you think /w does not work with the VER command word, but it works with DIR?

3 Write a one-page paper summarizing what you know about command-line user interfaces and answering the following questions:

a. Which DOS commands do you now know how to use?

b. How do you know which commands to use to accomplish a task?

c. How do you know what parameters work with each command?

d. What kinds of mistakes can you make that will produce an error message?

e. Can you enter valid commands that don't produce the results you want?

Using a Mouse

 A mouse is a standard input device on most of today's computers. You need to know how to use a mouse to manipulate graphical user interfaces and to use the rest of the Labs.

1 The Steps for the Using a Mouse Lab show you how to click, double-click, and drag objects using the mouse. Click the Steps button and begin the Steps. As you work through the Steps, answer all of the Quick Check questions that appear. When you complete the Steps, you will see a Summary Report that summarizes your performance on the Quick Checks. Follow the directions on the screen to print the Summary Report.

2 In Explore, demonstrate your ability to use a mouse and to control a Windows program by creating a poster. To create a poster for an upcoming sports event, select a graphic, type the caption for the poster, then select a font, font styles, and a border. Print your completed poster.

Using a Keyboard

 To become an effective computer user, you must be familiar with your primary input device—the keyboard.

1 The Steps for the Using a Keyboard Lab provide you with a structured introduction to the keyboard layout and the function of special computer keys. Click the Steps button and begin the Steps. As you work through the Steps, answer all of the Quick Check questions that appear. When you complete the Steps, you will see a Summary Report that summarizes your performance on the Quick Checks. Follow the directions on the screen to print the Summary Report.

2 In Explore, start the typing tutor. You can develop your typing skills using the typing tutor in Explore. Take the typing test and print out your results.

3 In Explore, try to improve your typing speed by 10 words per minute. For example, if you currently type 20 words per minute, your goal would be 30 words per minute. Practice each typing lesson until you see a message that indicates you can proceed to the next lesson. Create a Practice Record as shown here to keep track of how much you practice. When you have reached your goal, print out the results of a typing test to verify your results.

Practice Record

Name: _____

Section: _____

Start Date: _____ Start Typing Speed: _____ wpm

End Date: _____ End Typing Speed: _____ wpm

Lesson #: _____ Date Practiced/Time Practiced _____

SOFTWARE AND MULTIMEDIA APPLICATIONS

2

The quest for multipurpose machines has always enchanted inventors. Soon after the first "horseless carriages" appeared, some inventors dreamed about creating a multipurpose car-boat—a vehicle for both water and land. Car-boats never really caught on. Today, we have a multipurpose machine that is far more useful—the computer.

The computer is the most successful and versatile machine in history. The same computer can produce professionally typeset documents, translate French into English, produce music, diagnose diseases, control machinery, keep track of airline reservations, and much more. A computer's versatility is possible because of software. But what does software do that gives a computer such versatility? What kinds of software can you buy? How do you know what software works with your computer?

In this chapter you will learn how the computer uses software and how you can legally use software. You will learn the difference between system software and application software, and find out about trends in multimedia computing. This chapter ends on a practical note with information about how to install new software on your computer system.

CHAPTER PREVIEW

This chapter contains concepts that help you get started using computer software. Once you understand what kind of software is available, you can select the software that will help you with your work. You can then begin learning how to use it. You also will find out how to use a format utility—an important step if you want to save data on a disk. When you have completed this chapter, you should be able to:

- Determine the legal restrictions placed on your use of software by copyright laws and license agreements
- Describe the purpose of a computer operating system
- Recognize DOS, Windows, UNIX, and Mac OS
- Categorize software as either system software or application software
- Determine the best type of software to use for a specific task
- List the computer equipment you need for multimedia applications
- Determine if a software package is compatible with your computer system

LABS

Multimedia

Computer History Hypermedia

Ⓐ Computer Software Basics

Computer software determines what a computer can do. In a sense, software transforms a computer from one kind of machine to another—from a drafting station to a typesetting machine, from a flight simulator to a calculator, from a filing system to a music studio.

Computer Programs

Do I need to write programs for my computer? A **computer program** is a set of detailed, step-by-step instructions that tells a computer how to solve a problem or carry out a task. Some computer programs handle simple tasks, such as converting feet and inches to centimeters. Longer and more complex computer programs handle very complicated tasks, such as maintaining the accounting records for a business.

The steps in a computer program are written in a language that the computer can interpret and process. As you read through the simple computer program in Figure 2-1, notice the number of steps required to perform a relatively simple calculation.

Figure 2-1

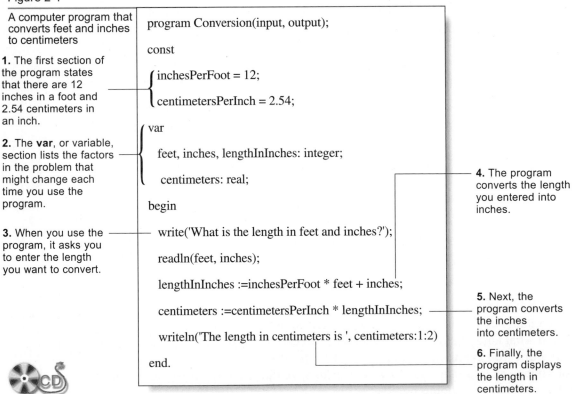

A computer program that converts feet and inches to centimeters

1. The first section of the program states that there are 12 inches in a foot and 2.54 centimeters in an inch.

2. The **var**, or variable, section lists the factors in the problem that might change each time you use the program.

3. When you use the program, it asks you to enter the length you want to convert.

4. The program converts the length you entered into inches.

5. Next, the program converts the inches into centimeters.

6. Finally, the program displays the length in centimeters.

```
program Conversion(input, output);

const
  inchesPerFoot = 12;
  centimetersPerInch = 2.54;

var
  feet, inches, lengthInInches: integer;
   centimeters: real;

begin
  write('What is the length in feet and inches?');

  readln(feet, inches);

  lengthInInches :=inchesPerFoot * feet + inches;

  centimeters :=centimetersPerInch * lengthInInches;

  writeln('The length in centimeters is ', centimeters:1:2)

end.
```

At one time organizations and individuals had to write most of the computer programs they wanted to use, but today most organizations purchase commercially written programs to avoid the time and expense of writing their own. Individuals rarely write computer programs for their personal computers, preferring to select from thousands of commercially written programs, sold as software. Although most computer users do not write their own programs, working as a computer programmer for a business, government agency, or software publisher is a challenging career.

Computer Software

Are computer programs, data, and software the same thing? Software is a basic part of a computer system, but "software" is a term that has more than one definition. In the early days of the computer industry, it became popular to use the term "software" for all the non-hardware components of a computer. In this context, software referred to computer programs and to the data used by the programs.

The U.S. Copyright Act of 1980 defines software as "a set of statements or instructions to be used directly or indirectly in a computer in order to bring about a certain result." This definition implies that computer software is essentially the same as a computer program. It also implies that a collection of data, such as a list of dictionary words, is not software.

In practice, the term "software" is usually used to describe a commercial product, which might include more than a single program and might also include data, as shown in Figure 2-2.

Figure 2-2

A software product

A **software package** contains disks or a CD-ROM and a reference manual.

The CD-ROM contains one or more **programs**, and possibly some data. For example, the Microsoft Office 97 software includes programs that help you draw graphics, write documents, and make calculations. The software also includes some data, such as a thesaurus of words and their synonyms.

In this textbook, we define **software** as instructions and associated data, stored in electronic format, that direct the computer to accomplish a task. Under this definition, computer software may include more than one computer program, if those programs work together to carry out a task. Software also can include data, but data alone is not software. For example, word-processing software might include the data for a dictionary, but the data *you create* using a word processor is not called software. Suppose you write a report using a software package, then store the report on a disk. Your report consists of data rather than instructions for the computer to carry out. Because your report does not contain instructions, it is not software.

"Software" is a plural noun, so there is no such thing as "softwares" or "one software." How, then, do we talk about software in the singular? We often use the term "software package" when we want to talk about a particular example of software.

Copyright
1

Copyrighted Software

Is it illegal to copy software?   Just because you can copy software doesn't make it legal to do so. Like books and movies, most computer software is protected by a copyright. A **copyright** is a form of legal protection that grants certain exclusive rights to the author of a program or the owner of the copyright. The owner of the copyright has the exclusive right to copy the software, to distribute or sell the software, and to modify the software.

When you purchase copyrighted software, you do not become the owner of the copyright. Instead, you have purchased only the right to use the software. Your purchase allows you to use the software on your computer, but you cannot make additional copies to give away or sell. People who illegally copy, distribute, or modify software are sometimes called **software pirates**, and the illegal copies they create are referred to as **pirated software**.

Copyrighted software displays a copyright notice such as "© 1998 Course Technology, Inc." When you start a computer program, the copyright notice usually appears on the first screen; it is also usually printed in the reference manual. Most countries have copyright laws that allow you to copy or modify software only under certain circumstances. If you read the sections of the U.S. Copyright Act shown in Figure 2-3, you will discover under what circumstances you can and cannot legally copy copyrighted software.

Figure 2-3

Sections 106 and 117 of the 1980 U.S. Copyright Act

Section 106. Exclusive Rights in Copyrighted Works
Subject to sections 107 through 118, the owner of copyright under this title has the exclusive rights to do and to authorize any of the following:

(1) to reproduce the copyrighted work in copies or phonorecords;
(2) to prepare derivative works based upon the copyrighted work;
(3) to distribute copies or phonorecords of the copyrighted work to the public by sale or other transfer of ownership, or by rental, lease, or lending…

> Only the copyright owner can reproduce, sell, or distribute the copyrighted software.

Section 117 - Right to Copy or Adapt Computer Programs in Limited Circumstances
Notwithstanding the provisions of section 106, it is not an infringement for the owner of a copy of a computer program to make or authorize the making of another copy or adaptation of the computer program provided:

1. that such a new copy or adaptation is created as an essential step in the utilization of the computer program in conjunction with a machine that is used in no other manner; or

2. that such new copy or adaptation is for archival purposes only and that all archival copies are destroyed in the event that continued possession of the computer program should cease to be rightful. Any exact copies prepared in accordance with the provisions of this section may be leased, sold or otherwise transferred, along with the copy from which such copies were prepared, only as part of the lease, sale, or other transfer of all rights in the program. Adaptations so prepared may be transferred only with the authorization of the copyright owner.

> It is legal to copy the software from the distribution disks to the hard disk of your computer.

> It is legal to make an extra copy of the software in case the copy you are using becomes damaged.

> If you give away or sell the software, you cannot legally keep a copy.

> You cannot legally sell or give away modified copies of the software without permission.

Licensed Software

Do I need to read the small print before I buy software? In addition to copyright protection, computer software is often protected by the terms of a software license. A **software license** is a legal contract that defines the ways in which you may use a computer program. For micro-computer software, you will find the license on the outside of the package, on a separate card inside the package, or in the reference manual. Mainframe software licenses are usually a separate legal document, negotiated between the software publisher and a corporate buyer.

A software license often extends the rights given to you by copyright laws. For example, although copyright law makes it illegal to copy software for use on more than one computer, the license for Claris Works software allows you to buy one copy of the software and install it on your home computer and your office computer as long as you are the primary user of both computers.

Software licenses are often lengthy and written in "legalese," but they are generally divided into manageable sections that you can understand by reading them carefully. Your legal right to use the software continues only as long as you abide by the terms of the software license. Therefore, you should understand the software license for any software you use. To become familiar with a typical license agreement, you can read through the "No-Nonsense License Statement" used for software published by Borland International, shown in Figure 2-4.

Figure 2-4

A software license

This section explains that you can use the software "like a book" meaning that more than one person can use it, but only one at a time.

These sections make provisions for multiple users.

Here, Borland essentially says that you use this software at your own risk.

This software is protected by both United States copyright law and international copyright treaty provisions. Therefore, you must treat this software just like a book, except that you may copy it onto a computer to be used and you may make archival copies of the software for the sole purpose of backing-up our software and protecting your investment from loss.

By saying "just like a book," Borland means, for example, that this software may be used by any number of people, and may be freely moved from one computer location to another, so long as there is no possibility of it being used at one location while it's being used at another or on a computer network by more than one user at one location. Just like a book can't be read by two different people in two different places at the same time, neither can the software be used by two different people in two different places at the same time. (Unless, of course, Borland's copyright has been violated or the use is on a computer network by up to the number of users authorized by additional Borland licenses as explained below.)

LAN PACK MULTIPLE-USE NETWORK LICENSE

If this is a LAN Pack package, it allows you to increase the number of authorized users of your copy of the software on a single computer network by up to the number of users specified in the LAN Pack package (per LAN Pack — see LAN Pack serial number).

USE ON A NETWORK

A "computer network" is any electronically linked configuration in which two or more users have common access to software or data. If more than one user wishes to use the software on a computer network at the same time, then you may add authorized users either by (a) paying for a separate software package for each additional user you wish to add or (b) if a LAN Pack is available for this product, paying for the multiple-use license available in the LAN Pack. You may use any combination of regular software packages or LAN Packs to increase the number of authorized users on a computer network. (In no event may the total number of concurrent users on a network exceed one for each

software package plus the number of authorized users installed from the LAN Pack(s) that you have purchased. Otherwise, you are not using the software "just like a book.") The multiple-use network license for the LAN Pack may only be used to increase the number of concurrent permitted users of the software logged onto the network, and not to download copies of the software for local workstation use without being logged onto the network. You must purchase an individual copy of the software for each workstation at which you wish to use the software without being logged onto the network.

FURTHER EXPLANATION OF COPYRIGHT LAW PROVISIONS AND THE SCOPE OF THIS LICENSE STATEMENT

You may not download or transmit the software electronically (either by direct connection or telecommunication transmission) from one computer to another, except as may be specifically allowed in using the software on a computer network. You may transfer all of your rights to use the software to another person, provided that you transfer to that person

(or destroy) all of the software, diskettes and documentation provided in this package, together with all copies, tangible or intangible, including copies in RAM or installed on a disk, as well as all back-up copies. Remember, once you transfer the software, it may only be used at the single location to which it is transferred and, of course, only in accordance with the copyright laws and international treaty provisions. Except as stated in this paragraph, you may not otherwise transfer, rent, lease, sub-license, time-share, or lend the software, diskettes, or documentation. Your use of the software is limited to acts that are essential steps in the use of the software on your computer or computer network as described in the documentation. You may not otherwise modify, alter, adapt, merge, decompile or reverse-engineer the software, and you may not remove or obscure Borland copyright or trademark notices.

L I M I T E D   W A R R A N T Y

Borland International, Inc. ("Borland") warrants the physical diskette(s) and physical documentation enclosed herein (but not any diskettes or documentation distributed by the Paradox Runtime Licensee) to be free of defects in materials and workmanship for a period of sixty days from the purchase date. If Borland receives notification within the warranty period of defects in materials or workmanship, and such notification is determined by Borland to be correct, Borland will replace the defective diskette(s) or documentation. DO NOT RETURN ANY PRODUCT UNTIL YOU HAVE CALLED THE BORLAND CUSTOMER SERVICE DEPARTMENT AND OBTAINED A RETURN AUTHORIZATION NUMBER.

The entire and exclusive liability and remedy for breach of the Limited Warranty shall be limited to replacement of defective diskette(s) or documentation and shall not include or extend to any claim for or right to recover any other damages, including but not limited to, loss of profit, data, or use of the software, or special, incidental, or consequential damages or other similar claims, even if Borland has been specifically advised of the possibility of such damages. In no event will Borland's liability for any damages to you or any other person ever exceed the lower of suggested list price or actual price paid for the license to use the software, regardless of any form of the claim.

BORLAND INTERNATIONAL, INC. SPECIFICALLY DISCLAIMS ALL OTHER WARRANTIES, EXPRESS OR IMPLIED, INCLUDING BUT NOT LIMITED TO, ANY IMPLIED WARRANTY OF MERCHANTABILITY OR FITNESS FOR A PARTICULAR PURPOSE. Specifically, Borland makes no representation or warranty that the software is fit for any particular purpose and any implied warranty of merchantability is limited to the sixty-day duration of the Limited Warranty covering the physical diskette(s) and physical documentation only (and not the software) and is otherwise expressly and specifically disclaimed.

This limited warranty gives you specific legal rights; you may have others which may vary from state to state. Some states do not allow the exclusion of incidental or consequential damages, or the limitation on how long an implied warranty lasts, so some of the above may not apply to you.

BUSINESS PRODUCTS (With Network Provisions): NO-NONSENSE LICENSE STATEMENT

BUSINESS PRODUCTS (With Network Provisions): NO-NONSENSE LICENSE STATEMENT

This section restates the basic copyright restrictions about transferring software.

Shrink-Wrap Licenses

Do I have to sign a software license for it to be valid? Signing and submitting a license agreement every time you purchase software would be inconvenient, so the computer industry makes extensive use of **shrink-wrap licenses**. When you purchase computer software, the disks or CD-ROM in the package are usually sealed in an envelope or plastic shrink wrapping. A notification, such as the one in Figure 2-5, states that opening the wrapping signifies your agreement to the terms of the software license.

Figure 2-5

When software has a shrink-wrap license, you agree to the terms of the license agreement by opening the package. If you do not agree with the terms, you should return the software unopened.

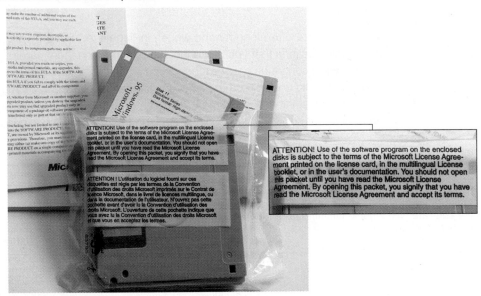

ATTENTION! Use of the software program on the enclosed disks is subject to the terms of the Microsoft License Agreement printed on the license card, in the multilingual License booklet, or in the user's documentation. You should not open this packet until you have read the Microsoft License Agreement. By opening this packet, you signify that you have read the Microsoft License Agreement and accept its terms.

With a shrink-wrap license, the software publisher avoids the lengthy process of negotiating the terms of the license and obtaining your signature. It is essentially a "take it or leave it" approach to licensing. Court rulings in 1996 and 1997 have upheld the validity of shrink-wrap licensing, one of the most frequently used methods for providing legal protection for computer software.

Licenses for More Than One User

If my company has a computer network, does it still have to pay for a license for each user? Most software publishers offer a variety of license options; some are designed for a single user, others for more than one user. A **single-user license** limits the use of the software to one user at a time. Most commercial software is distributed under a single-user license.

A **multiple-user license** allows more than one person to use a particular software package. This type of license is useful in cases where users each have their own personalized version of the software. An electronic mail program would typically have a multiple-user license because users each have their own mailbox. Multiple-user licenses are generally priced per user, but the price for each user is typically less than the price of a single-user license.

A **concurrent-use license** allows a certain number of copies of the software to be used at the same time. For example, if an organization with a computer network has a concurrent-use license for five copies of a word processor, at any one time as many as five employees may use the software. Concurrent-use licenses are usually priced in increments. For example, a company might be able to purchase a concurrent-use license for up to 50 users for $2,500, or up to 250 users for $10,000.

A **site license** generally allows the software to be used on any and all computers at a specific location, such as within a corporate office building or on a university campus. A site license is priced at a flat rate, for example, $5,000 per site.

Shareware

My friend gave me a copy of something called "shareware." Was that illegal?

InfoWeb

Shareware
2

Shareware is copyrighted software marketed under a "try before you buy" policy. Shareware usually includes a license that allows you to use the software for a trial period. If you want to continue to use it, you must send in a registration fee. A shareware license typically allows you to make copies of the software and distribute them to others. This is a fairly effective marketing strategy that provides low-cost advertising. Unfortunately, registration fee payment relies on the honor system, so many shareware authors collect only a fraction of the payment they deserve for their programming efforts. Take a look at the shareware license in Figure 2-6 and notice the rights it includes.

Figure 2-6

A typical shareware license

You can legally make copies and give them away, but you cannot sell them.

You cannot distribute modified copies.

You can become a registered user for $20.

For $45, you will receive the next update of the software.

License

Copyright (c) 1997, 1998 GuildWare, Inc. All Rights Reserved.

You are free to use, copy and distribute TYPER'S TOOLKIT for noncommercial use IF:

    NO FEE IS CHARGED FOR USE, COPYING OR DISTRIBUTION.

    IT IS NOT MODIFIED IN ANY WAY.

Clubs and user groups may charge a nominal fee (less than $10) for expenses and handling while distributing TYPER'S TOOLKIT.

Site licenses, commercial licenses and custom versions of TYPER'S TOOLKIT are available. Write to the address below for more information.

This program is provided AS IS without any warranty, expressed or implied, including but not limited to fitness for a particular purpose.

If you find TYPER'S TOOLKIT fast, easy, and convenient to use, a contribution of $20 would be appreciated. With each contribution of $45 or more you will be registered to receive a diskette with the next version of TYPER'S TOOLKIT when available. Please state the current version of TYPER'S TOOLKIT that you have. Send contributions to:

GuildWare, Inc.
Box 391
Glendale, WI 53209

Public Domain Software

Isn't some software free? Sometimes an author abandons all rights to a particular software title and places it in the public domain, making the program available without restriction. Such software, referred to as **public domain software**, is owned by the public rather than by the author.

Public domain software may be freely copied, distributed, and even resold. The primary restriction on public domain software is that you are not allowed to apply for a copyright on it. Public domain software is fairly rare. It is frequently confused with shareware because it is legal to copy and distribute both public domain software and shareware.

Software Categories

What's the difference between system software and application software? Because there are so many software titles, categorizing software as either system software or application software is useful. **System software** helps the computer carry out its basic operating tasks. **Application software** helps the human user carry out a task.

System software and application software are further divided into subcategories. As you continue to read this chapter, use Figure 2-7 to help you visualize the hierarchy of software categories.

Figure 2-7

Software categories

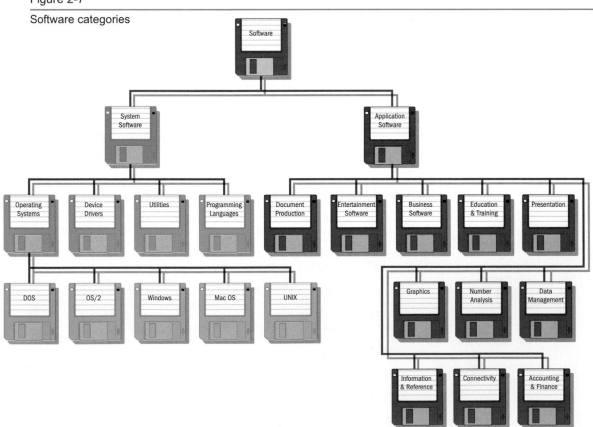

To many computer users, the difference between system software and applications software seems somewhat arbitrary. To clarify the difference, you can generally classify software as system software if the only reason you need that software is because you have a computer. For example, if you didn't have a computer, you would not need an operating system, or device drivers, or computer programming languages.

You would put software in the application software category if it computerizes something you might do even without a computer. For example, you would write letters and papers even if you didn't have a computer, so the software you use to create documents would be classified as application software.

Admittedly, some software is still difficult to classify. For example, the software you use to connect your computer to the Internet is called communications software. You would not be connecting to the Internet if you did not have a computer, and yet communications software has additional features such as voice calls, voice mail, and faxing that you might do without a computer. As you read the next section of this chapter on application software you'll develop a better idea of how it differs from system software.

QuickCheck A

1. If you use a computer to write a report, the report is considered software. True or false? _____

2. To use a computer effectively, you need to be a computer programmer. True or false? _____

3. When you type a report or enter the information for a mailing list, you are creating _____.

4. The instructions that tell a computer how to convert inches to centimeters are a computer _____.

5. To use a computer to write and edit documents, you need word-processing _____.

6. The "try before you buy" policy refers to _____ licenses.

7. A(n) _____ for microcomputer or mainframe software is a contract by which the software publisher grants the buyer permission to use the software.

8. _____ software helps the *computer* carry out its basic operating tasks, whereas _____ software helps a human user carry out tasks.

⅛ System Software

System software is the category of software containing programs that perform tasks essential to the efficient functioning of computer hardware. System software includes the programs that direct the fundamental operations of a computer, such as displaying information on the screen, storing data on disks, sending data to the printer, interpreting commands typed by users, and communicating with peripheral devices.

Let's look at some of the specific functions of the four subcategories of system software: operating systems, utilities, device drivers, and computer programming languages.

Operating Systems

| Why does a computer need an operating system? | An **operating system** is the software that controls the computer's use of its hardware resources such as memory and disk storage space. You might be familiar with the names of the most popular microcomputer operating systems: Microsoft Windows, DOS, OS/2, and Mac OS. Minicomputer and mainframe operating systems include UNIX, VMS, and MVS.

An operating system works like an air traffic controller to coordinate the activities within the computer. Just as an airport cannot function without air traffic controllers, a computer cannot function without an operating system. When you purchase a microcomputer, the operating system is usually pre-installed on the hard disk and ready to use. You "see" the operating system each time you turn on your computer, and the operating system provides a variety of services that you can use to run programs and manage your data.

If you envision computer hardware as the core of your computer system, then the operating system provides the next layer of functionality by assisting the computer with its basic hardware operations. The operating system also interacts with the next layer—application software—to carry out application tasks such as printing and saving data. Figure 2-8 helps you envision the relationship between your computer hardware, the operating system, and application software.

Figure 2-8

Application software requires the operating system to carry out hardware related tasks such as printing reports and storing data on disks.

The **operating system** acts as a liaison between the computer hardware and application software.

The **computer hardware** is the core of the system, but the hardware cannot function without an operating system.

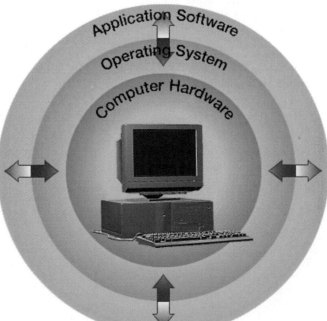

Let's look at a specific example of how the operating system works as a liaison between the computer hardware and application software. Suppose you use application software to write a letter and then you want to print it. The operating system helps the application software communicate with your computer's printer, as shown in Figure 2-9.

Figure 2-9

The operating system helps the application software print a document.

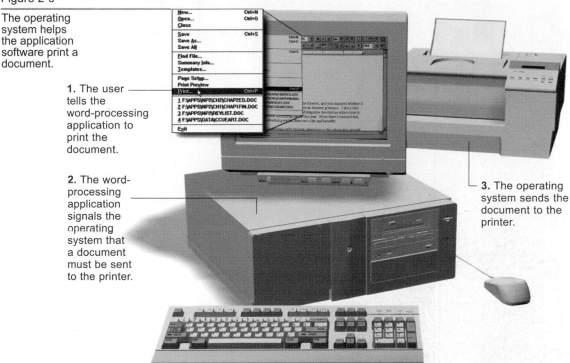

1. The user tells the word-processing application to print the document.

2. The word-processing application signals the operating system that a document must be sent to the printer.

3. The operating system sends the document to the printer.

Operating systems for micro, mini, and mainframe computers perform many similar services. These services can be classified either as "external" or "internal."

The operating system provides **external services** that help users start programs, manage stored data, and maintain security. You, as the computer user, control these external functions. Using a command-line, menu-driven, or GUI user interface, an operating system provides you with a way to select the programs you would like to use. The operating system also helps you find, rename, and delete documents and other data stored on disk or tape. On many, but not all computer systems, the operating system helps you maintain security by checking your user ID and password, as well as protecting your data from unauthorized access and revisions.

The operating system provides **internal services** "behind the scenes" to ensure that the computer system functions efficiently. These internal services are not generally under your control, but instead are controlled by the operating system itself. The operating system controls input and output, allocates system resources, manages the storage space for programs and data, and detects equipment failure without any direction from you. Study Figure 2-10 on the next page to discover more about what an operating system does.

Figure 2-10

Operating system services

Control Basic Input and Output

An operating system controls the flow of data into and out of the computer, as well as the flow of data to and from peripheral devices. It routes input to areas of the computer where it can be processed and routes output to the screen, a printer, or any other output device you request.

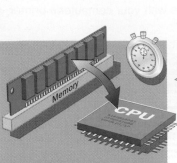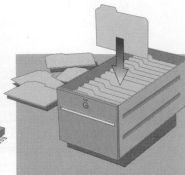

Allocate System Resources

A **system resource** is any part of a computer system, such as a disk drive, memory, printer, or processor time, that can be used by a computer program. The operating system allocates system resources so programs run properly.

For example, each program instruction takes up space inside the computer and each instruction requires a certain amount of time to complete. The operating system ensures that adequate space is available for each program that is running and makes sure the processor quickly performs each program instruction.

The operating system also manages the additional resources required for using multiple programs or for providing services to more than one user at the same time. For example, if you want to run two or more programs at the same time, a process called **multitasking**, the operating system ensures that each program has adequate space and that the computer devotes an appropriate amount of time to the tasks prescribed by each program.

To accommodate more than one user at a time, an operating system must have multiuser capabilities. You typically find **multiuser** operating systems on mainframe and minicomputer systems, where users each have their own terminal but share the processing capability of a single main computer. Multiuser operating systems typically provide speedy service so users each think they are the only ones using the computer.

Manage Storage Space

The operating system keeps track of the data stored on disks and CD-ROMs. Think of your disks as filing cabinets, your data as papers stored in file folders, and the operating system as a filing clerk. The filing clerk takes care of filing a folder when you finish using it. When you need something from your filing cabinet, you ask the filing clerk to get it. The filing clerk knows where to find your folder. On your computer system, the operating system stores your data at some location on a disk. Although you might not know exactly where your data is stored on the disk, when you need the data again, you only need to ask the operating system to retrieve it.

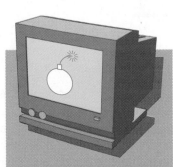

Detect Equipment Failure

The operating system monitors the status of critical computer components to detect failures that affect processing. When you turn on your computer, the operating system checks each of the electronic components and takes a quick inventory of the storage devices. For example, if an electrical component inside your computer fails, the operating system displays a message identifying the problem and does not let you continue with the computing session until the problem is fixed.

Maintain Security

The operating system also helps maintain security for the data on the computer system. For example, the operating system might not allow you to access the computer system unless you have a user ID and password.

Operating
Systems
3

Microcomputer Operating Systems

> As a computer user, why is it important for me to know which operating system is on my computer?

Today's popular operating systems for the PC platform include DOS, Windows, and OS/2. The Macintosh operating system is called Mac OS. UNIX is available for both PCs and Macintosh computers. Versions of UNIX and Windows are also available for minicomputers and mainframes.

You interact directly with your computer's operating system to start programs and manage the data on your disks. You need to know which operating system your computer uses so you can enter the appropriate instructions to accomplish these tasks. How can you tell which operating system your computer uses? Many microcomputer users can recognize an operating system by looking at the first screen that appears when they turn the computer on or by recognizing the operating system prompt. If you study Figures 2-11 through 2-15, you can identify the DOS, Mac OS, Windows 3.1, Windows 95, and UNIX operating systems when you encounter them in the future.

Figure 2-11

DOS

The **DOS prompt** is a distinguishing feature of MS-DOS and PC-DOS.

The **cursor** shows your place on the screen.

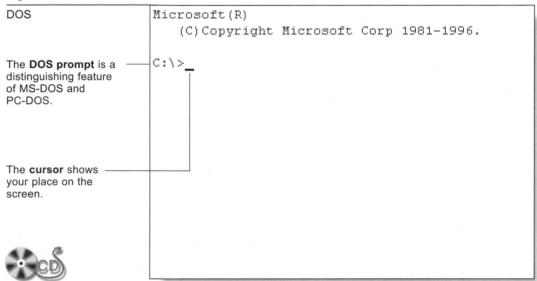

```
Microsoft(R)
      (C)Copyright Microsoft Corp 1981-1996.

C:\>_
```

DOS, which stands for Disk Operating System, is marketed under the trade names PC-DOS and MS-DOS. Both PC-DOS and MS-DOS were developed primarily by Microsoft Corporation and are essentially the same operating system.

DOS was introduced in 1981 with IBM's first personal computer. Since the first version of DOS appeared, this operating system has gone through six major versions.

DOS has been replaced by the Windows operating system on most of today's computers.

Figure 2-12

Microsoft
Windows 3.1
operating
system

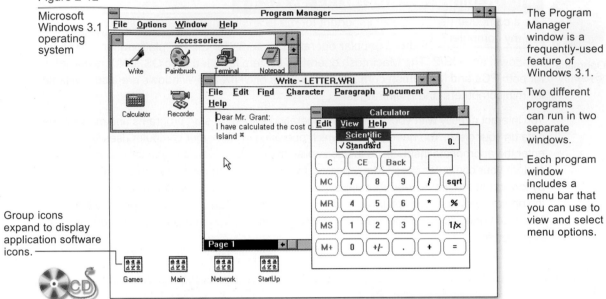

The Program
Manager
window is a
frequently-used
feature of
Windows 3.1.

Two different
programs
can run in two
separate
windows.

Each program
window
includes a
menu bar that
you can use to
view and select
menu options.

Group icons
expand to display
application software
icons.

Microsoft took a more graphical approach to operating systems when it designed Windows. **Microsoft Windows 3.1** provides icons that you can directly manipulate on the screen using a pointing device, and pull-down menus you can use to easily issue a command. The applications you use with Windows 3.1 all have a consistent look, so it is easy to learn how to use new software.

Windows 3.1 also lets you run more than one program at a time in separate windows on the screen, and lets you easily transfer data between them. While using Windows 3.1, you can still run DOS software.

Figure 2-13

Microsoft Windows 95
and Windows 98
operating systems

Icons represent
computer hardware
components and
software.

Two
different
programs
can run
in two
separate
windows.

Each
program
window
includes a
menu bar
that you
can use
to view
and
select
menu
options.

The Start button is a
unique feature of
Windows 95 and
Windows 98.

The task
bar
shows
which
programs
are
running.

In 1995, Microsoft introduced Windows 95, an operating system that offered better operating efficiency than Windows 3.1. In 1998, Microsoft introduced Windows 98 to add

enhanced Internet features. The **Windows 95** and **Windows 98** interfaces are similar. They use icons to represent objects such as computers, disk drives, and documents. These operating systems

run software designed for Windows 3.1 and DOS. In addition, they support multitasking, networking, and Internet access.

Figure 2-14

Mac OS

Apple icon

Pull down
menu

Windows

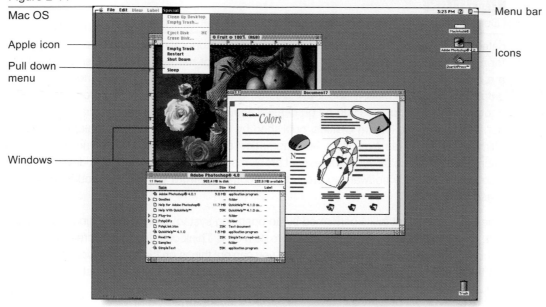

Menu bar

Icons

In 1984, Apple Computer, Inc.
took a revolutionary step when it
introduced the Apple Lisa computer
with a new operating system based
on a graphical user interface featuring pull-down menus, icons, and a
mouse.

The Lisa computer was not a commercial success, but Apple's next
product, the Macintosh computer,
was very successful and defined a
new direction in operating system
user interfaces that became an
industry standard.

The **Macintosh operating system**
is usually referred to by its version
number. For example, version
eight of the operating system is
called Mac OS 8. The Macintosh
operating system has multitasking
capability and offers network
support.

Figure 2-15

UNIX operating
system

UNIX prompt

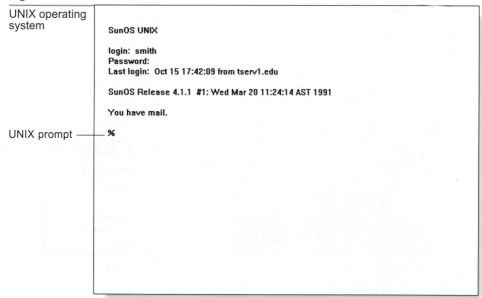

UNIX is an operating system
that was developed at AT&T's
Bell Laboratories in 1969. UNIX
was originally designed for minicomputers, but is now also
available for microcomputers
and mainframes.

UNIX features a command-line
user interface, but you can purchase add-on software that provides a graphical user interface
with direct object manipulation
and pull-down menus.

UNIX is a multiuser operating
system, which means that many
users can run programs on a
single computer at the same
time. UNIX also supports multitasking. UNIX is popular with
companies that provide information on the Internet.

Utilities

Does the operating system include all the system software I need? **Utilities** are a subcategory of system software designed to augment the operating system by providing a way for a computer user to control the allocation and use of hardware resources. Some utilities are included with the operating system; they perform tasks such as preparing disks to hold data, providing information about the files on a disk, and copying data from one disk to another. Additional utilities can be purchased separately from software publishers and vendors. For example, Norton Utilities, published by Symantec, is a very popular collection of utility software. It retrieves data from damaged disks, makes your data more secure by encrypting it, and helps you troubleshoot problems with your computer's disk drives. You can also purchase utility software to protect your computer from viruses that could damage or erase your data.

One of the important tasks performed by an operating system utility is formatting a disk. Each disk must be formatted before you can store data on it. Think of formatting as creating the electronic equivalent of storage shelves. Before you can put things on the shelves, you must assemble the shelves. In a similar way, before you can store data on a disk, you must make sure the disk is formatted.

You can buy preformatted disks, but you still might need a disk format utility if you use a disk that has not been preformatted or a disk that was formatted previously for a different type of computer. Figure 2-16 shows how to use the format utility for Windows 95.

Figure 2-16

Using the Windows 95 format utility

1. Insert the disk you want to format and click the **My Computer** icon to select it, then press **Enter**.

3. Click **File** on the menu bar, then click **Format** to open the Format window.

2. Click the **3½ Floppy (A:)** icon in the My Computer window.

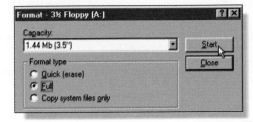

4. Make sure the Capacity box matches the size of the disk you want to format, then click the **Start** button.

Device Drivers

How do I use a device driver? In Chapter 1, you learned that when you purchase a new peripheral device, such as a CD-ROM drive or a mouse, you often need to install software that tells your computer how to use the device. The system software that helps the computer control a peripheral device is called a **device driver**.

When you purchase a new peripheral device, its installation instructions usually tell you how to install both the device and the necessary device drivers. The way you "use" a device driver is to install it according to the instructions. Once the device driver is installed correctly, the computer uses it "behind the scenes" to communicate with the device.

Computer Programming Languages

Is a computer programming language included with a basic computer system? As you know, a computer program is a series of instructions that the computer follows to perform a task. However, the list of instructions written by a human programmer is quite different from the instructions that the computer actually follows. The programmer's instructions must be translated into electrical signals that the computer can manipulate and process.

A **computer programming language** allows a programmer to write programs using English-like instructions, such as those you saw in Figure 2-1. These instructions are translated into a format the computer can interpret and directly process.

As mentioned earlier in this chapter, most computer users do not need to write programs. Therefore, most computers do not include a computer programming language. If you want to write programs, you must purchase programming language software. Today some of the most popular programming languages are BASIC, Visual Basic, C, C++, COBOL, Ada, and FORTRAN. Programming languages such as Java, JavaScript, J++, VBscript, CGI, and Perl are optimized to provide additional interactivity and animations on Web pages.

QuickCheck B

1. If you want to run more than one program at a time, you must use an operating system with _____ capability.

2. _____ is a multiuser operating system.

3. The DOS, Windows, and Mac OS operating systems are typically used on _____ computer systems.

4. The _____ operating system is popular with companies that supply information on the Internet.

5. _____ software helps the computer accomplish such tasks as preparing a disk for data, providing information about the files on a disk, copying data from one disk to another, and retrieving data from damaged disks.

6. You install a(n) _____ to tell the computer how to use a new peripheral device.

7. A(n) _____ allows you to write computer programs using English-like instructions.

C Application Software

Now let's return to the idea presented at the beginning of this chapter—that the computer is a multipurpose machine. Although system software handles internal computer functions and helps the computer use peripheral devices, it doesn't transform the computer into the different kinds of machines you need to write reports, "crunch" numbers, learn how to type, or draw pictures. It is application software that enables the computer to become a multipurpose machine and to perform many different tasks.

Software categorized as **application software** helps you accomplish a specific task using the computer. Application software helps you produce documents, perform calculations, manage financial resources, create graphics, compose music, play games, maintain files of information, and so on. Application software packages are sometimes referred to simply as **applications**.

Software Jargon

What's all this talk about groupware, suites, and productivity software? When you shop for computer software in catalogs or stores, you might encounter terms such as "productivity software," "suites," and "groupware." These terms describe broad categories of applications software.

InfoWeb

Application Software 4

As you might expect from its name, **productivity software** helps you work more effectively. Used by individuals, businesses, or organizations, the most popular types of productivity software include word-processing, spreadsheet, data management, and scheduling. The term **suite** or **office suite** refers to a number of applications that are packaged together and sold as a unit. A typical suite includes software you would use to write documents, work with numbers, create graphics, and keep track of data. **Groupware** provides a way for more than one person to collaborate on a project. It facilitates group document production, scheduling, and communication. Often it maintains a pool of data that can be shared by members of the workgroup.

Software is also categorized by how it is used. For example, document production software helps you create, edit, and publish documents. Software in the connectivity software connects your computer to the Internet, to other computers, and to networks. The names of these functional categories are not consistent. For example, browsing through different software catalogs and perusing the shelves of computer stores, you might notice that connectivity software is sometimes referred to as communications software. As with much of the terminology that is in daily use by non-technical people, software categories might seem somewhat imprecise, but you often can figure out by using common sense.

Figure 2-17

The array of application software is extensive.

How much you use a computer, how much time it helps you save, and how much it improves the quality of your work depends on the software you select and use. The array of software applications is extensive, as you can see from Figure 2-17 and as you read on.

Document Production Software

What software should I use to produce documents? Whether you are writing a 10-page term paper, writing software documentation, designing a brochure for your new start-up company, or laying out the school newspaper, you will probably use some form of document production software. **Document production software** as the term implies, assists you with composing, editing, designing, and printing documents. The three most popular types of document production software are word-processing, desktop publishing, and Web authoring software.

Word-processing software has replaced typewriters for producing documents such as reports, letters, papers, and manuscripts. Individuals use word-processing software for correspondence, students use it to write reports and papers, writers use it for novels, reporters use it to compose news stories, scientists use it to write research reports, and business people use it to write memos, reports, and marketing materials. Because documents are in an electronic format, it is easy to reuse them, share them, and even collaborate on them.

Word-processing software gives you the ability to create, spell check, edit, and format a document on the screen before you commit it to paper. When you are satisfied with the content of your document, you can use formatting and page layout features of your word-processing software to create a professional-looking printout. Today's best-selling word-processing software includes Microsoft Word, Claris WordPerfect, and Lotus Word Pro.

InfoWeb

Desktop
Publishing
5

Desktop publishing software takes word-processing software one step further by helping you use graphic design techniques to enhance the format and appearance of a document. Although many page layout and design features are available in today's word-processing software, desktop publishing software provides more sophisticated features to help you produce professional quality output for newspapers, newsletters, brochures, magazines, and books. Figure 2-18 illustrates the professional results you can achieve with desktop publishing software such as Quark XPress, Adobe Pagemaker, Corel VENTURA, and Microsoft Publisher.

Figure 2-18

For documents with many graphics that will be produced by a professional printer, you should consider using desktop publishing software instead of word-processing software. Desktop publishing software is typically the tool of choice for newspapers, magazines, and books, such as the one you are reading.

Web page authoring software helps you design and develop customized Web pages that you can publish electronically on the Internet. Only a few years ago, creating Web pages was a fairly technical task that required authors to use hypertext markup language (HTML) "tags" such as <A HREF = "contents.htm">. Now, Web page design software helps authors avoid HTML by providing tools to compose the text for a Web page, assemble graphical elements, and automatically generate HTML tags. Best-selling software in this category includes Claris Home Page and Microsoft Front Page.

Graphics Software

What's the best graphics software? | **Graphics software** helps you create, edit, and manipulate images. These images could be photographs that you're planning to insert in a real estate brochure, a freehand portrait, a detailed engineering drawing of a Harley-Davidson motorcycle, or a cartoon animation. The graphics software you select depends on the type of image you're creating. Although best-selling graphics packages such as Adobe Illustrator, CorelDRAW, and Micrografx Graphics Suite handle more than one type of image, few graphics packages handle all image types. Once you know the type of image you need, you can read software descriptions and reviews to find the graphics software that's right for you.

Photos. Suppose you want to include photos in a document, brochure, greeting card, poster, or presentation. Photo editing features of graphics software help you crop photos, modify colors, remove red eye, combine elements from more than one photo, and apply special effects.

Paintings. If you have artistic talent and you want to use the computer to create sketches and paintings, you'll be working with a **bitmapped image**. Painting features allow you to create and edit bitmapped images on screen that look like water colors, oil paint, chalk, ink, or charcoal.

InfoWeb

3-D
Graphics
6

Drawings and 3-D objects. Images composed of lines and filled shapes are called **vector graphics**. Their advantage is the relatively small amount of storage space they require. Vector graphics images are easy to manipulate as shown in Figure 2-19.

Figure 2-19

You can create a wireframe drawing of a car, then rotate it to view it from the back, sides, or front. A process called **rendering** creates a 3-D solid image by covering the wireframe and applying computer-generated highlights and shadows.

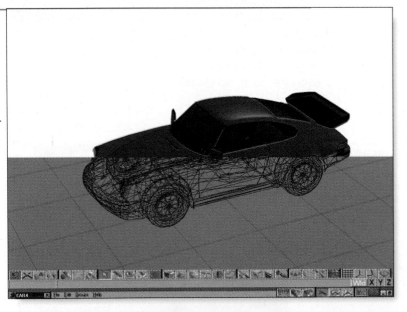

Animations and videos. You can spark up computer presentations by adding animated cartoons or video clips. You can also use animations and videos to illustrate educational tutorials or reference materials. Animation software streamlines the process of creating a series of still frames that produce an animated sequence. You can use graphics software to capture videos from your television, camcorder, or VCR. The software helps you edit the video by cutting out unwanted footage and adding a sound track. The process of converting videos into a format that can be stored on a computer disk is called **digitizing.**

Presentation Software

How do I use the computer to create snazzy speeches and presentations? Suppose you are taking an art history course. Fifty percent of your grade will be based on an in-class presentation. Is there software that can help you? Yes, it's called presentation software. Two of the most popular applications are Microsoft PowerPoint and Lotus Freelance Graphics.

Figure 2-20

A slide typically contains a title, a bulleted list, and a graphic.

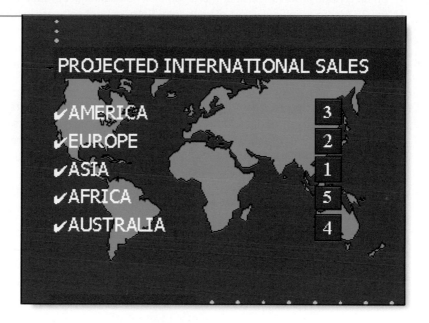

Presentation software provides all the tools you need for combining text, graphics, graphs, animations, and sound into a series of electronic **slides** like the one shown in Figure 2-20. Most presentation software includes collections of graphics and sounds that can enhance your presentation. After you create your slides, use the presentation software to organize them into a compelling visual story for your audience.

InfoWeb

Presentations 7

You can output the presentation as overhead transparencies, paper copies, or 35mm slides. You can display the slides on a color monitor for a one-on-one presentation or run the slide show for a group using a computer projection device as shown in Figure 2-21.

Figure 2-21

A projection device displays slides on a large wall screen.

Numeric Analysis Software

What kind of software do I use for number crunching? **Numeric analysis software** simplifies tasks such as constructing numeric models of physical and social systems, then analyzing those models to predict trends and understand patterns. Numeric analysis software includes spreadsheets, graphing packages, and statistical packages.

Spreadsheet software performs calculations based on numbers and formulas that you enter. A handy tool for quick or more complex calculations, spreadsheet software also allows you to create graphical views of your data. Spreadsheet software is frequently used by financial analysts to examine investment opportunities, by managers to create budgets, and even by educators to keep track of student grades, and by individuals to track household budgets, analyze retirement investments, and balance checkbooks. Top-selling packages include Microsoft Excel and Lotus 1-2-3.

Graphing software transforms complex data into meaningful graphs that allow you to visualize and explore data. When you put numerical data into a graphical format, you can see patterns and relationships that might not otherwise be apparent. Graphing software performs basic calculations and statistical procedures similar to those in spreadsheet or statistical software, but gives you added formatting flexibility to create more visually attractive graphs. Consider using graphing software if your spreadsheet or statistical package does not produce the kind or quality of graph you require.

Statistical software helps you analyze large sets of data to discover patterns and relationships. It is a helpful tool for summarizing survey results, test scores, experiment results, or population data. Most statistical software includes graphing capability so you can display and explore your data visually. Software such as SPSS, JMP, and Data Desk offer a full line of sophisticated statistical analysis tools (Figure 2-22).

Figure 2-22

To use statistical software, you first enter your data, then select a statistical procedure. The software displays your results as a table or graph.

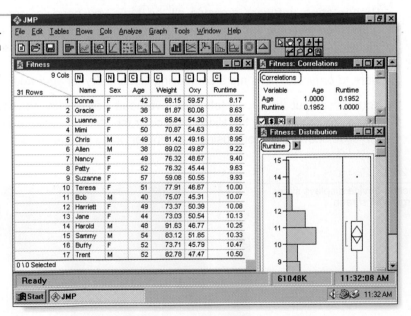

Data Management Software

How can I keep track of information? We live in an information society. We value information and we collect information—tons of it. **Data management software** helps us store, find, update, organize, and report information.

In computer jargon, a **flat file** stores information in records similar to the 3 x 5 cards or Rolodex cards. **File management software** helps you organize these records, find records that match specific criteria, and print lists based on the information. File management software is ideal for working with simple lists of information such as holiday card addresses, doctor visits, and household inventory.

Unlike a single flat file, a **database** is a collection of related files. **Database management software** or **database software** provides a flexible way to join and summarize the information in more than one file. For example, suppose you are the curator for an extensive collection of classic rock videos for MTV. You have a computer file of all the videos. You also have a file of the performers. While looking at the information on Michael Jackson's *Thriller* video, you wonder how old he was when the video was recorded. Instead of closing the video file and opening the performer file, you can use your database software to, in effect, join the two files together so you can see all the information about *Thriller* and Michael Jackson at the same time.

Database software is probably used more frequently by business, government, and education than by individuals. Microsoft Access, Lotus Approach, and Claris File Maker Pro are popular examples of database software for microcomputers. If you're using a database on a mainframe computer, it is likely to be Oracle 7 or IBM's DB2.

A **search engine** helps you find information. File management and database software both include a search engine capable of finding any record you specify in a fraction of a second. You can also purchase separate search engine software that is designed specially to help you find information from the huge pool of documents on the Web. Search engine software that runs on your computer is sometimes dubbed a **personal search engine** to distinguish it from the search engines that are provided at Web sites (Figure 2-23). Popular personal search engines include ForeFront, WebSeeker, and Symantec FastFind.

Figure 2-23

The advantage of a personal search engine is that it can automatically search through more than 20 Web site indexes, delete duplicate results, then provide you with the links you need to go directly to the relevant information.

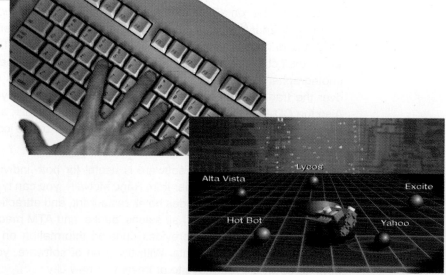

Information and Reference Software

How do I locate facts, figures, and other information? **Information and reference software** provides you with a collection of information and a way to access that information. The fact that this software includes massive amounts of data distinguishes it from data management software, which contains no data. The information and reference software category spans a broad range of applications from encyclopedias to medical reference, from map software to trip planners, and from cookbooks to telephone books. The options are as broad as the full range of human interests.

Information and reference software is generally shipped on a CD-ROM disk because of the quantity of information it includes. With many of these products, links between the CD-ROM and a Web site provide updates to information that has gone out of date. Other software publishers have eliminated the CD-ROM entirely and placed all their reference materials on the Web. Access to that information often requires a fee or a subscription.

Figure 2-24

Listings Deluxe bills itself as the "largest warehouse of reference data ever compiled in a single box." It claims to help you find phone numbers for any home or business in the U.S. or Canada, print street maps of every city in the U.S., look up 450,000 Web addresses, and summarize census data for any region of the U.S.

The most popular software in this category—encyclopedias—contain text, graphics, audio, and video on a full range of topics from apples to zenophobia. Best sellers include Microsoft's Encarta, IBM's World Book encyclopedia, Grolier's encyclopedia, Compton's encyclopedia, and Britannica's CD. All these titles contain the standard information you would expect from an encyclopedia—articles written by experts on various topics, maps, photographs, and timelines. There are several advantages to a CD-ROM encyclopedia over the traditional print versions. Finding the information you are looking for is easier. Also the CD-ROM takes up less space, is more affordable, and includes video and audio clips. The lower cost allows the average person to own a comprehensive encyclopedia, an invaluable resource for research and learning.

Mapping and trip planning software is useful for both individuals and business people. With software like Streetfinder from Rand McNally, you can type an address, and view and print a detailed map. It includes hotel, restaurant, and attraction information; business listings, such as dry cleaners, hair salons, banks, and ATM machines; and links to the Rand McNally Web site, which provides updated information on road construction, weather reports, and seasonal events. With this type of software, you never again need to feel bewildered when you move to or travel to a new city.

Connectivity Software

Do I need special software to connect to other computers and the Internet? By now, most people know that networks and the Internet are the hot technology tickets to an amazing world of information and interaction. **Connectivity software** connects your computer to a local computer network or the Internet and provides you with tools to take advantage of the information and communications they offer. Connectivity software includes basic communications software, remote control software, e-mail, and Web browsers.

Communications software interacts with your computer's modem to dial and establish a connection with a remote computer. Basic communications software is now built into most microcomputer operating systems and is sometimes classified as system utility software.

Suppose you have a computer in your office and a notebook computer at home. You're home one evening and need some information that's stored on your office computer. If both computers have modems and the computer in your office is on, you can use **remote control software** to establish a connection between the two machines. Using the keyboard of your notebook computer, you can control your office computer to locate and view the information you need. Popular remote control applications include Procomm Rapid Remote, pcANYWHERE, ReachOut, LapLink, and Remotely Possible.

E-mail is, perhaps, the heart of Internet activity. It helps you stay in touch with friends, relatives, colleagues, and business associates. **E-mail software** manages your computer mailbox. The preferred e-mail software with over 10 million users, is Eudora from Qualcomm, but Microsoft Internet Mail and Lotus Notes are popular alternatives.

InfoWeb

Web
Browsers
8

To access information on the Web, you need communications software and an additional software package called a Web browser. **Web browser software** allows you to view Web pages and manages the links that you use to jump from one document to the next. The two leading Web browsers are Netscape Navigator and Microsoft Internet Explorer. A coming trend, shown in Figure 2-25, is to combine browser-like capabilities with the operating system user interface so you can browse and manage files on your PC in much the same way that you surf through pages on the Web.

Figure 2-25

Microsoft's Internet Explorer 4.0 Web browser turns familiar desktop elements, such as the My Computer icon, into clickable links.

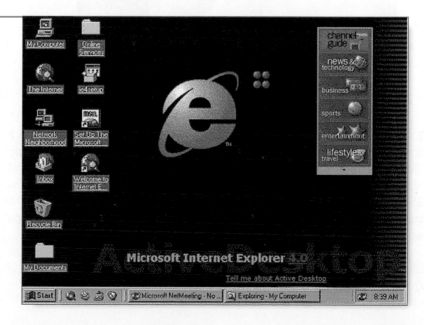

Education and Training Software

Can I use software to improve my grades? Do your keyboarding skills need a bit of polish? Do you want to help your children learn and have fun at the same time? Are you the head of human resources and find that your company's managers don't understand all the fuss about diversity? Where will you turn for help? You might very well find your answers in education and training software.

Education and training software helps you learn and perfect new skills. For the youngest ages, educational software, such as The Learning Company's Reader Rabbit and Math Rabbit, teach basic reading and counting skills. Instruction is presented as games that children can play, and different levels of play adapt to the child's age and ability.

For older students and adults, software is available to help learn languages, learn how to play the piano, prepare for standardized tests, improve keyboarding skills, and even learn about managing in a diverse workplace. Exam preparation software is available for standardized tests such as the SAT, GMAT, and LSAT. Although little research is available on the effectiveness of this software, experts believe the results should be similar to those of in-person coaching courses that improve composite SAT scores by about 100 points. Figure 2-26 explains more about exam preparation software.

Figure 2-26

Exam preparation software assesses your skill level, coaches you on your weak skills, and provides test-taking tips.

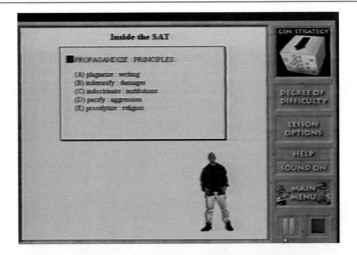

Education and training software is often called **edutainment software** because it blurs some of the lines between learning and game playing. By far, the most active segment of the edutainment industry is childrens' software. In 1996, entertainment and education software titles accounted for about 60 percent of all software sold, and retail sales were about $550 million. There are about 15,000 titles available, and the average price of an edutainment program is $40. Experts expect the edutainment industry to grow to $8 billion worldwide by the year 2000.

Entertainment Software

Are computers changing the way we spend our spare time? Worldwide computer and video game software sales annually exceed $10 billion. Publishers invest 18 months and up to $2 million to create and produce a successful entertainment software title. Overall, the entertainment software industry employs about 90,000 workers and is increasing its employees by 26 percent per year—better than most Fortune 500 companies. Clearly, entertainment software is big business as well as fun business. What is entertainment software? It includes games of all sorts, software toys, simulations, and software designed to help you enjoy hobbies and leisure activities.

InfoWeb

Games Galore 9

Generally, **game software** is divided into six main categories: action, adventure/role playing, classic/puzzle, simulations, and strategy/war games. Many of the most popular games are available in multiple formats. You can play them alone on your PC, in multiplayer environments via the Internet, or on a stand-alone game console such as Sega or Nintendo.

Adventure/role playing software has realistic 3-D graphics, allows players to interact with the environment, and has weapons and monsters galore. Some of the most popular adventure/role playing titles are Duke Nukem, Doom, Diablo, Quake, and Tomb Raider. Games vary in their level of violence, and many new games come with password options that allow parents to reduce the amount of R-rated material. **Action games** like the one shown in Figure 2-27 are similar to arcade games.

Figure 2-27

Guiding an action figure past obstacles requires fast thinking and good reflexes.

Simulation software covers a broad range of interests. With SimCity you develop a city. The computer populates your city with "Simmies" that clog your streets, trash your parks, and threaten to remove you from office if you don't supply better city services. With Nascar Racing 2, you can get in the driver's seat of a stock car and test your driving skills on one of 16 authentic Nascar tracks. You can shoot a round of golf with Tiger Woods, fly fighter planes, attack helicopters, or even strap into the pilot's seat of an X-wing fighter from Star Wars.

With the industry growing at a rapid pace and new technology creating ever more sophisticated multimedia capabilities, the future of entertainment software appears to be limited only by how much money consumers are willing to spend.

Accounting and Finance Software

Can software help me manage my money? If you've been reading the newspapers, then you are probably aware of the predictions that social security is likely to run out of money sometime in the next 50 years. It is never too early to start saving and investing money. The earlier you start, the more likely you will be able to have financial security by the time you are ready to retire. If retirement seems too far away to worry about, you probably have some other short-term financial goals such as earning enough money for next year's tuition, buying a new multimedia PC, or saving $2,000 for a trip to Australia. Without a financial plan, you might never reach these goals. Software can help you keep track of your money and progress toward financial goals.

Money Management 10

Accounting and finance software keeps a record of monetary transactions and investments. In this category, **personal finance software** is geared toward individual finances by helping you keep track of bank accounts, credit cards, investments, and your bills. Some packages support **online banking**—a way to use your computer and modem to download transactions directly from your bank, transfer funds among accounts, and pay bills. The best selling personal finance software program is Intuit's Quicken shown in Figure 2-28.

Figure 2-28

Personal finance software can help you track your money and investments.

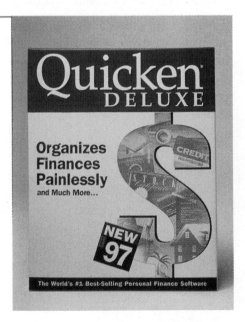

Some accounting and finance software is geared toward business. If you're an entrepreneur—even if you have a small business while you're in college—**small business accounting software** can be a real asset. These programs are easy to use and don't require more than a basic understanding of accounting and finance principles. Best-sellers include Peachtree Complete Accounting, Intuit QuickBooks, and Best!Ware M.Y.O.B. This software helps you invoice customers and keep track of what they owe. It stores additional customer data, such as contact information and purchasing history. Inventory functions keep track of the products you carry. Payroll capabilities automatically calculate wages and deduct federal, state, and local taxes.

Business Software

What's the difference between horizontal-market and vertical-market software? **Business software**, helps organizations efficiently accomplish routine tasks. Often, business software is divided into two categories: horizontal-market software and vertical-market software.

The term "horizontal market" refers to different types of businesses that, despite their differences, have some of the same software needs. **Horizontal-market software** is any generic software package that can be used by many different kinds of businesses. Much of this software comes from other software categories, such as accounting and finance. Payroll software is a good example of horizontal-market software. Almost every business has employees and needs to maintain payroll records. Payroll software keeps track of employee hours and produces the reports required by the government for income tax reporting.

A vertical market is a group of similar businesses that need specialized software. **Vertical-market software** is designed for specialized tasks in a specific market or business. For example, tasks in the construction industry include estimating the cost of labor and materials for a new building and providing the customer with a bid or estimate of the price for the finished building. Vertical-market estimating software for the construction industry would automate the task of gathering labor and materials costs and perform the calculations needed to arrive at an estimate. Other examples of vertical market software include the software that handles billing and insurance for medical practices and software that tracks the amount of time attorneys spend on each case. Advertisements for vertical-market software can be found in trade journals and on the Web.

Figure 2-29

Vertical-market software targets specific businesses and industries.

QuickCheck C

1. If you purchase a software _____, you will get several applications in one package.

2. _____ software provides sophisticated features for producing professional quality newspapers, magazines, and books.

3. You need graphics software that manipulates _____ graphics if you want to create wireframe drawings and rotate them.

4. The main characteristic of data management software such as a search engine is that it contains data. True or false? _____

5. _____ software allows you to browse Web pages and link to other Web documents.

6. _____-market software is designed for specialized tasks in a specific market or business.

D Multimedia

LAB

Multimedia

In the 1960s, a group of mop-haired musicians called the Beatles burst onto the music scene. Millions of screaming fans sent "I Want to Hold Your Hand" rocketing to the top of the charts. The Beatles formed their own record company called Apple Corps, Ltd.

In 1976, two young Californians, Steve Jobs and Steve Wozniak, started a computer company in a garage. Before the decade was out, both Wozniak and Jobs had become millionaires. Their company, Apple Computers, was wildly successful.

Two totally different companies with similar names? Today, the distinction between computer technology and record companies is not so clear. Consumer electronic inventions—radio, telephone, photography, sound recording, television, video recording, and computers— have merged to create a new technology called multimedia.

Multimedia's Roots

Is multimedia the same as CD-ROM? The term "multimedia" isn't new—it refers to the integrated use of multiple media, such as slides, videotapes, audiotapes, records, CD-ROMs, and photos. Now, however, the computer is replacing or controlling the slide projectors, tape recorders, and record players previously used for multimedia presentations. Advances in computer technology have made it possible to combine text, photo images, speech, music, animated sequences, and video into a single interactive computer application. A new definition of multimedia has emerged from this blend of technology. Today, **multimedia** is defined as an integrated collection of computer-based media including text, graphics, sound, animation, photo images, and video.

Envision a multimedia encyclopedia, for example. Like a traditional encyclopedia, it contains articles and pictures on a wide range of topics. But a multimedia encyclopedia has more. Suppose you're writing a research paper on space. You can pull up an article about space exploration, look at photos of spacecraft, and watch a video of the Hubble Space Telescope. As you read the article you can instantly link to related articles as shown in Figure 2-30.

Figure 2-30

A multimedia encyclopedia provides you with a rich selection of text, graphics, sound, animation, and video.

To locate information, use the Find button.

You control the video clip using on-screen controls modeled after a VCR.

These buttons display a topic outline and information on related topics.

Click here to see a photo of the Voyager spacecraft.

Click here to see a video clip about the Hubble Telescope.

Additional links to related topics are shown in red.

Most multimedia applications are shipped on a CD-ROM because the graphics, sound, and video require large amounts of storage space. However, not everything shipped on CD-ROM is multimedia. Many software publishers distribute large data files and non-multimedia software on CD-ROM because one CD-ROM is more convenient and more cost-effective than 20 or 30 floppy disks. For example, the CD-ROM shown in Figure 2-31 contains an archive of articles from back issues of *Visual Basic Programmers Journal*. In this case, the CD-ROM contains data, but no multimedia sounds, video, or animations.

Figure 2-31

Not all CD-ROMs contain multimedia. Some CD-ROMs, such as this one, contain data, but not multimedia elements.

Multimedia Applications

Are multimedia applications better than plain old software? Multimedia technology adds pizzazz to all types of computer applications. For example, a multimedia scheduler might remind you of appointments by displaying a video image of a "personal assistant." "Excuse me," your personal assistant might say, "but I believe you have an appointment in five minutes."

InfoWeb

Multimedia
11

You can use multimedia entertainment applications to have an animated adventure in the far reaches of space. You'll control the animated instrument panel of your spacecraft from your computer keyboard, discuss tactics with video images of your crew members, and hear the sounds of your engines, instrument warnings, and weapons.

You can use multimedia computer-aided instruction to learn a foreign language. You'll watch and listen to a short foreign-language video segment and view a synchronized translation. Then you can practice your pronunciation by speaking into a microphone so the computer can compare your pronunciation with a native speaker's.

You can even create multimedia applications of your own using **multimedia authoring tools** such as Macromedia Director or MicroMedium Digital Trainer Professional. This software helps you create lessons or reference books that include text, videos, animations, and sound tracks.

Multimedia technology opens possibilities for new and creative applications. However, all multimedia products do not necessarily make effective use of multimedia technology. Multimedia product designers have not always considered which technologies would actually enhance their product.

Some multimedia products can be faulted for an incomplete use of multimedia technology. For example, one multimedia product was criticized for including "photos with brief titles but no explanatory text…sketchy text, discontinuity, and almost total lack of sound." On the other hand, overuse of multimedia elements can sometimes detract from the contents. A reviewer pans one multimedia encyclopedia as "big on photos and animations, small on info." So, multimedia has the *potential* to improve an application, if the multimedia product is well designed.

Hypertext and Hypermedia

LAB

Computer
History
Hypermedia

How do hypertext and hypermedia help me use multimedia applications? Hypertext, a key element of many multimedia products, has been used effectively in non-multimedia products as well. Because you are likely to use hypertext with many computer applications and on the Web, it is useful to learn what it's all about. The term **hypertext** was coined by Ted Nelson in 1965 to describe the idea of documents that could be linked to each other. Linked documents make it possible for a reader to jump from a passage in one document to a related passage in another document. Figure 2-32 will help you visualize a hypertext.

Figure 2-32

A hypertext
of linked
documents

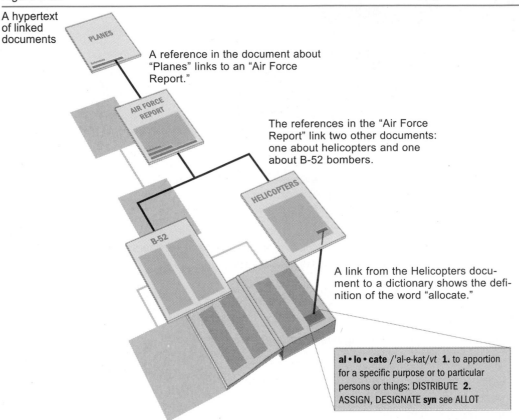

A reference in the document about "Planes" links to an "Air Force Report."

The references in the "Air Force Report" link two other documents: one about helicopters and one about B-52 bombers.

A link from the Helicopters document to a dictionary shows the definition of the word "allocate."

al•lo•cate /ˈal-e-kat/*vt* **1.** to apportion for a specific purpose or to particular persons or things: DISTRIBUTE **2.** ASSIGN, DESIGNATE **syn** see ALLOT

InfoWeb

Hypertext
12

Nelson wanted to create a giant hypertext that encompassed virtually every document on library shelves. His goal was not achievable with the technology of the sixties, and little was heard about hypertext for about 20 years. Then in 1987 Apple shipped a software product called Hypercard. It provided a way to create the electronic equivalent of a stack of note cards. Each card could contain text, graphical images, and sounds. Also, the cards could be linked to each other. Users jumped from one card to another by clicking buttons, underlined **links**, or specially marked **hot spots** in the text or graphics. The Hypercard-style implementation of hypertext developed over the next 10 years and became an important element of online help, computer-based learning systems, multimedia applications, and the Web.

The links in today's applications often involve graphics, sound, and video, as well as text. This type of multimedia hypertext is referred to as **hypermedia**. Hypertext and hypermedia are important computer-based tools because they help you easily follow a path that makes sense to you through a large selection of text, graphical, audio, and video information. Figure 2-33 shows you how to use hypermedia links to view film clips, compare critical reviews, and listen to sections of dialog with Microsoft Cinemania software.

Figure 2-33

Using hypermedia

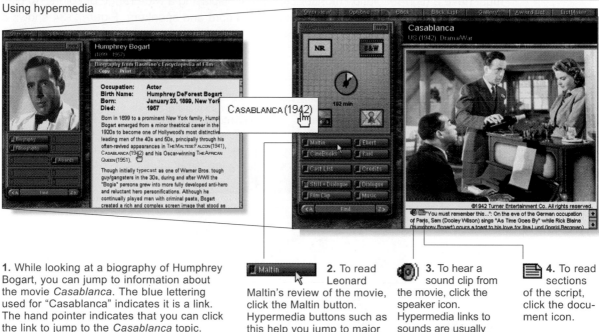

1. While looking at a biography of Humphrey Bogart, you can jump to information about the movie *Casablanca*. The blue lettering used for "Casablanca" indicates it is a link. The hand pointer indicates that you can click the link to jump to the *Casablanca* topic.

2. To read Leonard Maltin's review of the movie, click the Maltin button. Hypermedia buttons such as this help you jump to major sections of the hypermedia.

3. To hear a sound clip from the movie, click the speaker icon. Hypermedia links to sounds are usually indicated by a speaker icon.

4. To read sections of the script, click the document icon.

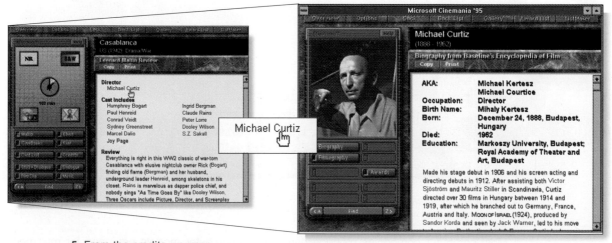

5. From the credits, you can select any topic indicated by blue lettering. For example, select the director's name to see his biography.

Multimedia Equipment

How do I know if my computer can use multimedia applications?   Today's multimedia applications require a computer system that can display graphic images, run video clips, and play sounds. Because most multimedia applications are shipped on a CD-ROM disk, your computer needs to have a CD-ROM drive. Your computer system must be able to quickly manipulate and transfer large amounts of data so you need a fast computer with a lot of memory. To display realistic graphical and video images, your computer system must have a high-resolution monitor capable of displaying a wide range of colors. To play realistic sounds, your computer needs a sound card and speakers. Figure 2-34 shows a computer well equipped for multimedia.

Figure 2-34

A multimedia PC

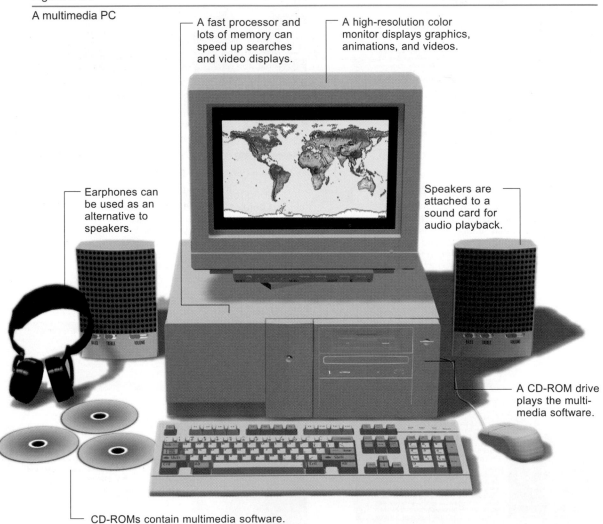

A fast processor and lots of memory can speed up searches and video displays.

A high-resolution color monitor displays graphics, animations, and videos.

Earphones can be used as an alternative to speakers.

Speakers are attached to a sound card for audio playback.

A CD-ROM drive plays the multimedia software.

CD-ROMs contain multimedia software.

Most computer companies produce one or more computer models equipped for multimedia applications. If you are in the market for a new computer, it makes sense to get one equipped for multimedia because of the many excellent multimedia applications available today. If you already have a computer, but it is not equipped for multimedia, you can add multimedia capabilities by purchasing a multimedia kit that contains a CD-ROM drive and sound card.

Figure 2-35

A multimedia kit is designed for non-technical users and usually can be installed in a few hours. Instead of using a multimedia kit, you can purchase a CD-ROM drive and sound card individually, but installing these individual components usually requires more technical expertise.

Speakers

Sound card

CD-ROM drive

Disk containing device drivers

InfoWeb

MMX
13

Multimedia has become so popular that many of today's computers have a Pentium® processor with special multimedia enhancements called **Intel MMX™ technology**. This chip speeds up multimedia features such as sound and video. However, only specially-written software can take advantage of the special multimedia features on the chip. The MMX Logo shown in Figure 2-36 on a software package indicates that the software is optimized for the Intel MMX technology.

Figure 2-36

MMX Logo

QuickCheck D

1 Multimedia is a blend of technologies, such as text, photo images, speech, music, animated sequences, and video. True or false? _____

2 Multimedia is the same as CD-ROM. True or false? _____

3 When you add multimedia to hypertext you get _____.

4 The _____ logo means a software program has been specially designed to handle multimedia commands.

UserFocus

E Installing Software

Many microcomputers are sold with pre-installed system and application software, but eventually most computer users want to install additional software.

Software Compatibility

How do I know what software will work on my computer? Before you install software or a multimedia application, you must make sure it is compatible with your computer system. To be compatible, the software must be written for the type of computer you use and for the operating system installed on your computer. You must also make sure your computer meets or exceeds the system requirements specified by the software. **System requirements** specify the operating system type and minimum hardware capacity needed for a software product to work correctly. The system requirements are usually listed on the outside of a software package, as shown in Figure 2-37. They might also be explained in more detail in the software reference manual.

Figure 2-37

The system requirements on a software package describe the equipment and operating system required to run the software.

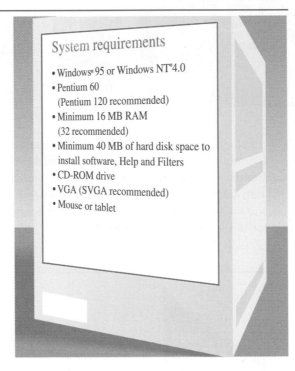

System requirements

- Windows® 95 or Windows NT® 4.0
- Pentium 60
  (Pentium 120 recommended)
- Minimum 16 MB RAM
  (32 recommended)
- Minimum 40 MB of hard disk space to install software, Help and Filters
- CD-ROM drive
- VGA (SVGA recommended)
- Mouse or tablet

Determining Compatibility

Does the version of my computer's operating system affect compatibility? Suppose you want to purchase software for your PC. First, you need to make sure the software is written for PCs, rather than for the Apple Macintosh. Sometimes the same software title is available for more than one type of computer. For example, Microsoft Word is available for both PCs and Macs, but these are two distinct versions of the software. You cannot use the Macintosh version of Microsoft Word on your PC.

Once you know the software is compatible with your computer, you must make sure the software will work with your operating system. If your PC uses the DOS operating system, you must select DOS software. If your computer uses the Microsoft Windows operating system, you can select DOS or Windows software because Windows can run software designed for both of these operating systems. If your computer uses OS/2, you can select OS/2, DOS, or Windows software because OS/2 can run software designed for all three operating systems.

Operating systems go through numerous revisions. A higher version number indicates a more recent revision; for example, DOS 6.0 is a more recent version than DOS 5.0. Windows 95 and Windows 98 are more recent versions than Windows 3.1. Operating systems are usually **downwardly compatible**, which means that you can use application software designed for earlier versions of the operating system, but not those designed for later versions. For example, if Windows 95 is installed on your computer, you can generally use software designed for earlier versions of Windows, such as Windows 3.1. However, your software might not work correctly if it requires Windows 95 but you have Windows 3.1 on your computer. If you want to use software that requires a newer version of your operating system, you must first purchase and install an operating system upgrade. Figure 2-38 summarizes the concept of downward compatibility.

Figure 2-38

Downward compatibility

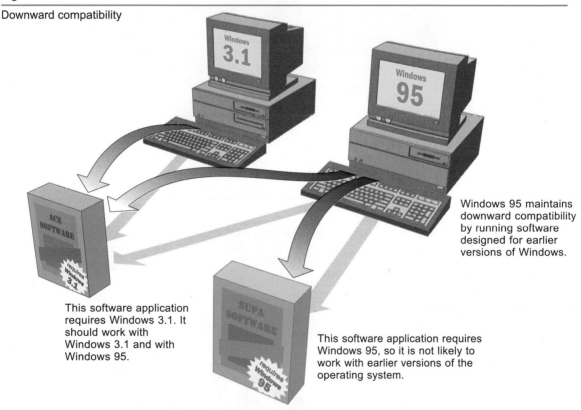

Windows 95 maintains downward compatibility by running software designed for earlier versions of Windows.

This software application requires Windows 3.1. It should work with Windows 3.1 and with Windows 95.

This software application requires Windows 95, so it is not likely to work with earlier versions of the operating system.

Software Setup

When I purchase software, what do I do with the disks? Computer software is usually shipped on floppy disks, called **distribution disks**, or on CD-ROMs. In the years when personal computers first appeared on the market, you could often use the software directly from the distribution disk. Now, that is rarely possible because the programs are so large they take up many disks. Today, instead of using software directly from the distribution disk, you usually install it on your hard disk. During the **installation process**, programs and data for the software are copied to the hard disk of your computer system.

When you install software using a command-line operating system, such as DOS, you should carefully follow the installation instructions provided in the reference manual. There is no consistent installation procedure for DOS software, so each software application might require different steps. On the other hand, for Microsoft Windows applications, the installation process is more consistent and usually much easier. Figure 2-39 shows you how to install Windows applications.

Figure 2-39

The installation process

1. Insert the setup disk and start the setup program.

2. Select full or customized installation. For a full installation, the setup program copies all the files and data from the distribution disks to the hard disk of your computer system. A full installation provides you with access to all the features of the software.

During a customized installation, the setup program displays a list of software features for your selection. After you select the features you want, the setup program copies only the selected program and data files to your hard disk. A customized installation can save space on your hard disk.

☒ **Full Installation**
☐ **Customized Installation**

3. If the software includes multiple disks, insert each disk in the specified drive when the setup program tells you to do so.

4. When the setup program is finished, start the program you have just installed to be sure it works.

5. Fill out the registration card and send it in. When you send in the card, you become a registered user. The perks of being a registered user vary with each software publisher, but they might include receiving free technical support, product information, or discounts on new versions of the software.

When you install non-multimedia applications such as word-processing or accounting software, the computer copies all the program modules from the distribution disks or CD-ROM to the hard disk of your computer. You do not need to insert the disk or CD-ROM every time you want to use the program because everything you need is on your hard disk. For multimedia applications, this is not always the case. You generally copy only a small start-up program to your hard disk, leaving most of the multimedia images, videos, and sounds on the CD-ROM.

Why wouldn't you copy all the multimedia components to your hard disk? The answer is to save hard disk space. Multimedia applications require lots of storage space. For example, Microsoft's Encarta encyclopedia takes up about three times as much space as Microsoft Office 97, which includes word-processing, spreadsheet, presentation, and database software applications. You are likely to have many multimedia applications, but use them infrequently. Rather than devoting a large portion of your hard disk space to a multimedia application, you must insert its CD-ROM into the CD-ROM drive so that you have access to the images, animations, videos, and sound.

EndNote

InfoWeb

Anti-Piracy
14

Software is the key to the computer's versatility. System software and application software work together to help you accomplish an incredible variety of tasks. You might think it is "corny" to follow copyright laws and license restrictions, but ethical software use benefits everyone. Software publishers use revenues from software sales to improve current software, provide technical support, and develop new applications. By resisting the temptation to use illegal copies of software, you can help provide software publishers with the resources they need to develop more of the software that makes the computer such a versatile machine.

InfoWeb

Chapter Links

The InfoWeb is your guide to print, film, television, and electronic resources. Use it to obtain updates on quickly changing technical information and to locate information for research papers. If you're using the New Perspectives CD-ROM, click the InfoWeb icon on the left side of this paragraph to access the online InfoWeb links. Otherwise, use your Web browser and type in the address of the New Perspectives site: www.cciw.com/np3. At the New Perspectives site you'll find up-to-date links to the topics covered in this chapter.

1 Copyright and Software Law

Software copyright law is the focus of an ongoing discussion among American legal experts, American law makers, software publishers, and consumers' rights advocacy groups. There seems to be general agreement that current laws should be updated. Cornell University provides a hypertext version of the U.S. Copyright Act that is currently in effect at **www.law.cornell.edu/uscode/17**. For Canadian copyright law, connect to **www.perlaw.ca/copyright_index.html**. If you have questions about what's legal and what's not, you'll find Copyright FAQs at the Electronic Frontier Foundation site **eff.org/pub/ Intellectual_property**. For "plain speak" information on the difference between copyrighted, licensed, shareware, and public domain software connect to The Copyright Website at **www.benedict.com**.

2 Shareware: Try Before You Buy

The Internet provides an ideal distribution channel for shareware. You can connect to a shareware site, select the program that you want to try and "download it" by transferring it to your computer. The Shareware Trade Association and Resources' Web site **www.shareware.org** distributes software from over one hundred North American and European programmers. At a similar site, **www.shareware.com** you can search for, browse, and download freeware, shareware, demos, fixes, patches, and upgrades from various software archives and computer vendor sites on the Internet. Before you download shareware, be sure that you understand the copyright and license. Also make sure your shareware source is reputable and guarantees that its software is virus free.

3 Operating Systems

To learn more about operating systems, head for the Web sites of the companies that produce them. DOS and Windows operating systems are at **www.microsoft.com**, the Mac OS is at **www.apple.com**, OS/2 is at **www.ibm.com**, and UNIX is at **www.sco.com**. A good desktop reference if you're using Windows is **Inside Windows 95** by Jim Boyce, et al (New Riders Publishing, 1996) or **Windows 95 Secrets Gold** by Brian Livingston and Davis Straub (IDG Books Worldwide, 1996). Most computer curricula include an operating systems course in which students learn about operating system services and the specific ways an operating system controls computer hardware. One of the standard texts for this course is **Operating Systems: Design and Implementation** by Andrew S. Tanenbaum and Albert S. Woodhull (Prentice Hall, 1997).

4 Shopping for Application Software

These days you can buy software without leaving your house—as long as you have Internet access and a credit card. Egghead Computer is a chain of retail stores that also has a Web site at **www.egghead.com**. Here you will find the descriptions and system requirements for software packages, as well as articles and reviews detailing their strengths and weaknesses. Micro Warehouse Inc. offers catalog sales of hardware and software and also has a Web site at **www.warehouse.com**. At the ComputerESP Web site **www.computeresp.com** you can choose a software package and compare prices from stores and catalogs across the country. Students can often get discounts on software at sites, such as **www.studentdiscount.com** or **www.micromaster.com**.

Computer magazines are good sources of information about software—look for them in your library, on newsstands, or on the Web. Two of the biggest computer magazine publishers are Ziff Davis and CMP. Ziff Davis publications include *PC Week, PC Computing, Mac Week*, and *Computer Shopper*. CMP publishes *Computer Reseller News, Home PC, InformationWeek, NetGuide*, and *Windows Magazine*. You can find their magazines online at the ZDNet Web site, **www.zdnet.com**, and the TechWeb site, **techweb.cmp.com**. *BYTE* magazine at **www.byte.com** has excellent product reviews, but the focus is somewhat technical. *Computerworld* at **www.computerworld.com** has great product comparisons as does *InfoWorld* at **www.infoworld.com**.

5 Desktop Publishing

The popularity of desktop publishing increases every year. Why? Find out how companies save money, improve their image, and publicize their message at **www.adobe.com/studio/casestudies/main.html**, the Web site maintained by the publisher of the popular PageMaker DTP software. You can download your own trial version of the Quark desktop publishing software at **www.quark.com**. The Quark site, home of the highly-rated Quark Xpress software, also contains a detailed list of software features, useful if you want to know what desktop software really does. You'll find links to many DTP sites at **www.teleport.com/~eidos/dtpij/**. For DTP professionals, the online magazine **www.publish.com** is a must read for design tips and the latest on DTP technology.

6 3-D Graphics

One of the most exciting developments in graphics is 3-D rendering. Premier packages include AutoCad and Caligari trueSpace. To find out more about 3-D software, click the Gallery link on the Caligari site at **www.caligari.com**. This site also features a great collection of samples and a free trial version of the software. Persistance of Vision also hosts a site, **www.povray.org/java-index.html**, that contains stunning 3-D samples. While at the site, you can download a well-regarded free ray tracing program. Want to see what kind of graphics you can generate with a supercomputer? Connect to **www.ncsa.uiuc.edu/SDG/DigitalGallery/DG_science_theater.html**.

7 Presentations

Using Microsoft PowerPoint software to create presentations? Your local bookstore might have just the desk reference you need to master all its features. The 400 pages and CD-ROM for **Creating Cool Powerpoint 97 Presentations** by Glenn E. Weadock and Emily Sherrill Weadock (IDG Books Worldwide, 1997) are chock full of great hints. Using presentation software won't guarantee a successful presentation. For tips on how to plan, prepare, and deliver a presentation check your library for books such as **Business Presentations and Public Speaking** by Peter H. Engel (Harvard Business School Press, 1996) and **How to Give A Terrific Presentation** by Karen Kalish (Amacom, 1996). Online you can connect to *Presentations* magazine at **www.presentations.com** for tips on making presentations, selecting presentation hardware and making effective use of presentation software.

8 Web Browsers

To access the Web, you need Web browser software. Two companies, Netscape Communications and Microsoft, are in stiff competition to see who can capture and hold the lion's share of the browser market. At the Microsoft site, check out **www.microsoft.com/ie** for a description of the Internet Explorer browser and plug-in Internet tools. Information about Netscape Navigator can be found at **www.netscape.com**.

9 Games Galore

Most software publishers give away free playable demos of their game software. A fun site with downloads, including children's games, is **www.happypuppy.com**. "Serious" and more violent game demos are supplied by **www.avault.com**.

10 Money Management

Money problems? Personal financial management can't promise to solve them, but can supply the software tools you need to get your finances in order. Visit the Intuit Web site at **www.intuit.com** where you can read about the popular Quicken and QuickBooks software, then download a free trial version. A related site, the Quicken Financial Network at **www.qfn.com**, has articles about retirement planning, managing a stock portfolio, and online banking. Click the Debt Survey link and respond to the questionnaire, then compare your results with others.

11 Multimedia

Interacting with multimedia products can be fascinating and will keep you engaged, learning, and having fun for many hours. However, at $50 to $60 a title, you don't want to just browse the titles, read the package copy, and take one home. Fortunately, many magazines review current titles, and some publications and Web sites rate titles. *Publisher's Weekly*, the publishing industry's trade magazine, periodically presents reviews of multimedia titles and a multimedia title bestsellers list, comparable to their book bestsellers lists. You can find their PW Multimedia Directory Web site at **www.bookwire.com/PW/mmd/directory/html**.

12 Hypertext

Although Ted Nelson coined the term "hypertext" he claims to have been inspired by an article by Vannevar Bush called "As We May Think" (find it at **www.isg.sfu.ca/~duchier/misc/vbush**) that describes a personal information retrieval device called Memex. Ted Nelson originally envisioned hypertext as the underlying technology for project Xanadu, a vast repository of linked documents that readers could easily peruse and even add their own annotations. You'll find the Xanadu Web site at **www.cinemedia.net/xanadu**. Your library might have Nelson's books, **Literary Machines** (1981) and **Computer Lib** (Microsoft Press, 1987). For information on how hypertext has impacted the Internet and literature, try The Electronic Labyrinth Web site at **jefferson.village.virginia.edu/elab/elab.html**.

13 MMX

Multimedia has become so popular that many new computers include a processing chip specially designed to optimize video and sound. However, only specially written software can take advantage of the MMX instruction set. PC Webopaedia at **www.webopaedia.com/MMX.htm** has a definition of MMX and links to related articles.

14 Anti-Piracy

According to a May 1995 *Computerworld* survey of information systems professionals, 47 percent of the respondents admitted to copying commercial software illegally, despite the fact that 78 percent agreed it should never be done. Find this and other facts about software piracy at the Business Software Alliance Web site, **www.bsa.org/piracy/diduknow.html**. What should you do if you discover a software pirate? The Software Publisher's Association (SPA) has an Anti-Piracy Hotline at (800) 388-7478. Visit the SPA's Anti-Piracy site for information on software law in U.S. and Canada, answers to your questions about legal copying, and guidelines for schools and businesses at **www.spa.org/piracy/info.htm**.

Review

1 Write a sentence or two explaining the most important concept from each of the five sections of this chapter.

2 Below each heading in this chapter, there is a question. Look back through this chapter and answer each of these questions using your own words.

3 Select 10 terms in this chapter that you believe are most important, then use your own words to write a definition of each term.

4 Under U.S. copyright law, what are the two major rights granted to the copyright holder? What are the three rights granted to the user of copyrighted materials?

5 Complete the following "legal" matrix to clarify the difference between copyrighted software, licensed software, shareware, and public domain software.

Suppose you are not the author of a software package. Is it...	Copyrighted Software	Licensed Software	Shareware	Public Domain Software
Legal to make a backup copy?				
Legal to sell a copy?				
Legal to give a copy to a friend?				
Protected by U.S. Copyright Law?				

6 For each of the following descriptions, indicate whether the software is copyrighted, licensed, shareware, or public domain. For some descriptions, there is more than one answer.

　a. The software does not have a copyright notice

　b. You must send in money to become a registered user

　c. The software is shrink wrapped and there is a message about your rights and responsibilities

　d. When you start the software you see a message "© 1998 Course Technology, Inc."

　e. When you start the program you see a message, "Copyright 1996, 1997 SupRSoft, Inc. All Rights Reserved. You are free to use, copy, and distribute this software for non-commercial use if no fee is charged for use, copying, or distribution, and if the software is not modified in any way."

7 Create a sentence outline of Section B System Software. Your outline should have at least three levels. You can use I., A., and 1. for the outline levels. Be sure that the sentence you write for each outline level focuses on a single, important point.

8 Fill in the following table by using a check mark to indicate which operating systems are available for each type of computer.

Operating System	IBM Compatible	Macintosh	Minicomputer	Mainframe
DOS				
WINDOWS				
OS/2				
MVS				
VMS				
UNIX				

9 Indicate what software tool(s) you could use to accomplish the following tasks. If you could use more than one tool for the task, indicate which you think would be best.

　a. Working with numbers and examining "what-if" scenarios

　b. Producing documents

　c. Working with facts and figures, such as customer names and addresses

d. Drawing pictures, 3-D images, and animations

e. Sending electronic messages between two computers

f. Producing professional-looking brochures and newsletters

g. Creating pie charts, line graphs, and bar graphs

h. Determining times for meetings, tracking special events, and maintaining employee schedules

10 Make a two-column list to summarize multimedia. The left column of the list should include multimedia features such as sound, animation, and so on. The right column should indicate the computer equipment that is needed to implement the features you listed in the left column.

11 Suppose you're thinking of purchasing Microsoft Excel for Windows. The software requires "an IBM-PC/AT, PS/2, or compatible; graphics compatible with Microsoft Windows version 3.0 or later; MS-DOS version 3.1 or later; optional printer; a mouse or compatible pointing device is recommended." You have a Compaq computer with Windows 95, a Hewlett-Packard printer, and a Microsoft mouse. Explain whether you can expect the Microsoft Excel spreadsheet software to work on your computer after you install it.

12 Use the New Perspectives CD-ROM to take a practice test or to review the new terms presented in this chapter.

Projects

1 Format a Disk In this chapter you learned how utility software helps you direct the operating system to accomplish tasks such as formatting a disk. This is a good time to try it out. If your lab computers have the

Windows 95 operating system, you can do this project on your own by referring to Figure 2-39. Otherwise, your instructor will need to help you.

2 The Operating System in Your School's Lab In this chapter you learned how to identify microcomputer operating systems by looking at the main screen and prompt. In this project you will explore more about the operating system in your school computer lab. If you have more than one lab or your computer uses more than one operating system, your instructor should tell you which one to use for this project.

Find out which operating system is used in your school computer lab. Be sure you find out the type and version. You can go into the lab and obtain this information from one of the computers. If you see a command-line user interface, try typing "ver" and then pressing the Enter key. If you see a graphical user interface, try clicking the Apple menu, or click the Help menu, then select Help About. Once you know the operating system used in your school lab, use the operating system reference manual and library resources to answer the following questions:

a. Which operating system and version are used in your school lab?

b. What company publishes the operating system software?

c. When was the first version of this operating system introduced?

d. Does this operating system have a command-line user interface or a graphical user interface?

e. Does this operating system support multitasking?

f. Do you need a password to use the computers in your school lab? Even if you do not need to use a password, does the operating system provide some way to secure access to the computers?

g. What is the anticipated arrival date for the next version of this operating system?

h. How much does the publisher of this operating system usually charge for upgrades if you are a registered user?

3 **The Legal Beagle: Analyzing a License Agreement** When you use a software package, it is important to understand the legal restrictions on its use. In this project you have an opportunity to practice reading a real software license agreement and making decisions based on how you interpret what it says. You can do this project on your own or discuss it in a small group, as specified by your instructor. Read the IBM Program License Agreement (on the previous page) then answer these questions:

a. Is this a "shrink wrap" license? Why or why not?

b. After you pay your computer dealer for the program this license covers, who owns the program?

c. Can you legally have one copy of the program on your computer at work and another copy of the program on your computer at home if you use the software only in one place at a time?

d. Can you legally sell the software? Why or why not?

e. Under what conditions can you legally transfer possession of the program to someone else?

f. If you were the owner of a software store, could you legally rent the program to customers if you were sure they did not keep a copy after the rental period was over?

g. Can you legally install this software on one computer, but give more than one user access to it?

h. If you use this program for an important business decision and you later find out that a mistake in the program caused you to lose $500,000, what legal recourse is provided by the license agreement?

International Business Machines Corporation *Armonk, New York 10504*

IBM Program License Agreement

BEFORE OPENING THIS PACKAGE, YOU SHOULD CAREFULLY READ THE FOLLOWING TERMS AND CONDITIONS. OPENING THIS PACKAGE INDICATES YOUR ACCEPTANCE OF THESE TERMS AND CONDITIONS. IF YOU DO NOT AGREE WITH THEM, YOU SHOULD PROMPTLY RETURN THE PACKAGE UNOPENED AND YOUR MONEY WILL BE REFUNDED.

This is a license agreement and not an agreement for sale. IBM owns, or has licensed from the owner, copyrights in the Program. You obtain no rights other than the license granted you by this Agreement. Title to the enclosed copy of the Program, and any copy made from it, is retained by IBM. IBM licenses your use of the Program in the United States and Puerto Rico. You assume all responsibility for the selection of the Program to achieve your intended results and for the installation of, use of, and results obtained from, the Program.

The Section in the enclosed documentation entitled "License Information" contains additional information concerning the Program and any related Program Services.

LICENSE
You may:
1) use the Program on only one machine at any one time, unless permission to use it on more than one machine at any one time is granted in the License Information (Authorized Use);
2) make a copy of the Program for backup or modification purposes only in support of your Authorized Use. However, Programs marked "Copy Protected" limit copying;
3) modify the Program and/or merge it into another program only in support of your Authorized Use; and
4) transfer possession of copies of the Program to another party by transferring this copy of the IBM Program License Agreement, the License Information, and all other documentation along with at least one complete, unaltered copy of the Program. You must, at the same time, either transfer to such other party or destroy all your other copies of the Program, including modified copies or portions of the Program merged into other programs. Such transfer of possession terminates your license from IBM. Such other party shall be licensed, under the terms of this Agreement, upon acceptance of the Agreement by its initial use of the Program.

You shall reproduce and include the copyright notice(s) on all such copies of the Program, in whole or in part.

You shall not:
1) use, copy, modify, merge, or transfer copies of the program except as provided in this Agreement;
2) reverse assemble or reverse compile the Program; and/or
3) sublicense, rent, lease, or assign the Program or any copy thereof.

LIMITED WARRANTY
Warranty details and limitations are described in the Statement of Limited Warranty which is available upon request from IBM, its Authorized Dealer or its approved supplier and is also contained in the License Information. IBM provides a three-month limited warranty on the media for all Programs. For selected Programs, as indicated on the outside of the package, a limited warranty on the Program is available. The applicable Warranty Period is measured from the date of delivery to the original user as evidenced by a receipt.

Certain Programs, as indicated on the outside of the package, are not warranted and are provided "AS IS."
Z125-3301-02 4/87

SUCH WARRANTIES ARE IN LIEU OF ALL OTHER WARRANTIES, EXPRESS OR IMPLIED, INCLUDING, BUT NOT LIMITED TO, THE IMPLIED WARRANTIES OF MERCHANTABILITY AND FITNESS FOR A PARTICULAR PURPOSE.

Some states do not allow the exclusion of implied warranties, so the above exclusion may not apply to you.

LIMITATION OF REMEDIES
IBM's entire liability and your exclusive remedy shall be as follows:
1) IBM will provide the warranty described in IBM's Statement of Limited Warranty. If IBM does not replace defective media or, if applicable, make the Program operate as warranted or replace the Program with a functionally equivalent program, all as warranted, you may terminate your license and your money will be refunded upon the return of all your copies of the Program.
2) For any claim arising out of IBM's limited warranty, or for any other claim whatsoever related to the subject matter of this Agreement, IBM's liability for actual damages, regardless of the form of action, shall be limited to the greater of $5,000 or the money paid to IBM, its Authorized Dealer or its approved supplier for the license for the Program that caused the damages that is the subject matter of, or is directly related to, the cause of action. This limitation will not apply to claims for personal injury or damages to real or tangible personal property caused by IBM's negligence.
3) In no event will IBM be liable for any lost profits, lost savings, or any incidental damages or other consequential damages, even if IBM, its Authorized Dealer or its approved supplier has been advised of the possibility of such damages, or for any claim by you based on a third party claim.

Some states do not allow the limitation or exclusion of incidental or consequential damages so the above limitation or exclusion may not apply to you.

GENERAL
You may terminate your license at any time by destroying all your copies of the Program or as otherwise described in this Agreement.

IBM may terminate your license if you fail to comply with the terms and conditions of this Agreement. Upon such termination, you agree to destroy all your copies of the Program.

Any attempt to sublicense, rent, lease or assign, or, except as expressly provided herein, to transfer any copy of the Program is void.

You agree that your are responsible for payment of any taxes, including personal property taxes, resulting from this Agreement.

No action, regardless of form, arising out of this Agreement may be brought by either party more than two years after the cause of action has arisen except for the breach of the provisions in the Section entitled "License" in which event four years shall apply.

This agreement will be construed under the Uniform Commercial Code of the State of New York.

4  **INTERNET Optional**

Software Applications: What's Available? There are so many software packages that it is difficult to get an idea of what's available unless you take a look through current computer magazines and software catalogs. Use computer magazines and/or the Web to complete the following tasks:

1. Find an ad for a computer vendor that sells a large variety of software. Jot down the name of the vendor and where you found the ad. List the categories the vendor uses to classify software and the number of software packages in each category.

2. Select one type of software from the following categories: operating systems, disk utilities, word-processing, graphics, presentation graphics, electronic mail, desktop publishing, spreadsheets, database, accounting, or scheduling. Read a comparison review of software packages in the category you select. Next locate and photocopy ads for each of the products in the review. Look through the software vendor ads to find the best price for each product. Finally, write a one- or two-page summary explaining your purchase recommendation.

5 **What Software Tool Would You Recommend?** Folk wisdom tells us to use the appropriate tool for a job. This is true for software tools, too. In this project you decide what software tool is most appropriate for a task. You can do this project on your own or discuss it in a small group.

For each of the scenarios that follow, decide which software tool (i.e., word-processing) would accomplish the task most effectively.

a. You want to keep track of your monthly expenses and try to figure out ways to save some money.

b. As the leader of an international team of researchers studying migration patterns of Canadian geese, you want all the team members to communicate their findings to each other quickly.

c. You are the office manager for a department of a large Fortune 500 company. One of your responsibilities is to arrange meetings and schedule facilities for the employees in your department.

d. As a partner in a law firm, you need to draft and modify legal briefs.

e. You are in charge of a fund-raising campaign and you need to track the names, addresses, phone numbers, and donations made by contributors.

f. You are going to design and produce the printed program for a community theater play listing the actors, director, lighting specialists, and so on.

g. A sales manager for a cosmetics company wants to motivate the sales force by graphically showing the increases in consumer spending in each of the past five years.

h. The marketing specialist for a new software company wants to send out announcements to 150 computer magazines.

i. The owners of five golf courses in Jackson County want to design a promotional brochure that can be distributed to tourists in restaurants and hotels.

j. The owner of a small business wants to keep track of ongoing income and expenses and print out monthly profit and loss statements.

k. The superintendent of a local school system wants to prepare a press release explaining why student test scores were 5 percent below the national average.

l. A contractor wants to calculate his cost for materials needed to build a new community center.

m. A college student wants to send out customized letters addressed to 20 prospective employers.

n. The parents of three children want to decide whether they should invest money for their children's education in the stock market or whether they should buy into their state's prepaid tuition plan.

o. The director of fund-raising for a large nonprofit organization wants to keep a list of prospective donors.

6 Multimedia "Top 10" In the last two years the multimedia market has exploded. For this project, create your own list of "top 10" multi-media titles. Look in recent editions of computer magazines or on the Web and select the 10 multi-media applications that are most interesting or useful to you. For each multimedia application you select, list its title, publisher, and a short description of what it does. Also list the name of the computer magazine you used and the page on which you found the information about each multi-media application.

7 Productivity, Suites, and Groupware Use computer magazines or the Web to find the name or one productivity software package, one office suite package, and one groupware package. For each example, list the title, publisher, and price. Also, write one paragraph about each package describing the kinds of tasks it is designed to accomplish.

8 Where's the Shareware? You learned in this chapter that shareware can be less expensive than commercial software; it also lets you try the software before you buy it. But is shareware as available as commercial software? In this project you will find out.

Use computer magazines and/or Internet sites to find a shareware program and a commercial program for each of the categories in the table that follows. For each shareware package, indicate the program name, the name of the retailer

or vendor, and the selling price. In the reference column, indicate the name, date, and page of the magazine, or the Internet site, where you found the information. Shareware vendors frequently advertise in the back pages of computer magazines.

Software Type	Title	Price	Vendor	Reference
Shareware productivity				
Commercial productivity				
Shareware system utility				
Commercial system utility				
Shareware education				
Commercial education				
Shareware games				
Commercial games				

Lab Assignments

Computer History Hypermedia

The Computer History Hypermedia Lab is an example of a multimedia hypertext, or hypermedia that contains text, pictures, and recordings that trace the origins of computers. This Lab provides you with two benefits: first, you learn how to use hypermedia links, and second, you learn about some of the events that took place as the computer age dawned.

1 Click the Steps button to learn how to use the Computer History Hypermedia Lab. As you proceed through the Steps, answer all the Quick Check questions that appear. After you complete the Steps, you

will see a Quick Check Summary Report. Follow the instructions on the screen to print this report.

2 Click the Explore button. Find the name and date for each of the following:

a. First automatic adding machine.

b. First electronic computer.

c. First fully electronic stored-program computer.

d. First widely used high-level programming language.

e. First microprocessor.

f. First microcomputer.

g. First word-processing program.

h. First spreadsheet program.

3 Select one of the following computer pioneers and write a one-page paper about that person's contribution to the computer industry: Grace Hopper, Charles Babbage, Augusta Ada, Jack Kilby, Thomas Watson, or J. Presper Eckert.

4 Use this Lab to research the history of the computer. Based on your research, write a paper explaining how you would respond to the question, "Who invented the computer?"

Multimedia

Multimedia brings together text, graphics, sound, animation, video, and photo images. If you are using the CD version of this book, you have already seen multimedia in action. In this Lab you will learn how to apply multimedia and then have the chance to see what it might be like to design some aspects of multimedia projects.

1 Click the Steps button to learn about multimedia development. As you proceed through the Steps, answer the Quick Check questions. After you complete the Steps, you will see a Quick Check Report. Follow the instructions on the screen to print this report.

2 In Explore, browse through the STS-79 Multimedia Mission Log. How many videos are included in the Multimedia Mission Log? The image on the Mission

Profile page is a vector drawing, what happens when you enlarge it?

3 Listen to the sound track on Day 3. Is this a WAV file or a MIDI file? Why do you think so? Is this a synthesized sound or a digitized sound? Listen to the sound track on page 8. Can you tell if this is a WAV file or a MIDI file?

4 Suppose you were hired as a multimedia designer for a multimedia series on targeting fourth- and fifth-grade students. Describe the changes you would make to the Multimedia Mission Log so it would be suitable for these students. Also, include a sketch showing a screen from your revised design.

5 When you view the Mission Log on your computer, do you see palette flash? Why or why not? If you see palette flash, list the images that flash.

6 Multimedia can be effectively applied to projects such as Encyclopedias, atlases, and animated storybooks; to computer-based training for foreign languages, first aid, or software applications; for games and sports simulations; for business presentations; for personal albums, scrapbooks, and baby books; for product catalogs and Web pages.

Suppose you were hired to create one of these projects. Write a one-paragraph description of the project you would be creating. Describe some of the multimedia elements you would include. For each of the elements indicate its source and whether you would need to obtain permission for its use. Finally, sketch a screen or two showing your completed project.

DOCUMENTS, WORKSHEETS, and DATABASES

3

The news in 1979 and 1980. The Shah of Iran flees into exile. A partial meltdown at the Three Mile Island nuclear power plant horrifies environmentalists. Members of the U.S embassy in Teheran are taken hostage and will remain in captivity for over a year. The Mount St. Helens volcano erupts, leveling 120 square miles of Washington State forest. John Lennon is murdered.

For microcomputer owners, however, the news in 1979 and 1980 is more positive. Three super software packages arrive on the market. They quickly become best sellers and form the bedrock of microcomputer software. Computer users gladly tackle the complex interface of the WordStar word-processing software so they can create professional-looking documents. VisiCalc, a totally new invention in a category dubbed "spreadsheet software," seems to make it relatively painless for novices to set up complex numerical calculations. A third product, dBase, helps computer users organize their information by creating and maintaining databases. This chapter takes a look at how these software tools affect the computing you do today and how they have affected our society.

CHAPTER**PREVIEW**

This chapter is filled with tips about working with computerized documents, worksheets, and databases. The tips will help you use software to improve the quality of your work, to get better grades, and to enhance your career. The *User Focus* section explains how to integrate software tools to create great reports and presentations. After you have completed this chapter you should be able to:

- List examples of how document production software is used in different career fields
- Discuss and demonstrate how document production software can help you improve the quality of your writing and the format of your documents
- Compare and contrast electronic publishing with traditional paper-based publishing
- Discuss some of the ways spreadsheet software affects politics, business, and education in a technologically advanced society
- Describe how spreadsheets work, and how you create, format, and audit a worksheet
- Discuss your responsibilities for creating accurate worksheets and graphs
- Describe the database skills you need to be productive in today's Information Age
- Differentiate between a structured database and a free-form database
- Describe the techniques you can use to search for data in databases
- Describe how to integrate word-processing, spreadsheet, and database software

LABS

Word Processing

Spreadsheets

Databases

A Documents

LAB

Word
Processing

Documents are an integral part of our society and culture. Historical documents such as the Declaration of Independence and the U.S. Constitution promote social and political philosophies. Literary documents, such as *To Kill a Mockingbird* and *War and Peace,* record the issues and dilemmas facing societies and cultures. Fiction entertains. Weekly magazines and daily newspapers provide information on current events. Contracts record agreements for corporations and individuals.

Despite the popularity of radio, television, and film, documents remain an important component of our everyday lives. Historically, growing literacy rates reflect the importance of reading and writing and seem to correspond to social and economic progress.

InfoWeb

Literacy
1

As literacy increased throughout the world, the tools of document production changed. Hand-copied manuscripts were produced too slowly to satisfy the demands of a literate populace. The printing press, and later the photocopier, made it easy to produce and distribute books, magazines, newspapers, pamphlets, and newsletters. The quill pen was inconvenient because it required the writer to pause every few words to dip the pen into an inkwell. Fountain pens, and later ball-point and felt-tip pens, provided writers with more free-flowing writing tools. The pencil and erasable ink were notable innovations for providing writers with editing capabilities. The typewriter became what might now be called a personal printing device and enabled individuals to produce professional-looking documents without using an expensive printing press (Figure 3-1).

Figure 3-1

Technology has
had a significant
impact on document
production tools.

For most of today's document production tasks, computers with document production software have replaced pencils with chewed-up erasers, smudgy ball-point pens, and clacking typewriters. **Document production software** includes word-processing software, desktop publishing software, e-mail editors, and the software that helps you create home pages and hypertext documents for the Internet's World Wide Web.

Today, it seems that everyone uses computers to produce documents. Using computers, college students write research papers, elementary school students write short essays, secretaries write memos, grandmothers write thank-you notes, executives write corporate reports, job-hunters produce resumes, novelists write books, reporters write news stories, and the list goes on. Should you use a computer for your writing? Check out some good and bad reasons in Figure 3-2.

Figure 3-2

Using a
computer for
your
writing—
good and
bad reasons

**Good reasons to use a computer
for your writing**

- You don't trust your spelling.

- You want to improve your grammar and
writing style.

- When you proofread your work, you see
scotions that you know you can improve.

- You have good ideas and you want people
(including your instructors) to pay
attention to them.

- You're a perfectionist.

- You're not a good typist.

- You can't afford to hire a good typist.

**Bad reasons to use a computer
for your writing**

- You never get started until the last minute.

- You're too lazy to proofread your
document.

- You want to "borrow" your roommate's
report from last semester.

- You hope your readers will be so
impressed with your graphics and layout
that they don't read what you have written.

A Nation of Typists

Do I really have to know how to type? Typing was once a specialized skill practiced mainly by women in secretarial positions, but it is now a skill possessed to some degree by a sizable percentage of the population in highly literate nations. The pervasiveness of this skill stems from the popularity of computerized document production.

InfoWeb

Typing
2

To use a computer to produce documents, typing on a keyboard is pretty much required. Surprisingly, enrollments in typing classes have not increased. Although there are advantages to being a good keyboarder, you don't need to be an expert typist to create documents. Document production software has a variety of features that help you create error-free documents. In addition, many people are finding that their typing skills quickly improve beyond hunt-and-peck just by using computers from day to day. Typing tutor software can help you quickly increase your typing speed and accuracy without taking a course.

Typically, creating a document requires several steps. To begin, you type the text using a word processor. Next, you edit the document until you are satisfied with the content and writing style. Then, you might use the word-processing software to format and print the document. Alternatively, you might transfer your document to desktop publishing software to complete the layout and printing.

As you type your document, don't get distracted by how your final product will look. Instead, concentrate on expressing your ideas. Later, when you're satisfied with the content of your document, you can shift your focus to the details of how your document will look on paper.

When you use document production software correcting typing and spelling errors is easy. Some word-processing software features **in-line spell checking** that checks the spelling of each word as you type, as shown in Figure 3-3.

Figure 3-3

In-line spell check

A wiggly red line indicates a possible spelling error.

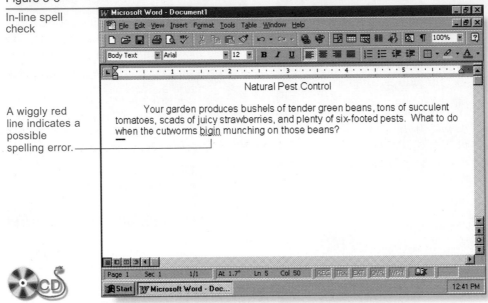

Correcting obvious typographic errors as you're writing is a real benefit, but don't fall into the "tweaking trap." Many writers dither around while writing their first draft, trying to perfect each sentence before continuing. Writing instructors suggest that you can produce better documents faster if you just let your words flow. When you get to a tricky spot, mark the place with a few question marks or asterisks, then continue. You can return to these spots later to select the exact words you want to use.

Word processors make it easy to let your ideas flow because they automatically handle many of the tasks that distracted writers who used typewriters. For example, you don't need to worry about typing off the edge of the paper. With document production software, a feature called **word wrap** takes care of where to break lines. Imagine that the sentences in your document are ribbons of text and word wrap bends the ribbons. Changing margins just means bending the ribbon in different places. Even after you have typed an entire document, adjusting the size of your right, left, top, and bottom margins is simple.

Writing Quality

Does document production software improve writing quality? Computers have been accused of dumping a mountain of poor quality documents into circulation. To anyone who reads electronic mail it soon becomes painfully clear that many literate people still have trouble with spelling and grammar. Some observers characterize the material exchanged in online discussions and newsgroups as crude, silly, uninformed, and self-serving. This criticism implies that instead of helping writers, computers have somehow lowered literary standards.

InfoWeb

Improve
Your
Writing
3

Perhaps much of this criticism is misplaced. Pulp fiction lined bookstore shelves long before computers graced the drawing boards of IBM and Apple. In any case, people—not computers—create documents. Those spelling errors, grammatical blunders, incoherent arguments, and unverified assertions are probably attributable to human fallibility, rather than to some computer-sponsored plot to subvert literature as we know it.

When used skillfully, computerized document production tools can help you improve the quality of your writing. With such tools, it is easy to edit the first draft of your document to refine its overall structure, then zero in to make detailed improvements to your sentence structure and word usage.

Figure 3-4

The late Isaac Asimov was one of this century's most prolific writers. When describing the writing process, he said, "My routine was (and still is) to write a story in its first draft as fast as I can. Then go over it, and correct errors in spelling, grammar, and word order."

Using document production tools, you can easily insert text, cut sections of text, and move entire paragraphs or pages to improve the structure and logical flow of a document. In document production terminology, sections of your document are referred to as **blocks**. Deleting or moving blocks are sometimes referred to as **block operations**.

Although document production software simplifies block operations, you first need to decide how to rearrange your document for a more effective progression of ideas. Some writers find that the limited amount of text displayed on the screen prevents them from getting a good look at the overall flow of ideas throughout the document. One solution is to use the outline feature of your software.

An **outliner** helps you develop a document as a hierarchy of headings and subheadings. This textbook, for example, is structured into chapters, sections, and subsections. When you create a hierarchical document you "tag" each heading to identify whether it starts a chapter, section, or subsection. To get an overall view of the document your software can show only the chapter headings. Or, to view the structure in more detail, the outliner can display the chapter headings and the section headings. When you move a heading in outline view, the outliner automatically moves all its subheadings and paragraphs.

As an alternative to outlining, you might try a time-tested, low-tech technique that works for creative writing as well as hierarchically structured documents. Print out your first draft, then cut it into pieces, paragraph by paragraph. Spread these paragraphs out on the floor and rearrange them until you're satisfied that you have the most logical, effective, and compelling organization. Finally, you can use the block move feature of your software to duplicate your new organization.

Once you have taken care of the overall structure of your document, you can turn to the details of word usage, spelling, and grammar. For example, you might use your software's **thesaurus** to help you find more descriptive words to clarify and enliven your writing.

Some writers know that they tend to overuse certain words or use them incorrectly. For instance, you might tend to overuse the word "however." If you have specific writing problems such as this, you might use the **search feature** to hunt for all the occurrences of your problem word. For each occurrence, you can decide to leave it or revise it. Another feature, **search and replace**, is handy if you want to substitute one word or phrase for another. For example, after you finish the first draft of a short story, you might change its location by using search and replace to change every occurrence of "Texas" to "New Mexico."

Now, what about spelling? A document with spelling errors reflects poorly on the writer. Most document production tools, including newer e-mail editors, have some type of spell check feature. An **in-line spell checker** shows you errors as you type. A less sophisticated, but equally useful, spell checker looks through your entire document any time you activate it. You would generally use this type of spell checker when you have completed your first draft, then again just before you print (Figure 3-5).

Figure 3-5

Using a full-document spell checker

The spell checker finds a misspelled word and highlights it.

The speller checker offers some correctly spelled options.

You can select one of the options to replace the misspelling using the Change button. To leave the word as is, you would click the Ignore button.

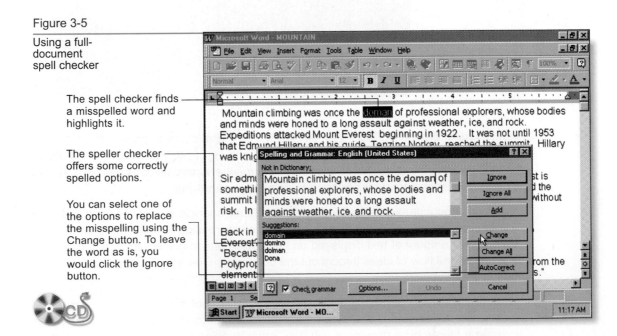

Don't depend on a spell checker to proofread your document. A spell checker works by looking for each word from your document in a list called a **dictionary**. If the word from your document is in the dictionary, the spell checker considers the word correctly spelled. If the word is not in the dictionary, the word is counted as misspelled. Sounds OK, right? Well, suppose your document contains a reference to the city of "Negaunee." This word is not in the dictionary, so the spell checker considers it misspelled. It might even suggest that you change the word to "negate"—a word that does appear in the dictionary. Because they are not in the dictionary, proper nouns and scientific, medical, and technical words are likely to be flagged as misspelled, even if you have spelled them correctly. If you plan to use such words often, you can add them to the dictionary.

Now suppose that your document contains the phrase "a pear of shoes." Although you meant to use "pair," not "pear," the spell checker will not catch your mistake because "pear" is a valid word in the dictionary. Your spell checker won't help if you have trouble deciding whether to use "there" or "their," "its" or "it's," "too" or "to." Remember, then, that a spell check will not substitute for a thorough proofread.

InfoWeb

Grammar
4

All languages are complex. English, for example, is characterized by many linguists as having an exception to every rule. You can clear up many grammatical questions by using a **grammar checker**, a feature of most word processors that coaches you on correct sentence structure and word usage. Think of a grammar checker as an assistant that will proofread your document, point out potential trouble spots, and suggest alternatives. If English is your second language, a grammar checker might be especially helpful.

A grammar checker will not change your document for you. Instead it points out possible problems, suggests alternate words or phrases, and gives you the option of making changes. For example, if a document contains the sentence, "Did the plot turn out like you expected?" a grammar checker might point out that you should consider using "as" instead of "like." Refer to Figure 3-6.

Figure 3-6

A grammar checker suggests a change, but you decide whether to accept the suggestion.

The grammar checker highlights the sentence it is currently checking.

The problem is indicated in green.

A suggestion for improvement.

If requested, the grammar checker explains the basis for its suggestion.

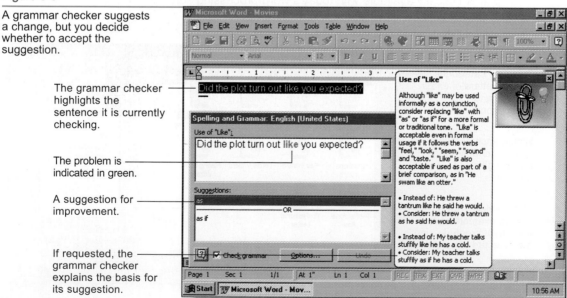

Formatting a Document

How does document production software help create documents that look great?

Before the printing press, documents were hand copied. In the Middle Ages, artists and monks huddled in cavernous rooms called "scriptoria" to painstakingly hand copy religious documents. Many of these hand-copied documents, called "illuminated manuscripts," were works of art in addition to a means of communicating information. These manuscripts often contained illustrations, elaborately detailed initial letters on each page, and decorative borders. Most of these manuscripts were commissioned by wealthy aristocrats. Figure 3-7 shows an example of an illuminated manuscript.

Figure 3-7

Vatican library illuminated manuscript

Beautifully crafted documents are no longer a special perk of wealth. Modern printing techniques make it cost-effective to produce beautiful documents that are available to everyone in libraries, bookstores, and newsstands. In addition, today's document production software provides individuals with the tools necessary to produce professionally formatted and illustrated documents. When you create documents, you'll want to take advantage of formatting tools such as document templates, wizards, fonts, styles, borders, and clip art.

A **document template** is a preformatted document into which you type your text. Most document production software encourages you to select a template before you type the text for your first draft. If you don't select a template, the software will select one for you—usually a plain template suitable for letters and reports. Format settings such as margins, line spacing, heading fonts, and type size have all been set up for you. Figure 3-8 shows some of the document templates typically available with today's word-processing software.

Figure 3-8

Document templates

Template categories include letters, memos, reports, and publications.

Within each category you can choose from several different templates.

The preview shows you an example of a document created using the selected template.

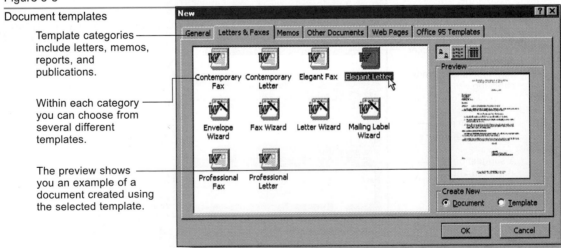

You might wonder if selecting a template before you begin to type contradicts the conventional advice to ignore formatting issues for your first draft. In practice, you'll want to select a template and perhaps format your headings as you type. You can postpone the rest of your formatting activities until you're satisfied with the content.

Some software goes a step further than templates by furnishing you with **document wizards** that not only provide you with a document format, but take you step by step through the process of entering the text for a wide variety of documents. You'll want to check out the templates and wizards provided by your software before you struggle with creating your own formats. For example, to create an entry-level resume, you might find it easy to use a resume wizard like the one shown in Figure 3-9.

Figure 3-9

Entry-level resume wizard

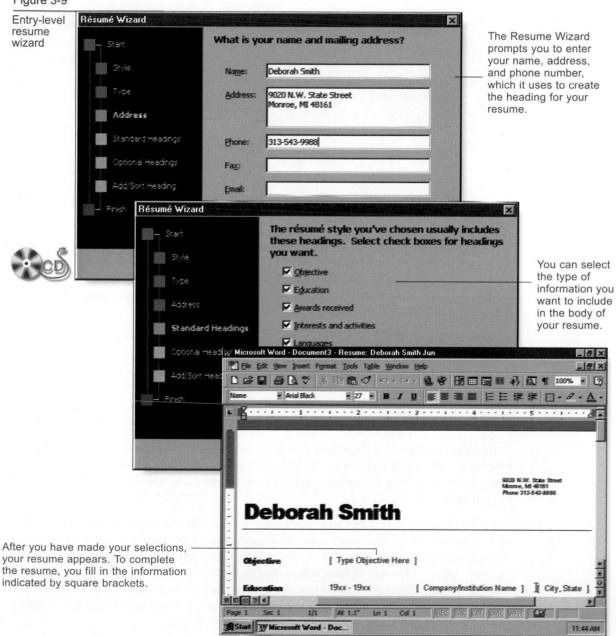

The Resume Wizard prompts you to enter your name, address, and phone number, which it uses to create the heading for your resume.

You can select the type of information you want to include in the body of your resume.

After you have made your selections, your resume appears. To complete the resume, you fill in the information indicated by square brackets.

InfoWeb

Fonts
5

The **font** you select has a major impact on the look of your document. Fonts are designed by typesetters and artists. Your document production software generally supplies you with many fonts. If you want even more variety, you can purchase and install additional font collections.

Typeset fonts such as Times New Roman and Arial make your document look formal and professionally produced. Research studies show that serif fonts are easier to read on the printed page, whereas sans serif fonts are easier to read on the computer screen. In addition, a kerned font is easier to read than a monospaced font. Figure 3-10 shows you the difference between a serif and a sans serif font, and the difference between a kerned font and a monospaced font.

Figure 3-10

Serifs and kerning

Each character of a monospaced font takes up the same amount of space.	Wow, look at this!
A kerned font provides a wider space for wide letters such as "w," but reduces the amount of space allotted to narrow letters such as "t."	Wow, look at this!
A serif font has small embellishments called "serifs" on the ends of the lines that form the characters.	**Wow, look at this!**
A sans serif font lacks serifs.	Wow, look at this!

You can also use simulated **handwriting fonts** to give your document a more personal appeal. Why not just write the document by hand? You can spell check your work—something you can't do if you just scribble a note—and you can mix the handwriting fonts with more conventional, typeset fonts. Some companies will scan in your handwriting and convert it into your own personal handwritten font for use on your computer.

In addition to selecting fonts, you can manipulate the look of your document by adjusting the line spacing, margins, indents, tabs, borders, and frames. Additional space makes a document easier to read. Larger margins and double-spacing generate white space, make your document appear less dense, and make reading seem easier. The margins for most papers and reports should be set at 1 inch or 1.5 inches. Unless double spacing is required, most word processors set the line spacing at an appropriate distance for the font size.

Justification defines how the letters and words are spaced across each line. Typeset documents are often fully justified so the text on the right margin as well as on the left margin is aligned evenly. Your document will look more formal if it is fully justified than if it has a ragged right margin.

Columns enhance readability and tables organize data. In document production terminology, **columns** generally mean newspaper-style layout of paragraphs of text. **Tables** arrange data in a grid of rows and columns. Tables are more appropriate than columns for numeric data and for lists of information. For example, if you are creating a "two-column" resume, you should use the table function in your word-processing software. Don't waste your time trying to arrange columns or tables using the tab key and space bar. Instead, use your software's automatic table feature or column format.

When you summarize or list information, or even when you type your answers to homework questions, your points will stand out if you use hanging indents, bulleted lists, or numbered lists as shown in Figure 3-11.

Figure 3-11

Hanging indent

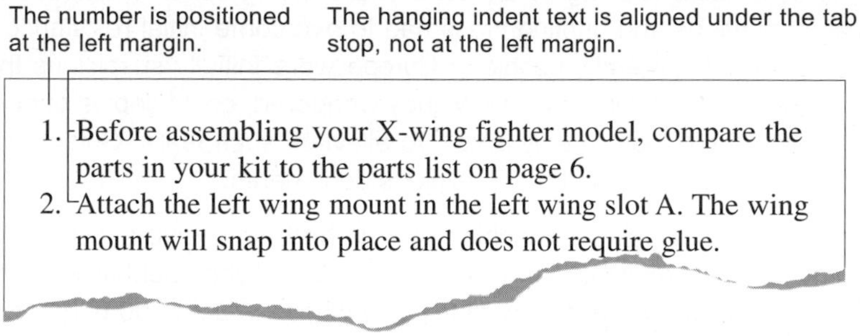

The number is positioned at the left margin.

The hanging indent text is aligned under the tab stop, not at the left margin.

1. Before assembling your X-wing fighter model, compare the parts in your kit to the parts list on page 6.
2. Attach the left wing mount in the left wing slot A. The wing mount will snap into place and does not require glue.

To add visual interest to your documents, incorporate borders, rules, and graphics. A **border** is a box around text or graphics—usually around a title, heading, or table. A **rule** is a line, usually positioned under text. Rules can be horizontal, vertical or diagonal. The thinnest rule is one pixel thick and called a **hairline rule**.

Graphics are pictures and illustrations. Clip-art collections provide hundreds of images that you have permission to use in non-commercial works. You can also find graphics on the Internet. With the right equipment, you can scan pictures from books and magazines. Just be sure you check for permission before you use any graphic in your documents.

Most document production software uses frames as containers for graphics. A **frame** is an invisible box that you can position anywhere on the page. Generally you can flow text around the frame and layer frames one on top of another to achieve complex layout effects as shown in Figure 3-12.

Figure 3-12

Frames

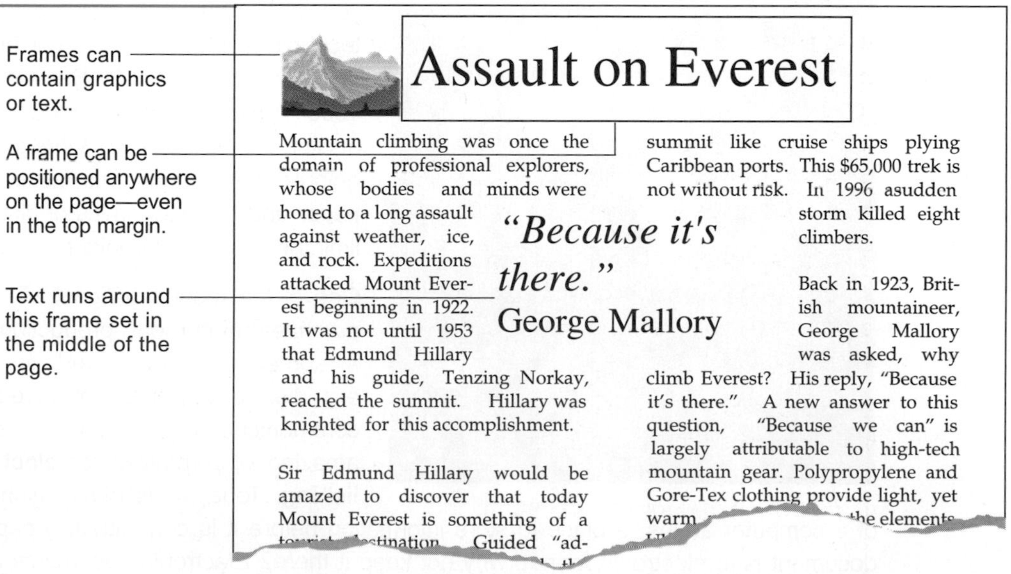

Frames can contain graphics or text.

A frame can be positioned anywhere on the page—even in the top margin.

Text runs around this frame set in the middle of the page.

Assault on Everest

Mountain climbing was once the domain of professional explorers, whose bodies and minds were honed to a long assault against weather, ice, and rock. Expeditions attacked Mount Everest beginning in 1922. It was not until 1953 that Edmund Hillary and his guide, Tenzing Norkay, reached the summit. Hillary was knighted for this accomplishment.

Sir Edmund Hillary would be amazed to discover that today Mount Everest is something of a tourist destination. Guided "ad-

"Because it's there."
George Mallory

summit like cruise ships plying Caribbean ports. This $65,000 trek is not without risk. In 1996 a sudden storm killed eight climbers.

Back in 1923, British mountaineer, George Mallory was asked, why climb Everest? His reply, "Because it's there." A new answer to this question, "Because we can" is largely attributable to high-tech mountain gear. Polypropylene and Gore-Tex clothing provide light, yet warm the elements.

The Power of the Printed Word

What are the options for printing and publishing documents? Printing with moveable type existed in Asia as early as 1000 A.D. However, until Johann Gutenberg demonstrated his moveable type printing press in 1448, this technology did not exist in Europe. Printing eventually replaced hand copying as a means of producing documents, but as with many technological innovations, the printing press had to overcome initial resistance from some segments of society. Apparently, people in Europe were initially suspicious that the new printing techniques were black magic. How, they wondered, could copies of documents be produced so quickly and look exactly alike? To alleviate such fears, Gutenberg and other early printers produced Bibles and other religious documents.

InfoWeb

Publishing
6

The change from hand copying to machine printing had a massive effect on Western culture and civilization by making information available to all who could read. Thomas Paine harnessed the power of the printed word in 1776 when he sold 500,000 copies of a 50-page pamphlet, *Common Sense*. This document asserted that it was just common sense for the American colonies to become independent from Great Britain. Six months later, the Declaration of Independence was signed. Thomas Paine and his compatriot, Thomas Jefferson, envisioned a free press as the cornerstone of a free society. They hoped that publishing would spread ideas, foster dialogs between diverse interest groups, and help to establish a common social agenda (Figure 3-13).

Figure 3-13

When Thomas Paine sold 500,000 copies of *Common Sense*, the colonies had a population of only four million.

Early expectations were that computerized document production would make it easy for individuals, not just publishing companies, to produce professional-quality books and pamphlets. Word processors have made it possible for individuals to create more documents, such as newsletters and manuscripts. However, computerized document production has had only a moderate effect on traditional paper-based publishing. If you assumed that document production technology would produce a huge glut of new books, think again. Between 1993 and 1995 American book production actually declined by 5,000 titles. Although computers help produce documents faster, the cost of paper and the economics of distribution still limit the number of books published.

One of the most significant effects of computerized document production came as a somewhat unexpected surprise. The expedient development of a worldwide data communications network has opened up amazing opportunities for **electronic publishing**. Today, it is old fashioned to think of a computer as just a place to store information before it is committed to paper. Once a document is in electronic format, why not keep it there? Electronic documents are easy to send, store, and manipulate. They might even bring us closer to the global democracy that Thomas Paine envisioned. Today virtually anyone can post a document on the World Wide

Web, send an e-mail message, or participate in online discussion groups. The power of the printed word seems to be evolving into the power of the electronically published word (Figure 3-14).

Figure 3-14

Many activists believed that certain provisions of the U.S. Telecommunications Act of 1996 would limit freedom of speech on the Internet. Massive protests on electronic forums and a well-engineered lawsuit prompted the Supreme Court to declare that many parts of the Act were unconstitutional.

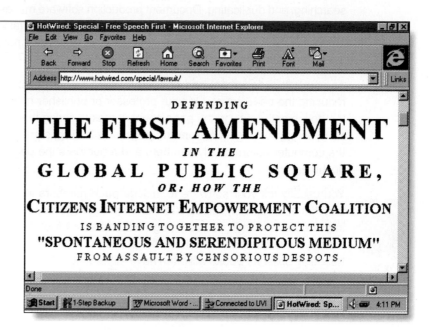

To create Web pages, many word processors and desktop publishers automatically generate an HTML formatted document from any document you have entered and stored. When you create a Web page, your goal should be to effectively combine and format basic Web elements to create a visual display that enhances the content of your page. The basic elements of a Web page are shown in Figure 3-15.

Figure 3-15

Web page elements

Web page title

URL

Two separately scrolling frames

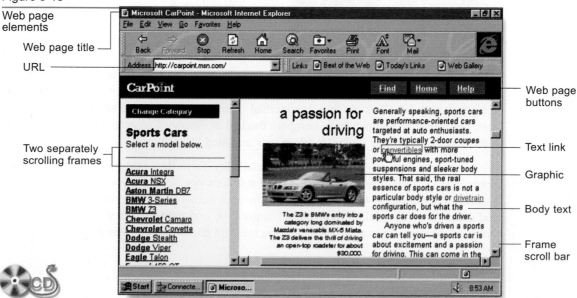

Automating Document Production

How can I harness the power of a computer to automate document production tasks?

Computers are pretty talented when it comes to repetitive tasks such as counting, numbering, searching, and duplicating. Document production software makes clever use of the computer's talents in these areas to automate many of the repetitive tasks associated with document production. Automating such tasks saves time and increases productivity. Let's look briefly at a few of the more useful tasks in this category.

As you edit a document and change its format, you might remove large sections of text, reducing the page count. Or, your professor or publisher might insist that you double space the document, doubling the page count. It makes sense then to let the software take care of numbering your pages. **Automatic page numbering**, sometimes called **pagination**, means the computer automatically numbers and renumbers the pages as you edit and format your document.

InfoWeb

Who Wrote It? 7

You usually tell your software to include page numbers in a header or footer. A **header** is text that automatically appears in the top margin of every page. A **footer** is text that appears in the bottom margin of every page. Headers and footers help identify the document and make your documents look more like published works. Look at a page in this book. It has a header. Published books will often have either a header, a footer, or both on each page. Your documents can easily have these professional elements. A simple footer might be the word "Page," followed by the current page number. For identification purposes, you might put your name in the header of your documents.

Figure 3-16

Joe Klein, the "anonymous" author of *Primary Colors*

Does your English professor want a 1,000-word essay? Your computer can count the words in a document with the **automatic word count** feature of your document production software. Another use for a computer's ability to count words is for literary analysis. A **concordance** is an alphabetized list of words in a document and the frequency with which each word appears. Concordance has been used to determine authorship of historical and contemporary documents by comparing the frequencies of words used in a document by an unknown author to the frequencies of words used in a document of known authorship. The anonymously authored novel, *Primary Colors*, was widely speculated to be based on behind-the-scenes wheeling and dealing during Bill Clinton's first presidential campaign. Vassar professor Donald Foster used concordance techniques to compare the text of *Primary Colors* to a series of columns written by journalist Joe Klein. Mr. Klein later admitted his authorship.

Most grammar checkers have built in **readability formulas** that count the number of words in each sentence and the number of syllables per word. As you write, you can use readability formulas to target your writing to your audience. The longer your sentences and words, the higher the reading level required to understand your writing. Most writers aim for a seventh- or eighth-grade reading level on documents for the general public.

Scholarly documents often require **footnotes** that contain citations for works mentioned in the text. As you revise your text, the footnotes need to stay associated with their source in the text and must be numbered sequentially. Your document production software includes footnoting facilities that correctly position and number the footnotes even if you move blocks of text. Need end notes instead of footnotes? Your software can gather your citations at the end of your document and print them in order of their appearance in the document or in alphabetical order. Some word processors even have wizards that help you enter your citations in the correct format depending on whether they are books or magazine articles.

Longer documents benefit from a **table of contents** and an **index**. Because of document production technology, many people have come to expect that all documents, not just those created by professional publishers, have indexes and tables of contents. Most document production software will automatically generate an index and table of contents, then automatically update them as you edit your document.

Boilerplating refers to the process of merging standard paragraphs to create a new document. Law offices frequently use boilerplating to draw up legal documents for wills, divorces, trusts, and so on.

Mail merge automates the process of producing customized documents such as letters and advertising flyers. You might use mail merge to send out application letters when you're searching for a job. Figure 3-17 explains how it works.

Figure 3-17

To set up a mail merge, you create a document containing specially marked "blanks." You also create a file of information that goes in the blanks each time the document is printed. Your document production software will merge the document and the information.

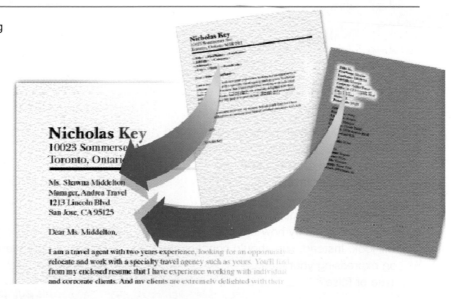

Document Production Technology

Now I'm convinced that I need a word processor—what are my options? In a consumer society, the name of the game is "variety." Consumers who shop for document production technology have a dazzling variety of hardware and software options. To get the right product and stay within your budget, you should be aware of the major product categories.

Word-processing technology includes inexpensive electronic typewriters, personal word processors, and personal computers. In Figure 3-18 you can compare the price and features of today's word-processing technologies.

Figure 3-18

Word-processing technology

A **personal computer** set up for word-processing includes hard and floppy disk drives, and a screen. Word-processing software and a printer might need to be purchased separately. $1,500 to $2,000 including printer and software.

An **electronic typewriter** has a 3–5 line screen display, stores a few pages in memory, and has a built in printer. $200.

A **personal word processor** includes a larger screen, floppy disk drive, and printer, but does not run a large variety of other software. $400.

QuickCheck A

1 The spread of literacy went hand-in-hand with technology developments, culminating in today's use of computers and _____ software.

2 When you type a document, it is best not to get distracted by how the final product will look. Instead, you should concentrate on expressing your ideas. True or false? _____

3 A feature of word-processing software called _____ takes care of where to break lines of text.

4 The spell check feature of word-processing software would alert you if you accidentally used the word "see" instead of "sea" when referring to a large body of water. True or false? _____

5 A(n) _____ provides preset formats for a document, whereas a(n) _____ is a feature that coaches you step-by-step through the process of entering text into a document.

6 One of the most significant effects of computerized document production has been to encourage _____ publishing.

7 _____ has been used to establish the authorship of historical and contemporary documents.

8 Documents that are posted on the World Wide Web must be in _____ format.

B Spreadsheets and Worksheets

Mathephobia /maθ(ə) 'fəʊbiə/ mathe after Fr *mathematiques* the abstract deductive science of number and quantity + phobia L f. Gk,f. `phobos` denoting fear, dislike, antipathy as in hope to never take another math class again.

Spreadsheets

The United States is one of the most technological societies on earth. Therefore, the population's resistance to math, as evidenced by standardized test scores, is somewhat surprising. People with mathephobia hate to balance their checkbooks, calculate their tax returns, work out expense budgets, or decide what to do about financing their retirement.

Sensing financial opportunity, entrepreneurs have devised a number of tools to ease the burden of making calculations. To date, the most ambitious of these tools is the computerized spreadsheet. A **spreadsheet** is a numerical model or representation of a real situation. For example, your checkbook register is a sort of spreadsheet because it is a numerical representation of the cash flowing in and out of your bank account. One expert describes spreadsheets as "intuitive, natural, usable tools for financial analysis, business and mathematical modeling, decision making, simulation, and problem solving."

Using a spreadsheet is fairly straightforward. You enter the numbers you want to calculate and then indicate how you want the computer to manipulate those numbers. For example, suppose you're planning a one-week trip to Mexico to see the Mayan ruins at Chichen Itza (Figure 3-19).

Figure 3-19

Caracol at Chichen Itza

You're interested in the total cost of the trip. Using spreadsheet software, you can enter the cost of transportation, food, and lodging. Then, you can tell the computer to add these numbers together to give you a total. Does this sound like a job you can do with your trusty handheld calculator? You can, but spreadsheet software has advantages your calculator just can't provide.

A handheld calculator might be useful for simple calculations, but it becomes less convenient as you deal with more numbers and as your calculations get more complex. For example, the food and lodging calculation for the Mexico trip requires several steps as shown in Figure 3-20.

Figure 3-20

Calculations for
the Mexico Trip

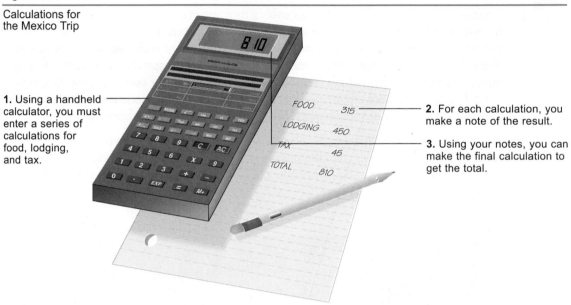

1. Using a handheld calculator, you must enter a series of calculations for food, lodging, and tax.

FOOD   315

LODGING   450

TAX   45

TOTAL   810

2. For each calculation, you make a note of the result.

3. Using your notes, you can make the final calculation to get the total.

The biggest disadvantage of most calculators is that the numbers you entered are stored, but you can't see them. You can't verify if they're accurate. Also, it is difficult to change the numbers you have entered without starting the whole calculation over again. By contrast, if you use spreadsheet software, all your numbers are visible on the screen, and they are easy to change. You can print your results as a nicely formatted report, you can convert your numbers into a graph, and you can save your work and revise it later. You can easily incorporate your calculations and results into other electronic documents, post them as Web pages, and e-mail them to your colleagues.

Spreadsheet Basics

What does a spreadsheet look like? A company that publishes spreadsheet software estimates that today there are more than 20 million people in the world busily using spreadsheets. Certainly this software has had a major effect on the way people work with numbers. What's the big attraction? To answer this question, it's important to understand how spreadsheets work.

You use spreadsheet software to create an on-screen spreadsheet called a **worksheet**. A worksheet is based on a grid of **columns** and **rows.** Each column is lettered and each row is numbered. The intersection of a column and row is called a **cell**. Each cell has a unique **address** derived from its column and row location. For example, the upper-left cell in a worksheet is cell A1 because it is in column A of row 1.

A cell can contain a number, text, or a formula. A **number** is a value that you want to use in a calculation. **Text** is used for the worksheet title and for labels that identify the numbers. For example, suppose your worksheet contains the number $2,559.81. You could use text to identify this number as "Income." A **formula** tells the computer how to use the contents of cells in calculations. You can use formulas to add, subtract, multiply, and divide numbers. Figure 3-21 illustrates a simple spreadsheet that performs subtraction to calculate savings.

Figure 3-21

A typical worksheet displays numbers and text in a grid of rows and columns. Cell B6 contains the result of a calculation performed by the spreadsheet software.

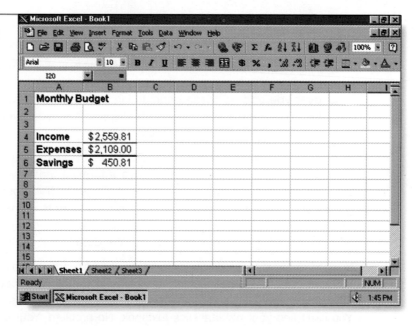

Calculations

How does spreadsheet software work? The value of spreadsheet software is the way it handles the numbers and formulas in a worksheet. Think of the worksheet as having two layers—the layer you see and a hidden layer underneath. The hidden layer can hold formulas, but the result of these formulas appears on the visible layer. Figure 3-22 shows how this works.

Figure 3-22

The formula =B4-B5 works behind the scenes to tell the computer to subtract the number in cell B5 from the number in cell B4. The formula is located in cell B6, but what appears in cell B6 is not the formula but its results.

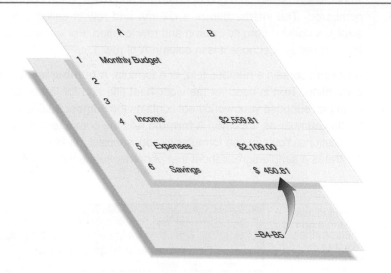

Whenever you add or change something in a cell, the spreadsheet calculates all the formulas. This means that the results displayed on your worksheet always reflect the current figures contained in the cells.

Formulas can include numbers and references to other cells. This is what gives a spreadsheet such flexibility. If you have a formula that says "subtract the contents of cell B5 from the contents of B4" it doesn't matter what those cells contain. The result will be accurate even if you later change the contents of these cells. Using **cell references** such as B5 and B4, you can create generic formulas such as =B4-B5 that work no matter how many times you change the data in these cells.

You can enter your own formulas to specify how to carry out calculations. As another option, you can select a predefined formula called a **function**. Suppose you've got a research assignment and you need to find the standard deviation of test scores for a school district. You can't find your old statistics textbook. No problem. Your spreadsheet software has a built-in function to calculate standard deviations. You just enter the test scores in a series of cells and tell the computer to use the standard deviation function for the calculation. Most spreadsheet software includes hundreds of functions for mathematical, financial, and statistical calculations.

Creating a Simple Worksheet

How do I create a simple worksheet? Building a worksheet from scratch requires thought and planning so that you end up with an accurate and well-organized worksheet. When you create your own worksheets, use these seven steps as guidelines:

InfoWeb

Spreadsheet Tips 8

1. **Determine the main purpose of the worksheet.** Write down the purpose to make sure it is clear. For example, if you were going to make a worksheet for the Mexico trip, you might write, "The purpose of this worksheet is to calculate the total cost of a trip to Chichen Itza for one person next October."

2. **List the information available to solve the problem.** In the case of the Mexico trip, your list might include cost of airfare, number of days for the trip, daily lodging cost, the lodging tax percent, and daily food costs. Consider which of your numbers might be variable. For example, if you're planning a trip to Mexico, the number of days you'll stay might be variable—depending on what you can afford.

3. **Make a list of the calculations you'll need.** For example, your Mexico trip calculations include adding up the cost of food, lodging, and tax.

4. **Enter numbers and labels in the cells.** When you enter the numbers, make sure you put a descriptive label in an adjoining cell, usually to the left of the data. It's also a good idea to include a title at the top of the worksheet.

5. **Enter the formulas.**

6. **Test the worksheet.** There are various ways to do this that you'll learn about later, but the first question to ask yourself is "Do these results make sense?" If the results shown on the worksheet don't seem to be "in the ballpark" of what you expected, maybe you've made a typo when entering a formula. You'll need to check your numbers and formulas and make revisions until the worksheet produces correct results.

7. **Save and print the worksheet.** Figure 3-23 shows the Mexico worksheet before printing.

Figure 3-23

Mexico trip worksheet

Every worksheet should have a title.

Documentation helps you keep track of revisions and explains how the sheet was created in case someone else needs to revise it.

Labels identify data.

These numbers are used in the formulas in column C.

In the cells that contain formulas, only the results appear.

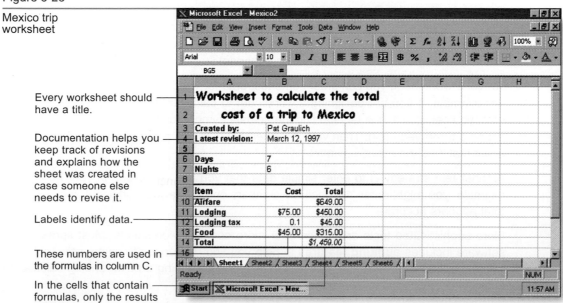

Worksheet Templates

What if I'm not sure how to set up a worksheet? If you have trouble creating a worksheet from scratch, you might find a predefined template that meets your needs. A template is essentially a worksheet form created by professionals who have done all the formatting and formulas for you. If you decide to use a template, you simply select the template you want and then fill it in with your numbers. One popular spreadsheet program offers templates for the following tasks:

- Tracking a household budget

- Deciding on the best car lease option

- Creating a business plan

- Invoicing customers

- Providing customers with a sales quote

- Creating purchase orders

- Calculating monthly loan payments

- Recording business expenses while you travel

- Tracking the time you work on various projects

Who's Responsible?

How do I know if my spreadsheet is producing correct results? The United States has more lawyers per capita than any other country in the world. In a society where lawsuits seem as common as weddings, it might be prudent to consider who is responsible for the accuracy of a spreadsheet. For example, who's fault is it when a project runs over budget because the formula to total up all the costs was not accurate?

InfoWeb

Errors
9

In a well-publicized case, a company discovered that an incomplete worksheet formula resulted in a loss of several hundreds of thousands of dollars. The company sued the spreadsheet publisher, claiming that the software was faulty. The lawsuit was dropped. Responsibility for the accuracy of a worksheet lies with the person who creates it.

In a business situation, an error in a worksheet formula can cost a company hundreds of thousands of dollars. But even if the stakes are not that high for the worksheets you create, you should make an effort to verify the accuracy of your data and formulas. The prime directive of worksheet design is "Don't rely on your worksheet until you test it." Testing, called **auditing** in spreadsheet jargon, is important.

To test a worksheet, you can enter some test data for which you already know the result. For example, if you are designing a worksheet to calculate monthly payments for a car loan, you can use a loan table to find the actual payment for a $12,000 car at 8.5% interest on a three-year loan. Then you can enter this data into your worksheet and see if the result matches the actual payment.

Another test strategy is to enter simple data that you can figure out "in your head." For example, you might enter "1" for all the numbers on the Mexico worksheet and see if the total appears accurate.

More sophisticated tests are required for more complex worksheets. Most spreadsheet software includes **auditing features** to help you find references to empty cells, cells not referenced, and formulas that reference themselves, causing a never-ending calculating loop.

Modifying Worksheets

Can I modify my spreadsheets? Modifying the text, numbers, and formulas on a worksheet is as easy as using a word processor's insert and delete features. As soon as you enter new numbers in a worksheet, the computer recalculates all the formulas, keeping the results up-to-date.

You can also modify the structure of a worksheet by inserting rows and columns, deleting rows and columns, or moving the contents of cells to other cells. Many inexperienced spreadsheet users might hesitate to make such structural changes. Why? Suppose you've created a spreadsheet and have tested all its formulas. You decide to delete row 3, which is currently blank. All the labels, numbers, and formulas move up one row. But what's happened to that formula that used to reference cells B4 and B5? Now those numbers have moved up to cells B3 and B4. Do you have to revise all the formulas on your worksheet? Happily, the answer is no.

When you insert, delete, or move cells, the spreadsheet software attempts to adjust your formulas so the cell references they contain are still accurate, as shown in Figure 3-24.

Figure 3-24

Spreadsheet software adjusts formulas when you insert or delete cells.

1. A formula in cell B6 calculates savings based on numbers in cells B4 and B5.

2. The spreadsheet software automatically changes the formula to reflect the new location of the Income and Expenses numbers.

What if you don't want the formula to change? You can define any reference in a formula as an absolute reference. An **absolute reference** never changes when you insert rows or copy or move formulas. Understanding when to use absolute references is one of the key aspects to developing spreadsheet design expertise.

Spreadsheet "Intelligence"

In what sense is spreadsheet software intelligent? When mainframe computers first made the headlines in the 1950s, they had an unsettling effect on the American public. And no wonder. Headlines dubbed these computers "Giant Brains," and journalists speculated how long it might be until computers "took over." The public was pacified when word spread that computers could only follow the instructions of their human programmers.

Fifty years have passed since the Giant Brain headlines appeared. Computer technology has improved to the point where it sometimes seems that computers do have some sort of intelligence—or at least they seem to anticipate what you want them to do. You'll run into some examples of this when you use spreadsheet software.

An example that you'll recognize as soon as you begin to use spreadsheet software is its ability to distinguish between the data you're using for text and the data you're using for numbers. At first this might seem easy—text is letters and numbers are, well, numbers. But suppose that you want to enter a social security number in a cell. When you enter 375-80-9876 should the spreadsheet regard this as the subtraction formula—375 minus 80 minus 9876? Should the spreadsheet regard this as a single number 375809876 that can be used for mathematical operations? Or should the spreadsheet regard this as text that can not be mathematically manipulated? The answer is that your spreadsheet software will regard 375-80-9876 as text. If you think about this, you'll see that is correct. Even though we call these social security numbers, we don't add, subtract, multiply, or divide them. We treat them as text.

Shortcuts are another example of spreadsheet "intelligence." Spreadsheet software contains many handy shortcuts to help simplify the process of creating, editing, and formatting a worksheet. For example, fill operations continue a series you have started. Type "January" in one cell and "February" in the next, then use a fill operation and the spreadsheet will automatically enter the rest of the months in the next 10 cells. Fill operations also complete numerical sequences such as "1, 2, 3, 4.." or "1990, 1995, 2000…". Figure 3-25 shows how a fill operation works.

Figure 3-25

Filling cells with data

1. Type the first few numbers in a series.

2. The spreadsheet software will fill in the rest of the series.

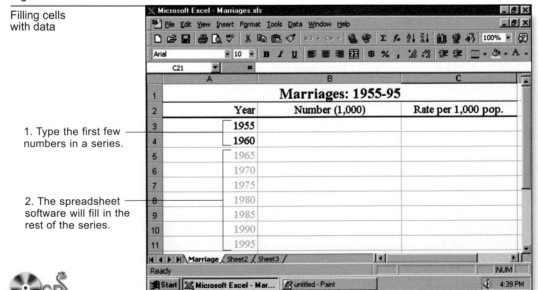

Formatting Worksheets

Does spreadsheet software provide formatting options similar to those provided by word-processing software? As the business world embraced spreadsheets, sharing them with colleagues, employees, and customers became important. Today, business meetings have an element of theater as computer projection devices display full-screen, full-color, beautifully formatted worksheets.

Spreadsheet software provides you with formatting options to improve the appearance of your worksheet. The formatting you use for a spreadsheet depends on your output plan. Worksheets that you intend to print might be formatted differently from worksheets that you intend to view only on the screen. Worksheets that you want to project for presentations often require a format different from printed worksheets.

Worksheets for routine calculations are much handier to use if you can see all the information without scrolling, so try to place all the labels, numbers, and formulas on one screen. If necessary, you can make the columns narrow so that more of them fit on the screen. If you're creating a worksheet for your own use, there's probably no need to spend time making it look attractive.

If you are going to print your spreadsheet, you'll want to spend some time creating an attractive format. Use a larger font for the title, and consider italicizing or boldfacing important numbers and their labels. Your worksheet will look more polished if you omit the grid lines between rows and columns. As when you format documents with a word processor, maintain a liberal amount of white space on the page. However, don't try to skip every other row to give the appearance of double spacing. If you do this, you'll have trouble graphing this data. Figure 3-26 provides some tips for improving the Mexico worksheet.

Figure 3-26

Formatting for a printed worksheet

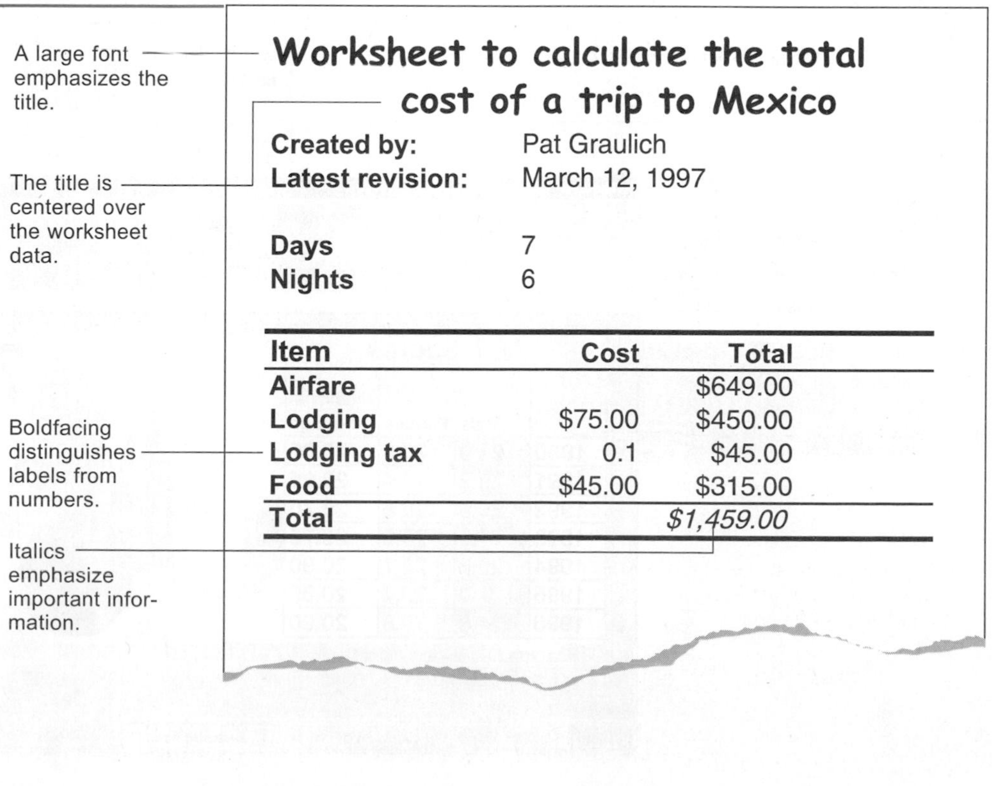

A large font emphasizes the title.

The title is centered over the worksheet data.

Boldfacing distinguishes labels from numbers.

Italics emphasize important information.

Worksheet to calculate the total cost of a trip to Mexico

Created by: Pat Graulich
Latest revision: March 12, 1997

Days 7
Nights 6

Item	Cost	Total
Airfare		$649.00
Lodging	$75.00	$450.00
Lodging tax	0.1	$45.00
Food	$45.00	$315.00
Total		*$1,459.00*

Spreadsheets for presentations must be legible when displayed by a projection device. You might consider a larger type size—one that can be easily viewed from the back of the room in which your worksheet will be projected. Scrolling is usually not desirable in a presentation situation, so try to fit the worksheet on one screen. You might have to move the documentation to another worksheet of the workbook to make room for the data and results that are important to your audience. Place your graphs on other pages of your workbook so you don't have to scroll to display them.

The use of color will make your presentation more interesting and help to highlight important data on the worksheet. However, if you are also planning to print your worksheet in black and white, select your colors carefully. Colors appear in shades of gray on a black-and-white printout. Some colors produce a dark shade of gray that obscures labels and numbers. Figure 3-27 provides some tips for formatting worksheets for presentations.

Figure 3-27

Spreadsheets for presentations should use large fonts and colors.

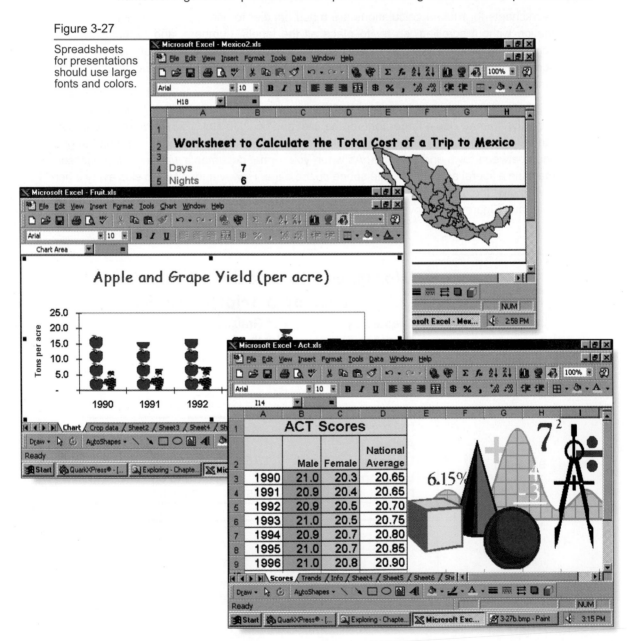

The Monkey's Paw

What about graphs and charts? During the 1992 Presidential election, the candidates jumped on the "one picture is worth a thousand words" bandwagon. This precipitated a parade of media events in which candidates spoke with great solemnity about trend lines, investments, and deficits against a backdrop of colorful charts and graphs. Especially noteworthy was Ross Perot brandishing a mummified monkey's paw to explain his opponent's policy of "voodoo economics" on a series of graphs (Figure 3-28).

Figure 3-28

Ross Perot used graphs during campaign '92.

Spreadsheet software is characterized by its ability to easily create professional-looking graphs and charts. Remember the unsatisfactory results you got by using graph paper and colored pencils? With spreadsheet software it is simple to create an attractive pie graph that illustrates opinion poll data, a line graph that drives home the alarming increase in the national debt, or a bar graph that compares market share for U.S. and foreign automobile manufacturers.

InfoWeb

Lie
11

Graphs, as you know, provide a quick summary or overview of a set of data. Trends that might be difficult to detect in columns of figures come into focus when skillfully graphed. Graphs are an effective presentation tool because they are simple to understand and visually interesting. However, when you design graphs, you have a responsibility to your audience to create a visual representation of the truth. Although you might not intentionally design a graph to "lie" it is all too easy to design a graph that implies something other than the truth. For example, which of the two graphs from Figure 3-29 do you think a sales manager would prefer to show?

The sales figures represented by the graph on the right certainly look better than those on the left. Look closely. The sales figures on both graphs are the same, but by changing the shape of the graph, the trend in sales can look either pretty tame or very dramatic. When you design a graph, try to consider how the average person would interpret it, then make sure that interpretation coincides with reality.

Figure 3-29

Graphs can "stretch the truth."

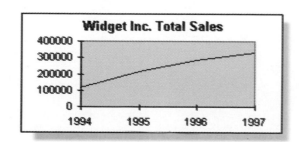

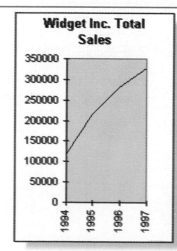

Claw Your Way to the Top with Spreadsheet Software

In what situations can I use spreadsheet software? Computerized spreadsheet software was invented in 1978 by a Harvard Business School student, Dan Bricklin. Many computer historians believe that his software, called VisiCalc, not only launched a new genre of computer software, but also put a rocket under the fledgling microcomputer industry and launched the Digital Age. Before the availability of VisiCalc, consumers couldn't think of much use for a personal computer. VisiCalc provided business people with a handy tool for making calculations without visiting a statistician or accountant. It contained all the basic elements of today's electronic spreadsheets—a screen-based grid of rows and columns, predefined functions, automatic calculations, formatting options, and rudimentary "intelligence" for copying and replicating formulas.

A spreadsheet works well for recording and graphing data, for making calculations, and for constructing numerical models of the real world. The main advantage of spreadsheet software is the time it saves—once you create a worksheet, you can change your data without redoing all your calculations. In addition, worksheet data is stored in electronic format so it can be merged with word-processing documents, posted on the Internet, or transmitted as part of an e-mail message.

Figure 3-30

Claw Your Way to the Top

CLAW YOUR WAY TO THE TOP
How to Become the Head of a Major Corporation in Roughly a Week
BY DAVE BARRY
Author of Babies and Other Hazards of Sex

In his tongue-in-cheek book, *Claw Your Way to the Top* (Figure 3-30), Dave Barry defines a spreadsheet as "a kind of program that lets you sit at your desk and ask all kinds of neat 'what if?' questions and generate thousands of numbers instead of actually working." The what-if questions are part of a process called spreadsheet modeling.

Spreadsheet modeling means setting up numbers in a worksheet to describe a real-world situation. For example, spreadsheets are often used for business modeling. The worksheet data represents or describes the financial activities in a business—products sold, expenses for employees, rent, inventory and so forth. By looking at the numbers in such a business model, you can get an idea of its current profitability. You can also experiment with changing some of the numbers in the model to see how changes in business activities might affect profitability. The process of setting up a model and experimenting with different numbers is often referred to as **what-if analysis**.

What-if analysis is certainly a useful tool. Imagine having answers to questions such as "What if I get an A on my next two economics exams? But what if I get Bs?"; "What if I invest $100 a month in my retirement plan? But what if I invest $200 a month?"; "What if our sales reps increase sales by 10%? But what if sales decline by 5%?"; "What if I take out a 30-year mortgage at 8.5%? But what if I take out a 15-year mortgage at 7.75%?". Spreadsheets make these questions easy to answer.

Spreadsheet software is applicable in just about every profession. Educators use spreadsheets for grade books and analyzing test scores. Farmers use spreadsheets to keep track of crop yield, to calculate the amount of seed to purchase, and to estimate expenses and profits for the coming year. At home, spreadsheets help you balance your checkbook, keep track of household expenses, track your savings and investments, and calculate your taxes.

Entrepreneurs use spreadsheets to define business plans. Corporate executives use spreadsheets to keep tabs on finances. Athletes use spreadsheets to track training programs and sports statistics. Contractors use spreadsheets to make bids on construction projects. Scientists use spreadsheets to analyze data from experiments. The list goes on and on. You'll want to consider how spreadsheets can help you in your career field.

QuickCheck B

1. In a spreadsheet grid, each _____ is lettered, each _____ is numbered.

2. B3 and B4 are called cell _____.

3. Most spreadsheet software includes hundreds of predefined formulas called _____ for mathematical, financial, and statistical calculations.

4. A worksheet that will be viewed on the screen would generally be formatted differently than a worksheet that will be printed in black and white. True or false? _____

5. When you move or copy a cell, a spreadsheet typically adjusts any formulas in that cell relative to their original position. You must use an absolute reference if you don't want the formula to change. True or false? _____

6. The spreadsheet software publisher is responsible for the validity of the figures and formulas in your worksheets. True or false? _____

7. The process of setting up a model and experimenting with different numbers is often referred to as _____ analysis.

C Databases

LAB

Databases

Sometime in the middle of this century our industrial society began to evolve into an information society. The way we live has changed in many ways. We more frequently interact with information, we enter careers connected to information management, we increasingly attach a cash value to information, we tend to depend on information, and we are becoming aware of the potential problems that can occur when information is misused.

The Information Age is fueled by an explosion of data that is collected and generated by individuals, corporations, and government agencies. Some experts estimate that the amount of information doubles every year. This information is stored in an uncountable number of databases, most of them computerized. In the course of an ordinary day, you're likely to interact with more than one of these databases. It's pretty clear, then, that understanding and using databases is an important skill for living in the Information Age (Figure 3-31).

Figure 3-31

The rock group Police sings "Too much information running through my brain. Too much information, driving me insane."

The term "database" is a slippery thing. There is a technical definition of the term, but it is largely ignored in popular usage. In this section, we'll focus on the popular rendition of databases, using a broad, non-technical definition. We'll define a **database** as a collection of information stored on one or more computers.

In this section, we'll also focus on software that's designed to search for information in databases, rather than on database management software that's designed to create and manipulate databases. You might like this approach because it's so practical. Of 100 times that you encounter a database, 95 of those times you'll be looking for information, not creating or adding information.

Structured and Free-Form Databases

What kind of databases am I likely to use? In a typical day, you're likely to encounter many types of databases such as a library card catalog, your bank's database of checking and savings account balances, CD-ROM encyclopedias, the computer's directory of files, and your e-mail address book. You might also have experience interacting with collections of information accessed via the Internet such as Web sites devoted to hip-hop music, the stock market, the job market, or travel.

Databases come in two flavors: structured databases and free-form databases. A **structured database** (also called a **structured data file**) is a file of information organized in a uniform format of records and fields. Figure 3-32 shows an example of a record from a structured database for a library card catalog.

Figure 3-32

A structured database

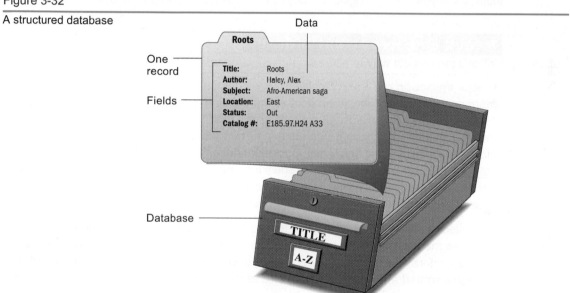

Structured databases typically store data that describes a collection of similar entities. A medical database stores data for a collection of patients. An inventory database stores data for a collection of items stocked on store and warehouse shelves.

A **free-form database** is a loosely structured collection of information, usually stored as documents, rather than as records. You might consider the collection of word-processing documents stored on your computer to be a free-form database of your own writing. A CD-ROM containing documents and videos of the Civil War would be another example. The World Wide Web, with its millions of documents stored worldwide, is another example of a free-form database. Whether stored on your hard disk, a CD-ROM, or the Internet, free-form databases have the potential to contain varied and useful information for you as a student or as a career professional.

Searching for Information

How do I find the information I'm looking for in a database? When you're searching for information, as opposed to creating and maintaining a database, you typically don't need to know whether you're accessing a structured database or a free-form database because your data access software hides the details of the database structure. **Data access software** is the interface you use to search for information in a database. You tell the data access software what you're looking for, and it will attempt to find it. The data access software understands the structure and details of the database, so you don't need to.

Different databases inevitably use different data access software. Therefore, becoming an effective information gatherer in the Information Age requires you to be flexible and willing to learn different searching procedures for different data access software. Depending on your data access software, you might enter your search specifications using a menu, a hypertext index, a keyword search engine, a query by example, a query language, or a natural language.

Menus and Hypertext Indexes

What's the easiest way to access database information? The Information Age has had a major impact on our lives. Consider how it has changed the way we do our banking. Information is now the basic product of the banking industry. As one expert points out, "Money is today only a special case of information." You've probably used your bank's phone-in automated account information system that asks you to "press 1 for account information, press 2 for help with your PIN number" and so on. Such a system is your interface to the bank's database of checking and savings account information. With so many people using this type of database, access must be simple. Therefore, most access software for bank customers is based on menus.

The collection of choices you're given to interact with a database is referred to as a **menu**. Database menus are similar to those you use in most other software. Menus that access database information can be screen-based or audio. Menus are typically arranged as a hierarchy, so that after you make a choice at the first level of the menu, a second series of choices appears.

The trick to using telephone menus is to put your finger over the best choice as you hear it. Leave your finger there until you hear a better choice. Then when the voice is through explaining the menu options, you don't have to recall the number of the one you want. Screen-based menus are easier to use because you always have all the options in view. For this reason, they can also be more complex, displaying many options on multiple levels. If you frequently use the same menu-based data access software, you'll become more proficient at gathering information if you try to envision the hierarchy of menus.

Screen-based menus have become a popular format for providing access to information via the Internet. Yahoo!, one of the most popular indexes to the Internet World Wide Web, features what is sometimes called a **hypertext index** that links you to information in categories such as education, entertainment, and business. To use a hypertext index such as Yahoo!, you select a general category such as News. Yahoo! then presents you with a list of news topics. You might select Politics from this list. Yahoo! will then show you another list from which to choose. Eventually, after you have navigated enough lists, you'll see a document containing the information you were seeking. Figure 3-33 shows Yahoo!'s hypertext index.

Figure 3-33

Yahoo!'s hypertext index

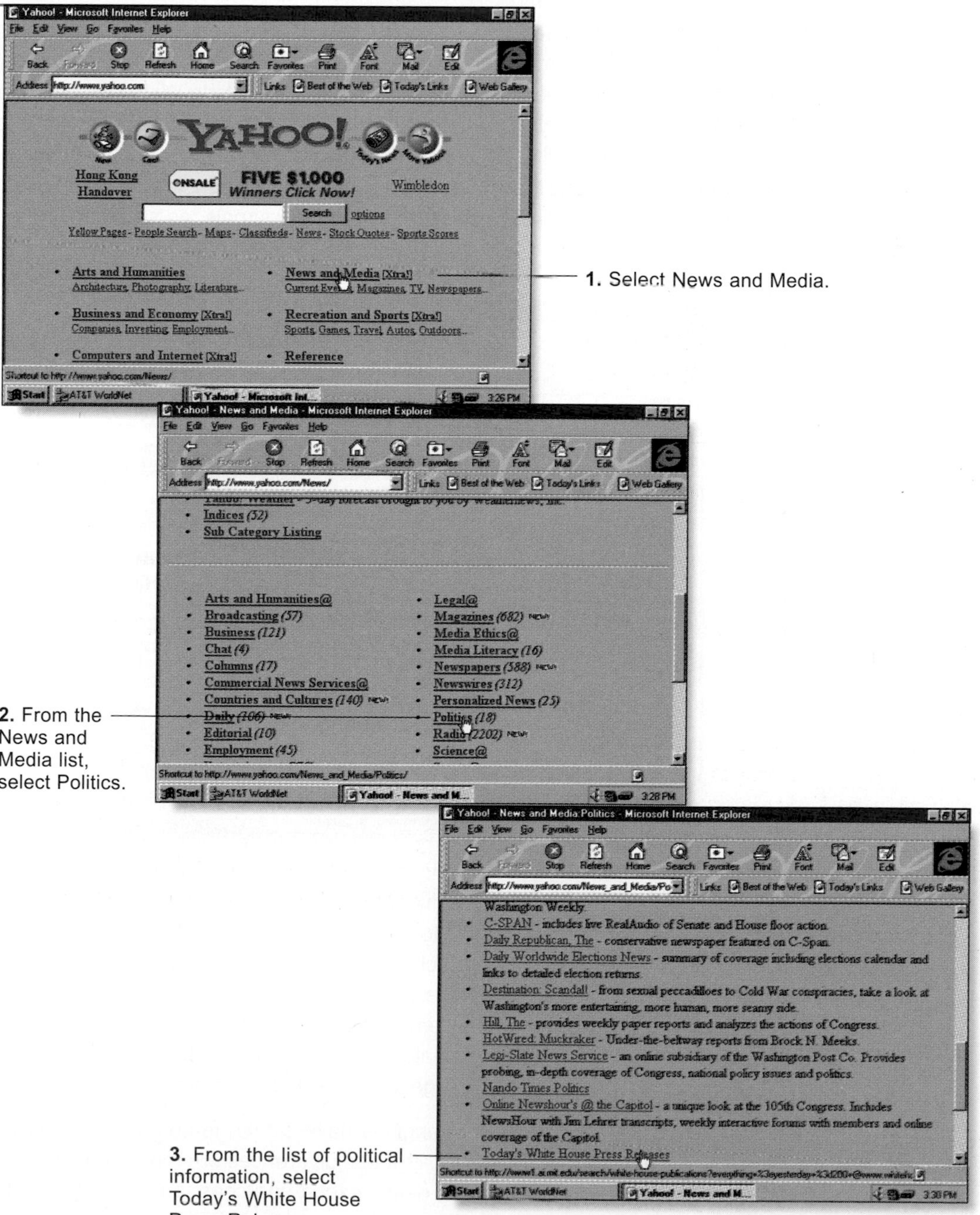

1. Select News and Media.

2. From the News and Media list, select Politics.

3. From the list of political information, select Today's White House Press Release.

Keyword Searches

What if I don't want to wander through all the levels of a menu to find information?

Information
Science
11

Libraries have influenced the way we organize information. Traditionally, we have found it handy to place information into categories, for example, following John Dewey's classifications or those of the Library of Congress. Therefore, it seems natural to use similar classifications to organize electronic information, such as World Wide Web documents. Yahoo!'s menu structure, for example, reflects such a classification scheme. However, not everything can be neatly classified. Now, using the power and speed of computers, you can search for information by keyword, instead of by topic.

A **keyword search engine** lets you access data without slogging through a menu of subject categories. Keyword search engines are especially popular for searching through the many documents stored in a free-form database such as the World Wide Web. To use a keyword search engine, you simply type in a word such as "parties" and the search engine locates related information. Usually, it shows you short summaries of the documents that contain the word you typed. You can then select those documents you think are most useful. The user interface for a keyword search engine is usually very simple, as shown in Figure 3-34.

Figure 3-34

A keyword search engine has a simple user interface.

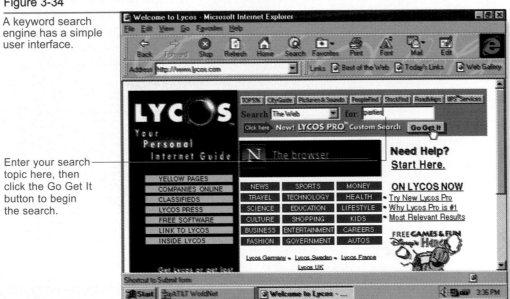

Enter your search topic here, then click the Go Get It button to begin the search.

Search
Engines
12

A search for a broad topic such as "parties" generally provides too much information. Therefore, search engines allow you to compose "expert" searches using more specific search criteria. For example, you could search for the *phrase* "political parties" to limit your search to the political arena. You could use *operators* such as "and" and "or" to look for more than one specific item as in the search for "democratic party *and* political conventions." You can also specify whether you want an exact match or an "in the ballpark" match. If you ask for an exact match to "political parties" you won't get articles on party politics.

Although different keyword search engines have similar features, their user interfaces are likely to be somewhat different. Happily, these differences are mostly cosmetic. Almost every search engine lets you enter topics, define expert searches, and specify the strength of the match. Therefore, many of the general skills you learn using one search engine apply when you use other search engines.

Query by Example (QBE)

What about finding data in structured databases? Remember the scene at the end of the film *Raiders of the Lost Ark*? Indiana Jones' valuable archeological discovery is unloaded from a forklift in a cavernous government warehouse full of crates and boxes. How long would it take to find it again?

Today, we expect to have information instantly. We want to know our bank balance right away. We want our Social Security checks on time. We want our tax refunds sooner, rather than later. We don't want to wait for a clerk to run back to the dairy aisle to check the price of a carton of yogurt.

When the information in a database needs to be accessed quickly, it is usually stored as a structured database. Because of its structure, a computer can generally locate data in a structured database faster than it can locate information in a free-form database. For example, in a warehouse database, the description of an item is stored in a particular field. Suppose you tell the computer to find the records for any item described as "Lost Ark." The computer will look at the description field of each record until it finds a record containing the words "Lost Ark."

Although computers can more easily find information in structured databases, the structure can cause a problem for humans. The problem is that users might not know the format for the records in a database. For example, how would you know whether an online library card catalog stores book titles in a field called Title, BookTitle, or T? Is the title the first field? Or does the first field contain the name of the author? One way to help users search structured databases is by providing a **query by example** (QBE for short) user interface like the one shown in Figure 3-35.

Figure 3-35

When you use a QBE interface, you see a blank record on the screen. Into this record you enter examples of what you want the computer to find. In this case, the user is looking for a book published in 1993 or later that includes "Economics" in the title.

Granville State University Library
Books On-Line
Public Access Card Catalog

Instructions: Fill in one or more of the blanks below to describe the materials you are trying to find. If you need more help , click [?]

Author:

Title: *Economics*

Date: 1993-

Publisher:

ISBN:

In Figure 3-35 the user has entered *Economics* in the title field to indicate the word economics should appear somewhere in the title of the book. "Economics" (without the asterisks) would tell the computer to find books titled only "Economics." As you might guess from this example, using QBE requires you to learn a few "tricks" such as the use of the asterisk and dash. Different QBE software might use different symbols. Your best bet when using a new QBE is to read the help instructions carefully before you set up your query.

Query Languages and Natural Language

Can I just type in a question to find information? Many science fiction writers and film-makers have speculated about the impact on society of intelligent computers and robots. Of course, one aspect of such intelligence would be the ability to understand human speech. It would be handy if we could access databases in the same way we describe the type of data we wanted to find to a research librarian (Figure 3-36). The first step in this direction is the use of query languages.

Figure 3-36

Robots with intelligence are a common theme in science fiction and films. When will computers respond to our database queries with the insight of a skilled reference librarian?

A **query language** is a set of command words that you can use to direct the computer to create databases, locate information, sort records, and change the data in those records. In situations where fairly sophisticated users want to access a structured database, a query language provides good flexibility for pinpointing information.

To use a query language, you need to know the command words and the grammar or syntax that will let you construct valid query "sentences." For example, the SQL query language command word to find records is "select." When you type the command "select *" the computer will look for all records. To locate all the Byzantine statues in an art museum database you would enter an SQL query something like this:

Select * from artworks where style = 'Byzantine' and media = 'statue'

Before you can compose such a query, you must have a fairly extensive knowledge of the database and its structure. You must know that the name of the database is "artworks." You must also know that the artistic style of each work is stored in a field called "Style" and that works are categorized as painting, statue, pottery, and so on, in a field called "Media." You can see that this interface is not suitable for casual users. Imagine if you had to compose SQL queries to use your library card catalog! Many people would find it easier to just wander around the stacks.

Advances in artificial intelligence have made some progress in the ability of computers to understand queries formulated in a **natural language** such as English, French, or Japanese. To make such natural language queries you don't need to learn an esoteric query language. Instead, you just enter questions such as:

What Byzantine statues are in our museum collection?

Computers still have some interpretation difficulties arising from ambiguities in human languages, so the use of natural language query software is not yet widespread.

Using Search Results

What can I do with the information I find? The power of information comes not only from finding it, but from using it. In an information-rich society, finding information that is astonishing, amusing, and informative is not difficult. Finding information that is bizarre, offensive, destructive, and confidential is not difficult either. Keep in mind that the information you seek, collect, and disperse is a reflection of your values and ethics. It seems that laws and regulations on the publication and use of information in electronic form have not kept up with the technology. Therefore, it is up to you to "use it, but don't abuse it." Once you find information in a database, you can use it in a number of ways.

Print it. When you find information in a structured database, you can generally print out a single record or a list of selected records. You might want to print a particular record, for example, if you're looking through a real estate database and find your dream house. In another scenario, suppose you were looking in the ERIC database to find some academic articles for a paper you're writing about male role models in elementary schools. You could print out a list of article titles and the journals in which they appeared. If call numbers for the journals are available, including that information on the printout would make it much easier to locate the articles in your library.

Copy and Paste. Most of today's graphical user interfaces provide a way to highlight database information you see on the screen and copy it to a worksheet or document. This technique is especially useful with the information you find in free-form databases because often you want just the information from one section of one document. For example, suppose you've been cruising the Internet for information on forest canopies for your botany seminar. You locate a Green Peace document that contains relevant information. Figure 3-37 shows you how to copy this information from the Web to one of your own word-processing documents.

Figure 3-37

Copy and paste

1. Highlight the text you want to copy.

2. Then, click the Edit menu, then select Copy. The text is copied to a special area of computer memory called the Clipboard. You can now switch to your word-processing software and paste the text into a document.

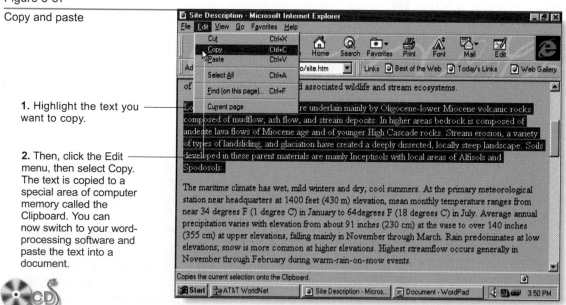

Export it. You might find some data that you want to analyze or graph using spreadsheet software. Many databases automatically **export data** by transforming it into a format that's acceptable to your spreadsheet software. If your database does not have this capability, your spreadsheet software might be able to **import data** by reading the database data and translating it into a worksheet. As another option, your spreadsheet software might include a wizard to help you transport data between databases and worksheets.

Save it. When you find a group of records in a structured database that you want to work with later, your database software might provide you with an option to save the records as a file on a hard or floppy disk. If you opt for this route, you should be aware that to manipulate the records later you are likely to need the same database software that was originally used to enter and create the records. This is not always practical, so you might have to use export or copy options instead. If you find data on the Web, the software you're using to access the information usually provides you with a way to save it on your own computer. This is particularly useful if you find a long document that you want to read at your leisure.

Transmit it. Today, we're plugged into a "global village" where e-mail arrives just minutes after it was sent and where you can "chat" online with people from countries all over the world. You can electronically distribute the information you collect; an easy way is to insert information into e-mail messages. A more ambitious project would be to develop your own World Wide Web site from which people could view Web pages and download databases.

Whether you print, import, copy, save, or transmit the data you find in databases, it is your responsibility to use it appropriately. Respect copyrights by giving credit to the original author in a footnote or end note. The information in corporate and government databases is often confidential. When you have access to such data, respect the privacy of the individuals who are the subject of the data. Don't divulge the information you find or introduce inaccuracies into the database.

QuickCheck C

1. In popular terminology, a(n) _____ is a collection of information stored on one or more computers.

2. A(n) _____ database is a file of information organized in a uniform format of records and fields, whereas a(n) _____ database is a loosely structured collection of information.

3. Menus, keyword searches, query by example, a query language, and natural language are all methods used to _____ information in a database.

4. To use a keyword search engine, you simply type in a word such as "music" and the search engine locates all related information in the database. True or false? _____

5. When using a(n) _____ user interface to search a database, you use a blank record to enter examples of the data you want the computer to find.

6. A(n) _____ such as SQL consists of a set of command words that you can use to direct the computer to create databases, locate information, sort records, and change the data in those records.

7. Once you locate information in a database, you can print it, export it to other software packages, copy and paste it into other software, save it for future reference, or transmit it. True or false? _____

UserFocus

D Putting It All Together

You shouldn't finish this chapter with the impression that you use only one software tool per project. It is true that word-processing, spreadsheet, and database software tools each have their own strengths. But you often can be more productive if you use the tools together. Suppose you are writing a report. How can you use the tools you've learned about to gather information, organize it, analyze it, and report your results?

Researching a Topic

Where do I start? Got to write a paper, but you find yourself staring at a blank sheet of paper or a blank computer screen? Just take one step at a time. Use your technology tools. You'll be surprised at how fast your paper materializes.

InfoWeb

Online Card Catalogs 13

First, choose your topic. Then browse around your library and the Internet to find sources of information. Whereas most research once took place in library buildings, the trend today is to use a computer to search online. From your home or office you can look through millions of Web documents and search through the card catalogs of many libraries, including the Library of Congress.

You might want to make photocopies of interesting articles, check out relevant books, and save any information you find on the Web. If you seem to be finding bits and pieces of information on the Web, copy and paste these bits into a document you create with word-processing software. Don't worry about the organization of the document for now. Just think of it as notes that you can use later.

Make sure you keep track of where you obtain your information. Make a note of the magazine name and issue date on any photocopies you make. For information you gather from the Internet, make note of its source. Every document on the World Wide Web has a unique address called a URL. Most Web browser software has a setting to include the URL on any Web pages you send to your printer. If you note the URL for every bit of information you gather, you will be able to give credit to the authors in your final report. Figure 3-38 illustrates a Web page URL.

Figure 3-38

A Web page URL

Make sure that as part of your information-gathering activities, you have a way to distinguish which information you copy verbatim and which information you have paraphrased using your own words. You might simply put quotes around the material that you copied verbatim, as you would in your final draft. This will help keep you honest about which parts of the report are your own work.

Organizing and Analyzing Information

How do I add my own viewpoint and analysis to the report? After you collect information, you need to read through it and think about what it means. What are the trends? What are the controversies? What stands out as interesting? With this background, you can determine what you want to say.

Begin a new document using your word-processing software and type in your main point. You should be able to write this as a single, clear sentence. Use the editing features of your software to work on this sentence until it is perfect.

The next step is to create an outline of items that will support your main point. Use the outlining feature of your word processor to type in the headings and subheadings for your report. Refer back to the information you have gathered when you need to. You can have two or more documents open at the same time when you use word-processing software, so it's easy to flip back and forth between the document that contains your outline and the one that contains your research notes.

With your outline in place you can begin to move your research notes into the appropriate places in your outline. Use the copy and paste feature while both documents are open to make this process a breeze.

Figure 3-39

Don't forget to proofread your work!

Of course, you don't want your paper to simply be a collage of other people's work. As a rule of thumb, in your final paper at least 8 of every 10 paragraphs should be your own words. Now is your chance to add your viewpoint and skillfully weave together the facts. Don't be misled into thinking that paraphrasing just means rearranging a few words in each of the sentences you copied from someone else's work. If you're tempted to do this, read your research note, then delete it and rewrite it completely using your own words.

Work on your document until you're satisfied, then run a spell check and a grammar check if one is available. Don't forget to proofread it (Figure 3-39)!

Before you finalize the content of your paper, you might consider if some sections would be clearer if you included a graph or other illustration. You can use spreadsheet software to create graphs for data you have gathered. You can use your copy and paste commands to insert the graphs into your document.

When you're happy with the content of your document save it on disk. Make an extra copy of your work on a different disk, just to be safe. You might also want to print your paper, even though you have not formatted it yet. If you lose your electronic copies, you can then still reconstruct it from the printout.

Following a Style Guide

How do I know how to format my paper? If you have not been provided with style guidelines from your instructor or boss, you should follow a standard style manual such as the *Publication Manual of the American Psychological Association*, *The Chicago Manual of Style*, or Turabian's *Guide to Style*. These manuals tell you how large to make your margins, what to include in headers and footers, how to label graphs and illustrations, how to format your footnotes or end notes correctly, and so forth. You'll use the formatting features of your word-processing software to follow the style guidelines.

InfoWeb

Internet Citations 14

A style guide devotes many pages to the correct format for the book and magazine citations you include at the end of a paper or in footnotes. But what is the correct citation format for materials you use from Web pages or other Internet sources? Most style guides are now including this information. If your style guide does not, you can access one of several Web sites that provide formats for electronic citations.

Presentations

What if I have to give a speech? If you're going to present your report, you need some speaking notes and some visual aides. Create your speaking notes using your word-processing software. Use a large boldface font and double or triple spacing. After you print these notes, use different color highlighters to mark the first word in each paragraph. This will help you keep your place as you speak.

Visual aids could mean handouts or computer-generated "slides." Consider whether an outline, graph, list of important points, or graphics would be most useful for your audience. Your word-processing software can help you produce printed handouts. Your spreadsheet software might help you put together a few graphs to support your main point. You could also consider using **presentation software** to create a computer-generated slide presentation (Figure 3-40). You could include an opening graphic, a list of important points, and a graph. Don't forget to practice before you're "on stage!"

As you continue to work with electronic documents, you'll discover even more "tricks" for harnessing their features to increase your productivity and the quality of your work. Watch for tips in magazines and newspapers, on computer TV shows, and on the Web.

Figure 3-40

Use presentation software to create effective visual aids.

EndNote

In today's computing environment, you can hardly avoid using computer-based documents, worksheets, and databases. The software you use to manipulate these documents provides you with tools that can improve the quality of your work. It also can provide considerable savings for previously tedious tasks such as typing the final draft of a document—and getting it perfect!

But don't expect to pare down the time you spend on projects such as a written report or essay. It seems that because your tools allow you to do more, you *will* do more. You'll spend more time gathering information because now with the Internet much more information is available. You'll do more editing because it's so easy. You'll grammar check your documents because you end up with clearer writing. And you'll spend a little time creating a graph because it adds a professional touch to your final package.

With today's software tools, you'll work smarter and produce better work, but your time commitment will remain about the same. Get yourself a scheduler if you don't have one already. Procrastination doesn't work today—any more than it worked before you used word-processing, spreadsheet, and database tools.

InfoWeb

InfoWeb
Chapter
Links

The InfoWeb is your guide to print, film, television, and electronic resources. Use it to obtain updates on quickly changing technical information and to locate information for research papers. If you're using the New Perspectives CD-ROM, click the InfoWeb icon on the left side of this paragraph to access the online InfoWeb links. Otherwise, use your Web browser and type in the address of the New Perspectives site: www.cciw.com/np3. At the New Perspectives site you'll find up-to-date links to the topics covered in this chapter.

1 Literacy

We assume that everyone can read and write, but that is not true in either North America or around the world. According to the UN, almost 97% of adult populations in Western developed countries are literate. But the media in the U.S. often claims that 20 to 30% of Americans are functionally illiterate—they cannot read well enough to understand a newspaper, understand a paycheck stub, or complete a simple form. What is the cause of this discrepancy? It all depends on how you measure literacy and illiteracy, and there are many ways to do so. "Measuring the Nation's Literacy: Important Considerations" by Terrence Wiley from the ERIC Digest at **www.ed.gov/databases/ERIC_Digests/ed334870.html** will fill you in on the problems of defining and measuring illiteracy. Literacy is important because how well you read and write influences your ability to participate in economic, social, and political life. Although nearly 10 years old, the classic book **Illiterate America** by Jonathan Kozol (New American Library Trade, 1988) will give you a good start in understanding the problems of illiteracy, why literacy is critical to success in life, and what you can do about illiteracy. On the World Wide Web, connect to Summer Institute of Linguistics at **www.sil.org** where you can find information about literacy around the world and the connection between economic development and literacy. At the Laubach Literacy Web site, **www.laubach.org**, you can find information about volunteer-based literacy programs around the world.

2 Typing

Gregory Arakelian holds the record as the world's fastest typist at 158 words per minute. A "good" typist's speed is around 60 words per minute. If you are still hunting and pecking, you might want to try working with a typing tutor, such as **Typing Tutor VII** or **Typing Instructor Deluxe CD**. To learn more about typing tutorial software and some tidbits about typewriters and typing, read the article "Time to Start Typing?" at **www.zdnet.com/familypc/content/960819/columns/parental/960819.html**. Some researchers claim that the arrangement of keys on the QWERTY keyboard limits typing speed. Read the article "Typing Errors" at the Reason Online site, **www.reasonmag.com/9606/Fe.QWERTY.html**, for a different discussion of the facts. At the Mavis Beacon Teaches Typing Web site, **www.mavisbeacon.com**, you can find information about the history of typing, links to information on repetitive stress injuries, and more.

3 Improve your Writing

The World Wide Web has many, many resources for writers of all experience and talents. A number of universities have online writing labs that offer writing tips, style guidelines, and advice about conducting research for and writing term papers. An excellent example is The Writing Place at Northwestern University which offers the Working Writers Project at **www.writing.nwu.edu/wwriters/heller.html**. This project is a collection of talks given by professional writers at Northwestern University on the art and craft of writing. For non-fiction writing, the book **The Complete Guide to Writing Nonfiction** by the American Society of

Journalists and Authors (Harper & Row, 1988) provides a broad and candid look at the writing business from the research process to writing for specific markets. You might also want to read the classic book on writing fiction, **The Art of Fiction**, by John Gardner (Alfred A. Knopf, 1984). And if you need inspiration, connect to the Isaac Asimov Home Page at **www.clark.net/pub/edseiler/WWW/ asimov_home_page.html** where you'll find advice from one of the world's most prolific and broad-based writers.

4 Grammar

How's your grammar? You can take a grammar quiz (more interesting than it sounds) at **w3.one.net/ ~sparks25/quizcht.html**. If you want to avoid the 11 most commonly violated rules of writing, check them out at **www.concentric.net/~rag/writing.shtml**. For an entertaining viewpoint on grammar, read the Grammar Lady's column at **www.grammarlady.com**. At this site you can also submit questions to the grammar hotline. A good desk reference is **Webster's New World Guide to Current American Usage** by Bernice Randall (Prentice Hall, 1988).

5 Fonts

Fonts or typefaces are the clothes that your words wear. The book **Typographic Design: Form and Communication** by Rob Carter, Ben Day, and Philip Meggs (Van Nostrand Reinhold, 1985) provides a good introduction to typeforms, their organization, and their relationship to content. At the Graphion's Online Type

Serif

Serif

Museum Web site, **www.slip.net/~graphion/museum.html**, you can learn about the history and practice of typesetting. At the typoGRAPHIC Web site, **www.subnetwork.com/typo**, you can learn about the evolution and development of letterforms, view a timeline of the recent history of typography, find a glossary of typographic terms, and browse a gallery of typographic imagery. Microsoft Typography at **www.microsoft.com/ truetype** contains free TrueType fonts and a discussion of the future of typography on the Web. At the Shareware and Freeware Fonts Web page, **desktoppublishing.com/fonts-free.html**, you can find links to many Web sites that provide electronic fonts either for free or for a small fee. Brendan's Font Collection at **www.geocities.com/Athens/8368** claims to be one of the Web's largest sources of free fonts for downloading.

6 Publishing: Electronic New Frontiers

Some inventions and discoveries have not only changed the trajectory of human endeavor, but have also changed the way we see the world around us. Printing and, as many suspect, electronic publishing are inventions with such impact. At The Media History Project Web site, **www.mediahistory.com/ histhome.html**, you can contemplate these types of questions. You can also find at that site a timeline of media from 5,000 B.C.E. to the present, reviews of books, archives of the Dead Media Project, and links to Internet resources on various media from oral history to the printing press to digital media. You can find a discussion of Thomas Paine as the moral father of the Internet at "The Age of Paine," by Jon Katz at **wwww.wired.com/wired/3.05/features/paine.html/**. For some speculation about the future of books and electronic publishing, read "The Future of the Book" by Nicholas Negroponte at **wwww.wired.com/wired/ 4.02/negroponte.html**.

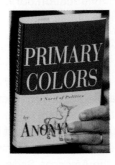

7 Who Wrote It?

A concordance was the key tool used to unmask the anonymous author of *Primary Colors*. To learn more about concordances, connect to the Web Concordances and Workbook Web site at **www.dundee.ac.uk/english/wics/wics.htm**, a site in Dundee, Scotland, which includes concordances of selected poems of Shelley, Coleridge, Keats, Blake, and other poets. Concordances and Corpora at **www.georgetown.edu/cball/ corpora/tutorial3.html** discusses how computerized concordances work and presents information on several programs. You might also want to read **"End of the Game"** by L. Reilbstein (*Newsweek*, July 29, 1996), which summarizes the controversy over the authorship of *Primary Colors*.

8 Spreadsheet Tips

For tips on how to get the most out of spreadsheet software, connect to *PC World's* Spreadsheet site at **www.pcworld.com/software/spreadsheet**. The Spreadsheet Page at **www.j-walk.com/ss** contains information, files, and FAQs, about Excel, Lotus 1-2-3, and Quattro Pro. At the Unofficial Microsoft Excel Page, **www.vex.net/~negandhi/excel**, you can find tips, reports on bugs, and files to download. You can link to tutorials, tips, free software and templates at both the Microsoft Excel site, **www.microsoft.com/excel/**, and the Lotus 1-2-3 site, **www2.lotus.com/123.nsf**. For some tips and guidance on how to create a well-designed spreadsheet, connect to Spreadsheet Etiquette at **www.melbpc.org.au/pcupdate/9409/409sset.htm**.

9 Errors

In 1986, Joseph A. Cummings, Inc. a construction firm, unsuccessfully tried to sue Lotus Development Corporation because a spreadsheet they used generated a $250,000 contract error. Research on spreadsheet errors has been carried out by Raymond R. Panko at the University of Hawaii. You can find out more about the alarming rate of spreadsheet errors at **www.cba.hawaii.edu/panko**.

10 Lie: Don't Do it With Statistics or Graphs

You should avoid the temptation to tell tall tales with statistics. Find out how with the video **How Numbers Lie: Self-Defense Against Misleading Statistics** (1996). If you need to brush up on statistics, head for **nilesonline.com/stats** where you'll find an entertaining tutorial. The updated 1954 classic, **How to Lie With Statistics** by Darrell Huff, (W W Norton & Co, 1993) is still a "must read." For information on creating effective and truthful graphs, read **The Visual Display of Quantitative Information** by Edward R. Tufte (Graphics Press, 1992).

11 Information Science

A career in information science is not new in the '90s, but this career has new challenges in the Information Age. What is information science? Is it the career for you? To learn more about information science, read Careers in Research Libraries and Information Science: The Dynamic Role of the Research Librarian at **arl.cni.org/careers/CareersPaper.html**. At the Education and Careers for the 21st Century Web site, **www-slis.lib.indiana.edu/21stCentury/**, you can learn more about careers for information professionals, in areas such as social informatics or content management. The American Society for Information Science (ASIS) was founded in 1937 and brings together information professionals from fields as diverse as computer science, linguistics, librarianship, engineering, and medicine. These professionals all share an interest in "improving the ways society stores, retrieves, analyzes, manages, archives and disseminates information." To learn more about ASIS, visit their Web site at **www.asis.org/**.

12 Search Engines

Search engines such as Yahoo! and Excite can help you locate information, and there are many search engines you can use. But how do you use them most effectively? For a basic introduction to searching for information, read "Secrets of the Super Searchers: Introduction," by Reva Basch at **www.onlineinc.com/pempress/secrets/intro.html**. "The Spider's Apprentice: How to Use Web Search Engines" at **www.monash.com/spidap4.html** provides helpful guidance about some of the Internet's main search engines, AltaVista, InfoSeek, Excite, WebCrawler, Lycos, Hotbot, OpenText, and Yahoo!. If you've ever asked yourself how these search engines work read the online article, "Seek and Ye Shall Find (Maybe)" by Steve G. Steinberg at **wwww.wired.com/wired/4.05/features/indexweb.html**. The Search Engine Watch Web site at **searchenginewatch.com/** includes reviews and tutorials, an overview of the major search engines and their history, and a search engine game. For a more in depth discussion of searching the Web, connect to "Beyond Surfing: Tools and Techniques for Searching the Web" by Kathleen Webster and Kathryn Paul at **magi.com/~mmelick/it96jan.htm**.

13 Online Card Catalogs

From your computer you can search through the four-million book card catalog of the Library of Congress. Just connect to **lcweb2.loc.gov/catalog**. Another great card catalog is at the U.S. National Archives and Records Administration at **www.nara.gov** where you'll find, among other things, the Kennedy Assassination Records Collection. The British Library also has an online card catalog that you can access at **opac97.bl.uk**.

14 Internet Citations

As you become an expert at locating information on the Web and Internet, you will want to start using that information in your term papers and reports. The **MLA Handbook for Writers of Research Papers** and the **APA Manual**, two books you can find in your library's reference department, present discussions and examples of how to cite source material from the Internet. "Beyond the MLA Handbook: Documenting Electronic Sources on the Internet" by Andrew Harnack and Gene Kleppinger of Eastern Kentucky University at **falcon.eku.edu/honors/beyond-mla/** provides a thorough discussion of citation style for Internet sources.

Review

1   Make a list of the boldface terms that appear in each section of this chapter. Make sure you understand the definition of each word. Select five words from each section. Write one sentence for each word (15 sentences total) to show that you know how to use the word in context.

2   Answer the questions below each heading in this chapter *using your own words*.

3   List the features of word-processing software that make it easy for you to enter the text of your documents.

4   Make a list of editing tasks that word-processing software can help you accomplish.

5   Explain the difference between a document template, a font, a style, and document wizard.

6   Explain the difference between the terms "kerning" and "serif" as they apply to fonts.

7   In document production terminology what is the difference between a column and a table?

8   Make a list of popular document automation features included with most word processors. Then describe a real-life situation in which each feature would be used effectively.

9   Write one or two paragraphs describing how a spreadsheet works to someone who has never seen one or used one.

10 Explain the difference between the following spreadsheet characteristics: a number, a formula, a function, and a cell reference.

11 Make a list of 10 careers, then write a brief description of a spreadsheet application that would be useful in each.

12 Make a list of tips for formatting worksheets. Divide your tips into three categories: on-screen, printed, and projected.

13 Explain what happens to the cell references in a formula when you copy that formula to a different column. How does this relate to absolute references?

14 Describe three techniques for auditing a worksheet.

15 Explain the difference between a structured database and a free-form database.

16 List and describe at least six search procedures that you might use to locate information in a database.

17 Describe five different ways you can use search results.

18 Outline the steps from the *User Focus* section of this chapter for using computer tools to create a research report.

19 Use the New Perspectives CD-ROM to take a practice test or to review the new terms presented in this chapter.

Projects

1   **Font Master** Do fonts make your document look formal or casual, simple or difficult, important or trivial? Look in magazines for samples of five different font treatments, including italics, serif, sans serif, mono-spaced, and kerned fonts. It is not necessary to find all five in a single article. Photocopy the best examples you find. After you study the documents that contain these fonts, write a one-page summary of how these different font treatments appear to be used to enhance readability, accentuate information, or add a certain personality to a document. Turn in your photocopies and your one-page summary.

2 INTERNET Optional

The March of Progress
The progress of document production, literacy, and civilization are closely linked. Create a timeline showing key developments in the history of document production. You should be able to find an abundance of information on this topic in your library and on the Internet. You can discuss the format for your timeline with your instructor. Depending on the time you have allocated for the project, you might simply use a word processor to list dates and events, you might incorporate graphics, or you might create a Web page.

3 **Who's pear of shoes our over their?**
Most word-processing software includes a grammar checker that helps you locate potential problems with sentence structure, punctuation, and word usage. When you use a grammar checker it is important to remember that you must evaluate its suggestions and decide whether to implement them. In this project you'll use a grammar checker to revise some of your own writing.

Begin with a first draft of at least one page of your writing. You can use something you have previously composed, or you can write something new. You'll need to type your document using word-processing software with grammar checking capabilities. Print out your first draft.

After you've printed your first draft, activate the grammar checker. Consider each of its suggestions and implement those you think will improve your writing. Make sure you proofread your document after you've completed the changes to make sure it still flows well.

Print out your revised document, then use a highlighter to indicate the changes you made. Turn in both drafts of your document.

4 **See Dick Run. See Jane. See Spot Play.**
Although close to 80% of the population for most industrialized countries has completed high school, journalists supposedly write for an audience with only an eighth-grade reading level. Is this true? To find out, you can use your word-processing

software to discover the reading level of typical articles in popular magazines and newspapers.

To complete this project, locate two articles you think are typical of the writing style for the magazines or newspapers you read. Using your word processor, enter at least 10 sentences from the first article. Use your word processor's reading-level feature to find the reading level for the passage you typed. Print out the passage and on it note the reading-level statistics you obtained from your word processor. Do the same with the second article. Turn in both of your printouts. Be sure to include full bibliographical data on both articles.

5 **True Lies** Arnold Schwarzenegger and Jamie Lee Curtis starred in an action-thriller spoof about a secret agent who pretended to be a nerdy computer technician. Another character in the film was actually a used car salesman, but pretended to be a secret agent. The theme of *True Lies*—that things are not always what they seem—applies to spreadsheet graphs as well. What graphs appear to show is not always what the data actually means.

For this project look through magazines, books, and newspapers to find an example of a misleading graph. You might find that the dimensions of the graph distort the true picture. Perhaps a line graph was used when a pie graph would have been more meaningful. Maybe some of the data was omitted.

Photocopy the graph, then write a paragraph describing how the graph is misleading and what you would suggest to make it better depict the real data.

6 INTERNET Required

Searching for Godot
Knowing how to use a search engine is becoming a pivotal skill for the Information Age. Most key word search engines include instructions or short tutorials on their use. For this project, you'll connect to one of the Web search engines and learn how to use it.

To do this project, you must have access to the Internet and you must have a Web browser such as Netscape or Microsoft Internet Explorer. Start your browser and connect to one of the following sites:

www.lycos.com   **www.altavista.com**

www.excite.com   **www.hotbot.com**

Read through the instructions carefully, paying close attention (and maybe taking notes) on the options available for advanced searches, exact matches, and Boolean operators (AND, OR, NOT). Next try a few searches to make sure you've got the hang of it.

Finally, write a mini-manual about how to use your keyword search engine, providing examples of different types of searches.

7   **Information Science Careers** Writing for *Wired* magazine, Steve Steinberg says, "The hard problems of knowledge classification and indexing are suddenly of commercial importance." Much has happened since Melvil Dewey set up the first formal training program for librarians in 1887. The field of library science has broadened to become information science and encompass the vast pool of electronic documents.

For this project, you will find information about training and careers in information science. You should use a variety of resources to gather information—you can interview librarians, check the Web sites for universities that offer information science degrees, and look in general reference books for background and historical information.

Summarize your findings by writing a pamphlet called "A Career Guide to Information Science." Anticipate that the audience will be high school seniors and college freshmen making career decisions.

8   **With Two You Get Egg Roll** Time was when the word "menu" evoked images of elegant restaurants—or at least Chinese take-out. Today, menus just as often mean electronic choices on automated phone systems and computer screens. Many times we use menus without really thinking about how they're organized or presented. But as a consumer in the Information Age you should take a more critical look at this ubiquitous tool.

For this project, pick an electronic menu that you use to access a database. It might be an ATM machine, a phone system at work, or an information kiosk. Draw a hierarchy diagram of the options available on the menus. To do this, you'll need to play around with the menus to examine all the options offered.

9   **Brave New World** Because computerized databases have become such an integral part of our society, we don't often consider what life would be like without them. However, without computerized databases, banking, shopping, communications, entertainment, education, and health care would probably be far different from what they are today. For this project, you should first make a list of assumptions about how your life would be different if there were no computerized databases. For example, one of your assumptions might be, "Without computerized databases, we would have to pay for everything in cash because banks couldn't process enough checks by hand, nor could credit card companies verify charges."

After you have a list of assumptions, write a short story about one day in the life of a person who lives in a society where there are no computerized databases. In your story, try to depict how this person's life is different from what we think of as "normal."

Turn in your list of assumptions and your short story.

10   **Edit Yourself** After reading the *User Focus* section of this chapter, you might have some ideas about how you can use software tools to collect facts, improve your writing, analyze numeric data, and give presentations. Select a report, paper, or presentation that you recently created. Think about specific ways in which you could improve it.

Make a list of improvements you could make, indicating the tools you would use. Be specific. For example, you might say "Gather additional facts about per capita coffee consumption using a Web search engine" or "Check the reading level using a word processor and make adjustments to bring it to the eighth- to tenth-grade level.

Turn in a photocopy of your original project as well as your list of improvements.

Lab Assignments

Word Processing

 Word-processing software is the most popular computerized productivity tool. In this Lab you will learn how word-processing software works. When you have completed this Lab, you should be able to apply the general concepts you learned to any word-processing package you use at home, at work, or in your school lab.

1. Click the Steps button to learn how word-processing software works. As you proceed through the Steps, answer all of the Quick Check questions that appear. After you complete the Steps, you will see a Quick Check Summary Report. Follow the instructions on the screen to print this report.

2. Click the Explore button to begin. Click File, then click Open to display the Open dialog box. Click the file **Timber.tex**, then press the Enter key to open the letter to Northern Timber Company. Make the following modifications to the letter, then print it out. You do not need to save the letter.
   a. In the first and last lines of the letter, change "Jason Kidder" to your name.
   b. Change the date to today's date.

c. The second paragraph begins "Your proposal did not include..." Move this paragraph so it is the last paragraph in the text of the letter.
   d. Change the cost of a permanent bridge to $20,000.
   e. Spell check the letter.

3. In Explore, open the file **Stars.tex**. Make the following modifications to the document, then print it out. You do not need to save the document.
   a. Center and boldface the title.
   b. Change the title font to size 16 Arial.
   c. Boldface the DATE, SHOWER, and LOCATION.
   d. Move the January 2-3 line to the top of the list.
   e. Double-space the entire document.

4. In Explore, compose a one-page double-spaced letter to your parents or to a friend. Make sure you date the letter and check your spelling. Print the letter and sign it. You do not need to save your letter.

Spreadsheets

 Spreadsheet software is used extensively in business, education, science, and humanities to simplify tasks that involve calculations. In this Lab you will learn how spreadsheet software works. You will use spreadsheet software to examine and modify worksheets, as well as to create your own worksheets.

1. Click the Steps button to learn how spreadsheet software works. As you proceed through the Steps, answer all of the Quick Check questions that appear. After you complete the Steps, you will see a Quick Check Summary Report. Follow the instructions on the screen to print this report.

2. Click the Explore button to begin this assignment. Click OK to display a new worksheet. Click File, then click Open to display the Open dialog box. Click the file **Income.xls**, then press the Enter key to

open the **Income and Expense Summary** worksheet. Notice that the worksheet contains labels and values for income from consulting and training. It also contains labels and values for expenses such as rent and salaries. The worksheet does not, however, contain formulas to calculate Total Income, Total Expenses, or Profit. Do the following:

a. Calculate the Total Income by entering the formula =sum(C4:C5) in cell C6.

b. Calculate the Total Expenses by entering the formula =sum(C9:C12) in C13.

c. Calculate Profit by entering the formula =C6-C13 in cell C15.

d. Manually check the results to make sure you entered the formulas correctly.

e. Print your completed worksheet showing your results.

3 You can use a spreadsheet to keep track of your grade in a class. In Explore, click File, then click Open to display the Open dialog box. Click the file **Grades.xls** to open the Grades worksheet. This worksheet contains all the labels and formulas necessary to calculate your grade based on four test scores.

Suppose you receive a score of 88 out of 100 on the first test. On the second test, you score 42 out of 48. On the third test, you score 92 out of 100. You have not taken the fourth test yet. Enter the appropriate data in the **Grades.xls** worksheet to determine your grade after taking three tests. Print out your worksheet.

4 Worksheets are handy for answering "what if" questions. Suppose you decide to open a lemonade stand. You're interested in how much profit you can make each day. What if you sell 20 cups of lemonade? What if you sell 100? What if the cost of lemons increases?

In Explore, open the file **Lemons.xls** and use the worksheet to answer questions a through d, then print the worksheet for question e:

a. What is your profit if you sell 20 cups a day?

b. What is your profit if you sell 100 cups a day?

c. What is your profit if the price of lemons increases to $.07 and you sell 100 cups?

d. What is your profit if you raise the price of a cup of lemonade to $.30? (Lemons still cost $.07 and assume you sell 100 cups.)

e. Suppose your competitor boasts that she sold 50 cups of lemonade in one day and made exactly $12.00. On your worksheet adjust the cost of cups, water, lemons, and sugar, and the price per cup to show a profit of exactly $12.00 for 50 cups sold. Print this worksheet.

5 It is important to make sure the formulas in your worksheet are accurate. An easy way to test this is to enter 1's for all the values on your worksheet, then check the calculations manually. In Explore, open the worksheet **Receipt.xls**, which calculates sales receipts. Enter 1 as the value for Item 1, Item 2, Item 3, and Sales Tax %. Now, manually calculate what you would pay for three items that cost $1.00 each in a state where sales tax is 1% (.01). Do your manual calculations match those of the worksheet? If not, correct the formulas in the worksheet and print out a *formula report* of your revised worksheet.

6 In Explore, create your own worksheet showing your household budget for one month. You may use real or made up numbers. Make sure you put a title on the worksheet. Use formulas to calculate your total income and your total expenses for the month. Add another formula to calculate how much money you were able to save. Print a formula report of your worksheet. Also, print your worksheet showing realistic values for one month.

Databases

The Database Lab demonstrates the essential concepts of file and database management systems. You will use the Lab to search, sort, and report the data contained in a file of classic books.

1. Click the Steps button to review basic database terminology and to learn how to manipulate the classic books database. As you proceed through the Steps, answer the Quick Check questions that appear. After you complete the Steps, you will see a Quick Check Summary Report. Follow the instructions on the screen to print this report.

2. Click the Explore button. Make sure you can apply basic database terminology to describe the classic books database by answering the following questions:

   a. How many records does the file contain?

   b. How many fields does each record contain?

   c. What are the contents of the Catalog # field for the book written by Margaret Mitchell?

   d. What are the contents of the Title field for the record with Thoreau in the Author field?

   e. Which field has been used to sort the records?

3. In Explore, manipulate the database as necessary to answer the following questions:

   a. When the books are sorted by title, what is the first record in the file?

   b. Use the Search button to search for all books in the West location. How many do you find?

   c. Use the Search button to search for all books in the Main location that are checked in. What do you find?

4. In Explore, use the Report button to print out a report that groups the books by Status and sorted by title. On your report, circle the four field names. Put a box around the summary statistics showing which books are currently checked in and which books are currently checked out.

COMPUTER FILES AND DATA STORAGE

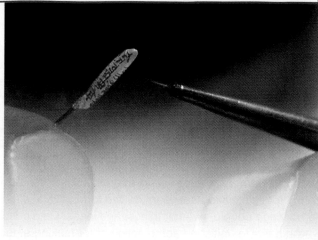

InfoWeb

World Records 1

How much data can you pack into a small area? In 1968, Frederick Watts hand-printed 9,452 characters on a piece of paper the size of a postage stamp. In 1983, Tsutomu Ishii of Tokyo, Japan wrote the Japanese characters for *Tokyo, Japan* on a human hair. A few years later, Surendra Apharya of Jaipur, India managed to squeeze 241 characters on a single grain of rice. That seems like a lot of data packed into a small area, but a computer can store hundreds of times as much data in the same area. For example, an entire encyclopedia can fit on a single 4.75-inch CD-ROM disk.

How can computers store so much data in such a small area? How can you search through all that data to find what you want? Can you change data once it is stored? What happens if you run out of space?

In this chapter you will learn the answers to these and many more questions. After learning the definitions of the terms *file*, *data*, and *information*, you will learn that there are different types of files, and you will find out how to use each type. You will see how the operating system provides a metaphor to help visualize and manipulate files and how this metaphor is quite different from the way the computer actually stores and keeps track of files. Finally you will learn about the speed, cost, and storage capacity of popular microcomputer storage media. With this information, you can make decisions about the storage devices that are right for your computing needs.

CHAPTER**PREVIEW**

This chapter provides a practical foundation for using a computer to manage your data. You will find out which disk drive to use when you store data and how to create a valid filename that the computer will accept. You will learn how to use DOS or Windows to organize the files on your disk so they are easy to locate. You will also learn what happens in the computer when you save, retrieve, or modify a file, so you will know what to do when the computer asks if you want to "Replace file?" After you have completed this chapter you should be able to:

- Correctly use the terms data and information
- Determine if a file is an executable file, data file, or source file
- Create valid filenames under DOS and Windows
- Explain how file extensions and wildcards simplify file access
- Describe the difference between logical and physical file storage

- Discuss how the directory and the FAT help you access files
- Select a storage device based on characteristics such as its capacity and access speed
- Describe the process of saving, retrieving, revising, deleting, and copying files

LABS

DOS Directories and File Management

Windows Directories, Folders, and Files

Defragmentation and Disk Operations

Using Files

A Data, Information, and Files

Computer professionals have special definitions for the terms *data*, *information*, and *file*. Although we might refer to these as technical definitions, they are not difficult to understand. Knowing these technical definitions will help you communicate with computer professionals and understand phrases such as "data in, information out."

Data and Information: Technically Speaking

Aren't data and information the same thing? In everyday conversation, people use the terms *data* and *information* interchangeably. However, some computer professionals make a distinction between the two terms. **Data** is the words, numbers, and graphics that describe people, events, things, and ideas. Data becomes information when you use it as the basis for initiating some action or for making a decision. **Information**, then, is defined as the words, numbers, and graphics used as the basis for human actions and decisions.

To understand the distinction between data and information, consider the following: AA 4199 ORD 9:59 CID 11:09. These letters, numbers, and symbols, which describe an event—a flight schedule—are typical of the *data* stored in a computer system. Now, suppose that you decide to take a trip from Chicago (ORD) to Cedar Rapids, Iowa (CID). Your travel agent sees the following on the computer screen:

Carrier	Flight Number	From	Departs	To	Arrives
AA	4199	ORD	9:59	CID	11:09

Here, the letters, numbers, and symbols displayed on the screen are considered *information* because your travel agent is using them to make your reservation.

The distinction between data and information might seem somewhat elusive, because "AA 4199 ORD 9:59 CID 11:09" can be both data and information. Remember that the distinction is based on usage. Usually, if letters, numbers, and symbols are stored in a computer, they are referred to as data. If letters, numbers, and symbols are being used by a person to complete an action or make a decision, they are referred to as information. Remember this: Data is used by computers; information is used by humans.

Incidentally, in Latin, the word *data* is the plural for *datum*. According to this usage, it would be correct to say "The January and February rainfall *data* are stored on the disk," and "The March *datum* is not yet available." Most English dictionaries accept the use of *data* as either singular or plural. In this text *data* is used with the singular verb, as in "The *data is* stored on the disk."

Computer Files

What kinds of files will I have on my computer? A **file** is a named collection of program instructions or data that exists on a storage medium such as a hard disk, a floppy disk, or a CD-ROM. Suppose you use a computer to write a memo to your employer. The words contained in the memo are stored on a disk in a file. The file has a name to distinguish it from other files on your disk. Although there are several kinds of files, a typical computer user deals mainly with executable files and data files. Understanding the difference between these two kinds of files is important because you use them in different ways.

Executable Files

How do I use executable files? An **executable file** contains the instructions that tell a computer how to perform a specific task. For example, the word-processing program that tells your computer how to display and print text is stored on disk as an executable file. Other executable files on your computer system include the operating system, utilities, and application software programs.

To use an executable file, you *run* it. In Chapter 1 you learned how to run programs. In DOS you type the name of the program, in Windows 3.1 you double-click a program icon, and in Windows 95 and Windows 98 you select the program from a menu. The programs you run are one type of executable file.

Your computer also has executable files that you cannot run. These files are executed at the request of a computer program, not the user. For example, a word-processing program may request that the computer use an executable file to check the grammar in a document.

Most operating systems help you identify the executable files you can run. DOS uses part of the filename to indicate an executable file. You will learn more about this later in the section "Filenaming Conventions." Windows uses icons to indicate which files you can run, as shown in Figure 4-1.

Figure 4-1

Program icons

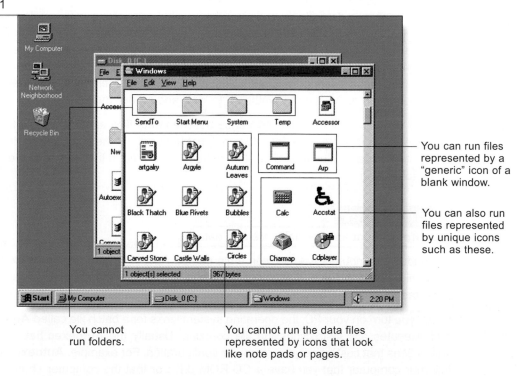

You can run files represented by a "generic" icon of a blank window.

You can also run files represented by unique icons such as these.

You cannot run folders.

You cannot run the data files represented by icons that look like note pads or pages.

The instructions in an executable file are directly executed by the computer. The instructions are stored in a format that the computer can interpret, but this format is not designed to be readable to humans. If you try to look at the contents of an executable file, the file will appear to contain meaningless symbols such as ☺□¬%■ŷ.

Data Files

How do I use data files? A **data file** contains words, numbers, and pictures that you can view, edit, save, send, and print. Typically, you create data files when you use application software. For example, you create a data file when you store a document you have written using word-processing software or a picture you have drawn using graphics software. You also create a data file when you store a spreadsheet, a graph, a sound clip, or a video.

You probably won't create all the data files you use. You might receive data files as part of a software package you purchase. For example, word-processing software often includes a dictionary data file that contains a list of words the software uses to check spelling.

You can also purchase specific data files that contain information you need. Suppose you own a business and want to mail product information to prospective customers. You could purchase a data file that contains the names and addresses of people in your geographical area who fit the age and income profile of consumers who are likely to buy your product.

Whether you create or purchase a data file, you typically use it in conjunction with application software. The application software helps you manipulate the data in the file. You usually view, revise, and print a data file using the same software you used to create it. For example, if you create a data file using word-processing software such as Microsoft Word, you would usually use Microsoft Word to edit the file.

If you purchase a data file, how do you know what application software to use it with? Usually, a software product that contains data files will also contain the program you need to manipulate the data. If the program that manipulates the data is not included, the user manual indicates which program you can use. For example, if you purchase a collection of data files that contain graphical images, the user manual might indicate that you need a program such as Microsoft Paintbrush to view and modify the images.

So how can you remember the difference between data files and executable files? Think of data files as passive—the data does not instruct or direct the computer to do anything. Think of executable files as active—the instructions stored in the file cause the computer to do something.

Source Files

Is Autoexec.bat an executable file or a data file? If you look at the files on most DOS or Windows computers, you will see a file named **Autoexec.bat**. This is an example of a batch file. A **batch file** is a series of operating system commands that you use to automate tasks you want the operating system to perform.

InfoWeb

Autoexec
2

When you turn on your PC, the operating system looks for a batch file called **Autoexec.bat** and executes any instructions the file contains. Usually the **Autoexec.bat** file contains instructions that customize your computer configuration. For example, **Autoexec.bat** might tell your computer that you have a CD-ROM drive or that the computer should establish connection with a network.

Because batch files contain instructions, you might assume that they are executable files. However, unlike most executable files, a batch file does not contain instructions in a format that the computer can directly carry out. Instead, a batch file contains instructions that computer users can read and modify. The commands in a batch file must go through a translation process before they can be executed. Batch files belong to a third category of files called **source files**, which contain instructions that the computer must translate before executing.

The Document-centric Approach to Files

How important is it for me to distinguish between executable files, data files, and source files? Understanding the difference between executable, data, and source files helps you understand how a computer works. Once you understand the characteristics of these file types, you understand that the computer performs the instructions in executable files to help you create data files. It follows, then, that the way you use a computer is to run an application program and use it to create data files. For example, first you run a word-processing program, then you use it to create a report.

The problem with this model is that to revise a document, you must remember what software you used to create it. Suppose you create a list of people who contributed to your organization's 1998 fund-raising campaign. The next year, you want to use this list again. You remember you called the file Contributors 98, but what program did you use to create it? Did you use Microsoft's Excel spreadsheet or Access database? Or did you use a word-processing program such as Microsoft Word?

An alternative approach to using files is referred to as the document-centric approach. The term is derived from two words: document and centric. **Document-centric** means that the *document* is *central* to the way you use a computer. Under the document-centric model, once you indicate the document you want to revise, the computer automatically starts the appropriate application program. For example, if you are using Windows, when you click the Contributors 98 document, the computer starts the Microsoft Word application, then retrieves the data file Contributors 98, as shown in Figure 4-2.

Figure 4-2

Windows supports a document-centric approach, as well as the traditional approach to using files. With the document-centric approach, you select the data file you want to revise. The operating system automatically starts the appropriate application software and opens the data file you selected.

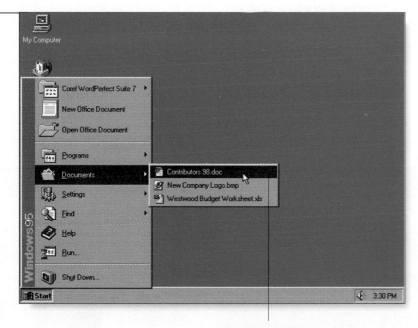

Clicking the document starts the appropriate program.

The operating system on your computer determines whether you can use the document-centric or traditional approach to files. To summarize the difference, under the document-centric approach, you select the data file you want to revise and the computer automatically runs the appropriate application program. Under the traditional approach, you run an application program first, then select the file you want to revise.

Filenaming Conventions

> May I use any name I want when I create my own files?

A **filename** is a unique set of letters and numbers that identifies a file and usually describes the file contents. For example, **Excel** is the name of one of the main files for the Microsoft Excel spreadsheet software.

The filename might be followed by a **filename extension** that further describes the file contents. Filename extensions are also referred to as *file extensions* or *extensions*. The filename **Excel.exe**, with the **.exe** extension, indicates it is an executable file. The extension is separated from the filename with a period, called a *dot*. So, if you were to tell someone the name of this file, you would say "Excel dot e-x-e."

As a computer user, you are not usually responsible for naming executable files. These files are included with the application software you purchase, and the files are named by the programmers who write them. When you look through a list of files on a disk, you can quickly identify executable files by their file extensions. See Figure 4-3.

Figure 4-3

The executable files you can run generally have either a **.com** (for *command*) extension or **.exe** (for *executable)* extension.

File Type	File Extension
Files you can run	.exe .com
FIles you cannot run	.sys .dll .drv .vbx .ocx

You must assign a valid filename to the data files you create. A **valid filename** adheres to specific rules, referred to as **filenaming conventions**. Each operating system has a unique set of filenaming conventions. You can use Figure 4-4 to determine whether **Aux**, **My File.doc**, and **Bud93/94.txt** are valid filenames under the operating system you use.

InfoWeb

Filename
Extensions
3

Figure 4-4

Filenaming conventions

	DOS and Windows 3.1	Windows 95	MacOS	UNIX
Maximum length of filename	eight character filename plus three character extension	255 character filename including the three character extension	31 characters No extensions used	14–256 characters (depends on the version of UNIX), including an extension of any length
Character to separate filename from extension	. (period)	. (period)	No extensions	. (period)
Spaces allowed	No	Yes	Yes	No
Numbers allowed	Yes	Yes	Yes	Yes
Characters not allowed	/[];="\:,|*?	\?:"<>|	None	!@#$%^&*()[]{}'"|;<>
Reserved words	AUX, COM1, COM2, COM3, COM4, CON, LPT1, LPT2, LPT3, PRN, or NUL	AUX, COM1, COM2, COM3, COM4, CON, LPT1, LPT2, LPT3, PRN, or NUL	None	Depends on version of UNIX
Case sensitive	No	No	Yes	Yes—use lowercase

Using DOS or Windows filenaming conventions, **Aux** is not a valid filename because it is a reserved word. **My File.doc** is not valid under DOS, Windows 3.1, or UNIX because it contains a space between My and File. The filename **Bud93/94.txt** would be valid only under Mac OS because it contains a slash. Filenames such as **Session**, **Report.doc**, **Budget1.wks**, and **Form.1** are valid under all the operating systems listed in Figure 4-4.

Filename extensions for data files fall into two categories: generic and application-specific. A **generic filename extension** indicates the type of data a file contains, but it does not tell you exactly which software application was used to create the file. For example, a **.bmp** extension tells you that the file contains graphical data, but the file might have been created by any of several graphics packages such as Microsoft Paint or MicroGraphx PicturePublisher. Figure 4-5 lists some generic filename extensions.

Figure 4-5

Generic filename extensions

File Type	File Extension
Text	.txt
Sound	.wav .mid
Graphics	.bmp .pcx .tif .wmf .jpg .gif
Animation/Video	.flc .fli .avi .mpg
Web documents	.html .htm

Figure 4-6

Application Software	File Extension
WordPerfect	.wpd
Microsoft Word and WordPad	.doc
Microsoft Works	.wps
Lotus Word Pro	.sam
Lotus 1-2-3	.wk4
Microsoft Excel	.xls
Corel Quattro Pro	.wb1
Lotus Approach	.apr
Microsoft Access	.mdb
Claris FileMaker Pro	.fm

An **application-specific filename extension** is associated with a particular application and indicates which software was used to create the file. For example, when you create a file with Microsoft Word for Windows, the software assigns a **.doc** extension to your filename. By automatically assigning an extension, the application helps you identify the files you created using that application.

Suppose that you had many files on a disk—some created using Word and others created using a spreadsheet program and a graphics program. Now you want to view or edit one of the files you created using Microsoft Word. The Word software searches through all the files on your disk and shows you a list of only those filenames that have a **.doc** extension. Because you see only the files you created using Word, you do not have to wade through a long list of files that include your spreadsheets and graphics. Figure 4-6 lists some application-specific filename extensions that you are likely to encounter.

Wildcards

What's *.* ? Files have unique names, but sometimes you want to refer to more than one file. For example, suppose you want to list all the files on your disk with an .exe extension. You can specify *.exe (pronounced "star dot e-x-e"). The asterisk is a **wildcard character** used to represent a group of characters. *.exe means all the files with an .exe extension. Suppose your disk contains the files: **Excel.exe**, **Spell.exe**, **Excel.cfg**, and **Budget.dat**. You could use Excel.* to represent **Excel.exe** and **Excel.cfg**.

. (pronounced "star dot star") means all files. When you use DOS, the command DEL *.* will delete all the files in a directory. Be careful if you use this command!

Most operating systems use wildcards to make it easier to manipulate a collection of files. For example, using wildcards, you can delete all the files on a disk in one operation, instead of deleting each file individually. You will use wildcards even with a graphical user interface, as shown in Figure 4-7.

Figure 4-7

Wildcards help you locate files in Microsoft Word for Windows.

The list includes only those files that begin with the letter R and have a .doc extension.

R* uses a wildcard to mean all files that begin with the letter R.

*.doc uses a wildcard to mean all files that have a .doc extension.

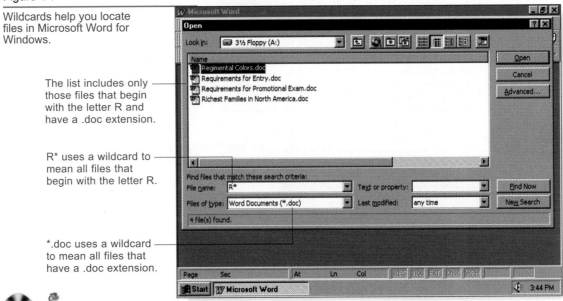

Logical File Storage

How do I keep track of all the files on my disks? Your computer system might contain hundreds, even thousands of files stored on disks and other storage devices. To keep track of all these files, the computer has a filing system that is maintained by the operating system. Once you know how the operating system manages your computer's filing system, you can use it effectively to store and retrieve files.

Most computers have more than one storage device that the operating system uses to store files. Each storage device is identified by a letter. Floppy disk drives are usually identified as A and B. The hard disk drive is usually identified as C. Additional storage devices can be assigned letters from D through Z. The drive letter is usually followed by a colon as in C:. Figure 4-8 shows some microcomputer configurations and the letters typically assigned to their storage devices. Does one of these match the configuration for the computer you use?

Figure 4-8

Storage device letter assignments

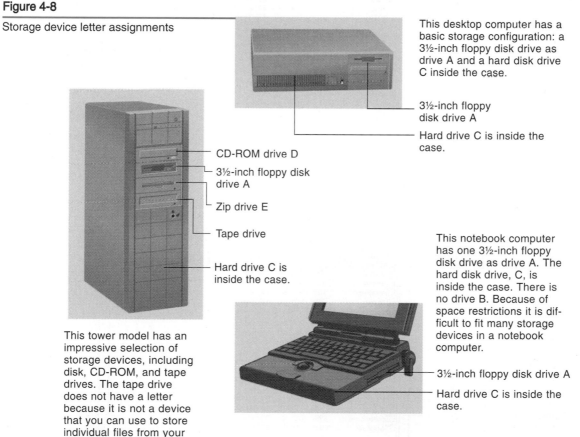

This desktop computer has a basic storage configuration: a 3½-inch floppy disk drive as drive A and a hard disk drive C inside the case.

3½-inch floppy disk drive A

Hard drive C is inside the case.

CD-ROM drive D

3½-inch floppy disk drive A

Zip drive E

Tape drive

Hard drive C is inside the case.

This tower model has an impressive selection of storage devices, including disk, CD-ROM, and tape drives. The tape drive does not have a letter because it is not a device that you can use to store individual files from your applicatons.

This notebook computer has one 3½-inch floppy disk drive as drive A. The hard disk drive, C, is inside the case. There is no drive B. Because of space restrictions it is difficult to fit many storage devices in a notebook computer.

3½-inch floppy disk drive A

Hard drive C is inside the case.

The operating system maintains a list of files called a **directory** for each disk or CD-ROM. The directory contains information about every file on a storage device such as the filename, the file extension, the date and time the file was created, and the file size. You can use the operating system to view the directory of a disk. Study the figures on this and the next page to compare different directory styles for DOS and Windows.

Figure 4-9

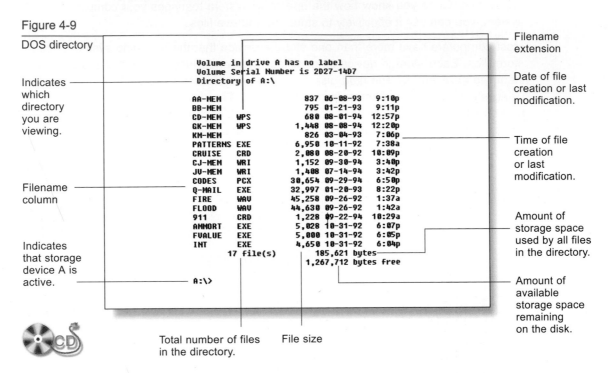

DOS directory

Indicates which directory you are viewing.

Filename column

Indicates that storage device A is active.

Filename extension

Date of file creation or last modification.

Time of file creation or last modification.

Amount of storage space used by all files in the directory.

Amount of available storage space remaining on the disk.

Total number of files in the directory.

File size

```
            Volume in drive A has no label
            Volume Serial Number is 2D27-14D7
            Directory of A:\

AA-MEM                    837  06-08-93    9:10p
BB-MEM                    795  01-21-93    9:11p
CD-MEM      WPS           680  08-01-94   12:57p
GK-MEM      WPS         1,448  08-08-94   12:20p
KM-MEM                    826  03-04-93    7:06p
PATTERNS    EXE        6,950  10-11-92    7:38a
CRUISE      CRD        2,080  08-20-92   10:09p
CJ-MEM      WRI        1,152  09-30-94    3:40p
JU-MEM      WRI        1,408  07-14-94    3:42p
CODES       PCX       30,654  09-29-94    6:50p
Q-MAIL      EXE       32,997  01-20-93    8:22p
FIRE        WAV       45,258  09-26-92    1:37a
FLOOD       WAV       44,630  09-26-92    1:42a
911         CRD        1,228  09-22-94   10:29a
AMMORT      EXE        5,028  10-31-92    6:07p
FVALUE      EXE        5,000  10-31-92    6:05p
INT         EXE        4,650  10-31-92    6:04p
       17 file(s)           185,621 bytes
                          1,267,712 bytes free

A:\>
```

Figure 4-10

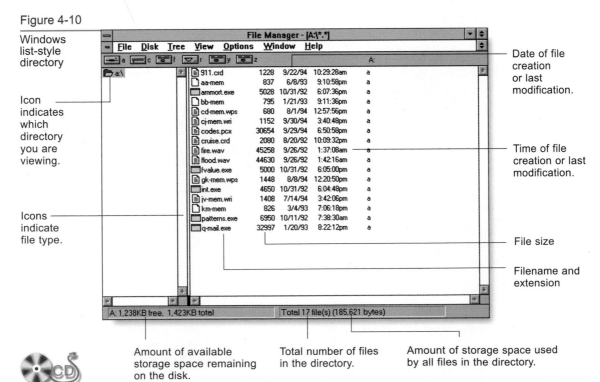

Windows list-style directory

Icon indicates which directory you are viewing.

Icons indicate file type.

Date of file creation or last modification.

Time of file creation or last modification.

File size

Filename and extension

```
                        File Manager - [A:\*.*]
  File  Disk  Tree  View  Options  Window  Help
 a   c   f   r   y   z                    A:
a:\        911.crd       1228   9/22/94  10:29:28am   a
           aa-mem         837   6/8/93    9:10:58pm   a
           ammort.exe    5028  10/31/92   6:07:36pm   a
           bb-mem         795   1/21/93   9:11:36pm   a
           cd-mem.wps     680   8/1/94   12:57:56pm   a
           cj-mem.wri    1152   9/30/94   3:40:48pm   a
           codes.pcx    30654   9/29/92   6:50:58pm   a
           cruise.crd    2080   8/20/92  10:09:32pm   a
           fire.wav     45258   9/26/92   1:37:08am   a
           flood.wav    44630   9/26/92   1:42:16am   a
           fvalue.exe    5000  10/31/92   6:05:00pm   a
           gk-mem.wps    1448   8/8/94   12:20:50pm   a
           int.exe       4650  10/31/92   6:04:48pm   a
           jv-mem.wri    1408   7/14/94   3:42:06pm   a
           km-mem         826   3/4/93    7:06:18pm   a
           patterns.exe  6950  10/11/92   7:38:30am   a
           q-mail.exe   32997   1/20/93   8:22:12pm   a

A: 1,238KB free, 1,423KB total       Total 17 file(s) (185,621 bytes)
```

Amount of available storage space remaining on the disk.

Total number of files in the directory.

Amount of storage space used by all files in the directory.

Figure 4-11

Windows icon-style
directory

Indicates that
directory is for
drive A.

Filenames,
extensions, and
icons

Amount of
storage space
used by all files
in the directory.

Total number of
files in the
directory.

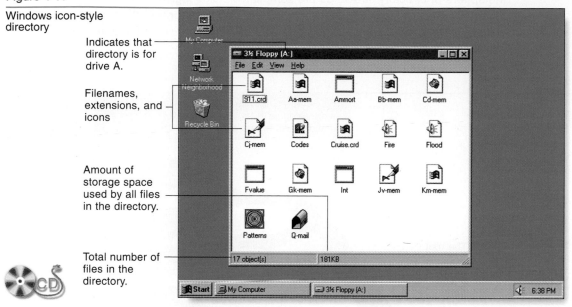

The main directory of a disk, sometimes referred to as the **root directory**, provides a useful list of files. It could be difficult, however, to find a particular file if your directory contains several hundred files. To help you organize a large number of files, most operating systems allow you to divide your directory into smaller lists called **subdirectories** or **folders**. For example, you can create one subdirectory to hold all your files that contain documents and another subdirectory to hold all your files that contain graphical images.

A subdirectory name is separated from a drive letter and a filename by a special symbol. In DOS and Microsoft Windows, this symbol is the backslash \. For example, the root directory of drive C might have a subdirectory called **Graphics**, written as **C:\Graphics**.

A **file specification** is the drive letter, subdirectory, filename, and extension that identifies a file. Suppose you create a subdirectory on drive A named Word for your word-processing documents. Now suppose you want to create a list of things to do called **To-do.doc** and store it on drive A in the Word subdirectory. The file specification is:

A:\Word\To-do.doc

Drive letter | | Extension
Subdirectory |
Filename

LAB

Windows
Directories,
Folders, and
Files

InfoWeb

Subdirectories can be further divided into what you might think of as *sub-subdirectories*. As you create more and more subdirectories on a disk, it becomes important to pay attention to the structure of the directories.

Directories
4

Metaphors of directory structures are sometimes called *logical models* because they represent the way you logically conceive of them. **Logical storage** is a conceptual model of the way data is stored on your disk. Figure 4-12 illustrates some metaphors for computer storage systems.

Figure 4-12

Metaphors of directory structures

You can mentally visualize the directory of a disk as a tree on its side. The trunk and branches are directories and the leaves are files.

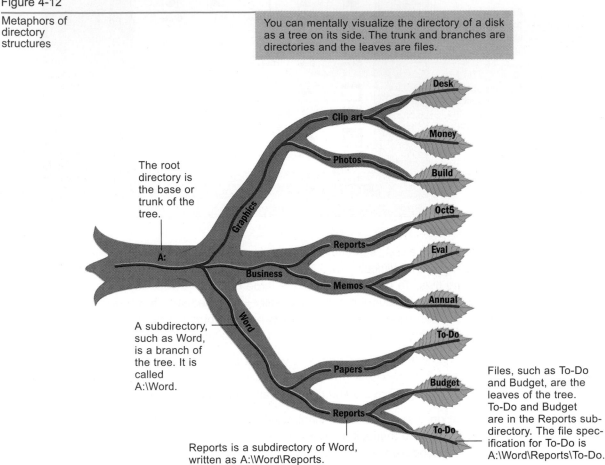

The root directory is the base or trunk of the tree.

A subdirectory, such as Word, is a branch of the tree. It is called A:\Word.

Reports is a subdirectory of Word, written as A:\Word\Reports.

Files, such as To-Do and Budget, are the leaves of the tree. To-Do and Budget are in the Reports subdirectory. The file specification for To-Do is A:\Word\Reports\To-Do.

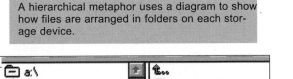

A hierarchical metaphor uses a diagram to show how files are arranged in folders on each storage device.

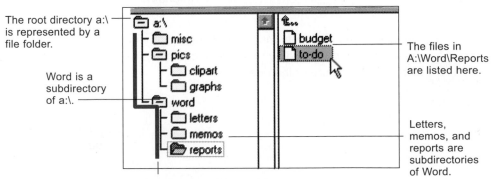

The root directory a:\ is represented by a file folder.

Word is a subdirectory of a:\.

The files in A:\Word\Reports are listed here.

Letters, memos, and reports are subdirectories of Word.

The red line shows the path for files in A:\Word\Reports.

Figure 4-12

Metaphors of directory structures (continued)

A boxes-within-boxes metaphor uses nested windows to represent the contents of folders.

The window for the root directory of 3½ Floppy (A:) holds the file folders Pics, Word, and Misc.

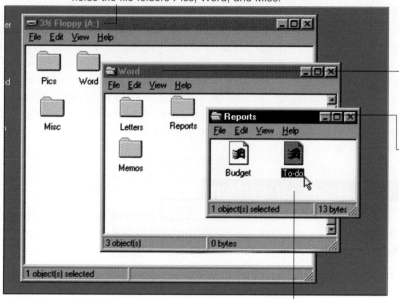

By clicking the Word file folder, you open the window for the Word directory.

By clicking the Reports folder, you open the window for the Reports directory.

The files in A:\Word\Reports are shown in the Reports window.

A logical view of storage is a convenient mental model that helps you understand the computer's filing system; however, it is not how the data is actually stored. **Physical storage** refers to how data is actually stored on the physical disk. To find out more about how computers physically store data, it is useful to understand a bit about storage media and storage devices. That is the topic of Section B.

QuickCheck A

1 To differentiate between data and information, use the rule: _____ is used by computers; _____ is used by humans.

2 What is the filename extension in the path: A:\Research\Primates\Jan5.Dat. _____

3 Files that you can run have _____ or .com extensions.

4 Nested file folders and directory trees are ways of representing _____ storage.

5 The main directory for a disk is called the _____ directory.

6 **Autoexec.bat** is an example of a(n) _____ file that needs to be translated by the computer before its instructions are executed.

B Storage Technologies

When it comes to computer storage, users have two questions: How much data can I store? How fast can I access it? The answers to these questions depend on the storage medium and the storage device. A **storage medium** (storage *media* is the plural) is the disk, tape, paper, or other substance that contains data. A **storage device** is the mechanical apparatus that records and retrieves the data from the storage medium. When we want to refer to a storage device and the media it uses, we can use the term **storage technology**.

The process of storing data is often referred to as **writing data** or **saving a file** because the storage device *writes* the data on the storage medium to *save* it for later use. The process of retrieving data is often referred to as **reading data**, **loading data**, or **opening a file**. The terms "reading" and "writing" make sense if you imagine that you are the computer. As the computer, you *write* a note and save it for later. You retrieve the note and *read* it when you need the information it contains. The terms *reading data* and *writing data* are often associated with mainframe applications. The terms *save* and *open* are standard Windows terminology.

Storage Specifications

How do I compare storage technologies? Knowing the characteristics of a storage device or storage medium helps you determine which one is best for a particular task. Storage technology comparisons are often based on storage capacity and speed.

Data is stored as bytes. Each **byte** usually represents one character—a letter, punctuation mark, space, or numeral. The phrase "profit margin" requires 13 bytes of storage space because the phrase contains 12 characters and the space between the two words requires an additional byte of storage space. **Storage capacity** is the maximum amount of data that can be stored on a storage medium and is usually measured in kilobytes, megabytes, or gigabytes. A **kilobyte** (KB) is 1,024 bytes, but this is often rounded to one thousand bytes. A **megabyte** (MB) is 1,048,576 bytes, approximately one million bytes. A **gigabyte** (GB) is 1,073,741,824 bytes, approximately one billion bytes. When you read that the storage capacity of a computer is 5.1 gigabytes, it means the hard disk on that computer can store up to 5.1 billion bytes of information. This is equivalent to approximately 1,350,000 single-spaced pages of text—that would be a stack of paper 450 feet high!

In addition to storage capacity, users are concerned with access time. **Access time** is the average time it takes a computer to locate data on the storage medium and read it. Access time for a microcomputer storage device, such as a disk drive, is measured in milliseconds. One **millisecond** (ms) is a thousandth of a second. When you read, for example, that disk access time is 11 ms, it means that on average, it takes the computer eleven thousandths of a second to locate and read data from the disk.

It is fairly easy to compare two storage technologies based on storage capacity and access time; these specifications are usually included in advertisements and product descriptions. However, additional characteristics of storage technologies must be considered. The durability and access methods of a storage technology are also important characteristics to compare.

Magnetic or Optical Storage?

Will the metal detector in an airport erase the data on my disks? Magnetic and optical storage technologies are used for the majority of today's micro, mini, and mainframe computers. Each of these technologies has advantages and disadvantages.

With **magnetic storage** the computer stores data on disks and tape by magnetizing selected particles of an oxide-based surface coating. The particles retain their magnetic orientation until that orientation is changed, thereby making disks and tape fairly permanent but modifiable storage media. Figure 4-13 shows how a computer stores data on magnetic media.

Figure 4-13

Storing data on magnetic media

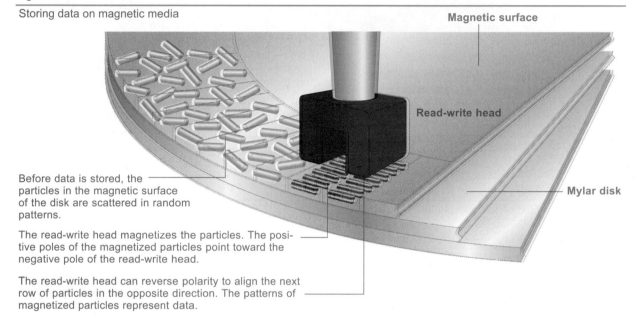

Magnetic surface

Read-write head

Mylar disk

Before data is stored, the particles in the magnetic surface of the disk are scattered in random patterns.

The read-write head magnetizes the particles. The positive poles of the magnetized particles point toward the negative pole of the read-write head.

The read-write head can reverse polarity to align the next row of particles in the opposite direction. The patterns of magnetized particles represent data.

You can intentionally change or erase files stored on magnetic media. If you run out of disk space, you can make more space available by erasing files you no longer need.

Data stored on magnetic media such as floppy disks can also be unintentionally altered by the environment and by device or media failure. In the environment, magnetic fields, dust, mold, smoke particles, and heat are the primary culprits causing data loss. Placing a magnet on your disk is a sure way of losing data. The metal detectors in an airport use a magnetic field, but the field is not strong enough to disrupt the data on your floppy or hard disks. You are more likely to damage your disks by leaving them on the dashboard of your car in the sun or carrying them around in your backpack where they will pick up dust and dirt. At many mainframe installations, magnetic media are stored in climate-controlled vaults to protect against environmental hazards such as dust, extreme temperatures, smoke, and mold.

Media failure is a problem with storage media that results in data loss. Magnetic media gradually lose their magnetic charge, resulting in lost data. Some experts estimate that the reliable life span of data stored on magnetic media is about three years, and they recommend that you refresh your data every two years by recopying it.

A device failure can damage a disk and result in data loss. A **device failure** is a problem with a mechanical device such as a disk drive. Storage devices fail as a result of power or circuitry problems.

With **optical storage**, data is burned into the storage medium using beams of laser light. The burns form patterns of small pits in the disk surface to represent data, as shown in Figure 4-14.

Figure 4-14

The pits on an optical storage disk as seen through an electron microscope. Each pit is 1 micron in diameter—1,500 pits lined up side by side would be about as wide as the head of a pin.

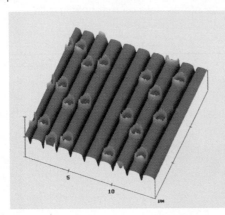

After creating a master, optical disks can be mass produced. During the manufacturing process copies of the disk are stamped out on a plastic disk. A thin layer of reflective aluminium is added, then a laquer coating for protection.

Optical media are very durable—the useful life of a CD-ROM is estimated to exceed 500 years. They are not susceptible to humidity, fingerprints, dust, or magnets. If you spill coffee on a CD-ROM disk, you can just rinse it off and it will be as good as new.

The data on optical media is permanent. Therefore, optical media do not give you the flexibility of magnetic media for changing data once it is stored. An optical drive that reads the data on an optical disk uses laser light, but less powerful than the laser that burns the pits in the original master. Figure 4-15 illustrates how light is used to read the data on an optical disk.

Figure 4-15

Reading data on an optical disk

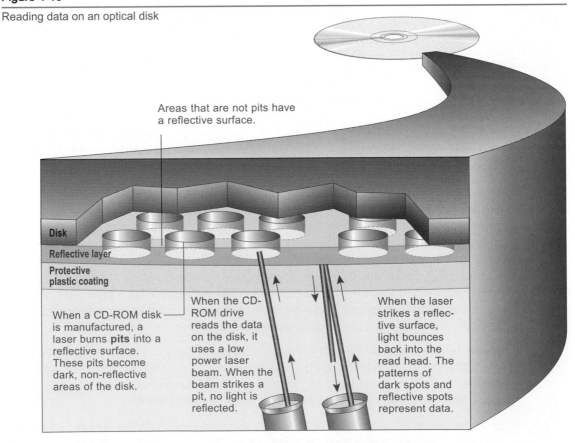

Areas that are not pits have a reflective surface.

Disk

Reflective layer

Protective plastic coating

When a CD-ROM disk is manufactured, a laser burns **pits** into a reflective surface. These pits become dark, non-reflective areas of the disk.

When the CD-ROM drive reads the data on the disk, it uses a low power laser beam. When the beam strikes a pit, no light is reflected.

When the laser strikes a reflective surface, light bounces back into the read head. The patterns of dark spots and reflective spots represent data.

Floppy Disk Storage

Floppies & Zips 5

Why is it called a floppy disk? A **floppy disk** is a round piece of flexible mylar plastic covered with a thin layer of magnetic oxide. The disk is sealed inside a protective casing. Those brightly colored computer disks that fit conveniently in your pocket or backpack are sometimes mistakenly called "hard disks" because of their rigid plastic casing. If you break open the disk casing (something you should never do unless you want to ruin the disk), you would see that the mylar disk inside is thin and, well, floppy. Floppy disks are also called **floppies** or **diskettes**. A special high capacity floppy disk manufactured by iomega, Corp. is called a **Zip disk**.

Floppy disks come in several sizes: 3½ inch, 5¼ inch, and 8 inch. The disk size most commonly used on today's microcomputers is 3½ inch. A 3½-inch circular disk made of flexible mylar is housed inside a protective case of rigid plastic. When the disk is inserted in the disk drive, the spring-loaded access cover slides to the side to expose the disk surface for reading and writing data. Figure 4-16 shows the construction of a 3½-inch disk.

Figure 4-16

3½-inch floppy disk

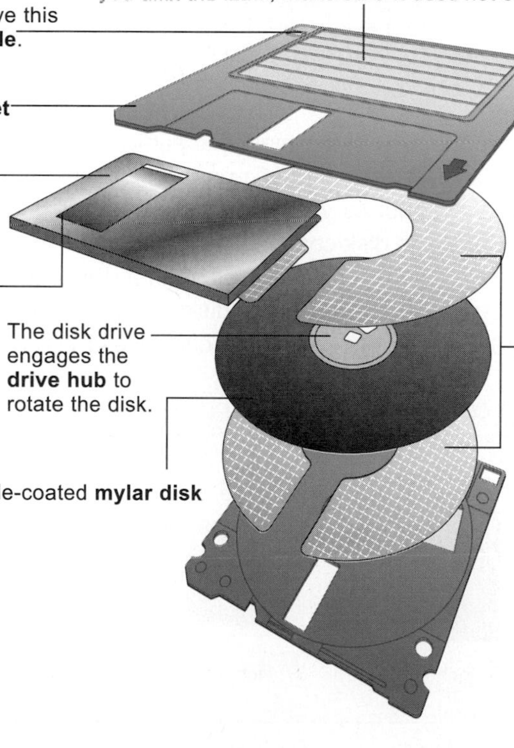

The **disk label** often wraps around to the underside of the disk. When you affix the label, make sure it does not stick to the access cover.

Only high-density disks have this **high-density indicator hole**.

The rigid plastic **disk jacket** protects the inner disk.

The spring-loaded **access cover** slides sideways when the disk is inserted in the drive.

When the disk is in the drive, this head aperture is aligned with the opening in the access cover to expose the disk surface to the read-write head.

The disk drive engages the **drive hub** to rotate the disk.

Oxide-coated **mylar disk**

When the **write-protect window** is open, the disk is write protected and the computer cannot write data on the disk. You usually keep the window closed so you can add, modify, and delete data on the disk.

The **disk liner** removes dirt and dust from the disk surface.

In the past, floppy disks stored data only on one side; but today most store data on both sides. As you might guess, a **double-sided disk**, sometimes abbreviated as DS, stores twice as much data as a single-sided disk.

The amount of data a computer can store on each side of a disk depends on the way the disk is formatted. In Chapter 2 you learned that a disk must be formatted before you can store data on it. The formatting process creates a series of concentric **tracks** on the disk, and each track is divided into smaller segments called **sectors**, as shown in Figure 4-17.

Figure 4-17

Tracks and sectors of a formatted disk

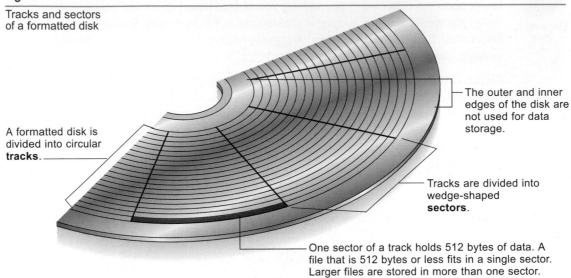

A formatted disk is divided into circular **tracks**.

The outer and inner edges of the disk are not used for data storage.

Tracks are divided into wedge-shaped **sectors**.

One sector of a track holds 512 bytes of data. A file that is 512 bytes or less fits in a single sector. Larger files are stored in more than one sector.

Disk density refers to the size of the magnetic particles on the disk surface. The higher the disk density, the smaller the magnetic particles it stores, and the more data it can store. Think of it this way: Just as you can put more lemons than grapefruit in a basket, you can store more data on a disk coated with smaller particles than with larger particles. A **high-density (HD) disk** can store more data than a **double-density (DD)** disk. Most of today's computers use high-density 3½-inch disks formatted with 18 sectors and 80 tracks per side. Figure 4-18 summarizes floppy disk capacities by size and density.

Figure 4-18

Floppy and Zip disk capacities

Size	5¼ inch	5¼ inch	3½ inch	3½ inch	3½ inch
Density	Double-density	High-density	Double-density	High-density	N/A
Capacity	360 KB	1.2 MB	720 KB	1.44 MB	100 MB
Sectors per side	9	15	9	18	32
Tracks per side	40	80	80	80	3065

The storage device that records and retrieves data on a floppy disk is a **floppy disk drive**. Figure 4-19 shows you a 3½-inch floppy disk drive and a Zip drive, along with the disks that they use.

Figure 4-19

Two popular disk drives

A 3½-inch disk drive has an eject button to release the disk and a drive light to indicate when the drive is in use. You insert the disk so the label goes in last. Virtually every computer has a 3½-inch disk drive.

A Zip drive uses special Zip disks that are slightly larger than a 3½-inch floppy disk. The green light indicates that the drive is ready. A yellow light indicates that the drive is in use. Insert the Zip disk so the label enters last. Zip disks are increasing in popularity and use.

In both a floppy disk drive and a Zip drive, the read-write head can read or write data from any sector of the disk, in any order. This ability to move to any sector is referred to as **random access** or **direct access**. Random access is a handy feature of disk-based storage that provides quick access to files anywhere on a disk. Even with random access, however, a floppy disk drive is not a particularly speedy device. It takes about 0.5 seconds for a 3½-inch drive to spin the disk up to speed and then move the read-write head to a particular sector. A Zip drive is about 20 times faster.

You don't usually run programs from floppy or Zip disks, so a 3½-inch or Zip drive would not be the main storage device in a computer system. Instead, floppies and Zip disks are typically used for transporting or shipping data files.

Newer technologies are decreasing the use of floppy disks. In the past, software was distributed on floppy disks. Now, most software vendors use CD-ROMs instead. Local computer networks and the Internet have made it easy to share data files, so floppy disks are shipped less frequently. Floppy disks have also been used to make duplicate copies of data files in case something happens to the originals, a process known as **backup**. The role of floppy disk storage for backup is being taken over, to some extent, by tape storage. Floppies are still used in many college computer labs so students can transport their data to different lab machines or to their home computers.

Hard Disk Storage

How can a hard disk be the same size as a floppy, but store so much more data? Hard disk storage is the preferred type of main storage for most computer systems because it provides faster access to files than floppy or Zip disk drives. A **hard disk platter** is a flat, rigid disk made of aluminum or glass and coated with a magnetic oxide. A **hard disk** is one or more platters and their associated read-write heads. You will frequently see the terms *hard disk* and *hard disk drive* used interchangeably. You might also hear the term *fixed disk* used to refer to hard disks.

Speed Update 6

Microcomputer hard disk platters are typically 3½ inches in diameter—the same size as the circular mylar disk in a floppy. However, the storage capacity of a hard disk far exceeds that of a floppy disk. Also, the access time of a hard disk is significantly faster than a floppy disk's. Hard disk storage capacities of 5 GB and access times of 10 ms (.001 seconds) are not uncommon. Figure 4-20 explains how is it possible to pack so much data on a hard disk and access it so quickly.

Figure 4-20

How a hard disk drive works

Each data storage surface has its own **read-write head**. Read-write heads move in and out from the center of the disk to locate a specific track. The head hovers only five micro inches above the disk surface so the magnetic field is much more compact than on a floppy disk. As a result, more data is packed into a smaller area on a hard disk platter.

The **drive spindle** supports one or more **hard disk platters**. Both sides of the platter are used for data storage. More platters mean more data storage capacity. Hard disk platters rotate as a unit on the drive spindle to position a specific sector under the read-write heads. The platters spin continuously making thousands of revolutions per minute.

The platter surfaces are formatted into cylinders and sectors. A **cylinder** is a vertical stack of tracks. A hard disk could have between 312 and 2,048 cylinders. To find a file, the computer must know the cylinder, sector, and platter in which the file is stored.

Like floppy disks, hard disks provide random access to files. Unlike floppy disks, which begin to rotate only when you request data, hard disks are continually in motion, so there is no delay as the disk spins up to speed. As a result, hard disk access is faster than floppy disk access.

It is important to keep track of how much space is available on your disk, so you don't inadvertently fill it up. You can ask your computer operating system to tell you the capacity of your hard disk and how much of the capacity is currently used for data. The screens in Figures 4-21, 4-22, and 4-23 show you how to find out your disk capacity and utilization under DOS, Windows 3.1, Windows 95 and Windows 98.

Figure 4-21

Hard disk capacity and utilization in DOS

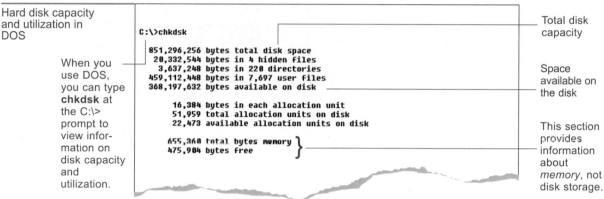

When you use DOS, you can type **chkdsk** at the C:\> prompt to view information on disk capacity and utilization.

Total disk capacity

Space available on the disk

This section provides information about *memory*, not disk storage.

Figure 4-22

Hard disk capacity and utilization in Windows 3.1

1. When you are using Windows 3.1, you must double-click the File Manager icon to open the File Manager window.

2. The File Manager window contains information about your computer's storage devices.

3. Click the icon for one of the storage devices shown in this row.

4. Capacity and utilization statistics are shown here.

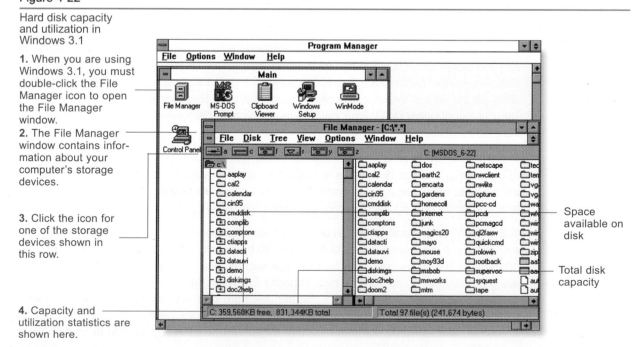

Space available on disk

Total disk capacity

Figure 4-23

Hard disk capacity and utilization
in Windows 95 and Windows 98

1. To view disk utilization statistics double-click the **My Computer** icon to open the My Computer window.

2. Click the storage device icon for which you want information.

3. Click File, then click **Properties** to display the properties of the storage device.

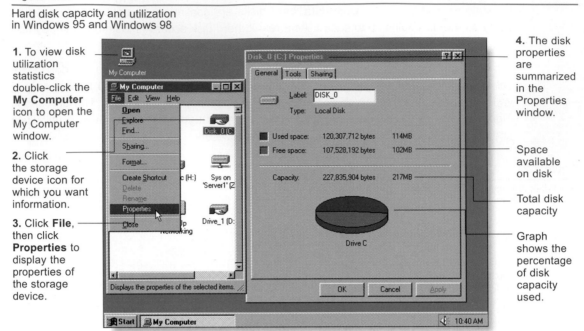

4. The disk properties are summarized in the Properties window.

Space available on disk

Total disk capacity

Graph shows the percentage of disk capacity used.

The read-write heads in a hard disk hover a microscopic distance above the disk surface. If a read-write head runs into a dust particle or some other contaminant on the disk, it might cause what is called a **head crash**. A head crash damages some of the data on the disk. To help eliminate contaminants from contacting the platters and causing head crashes, a hard disk is sealed in its case. A head crash can also be triggered by jarring the hard disk while it is in use. Although hard disks have become considerably more rugged in recent years, you should still handle and transport them with care.

Some hard disks are removable. **Removable hard disks** or hard disk cartridges contain platters and read-write heads that can be inserted and removed from the drive much like a floppy disk. Removable hard disks increase the potential storage capacity of your computer system, although the data is available on only one disk at a time. Removable hard disks also provide security for your data by allowing you to remove the hard disk cartridge and store it separately from the computer.

Mainframe users refer to disk storage as DASD (pronounced "daz-dee"). **DASD** stands for direct access storage device. As a direct, or random, access device, DASD can directly access data, much like a microcomputer hard disk drive. The DASD at most mainframe installations is either disk packs, high-capacity fixed disks, or RAID.

Many mainframe installations still use removable disk packs, although they are a fairly old technology. A **disk pack** contains from 6 to 20 hard disks. Each disk is a little larger than 10 inches. The entire pack can be removed and replaced with another pack. Disk packs are gradually being replaced by high-capacity fixed disk drives. **High-capacity fixed disk drive** technology is similar to a microcomputer hard disk with its platters and read-write heads, but with higher storage capacity. Each high-capacity fixed disk drive is housed in a cabinet. A mainframe computer system might include as many as 100 fixed disk drive cabinets.

RAID, another type of hard disk storage, is found in an increasing number of mainframe and microcomputer installations. RAID stands for redundant array of independent disks. A **RAID** storage device contains many disk platters, provides redundancy, and achieves faster data access than conventional hard disks. The **redundancy** feature of RAID technology protects data from media failures by recording data on more than one disk platter.

To further increase the speed of data access, your computer might use a disk cache. A **disk cache** (pronounced "cash") is a special area of computer memory into which the computer transfers the data you are likely to need from disk storage. Figure 4-24 shows how a disk cache works.

Figure 4-24

How disk caching works

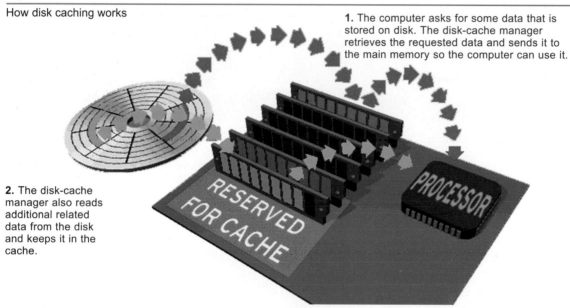

1. The computer asks for some data that is stored on disk. The disk-cache manager retrieves the requested data and sends it to the main memory so the computer can use it.

2. The disk-cache manager also reads additional related data from the disk and keeps it in the cache.

3. When the computer asks for more data, the disk-cache manager first checks the cache to see if the data is there. If the requested data is in the cache, it is immediately sent for processing. If the requested data is not in the cache, the disk-cache manager must take the time to locate the data on the disk, retrieve the data, then send it on to the main memory.

How does a disk cache help speed things up? Suppose your computer retrieves the data from a particular sector of your disk. There is a high probability that the next data you need will be from an adjacent sector—the remainder of a program file, for example, or the next section of a data file. The computer reads the data from nearby sectors and stores it in the cache. If the data you'll use next is already in the cache, the computer doesn't need to wait while the mechanical parts of the drive locate and read the data from the disk.

Tape Storage

Do they still use those big tape drives on computers that you see in old movies? In the 1960s, magnetic tape was the most popular form of mainframe computer storage. When IBM introduced its first microcomputer in 1981, the legacy of tape storage continued in the form of a cassette tape drive, similar to those used for audio recording and playback.

Using tape as a primary storage device instead of a hard disk would be slow and inconvenient because tape requires sequential, rather than random, access. With **sequential access**, data is stored and read as a sequence of bytes along the length of the tape. Study the diagram in Figure 4-25 to learn how computers store data on tape.

Figure 4-25

Sequential file access on magnetic tape

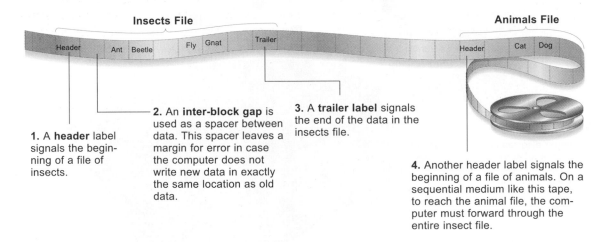

1. A **header** label signals the beginning of a file of insects.

2. An **inter-block gap** is used as a spacer between data. This spacer leaves a margin for error in case the computer does not write new data in exactly the same location as old data.

3. A **trailer label** signals the end of the data in the insects file.

4. Another header label signals the beginning of a file of animals. On a sequential medium like this tape, to reach the animal file, the computer must forward through the entire insect file.

Microcomputer users quickly abandoned tape storage for the convenience and speed of random access disk drives. Recently, however, tape storage for microcomputers has experienced a revival—not as a principal storage device, but for backing up data stored on hard disks. As you have learned in this chapter, the data on disks can be easily destroyed, erased, or otherwise lost. Protecting the data on the hard disk is of particular concern to users because it contains so much data—data that would be difficult and time-consuming to reconstruct. A **tape backup** is a copy of the data on a hard disk, stored on magnetic tape, and used to restore lost data. A tape backup is relatively inexpensive and can rescue you from the overwhelming task of trying to reconstruct lost data. If you lose the data on your hard disk, you can copy the data from the tape backup back to the hard disk. Typically, you do not use the data directly from the tape backup because the sequential access is too slow to be practical.

The large reels of computer tapes you might have seen in old movies are called **open reel tapes** and resemble spools of 16 mm film. Access speeds for open reel tapes are measured in seconds, not miliseconds. Open reel tapes are still used as a distribution medium for mainframe and microcomputer systems. Newer tape storage devices for these computers typically use half-inch tape cartriges. A **tape cartridge** is a removable magnetic tape module similar to a cassette tape.

InfoWeb

Tape
7

The most popular types of tape drives for microcomputers also use tape cartridges, but there are several tape specifications and cartridge sizes. **QIC** (quarter-inch cartridge) is a tape cartrige that contains quarter-inch wide tape. Depending on tape length, QIC tape capacities range from 340 MB to 2 GB. **DAT** (digital audio tape) was originally an audio recording format, but is now also used for data storage. The 4 mm wide DAT tape format storage capacity ranges from 2 GB to 12 GB. When you purchase tapes, check the tape drive manual to make sure the tapes you purchase are the correct type for your tape drive.

For a backup device, access time is less important than the time it takes to copy data from your hard disk to tape. Drive manufacturers do not usually supply such performance specifications, but most users can expect a tape drive to back up 100 MB in 15–20 minutes. Figure 4-26 shows a tape backup device that you might typically find in a microcomputer system.

Figure 4-26

Cartridge tape storage

Tape drives are typically incorporated in microcomputer systems to backup the contents of the hard drive. An external tape drive such as this one is a standalone unit that can be easily moved from one computer to another. Internal tape drives are installed in the system unit, similar to a floppy or CD-ROM drive.

The tape cartridge sequentially stores a backup of the data on the computer's hard disk drive

CD-ROM Storage

If CD-ROMs are read only, doesn't that limit their use? **CD-ROMs** are based on the same technology as the audio CDs you buy at your favorite music store. CD-ROM (pronounced "cee dee rom") stands for Compact Disc Read Only Memory. A computer CD-ROM disc, like its audio counterpart, contains data that has been stamped on the disk surface as a series of pits. To read the data on a CD-ROM, an optical read head distinguishes the patterns of pits that represent bytes. Figure 4-27 shows how you load a CD into the CD-ROM drive.

InfoWeb

CD-ROM
Update
8

Figure 4-27

CD-ROM storage

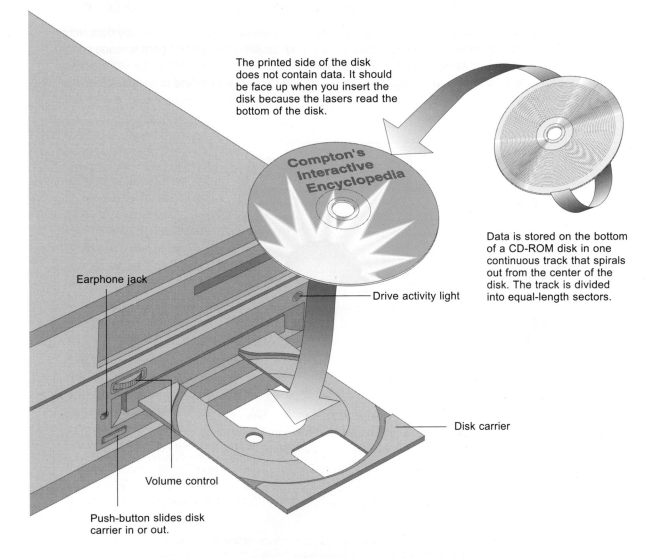

The printed side of the disk does not contain data. It should be face up when you insert the disk because the lasers read the bottom of the disk.

Compton's Interactive Encyclopedia

Data is stored on the bottom of a CD-ROM disk in one continuous track that spirals out from the center of the disk. The track is divided into equal-length sectors.

Earphone jack

Drive activity light

Disk carrier

Volume control

Push-button slides disk carrier in or out.

CD-ROMs provide tremendous storage capacity. A single CD-ROM disk holds up to 680 MB, equivalent to more than 300,000 pages of text, and is quite durable. The surface of the disk is coated with a clear plastic, making the data permanent and unalterable.

A CD-ROM drive supplements, rather than replaces, a hard disk drive because a CD-ROM is a read-only storage medium. **Read only** means that the computer can retrieve data from a CD-ROM but cannot save any new data on it. In this respect, CD-ROM technology differs from hard disk storage, on which you can write, erase, and read data.

A CD-ROM disk is relatively inexpensive to manufacture, making it an ideal way for software publishers to distribute large programs and data files. CD-ROM is the media of choice for delivery of multimedia applications because it provides the large storage capacity necessary for sound, video, and graphics files.

A recent technological development is the creation of CDs on which you can write data. **CD-R** (compact disc-recordable) technology allows the computer to record data on a CD-R disk using a special CD-R recording device. Disks that have been produced with the CD-R device can be used on a regular CD-ROM drive, like the one you might have on your computer. As with regular CD-ROMs the data on the disk cannot be erased or modified.

CD-R
9

CD-R is a useful technology for archiving data. **Archiving** refers to the process of moving data off a primary storage device when that data is not frequently accessed. For example, a business might archive its accounting data for previous years or a hospital might archive billing records once the accounts are paid. What's the difference between an archive and a backup? Archived data does not generally change, but the data you back up might change frequently.

Physical File Storage

What's the difference between physical and logical storage? Whether you store a file on a disk, CD-ROM, or tape, you have to know the filename and the letter of the device on which it was stored. That is the *logical* view of data storage, and it includes whatever desktop metaphor that makes it easy for you to view and select files. The *physical* view of data storage is how the computer keeps track of the location of your files on the physical disk, CD-ROM, or tape. To understand how the computer keeps track of your data, we'll look at how the computer manages data stored on a floppy disk.

Although a disk is formatted into tracks and sectors that provide physical storage locations for data, files are actually stored in clusters. A **cluster** is a group of sectors; it is the smallest storage unit the computer can access. The number of sectors that form a cluster depends on the type of computer and the capacity of the disk. For example, IBM-compatible microcomputers form a cluster from two sectors on a 360 K disk or 32 sectors on a 1 GB disk. Each cluster is numbered and the operating system maintains a list of which sectors correspond to each cluster.

When the computer stores a file on a disk, the operating system records the cluster number that contains the beginning of the file in a file allocation table (FAT). The **FAT** is an operating system file that maintains a list of files and their physical location on the disk. The FAT is such a crucial file that if it is damaged by a head crash or other disaster, you generally lose access to all the data stored on your disk. This is yet another reason to have a backup of the data on your hard drive.

FAT
10

When you want to store a file, the operating system looks at the FAT to see which clusters are empty. The operating system then puts the data for the file in empty clusters. The cluster numbers are recorded in the FAT. The name of the new file and the number of the first cluster that contains the file data are recorded in the directory.

A file that does not fit into a single cluster will spill over into the next adjacent or *contiguous* cluster unless that cluster already contains data. If the next cluster is full, the operating system stores the file in a noncontiguous (non-adjacent) cluster and sets up instructions called *pointers*. These "point" to each piece of the file, as shown in Figure 4-28.

Figure 4-28

How the FAT works

1. The directory is a file maintained by the operating system that contains a list of files on the disk and the number of the cluster that contains the start of the file. The directory and FAT work together to keep track of the files on a disk.

2. Here the directory shows that a file called **Jordan.wks** begins in cluster 7.

Directory	
Filename	**Starting Cluster**
Bio.txt	3
Jordan.wks	7
Pick.wps	9

3. The file allocation table (FAT) is a file maintained by the operating system to keep track of the physical location of files on a disk.

4. Each cluster is listed in the FAT, along with a number that indicates the status of the cluster. If status is "1," the cluster is reserved for technical files. If status is "0," the cluster is empty, so new data can be stored there. If the status is "999," the cluster contains the end of a file. Other status numbers indicate the sector that holds more data for a file.

5. Looking at the FAT entry for cluster 7, you see that the **Jordan.wks** file continues in cluster 8.

6. The FAT entry for cluster 8, shows that the **Jordan.wks** file continues in cluster 10. The file is stored in **non-contiguous** clusters 7, 8, and 10.

7. The FAT entry for cluster 10 shows that this is the end of the **Jordan.wks** file.

FAT		
Cluster	**Status**	*Comment*
1	1	*Reserved for operating system*
2	1	*Reserved for operating system*
3	4	*First cluster of Bio.txt. Points to cluster 4 which holds more data for Bio.txt.*
4	999	*Last cluster of Bio.txt*
5	0	*Empty*
6	0	*Empty*
7	8	*First cluster for Jordan.wks. Points to cluster 8 which holds more data for the Jordan.wks file.*
8	10	*Points to cluster 10 which holds more data for the Jordan.wks file.*
9	999	*First and last cluster containing Pick.wps*
10	999	*Last cluster of Jordan.wks*

When you want to retrieve a file, the operating system looks through the directory for the filename and the number of the first cluster that contains the file data. The FAT tells the computer which clusters contain the remaining data for the file. The operating system moves the read-write head to the cluster that contains the beginning of the file and reads it. If the file is stored in more than one cluster, the read-write head must move to the next cluster to read more of the file. It takes longer to access a file stored in noncontiguous clusters than one stored in contiguous clusters because the disk or head must move farther to find the next section of the file.

When you erase a file, the operating system changes the status of the appropriate clusters in the FAT. For example, if a file is stored in clusters 1, 2, 5, and 7 and you erase it, the operating system changes the status for those four clusters to "empty." The data is not physically removed or erased from those clusters. Instead, the old data remains in the clusters until a new file is stored there. This rather interesting situation means that if you inadvertently erase a file, you might be able to get it back using the operating system's **undelete utility**. Of course, you can only undelete a file if you haven't recorded something new over it, so undelete works only if you discover and correct mistakes immediately.

Storage
Basics
11

As you use random-access storage, files tend to become **fragmented**, that is, each file is stored in many noncontiguous clusters. Drive performance generally declines as the drive works harder to locate the clusters that contain the parts of a file. To regain peak performance, you can use a **defragmentation utility** to rearrange the files on a disk so that they are stored in contiguous clusters. Study Figure 4-29, which explains more about fragmentation and defragmentation.

Figure 4-29

Defragmenting a disk

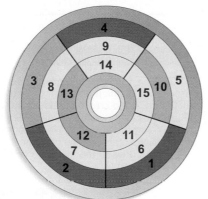

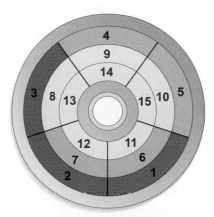

LAB

Defragmentation
and Disk
Operators

Fragmented disk

On this fragmented disk the purple, yellow, and blue files are stored in noncontiguous clusters. Accessing the clusters for these files is not efficient because of the time required to move the read-write head over the data.

Defragmented disk

When the disk is defragmented, the clusters of data for each file are moved to contiguous clusters. Data access becomes more efficient because drive head and disk movement are minimized.

QuickCheck B

1. Storage capacity is measured in _____, and access time is measured in _____.

2. A magnet can disrupt data on _____ storage, but _____ storage technology is more durable.

3. The formatting process creates a series of concentric _____ and triangle-shaped _____ on the disk.

4. The computer can move directly to any file on a(n) _____ access device, but must start at the beginning and read through all the data on a(n) _____ access device.

5. Two popular formats for microcomputer tape cartridges are _____ and DAT.

6. The primary storage device on a microcomputer is the _____.

7. The _____ keeps track of the physical location of files on a disk.

8. Data files that are entered by the user, changed often, or shared with other users are generally stored on optical media. True or false? _____

UserFocus

C Using Files

LAB

Now that you have learned about logical and physical file storage, let's apply what you've learned to how you typically use files when you work with application software. Using word-processing software to produce a document illustrates the way you use files on a computer, so look at the file operations for a typical word-processing session illustrated in Figure 4-30.

Using Files

Figure 4-30

File operations for a typical word-processing session

1   Running an Application

Suppose you want to create a document about the summer vacation packages your company offers. You decide to create the document using the word-processing software, Microsoft Word. Your first step is to start the Microsoft Word program. When you run Microsoft Word, the program file is copied from the hard drive to the memory of the computer.

2   Creating a File

You begin to type the text of the document. As you type, your data is stored in the memory of the computer. Your data will not be stored on disk until you initiate the Save command.

Word.exe is loaded into memory from hard disk

Your data is stored in memory while you type

3   Saving a Data File

When you create a file and save it on disk for the first time, the application or the operating system prompts you to name the file so you can later retrieve it by name. You know from earlier in this chapter that the name you give to a file must follow the naming convention for the operating system. You name the file A:Vacation.doc. By typing A: you direct the computer to save the file on the floppy disk in drive A. The computer looks for empty clusters on the disk where it can store the file. The computer then adds the filename to the directory, along with the number of the cluster that contains the beginning of the file. Once you have saved your file, you can exit the Word program or work on another document.

A:Vacation.doc is copied from memory to the floppy disk

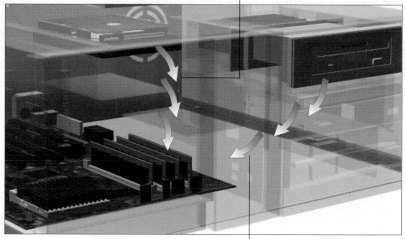

Word.exe is loaded into memory

A:Vacation.doc is copied from disk into memory

4 Retrieving a Data File

Now suppose that a few days later, you decide that you want to re-read Vacation.doc. You need to start Microsoft Word. Once the Word program is running, you can retrieve the Vacation.doc file from the disk on which it is stored.

When you want to use a data file that already exists on disk storage, you must tell the application to open the file. In Microsoft Word you either type the name of the file, A:Vacation.doc, or select the file-name from a list of files stored on the disk. The application communicates the filename to the operating system.

The operating system looks at the directory and FAT to find which clusters contain the file, then moves the read-write head to the appropriate disk location to read the file. The electronics on the disk drive transfer the file data into the main memory of the computer where your application software can manipulate it. Once the operating system has retrieved the file, the word-processing software displays it on the screen.

5 Revising a Data File

The changes you make to the document are stored in memory. When you save your revisions, they over-write the previous version of **Vacation.doc**.

When you see the Vacation.doc file on the screen, you can make modifications to it. Each character that you type and each change that you make is stored temporarily in the main memory of the computer, but not on the disk.

The Vacation.doc file is already on the disk, so when you are done with the modifications you have two options. Option one is to store the revised version in place of the old version. Option two is to create a new file for your revision and give it a different name, such as Holiday.

If you decide to go with option one—store the revised version in place of the old version—the operating system copies your revised data from the computer memory to the same clusters that contained the old file. You do not have to take a separate step to delete the old file—the operating system automatically records the new file over it.

If you decide to go with option two—create a new file for the revision—the application prompts you for a filename. Your revisions will be stored under the new filename. The original file, **Vacation.doc**, will still remain on the disk in its unrevised form.

Copying Files

Can I copy a file from the hard disk to my floppy disk and vice versa? You can copy a file from one storage medium to another. When you copy a file, the original file remains intact. You'll find that copying files is a task you will do frequently. Making copies of important files as backup, copying files from your hard disk to a floppy disk to share with a friend, or transferring files you receive on a floppy disk to your hard disk are only a few of the tasks that require you to know how to copy files.

LAB

DOS
Directories
and File
Management

Suppose you want to copy the **Vacation.doc** file from a floppy disk to your hard disk. The operating system is responsible for maintaining the list of files on your disk, so you usually use the operating system to copy files. With a graphical operating system such as Microsoft Windows, you can drag the icon that represents **Vacation.doc** from its place in the directory of drive A to the icon that represents drive C, as shown in Figure 4-31.

Figure 4-31

To copy the file
Vacation.doc to
drive C, drag the
file icon to the
drive C icon.

Drive C icon

File icon

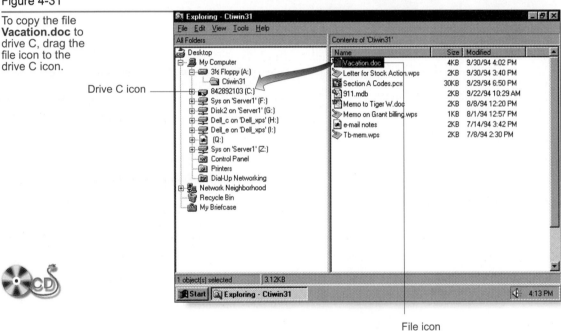

With the DOS operating system, you use the Copy command to copy a file. Let's assume that the disk containing **Vacation.doc** is in drive A and your hard disk drive is drive C. The DOS command to copy **Vacation.doc** from drive A to a subdirectory called Plans on drive C is:

COPY A:Vacation.doc C:\ Plans\Vacation.doc

Deleting Files

What if I run out of hard disk space? Eliminating files that you no longer need opens space for new files. If you want to eliminate a file that you have saved on disk, you **delete** or **erase** the file. As you know, when you delete a file, the operating system does not physically erase the cluster that contains the data belonging to that file. Instead, it changes the entries in the FAT to indicate that the clusters are available for storing other files. As additional files are stored on the disk, the sectors that formerly contained the deleted file are gradually overwritten.

To delete the file **Vacation.doc** from the disk in drive A using DOS, you type: DEL A:Vacation.doc. To delete a file using Windows 3.1, you highlight the file in the File Manager window, then press the Delete key. Using Windows 95 you delete a file by pressing the Delete key to delete the icon that represents the file.

EndNote

InfoWeb

Past & Future
12

Storage technology has dramatically advanced over the last 40 years. In 1956 IBM researchers introduced the world's first computer disk storage system. It stored 5 MB of data on fifty 24-inch disks. The disk drive's major advantage over tape storage was its ability to directly access any data on any of the disks, without sequentially reading all the data in between. Suddenly, computers could be used for interactive computing applications such as airline reservations and automated banking. In 1995 IBM researchers achieved a world record by storing 3 GB of data per square inch.

Such advances in storage technology did not eliminate tape storage. Quite to the contrary—tape drives have become faster and more efficient. By 1973, tapes were whizzing along at 200 inches per second, accelerating to that speed in less than 750 millionths of a second. Is that fast? You bet. At that rate of acceleration, tape speed would reach 12,000 mph in one second.

CD-ROMs, once thought to be the ultimate for multimedia storage are not large enough to store an entire two-hour feature film. Enter DVD (digital video disk). By increasing storage density, a DVD stores 4.7 GB of data on a disk the same size as a CD-ROM. Used in both the computing and entertainment industries DVD is designed to hold the data for a feature-length movie with theater-quality Dolby Surround Sound. DVD drives could be the next hot PC storage technology.

And what does the next 40 years hold for storage technology? How about holographic storage? Thinking in three-dimensions, instead of two-dimensional flat storage on disks and tapes, holographic storage is essentially a three-dimensional snapshot of data stored in a crystal medium. In the laboratory, researchers have achieved storage densities of 48 MB per cubic centimeter, but expected storage density is 10 GB per cubic centimeter. To put this in perspective, think about a couple of holographic storage cubes like a pair of dice that hold the contents of a half-mile high stack of books.

Researchers at the IBM Research Division's Zurich laboratory are working on another technology with the potential to revolutionize computer storage. They discovered that it is possible to manipulate individual molecules at room temperature. The researchers created a nano-abacus using microscopic soccerball-like carbon 60 molecules as the beads. A scanning tunneling microscope moves the beads along steps just one atom high. The process is similar to the earliest form of abacus in which the beads moved in groves instead of rods. These atoms could represent bits of stored data and eventually replace the much larger magnetic particles we use today on floppy and hard disks.

Figure 4-32

IBM's nano-abacus demonstrates that it might be possible in the future to use individual molecules to represent data bits for computer storage.

InfoWeb

InfoWeb

Chapter Links

The InfoWeb is your guide to print, film, television, and electronic resources. Use it to obtain updates on quickly changing technical information and to locate information for research papers. If you're using the New Perspectives CD-ROM, click the InfoWeb icon on the left side of this paragraph to access the online InfoWeb links. Otherwise, use your Web browser and type in the address of the New Perspectives site: www.cciw.com/np3. At the New Perspectives site you'll find up-to-date links to the topics covered in this chapter.

1 World Records

In 1951 a hunting party in Ireland shot at, but missed, some golden plovers. The hunters discussed at length whether the golden plover was Europe's fastest game bird. The managing director of Guinness breweries, Sir Hugh Beaver was a member of the hunting party. With sudden inspiration he realized that what the world needed was a book of records to settle such debates, and the *Guinness Book of World Records* was born. Now published annually, you can find it in your library or bookstore. There's even a *Guinness Disk of Records* published on CD-ROM by Grolier Electronic Publishing. For world record sites on the Web, connect to the Saxonia page **www.imn.htwk-leipzig.de/~saxonia/links.html**. You won't find records, but you will find lots of fun facts about computers in **The Official Computer Bowl Trivia Book** by Christopher Morgan (The Computer Museum, 1996).

2 Autoexec

To understand what the Autoexec.bat file is all about, you need to see an example. You can start the Sysedit program on your Windows computer to see what the Autoexec.bat file looks like, or you can look at an example online with explanations of what each line does at **www.ids.net/~jimwy/autoexec.html**.

3 Filename Extensions

You learned that much of today's software adds an application-specific filename extension to the files you save. Suppose you receive a file that has an unfamiliar extension. What software should you use to view the file? On the Web you'll find a list of filename extensions in alphabetical order at **stekt.oulu.fi/~jon/jouninfo/extension.html**.

4 Directories

To become more familiar with the terms associated with file management—such as directory, folder, root directory, and path—log on to the *Webopaedia* at **www.pcwebopaedia.com** and enter the term "directory." Follow the links for similar words, and check out the links to magazine articles.

5 Floppies & Zips

What if your floppy disk stops working? Get some hints on fixing it at **www.louisville.edu/~ajsmit01/floppy.html**. You'll learn more about the Zip drive at Iomega's site, **www.iomega.com**.

6 Speed Update

To find the latest information on disk drive storage capacities and access speeds, check out these manufacturer sites: Seagate at **www.seagate.com** and Western Digital Corporation at **www.wdc.com**. For RAID and mainframe storage solutions try **www.storage.ibm.com** and **www.storage.digital.com**.

7 Tape

What's new with tape drive capacity and tape technology? Check these manufacturers' sites: Hewlett Packard at **www.hp.com/storage/cms/index.html**, Exabyte at **www.exabyte.com**, and Seagate at **www.seagate. com/ tape/tapetop.shtml**.

8 CD-ROM Update

For the latest on CD-ROM access times and transfer rates, connect to manufacturer sites such as Mitsumi at **www.mitsumi.com** or NEC at **www.nec.com**.

9 CD-R Technology

Thinking of buying a CD-R drive and making your own CDs? There are pitfalls when you burn your own pits! See the advice from *PC Magazine* columnist Jim Seymour at **www8.zdnet.com/pcmag/ issues/1507/pcmg0043.htm**. For general information about CD-ROM drives, check out the CD Information Center at **www.cd-info.com/index.shtml**, sponsored by the CD-Info Company. Look for the CD-R FAQs and check out the latest on new packet writing software. Hewlett Packard manufactures one of the most popular CD-R drives. Connect to **www.hp.com** and search for CD-R. At HP's site you'll find a page "CDTechnology Introduction" that includes information on CD standards, data access, data formats, access speed, and more.

10 FAT

Learn about the FAT File System at **www.hptech.com/education.html**. FAT 32 allows your computer to use larger storage devices and provides more efficient storage with less wasted space. You can read about FAT 32 at **www.microsoft.com/windows/pr/fat32.htm**. You'll find additional information about the FAT, microcomputer storage, and a wide variety of other computer topics in Peter Norton's best-selling book, **Inside the PC** (Sams, 1995).

11 Storage Basics

Disk drive manufacturer Quantum maintains a Web site with an excellent overview of computer storage at **www.quantum.com/ssrc/storage_basics**. If you're looking for more information on mainframe and RAID storage, try the RAID Advisory Board Web site at **www.raid-advisory.com**. Another good source of basic information about disks and defragmentation is the complete online book *Fragmentation: the Condition, the Cause, the Cure* by Craig Jensen at **www.execsoft.com/fragbook/frame2.htm**.

12 Past & Future of Storage Technology

IBM maintains a visually stunning site about the history of computer storage at **www.almaden.ibm.com/ storage/firsts/n1956t.htm**. You'll find "believe it or not" factoids about how engineers pushed storage technology to its limits and beyond. What does the future have in store? You'll find an excellent introduction to DVD at **www.c-cube.com/technology/dvd.html#ES**. At the Creative Labs Web site, **www.creativelabs.com** you can follow the multimedia links to find the latest on DVD products. Learn about holographic storage by taking the easy-to-read tutorial at the Optitek Web site, **www.optitek.com/hdss_tutorial.htm**.

R e v i e w

1. Answer the questions below each heading in this chapter, *using your own words.*

2. List the three most *practical* things you learned from this chapter. Why do you think they are the most practical?

3. List each of the boldface terms used in this chapter, then *use your own words* to write a short definition of each term. If you would like clarification of one or more terms, refer to a computer dictionary or a computer science encyclopedia such as those listed in the InfoWeb section of Chapter 1. You can also refer to the Glossary/Index for this textbook.

4. Copy the following chart on paper. Place an X in the Data Files column if the feature applies to data files. Place an X in the Executable Files column if the feature applies to executable files. If a feature applies to both, put an X in both columns.

Feature	Data Files	Executable Files
Created by you, the user		
Created by programmers		
Use an application to view it		
Supplied with software		
Has an .exe or .com extension		
Referred to as a program or application		

5. Indicate which filenames in the following list are not valid under the operating system used in your school's computer lab. Which filenaming convention does each nonvalid filename violate?

Wp.exe	Ppr	Win.exe
Autoexec.bat	Results*.wks	Monthly.wk1
Report#1.txt	Smith&Smith.doc	Sep/94.wri
Asia map.doc	Ocean.tif	Mn43-44.dbf

6. Examine the directory listing below and answer the following questions:

a. What is the size of the file **Emergency.doc**?

b. On what date was **911.mdb** last modified?

c. How many program files are listed?

d. What is the name of the folder that contains these files?

e. What application was used to create **Memo to Tiger W?**?

f. How many of these files are data files?

g. What is the largest file on the disk?

h. Does **Section A Codes.pcx** contain text or graphics?

i. What type of data does the file **Fire.wav** contain?

j. How many of the files appear to be memos?

k. How would you use a wildcard to get a directory of all the files with .xls extensions?

l. How many files match the specification S*.*?

m. How many files match the specification *.*?

7 Suppose you have a disk with the following files:

Minutes.doc	Report.doc	Budget.xls
Jacsmemo.doc	Report1.doc	Shipjan.xls
Shipfeb.xls	Shipmar.xlx	Shipapr.xls
Minutes.txt	Roger.txt	Roadmap.bmp

If you could specify all the files with a .doc extension by *.doc. How would you specify the following files?

a. All the files with .txt extensions

b. All the files that contain "minutes"

c. All the files that begin with "Ship"

d. All the files on the disk

e. All the files that begin with the letter "R"

8 Suppose you need to retrieve a file from Sarah's computer. She tells you that the file is stored as D:\Data\Payables.xls.

a. What is the filename?

b. What is the file extension?

c. On which drive is the file stored?

d. In which directory is the file stored?

e. What type of file is it likely to be?

f. Will you need a specific software program to retrieve and view the file?

9 Suppose you need to defragment the files manually on the disk shown below. Using the disk on the right, show how the files are arranged after you complete the defragmentation. Use colored pencils or different patterns to show each file clearly.

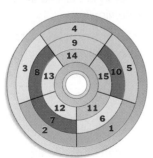 

10 Use the New Perspectives CD-ROM to take a chapter quiz or to review the new terms presented in this chapter.

Projects

1 **File Extensions** Many software applications use a specific file extension for data files created with that application. Determine the extensions used by five applications on your own computer or a lab computer. Run each software application and attempt to retrieve a file. If the software application uses a specific file extension, you will usually see the extension indicated in a box on the screen. For example, you might see *.doc if you are using Microsoft Word for Windows.

For each of the five programs you select:

a. Specify the program name.

b. Sketch a picture of the program icon (if you are using Windows) or indicate the executable filename (if you are using DOS).

c. Indicate the filename extension the program uses. If the program does not use a specific filename extension, indicate that this is the case.

2 **Storage Devices You Use** You should be aware of the storage devices on your computer so that you use the best device for each task. You will need to take a hands-on look at your computer at home or a computer in your school lab to answer the following questions:

a. Where is this computer located?

b. What is the hard disk capacity? (Hint: Refer to Figure 4-18.)

c. What is the hard disk drive letter?

d. What is the floppy disk size?

e. What is the floppy disk capacity?

f. What is the floppy disk drive letter?

g. Is there a tape storage device?

h. Is there a CD-ROM drive?

i. Which storage device do you usually use for the data files you create?

j. Which storage device holds most of the applications software that you use?

k. Which storage device would you use for backups?

3 Calculating Storage Requirements How much storage space would be needed to store this textbook? To calculate approximately how many bytes of storage space this text (not including pictures) requires:

a. Count the number of lines on a typical page.

b. Count the number of characters (including blanks) in the longest line of text on the page.

c. Multiply the number of lines by the number of characters in the longest line to calculate the number of characters (bytes) per page.

d. Multiply this figure by the number of pages in the book.

e. What do you estimate is the computer storage space required for this text?

4 Calculating Hard Disk Capacity Most manufacturers list the storage capacity of their hard disk drives on the drive itself or in the user manual. The manufacturer calculates storage capacity in bytes using the formula:

capacity = cylinders X surfaces X sectors X 512

The 512 in the formula is the number of bytes stored in each sector of each cylinder. Suppose you have a hard disk with 615 cylinders, 4 surfaces (two platters), and 17 sectors. What is the capacity in bytes of this disk?

5  **Shopping for Storage** Use a recent computer magazine or a Web site such as Computer Express at **www.cexpress.com** to fill in the following "shopping list:"

Item	Brand	Merchant	Price
Package of 10 3½-inch floppy disks			
High-density 3½-inch floppy disk drive			
850 MB, 10 ms hard disk drive			
Tape drive			
Quad-speed CD-ROM			

6 What's in That File? Earlier, you learned to distinguish between executable, data, and source files. In this project, you will look at the contents of each file type. When you view an executable file, you should see meaningless symbols. When you view a data file, you should be able to read the data. When you view a source file, you should be able to read the commands it contains. The Type command lets you view the contents of a file without changing it. You can use the Type command to look at the **Autoexec.bat** source file, the **Command.com** executable file, and the **Country.txt** data file.

If you are using DOS, make sure you are at the C:\> prompt. If you are using Windows 3.1, double-click the MS-DOS prompt icon in the Main window. If you are using Windows 95, click the Start button, select Programs, then select MS-DOS prompt. Do each of the following steps, and write down the first line you see on the screen:

a. Type the following command (including "type"), then press the Enter key:
   type c:\autoexec.bat|more

b. Type the following command, then press the Enter key:
   type c:\command.com

c. Type the following command, then press the Enter key:
   type c:\dos\country.txt|more

7 Troubleshooting a Storage Problem
Read the following scenario and determine what went wrong, then write a paragraph describing what you would do to correct the problem. Your instructor will indicate if you should do this project individually or discuss it in a small group.

Toni's 1 GB hard disk contained about 75 MB of files on February 18. On that day, she made a tape backup of the entire disk. On February 19, Toni moved to a company office one block away. The company maintenance staff moved the computer, along with Toni's paper files, in the late afternoon. The people on the maintenance crew left the computer on the desk in the new office.

On February 20, Toni set up the computer and tried to open a data file containing the names and addresses of her clients. The computer displayed a message—something about an error on drive C. Toni turned off her computer and then turned it back on, hoping the error would go away, but the computer wouldn't let her access any data on the hard disk.

8 **CD-Mania** What's the difference between the CDs that contain your favorite music album and the CD-ROMs you use in a computer? You might be surprised to learn that some computer

INTERNET
Optional

CD-ROM drives can play your music CDs. In fact, there are several CD formats, including CD-DA, CD-I, CD-ROM, PhotoCD, and CD-R. For this project, use your library and Internet resources to write a paper describing these CD formats. The length of your paper will depend on the scope of the project: a three-page paper is suitable for a short project, a term paper might require 10–15 pages. Be sure you include a bibliography.

Your paper can deal with CDs from the technical perspective or from the applied perspective. If you take the technical perspective, you should look for answers to questions such as, but not limited to:

a. What are the capacity and storage formats for each type of CD?

b. Why did these specifications originate?

c. What are the advantages and disadvantages of each?

If you take the applied perspective, you should try to find the answers to questions such as, but not limited to:

a. What are the primary uses for each type of CD?

b. What are the advantages and disadvantages of each?

c. How do the costs of each format compare?

9 Data Storage in Organizations
Organizations take different approaches to data storage, depending on the volume of their data, the value of their data, and the need for data security. The purpose of this project is to interview the person responsible for maintaining the data for an organization and discover the answers to the following questions:

a. What is the position title of the person responsible for this organization's data storage?

b. What preparation did this individual have to qualify for this position?

c. What are this individual's job responsibilities?

d. How does this individual keep up with trends that affect data storage?

e. What type of data does the organization store?

f. What percent of this data is stored on a computer system?

g. What types of storage devices are used in this organization?

h. What is the capacity of each storage device?

i. What happens when the storage devices are full?

j. What problems are associated with maintaining the data for this organization?

This project works well if the class is divided into teams and each team interviews a person from a different organization. Each team can then present a 15-minute report to the rest of the class, along with a two- to three-page written report of its findings.

10 **The Future of Computer Storage** Ten years ago, the idea of 4 GB of storage on a personal computer seemed incredible. But technology turned that dream into reality. What storage technologies might we use in the future? Will optical storage cubes the size of a nine-volt battery hold gigabytes of data? Will smart credit cards hold all our financial data? Will magneto-optical devices combine the flexibility of magnetic media with the permanence of optical media? Will data be stored as holograms?

Use recent computer magazines and journals to research trends and projections for computer storage technology. You might want to do a survey and write a paragraph or two on each new technology, or you might want to take an in-depth look at a technology that you find interesting.

The paper you write as the result of your research can be as short as three pages or as long as 25 pages, depending on the scope of the project specified by your instructor.

11 **Organizing Files and File Folders** How are you going to organize the information you plan to store on your hard drive? As you'll recall from reading the section on logical file storage, your hard disk storage is like a filing cabinet. You can create file folders in which to store your files. There is no one right way to organize your files, but it is important that your filing system work for you. Take time to think about the filing system you plan to create.

Read the following possibilities. Then comment on the advantages and disadvantages of each. Finally write a description and draw a picture to show how you plan to organize your folders.

a. Create a folder for each file that you make.

b. Create a folder for each application you plan to use and store only documents you generate with that application in that folder.

c. Create folders for broad topics such as Memos, Letters, BudgetItems, and Personal, and store documents that match those headings in the appropriate folder regardless of the application used to create these documents.

d. Create folders around specific topics such as Applications, Personal, Taxes, etc. and store all files related to that specific topic in the appropriate folder regardless of the application used to create these documents.

e. Basically the same as d. but create additional subfolders in each folder to help group similar files.

12 **Downsizing: Sizing up Future Storage Technologies** Storage always seems to be an issue with PCs. Just when you thought you couldn't possibly fill up that 1 GB hard drive, you find yourself scrambling to make disk space available. As you will recall from the *End Notes* section, there are several breakthroughs in storage technologies. Choose one of the following to research using the Internet and other available resources. Then create a presentation for the class.

a. Research how the size and capacity of storage technologies have changed over time. In your presentation, be sure to answer the following questions:

- What has the trend been? Why?

- How does the saying "Good things come in small packages" apply to storage technology?

- Is smaller better? Why? Is smaller more expensive? Why?

- What happens to the cost of new storage technologies when they are first introduced to the market and then over time? Why? Give examples.

b. Create a timeline to show past storage technologies including tape, floppies, Zip drives, and CD-ROMs. Then research and include in your timeline future storage technologies. You might use those mentioned in the *End Notes* section as a starting point.

c. Compare and contrast future storage technologies including holographic storage, molecule storage, and quantum-logic gate storage.

d. Suppose you are the head of a research and development department for a major computer company. The president of the company has come to your office to tell you that funds are running low and it is your responsibility to acquire more funds. Determine which future technology your company is pursuing and create a presentation for investors to convince them about why they should invest in the R & D project.

Lab Assignments

DOS Directories and File Management

DOS is an operating system used on millions of computers. Even if your computer has a graphical user interface, such as Microsoft Windows, understanding DOS commands helps you grasp the basic concepts of computer file management. In this Lab, you learn how to use basic DOS commands.

1 Click the Steps button to learn basic DOS commands. As you proceed through the Steps, answer all of the Quick Check questions that appear. After you complete the Steps, you will see a Quick Check Summary Report. Follow the instructions on the screen to print this report.

2 Go through the Steps for this Lab once again. This time, create a mini DOS manual by listing each DOS command and its function. For each command, you should also provide a sample of a valid command, for example:

DIR   Provides a listing of all the files on a disk

Example: DIR A:

3 Click the Explore button and make a new disk. (You can copy over the disk you used for the Steps.) Do each of the following tasks and record the command you used:

a. Display the directory for drive A.

b. Display only those files on drive A that begin with the letter "T."

c. Erase all the files that have names beginning with "New."

d. Create a directory called PAPERS.

e. Move all the files with .DOC extensions into the PAPERS directory.

f. Rename OPUS27.MID to SONG.MID.

g. Delete all the files with names that start with "Budget."

4 In Explore, make a new disk. (You can copy over the disk you used for earlier Lab activities.) Do each of the following tasks, then give your disk to your instructor. Don't forget to put your name on the disk label.

a. Make two subdirectories on your disk: PICS and BUDGETS.

b. Move all the files with .BMP extensions into the PICS directory.

c. Move all the files with .WKS extensions into the BUDGETS directory.

d. Delete all the files except README.TXT from the root directory. (Do not delete the files from PICS or BUDGETS.)

e. Rename the file README.TXT to READ.ME.

5 Use the TYPE command to view the contents of the START.BAT file. Describe the file contents. Use the TYPE command to view the contents of OPUS27.MID. Describe what you see. Explain the different results you obtained when you used the TYPE command with START.BAT and OPUS27.MID.

Windows Directories, Folders, and Files

Graphical user interfaces such as Mac OS, Windows 3.1, Windows 95, and Windows 98 use a filing system metaphor for file management. In this Lab, you will learn the basic concepts of these file system metaphors. With this background, you will find it easy to understand how to manage files with graphical user interfaces.

1 Click the Steps button to learn how to manipulate directories, folders, and files. As you proceed through the Steps, answer all of the Quick Check questions that appear. After you complete the Steps, you will see a Quick Check Summary Report. Follow the instructions on the screen to print this report.

2 Make sure you are in Explore. Change to drive C as the default drive. Double-click the c:\ folder to display its contents, then answer the following questions:

a. How many data files are in the root directory of drive C?

b. How many program files are in the root directory of drive C?

c. Does the root directory of drive C contain any subdirectories? How can you tell?

d. How many files are in the DOS folder?

e. Complete the diagram to show the arrangement of folders on drive C. Do not include files.

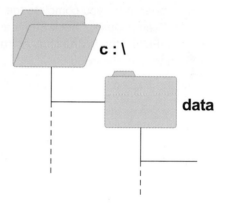

3 Click the Explore button. Make sure drive A is the default drive. Double-click the a:\ folder to display the folder contents, then answer the following questions:

a. How many files are in the root directory of drive A?

b. Are the files on drive a: data files or program files? How can you tell?

c. Does the root directory of drive A contain any subdirectories? How can you tell?

4 Open and close folders, and change drives as necessary to locate the following files. After you find the file, write out its file specification:

a. config.sys

b. win.ini

c. toolkit.wks

d. meeting.doc

e. newlogo3.bmp

f. todo.doc

Defragmentation and Disk Operations

In this Lab you will format a simulated disk, save files, delete files, undelete files to see how the computer updates the FAT. You will also find out how the files on your disk become fragmented and what a defragmentation utility does to reorganize the clusters on your disk.

1 Click the Steps button to learn how the computer updates the FAT when you format a disk and save, delete, and undelete files. As you proceed through the Steps, answer all of the Quick Check questions that appear. After you complete the Steps, you will see a Quick Check Summary Report. Follow the instructions on the screen to print this report.

2 Click the Explore button. Click the Format button to format the simulated disk. Try to save files 1, 2, 3, 4, and 6. Do they all fit on the disk?

3 In Explore, format the simulated disk. Try to save all the files on the disk. What happens?

4 In Explore, format the simulated disk. Save FILE-3, FILE-4, and FILE-6. Next, delete FILE-6. Now, save FILE-5. Try to undelete FILE-6. What happens and why?

5 In Explore, format the simulated disk. Save and erase files until the files become fragmented. Draw a picture of the disk to show the fragmented files. Indicate which files are in each cluster by using color, crosshatching, or labels. List which files in your drawing are fragmented. Finally, defragment the disk and draw a new picture showing the unfragmented files.

Using Files

In this Lab you manipulate a simulated computer to view what happens in memory and on disk when you create, save, open, revise, and delete files. Understanding what goes on "inside the box" will help you quickly grasp how to perform basic file operations with most application software.

1 Click the Steps button to learn how to use the simulated computer to view the contents of memory and disk when you perform basic file operations. As you proceed through the Steps, answer all of the Quick Check questions that appear. After you complete the Steps, you will see a Quick Check Summary Report. Follow the instructions on the screen to print this report.

2 Click the Explore button and use the simulated computer to perform the following tasks.

a. Create a document containing your name and the city in which you were born. Save this document as NAME.

b. Create another document containing two of your favorite foods. Save this document as FOODS.

c. Create another file containing your two favorite classes. Call this file CLASSES.

d. Open the FOOD file and add another one of your favorite foods. Save this file without changing its name.

e. Open the NAME file. Change this document so it contains your name and the name of your school. Save this as a new document called SCHOOL.

f. Write down how many files are on the simulated disk and the exact contents of each file.

g. Delete all the files.

3 In Explore, use the simulated computer to perform the following tasks.

a. Create a file called MUSIC that contains the name of your favorite CD.

b. Create another document that contains eight numbers and call this file LOTTERY.

c. You didn't win the lottery this week. Revise the contents of the LOTTERY file, but save the revision as LOTTERY2.

d. Revise the MUSIC file so it also contains the name of your favorite musician or composer, and save this file as MUSIC2.

e. Delete the MUSIC file.

f. Write down how many files are on the simulated disk and the exact contents of each file.

COMPUTER ARCHITECTURE

5

InfoWeb

April
Fools
1

An article in the April 1988 issue of *Scientific American* announced that "archaeologists had discovered the rotting remnants of an ingenious arrangement of ropes and pulleys thought to be the first working digital computer ever constructed." The article described in detail how the people of an ancient culture, known as the Apraphulians, built complex devices of ropes and pulleys, housed these devices in huge black wooden boxes, and used them to perform complex mathematical computations. Some of the devices were so colossal that elephants were harnessed to pull the enormous ropes through the pulley system.

A computer constructed of ropes and pulleys? As you might have guessed, this was an April Fools' article. And yet, such a device, if it were constructed, could accurately be called a digital computer. That you could build a computer out of ropes and pulleys reinforces the notion that a computer is, in many respects, a very simple device.

How does a computer work? This chapter, takes you on a tour inside the case of a modern computer system. The basic concepts you learn in this chapter apply to micro, mini, and mainframe computers.

LABS

Binary Numbers

CPU Simulator

Troubleshooting

CHAPTER**PREVIEW**

In this chapter you'll learn how a computer works, so you can troubleshoot problems you encounter in the lab, at work, or at home. You'll learn how, when, and why you should expand your computer system. You'll also learn terminology that will help you understand much of the jargon you read in computer ads and hear in conversations with computer professionals. When you have completed this chapter you should be able to:

- Identify the components that are on the main circuit board of a microcomputer
- Explain how RAM, virtual memory, CMOS, and ROM differ
- Explain how the CPU performs the instructions contained in a computer program
- List the factors that affect CPU performance
- Describe how the data bus and expansion bus work
- List the components necessary to connect a peripheral device to a computer and describe each component's role
- Trace the boot process of your computer system

A Digital Electronics

Computer architecture refers to the design and construction of a computer system. The architecture of any computer can be broadly classified by considering two characteristics: what the computer uses for power and how the computer physically represents, processes, stores, and moves data. Most modern computers are electronic devices, that is, they are powered by electricity. Also, a modern computer uses electrical signals and circuits to represent, process, and move data.

InfoWeb

Inside the Case 2

Inside the System Unit

What does the inside of a computer look like? If you have never looked inside a computer, you might stop reading for a moment and try to visualize the inside of a computer's system unit. Did you picture a maze of wires and other electronic gizmos? Many people do. But you might be surprised to find that the inside of a computer looks pretty simple. We took the cover off a microcomputer in Figure 5-1 to show you what's inside.

Figure 5-1

Inside the system unit

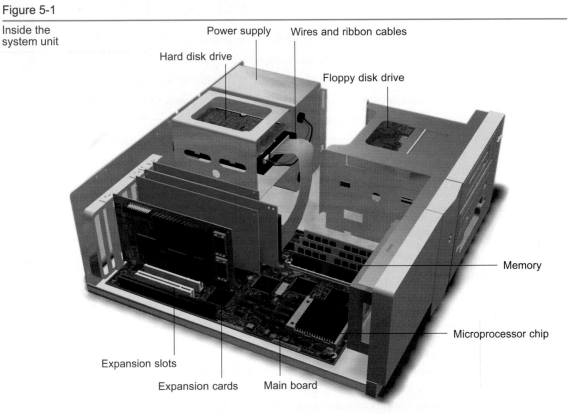

Power supply

Wires and ribbon cables

Hard disk drive

Floppy disk drive

Memory

Microprocessor chip

Expansion slots

Expansion cards

Main board

The arrangement of elements inside the case of a desktop computer differs somewhat from that inside a tower or notebook case. For example, the limited space inside of a notebook computer means that circuit boards and other components are more tightly packed together. Keep in mind, however, that the general componets of today's micro, mini, mainframe, and supercomputers are remarkably similar.

Integrated Circuits

InfoWeb

Integrated
Circuits
3

| Why isn't the system unit filled with a lot of wires? | Most of the components inside a computer are integrated circuits, commonly called **chips** or **microchips**. An **integrated circuit** (IC) is a thin slice of crystal packed with microscopic circuit elements such as wires, transistors, capacitors, and resistors.

Figure 5-2

A single integrated circuit less than a quarter-inch square could contain more than one million microscopic circuit elements.

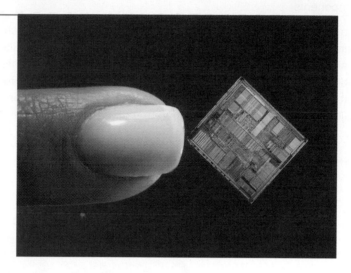

A chip is packaged in a ceramic carrier that provides connectors to other computer components. Inside of a computer you are likely to find several kinds of chip packages, including DIP, SIMM, SEC, and PGA, as shown in Figure 5-3.

Figure 5-3

Computer chip packages

A DIP (dual in-line pin) has two rows of connecting pins. Once used for memory, DIPs now contain specialized support circuitry.

A SIMM (single in-line memory module) is a small circuit board containing several chips typically used for memory.

A PGA (pin-grid array) is a square chip with pins arranged in concentric squares. Most of today's powerful microprocessors are housed in PGA packages.

An SEC (single edge contact) cartridge is a new IC package designed for the Pentium II processor created by Intel Corporation.

InfoWeb

Motherboards
4

The Motherboard

How do the chips fit together to make a computer? Inside the system unit, chips are housed on a circuit board called the **main board** or **motherboard**. If you look carefully at a computer circuit board you'll see that some chips are soldered, that is fused, to the board, but other chips are plugged into the board and can be removed. Soldered chips are permanent and aren't likely to work loose. Removable chips allow you to upgrade your computer components.

In a microcomputer, the motherboard contains the processor chip, the chips for computer memory, and chips that handle basic input and output. Circuits etched into the motherboard act like wires, providing a path so the computer can transport data from one chip to another as needed for processing. In addition, the motherboard contains expansion slots that allow you to connect peripheral devices to the computer. Figure 5-4 illustrates the major components of a microcomputer motherboard.

Figure 5-4

Microcomputer motherboard

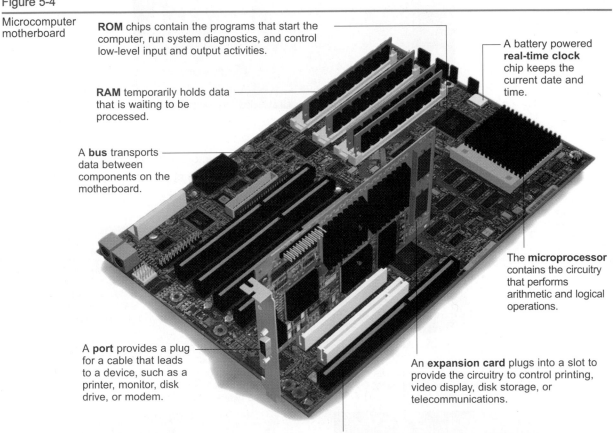

ROM chips contain the programs that start the computer, run system diagnostics, and control low-level input and output activities.

A battery powered **real-time clock** chip keeps the current date and time.

RAM temporarily holds data that is waiting to be processed.

A **bus** transports data between components on the motherboard.

The **microprocessor** contains the circuitry that performs arithmetic and logical operations.

A **port** provides a plug for a cable that leads to a device, such as a printer, monitor, disk drive, or modem.

An **expansion card** plugs into a slot to provide the circuitry to control printing, video display, disk storage, or telecommunications.

An **expansion slot** provides a way to add devices to a computer system.

Digital Data Representation

> But if a computer is just a bunch of electrical circuits, how can it manipulate numbers and letters?

Data representation refers to the form in which information is conceived, manipulated, and recorded. When people add a column of numbers or sort a list of names, they represent numbers and names by writing symbols such as 2, G, and 8. A computer is an electronic device, so it doesn't write down the data it works with. A computer somehow needs to use electrical signals to represent data.

The way a computer represents data depends on whether the computer is a digital or an analog device. A **digital device** works with discrete, that is, distinct or separate numbers or digits, such as 0 and 1. An **analog device** operates on continuously varying data. For example, a traditional light switch has two discrete states: off and on. The light switch is a digital device. A dimmer switch, on the other hand, has a rotating dial that increases or decreases brightness smoothly over a range from bright to dark. A dimmer switch is an analog device.

The circuits in a digital computer have only two possible states. For convenience let's say that one of those states is "on" and the other state is "off." If you equate the on state with 1 and the off state with 0, you can grasp the basic principle of how a digital computer works.

In a digital computer, each number or letter is represented by a series of electrical signals. Think about the way Morse code uses dashes and dots to represent letters. In a similar way, digital computers represent numbers, letters, and symbols with a code that uses a series of 0s (zeros) and 1s. Data that is represented digitally can be easily moved or stored electronically as a series of "ons" and "offs."

Each 1 or 0 that represents data is referred to as a **bit**. Most computer coding schemes use eight bits to represent each number, letter, or symbol. A series of eight bits is called a **byte**. Study Figure 5-5 to make sure you understand how the term *byte* is related to the terms *bits* and *characters*.

Figure 5-5

Bits, bytes, and characters

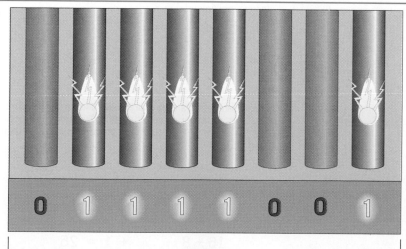

The smallest unit of information in a computer is a **bit**. A bit can be a 0 or a 1. The electronic circuits in a computer carry a 1 bit as a pulse of electricity.

A collection of eight bits is called a **byte**. This byte is composed of eight bits: 01111001.

A byte represents one **character**—a letter, numeral, or punctuation symbol. This byte, 01111001, represents a lowercase y.

LAB

Binary
Numbers

Data Representation Codes

Do all digital computers use the same code to represent data? Digital computers use many different coding schemes to represent data. The coding scheme the computer uses depends on whether the data is numeric data or character data.

Numeric data consists of numbers that represent quantities and that might be used in arithmetic operations. For example, your annual income is numeric data. You use it in arithmetic operations every April when you calculate your income taxes.

Digital computers represent numeric data using the **binary number system**, or base two. In the binary number system, there are only two digits: 0 and 1. The numeral 2 cannot be used in the binary number system, so instead of writing "2," you would write "10." The first eight numbers in the binary number system are 1, 10, 11, 100, 101, 110, 111, 1000. If you need to review binary numbers, study Figure 5-6.

Figure 5-6

Binary
numbers

Decimal		Binary			
Place	Place	Place	Place	Place	Place
10	**1**	**8**	**4**	**2**	**1**
	0				0
	1				1
	2			1	0
	3			1	1
	4		1	0	0
	5		1	0	1
	6		1	1	0
	7		1	1	1
	8	1	0	0	0
	9	1	0	0	1
1	0	1	0	1	0

1. In the decimal number system, there are ten digits: 0, 1, 2, 3, 4, 5, 6, 7, 8, 9. When we put one of these digits in the column for the 1's place, it represents a different number than when we put it in the column for the 10's place. For example, the digit 1 in the 1's column is worth 1, but the digit 1 in the 10's column is worth 10. As you know, after you use the digit 9, you must "carry" a one to the next column and use a zero as a placeholder to represent the number 10.

2. The columns or "places" for the binary number system are 1s, 2s, 4s, 8s, and so on. To find out the value of the next place, you double the value of the previous place. The next place to the left would be 16s.

3. In the binary number system there are only two digits: 0 and 1. When you are counting in binary, you run out of digits when you get to the number 2. To represent "2" in binary, you must move the digit 1 left into the next column and use a zero for a place holder. In binary, the number 10 (pronounced "one zero") means "2".

4. Suppose you want to convert the binary number 11001 into its decimal equivalent.

$$? \quad \overset{?}{\underset{?}{11001}} \quad ?$$

5. You can set up a conversion table like this one, using the the place values for the binary number system. Because the binary number 11001 has five places, our conversion table also needs five places: 16, 8, 4, 2, and 1.

16	8	4	2	1
1	1	0	0	1

16 + 8   + 1 = 25

6. Next, add the place values for any column that contains the digit 1. The sum is the decimal equivalent of the binary number. Here you see that binary 11001 is equivalent to the decimal number 25.

Character data is composed of letters, symbols, and numerals that will not be used in arithmetic operations. Examples of character data include your name, hair color, and Social Security number. Are you surprised that your Social Security *number* is considered character data? Because you are not going to use your Social Security number in arithmetic operations it is considered character data.

Digital computers typically represent character data using either the ASCII or EBCDIC codes. ASCII is the seven-bit data representation code used on most microcomputers, on many minicomputers, and on some mainframe computers. **ASCII** stands for American Standard Code for Information Interchange and is pronounced "ASK ee." The ASCII code for an uppercase "A" is 1000001.

IBM computers often use the EBCDIC code. **EBCDIC** stands for extended binary-coded decimal interchange code (pronounced "EB seh dick"). Figure 5-7 shows the EBCDIC codes in addition to the ASCII codes. See if you can spot some of the differences between the ASCII and EBCDIC coding schemes.

Figure 5-7

ASCII and EBCDIC codes

SYMBOL	ASCII	EBCDIC	SYMBOL	ASCII	EBCDIC	SYMBOL	ASCII	EBCDIC
(space)	0100000	01000000	?	0111111	01101111	^	1011110	
!	0100001	01011010	@	1000000	01111100	_	1011111	
"	0100010	01111111	A	1000001	11000001	a	1100001	10000001
#	0100011	01111011	B	1000010	11000010	b	1100010	10000010
$	0100100	01011011	C	1000011	11000011	c	1100011	10000011
%	0100101	01101100	D	1000100	11000100	d	1100000	10000100
&	0100110	01010000	E	1000101	11000101	e	1100101	10000101
'	0100111	01111101	F	1000110	11000110	f	1100110	10000110
(	0101000	01001101	G	1000111	11000111	g	1100111	10000111
)	0101001	01011101	H	1001000	11001000	h	1101100	10001000
*	0101010	01011100	I	1001001	11001001	i	1101001	10001001
+	0101011	01001110	J	1001010	11010001	j	1101010	10010001
,	0101100	01101011	K	1001011	11010010	k	1101011	10010010
–	0101101	01100000	L	1001100	11010011	l	1101100	10010011
.	0101110	01001011	M	1001101	11010100	m	1101101	10010100
/	0101111	01100001	N	1001110	11010101	n	1101110	10010101
0	0110000	11110000	O	1001111	11010110	o	1111111	10010110
1	0110001	11110001	P	1010000	11010111	p	1110100	10010111
2	0110010	11110010	Q	1010001	11011000	q	1110001	10011000
3	0110011	11110011	R	1010010	11011001	r	1110010	10011001
4	0110100	11110100	S	1010011	11100010	s	1110011	10100010
5	0110101	11110101	T	1010100	11100011	t	1110100	10100011
6	0110110	11110110	U	1010101	11100100	u	1110101	10100100
7	0110111	11110111	V	1010110	11100101	v	1110110	10100101
8	0111000	11111000	W	1010111	11100110	w	1110111	10100110
9	0111001	11111001	X	1011000	11100111	x	1111000	10100111
:	0111010	01111010	Y	1011001	11101000	y	1111001	10101000
;	0111011	01011110	Z	1011010	11101001	z	1111010	10101001
<	0111100	01001100	[	1011011	01001010	{	1111011	
=	0111101	01111110	\	1011100		}	1111101	
>	0111110	01101110	]	1011101	01011010			

Data Transport

What happens to the data in a computer? Typically, data travels from one location to another within the computer on an electronic pathway or circuit called a **data bus**. The data bus is a series of electronic circuits that connect the various electrical elements on the motherboard. The bus contains data lines and address lines. **Data lines** carry the signals that represent data. **Address lines** carry the location of data to help the computer find the data that it needs to process.

A computer data bus "picks up" a load of bits from one of the components on the motherboard, then transfers these bits to another motherboard component. After dropping off this load of bits, the bus collects another load, as shown in Figure 5-8.

Figure 5-8

How a data bus works

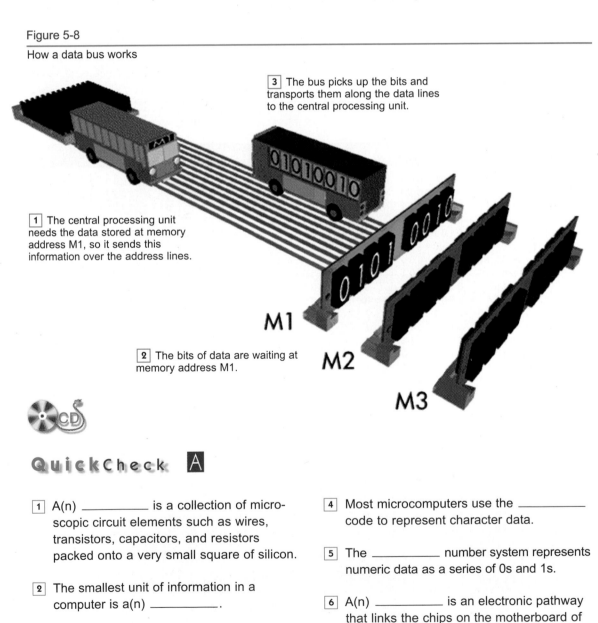

3 The bus picks up the bits and transports them along the data lines to the central processing unit.

1 The central processing unit needs the data stored at memory address M1, so it sends this information over the address lines.

2 The bits of data are waiting at memory address M1.

M1

M2

M3

QuickCheck A

1. A(n) _____ is a collection of microscopic circuit elements such as wires, transistors, capacitors, and resistors packed onto a very small square of silicon.

2. The smallest unit of information in a computer is a(n) _____.

3. A series of eight bits is referred to as a(n) _____.

4. Most microcomputers use the _____ code to represent character data.

5. The _____ number system represents numeric data as a series of 0s and 1s.

6. A(n) _____ is an electronic pathway that links the chips on the motherboard of a computer.

Ⓑ Memory

InfoWeb

Memory Technology 5

So far in this chapter you have learned that digital computers represent data using electronic signals. You know that the data bus transports these electronic signals from one place to another inside the computer. Now you will find out where the computer puts data when it is not in transit.

Memory is electronic circuitry that holds data and program instructions. Memory is sometimes called *primary storage*, but this term is easily confused with disk storage. It is preferable to use the term *memory* to refer to the circuitry that has a direct link to the processor and to use the term *storage* to refer to media, such as disks, that are not directly linked to the processor.

There are four major types of memory: random access memory, virtual memory, CMOS memory, and read-only memory. Each type of memory is characterized by the kind of data it contains and the technology it uses to hold the data.

Random Access Memory

How does RAM work? **Random access memory**, or **RAM**, is an area in the computer system unit that temporarily holds data before and after it is processed. For example, when you enter a document, the characters you type usually are not processed right away. They are held in RAM until you tell your software to carry out a process such as printing.

In RAM, microscopic electronic parts called **capacitors** hold the electronic signals for the ASCII, EBCDIC, or binary code that represents data. A charged capacitor represents an "on" bit. A discharged capacitor represents an "off" bit.

You can visualize the capacitors arranged in banks of eight. Each bank of capacitors holds eight bits, or one byte of data. A **RAM address** on each bank helps the computer locate the data contained in the bank, as shown in Figure 5-9.

Figure 5-9

RAM addresses and data

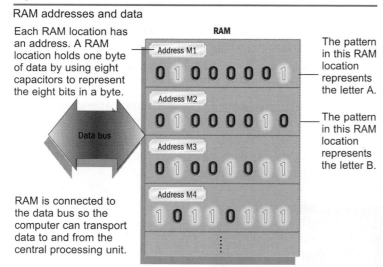

Each RAM location has an address. A RAM location holds one byte of data by using eight capacitors to represent the eight bits in a byte.

RAM is connected to the data bus so the computer can transport data to and from the central processing unit.

The pattern in this RAM location represents the letter A.

The pattern in this RAM location represents the letter B.

In some respects, RAM is like a chalkboard. You can use a chalkboard to write mathematical formulas, erase them, and then write an outline for a report. In a similar way, RAM can hold numbers and formulas when you use a spreadsheet, then hold the text of your English essay when you use a word processor. The contents of RAM can change just by changing the charge of the capacitors. Because its contents can be changed, RAM is a reusable resource.

Unlike hard disk or floppy disk storage, most RAM is *volatile*. In other words, if the computer is turned off or the power goes out, all data stored in RAM instantly and permanently disappears. When someone unhappily says, "I have lost all my data!" it often means that the person was entering data for a document or worksheet, and the power went out before the data was saved on disk.

RAM Functions

Why is RAM so important? RAM is the "waiting room" for the computer's processor. RAM holds raw data that is waiting to be processed. RAM holds the instructions that will process the raw data. RAM also holds processed data before it is stored more permanently on disk or tape. For example, when you use personal finance software to balance your checkbook, you enter raw data for check amounts, which is held in RAM. The personal finance software sends the instructions to process this data to RAM. The processor uses the instructions to process the data, then sends the results back to RAM. From RAM, the results can be stored on disk, displayed, or printed.

In addition to data and software instructions, RAM holds operating system instructions that control the basic functions of the computer system. These instructions are loaded into RAM every time you start your computer and remain there until you turn the computer off.

RAM Capacity and Speed

How much RAM does my computer need? The storage capacity of RAM is measured in megabytes. Today's microcomputers typically have between 16 and 64 megabytes of RAM, which means they can hold between 16 and 64 million characters of data or instructions.

InfoWeb

Grace
Hopper
6

The amount of RAM your computer needs depends on the software you use. RAM requirements are usually specified on the outside of the software box. What if the software you want to use requires more RAM than your computer has? You can purchase additional RAM to expand the memory capacity of your computer up to the limit set by the computer manufacturer.

The speed of RAM is also important. The processor works at a certain speed, but would be forced to slow down if it had to wait for data from RAM. Most RAM today has an access speed of 60 nanoseconds. Slower, older memory has access speeds of 70 or 80 nanoseconds. How long is a nanosecond? Figure 5-10 will give you an idea.

Figure 5-10

Grace Hopper, a pioneer in the early computer industry used a 12-inch piece of wire to illustrate the distance electricity could travel in a nanosecond—one billionth of a second. By contrast a microsecond would be a coil of wire nearly a thousand feet long.

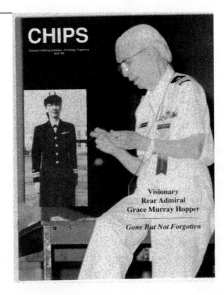

CHIPS

Visionary
Rear Admiral
Grace Murray Hopper

Gone But Not Forgotten

Virtual Memory

What if I run out of RAM? Suppose you use a word-processing program that requires 4 MB of RAM and a spreadsheet program that requires 2 MB of RAM. You might suspect that you would run out of RAM if you tried to run both programs at the same time. However, you need only 4 MB to run both programs. How can this be so?

With today's operating systems, you won't run out of RAM because the computer uses space on your computer's hard disk as an extension of RAM. A computer's ability to use disk storage to simulate RAM is called **virtual memory**. Figure 5-11 explains how virtual memory works.

Figure 5-11

How virtual memory works

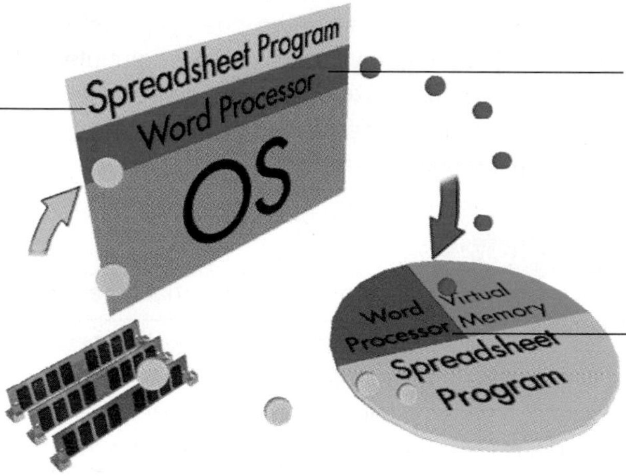

1. Your computer is running a word-processing program that takes up most of the program area in RAM, but you want to run a spreadsheet program at the same time.

3. The spreadsheet program can now be loaded into the RAM vacated by the least-used segment of the word-processing program.

2. The operating system moves the least-used segment of the word-processing program into virtual memory on disk.

Virtual memory allows computers without enough real memory to run large programs, manipulate large data files, and run more than one program at a time. Unfortunately, virtual memory is not as fast as RAM. It takes longer to retrieve data from virtual memory because the disk is a mechanical device. Disk access time of 10 milliseconds is quite a bit slower than RAM access speeds of 60 nanoseconds.

Like RAM, data in virtual memory becomes inaccessible if the power goes off. You might wonder why—normally disks do not lose data when the power goes off. Data in virtual memory is not erased from the disk if the power fails, but the computer cannot access it even after power is restored. The instructions that direct the computer to the location of virtual memory are stored in RAM and are lost when power fails.

Read-only Memory

If a computer has RAM, why does it need ROM? **Read-only memory**, or **ROM**, is a set of chips containing instructions that help a computer prepare for processing tasks. The instructions in ROM are permanent, and the only way to change them is to remove the ROM chips from the main board and replace them with another set. You might wonder why the computer includes chips with programs permanently stored in them. Why not use the more adaptable RAM?

The answer to this question is that when you turn on your computer, the central processing unit receives electrical power and is ready to begin executing instructions. But because the computer was just turned on, RAM is empty—it doesn't contain any instructions for the central processing unit to execute. This is when ROM plays its part. ROM contains a small set of instructions called the **ROM BIOS** (basic input output system). The BIOS is a small, but critical part of the operating system that tells the computer how to access the disk drives. When you turn on your computer, the central processing unit performs the instructions in the ROM BIOS to search the disk drive for the main operating system files. The computer can then load these files into RAM and use them for the remainder of the computing session.

CMOS Memory

If the boot instructions are permanent, does that mean I can't change any hardware on my computer system? The computer is not ready to process data until it has copied certain operating system files from the hard disk into RAM. But, the computer can only find data on the hard disk if it has some information about how the hard disk is formatted. The computer must know the number of tracks and sectors and the size of each sector, or it cannot know where to look for the operating system files.

If information about the hard disk was permanently stored in ROM, you would never be able to replace your hard disk drive with a larger one. The computer could not access the new hard disk using information about the old disk. Therefore, a computer must have some semipermanent way of keeping boot data, such as the number of hard disk drive cylinders and sectors. For this, a computer needs a type of memory more permanent than RAM, but less permanent than ROM.

CMOS memory (complementary metal oxide semiconductor, pronounced "SEE moss") holds data, but requires very little power to retain its contents. Because of its low power requirements, a CMOS chip can be powered by battery. The battery trickles power to the CMOS chip so that it can retain vital data about your computer system configuration, even when your computer is turned off.

When your system configuration changes, the data in the CMOS memory must be updated. Some operating systems have special utilities that help you update the CMOS settings. For example, most of today's computers have a **plug-and-play** feature that helps you update CMOS if you install a new hard drive. You can manually change the CMOS data, by running the CMOS configuration, or setup, program as shown in Figure 5-12.

Figure 5-12

CMOS holds computer configuration settings, such as date and time, hard disk capacity, number of floppy disks, and RAM capacity.

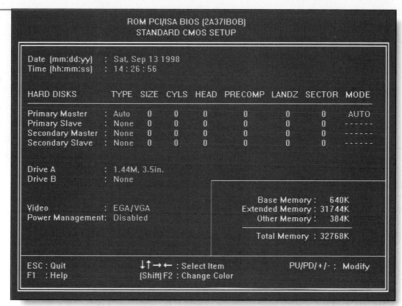

QuickCheck B

1 _____ is electronic circuitry that holds data and programs.

2 Having a steady power source is important for a computer because RAM is _____.

3 RAM capacity is measured in _____.

4 In RAM, microscopic electronic parts called _____ hold the electrical signals that represent data.

5 RAM speed is measured in _____.

6 If your computer does not have enough RAM to run several programs at once, your computer operating system might simulate RAM with disk-based _____ memory.

7 The series of instructions that a computer performs when it is first turned on are permanently stored in _____.

8 System configuration information, such as the number of the hard disk cylinders and sectors, is stored in battery-backed _____ memory.

C Central Processing Unit

So far in this chapter you have learned that digital computers represent data using a series of electrical signals. You know that data can be transported over the data bus or held in memory. But a computer does more than transport and store data. A computer is supposed to process data—perform arithmetic, sort lists, format documents, and so on.

The **central processing unit** is the circuitry in a computer that executes instructions to process data. The central processing unit retrieves instructions and data from RAM, processes those instructions, then places the results back into RAM so they can be displayed or stored. Figure 5-13 will help you visualize the flow of data and instructions through the processor.

Figure 5-13

The data bus transports data and instructions between RAM and the CPU.

The data bus transports data and instructions from RAM to the CPU for processing.

The CPU processes data.

RAM contains data and instructions about how to process the data.

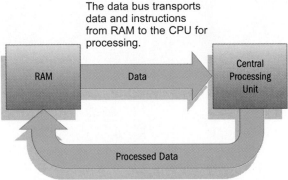

The data bus transports the processed data to RAM so it can be displayed, output, or stored on disk.

InfoWeb

CPUs
7

Central Processing Unit Architecture

What does the CPU look like? At one time, computer CPUs were huge, unreliable expensive devices that guzzled a tremendous amount of electrical power. In 1945, the size of a CPU was measured in feet (Figure 5-14), whereas today it is measured in **mils** (.001 inch).

Figure 5-14

The ENIAC, built in 1944 had 20 processing units, each about two feet wide and eight feet high. Today, this circuitry fits on an integrated circuit less than 560 mils (.56 inches) square.

The central processing unit of a mainframe computer usually contains several integrated circuits and circuit boards. In a microcomputer the central processing unit is a single integrated circuit called a **microprocessor**. Figure 5-15 shows a microprocessor similar to the one that is probably in the computer you use.

Figure 5-15

A microprocessor

The central processing unit has two main parts: the arithmetic logic unit and the control unit. Each of these units perform specific tasks to process data. The **arithmetic logic unit (ALU)** performs arithmetic operations such as addition and subtraction. It also performs logical operations such as comparing two numbers to see if they are the same. The ALU uses **registers** to hold data that is being processed. In the ALU the result of an arithmetic or logical operation is held temporarily in the **accumulator**, as shown in Figure 5-16.

Figure 5-16

How the ALU works

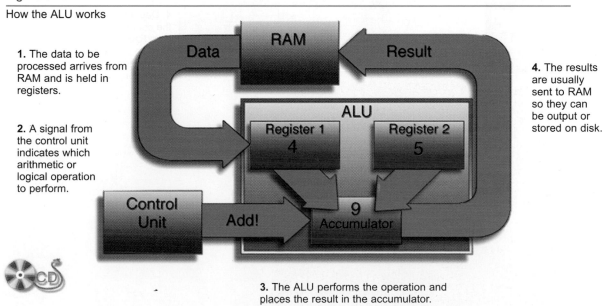

1. The data to be processed arrives from RAM and is held in registers.

2. A signal from the control unit indicates which arithmetic or logical operation to perform.

RAM
Data — Result

ALU
Register 1 — 4
Register 2 — 5

Control Unit — Add! — 9 Accumulator

4. The results are usually sent to RAM so they can be output or stored on disk.

3. The ALU performs the operation and places the result in the accumulator.

How does the ALU get its data, and how does it know which arithmetic or logical operation it must perform? The **control unit** directs and coordinates processing.

The control unit retrieves each instruction in sequence from RAM and places it in a special **instruction register**. The control unit then interprets the instruction to find out what needs to be done. According to its interpretation, the control unit sends signals to the data bus to fetch data from RAM, and to the arithmetic logic unit to perform a process.

The control unit makes a significant contribution to processing efficiency. It is analogous to the director on a movie set, because it executes a series of instructions just as a director follows a script. The control unit directs the movement of data just as a director positions actors and props on the set. A movie director schedules production to make sure that the camera operators, actors, sound technicians, and lighting crew are ready to film each scene. The control unit schedules processing by making sure that the data and instructions arrive in the ALU where they are processed. Figure 5-17 diagrams the role of the control unit.

Figure 5-17

How the control unit works

2. The RAM address of the instruction is kept in the **instruction pointer**. When the instruction has been executed, the address in the instruction pointer changes to indicate the RAM address of the next instruction to be executed.

1. The control unit retrieves an instruction from RAM and puts it in the **instruction register**.

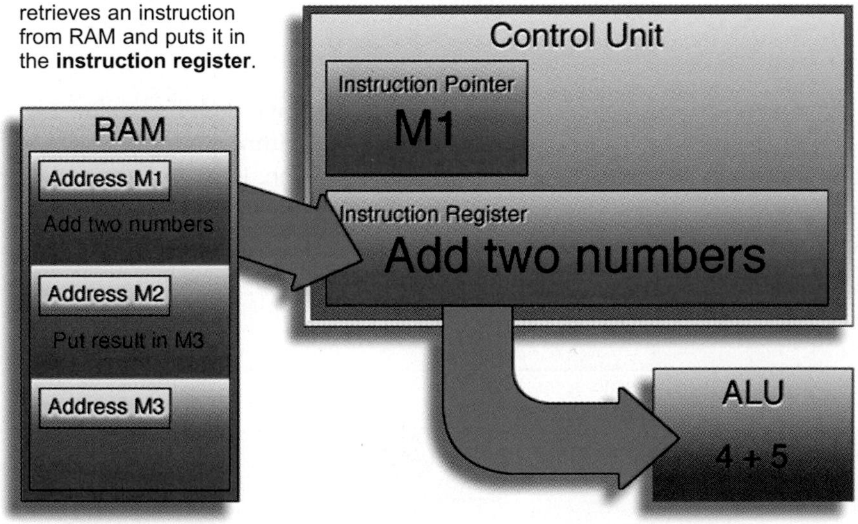

RAM

Address M1

Add two numbers

Address M2

Put result in M3

Address M3

Control Unit

Instruction Pointer

M1

Instruction Register

Add two numbers

3. The control unit interprets the instruction in its instruction register.

ALU

4 + 5

4. Depending on the instruction, the control unit will get data from RAM, tell the ALU to perform an operation, or change the memory address in the instruction pointer.

InfoWeb

Instruction
Sets
8

Instructions

What specifies the steps that the CPU must perform to accomplish a task? A computer accomplishes a complex task by performing a series of very simple steps, referred to as instructions. An **instruction** tells the computer to perform a specific arithmetic, logical, or control operation.

An instruction has two parts: the op code and the operands. An **op code**, which is short for operation code, is a command word for an operation such as add, compare, or jump. The **operands** for an instruction specify the data or the address of the data for the operation. Let's look at an example of an instruction:

op code ──────→ JMP M1 ←────── operand

LAB

CPU
Simulator

In the instruction JMP M1, the op code is JMP and the operand is M1. The op code JMP means *jump* or go to a different instruction. The operand M1 is the RAM address of the instruction to which the computer is supposed to go. The instruction JMP M1 has only one operand, but some other instructions have more than one operand. For example, the instruction to add the contents of register 1 and register 2 has two operands:

op code ──────→ ADD REG1 REG2 ←────── second operand
↑
first operand

The list of instructions that a central processing unit performs is known as its **instruction set**. Every task a computer performs must be described in terms of the limited list of instructions in the instruction set. As you look at the list of instructions in Figure 5-18, consider that the computer must use a set of instructions such as this for all the tasks it helps you perform—from word-processing to database management.

Figure 5-18

A simple microcomputer instruction set

Op Code	Operation	Example
INP	Input the given value into the specified memory address	INP 7 M1
CLA	Clear the accumulator to 0	CLA
MAM	Move the value from the accumulator to the specified memory location	MAM M1
MMR	Move the value from the specified memory location to the specified register	MMR M1 REG1
MRA	Move the value from the specified register to the accumulator	MRA REG1
MAR	Move the value from the accumulator to the specified register	MAR REG1
ADD	Add the values in two registers, place result in accumulator	ADD REG1 REG2
SUB	Subtract the value in the second register from the value in the first register, place the result in the accumulator	SUB REG1 REG2
MUL	Multiply the values in two registers, place the result in the accumulator	MUL REG1 REG2
DIV	Divide the value in the first register by the value in the second register, place the result in the accumulator	DIV REG1 REG2
INC	Increment the value in the register by 1	INC REG1
DEC	Decrement the value in the register by 1	DEC REG1
CMP	Compare the values in two registers; if values are equal, put 1 in the accumulator, otherwise put 0 in the accumulator	CMP REG1 REG2
JMP	Jump to the instruction at the specified memory address	JMP P2
JPZ	Jump to the instruction at the specified address if the accumulator holds a 0	JPZ P3
JPN	Jump to the instruction at the specified address if the accumulator does not hold a 0	JPN P2
HLT	Halt program execution	HLT

Figure 5-19

Instruction cycle

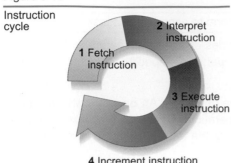

Instruction Cycle

How does a computer process instructions? The term **instruction cycle** refers to the process in which a computer executes a single instruction. The instruction cycle is repeated each time the computer executes an instruction. The steps in this cycle are summarized in Figure 5-19.

You have all the pieces you need to understand the details of the instruction cycle. You know how the ALU performs arithmetic and logical operations and how the control unit retrieves data from RAM and tells the ALU which operation to perform. Figure 5-20 shows how the ALU, control unit, and RAM work together to process instructions.

Figure 5-20

Processing an instruction

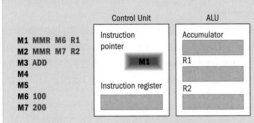

1. The instruction pointer indicates the memory location that holds the first instruction (M1).

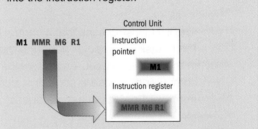

2. The computer fetches the instruction and puts it into the instruction register.

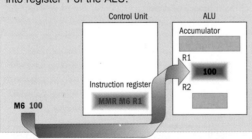

3. The computer executes the instruction that is in the instruction register; it moves the contents of M6 into register 1 of the ALU.

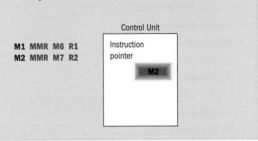

4. The instruction pointer changes to point to the memory location that holds the next instruction.

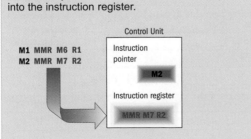

5. The computer fetches the instruction and puts it into the instruction register.

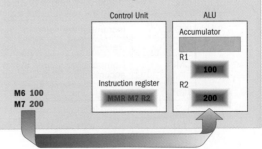

6. The computer executes the instruction; it moves the contents of M7 into register 2 of the ALU.

Figure 5-20

Processing an instruction (continued)

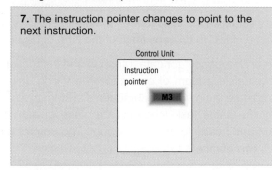

7. The instruction pointer changes to point to the next instruction.

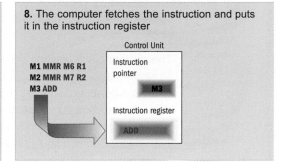

8. The computer fetches the instruction and puts it in the instruction register

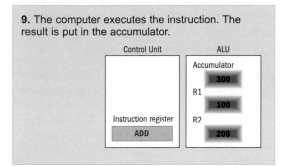

9. The computer executes the instruction. The result is put in the accumulator.

CPU Performance

How does the architecture of a computer contribute to its performance? Integrated circuit technology is the basic building block of CPUs in today's micro, mini, mainframe, and supercomputers. Remarkable advances in this technology have produced exponential increases in computer speed and power. In 1965, Gordon Moore, co-founder of chip-production giant, Intel Corporation, predicted that the number of transistors on a chip would double every 18 to 24 months. Much to the surprise of engineers and Moore himself, "Moore's Law," accurately predicted 30 years of chip development. In 1958, the first integrated circuit contained two transistors. The Pentium II processor, introduced in 1997, has 7.5 million transistors.

More transistors mean more processing power, so on the whole, today's CPU chips are faster than those of the past. However, all CPUs are not created equal; some process data faster than others. CPU speed is influenced by several factors including clock rate, word size, cache, and instruction set size. Specifications for these factors allow you to compare different CPUs.

Before you learn more about the factors that affect CPU performance, you should understand that a computer system with a high-performance CPU might not necessarily provide great overall performance. You know the old saying that a chain is only as strong as its weakest link. A computer system might also have weak links. Even with a high-performance processor, a computer system with a slow hard disk, no disk cache, and a small amount of RAM is likely to be slow at tasks such as starting programs, loading data files, printing, and scrolling through long documents.

Clock Rate

What does the date and time have to do with CPU performance? A computer contains a **system clock** that emits pulses to establish the timing for all system operations. The system clock is not the same as a "real-time clock" that keeps track of the time of day.

The system clock sets the speed or "frequency" for data transport and instruction execution. To understand how this works, visualize a team of oarsmen on a Viking ship. The ship's coxswain beats on a drum to coordinate the rowers. A computer's system clock and a ship's coxswain accomplish essentially the same task—they set the pace of activity. Boom! A stream of bits takes off from RAM and heads to the CPU. Boom! The control unit reads an instruction. Boom! The ALU adds two numbers together.

The clock rate set by the system clock determines the speed at which the computer can execute an instruction and, therefore, limits the number of instructions the computer can complete within a specific amount of time. The time to complete an instruction cycle is measured in **megahertz** (MHz), or millions of cycles per second.

The microprocessor in the original IBM PC performed at 4.77 MHz. Today's processors perform at speeds exceeding 300 MHz. If all other specifications are identical, higher megahertz ratings mean faster processing.

Word Size

Which is faster, an 8-bit processor or a 64-bit processor? **Word size** refers to the number of bits the central processing unit can manipulate at one time. Word size is based on the size of the registers in the CPU and the number of data lines in the bus. For example, a CPU with an 8-bit word size is referred to as an 8-bit processor; it has 8-bit registers and manipulates 8 bits at a time.

Computers with a large word size can process more data in each instruction cycle than computers with a small word size. Processing more data in each cycle contributes to increased performance. For example, the first microcomputers used 8-bit microprocessors, but today's faster computers use 32-bit or 64-bit microprocessors.

Cache

Disk cache speeds up access to data on disk; is there a similar process that speeds access to data from RAM? Another factor that affects CPU performance is cache. **Cache**, sometimes called **RAM cache** or **cache memory**, is special high-speed memory that gives the CPU more rapid access to data. A high-speed CPU can execute an instruction so quickly that it often waits for data to be delivered from RAM; this slows processing. The cache ensures that data is immediately available whenever the central processing unit requests it.

As you begin a task, the computer anticipates what data the central processing unit is likely to need and loads this data into the cache area. When an instruction calls for data, the central processing unit first checks to see if the required data is in the cache. If so, the central processing unit takes the data from the cache instead of fetching it from RAM, which takes longer. All other factors being equal, more cache means faster processing.

RISC
9

Instruction Set Complexity

What's the difference between CISC and RISC? As programmers developed various instruction sets for computers, they tended to add more and more complex instructions that took up many bytes in memory and required several clock cycles for execution. A computer based on a central processing unit with a complex instruction set came to be known as a **complex instruction set computer**, or **CISC**.

In 1975 John Cocke, an IBM research scientist, discovered that most of the work done by a microprocessor requires only a small subset of the available instruction set. Further research showed that only 20 percent of the instructions of a CISC machine do about 80 percent of the work. Cocke's research resulted in the development of microprocessors with streamlined instruction sets, called RISC machines.

The microprocessor of a **reduced instruction set computer**, or **RISC**, has a limited set of instructions that it can perform very quickly. In theory, therefore, a RISC machine should be faster than a CISC machine for most processing tasks. Some computer scientists believe, however, that a balance or hybrid of CISC and RISC technologies produce the most efficient and flexible computers.

Parallel
&
Pipelining
10

Pipelining and Parallel Processing

Can a CPU increase its performance by executing more than one instruction at a time?

Computers with a single processor execute instructions "serially," that is, one instruction at a time. Usually, the processor must complete all four steps in the instruction cycle before it begins to execute the next instruction. However, with a technology called **pipelining**, the processor begins executing an instruction before it completes the previous instruction. Pipelining speeds up processing, as shown in Figure 5-21.

Figure 5-21

How pipelining works

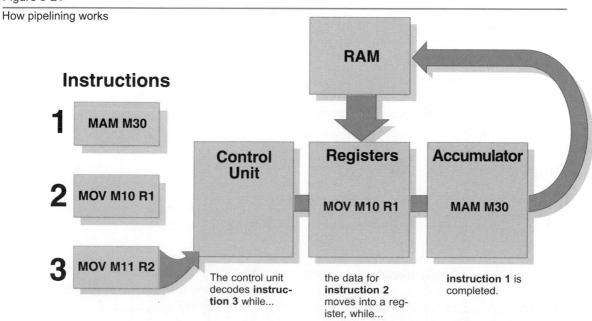

A computer that has more than one processor can execute multiple instructions at the same time. **Parallel processing** increases the amount of processing a computer can accomplish in a specific amount of time. Computers that are capable of parallel processing are called **parallel computers** or **non-von Neumann machines**. Figure 5-22 explains the concept of parallel processing.

Figure 5-22

How parallel processing works

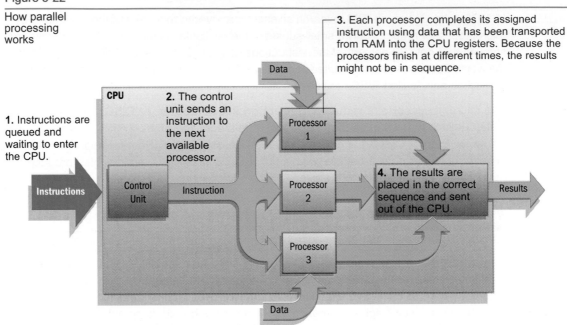

1. Instructions are queued and waiting to enter the CPU.

2. The control unit sends an instruction to the next available processor.

3. Each processor completes its assigned instruction using data that has been transported from RAM into the CPU registers. Because the processors finish at different times, the results might not be in sequence.

4. The results are placed in the correct sequence and sent out of the CPU.

To get a clearer picture of serial, pipelining, and parallel processing techniques, consider an analogy in which computer instructions are pizzas. Serial processing executes only one instruction at a time, just like a pizzeria with only one oven that can bake only one pizza (instruction) at a time. Pipelining is similar to a pizza conveyor belt. A pizza starts moving along the conveyor belt, but before it reaches the end of the belt, another pizza starts moving along the belt. Likewise, a pipelining computer starts processing an instruction; but before it completes the instruction, it begins processing another instruction. Finally, parallel processing is similar to a pizzeria with many ovens. Just as these ovens can bake more than one pizza at a time, a parallel processor can execute more than one instruction at a time.

QuickCheck C

1. A microcomputer uses a(n) _____ chip as its CPU.

2. The _____ in the CPU performs arithmetic and logical operations.

3. The _____ in the CPU directs and coordinates the operation of the entire computer system.

4. A computer instruction has two parts: the op code and the _____.

5. CPU speed is measured in _____.

6. The timing in a computer system is established by the _____.

Ⓓ Input/Output

When you purchase a computer, you can be fairly certain that before its useful life is over, you will want to add equipment to expand its capabilities. If you understand computer input/output, you will see how it is possible to expand a computer system. **I/O**, pronounced "eye-oh," is computer jargon for input/output. I/O refers to collecting data for the microprocessor to manipulate, and transporting results to display, print, and storage devices.

You already learned that a data bus transports data between RAM and the CPU. The data bus also extends to other parts of the computer. The segment of the data bus that transports data between RAM and peripheral devices is called the **expansion bus**. I/O between the central processing unit and peripheral devices often involves a long path that moves data over the expansion bus, slots, cards, ports, and cables. Figure 5-23 is an overview of the I/O architecture described in the rest of this section.

Figure 5-23

I/O architecture

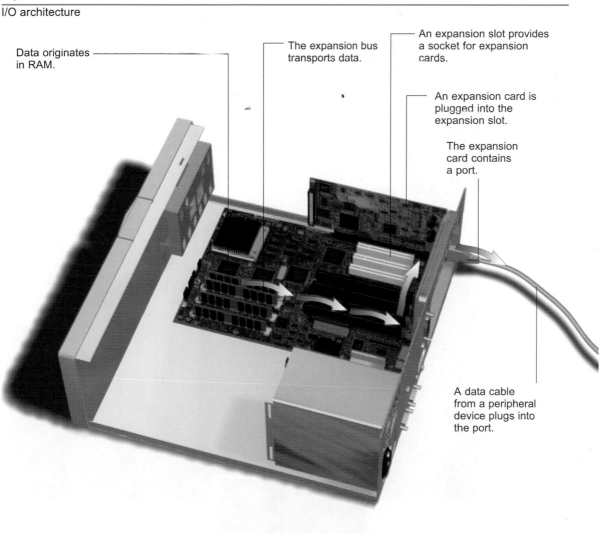

Data originates in RAM.

The expansion bus transports data.

An expansion slot provides a socket for expansion cards.

An expansion card is plugged into the expansion slot.

The expansion card contains a port.

A data cable from a peripheral device plugs into the port.

Expansion Slots

How do I use expansion slots? On the main board, the expansion bus terminates at an expansion slot. An **expansion slot** is a socket into which you can plug a small circuit board called an expansion card. The expansion slots on mainframes, minicomputers, and microcomputers provide a way to connect a large variety of peripheral devices.

Most microcomputers have four to eight expansion slots, but some of these slots usually contain expansion cards when you purchase the computer. The number of empty slots in your computer dictates its expandability.

Suppose that a few months after you purchase your computer, you decide you want to add sound capability. To find out if you have adequate expansion capability, turn your computer off, unplug it, then open the system unit case. Some computers contain more than one type of expansion slot, so the slots in your computer might appear to be different sizes. If you have an empty expansion slot, you can insert an expansion card, as shown in Figure 5-24.

Figure 5-24

Inserting an expansion card into a slot

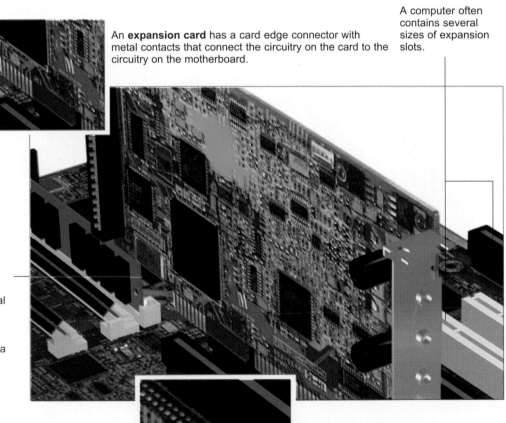

An **expansion card** has a card edge connector with metal contacts that connect the circuitry on the card to the circuitry on the motherboard.

A computer often contains several sizes of expansion slots.

When the card is inserted into the slot, the metal card edge connector contacts the connector in the slot to make a circuit for data transport.

An **expansion slot** contains metallic contacts that connect to the expansion bus.

Expansion Cards

What kinds of expansion cards are available? An **expansion card**, also referred to as an **expansion board** or a **controller card**, is a circuit board that plugs into an expansion slot. An expansion card provides the I/O circuitry for peripheral devices and sometimes contains an expansion device. For example, if you want to add sound capability, you would purchase and install an expansion card called a sound card. The sound card contains the circuitry to convert digital signals from your computer to sounds that play through speakers. Once you have inserted the sound card into an expansion slot, you can connect speakers or headphones. Microcomputer users can select from a wide variety of expansion cards, such as those shown in Figure 5-25.

Figure 5-25

Expansion cards

A **graphics card** connects your monitor and computer.

A **network card** connects your computer to the other computers on a local area network.

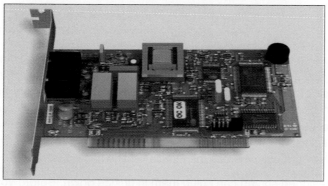

A **modem card** connects your computer to the telephone system so you can transport data from one computer to another over phone lines.

Expansion Ports

How do I connect a peripheral device to an expansion card? | To connect a peripheral device to an expansion card, you plug a cable from the peripheral device into the expansion port on the expansion card. An **expansion port** is a location that passes data in and out of a computer or peripheral device. An expansion port is often housed on an expansion card so that it is accessible through a hole in the back of the computer system unit. A port might also be connected directly to the main board, instead of to an expansion card.

To many computer users, the back of a computer is a confusing array of unlabeled ports, connectors, and cables. Study Figure 5-26 to become familiar with the shapes of the most frequently used expansion ports.

Figure 5-26

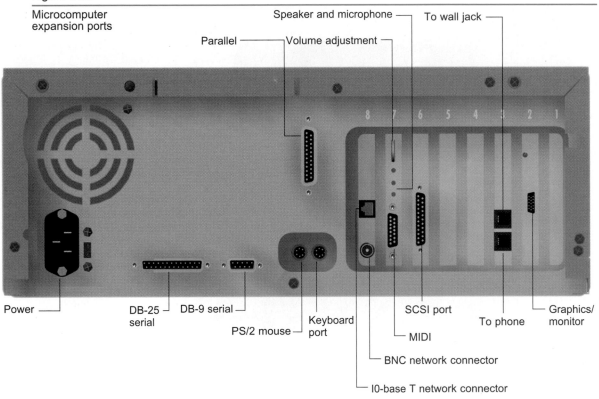

Microcomputer expansion ports

Speaker and microphone — To wall jack —

Parallel ——————— Volume adjustment —

Power ——— | DB-25 serial | DB-9 serial | PS/2 mouse — Keyboard port | SCSI port | MIDI | To phone | Graphics/ monitor

BNC network connector

I0-base T network connector

InfoWeb

Connectors
11

The cable that you plug into the computer port will contain a corresponding **connector**. Each type of connector has a designation such as DB-9 or C-50. The first part of the designation indicates the shape of the connector. For example, DB and C connectors are trapezoidal, whereas DIN connectors are round. The second part of the designation indicates the number of pins. A DB-9 connector has nine pins. In general, larger size connectors have more pins than smaller connectors. Most types of connectors have male and female versions. The male version has pins that stick out, whereas the female version has holes.

Connectors are designed so you can't plug them in upside down. Before you plug a cable into a port, make sure you have the correct connector and it is aligned with the pins. Figure 5-27 describes the cable connectors you'll typically find on a PC.

Figure 5-27

Cables and connectors

Cable/Connector	Description	Devices
DB9F or DB25F	Serial port sends data over a single data line one bit at a time at speeds of .005 MB/second	Mouse or modem
USB A	Universal serial bus (USB) port sends data over a single data line at speeds of 1.5 MB/second; connects up to 127 devices	Modem, keyboards, joystick, scanner, mouse
DB-25M	Standard parallel port sends data simultaneously over eight data lines at speeds of 1.5 MB/second	Printer
IEEE 1284 A-B cable (DB25M)	Enhanced parallel port sends data simultaneously over eight data lines, bi-directional, .5 MB/second	Printer, external CD-ROM drive, Zip drive, external hard disk drive, or tape backup
C50F	SCSI ("scuzzy") port sends data simultaneously over eight or 16 data lines at speeds from 5 MB/ seconds to 40 MB/second. May daisychain eight or 16 peripheral devices, depending on SCSI type.	Hard disk drive, scanner, CD-ROM drive, tape drive
HDB15	VGA port transfers data from the computer to the monitor	Monitor

QuickCheck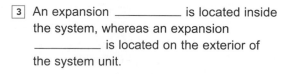

1 A(n) _____ is an electronic path that transports data between RAM and expansion slots.

2 A(n) _____ is a small circuit board that plugs into an expansion slot.

3 An expansion _____ is located inside the system, whereas an expansion _____ is located on the exterior of the system unit.

4 A(n) _____ port allows you to connect up to 127 peripheral devices to a single port.

User Focus

E The Boot Process

LAB

Trouble-shooting

Now that you have an understanding about how I/O, RAM, ROM, and the CPU operate, you're ready to learn how they all work together to prepare a computer for accepting commands each time you turn it on.

The sequence of events that occurs between the time you turn on a computer and the time it is ready for you to issue commands is referred to as the **boot process**. Micro, mini, and mainframe computers all require a boot process. In this section of the chapter you'll learn about the microcomputer boot process because that is the type of computer you are most likely to use.

You'll find out what happens during each step of the boot process for a typical PC and what you should do when the boot process doesn't proceed smoothly. Of course, even when you know how to troubleshoot computer problems, you should always follow the guidelines provided by your school or employer when you encounter equipment problems.

An Overview

If the computer memory is blank when I turn it on, how does it know how to start up?

As you learned earlier, one of the most important components of a computer—RAM—is volatile, so it cannot hold any data when the power is off. It also cannot hold the operating system instructions when the power is off. Therefore, the computer cannot use RAM to "remember" any basic functions, such as how to deal with input and communicate output to the external world. A computer needs some way to get operating system files into RAM. That's one of the main objectives of the boot process. In general, the boot process follows these six steps:

1. **Power Up**—When you turn on the power switch, the power light is illuminated, and power is distributed to the internal fan and main board.

2. **Start Boot Program**—The microprocessor begins to execute the instructions stored in ROM.

3. **Power-On Self-Test**—The computer performs diagnostic tests of crucial system components.

4. **Load Operating System**—The operating system is copied from a disk to RAM.

5. **Check Configuration and Customization**—The microprocessor reads configuration data and executes any customized start-up routines specified by the user.

6. **Ready for Commands and Data**—The computer is ready for you to enter commands and data.

Power Up

What's the first thing that happens when I turn the power on? The first stage in the boot process is the power-up stage. The fan in the power supply begins to spin, and the power light on the case of the computer comes on, as shown in Figure 5-28.

Figure 5-28

Power up

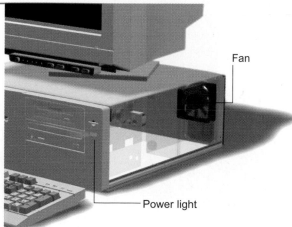

Fan

Power light

If you turn on the computer and the power light does not come on, the system is not getting power. You should check the power cord at the back of the computer to make sure it is firmly plugged into the wall and into the system unit. Also, make sure that the wall outlet is supplying power. If the power light still does not come on, then the computer's power supply might have failed. If you encounter this problem, you need to contact a technical support person for assistance.

Start Boot Program

What happens if the ROM is malfunctioning? When you turn on the computer, the microprocessor begins to execute the boot program stored in ROM, as shown in Figure 5-29.

If the ROM chips, RAM modules, or microprocessor are malfunctioning, the microprocessor is unable to run the boot program and the computer stops or "hangs." You know you have a problem at this stage of the boot process if the power light is on and you can hear the fan, but there is no message on the screen and nothing else happens. This problem requires the assistance of a technical support person.

Figure 5-29

ROM boot program activated

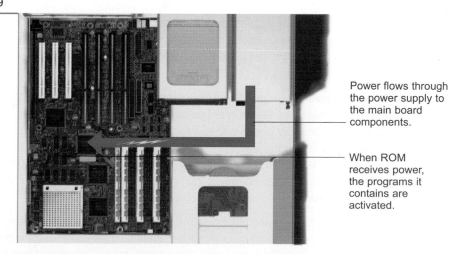

Power flows through the power supply to the main board components.

When ROM receives power, the programs it contains are activated.

Power-On Self-Test

Can the computer check to determine if all its components are functioning correctly?

The next step in the boot process is the **power-on self-test (POST)**, which diagnoses problems in the computer, as shown in Figure 5-30.

Figure 5-30

Power-on self-test

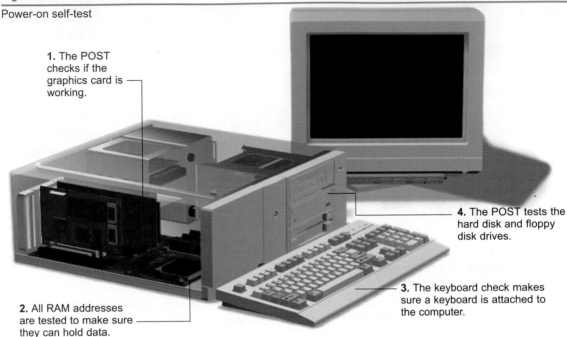

1. The POST checks if the graphics card is working.

2. All RAM addresses are tested to make sure they can hold data.

4. The POST tests the hard disk and floppy disk drives.

3. The keyboard check makes sure a keyboard is attached to the computer.

The POST first checks the graphics card that connects your monitor to the computer. If the graphics card is working, you'll see a message such as "Video BIOS ver 2.1 1997." If your computer beeps and does not display the video BIOS message, the graphics card is probably malfunctioning. You should contact a technical support person to have the graphics card checked.

The computer next tests RAM by placing data in each memory location, then retrieving that data to see if it is correct. The computer displays the amount of memory tested. If any errors are encountered during the RAM test, the POST stops and displays a message that indicates a RAM problem.

The POST then checks the keyboard. On most computers you can see the keyboard indicator lights flash when the keyboard test is in progress. If the keyboard is not correctly attached or if a key is stuck, the computer beeps and displays a keyboard error message. If a keyboard error occurs, you should turn the computer off and make sure that nothing is holding down a key on the keyboard. Next, unplug the keyboard and carefully plug it back into the computer. Finally, turn on the computer again to repeat the boot process. If the problem recurs, you might need to have your keyboard repaired or replaced.

The final step in the POST is the drive test. If you watch the hard disk drive and floppy disk drives during this test, you will see the drive activity lights flash on for a moment, and you will hear the drives spin. The drive test should only take a second or two to complete. If the computer pauses on this test, there might be a problem with one of the drives, and you should consult a technical support person.

Load Operating System

How does the computer load the operating system into RAM? After successfully completing the POST, the computer continues to follow the instructions in ROM to load the operating system, as shown in Figure 5-31.

Figure 5-31

Loading the operating system

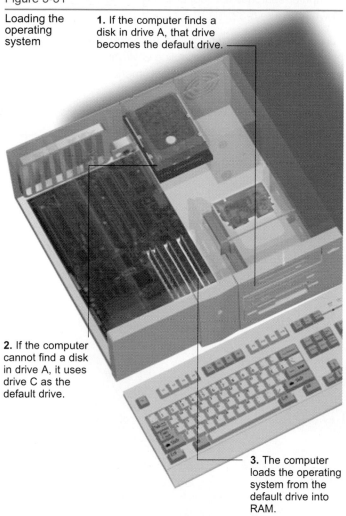

1. If the computer finds a disk in drive A, that drive becomes the default drive.

2. If the computer cannot find a disk in drive A, it uses drive C as the default drive.

3. The computer loads the operating system from the default drive into RAM.

The computer first checks drive A to see if it contains a disk. If there is a disk in this drive, drive A becomes the **default drive**. The computer uses the default drive for the rest of the computing session unless you specify a different one.

If there is no disk in drive A but the computer has a drive C, the computer uses drive C as the default drive. If your computer has a hard disk, you generally want drive C to be the default drive, so it is best not to put disks in any of the floppy disk drives until the boot process is complete. Otherwise, the computer recognizes the floppy disk drive as the default.

Next, the computer tries to locate and load operating system files from the default drive. First, the computer looks for two operating system files: **Io.sys** and **Msdos.sys**. If these files do not exist on the disk, the boot process stops and displays a message such as "Non-system disk or disk error" or "Cannot load a file." If you see one of these messages, there is probably a disk in drive A that should not be there. Remove the disk from drive A so your computer looks on the hard drive for the operating system files.

The microprocessor next attempts to load another operating system file, **Command.com**. Two problems could occur at this stage of the boot process, and both problems have the same error message—"Bad or missing command interpreter." First problem: the file **Command.com** might be missing because someone inadvertently erased it. Second problem: your disk might contain the wrong version of **Command.com** because someone inadvertently copied a different version onto the computer.

If you encounter either problem, you should turn the computer off, then find a bootable floppy disk. A **bootable floppy disk**, such as the one that came with the computer, contains operating system files. Put this floppy disk in drive A and turn on the computer again. Even if you are successful using a floppy disk to boot your system, you need to correct the **Command.com** problem on your hard disk. A technical support person or experienced user can help you do this.

Check Configuration and Customization

| Does the computer get all its configuration data from CMOS? | Early in the boot process, the computer checks CMOS to determine the amount of installed RAM and the types of available disk drives. Often, however, more configuration data is needed for the computer to properly access all available devices and set up your screen-based desktop. In the next stage of the boot process, the computer searches the root directory of the boot disk for configuration and setup files, as shown in Figure 5-32.

On some computers these instructions are stored in a file called **Autoexec.bat** or a Windows startup group, which you can modify to customize your computing environment. For example, you might customize the startup instructions so your To-do list document appears every time you start your computer.

Figure 5-32

Load configuration data

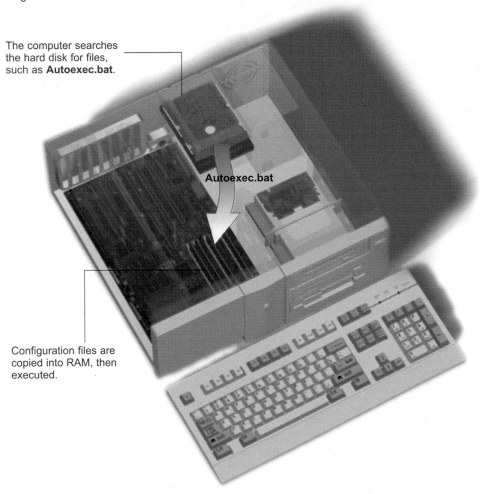

The computer searches the hard disk for files, such as **Autoexec.bat**.

Autoexec.bat

Configuration files are copied into RAM, then executed.

Ready for Commands and Data

How do I know when the computer has finished booting? The boot process is complete when the computer is ready to accept your commands. Usually the computer displays the operating system main screen or prompt at the end of the boot process. If you are using Windows, you will see the Windows desktop or, if you are using DOS, you will see the operating system prompt (Figure 5-33).

Figure 5-33

You can enter commands and launch programs when the computer displays the DOS operating system prompt C:\>, or the Windows desktop.

EndNote

Today's computers are digital electronic devices that accomplish complex tasks by performing a fairly limited set of instructions at breakneck speed. Understanding how a computer manipulates data coded as 1s and 0s should help dispel some of the mystery about what goes on "under the hood" of a microcomputer. Also, you can apply this understanding to troubleshooting your way past computer equipment problems.

Trouble-
shooting
12

Troubleshooting is not difficult if you follow a logical procedure and think creatively. When you have a problem with a computer, first try to make a specific statement that describes the problem. Saying "It's broken!" is not very useful. A more specific description might be something like, "I turned my computer on, but the screen is blank."

Try to make some hypotheses, or guesses, about the cause of the problem. Be creative—try to think of at least three potential causes. If your screen is blank, you might hypothesize that the monitor isn't getting power, that it is not getting a video signal, or that it has somehow "burned out."

Ask yourself which of these potential causes would have the simplest solution. Start with the simple solution first—the monitor might not be getting power because it's not turned on or because the power cable isn't plugged in. These are the things you check first. Of course, you should follow the repair policies of your school or place of employment by not trying to fix equipment that must be repaired by a qualified service agent. And remember the golden rule of troubleshooting: Don't panic.

InfoWeb

InfoWeb

**Chapter
Links**

The InfoWeb is your guide to print, film, television, and electronic resources. Use it to obtain updates on quickly changing technical information and to locate information for research papers. If you're using the New Perspectives CD-ROM, click the InfoWeb icon on the left side of this paragraph to access the online InfoWeb links. Otherwise, use your Web browser and type in the address of the New Perspectives site: www.cciw.com/np3. At the New Perspectives site you'll find up-to-date links to the topics covered in this chapter.

1 April Fools

The Apraphulian computer was the subject of A. K. Dewdney's article, **Computer Recreations: An ancient rope-and-pully computer is unearthed in the jungle of Apraphul** published in *Scientific American*, April 19, 1988. What begins as an April Fools' joke turns out to be an excellent explanation on the basic circuitry in a digital computer. Although this article is not online, you'll find more recent editions of *Scientific American* at **www.sciam.com**. Each issue contains at least one article about computers and don't miss "Ask the Experts" where you'll find authoritative answers to questions such as "Can computers be made from strands of DNA?"

2 Inside the Case

If you have a chance to visit the Computer Museum in Boston, make sure you tour the Walk-through Computer 2000 exhibit where you'll walk inside the system unit of a gigantic PC to get an up-close view of the computer components discussed in this chapter. The Computer Museum Web site at **www.tcm.org** contains a text-based description of the exhibit; select Resources, then click "The Walk-through Computer 2000."

3 Integrated Circuits

Without the invention of the integrated circuit, computers would still be room-sized devices affordable to only the largest and most powerful governments and organizations. You can see a picture of the first IC and read the inventor's original notes at the Texas Instruments site at **www.ti.com/corp/docs/history/firstic.htm**. For information on Ted Hoff and other inventors, visit the Invention Dimension site at **web.mit.edu/invent** and go to the Inventor of the Week archives. To get an idea of how many ICs have been manufacturered and to see what kinds of products they're in, check out the QuestLink Technology site **www.questlink.com**.

4 Motherboards

For an update on what's new in motherboard technology look for the Mainboard Guide site at **sysdoc.pair.com/mainboard.html** where you'll find FAQs and recommendations for selecting a motherboard. A more technical site with links to motherboard manufacturers and other motherboard sites is the Motherboard Homeworld at **web2.superb.net/motherboard**. Intel recently introduced a new motherboard "form factor" design called NLX. You'll find a picture and description at **www.intel.com/design/motherbd/nlx.htm**.

5 Memory Technology

Bob Campbell has kindly posted the first chapter of his excellent book, *Beyond the Limits: Secrets of PC Memory Management* (Sybex, 1993) on the Web at **www.well.com/user/memory/memtypes.htm**. Another Web site worth browsing is the Memory Manual at **pdsys.com/mem_man.htm**. Here you can search an acronym dictionary to discover the meaning of memory terms such as EDO and FPM. In addition you will find up-to-date information on memory speed and capacity.

6 Grace Hopper

Never one to follow gender stereotypes, Grace Hopper graduated with a Ph. D. in mathematics, joined the United States Naval Reserves, and in 1944 became one of the first computer programmers. Until her death in 1992, Dr. Hopper presented fascinating lectures peppered with her particular brand of wit and wisdom. Read about her at **www.cs.yale.edu/HTML/YALE/CS/HyPlans/tap/Files/hopper-wit.html**. In 1997 the U.S. Navy commissioned a destroyer in her honor, the U.S.S. Hopper. It is the first time a destroyer has been named after a woman. The navy maintains a site with information on the woman and the ship at **www.navysea.mil/hopper**. You'll find additional information at **www.sdsc.edu/Hopper/hopper_links.html**.

7 CPUs

A microprocessor is a fascinating microworld of nearly invisible circuitry. To get a glimpse into this world, visit **micro.magnet.fsu.edu/chipshot.html.cards**, where you'll see excellent pictures of microprocessors taken through an electron microscope. There are more pictures at **infopad.eecs.berkeley.edu/CIC/die_photos**. Don't leave without looking at some of the photos with overlays—they show you the location of the microscopic ALU, registers, and control unit. For updates on current microprocessor technology, follow the site links for microprocessor manufacturers, such as **www.intel.com**, **www.amd.com**, **www.cyrix.com**, **www.motorola.com**, and **www.ibm.com**.

8 Instruction Sets

For a more in-depth look at what happens in a microprocessor, read *How Microprocessors Work* by Wyant and Hammerstrom (Ziff-Davis Press, 1994). This book has many excellent illustrations that help you visualize what happens within the microprocessor circuitry. Microprocessor instruction sets are a pretty esoteric subject. The instruction set you saw in Figure 5-18 is very small, compared to those of most CISC processors. To get a taste of a real instruction set, take a quick browse through the instruction set cards at **ftp.comlab.ox.ac.uk/archive/cards**.

9 RISC

Read an interview with the founder of RISC technology, John Cocke, at **www.rs6000.ibm.com/resource/interviews**. A good comparison table of CISC vs. RISC architectures is available at the Seoul National University Architecture Courseware Home page, **archi.snu.ac.kr/course**, where you need to scroll down and select "Instruction Set Architecture."

10 Parallel and Pipelining

Parallel processing technology is a key to today's supercomputer architecture. In a test run, an Intel computer using 9,200 Pentium Pro microprocessors running in parallel clocked a new record by performing 1.34 trillion operations per second. Read more about it at **www.intel.com/pressroom/archive/releases/CN0611B.HTM**.

Spend a few minutes with an easy-to-understand basic tutorial on pipelining by Tony Wesley at **www.acs.oakland.edu/~awesley/pipetop.htm**. To get an idea of how parallel architecture is applied in the real world, visit the Lawrence Livermore National Laboratory Web site on parallel computing at **www.llnl.gov/liv_comp/parcomp**.

11 Connectors

You'll find everything you wanted to know about ports, cables, and connectors in the *Hardware Book*, and its online site at **www.blackdown.org/~hwb/hwb.html**. Also check out the pictures of PC cables and connectors at ConnectPro's online catalog at **www.connectpro.com/pccable.htm**. For a tour of USB technology, link to Intel's USB page at **www.intel.com/design/usb/index.htm**.

12 Troubleshooting

The PC Mechanic site at **www.geocities.com/SiliconValley/Lakes/3553** is where to go if you want to learn more about the parts of a PC. You'll find all sorts of handy information, such as the meaning of those beeps you hear when your computer doesn't boot up. If you really get into computer hardware, you might want to build your own computer. Before you get started, visit the Build Your Own PC site at **www.verinet.com/pc**. You'll love the graphics here and the casual easy-to-understand style. If you're having trouble with a computer, try A:1 Computer's site at **aloha-mall.com/a-1/START.HTM** where you can click the links to Preventive Maintenance Tips or Troubleshooting Tips. The Troubleshooting Flowchart is particularly useful. Successful troubleshooting begins with an organized approach to problem solving. Read tips from an expert at the Troubleshooters.Com site, **www.troubleshooters.com**. Another source of good troubleshooting information might be a users group near you. Search for "users groups" on Yahoo! for a group you might visit or join.

Review

1 Below each heading in this chapter, there is a question. Look back through this chapter and answer each of these questions using your own words.

2 Make a list of the boldface terms in this chapter, and use your own words to define each term.

3 Place an X in the following table to indicate which characteristics apply to each type of memory.

	RAM	Virtual Memory	ROM	CMOS
Holds user data such as documents				
Holds program instructions such as word processor				
Holds boot program				
Holds configuration data for hard disk type				
Temporary				
Permanent				
Battery powered				
Disk-based				

4 Use Figure 5-7 to write out the ASCII code for the following phrase: **Way Cool!**

5 Create a conceptual diagram like the one in Figure 5-9 to show how the phrase **Way Cool!** is stored in RAM.

6 Label the microcomputer components shown in a through g.

a.
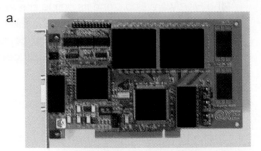

b.
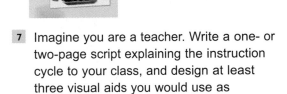

c. 　　　d.

e. 　　　f.

g.

7 Imagine you are a teacher. Write a one- or two-page script explaining the instruction cycle to your class, and design at least three visual aids you would use as illustrations.

8 Compare the ASCII and EBCDIC coding schemes in Figure 5-7 and describe some of the differences between them.

9 After the processor executes the three instructions in RAM, what are the final values in Register 1, Register 2, and the accumulator? (Hint: Refer to Figure 5-18.)

Program			
P1	MMR	M1	REG1
P2	MMR	M2	REG2
P3	ADD	REG1	REG2
P4	MAM	M3	
P5	HLT		

Data			
M1	5		
M2	3		
M3	0		

CONTROL UNIT	
INSTRUCTION POINTER	P1
INSTRUCTION REGISTER	

ALU	
ACCUMULATOR	
REG1	
REG2	

10 What are the values in Register 1, Register 2, and the accumulator when the computer has completed the instructions in the RAM shown below?

Program			
P1	MMR	M1	REG1
P2	MMR	M2	REG2
P3	INC	REG1	
P4	DEC	REG2	
P5	MUL	REG1	REG2
P6	MAM	M3	
P7	HLT		

Data			
M1	7		
M2	4		
M3	0		

CONTROL UNIT	
INSTRUCTION POINTER	P1
INSTRUCTION REGISTER	

ALU	
ACCUMULATOR	
REG1	
REG2	

11 Use your own words to write a one-paragraph description of pipelining.

12 Compare the specifications for Computer 1 and Computer 2 below. Circle the best performance rating in each category.

Performance Factor	Computer 1	Computer 2
Clock Rate	266 MHz	200 MHz
Word Size	32 bit	64 bit
Cache	256 K	32 K
Instruction Set	CISC	RISC
Pipelining	Yes	No
Parallel Processing	No	Yes

13 Label each of the components illustrated below:

14 Think about the concepts in the first four sections of this chapter: Digital Electronics, Memory, Central Processing Unit, and I/O. Using these concepts, put together your own description of how a computer processes data. You can use a narrative description and/or sketches.

15 Use the New Perspectives CD-ROM to take a practice test or to review the new terms presented in this chapter.

Projects

1 **The Apraphulians' Computer** Read the article about the Apraphulian computer in the April 19, 1988 issue of *Scientific American*, entitled "An Ancient Rope-and-Pulley Computer is Unearthed in the Jungle of Apraphulia," then answer the following questions:

a. The Apraphulians did not use electricity. How then did they represent 0s and 1s?

b. What did the Apraphulian's *inverter box* accomplish?

c. The archaeologists excavating the Apraphulian site found a large overgrown field where several thousand rotting flip-flop boxes were buried. What part of the computer was at this site?

d. Redraw the flip-flop diagram from the article and label it to show how it worked.

2 **Looking From the Inside Out** After disconnecting the power cable, carefully open the case of a computer system unit. Draw a sketch and label each of the components you see inside. Try to locate and label all the components shown in Figure 5-1.

3 **The History of the IC** Computers would not be available to individuals today if not for the invention of the integrated circuit. Just four months apart in 1959, Jack Kilby and Robert Noyce independently created working models of the circuit that was to transform the computer industry. Jack Kilby worked at Texas Instruments, and you can find reproductions of his original research notes on the Web site, **www.ti.com/corp/docs/history/firstic.htm.** Robert Noyce developed the integrated circuit while CEO of Fairchild Semiconductor, but he left Fairchild to form Intel.

Use your library and Internet resources to research the impact of the integrated circuit on the computer industry, then do one of the following:

a. Write a two- to three-page paper summarizing how the integrated circuit was used in the first five years after it was invented.

b. Write two one-page biographical sketches; one of Jack Kilby and one of Robert Noyce.

c. Create a diagram of the "family tree" of computer technologies that resulted from the development of the integrated circuit.

d. Based on the facts you have gathered about the development of the computer industry, write a two- to three-page paper describing the computer industry today if the integrated circuit had not been invented.

4 **Scanning a Computer Ad for Key Terms** Photocopy a full-page computer ad from a current issue of a computer magazine, such as *Computer Shopper*. On the copy of the ad use a colored pen and circle any of the key terms that were presented in this chapter. Make sure you watch for abbreviations; they are frequently used in computer ads. On a separate sheet of paper, or using a word processor, make a list of each term you circled and write a definition of each.

5  **Researching and Writing about RAM** Suppose you are a computer industry analyst preparing an article on computer memory for a popular computer magazine. Gather as much information as you can about RAM, including current pricing, the amount of RAM that comes installed in a typical computer, tips for adding RAM to computers, and so forth. Use a word processor to write a one- to two-page article that would help your magazine's readers understand all about RAM.

INTERNET Optional

Researching and Writing about RISC Write a one- to two-page paper about RISC technology. You might want to explore the history of the concept beginning with John Cocke's research. You can also look at the use of RISC processors for the type of powerful workstations typically used for engineering and CAD applications. You might also research Apple's PowerPC computer that uses the PowerPC RISC chip. If you have Internet access, start your research with the resources listed in InfoWeb 9.

7 Expansion Ports Look in computer magazines to find advertisements for three peripheral devices that connect to a computer using different ports or buses. For example, you might find a modem that connects to the serial port. Photocopy each of these three ads. For each device circle on the photocopy the device's brand name, model name and/or number, and the port or bus it uses. Also make sure you provide your instructor with the name and publication date of the magazine and the page number on which you found the information.

8 Interview with a Computer User Complete the following steps to interview one of your friends who has a computer, and write a report that describes how your friend could expand his or her computer system.

a. Find out as many technical details as you can about your friend's computer, including the type of computer, the type and speed of the microprocessor, the amount of memory, the configuration of disk drives, the capacity of the disk drives, the resolution of the monitor, and so on.

b. Find out how your friend might want to expand his or her computer system either now or sometime in the future. For example, your friend might want to add a printer, a sound card, CD-ROM drive, memory, or a monitor.

c. Look through computer magazines to find a solution for at least one of your friend's expansion plans. What would you recommend as a solution? If money was no object would your recommendation change? Why or why not?

d. Write a two-page report describing your friend's computer and his or her expansion needs. Then describe the solution(s) you found.

9 Observing the Boot Process Using the *User Focus* section of this chapter as your guide, make a detailed list of each step in the boot process. Take your list into the computer lab and boot one of the computers. As the computer boots, read your list to make sure it is correct. For which steps in the boot process can you see or hear something actually happening?

INTERNET Optional

Can a Computer Make Errors? In 1994 Intel released the Pentium microprocessor. Within a matter of weeks, rumors began to circulate that the Pentium chip had a bug that caused errors in some calculations. As the rumors spread, corporate computer users became nervous about the numbers that appeared on spreadsheets calculated on computers with the Pentium processor. How can a computer make such mistakes? Are computers with Pentium processors destined for the dumpster? Is there any way users can save the money they have invested in their Pentium computers?

Suppose you own a computer store that sold many computers with the flawed Pentium microprocessor. Your customers are calling you to get the straight facts. Use your library and Internet resources to gather as much reliable information as you can about the Pentium flaw. Use this information to write a one-page information sheet for your customers. You might find the following resources useful:

- Intel's Internet site: **www.intel.com**
- "The Truth Behind the Pentium Bug" *Byte*, March 1995.

11 Troubleshooting Scenarios—What Would You Do? Your instructor might want you to do this project individually or in a small group. For each of the following scenarios, indicate what might be wrong.

a. You turn on the computer's power switch and nothing happens—no lights, no beep, nothing. What's the most likely problem?

b. You turn on your computer and the computer completes the POST test. You see the light on drive A and you hear the drive power up, but you get a message on the screen that says "Cannot load file." Explain what caused this message to appear and explain exactly what you should do to complete the boot process.

c. You are using a word processor to write an essay for your English composition course. You have completed eight pages, and you have periodically saved the document. Suddenly, you notice that when you press a key nothing happens. You try the mouse, but it no longer moves the pointer on the screen. What should you do next?

d. You turn on your computer, see the power light, and hear the fan. Then, the computer begins to beep repeatedly. What would you suspect is the problem?

Lab Assignments

Binary Numbers

Computers process and store numbers using the binary number system. Understanding binary numbers helps you recognize how digital computers work by simply turning electricity on and off. In this Lab, you learn about the binary number system and you learn how to convert numbers from binary to decimal and from decimal to binary.

1 Click the Steps button to learn about the binary number system. As you proceed through the Steps, answer all of the Quick Check questions that appear. After you complete the Steps, you will see a Quick Check Summary Report. Follow the instructions on the screen to print this report.

2 Click the Explore button, then click the Conversions button. Practice converting binary numbers into decimal numbers. For example, what is the decimal equivalent of 00010011? Calculate the decimal value on paper. To check your answer, enter the decimal number in the decimal box, and then click the binary boxes to show the 1s and 0s for the number you are converting. Click the Check It button to see if your conversion is correct.

Convert the following binary numbers into decimals:

a. 00000101

b. 00010111

c. 01010101

d. 10010010

e. 11111110

3 In Explore, click the Conversions button. Practice converting decimal numbers into binary numbers. For example, what is the binary equivalent of 82? Do the conversion on paper. To check your answer, enter the decimal number in the decimal box, and then click the binary boxes to show the 1s and 0s of its binary equivalent. Click the Check It button to see if your conversion is correct.

Convert the following decimal numbers to binary numbers:

a. 77

b. 25

c. 92

d. 117

e. 214

4 In Explore, click the Binary Number Quiz button. The quiz provides you with ten numbers to convert. Make each conversion and type your answer in the box. Click the Check Answer button to see if you are correct. When you have completed all ten quiz questions, follow the instructions on the screen to print your quiz results.

CPU Simulator

 In a computer central processing unit (CPU), the arithmetic logic unit (ALU) performs instructions orchestrated by the control unit. Processing proceeds at a lightning pace, but each instruction accomplishes only a small step in the entire process. In this Lab you work with an animated CPU simulation to learn how computers execute assembly language programs. In the Explore section of the Lab, you have an opportunity to interpret programs, find program errors, and write your own short assembly language programs.

1 Click the Steps button to learn how to work the simulated CPU. As you proceed through the Steps, answer all of the Quick Check questions that appear. After you complete the Steps, you will see a Quick Check Summary Report. Follow the instructions on the screen to print this report.

2 Click the Explore button. Use the File menu to open a program called **Add.cpu**. Use the Fetch Instruction and Execute Instruction buttons to step through the program. Then answer the following questions:

a. How many instructions does this program contain?

b. Where is the instruction pointer after the program is loaded but before it executes?

c. What does the INP 3 M1 instruction accomplish?

d. What does the MMR M1 REG1 instruction accomplish?

e. Which memory location holds the instruction that adds the two numbers in REG1 and REG2?

f. What is in the accumulator when the program execution is complete?

g. Which memory address holds the sum of the two numbers when program execution is completed?

3 In Explore, use the File menu to open a program called **Count5.cpu**. Use the Fetch Instruction and Execute Instruction buttons to step through the program. Then answer the following questions:

a. What are the two input values for this program?

b. What happens to the value in REG1 as the program executes?

c. What happens when the program executes the JPZ P5 instruction?

d. What are the final values in the accumulator and registers when program execution is complete?

4 In Explore, click File, then click New to make sure the CPU is empty. Write a program that follows these steps to add 8 and 6:

a. Input 8 into memory address M3.

b. Input 6 into memory address M5.

c. Move the number in M3 to Register 1.

d. Move the number in M5 to Register 2.

e. Add the numbers in the registers.

f. Move the value in the accumulator to memory address M1.

g. Tell the program to halt.

Test your program to make sure it produces the answer 14 in address M1. When you are sure your program works, use the File menu to print your program.

5 In Explore, use the File menu to open a program called **Bad1.cpu**. This program is supposed to multiply two numbers together and put the result in memory location M3. However, the program contains an error.

a. Which memory location holds the incorrect instruction?

b. What instruction will make this program produce the correct result?

6 In Explore, use the CPU simulator to write a program to calculate the volume, in cubic feet, of the inside of a refrigerator. The answer should appear in the accumulator at the end of the program. The inside dimensions of the refrigerator are 5 feet, by 3 feet, by 2 feet. Make sure you test your program, then print it.

Troubleshooting

Computers sometimes malfunction, so it is useful to have some skill at diagnosing, if not fixing, some of the hardware problems you might encounter. In this Lab, you use a simulated computer that has trouble booting. You learn to make and test hypotheses that help you diagnose the cause of boot problems.

1 Click the Steps button to learn how to make and test hypotheses about hardware malfunctions during the boot process. As you proceed through the Steps, answer all of the Quick Check questions that appear. After you complete the Steps, you will see a Quick Check Summary Report. Follow the instructions on the screen to print this report.

2 Click the Explore button. Use the File menu to load **System11.trb**. Click the Boot Computer button and watch what happens on the simulated computer (in this case, actually, what does not happen!). Make your hypothesis about why this computer does not boot. Use the Check menu to check the state of various cables and switches. When you think you know the cause of the problem, select it from the Diagnosis list. If you correctly diagnosed the problem, write it down. If your diagnosis was not correct, form another hypothesis and check it, until you have correctly diagnosed the problem.

3 Sometimes problems that appear very similar, result from different causes. In Explore, use the File menu to load **System03.trb**, then diagnose the problem. Do the same for **System06.trb**. Describe the problems with these two systems. Then describe the similarities and differences in their symptoms.

4 In Explore, use the File menu to load System02 and System08. Both systems produce keyboard errors, but these errors have different causes. Describe what caused the problem in System02, and what caused the problem in System08. Once you have diagnosed these problems, what can you do about them?

5 In Explore, use the File menu to load Systems 04, 05, 07, 09, and 14. These systems produce similar symptoms on boot up. However, these systems have different problems. Diagnose the problem with each of these systems and indicate the key factor (the symptom or what you checked) that led to your diagnosis.

THE COMPUTER MARKETPLACE

6

I t is one of those dreary afternoons when the rain fogs up the windows. Your friend Matt is sprawled on the floor amidst a small mountain of computer magazines. Now and then he tags a page with a Post-it note or jots down the price of a computer system. You munch on a sandwich while browsing employment sites on the Web.

"Hey, what's up?" you ask.

"See all these magazines! See all these ads! How's a person supposed to know what to buy? The more I look, the more confused I get!" He opens the latest issue of *Computer Shopper*— all 800 pages of it—and you see that he has marked at least 30 ads with Post-it notes!

"Look," he says, "here's a computer with a Pentium processor…$1,995. Here's another one from a different company…$2,195."

"There's got to be some difference between them." You try to help.

Matt frowns. "Yeah. That's the trouble. One has more RAM, but the other one has a better monitor. I could spend $2,295 and get Surround Sound plus a larger hard drive, but that would wreck my budget. What am I going to do!"

Whether you're shopping for a computer or considering a career, the computer industry offers a huge variety of choices. As a consumer, understanding the computer industry is just as important as understanding world events. In fact, much of the news about the computer-industry has global significance for today's information age. You'll see increasing coverage of computers and the computer industry on the evening news, in magazines, on the Internet, and on TV.

The purpose of this chapter is to help you learn about the computer industry. You'll discover what you need to know to be a smart computer shopper. You'll discover who does what in the computer industry, and maybe you'll even identify a computer career that appeals to you.

LABS

Buying a
Computer

A Consumer's Guide to Computer Systems

Sometime in the not-too-distant future you are likely to participate in a computer purchase decision—if not for your own computer, then one for your friend, your parents' small business, your employer, or your children. Buying the right computer and keeping within your budget are challenges.

Suppose you decide to buy a computer. You'll probably look at computer ads to get an idea of features and prices. Most computer ads list technical specifications describing the computer's components, capabilities, and special features. Do you need to understand the technical specifications to make an intelligent purchase decision? The answer is definitely "yes!" Suppose that you see a computer ad such as the one in Figure 6-1. This computer system costs $2,295. Would it be a good "deal"?

Figure 6-1

MicroPlus computer ad

MicroPlus HomePC

MicroPlus award-winning computers offer strong performance at a reasonable price. Simply the fastest Windows machines you can buy. MicroPlus computers feature superior engineering, starting with a genuine Intel processor and a motherboard designed specifically to take advantage of the latest technological advancements. Of course, you are covered by our one-year on-site parts and labor warranty.*

*ON-SITE SERVICE AVAILABLE FOR HARDWARE ONLY AND MAY NOT BE AVAILABLE IN CERTAIN REMOTE AREAS. SHIPPING AND HANDLING EXTRA. ALL RETURNS WILL BE EXCHANGED FOR LIKE PRODUCT ONLY. ALL RETURNS MUST BE IN ORIGINAL BOX WITH ALL MATERIALS. CALL FOR AN RMA NUMBER. DEFECTIVE PRODUCTS WILL BE REPAIRED AT MICROPLUS DISCRETION. THE COST FOR RETURNED MERCHANDISE IS NOT INCLUDED WITH ANY MONEY-BACK GUARANTEE. PRICES AND AVAILABILITY SUBJECT TO CHANGE WITHOUT NOTICE.

- Intel Pentium II 266 MHz, 512 KB cache
- 32 MB EDO RAM expandable to 128 MB
- 6.4 GB 10 ms EIDE hard drive with 512 K cache
- 16X variable CD-ROM drive
- 3.5" 1.44 MB floppy drive
- Creative Labs stereo sound card and speakers
- 64-bit video card with 4 MB RAM
- 17" 1600 x 1200 .26 dp color monitor (15.7" vis)
- Six-bay tower case
- Mouse
- Microsoft Windows 98
- Three PCI and four ISA slots
- RS-232, USB, and parallel ports
- 33.6 bps fax/modem

1997 BEST TECH!

COMPUTER CHOICE TOP AWARD

QUALITY PICK 1997

All Credit Cards Welcome Call Toll Free 1-800-555-0000 and order today!

You can't tell if the MicroPlus computer is a good deal unless you can compare its specifications to those of computers from other vendors. Let's take a closer look at what the specifications mean in terms of price and performance.

Selecting a Microprocessor

InfoWeb

Which Chip?
1

Does the processor affect the price of a computer? The microprocessor is the core component in a computer and is featured prominently in product descriptions. Computer ads typically indicate the type of microprocessor and its speed. Most of today's microcomputers are designed around a microprocessor from one of two product families: x86, or PowerPC.

The original IBM PC used the Intel 8088 microprocessor, one of the first models in the **x86 family** of microprocessors. Today's PCs still contain x86 processors such as the **Pentium**. Most of these processors are manufactured by Intel, but companies such as Cyrix and AMD have produced what are called "work-alike" processors. Computers with work-alike processors are generally less expensive than an equivalent computer with an Intel processor. Most computer ads specify which company manufactured the microprocessor. If you want to run Windows software, choose a computer with an x86 processor.

If you would rather run Macintosh software, select a computer with a 68000-series or PowerPC microprocessor. Until 1994, Macintosh computers contained a **68000-series microprocessor** manufactured by Motorola. More recent models, called "Power Macs" contain a **PowerPC microprocessor** that implements RISC architecture to provide relatively fast performance at a low cost.

Computers that contain recent-model microprocessors are more expensive than computers that contain older microprocessor technology. The geneology tree in Figure 6-2 will help you determine if the microprocessor technology in a PC is new or old.

Figure 6-2

PC processor
geneology

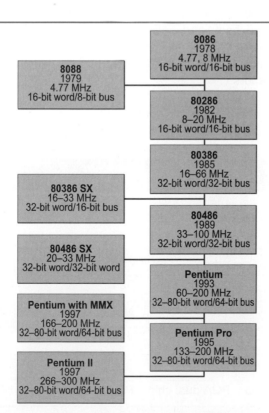

Comparing Pentiums

Which Pentium is right for me? The x86 chip family descended from Intel's 8086 microprocessor. The 80286, 80386, and 80486 models that followed were usually referred to by the last three digits, 286, 386, and 486. For the next generation, however, Intel broke with tradition. Initially, the 80586 chip was dubbed the P5, until it was officially christened the **Pentium**. Intel introduced the Pentium processor in 1993. This processor packed an impressive 3.3 million transistors on a chip .36-inch square. Using **dual-pipeline architecture**, the chip could execute two instructions at a time.

In 1995, Intel produced the P6 generation of processors called the **Pentium Pro**. With five execution pipelines and 5.5 million transistors, the Pentium Pro was optimized for the 32-bit instruction set that Microsoft had used to develop the Windows NT operating system. A Level 2 cache contributes to the speed of this chip and is often referred to in computer ads. A **Level 2 cache** (L2 cache) is memory circuitry housed off the processor on a separate chip. The cache chip connects to the main processor by a dedicated high-speed bus. Level 2 cache is much faster than RAM and almost as fast as cache built into the processor chip.

In 1997, Intel launched two new processors. The **Pentium with MMX technology** was a jazzed-up version of the original Pentium chip and contained circuitry to speed the execution of multimedia applications. A second chip, the **Pentium II**, added MMX technology to the Pentium Pro chip.

InfoWeb

Benchmarks
2

Most experts agree that the Pentium with MMX technology provides the most processing power for your dollar. The Pentium with MMX technology is less expensive than the Pentium Pro but has similar performance levels on tests such as SYSmark32. **SYSmark32** is a standard benchmark test that measures computer speed for word-processing, graphics, spreadsheet, and database tasks. If cost is not a factor, the Pentium II is a more expensive chip but will provide you with the highest level of performance. The chart in Figure 6-3 summarizes features and performance factors for each of the Pentium processors.

Figure 6-3

Pentium feature summary

	Pentium	Pentium Pro	Pentium with MMX technology	Pentium II
Speed	75–200 MHz	166–200 MHz	166–233 MHz	233–300 MHz
SySmark 32	175	214	203	249
MMX	No	No	Yes	Yes
On-chip cache	16 K	16 K	32 K	32 K
L2 cache	No	Yes	No	Yes
Transistors	3.3 million	5.5 million	4.5 million	7.5 million
Execution pipelines	2	5	2	5
Chip package	PGA single chip	PGA dual chip	PGA single chip	SEC cartridge
Introduced	1993	1995	1997	1997

RAM: Requirements and Cost

How much RAM is enough? The amount of RAM a computer needs depends on the operating system and applications software you plan to use. RAM costs have dropped in recent years. Today, RAM costs about $10 per megabyte, so it doesn't have a major impact on the price of a computer system. To run Windows software effectively, your computer should have at least 32 MB of RAM.

If a computer features **EDO** (Extended Data Out) RAM technology, you can expect better perfomance from it than from computers with standard memory technology.

It is possible to add RAM after you purchase a computer system. For example, the MicroPlus computer includes 32 MB of RAM, but additional memory modules can be added up to a maximum of 128 MB. Most consumer advocates recommend that you get as much RAM as you can afford with your initial purchase.

Floppy Disk Drives: How Many?

Do I need more than one floppy disk drive? Most microcomputers today are configured with a single 3½-inch high-density floppy disk drive. Older computers often included an additional 5¼ inch drive. These two disk drive sizes were useful during the transition from the earlier 5¼-inch disks to the newer 3½-inch disks. Today, most software is shipped on 3½-inch disks or on CD-ROMs, so a 5¼-inch drive is unnecessary.

A popular misconception is that a computer needs two disk drives to copy the contents of one disk to another, but this is not the case. Both Windows and DOS allow you to make a copy of an entire disk by reading data from the original disk into memory, then inserting the destination disk and copying the data from memory to the destination disk. One 3½-inch floppy disk drive should be sufficient for your computing needs.

Hard Drive Specifications

What's the difference between SCSI and EIDE? The factors that influence hard drive performance and price include storage capacity, access time, and controller type. The more storage space you have, the better. So when comparing computer systems, the hard drive capacity is a significant factor. Most computers today are shipped with at least 5 GB of hard disk capacity.

Computer ads usually specify hard disk access time as an indication of drive performance. Access times of 9, 10, or 11 ms are typical for today's microcomputer hard drives.

The two most popular types of hard drives are EIDE and SCSI. A hard drive mechanism includes a circuit board called a **controller** that positions the disk and read-write heads to locate data. Disk drives are categorized according to the type of controller they have. An **EIDE** (Enhanced Integrated Device Electronics) drive features high storage capacity and fast data transfer. **SCSI** (Small Computer System Interface) drives provide a slight performance advantage over EIDE drives and are recommended for high-performance microcomputer systems and minicomputers.

CD-ROM Drive: Worth the Cost?

Do I need a CD-ROM drive? A CD-ROM drive is a worthwhile investment that lets you use multimedia, game, educational, and reference applications that are available only on CD-ROM disks.

Today, most microcomputers are configured with a CD-ROM drive. Compared to a floppy disk drive, a CD-ROM drive delivers data at a faster rate and provides better performance, especially with multimedia applications. You should purchase the fastest CD-ROM drive that you can afford.

The access time of today's CD-ROM drives is 100 to 200 ms, ten times slower than a hard disk drive. In ads, however, the speed of a CD-ROM drive is measured by comparing its data transfer rate to the rate of the original CD-ROM drive technology. For example, the original CD-ROM drives had a data transfer rate of 150 KB per second. Dual speed or 2X CD-ROM drives have a data transfer rate of 300 KB per second.

Today's 12X CD-ROM drives have a data transfer rate of 1.8 MB per second. As a point of reference, the data transfer rate of a hard drive is about 3 MB per second. The computer ad in Figure 6-1 describes the CD-ROM drive as "16X variable." This means that the data transfer rate of the CD-ROM drive varies between a minimum transfer rate of 1.8 MB per second (12X) and a maximum speed of 2.4 MB per second (16X). Alternative terminology for 16X variable includes 12–16X and 16X max. The table in Figure 6-4 will help you compare the actual data transfer rates and access times of CD-ROM drives.

Figure 6-4

CD-ROM drive
data-transfer
rates

Speed	Seek Time (ms)	Data Transfer Rate
Single-speed	600	150 KB per second
2X	320	300 KB per second
3X	250	450 KB per second
4X	135–180	600 KB per second
6X	135–180	900 KB per second
8X	135–180	1.2 MB per second
10X	135–180	1.6 MB per second
12X	100–180	1.8 MB per second
16X	100–180	2.4 MB per second

Selecting a Sound System

What's wave table synthesis, and do I need it? With the proliferation of multimedia applications, a sound system has become an essential part of a computer system. A basic computer sound system includes a sound card and a set of small speakers; but if you want your computer-generated tunes to blow you away, you will want to invest in a more sophisticated sound system.

InfoWeb

Sound Systems 3

A sound card converts the digital data in a sound file into analog signals for instrumental, vocal, and spoken sounds. In addition, a sound card lets you make your own recordings by converting analog sounds into **digitized sound files** that you can store on disk. To record your own sounds, you'll need to add a good quality microphone to your sound system. Digitized sound files require lots of storage space. Ten seconds of digitized stereo sound can consume up to 5 MB of disk space.

A more compact alternative to digitized sound is to store music as **MIDI sound**. A sound card generally supports one of two MIDI standards. **FM synthesis** provides instructions for the computer to synthesize sounds by simulating the sounds of real musical instruments. **Wave table synthesis** creates music by playing digitized sound samples of actual instruments. Wave table synthesis provides better quality sound, but at a higher price than FM synthesis.

Most multimedia software specifies the type of sound required. A basic sound card with FM synthesis is usually sufficient for most reference software and educational software. Some games require Sound Blaster compatible sound. If you own such software, make sure your sound card is described as "Sound Blaster compatible."

A sound card outputs sound to speakers or earphones. As with any audio system, higher quality speakers provide richer sound and enhanced volume. If you're really serious about sound, consider a subwoofer for big bass sound. An Altec Lansing sound system with Dolby Surround Sound such as the one in Figure 6-5 uses only two speakers but envelops you in a 3-D soundscape for a price of about $300.

Figure 6-5

Altec Lansing's ACS500 produces a Dolby Surround Sound environment.

Computer Display Systems

| What is the relationship between the graphics card and the monitor? | A computer display system consists of a monitor and a **graphics card**, also called a **video display adapter** or **video card**. A graphics card is an expansion card that controls the signals that the computer sends to the monitor. The clarity of a computer display depends on the quality of the monitor and the capability of the graphics card. As a consumer, your goal is to buy the best display system that fits your budget.

InfoWeb

Display System 4

Factors that influence the quality of the monitor include screen size, maximum resolution, and dot pitch. **Screen size** is the measurement in inches from one corner of the screen diagonally across to the opposite corner. Most computer systems are packaged with a 14-inch or 15-inch screen. You might want to consider paying an additional $300 to $500 for a 17-inch monitor if you have a vision problem or if you often work with more than one program at the same time. With a 17-inch monitor you can switch to a high resolution to fit more windows on the screen, and the text will still be reasonably large.

Figure 6-6

As with a TV, the monitor's viewable image size is less than the screen size.

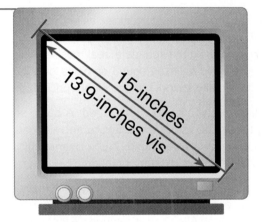

13.9-inches vis 15-inches

On most monitors, the viewable image does not stretch to the edge of the screen. Instead a black border makes the image smaller than, for example, the 15-inch size specified. Many computer vendors now include a measurement for the **viewable image size (vis)**. A 15-inch monitor has approximately a 13.9-inch vis as shown in Figure 6-6.

Dot pitch is a measure of image clarity; a smaller dot pitch means a crisper image. Technically, dot pitch is the distance in millimeters between like-colored pixels. A .28 or .26 dot pitch is typical for today's monitors.

The specifications for a monitor include its **maximum resolution**—the maximum number of pixels it can display. Standard resolutions include 640 x 480, 800 x 600, 1024 x 768, 1280 x 1024, and 1600 x 1200. Today's monitors typically have a maximum resolution of 1280 x 1024; but most people continue to use 640 x 480 resolution because it provides large, easy to read text. At higher resolutions the text appears smaller; but you can display a larger work area—for example, an entire page of a document.

It is important to realize that the maximum resolution you can use is determined by both the graphics card and the monitor. If your graphics card supports 1600 x 1200 resolution, but your monitor supports only 1280 x 1024, the maximum resolution you can use will be 1280 x 1024.

Most graphics cards use special graphics chips to boost performance. These **accelerated graphics cards** can greatly increase the speed at which images are displayed. An accelerated graphics card connected to a fast **PCI bus** can move data between the microprocessor and the graphics card as fast as the microprocessor can process it.

You can set your computer to display either 16, 256, 65,000, or 16 million colors. More colors provide more realistic images, but also require more computer resources. For higher resolutions and more colors, your graphics card needs more memory. To display photographic-quality images at 640 x 480 resolution, a graphics card should have at least 1 MB of memory. If you plan to display such images at 800 x 600 or 1024 x 768 resolutions, the graphics card should have 2 MB to 4 MB of memory. Figure 6-7 shows you how to change your display settings.

Figure 6-7

Change your display settings using Windows Control Panel.

Open the Display Properties dialog box.

Number of colors

Monitor resolution

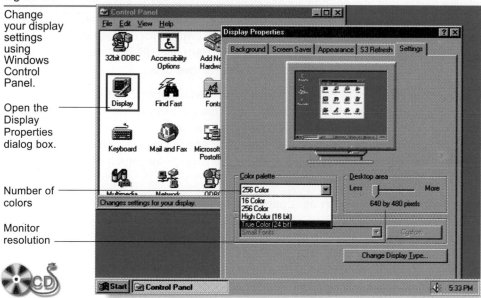

Comparing Notebook Displays

Is it true that the screen image on a notebook computer is not as good as the image on a desktop computer? Notebook computers do not use monitors, which are big, heavy, and require too much electrical power to run on batteries. Instead, notebooks have a flat panel liquid crystal display. A **liquid crystal display** (LCD) uses a technically sophisticated method of passing light through a thin layer of liquid crystal cells to produce an image. The resulting flat panel screen is lightweight and compact.

InfoWeb

Notebooks
5

Many older notebooks have a passive matrix screen, sometimes referred to as *dual-scan*. A **passive matrix screen** relies on timing to make sure the liquid crystal cells are illuminated. As a result, the process of updating the screen image does not always keep up with moving images, and the display can appear blurred. Passive matrix technology is not suitable for multimedia applications that include animations and videos.

An **active matrix screen**, referred to as **TFT** (thin film transistor), updates more rapidly and provides image quality similar to that of a monitor. Active matrix screens are essential for a crisp display of animations and video. However, active matrix screens are difficult to manufacture—approximately 50 percent are rejected due to defects—and add significantly to the price of a notebook computer.

Most notebook computers have a port to connect an external monitor. The advantage of an external monitor is the high-quality display. The disadvantage is that you need to disconnect the external monitor when you transport the computer.

Planning for Expansion

How can I make sure that I can expand my computer system? No matter how many bells and whistles your new computer system includes, you'll want to add to it in the future. Before you purchase a computer, make sure it has empty bays and unused expansion slots for additional storage devices and expansion cards.

The system unit case holds the main board and provides openings, called **bays**, for mounting disk, CD-ROM, and tape drives. An **external bay** provides an opening for installing a device that you need to access from the outside of the case. For example, you would install a floppy disk drive in an external bay because you need to insert and remove the floppy disks. An **internal bay** provides a mounting bracket for devices that do not need to be accessible from outside the system unit case. Hard disk drives typically use internal bays because they don't require you to insert and remove disks.

A system unit with many bays provides greater expansion capability. Notice in Figure 6-1 that the MicroPlus computer tower case has six bays. From the picture in the ad, it appears that there are five external bays, so one of the bays must be internal. The hard disk drive occupies one internal bay, while the floppy disk drive and CD-ROM each occupy one external bay. That leaves three external bays for expansion—probably enough for most home and business uses.

To add peripheral devices such as a printer, scanner, or graphics tablet, your computer needs an open port or expansion slot. In Chapter 5 you learned that you can plug an expansion card for a peripheral device into an expansion slot on the motherboard, or you can plug it into a serial, parallel, USB, or SCSI port. When you purchase a new computer, some ports and slots will already be connected to peripheral devices. Be sure to ask how many slots are free for later expansion.

Expanding a Notebook Computer

There doesn't seem to be much room in a notebook computer case—how do I add expansion cards? A **PCMCIA slot** (Personal Computer Memory Card International Association) is a special type of expansion slot developed for notebook computers, which do not have space in the case for full-size expansion slots and cards. A PCMCIA slot is a small, external slot into which you can insert a PCMCIA card, as shown in Figure 6-8.

Figure 6-8

To add a modem, sound card, or a hard disk to a notebook computer, plug in a PCMCIA card.

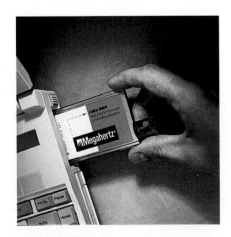

PCMCIA
6

PCMCIA cards, also called **PC cards**, are credit-card-sized circuit boards that incorporate an expansion card and device. So, for example, some PCMCIA cards contain a modem, others contain memory expansion, and others contain a hard disk drive. You can plug in and remove PCMCIA devices without turning the computer off, unlike desktop computer expansion cards. In this way you can switch from one PCMCIA device to another without disrupting your work.

PCMCIA slots are categorized by size. Type I slots accept only the thinnest PCMCIA cards such as memory expansion cards. Type II slots accept most of the popular PCMCIA cards—those that contain modems, sound cards, and network cards. Type III slots accept the thickest PCMCIA cards, which contain devices such as hard disk drives. Many notebooks provide a multipurpose PCMCIA slot that will accept two Type I cards, two Type II cards, or one Type III card.

Notebook computer expansion devices tend to be more expensive than those for desktop computers, but it is possible to use desktop peripherals with notebook computers if you have a docking station or a port replicatior.

A **docking station** is essentially an additional expansion bus into which you plug your notebook computer. The notebook provides the processor and RAM. The docking station provides expansion slots for cards that would not fit into the notebook case. It allows you to purchase inexpensive expansion cards and peripherals designed for desktops, instead of the more expensive devices designed specifically for notebooks. You sacrifice portability—you probably won't carry your docking station and external CD-ROM drive with you—but you gain the use of low-cost, powerful desktop peripherals. Figure 6-9 illustrates how a docking station works.

Figure 6-9

Notebook docking station

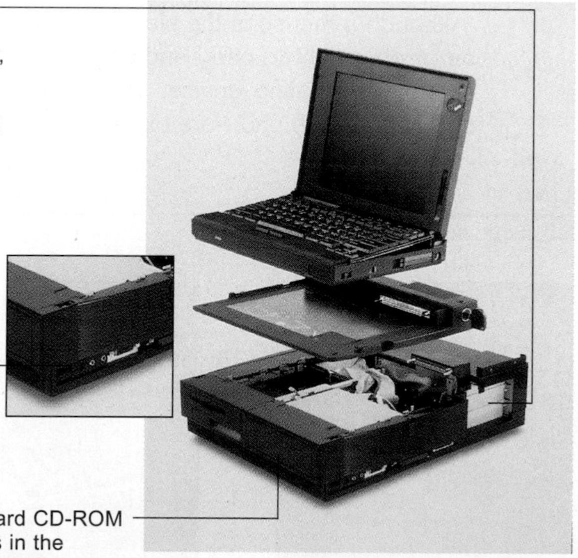

A docking station rests under or behind the notebook computer, and has room for speakers as well as other devices designed for full size desktop computers.

The docking station's external keyboard connector lets you use the keyboard from your desktop computer.

A standard CD-ROM drive fits in the docking station.

A **port replicator** is an inexpensive device that connects to a notebook computer by a bus connector plug; it contains a duplicate of the notebook computer's ports and makes it more convenient to connect and disconnect your notebook computer from devices such as an external monitor, mouse, and keyboard. Port replicators do not include expansion slots and typically cannot be used to add a sound card or CD-ROM drive to your notebook computer.

Selecting Input Devices

Should I settle for a standard keyboard and mouse? Most desktop computers include a standard keyboard and a mouse, but you might want to consider alternative input devices. Cases of carpal tunnel syndrome, a stress-related wrist injury, are on the rise. Intensive keyboard and mouse use are the suspected culprits. Ergonomically designed keyboards, such as the one in Figure 6-10 may prevent computer-related injuries.

Figure 6-10

Microsoft claims that its Natural Keyboard was based on ergonomic and usability research.

Although a mouse is the standard pointing device used with desktop computers, it can be inconvenient to carry and use while traveling. Most notebook computers include an alternative pointing device. The three most popular options—built-in track ball, track point, and touch pad—are explained in Figure 6-11.

Figure 6-11

Notebook pointing devices

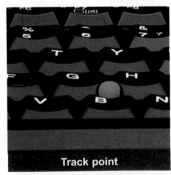

Track point

Track ball

Touch pad

A **track point** is a small eraser-like device embedded among the typing keys. To control the on-screen pointer, you push the track point up, left, right, or down. Buttons for clicking and double-clicking are located in front of the spacebar.

A **track ball** is like an upside-down mouse. By rolling the ball with your fingers, you control the on-screen pointer. Buttons for clicking are often located above or to the side of the track ball.

A **touch pad** is a touch-sensitive device. By dragging your finger over the surface, you control the on-screen pointer. Two buttons equivalent to mouse buttons are located in front of the touch pad.

Considerations for Notebook Power Sources

How long will a notebook computer run on batteries? Most notebook computers operate on power from either rechargeable batteries or a wall outlet. Because notebooks are designed for portability, the computing time provided by batteries is important. For example, an executive who frequently travels to Asia might want at least six hours of computing time during the 14-hour flight.

The length of time a notebook computer can operate from battery power depends on many factors. Fast processors, active matrix LCDs, and additional peripheral devices demand significant power from notebook computer batteries. Notebook manufacturers attempt to reduce power consumption by building power-saving features into their computers. These features automatically switch off the hard disk drive, LCD display, or even the processor if you do not interact with the computer after a short period of time. These devices are reactivated when you press a key or move the mouse.

On battery power, notebook computers typically provide two to four hours of operating time before the batteries need to be recharged. Most notebook computers use one of three types of batteries: Nicad (nickel cadmium), NiMH (nickel-metal hydride), or Lithium ion. Nicad batteries typically store less power than NiMH or Lithium ion batteries of equivalent size and weight. Therefore, Nicad batteries provide the shortest operating times. Most ads for notebook computers indicate the battery type and estimated computing times. Consumers need to be aware that many ads indicate maximum operating times. An ad that proclaims "Runs *up to* four hours!" might mean that the battery can supply four hours of operating time with no additional devices attached and with minimal use of the hard disk drive. Under typical working conditions the computer with fully charged batteries may run for significantly less than four hours.

The easiest way to extend the operating time of your notebook computer is to purchase extra batteries. When the first battery wears down, you can swap in a new battery and get back to work. Some notebook computers allow you to insert several batteries at the same time; as soon as one is discharged, the notebook switches to the next. Switching batteries while the computer is on is called a **hot swap** (Figure 6-12).

Figure 6-12

Notebook batteries are specially designed modules, made to slip into the notebook battery port.

Most notebook computers require an external AC adapter to plug into a wall outlet or to recharge the batteries. This adapter—about the size and weight of a small brick—can add significantly to the traveling weight of the notebook. Some notebook computers have eliminated the external adapter and require only a power cable to plug into a wall outlet. It is a good idea to use AC power whenever possible, such as when you use your notebook at home. Using AC power saves your batteries for when AC power is not available.

Choosing the Right Printer

InfoWeb

Printers
7

What kind of printer should I buy?   Occasionally a computer vendor offers a *hardware bundle* that includes a computer, printer, and software. More often, however, printers are sold separately so consumers can choose the quality, features, and price they want. Ink–jet and personal laser printers are most popular with today's consumers because they provide high-quality print on plain paper. Figure 6-13 is a guide to the features of laser and ink-jet printers. A dot-matrix printer is an older technology that creates letters and graphics by striking an inked ribbon with wires called pins. Athough these printers are inexpensive, their print-quality is not as crisp as an ink-jet or a laser printer. Today, dot-matrix printers are used mainly for applications that require multi-part forms.

Figure 6-13

Laser printers use the same technology as duplicating machines. A laser charges a pattern of particles on a drum which picks up a powdery black substance called toner. The toner is transferred onto paper that rolls past the drum. In the past, the price of laser printers limited their use to businesses and large organizations. Laser printer prices have decreased, however, making them affordable for individuals.

Color laser printers work by reprinting each page for each primary color. For each reprint, the paper must be precisely positioned so each color is printed in exactly the right spot. This dramatically increases the complexity of the print mechanism and the amount of time required to print each page.

Operating costs of laser printers include replacement toner cartridges and print drums. The estimated cost of laser printing is about $.05 per page.

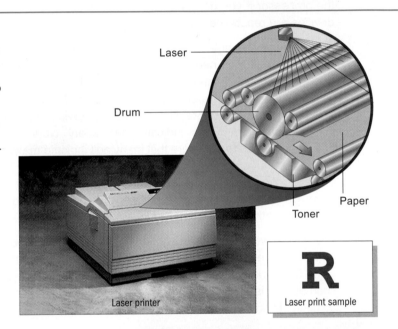

Laser printer

Laser print sample

Characteristics	
✓	Moderate to high price
✓	High-quality output
✓	More expensive to operate
✓	Cannot print multipart forms
✓	Fast
✓	Quiet
✓	Expensive, high-quality color
✓	Durable

Ink-jet printers produce characters and graphics by spraying ink onto paper. The print head is a matrix of fine spray nozzles. Patterns are formed by activating selected nozzles. An ink-jet printer typically forms a character in a 20 x 20 matrix, producing a high-quality printout.

Color ink-jet printers cost a little more, but produce much higher-quality output than color dot matrix printers. Using special paper, some color ink-jet printers can produce vivid, high-quality, color printouts. Ink-jet printers are inexpensive to operate, requiring only a new ink cartridge or ink refill. Estimated cost per page is about $.01.

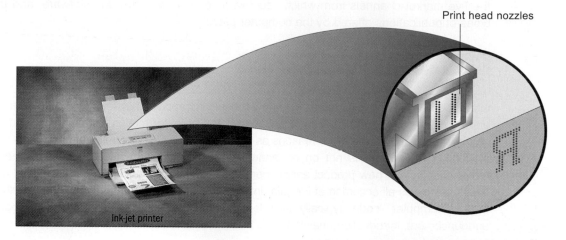

Print head nozzles

Ink-jet printer

R

Ink-jet print sample

Characteristics	
✓	Moderate price
✓	High-quality output
✓	Inexpensive to operate
✓	Cannot print multipart forms
✓	Slow
✓	Quiet
✓	Low-cost, low-quality color
✓	Durable

QuickCheck A

1. Most of today's PCs contain an Intel _____ model microprocessor.

2. If a computer features EDO RAM, you can expect better performance than from standard RAM. True or false? _____.

3. A SCSI hard drive has a slight performance advantage over a(n) _____ hard drive.

4. If you purchase a high-resolution monitor, the resolution of the graphics card is not important. True or false? _____.

5. Most notebook computers have either an active or passive matrix _____ display.

6. If you want to display photographic-quality images at 640 x 480 resolution, you need a graphics card with at least _____ of video memory.

7. A(n) _____ slot is important for adding peripheral devices to a notebook computer.

8. The best value for color printing is a(n) _____ printer.

☐ The Computer Industry

The **computer industry** consists of corporations and individuals that supply goods and services to people and organizations that use computers. The computer industry is in a continual state of change as new products appear and old products are discontinued; as corporations form, merge, and die; as corporate leadership shifts; as consumers' buying habits evolve; and as prices steadily continue to decrease. You will be a better informed consumer if you understand product life cycles, the tiered structure of computer vendors, the five market channels from which you can purchase hardware and software, and the types of publications offered by the computer press.

Hardware Product Life Cycle

Does the computer industry introduce new models annually? Automobile manufacturers introduce new models every year. The new models incorporate new and improved features and, therefore, give customers an incentive to buy. Computer manufacturers also introduce new models—and for the same reasons as their counterparts in the automotive industry. But the computer industry is not on an annual cycle so the computer marketplace seems rather chaotic with new product announcements and pre-announcements, ship dates, and availability dates all occurring at irregular intervals. In the computer industry, the life cycle of a new computer model typically includes five phases: product development, product announcement, introduction, maintenance, and retirement.

A **product announcement** declares a company's intention of introducing a new product. Products are announced at trade shows and press conferences. As a consumer, you should be wary of making purchasing decisions based on product announcements. A product announcement can precede the actual product by several years. Sometimes, products are announced but are never produced. These products are referred to as **vaporware**.

When a hardware product is first introduced, initial supplies of the product are generally low while manufacturing capacity increases to meet demand; consumers who want the scarce product must pay a relatively high price. As supply and demand for the product reach an equilibrium, the price of the product decreases slightly. Usually the price decrease is due to discounting by dealers, rather than a change in the manufacturer's list price. In Figure 6-14, you can see that the price of computers using the Pentium 133 MHz processor dropped significantly during the first year after their introduction.

Figure 6-14

The street price of the Compaq133 MHz Pentium computer shows a dramatic drop between April 1996 and June 1997.

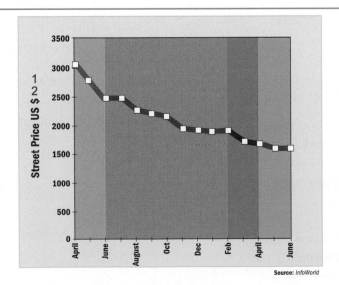

Source: *InfoWorld*

When a new product becomes available, it is usually added to the vendor's product line. The prices of products with older technology, such as Pentium 133 MHz processors, are reduced to keep them attractive to buyers. Gradually, the oldest products are discontinued as demand for them declines. As you can see from the ad in Figure 6-15 the less expensive products tend to have slower processors, less RAM, and lower-capacity hard disk drives. If your budget is not severely limited, a computer in the middle of a vendor's product line usually gives you the most computing power per dollar.

Figure 6-15

Microcomputer
product line

Gateway G-Series Multimedia PCs for the Home

G6-266 BEST BUY

- Intel 266MHz **Pentium II** Processor with 512K Cache
- 64MB DRAM
- **EV900 .26 Screen Pitch 19" Monitor** (18" viewable)
- 4MB 3-D 64-Bit Graphics
- 6.4GB 10ms Ultra ATA Hard Drive
- 12X min/24X max CD-ROM & 3.5" Diskette Drives
- Ensoniq Wavetable Audio
- **Boston Acoustics MicroMedia 3-Piece Speaker System**
- TelePath Modem *for Windows*, with x2 Technology™
- G-Series Mid-Tower Case
- 104+ Keyboard & MS IntelliMouse
- MS Windows 95
- Home Software Titles
- MMX Technology-Enhanced Software
- Gateway Gold Service & Support for G-Series PCs

$2999 As low as* $104/mo.

G6-300XL

- Intel 300MHz **Pentium II** Processor with 512K Cache
- 64MB DRAM
- **EV900 .26 Screen Pitch 19" Monitor** (18" viewable)
- 4MB 3-D 64-Bit Graphics
- TV/FM Tuner Card
- 8GB 8.5ms Ultra ATA Hard Drive
- **DVD-ROM Drive & DVD Decoder Card**
- 3.5" Diskette Drive
- Ensoniq Wavetable Audio
- **Boston Acoustics MicroMedia 3-Piece Speaker System**
- TelePath Modem *for Windows* with x2 Technology™
- G-Series Tower Case
- 104+ Keyboard & MS IntelliMouse
- MS Windows 95
- Home Software Titles
- MMX Technology-Enhanced Software
- Gateway Gold Service & Support for G-Series PCs

$3799 As low as* $132/mo.

G6-233

- Intel 233MHz **Pentium® II** Processor with 512K Cache
- 32MB DRAM
- CrystalScan700 .28 Screen Pitch 17" Monitor (15.9" viewable)
- 4MB 3-D 64-Bit Graphics
- 4GB 11ms Ultra ATA Hard Drive
- 12X min/24X max CD-ROM & 3.5" Diskette Drives
- Ensoniq Wavetable Audio
- **Boston Acoustics® MicroMedia™ 3-Piece Speaker System**
- TelePath Modem *for Windows*, with x2 Technology™
- G-Series Mid-Tower Case
- 104+ Keyboard & MS IntelliMouse
- MS Windows 95
- Home Software Titles
- MMX Technology-Enhanced Software
- Gateway Gold Service & Support for G-Series PCs

$2399 As low as* $84/mo.

*On-site service is available to most locations in the continental United States, Alaska, Hawaii, Puerto Rico and Canada after you and your Gateway technician determine an on-site visit is necessary. On-site service is provided by PC Technology Services, Inc. On-site is not available for any monitor, mouse, keyboard, E-1000 PC or portable system. Write or call for a free copy of the on-site service agreement.

GATEWAY2000
"You've got a friend in the business."®

800 - 846 - 2062

www.gateway.com

G-Series Multimedia PCs For The Home

Software Product Life Cycle

What's the difference between a version and a revision? Companies that produce computer software are referred to as **software publishers**. Software, like hardware, begins with an idea that is then shaped by a design team and marketing experts. For some software products, such as Windows 95, the software publisher orchestrates a glitzy rollout as described in Figure 6-16.

Figure 6-16

The glitzy roll-out of Microsoft Windows 95 included full-page ads in national newspapers, television ads, and product rallies.

Microsoft released Windows 95 on August 24, 1995. The Rolling Stones blast out their version of *Start me up!* during the product rollout. The Start button, a prominent new feature of Windows 95, is supposed to make the software easier to use.

The release of Windows 95 was a major event for investors as well as for consumers. It made front-page news in the *New York Times* (July 31, 1995).

James Dawson for The New York Times

Software Hype and Hopes

It is not a lunar landing or the cure for a disease. It is simply an improved version of a computer's operating system — like a more efficient transmission for a car. But 100 million personal computers use the Microsoft Corporation's software. And on Aug. 24, when Microsoft begins selling a new version of Windows, a multibillion-dollar economy will be set in motion. Besides deciding whether to buy the $100 Windows 95 software itself, consumers and corporations will need to consider whether to spend hundreds of dollars more on hardware and software that takes advantage of it — or thousands more to buy whole new machines. Meanwhile, the Justice Department is still considering whether to try to prevent Microsoft from including access to its new on-line service in Windows 95.

Coverage begins on page D1.

A new software product can be an entirely new product, a new **version** (also called a **release**) with significant enhancements, or a **revision** designed to add minor enhancements and eliminate bugs found in the current version. Before you buy software, you should be familiar with the difference between versions and revisions.

The original version of a software product is typically called version 1.0. Software publishers release a revision to fix bugs or make small changes to product features. The revision number is separated from the version number with a period. The first revision of a product will be 1.1. A major improvement to a software product would be indicated by a new version number, such as 2.0. You can usually find the revision and version numbers in a Windows program by clicking Help, then selecting About.

Software products undergo extensive testing before they are released. But even after testing, bugs inevitably remain. If you discover a software bug that effects usability, check with the software vendor to see if a revision of the product exists that includes with a "bug fix." The publisher will often supply a revision for free or nominal shipping costs.

"No one pays list price for software!" say industry analysts. A variety of discounts and special offers make it worth while to shop around. You can purchase a $495 software package for less than $100 if you're a smart shopper.

When a new software product first becomes available, the publisher often offers a special **introductory price** to entice customers. Several software products that now carry a list price of $495 were introduced at a special $99 price. Even after the introductory price expires, most vendors offer sizable discounts. The average dicounted price is referred to as the **street price**. Expect software with a list price of $495 to be offered for a street price of $299.

If you own an earlier version of a software package, you are probably eligible for the **version upgrade price**. By supplying the vendor with proof that you own the earlier version, you can get the new version at a discount. For example, if your word-processing software is version 7 and you want to upgrade to version 8, you can upgrade for $75 instead of paying the $299 street price.

A **competitive upgrade** is a special price offered to consumers who switch from one company's software product to the new version of a competitor's product. For example, suppose you've been using ClarisDraw, but you decide to switch to GRAFIX 7. You would pay $149 for a competitive upgrade, instead of paying the $399 street price as shown in Figure 6-17.

Figure 6-17

Competitive software upgrades provide an incentive for switching to a competitor's product.

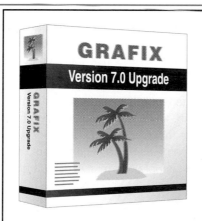

GRAFIX
Version 7.0 Upgrade

GRAFIX 7
Competitive Upgrade
for only
$149.95

• Windows qualifying products: Illustrator, Deneba Canvas, CorelDraw, ClarisDraw, or Freehand. Mail or fax a photocopy of either the user manual or the original program disk

(full price is $399)

Wholesale Computers 800-123-4567

Unlike computer hardware products, older versions of software do not remain in the vendor's product line. Soon after a new version of a software product is released, the software publisher usually stops selling earlier versions. When a publisher offers a new version of the software you are using, it is a good idea to upgrade; but you can wait for several months until the initial rush for technical support on the new product decreases. If you don't upgrade, you might find that the software publisher offers minimal technical support for older versions of the program. Also, if you let several versions go by without upgrading, you might have to purchase the software at full price when you eventually decide to upgrade.

Market Tiers

What accounts for price differences for computers with the same specifications from different vendors? Since 1981, hundreds of companies have produced personal computers. Industry analysts often refer to three tiers or categories of microcomputer companies, although not all analysts agree on which companies belong in each tier.

The top tier consists of large companies that have been in the computer business for more than ten years and have an identifiable percentage of total computer sales—companies such as IBM, Apple, Compaq, and Hewlett-Packard. The second tier includes newer companies with high sales volume, but with somewhat less financial resources than companies in the first tier. Most analysts place companies such as Gateway, Dell, and Packard Bell in the second tier. The third tier consists of smaller startup companies that sell primarily through mail order.

Computer prices vary by tier. Computers from the top-tier vendors generally are more expensive than computers offered by second-tier or third-tier vendors. For example, a computer with specifications similar to the MicroPlus computer featured in the ad at the beginning of this chapter might cost $2,699 from a first-tier vendor, $2,199 from a second-tier vendor, and $1,999 from a third-tier vendor.

Why do these prices vary by tier? Because first-tier companies often have higher overhead costs, management is often paid higher salaries, and substantial financial resources are devoted to research and development. The first-tier companies are responsible for many of the innovations that have made computers faster, more powerful, and more convenient. Also, many consumers believe that computers sold by first-tier companies are better quality and are a safe purchasing decision. They believe there is less risk that computers from first-tier companies will quickly become obsolete or that the vendor will go out of business.

Computers from second-tier companies are generally less expensive than those from the first tier, although the quality can be just as good. Most PCs are constructed from off-the-shelf circuit boards, cables, cases, and chips. This means that the components in the computers sold by second-tier companies are often the same as those in computers sold by the first tier. The quality of the off-the-shelf parts, however, is not uniform; it is difficult for the consumer to determine the quality of parts.

Second-tier companies often maintain their low prices by minimizing operating costs. These companies have a limited research and development budget. Also, they try to maintain a relatively small work force by contracting with another company to provide repair and warranty work.

Computers from third-tier companies often appear to be much less expensive than those in other tiers. Sometimes this reflects the low overhead costs of a small company, but other times it reflects poor-quality components. A consumer who is knowledgeable about the market and has technical expertise can often get a bargain on a good-quality computer from a third-tier company. But some consumers think it's risky to purchase computers from third-tier companies. Third-tier companies are smaller and perhaps more likely to go out of business, leaving their customers without technical support.

Marketing Channels

Is it safe to buy a computer by mail? Computer hardware and software are sold by marketing outlets or "channels," as shown in Figure 6-18.

Figure 6-18

Marketing channels

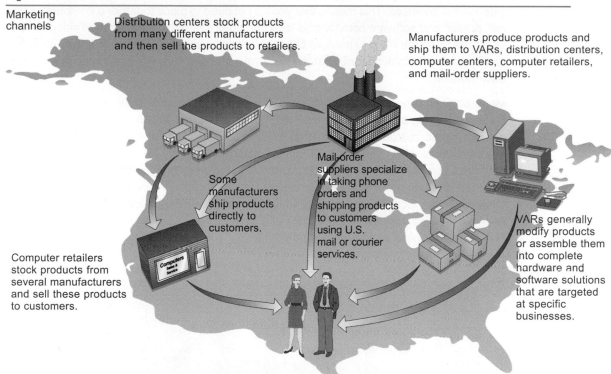

Distribution centers stock products from many different manufacturers and then sell the products to retailers.

Manufacturers produce products and ship them to VARs, distribution centers, computer centers, computer retailers, and mail-order suppliers.

Some manufacturers ship products directly to customers.

Mail-order suppliers specialize in taking phone orders and shipping products to customers using U.S. mail or courier services.

Computer retailers stock products from several manufacturers and sell these products to customers.

VARs generally modify products or assemble them into complete hardware and software solutions that are targeted at specific businesses.

A **computer retail store** purchases computer products from a manufacturer or distribution center and then sells the products to consumers. Computer retail stores are either small local shops or nationwide chains that specialize in the sale of microcomputer software and hardware. The employees at computer retail stores are often knowledgeable about a variety of computer products and can help you select a hardware or software product to fit your needs. Many computer retail stores also offer classes and training sessions, answer questions, provide technical support, and repair hardware products. A computer retail store is often the best source of supply for buyers who are likely to need assistance after the sale, such as beginning computer users or those with complex computer systems such as networks. But computer retail stores can be a fairly expensive channel for hardware and software. Their prices reflect the cost of purchasing merchandise from a distributor, maintaining a retail storefront, and hiring technically qualified staff.

Mail-order suppliers take orders by mail or telephone and ship the product directly to consumers. Mail-order suppliers generally offer low prices but provide limited service and support. A mail-order supplier is often the best source of products for buyers who are unlikely to need support or who can troubleshoot problems with the help of a technical support person on the telephone. Experienced computer users who can install components, set up their software, and do their own troubleshooting are often happy with mail-order suppliers. Inexperienced computer users might not be satisfied with the support and assistance they receive from mail-order suppliers.

Value-added resellers (VARs) combine commercially available products with specialty hardware or software to create a computer system designed to meet the needs of a specific industry. Although VARs charge for their expertise, they are often the only source for a system that really meets the needs of a specific industry. For example, if you own a video rental store and want to automate your store, the best type of vendor might be a VAR. The VAR can offer you a complete hardware and software package that is tailored to the video rental business. This means that you do not need to piece together a computer, scanner, printer, and software components for a computer system to keep track of video rentals. VARs are often the most expensive channel for hardware and software, but their expertise can be crucial in making sure that the hardware and software work correctly in a specific environment.

Manufacturer direct refers to hardware manufacturers that sell their products directly to consumers using a sales force or mail order. The sales force usually targets large corporate or educational customers where large volume sales can cover costs and commissions. Manufacturers also use mail order to distribute directly to individual consumers. Manufacturers can sell their products directly to consumers for a lower price than when they sell them through retailers, but they cannot generally offer the same level of support and assistance as a local retailer. In an effort to improve customer support, some manufacturers have established customer support lines and provide repair services at the customer's home or place of business as shown in Figure 6-19.

Figure 6-19

Many reputable mail-order vendors offer on-site service in the continental U.S., Alaska, Hawaii, and Canada. Make sure you ask about service policies. Some computer components are not covered by the on-site service plan.

The Computer Press

Where can I get reliable information about computers to help me make informed purchases? Computer publications provide information on computers, computing, and the computer industry. The type of computer publication you need depends on the kind of information you want.

InfoWeb

Publications
8

Computer magazines contain articles and advertisements for the latest computer products. One of the earliest computer magazines, *Byte*, began publication in August 1975 and still remains one of the most widely read sources of computer information. The success of *Byte* might be attributed to its wide coverage of computers and computing topics. Many magazines that featured only a single type of computer, such as the Apple II, had staying power only as long as the computer maintained good sales. There are exceptions, however, magazines for specific computers, such as *MacWorld*, have a healthy subscription list.

Computer magazines generally target users of both personal and business computers. Articles focus on product evaluations, product comparisons, and practical tips for installing hardware and using software. These magazines are full of product advertisements, which are useful if you want to keep informed about the latest products available for your computer. You can find computer magazines such as those in Figure 6-20 on virtually any newsstand and at the library.

Figure 6-20

Popular
computer
magazines

Computer industry trade journals have a different focus than computer magazines because they target computer professionals, rather than consumers. Computer trade journals, such as *InfoWorld* and *Computer Reseller News*, focus on company profiles, product announcements, and sales techniques. Often free subscriptions to trade journals are given to corporate decision makers because advertisers want them to be aware of their products. Trade journals are not always available on newsstands, and subscriptions are not always available to the general public.

Computing journals offer an academic perspective on computers and computing issues. Such journals focus on research in computing, with articles on such topics as the most efficient sorting technique to use in a database management system, the implication of copyright law for educational institutions, or the prevalence of spreadsheet use by executives in Fortune 500 companies. Academic journals rarely advertise hardware and software products because it might appear that advertisers could influence the content of articles.

An article in a computing journal is usually "refereed," which means that it is evaluated by a committee of experts who determine if the article is original and based on sound research techniques. The best place to find computing journals is in a university library. Some of the most respected journals in the computing field include *Communications of the ACM* (Association for Computing Machinery), *Communications of the IEEE* (Institute of Electrical and Electronics Engineers), *SIAM* (Society of Industrial and Applied Mathematics) *Journal on Computing*, and *Journal of Information Science*.

Web
Resources
9

Internet sites are an excellent source of information about the computer industry and computer products. Several computer magazines and trade journals maintain Internet sites with articles from back issues. Current issues are also available from some sites for a fee. Many computer companies have Internet sites where consumers can access up-to-date information about products and services. Here you can usually find product specifications, product announcements, sales literature, technical support forums, and pricing information.

Computer
TV
10

Television shows about computers provide hardware and software reviews, tips, and computer industry news for new and experienced users. The PCTV network produces shows such as *The Internet Cafe*, *Computer Chronicles* (Figure 6-21), *@Home*, and *User Group*. CNET produces *The Web*, *The New Edge*, and *CNET Central*. Jones Cable Network and Mind Extension University offer *Using the Computer in Business*, *The Home Computing Show*, and *New Media News*. CNN Financial Network includes a high tech overview called *Digital Jam*, also available in video format on the Internet. ZDTV, operated by Ziff-Davis, has teamed up with Microsoft to broadcast technology news on MSNBC. Most of these networks are carried on cable TV. Check your cable listings for airtimes.

Figure 6-21

For over 12 years, viewers have tuned into *Computer Chronicles* on the Public Broadcasting System. Hosted by Steward Chiefet, the show features demonstrations of new hardware and software products.

The computer industry has many **industry analysts** who monitor industry trends, evaluate industry events, and make predictions about what the trends seem to indicate. Computer industry analysts range from professional financial analysts, who report on the computer industry for the *Wall Street Journal* and *Forbes* magazine, to the "rumor-central" analysts, who spark up the back pages of trade journals and computer magazines with the latest gossip about new products.

If you want to invest in a computer corporation's stock, the financial analysts might offer some good insights. If you want to invest in a personal computer, rumor-central columns, such as the one in Figure 6-22 are the place to get the scoop about product shortages, hardware glitches, software bugs, and impending customer service problems.

Figure 6-22

Robert X. Cringely is one of the best known computer columnists. Look for his column, *Notes From the Field*, on the back pages of *InfoWorld* magazine.

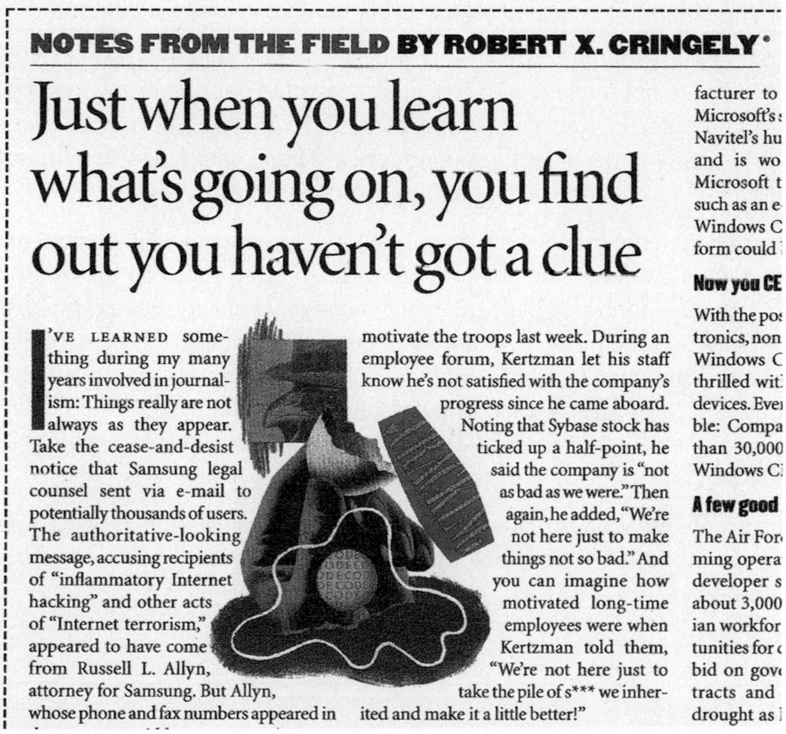

NOTES FROM THE FIELD BY ROBERT X. CRINGELY

Just when you learn what's going on, you find out you haven't got a clue

I'VE LEARNED something during my many years involved in journalism: Things really are not always as they appear. Take the cease-and-desist notice that Samsung legal counsel sent via e-mail to potentially thousands of users. The authoritative-looking message, accusing recipients of "inflammatory Internet hacking" and other acts of "Internet terrorism," appeared to have come from Russell L. Allyn, attorney for Samsung. But Allyn, whose phone and fax numbers appeared in

motivate the troops last week. During an employee forum, Kertzman let his staff know he's not satisfied with the company's progress since he came aboard. Noting that Sybase stock has ticked up a half-point, he said the company is "not as bad as we were." Then again, he added, "We're not here just to make things not so bad." And you can imagine how motivated long-time employees were when Kertzman told them, "We're not here just to take the pile of s*** we inherited and make it a little better!"

facturer to
Microsoft's
Navitel's hu
and is wo
Microsoft t
such as an e
Windows C
form could

Now you CE

With the po
tronics, non
Windows C
thrilled wit
devices. Eve
ble: Compa
than 30,000
Windows C

A few good

The Air For
ming opera
developer s
about 3,000
ian workfor
tunities for
bid on gov
tracts and
drought as

QuickCheck B

1. Products that are announced, but never shipped are called _____.

2. If your budget is not severely limited, a computer in the middle of a vendor's product line usually gives you the most computing power per dollar. True or false? _____

3. A(n) _____ upgrade is a special price offered to consumers who switch from one company's software product to a new version of a competitor's product.

4. Computer vendors are often categorized into three _____ based on market share and financial resources.

5. Computer books offer the most up-to-date information about computer products. True or false? _____

6. A(n) _____ sells complete computer solutions for a specific industry such as video stores or medical offices.

C Computer Industry Careers

InfoWeb

BLS 11

The $290 billion computer industry employs more than 1.5 million people. Over the past 50 years, it has created jobs that never before existed and financial opportunities for those with motivation, creative ideas, and technical skills. Since 1970, high-tech business has produced more than 7,000 millionaires and more than a dozen billionaires. According to the U.S. Bureau of Labor Statistics, computer and data processing services are projected to be third fastest growing industry; systems analysts, computer engineers, and data processing equipment repairers are expected to be among the 30 fastest growing occupations between now and 2005.

Computer Industry Job Categories

Does the computer industry include every job that involves a computer? It seems today that just about everyone uses computers at work. In fact it is difficult to find a job nowadays that does not make use of computers in some capacity. However, not everyone who uses a computer is employed in the computer industry. For a clear picture of computer jobs, it is useful to consider three categories. These categories can be somewhat loosely defined as computer-specific jobs, computer-related jobs, and computer-use jobs.

Computer-specific jobs—such as computer programming, chip design, and Webmaster— would not exist without computers. **Computer-related jobs**, on the other hand, are variations of more generic jobs that you might find in any industry. For example, jobs in computer sales, high-tech recruiting, and graphics design are similar to sales, recruiting and design jobs in the automobile or medical industries. **Computer-use jobs** require the use of computers to accomplish tasks in fields other than computing. Writers, reporters, accountants, retail clerks, medical technicians, auto mechanics, and many others use computers in the course of every day job activities.

Of the three categories, computer-specific jobs require the most preparation and will appeal to those who like working with, learning about, and thinking about computers (Figure 6-23).

Figure 6-23

Jay Nunamaker, a computer science professor and chairman of a computer consulting firm explores how computers can facilitate group interaction.

Computer-Specific Jobs

What are the qualifications for computer jobs? Jobs for people who design and develop computer hardware and software require a high degree of training and skill. A college degree is required for virtually any of these jobs, and many require a master's degree or doctorate.

College
Connection
12

Most colleges offer degrees in computer engineering, computer science, and information systems that provide good qualifications for computer-specific jobs. There is some overlap between these fields of study, but the emphasis for each is different.

Computer engineering degrees require a good aptitude for engineering, math, and electronics. Career opportunities for computer engineering graduates focus on the design of computer hardware and peripheral devices, often at the chip level (Figure 6-24).

Figure 6-24

Technicians in a chip fabrication plant wear "Bunny Suits" to maintain a sterile environment.

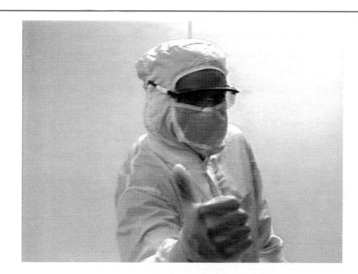

Computer science degrees require a good aptitude for math and computer programming. The main object of study in a computer science program is the digital computer, and the main objective is to make the computer work effectively and efficiently. Computer science graduates generally find entry-level jobs as programmers and Webmasters with good possibilities for advancement as software engineers, object-oriented/GUI developers, and project-leaders in technical applications development.

Information systems degree programs focus on the application of computers in a business or organizational environment. Coursework in business, accounting, computer programming, communications, systems analysis, and human psychology are usually required. For students who want to become computer professionals but lack strong math aptitude, most academic advisors recommend the information systems degree. An information systems degree usually leads to an entry-level programming or PC support job with good possibilities for advancement to systems analyst, project manager, database administrator, network manager, or other management positions.

Working Conditions

What are the advantages of working in the computer industry? Graduates with computer engineering, computer science, and information systems degrees generally work in a comfortable office or laboratory environment. Many high-tech companies offer employee-friendly working conditions that include childcare, flexible hours, and the opportunity to telecommute. As in any industry, the exact nature of a job depends on the company and the particular projects that are in the works. Some jobs and some projects are more interesting than others.

Many computer professionals like to pick and choose projects, which might account for the recent trend toward contract work and consulting. Contract programmers, consultants, and technical writers are self-employed, seek out short-term projects, and negotiate a per-project compensation rate. They set their own schedule, but often work 60-hour weeks. It takes motivation and discipline to be successful, but the rewards include control over your working environment.

In the computer industry, as in most industries, management positions command the highest salaries and salary levels increase with experience. Salaries vary by geographic location. In the Northeast and on the West Coast salaries tend to be higher than in the Southeast, Midwest, Southwest, and Canada. Figure 6-25 provides sample 1997 salaries for computer-related jobs in the Southeastern United States.

Figure 6-25

1997 computer industry salaries

Job Title	Salary (1997)	Job Title	Salary (1997)
Chief information officer	$122,000	Software engineer	$54,500
Information systems director	91,000	Senior database analyst	61,200
Manager of analysts and programmers	74,100	Object-orientated/GUI developer	58,100
Manager of systems programmers and technical support personnel	73,100	Web/Internet developer	51,700
Network manager	72,000	Network administrator	49,550
Project leader	62,000	Systems analyst/programmer	52,400
Database administration manager	69,800	PC applications specialist	41,900
Telecommunications manager	66,500	Technical writer	31,400
Data center manager	63,600	Consultant	58,100
PC workstation manager	48,500	Computer sales representative	74,100
Senior software engineer	64,000	Computer assembly worker	25,000

Preparing for a Computer Career

How do I prepare for a career in the computer industry? Education and experience are the keys to a challenging computer job with good potential for advancement. In addition to a degree in computer science, computer engineering, or information systems, think about how you can get on-the-job experience through internships, military service, government-sponsored training programs, or work-study programs. However, these experiences are only supplements to formal education. Most computer industry employers will not consider an applicant without a bachelor's degree in an appropriate field.

Figure 6-26

Not all computer science majors wear their computers around campus, but Computer Science and Information Systems degrees provide excellent credentials for a career in computing.

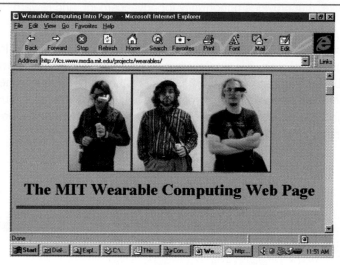

The MIT Wearable Computing Web Page

InfoWeb

Organizations
13

Owning your own computer, installing software, and troubleshooting provide good basic experience and familiarity with mass-market computing standards. You might pick up additional experience from projects sponsored by clubs and organizations. The three largest computer organizations in North America are the Association for Computing Machinery (ACM), the Association of Information Technology Professionals (AITP), and Institute of Electrical and Electronic Engineers - Computer Society (IEEE-CS).

InfoWeb

Certification
14

To beef up your credentials, you might also consider certification. The Institute for Certification of Computing Professionals (ICCP) has a regular schedule of comprehensive exams for computer jobs such as computer programming, systems analysis, and network management. If you are considering a career in computer network management, it might be worthwhile to complete the test for Novell NetWare or Microsoft NT certification. Certification for application software such as Microsoft Word, Excel, PowerPoint, and Access are also available.

Keep track of the job market in your area of specialty. You'll want to develop a good mix of generalized knowledge and specialized skills. Generalized knowledge, and your ability to apply it, will help you generate creative and feasible solutions to problems. Specialized skills such as experience with Visual Basic programming will give you marketable tools to match specific jobs. The trick is to anticipate which computer skills will be in demand when you next search for a job. By obtaining those skills, you put yourself in a good competitive position against other applicants.

Use Technology to Find a Job

How do I find a computer industry job? The first step in a job search is to realistically assess your qualifications and needs. Your qualifications include your computer skills, educational background, previous work experience, communications skills, and personality. By comparing your qualifications to the requirements for a job, you can assess your chances of being hired. Your needs include your preferred geographical location, working conditions, corporate lifestyle, and salary. By comparing your needs to the information you discover about a prospective employer, you can assess your chances of enjoying a job once you've been hired. Several excellent books and Web sites provide information to help you assess your qualifications and needs. It is an important step. Your goal is not to "get a job," but to get a job you like, that provides opportunity for advancement, and rewards you with a good salary.

InfoWeb

Career
Resources
15

Today, researching the job market has become much easier, thanks to the Internet. In 1997, an estimated one out of every five employers in North America used the Internet for recruiting. Popular Web-based "want ads" post descriptions of job openings. Usually the employers pay for these postings, so access is free to prospective employees. Web sites, such as the one in Figure 6-27, include general information about jobs, employment outlook, and salaries in computer-industry jobs.

Figure 6-27

One of the most popular career Web sites

Because the salaries for most jobs are vaguely stated as "commensurate with experience," it is useful to discover what you're worth by studying Web-based salary reports. If you're asked to name a figure during a job interview, you will then be able to provide your prospective employer with your salary requirements, based on occupation, experience, and geographic area. The Web is not the only source of job listings. You can and should consult newspaper want ads, attend job fairs, and consider using the services of a professional recruiter.

You will need to prepare a resume with your career goal, experience, skills, and education. Some career counselors suggest that high-tech candidates should not follow many of the rules delineated in traditional resume guidebooks. For example, if you have a substantial list of technical skills, you might not be able to limit your resume to a single page. Your resume should demonstrate technical savvy without appearing overly "packaged." For example, dot-matrix printing is hard to read and old fashioned, but would not automatically qualify for the wastebasket in a stack of engineering resumes. By contrast, unless you're applying for a job as a Web site or graphical designer, you don't want your resume to look like a page from *Wired* magazine. Such advice is interesting, but remember that corporate cultures differ. What might get your foot in the door at a shirt-and-tie corporation such as IBM could be different than at a jeans-and-sandals start-up such as Yahoo! Don't despair. You can use your word processor to tailor your resume to the corporate culture of each prospective employer.

Contact Prospective Employers

| How do I get my information out? | The standard procedure for mailing letters of application and resumes remains valid even in this age of high technology. However, alternatives sometimes prove even more effective. Many companies will accept resumes by fax to reduce the time it takes to process applicants. E-mail is another route that speeds up the process. Use it if you can, and make sure you include your e-mail address on your application materials. In addition to speeding communication, using e-mail demonstrates your familiarity with one of the most pervasive technology tools in the world today.

You can post your resume on a placement Web site where it can be viewed by corporate recruiters. Some of these Web sites charge a small fee for posting resumes; others are free. You can also post your resume along with your personal Web page, if you have one. This is particularly effective if you design these pages to showcase technical skills that are applicable to the job you're seeking. College students beware. Some employers have discovered much more than they bargained for by visiting the Web pages created by job applicants. If you are searching for employment, take a moment to look at your Web page through the eyes of a middle-aged, conservative, corporate recruiter. Remember that this page is public. Even if you don't include its Web address in your application materials, it is not difficult to find.

QuickCheck C

1. The U.S. Bureau of Labor Statistics estimates that computer and data processing services will be the fastest growing industry between now and 2001.
   True or false? _____

2. A(n) _____ degree program focuses on the application of computers in a business or organizational environment.

3. High-tech salaries tend to be highest on the West Coast and in the _____ section of the United States.

4. Education and _____ are the keys to a challenging computer job with good potential for advancement.

5. The AITP, ACM, and IEEE-CS are professional _____.

6. In addition to using Web-based job listings, you can consult newspaper want ads, attend _____, and use the services of a professional recruiter.

U s e r F o c u s

D Computer Shopping Strategies

If you are like most consumers in pursuit of a good computer value, you will talk to salespeople, read computer magazines, look through computer catalogs, and chat with your friends who own computers. Here are some shopping strategies that should help you purchase a computer that meets your needs within a budget you can afford.

Determine Your Needs and Budget

Buying a Computer

Where do I start? Start by setting a budget and stick to it! Computer vendors have very carefully priced the computers in their model line so that you will be tempted to spend "just a few hundred dollars more" to get a model with more features. The trouble is that if you decide to spend that few hundred dollars, you will be tempted to spend just a little more to get even more features.

Once you have established a budget, consider how you plan to use the computer. A computer can be a valuable tool for completing your college degree, it can be a useful educational tool for your children, and it can increase your competitive edge in your career. Consider these factors before you begin shopping for a computer:

Notebook or desktop? If you plan to carry your computer with you, a notebook computer is the optimal choice. However, a notebook costs more than a similarly configured desktop, so you will pay for portability or give up features.

Consumer Info 16

Multimedia? If you want to use multimedia applications, you should buy a system with a CD-ROM drive and sound card. Multimedia notebooks can be pricey, but a docking bay might allow you to add multimedia capabilities and still stay within your budget.

Compatibility? Most computers sold today are IBM compatible PCs. However, you should consider a Macintosh computer if most of the computers in your school are Macintoshes, if the computer is for your children who are using Macintosh computers in school, or if Macintosh is the major computer used in your career field.

Printer? Remember that you must include the cost of a printer in your budget. Unless you need to print multipart forms, you should not buy a dot matrix printer. A black-and-white ink jet printer is in the same price range, but it uses single-sheet paper and produces better print quality. Inexpensive laser printers, referred to as "personal laser printers," cost $100 to $300 more than a black-and-white ink-jet printer. Also consider a printer's operational cost. If you are on a very limited budget, it is easier to replace a $15 ink cartridge than a $100 toner cartridge.

Collect the Facts

What information do I need? Before you make a decision, shop around to collect information on pricing, features, and support. Although you might be tempted to buy the computer with the lowest price and best features, don't forget to consider the warranty and the quality of the support you are likely to get from the vendor. The checklist in Figure 6-28 will help you gather facts about pricing, features, and support.

Figure 6-28

Comparison data sheet

Computer Purchase Data Sheet
Specifications

Computer brand, model and manufacturer: _____

Processor type: _____

Processor speed: _____ MHz

MMX technology? ❑ Yes   ❑ No

RAM capacity: _____ MB

Number and size of floppy disk drives: _____

Capacity of hard disk drive: _____ GB

Speed of CD-ROM drive: _____

Capacity of tape drive: _____

Amount of cache memory: _____ KB

Monitor screen size: _____ vis or inches

Maximum monitor resolution: _____

Amount of memory on graphics card: _____ MB

Modem speed: _____ bps

Number of expansion slots: _____

Upgrade path for new processor? ❑ Yes   ❑ No

Operating system: _____

Mouse included? ❑ Yes   ❑ No

Sound card and speakers included? ❑ Yes   ❑ No

Value of bundled software: $_____

Service and Support

What is the warranty period? _____ years

Does the warranty cover parts and labor? ❑ Yes   ❑ No

Does the vendor have a good reputation for service? ❑ Yes   ❑ No

Are technical support hours adequate? ❑ Yes   ❑ No

Free 800 number for technical support? ❑ Yes   ❑ No

Can I contact technical support without waiting on hold for a long time? ❑ Yes   ❑ No

Are technical support people knowledgeable? ❑ Yes   ❑ No

Can I get my computer fixed in an acceptable time period? ❑ Yes   ❑ No

Are the costs and procedures for fixing the computer acceptable? ❑ Yes   ❑ No

Are other users satisfied with this brand and model of computer? ❑ Yes   ❑ No

Is the vendor likely to stay in business? ❑ Yes   ❑ No

Are the computer parts and components standard? ❑ Yes   ❑ No

Price: $_____

Evaluate the Facts

How do I make the decision?   After you have collected the facts, your decision might be obvious. In an ideal situation, a local vendor with a reputation for excellent support is selling a computer with features and price comparable to those sold by many reputable mail-order vendors. In the real world, however, your local vendor's price might be higher, and then your decision is not so clear. You might want to make a decision support worksheet like the one shown in Figure 6-29.

Figure 6-29

Decision support worksheet

1. List at least two possible options. This worksheet is designed to help you choose between Computer #1 and Computer #2.

2. List the factors that are important criteria for making your selection.

3. Assign a weight to each factor using a scale of 1 to 10.

4. After you research the options, assign a raw score for each factor.

5. Add a formula in the spreadsheet to multiply the raw score by the weighting factor to produce a weighted score.

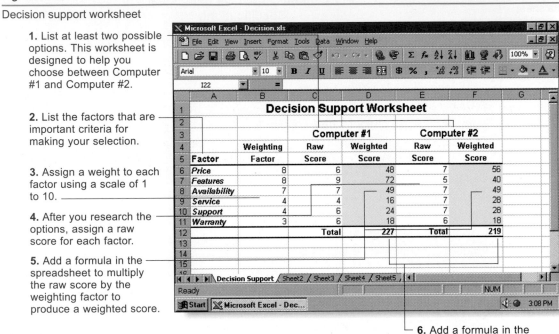

6. Add a formula in the spreadsheet to total the weighted scores for each option. The option that has the highest total is the best system for you to purchase.

EndNote   One strategy for buying a computer is to decide how much you want to spend and then buy whatever computer a major manufacturer offers at that price. You probably won't get a great deal. You might not even get a computer that really meets your needs. But you will have a computer. If you want to be a more effective consumer in today's computer marketplace, you must understand the terminology in computer ads and use magazines, journals, and the Internet to keep up-to-date on the latest computer models. If you are planning a career in computing, it is essential to keep track of current events in the computer industry so you can develop marketable skills and select an employer that produces state-of-the-art products and has an employee-friendly working environment.

InfoWeb

InfoWeb

Chapter
Links

The InfoWeb is your guide to print, film, television, and electronic resources. Use it to obtain updates on quickly changing technical information and to locate information for research papers. If you're using the New Perspectives CD-ROM, click the InfoWeb icon on the left side of this paragraph to access the online InfoWeb links. Otherwise, use your Web browser and type in the address of the New Perspectives site: www.cciw.com/np3. At the New Perspectives site you'll find up-to-date links to the topics covered in this chapter.

1 Which Chip?

Since 1993, Intel has introduced four versions of the Pentium processor. Competitors AMD and Cyrix have introduced additional work-alike chips. Which chip is best for your computing needs? Articles such as "Picking Your Processor" by Michael Slater (*Computer Shopper* May 1997; **www5.zdnet.com/cshopper/content/9705/cshp0083.html**) and "What's the Best CPU?" by Bill Howard (*PC Magazine*, June 10, 1997; **www8.zdnet.com/pcmag/issues/1611/bhoward.htm**) can help you answer that question. More information on the Web is in *The Link* newsletter article "The Silicon Shuffle" by Dinos Lambropoulos at the Earthlink Network site **www.earthlink.net/daily/tuesday/microprocessors**. You can get the offical party line about these chips at the Web sites for Intel at **www.intel.com**, AMD at **www.amd.com**, and Cyrix at **www.cyrix.com**.

2 Benchmarks

Want to test your own PC to see how it performs on standard benchmark tests? You can download benchmark tests and test your own PC using *PC Magazine's* Winstone 97 and WinBench 97 benchmark test files at **www8.zdnet.com/pcmag/pclabs/bench/bench.htm**. You'll find links to results of various benchmark tests at Scott Wainner's System Optimization site, **www.sysopt.com/bench.html**, and the Ideas International site at **www.ideasinternational.com/benchmark/bench.html**.

3 Sound Systems

You can purchase $10 speakers for your computer or you can purchase $500 speakers. What's the difference? The quality of sound you hear depends on the quality of your speakers, the capabilities of your sound card, and the quality of the sound file you're playing. To compare the quality of sound produced by expensive wave table synthesis, download the files at **pubweb.nwu.edu/~jll544/sndsmpl.html** and take the wavetable sound card test drive. Interested in Dolby Surround sound? CNET reports on the Altec's ACS500 speaker system at **w w w . c n e t . c o m / C o n t e n t / R e v i e w s / Compare/Speakers/ss02b.html**. For an update on the latest speaker technology, check out Altec Lansing's Web site at **www.altecmm.com** and click the Product Selector icon. Then check out the site of other popular speaker vendors: Creative Labs at **www.creativelabs.com**, Labtec at **www.labtec.com**, and Koss at **www.koss.com**.

4 Display System: Two to Tango

It takes two to tango and your display system is only as good as your monitor and graphics card. For advice on choosing a monitor, read page 123 of the October 7, 1996 issue of *Computerworld* magazine and search for "How to Select a PC Display System" at **www.techweb.com/encyclopedia**. At the TechWeb site you'll also find an article on "How to Buy a Video Card". Look for comparative reviews such as "Big Screens for Big Jobs" (*Byte* January 1997; **www.byte.com/art/9701/sec8/art1.htm**) and "13 Graphics Cards for Business" (*Byte* February 1997; **www.byte.com/art/9702/sec8/sec8.htm**) For an update on current monitor models, connect to vendor sites: NEC Technologies, Inc at **www.nec.com**, Sony Electronics Inc. at **www.sony.com**, Samsung Electronics America, Inc. at **www.samsung.com**, and Philips Electronics at **www.philips.com**. You can check out graphics card manufacturer's sites: Diamond Multimedia Systems Inc. at **www.diamondmm.com**, ATI Technologies Inc. at **www.atitech.com**, Matrox Electronic Systems Ltd. at **www.matrox.com**, and STB Systems, Inc. at **www.stb.com**.

5 Notebooks

Thinking of buying a notebook computer? *PC World* magazine has an excellent Web site just for you at **www.pcworld.com/hardware/t2010/noplus_nb.html**. If you're interested in the latest information of flat panel LCD displays, connect to the O'mara & Associates Web site at **www.omara-assoc.com**. An illustrated tutorial, *Introduction to Liquid Crystal Displays* at **abalone.phys.cwru.edu/tutorial/enhanced/files/lcd/Intro.htm** provides a good solid background in LCD technology. You might want to visit AT&T Bell Labs gallery of exquisite liquid crystal photos at **www.bell-labs.com/new/gallery/thumbnails.html**.

6 PCMCIA

The definitive site about PCMCIA is the PCMCIA Home Page at **www.pc-card.com**. Here you'll find links to PCMCIA FAQs, products, and press releases. You'll find a good primer on PCMCIA technology and markets at the Accurite Technologies site **www.accurite.com/PCMCIAprimer.html**.

7 Printers

Most computer users have heard of Epson, the printer manufacturer that set the standard for dot matrix printing. What many people don't know is that Epson's history spans over 100 years and includes the invention of the world's first quartz watch. In 1964, Epson created printing timers for the Tokyo Olympics. Epson (**www.epson.com**) competes for the lion's share of the computer printer market with Hewlett-Packard (**www.hp.com**). You can visit either Web site for an update on current printer technology. For buyer's guidelines look in recent editions of computer magazines, such as the April 1997 issue of *Windows* magazine (**www.winmag.com/library/1997/0401/featu153.htm**) or the April 1997 issue of *Byte* (**www.byte.com/art/9704/sec11/sec11.htm**).

8 Publications: Computer Industry Magazines and Journals

The number of computer publications reflects our interest in computing. On the Web, you can find listings of currently published computer magazines and journals at **www.amarillo.isd.tenet.edu/Computer_Journals.html** and **www.netvalley.com/netvalley/top100mag.html**. For PC users, the most popular hardware and software magazines are probably *Byte* (**www.byte.com**), *Computer Shopper* (**www.cshopper.com**), *InfoWorld* (**www.infoworld.com**), *PC Magazine* (**www.pcmag.com**), *PC Computing* (**www.pccomputing.com**), and *Windows* (**www.winmag.com**). The most readable academic journal is *Communications of the ACM*. For general commentary about the computer industry, check your newsstand or the Web for *Forbes* (**www.forbes.com**), *Upside* (**www.upside.com**), and the *Wall Street Journal* (**www.wsj.com**).

9 Web Resources: News and Views

For the latest breaking news about the computer industry, check out Yahoo! Technology Headlines at **www.yahoo.com/headlines/tech**, Infoseek's computer page at **www.infoseek.com/Computers**, or WebCrawler's computer page at **www.webcrawler.com/select/comput.new.html**. You can see live video of the CNN Financial Network Digital Jam show at **cnnfn.com/fnonair**. News at **www.computernewsdaily.com** includes articles from the *New York Times Syndicate*, a collection of excellent newspapers from North America, Europe, and Asia. Another great source of news and views on computing is Jeffrey Harrows' The Rapidly Changing Face of Computing at **www.digital.com/info/rcfoc**.

10 **Computer TV**

You'll have to check your local listings for the broadcast schedule for computer TV shows such as *Computer Chronicles* and *@Home*. To find out the topics on this week's shows, you can use the Web. Check the CNET site at **www.cnet.com** for information about The Web, The New Edge, and CNET Central. The PCTV Web site **www.pctv.com** provides information on *The Internet Cafe*, *Computer Chronicles*, *@Home*, and *UserGroup*. Jones Cable Network at **www.jec.com** gives you the run down on several high-tech shows, including *Computer Kids*, *Cyber City Diner*, *Digital Gurus*, *Home Computing*, and *Smart Alex*. Also, check out schedules for MSNBC at **www.msnbc.com**.

11 **BLS: Bureau of Labor Statistics**

The U.S. Bureau of Labor Statistics provides projections for computer industry employment at **stats.bls.gov/news.release/ecopro.table6.htm** and **stats.bls.gov/news.release/ecopro.table14.htm**. The BLS *Occupational Outlook Handbook* describes computer industry jobs, typical working conditions and salary levels at **stats.bls.gov.oco/oco10023.htm**.

Bureau of Labor Statistics BLS

12 **College Connection**

An excellent site that lets you interactively search for a college by major, location, size and tuition is CollegeNET at **www.collegenet.com**.

13 **Organizations**

What's up with computer professional organizations? Check out their Web sites or call for information. Your campus might have a student chapter of one or more of these organizations.

Association for Computing Machinery (**www.acm.org**) 212-626-0500

IEEE Computer Society (**www.computer.org**) 714-821-8380

Association for Women in Computing (**www.awc-hq.org/awc**) 415-905-4663

Association of Information Technology Professionals (**www.aitp.org**) 800-224-9371

14 **Certification**

The ICCP claims that "the CCP designation...Certified Computing Professional...from ICCP is recognized worldwide by employers and peers as validation of its holders' computing knowledge and experience." Find out more about the ICCP certification program for students and professionals at **www.iccp.org**. Information about preparing for and taking the Novell certification exams for computer networking is at **education.novell.com**. Connect to the Microsoft site **www.microsoft.com/train_cert/** to discover the benefits of becoming a Microsoft Certified Professional (MCP). To find out how to get certification for your expertise with Microsoft Office software, check out **www.microsoft.com/office/train_cert/default.htm**.

15 **Career Resources**

At the Resumix site **www.resumix.com/resume/resumeindex.html** you can fill in a form that will become an electronic resume. When you register for the High-Tech Career Alert at the HiTechCareers site **www.hitechcareer.com**, you will receive weekly e-mail of jobs in your career field. The comprehensive CareerBuilder site at **www.careerbuilder.com** contains tips for creating your resume, job listings, an interactive page that helps you compare the cost of living for different cities, and tips on successful job interviews. Another comprehensive site, *CareerMagazine's* **www.careermag.com**, includes job listings, a resume bank, employer profiles, and products and services to help you manage your career. One of the first and largest sources of career resources is the Monster Board at **www.monster.com**. Newer, but very active career sites include **www.headhunter.net** and **www.tcm.org**. A must-read for college students preparing for computing careers is *The No-Nonsense Guide to Computing Careers* published by the ACM in 1993. If you want inspiration, rent the video *Triumph of the Nerds*. Information and script for this video are available at **www.pbs.org/nerds**.

16 **Consumer Information: Buying a Computer**

The online *U-Geek* magazine includes a buyer's guide that features recommendations for selecting a processor, case, storage devices, sound system, and display system. *BusinessWeek* runs a great site at **www.maven.businessweek.com** where you can enter specifications for a computer system or printer to get information on its features, price, and performance. For comparison pricing connect to ComputerESP at **www.computeresp.com**, a site that claims to update over 100,000 prices

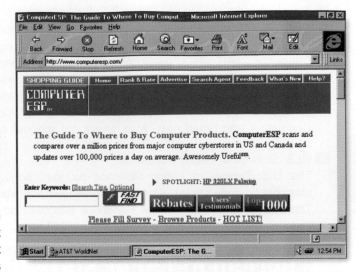

daily on computers, peripherals, and components. Pick the product you want to buy and Computer ESP shows you a list of vendors and current prices. Price Watch at **www.pricewatch.com** is a similar site for price comparisons. *PC Magazine* sponsors an annual survey that evaluates the service and reliability of PC vendors. You can find the results of the 1997 survey in the August issue or at **www8.zdnet.com/pcmag/features/perfectpc/surveypc/_open.htm**.

You can buy computers and components online at CompUSA's site **www.compusa.com**. In addition, computer vendors such as Dell and IBM offer online sales. Before you purchase anything by mail or online, read "Ten Tips for Direct Success" on page 80 of the July 1997 *Computer Shopper*. Connect to Consumer World at **www.consumerworld.org** for links to consumer information, the Better Business Bureau, and product reviews.

Review

1 Make a list of the key points you need to remember about buying a desktop computer.

2 Make a list of the additional factors you must consider when buying a notebook computer.

3 Demonstrate your understanding of the terminology and issues involved in purchasing a computer by answering the following questions about the computer ad in Figure 6-1.

a. The microprocessor in the MicroPlus computer would be categorized in which microprocessor family?

b. The software that you could run with the MicroPlus computer would not generally be compatible with which other types of computers?

c. Does the processor for the MicroPlus computer include MMX technology?

d. Does the MicroPlus computer have enough RAM to run Windows 95?

e. About how much would it cost to upgrade the MicroPlus computer to 64 MB of memory?

f. Why does the MicroPlus computer come with only one floppy disk drive?

g. How fast is the CD-ROM drive?

h. Can you add a second internal hard disk drive to the MicroPlus computer? Why or why not?

i. Would you be able to display photographic-quality images at 1024 x 768 resolution? Why or why not?

j. Would you be able to run multimedia software on the MicroPlus computer? Why or why not?

k. What bundled software, if any, is included with the MicroPlus computer?

l. If you purchase the MicroPlus computer and a week after you receive it, the monitor stops working, what is the MicroPlus company policy on repairs?

4 For each of the following computer components, indicate the unit of measurement used to describe the component's capacity:

a. microprocessor speed

b. microprocessor word size

c. hard disk capacity

d. disk drive access time

e. floppy disk capacity

f. CD-ROM drive speed

g. RAM capacity

h. video memory

i. disk cache capacity

j. screen resolution

k. image clarity

5 Draw a diagram to illustrate the life cycle of a computer hardware product.

6 Describe the difference between a version upgrade and a competitive upgrade.

7 Describe the characteristics of each of the three market tiers in the computer industry.

8 List the advantages and disadvantages of purchasing a computer from each computer industry market channel.

9 In your own words, describe the difference between computer-specific jobs, computer-related jobs, and computer-use jobs.

10 List the ways in which you can use technology to find a job.

11 Your parents are thinking of buying a computer. Because you are taking a computer course, they turn to you for advice. The first thing you tell them is to decide how much they want to spend. Think about everything you have learned in this chapter—especially the tips in the *User Focus* section. Based on what you have learned, compose a letter to your parents giving them advice about buying a computer.

12 Use the New Perspectives CD-ROM to take a practice test or to review the new terms presented in this chapter.

Projects

1 **The *Computer Shopper* Experience** The story about Matt at the beginning of this chapter is fairly realistic. Many people purchase mail-order computers, and *Computer Shopper* is the most popular source of information for mail-order prices. Suppose you decide to buy a computer, and you decide your budget is $2,000. You don't need to buy a printer because your friend is giving you a useable, but older printer. Look through the ads in a recent issue of *Computer Shopper* to find the best computer that fits your computing needs and your budget. Write the list of features, the price, and the vendor for the computer, as well as the month and page of the issue. Then explain why you think this computer is the best one for the money.

2 **Product Announcements** Find a product announcement in a computer magazine. How would you classify this announcement? Is it a trial balloon, an anticipated ship date, or a product release? How can you tell? Was it written by a vendor or by a reporter?

3 **Today's Microprocessors** Microprocessor technology changes rapidly. New models arrive every couple of years, and the clock speed for a particular model seems to increase every few months. As you learned in this chapter, computers that contain state-of-the-art microprocessors are usually priced at a premium. Because the latest microprocessors are so expensive, the most popular computers—those that are purchased by the most people—tend to contain a previous model microprocessor. When you are in the market for a computer, it is useful to be able to differentiate between the state-of-the-art microprocessors and previous models.

Browse through several computer magazines to determine which microprocessor is most popular and which microprocessor is currently state-of-the-art. Write a brief description of your findings. Include the following information:

a. The clock speed, processor model name or number, and word size for the most popular microprocessor.

b. The clock speed, processor model name or number, and word size for the state-of-the-art microprocessor.

c. A brief explanation of what factors helped you determine that these particular microprocessors are the most popular and the most state-of-the-art.

d. A bibliography of your sources.

4   **Comparison Shopping** Comparison shopping is a good strategy for finding the best deal in a computer system. Use the hardware checklist in Figure 6-29 to gather comparative information about two computer systems. You can gather the information from a computer magazine, the Internet, or from a local computer retail store. Be sure you exercise courtesy, especially if you visit a small retail store. Let the salesperson know that you are working on a class project, and recognize that the sales person's priority is shoppers who intend to actually buy a computer. Your instructor might assign this as a group project.

INTERNET Optional

5   **Computer Industry** Although the computer industry is less than half a century old, it has more than its share of good luck and hard luck stories. The history of each computer company has contributed in some way to the current state of the computer industry. Select a well-known company in the computer industry such as IBM, Digital, Microsoft, Apple, Compaq, Hewlett-Packard, Cray Research, or Toshiba. Use library and/or

INTERNET Optional

Internet resources to research the history of the company and trace the events that led to the company's current status in the computer industry. Write a report that summarizes your research. Follow your instructor's requirements for the length of your report.

6   **The Latest "Scoop"** Different industry analysts tend to give their readers the scoop on many of the same "hot topics." It's fascinating to see how the rumors spread and how analysts see events from different perspectives. Read at least 10 industry analysts' columns from several computer magazines published in the same month and year. Although 10 columns might sound like a lot, they are not long and many are fairly entertaining. Summarize what you read by indicating the topics that were "hot" that month and how the analysts agreed or disagreed.

7   **Your Dollar Buys a Lot More Today** You have probably heard that computer technology changes at an amazing speed. Today, your money buys much more computing power than it did in 1990. How much more? Look through the computer ads in back issues of computer magazines for June 1990, June 1993, and June 1995. Create a chart that shows the changes in the specifications for computers for a price of $2,000. Be sure you compare the processor type, processor speed, RAM capacity, hard disk drive capacity, screen resolution, and bus type.

8   **Product Comparison Reviews** Many computer magazines feature extensive product comparison reviews in which several hardware or software products are evaluated and compared. Suppose you are working for an organization and your job is to select hardware and software products.

a. Describe the organization for which you work, then specify which type of product (notebook computers, word-processing software, group scheduler, and so on) you are looking for and why.

b. Explain the important factors that will influence your decision, such as budget or special features that your organization requires from the product.

c. Find and read an appropriate comparative review in a recent computer magazine.

d. Based on the comparative review, which product would you recommend? Why?

9 **Career Research** Books, magazines, and the Web supply plenty of resources to help you choose a career. Or, if you're considering a career change, these resources can help you decide if it is the right thing to do. Use the resources in your library and on the Web to gather information about a career in which you are interested. Unless your instructor requires it, you do not need to limit yourself to computing careers. Answer the following questions:

a. In one paragraph, how would you describe the nature of the work you would perform in this career?

b. What types of businesses and organizations typically hire people in your chosen career field?

c. What are the working conditions?

d. What specific qualifications would you need to successfully compete in this career?

e. What is the employment outlook for this career?

f. What is a typical starting salary? What is the salary range?

g. What sources did you use to locate information about this career?

10
INTERNET Required

Web Resume The Web provides a way to publish your resume where it might be seen by prospective employers. But like a stack of resumes on a recruiter's desk, your Web resume can get quickly rejected for spelling and grammar errors, if it is difficult to read, or if your credentials are not presented in a logical format. It takes several drafts to produce a good resume.

Begin by creating your resume using a word-processing program. Use a reference book or Web site about resumes to help organize your content. Spell check this first draft and print it.

Next show the first draft to at least three friends, colleges, or instructors. Make revisions based on their comments. When you are satisfied with your resume, generate a Web page. Store the page on a floppy disk and hand it in.

11 **Your Compatibility Needs** When you purchase a computer, it is likely you will want to maintain compatibility with the type of computers used in your field. For example, if most elementary schools use Apple computers and your field is elementary education, you might have a strong reason for purchasing an Apple computer instead of an IBM compatible. For this project, research the type of computers most typically used in your field or major. Keep a lookout for hard data, such as the number of Apple II computers still in use in schools. Write a one- to two-page report describing your findings; conclude with the computer you would purchase today to prepare for your career of the future. Your instructor might suggest that you do this project in a small group with other students who have similar career goals.

12 **Using a Decision Support Spreadsheet for Buying a Computer** A decision support spreadsheet like the one in Figure 6-30 helps you prioritize your computing needs and compare the value of several computers based on these priorities. For this Project, do the following:

a. Create a spreadsheet like the one shown in Figure 6-30.

b. Modify the factors listed in column A to reflect your computing needs.

c. Modify the weighting factors in column B to reflect their importance to you.

d. Gather information about two different computer systems that you might consider purchasing.

e. Give each computer a raw score for each factor. For example, if Computer #1 has all the features you seek, enter a 10 in cell B7. If Computer #2 only has half the features you want, enter a 5 in cell E7.

f. Notice which computer has the highest total score. This should be the best computer for your needs.

g. Somewhere on the spreadsheet include a short description of each computer, including its brand name, price, and model.

h. Print out your spreadsheet. Be sure to include your name.

Computer Companies on the Internet Many hardware and software companies maintain Internet sites. A major purpose of these sites is to distribute information to potential and existing customers. Access the Web page for one of the following companies, then answer questions a through d:

http://www.microsoft.com
http://www.ibm.com
http://www.intel.com
http://www.apple.com

a. How would you characterize the information at this site? Is it primarily sales, technical, and/or company background?

b. Give an example of information at this site that would help you decide whether you wanted to buy a particular product.

c. Would you be able to use this site to contact a company representative? If so, how would you do this?

d. Even if you weren't thinking of purchasing a product from this company, describe in detail something at the site you found to be interesting.

Lab Assignments

Buying a Computer

When buying from a mail-order or Internet computer vendor, consumers don't have an opportunity to take various computer models for a "test drive." They make a computer purchase decision based solely on a list of specifications. Thus, it is essential to understand the specifications in computer ads. In this Lab, you will find out how to use a Shopping Glossary to interpret the specifications.

1 Click the Steps button to learn how to use the Shopping Glossary. As you proceed through the Steps, answer all of the Quick Check questions that appear. After you complete the Steps, you will see a Quick Check Summary Report. Follow the instructions on the screen to print this report.

2 Click the Explore button and read the ad for the VectorMicro Computer system. Use the Shopping Glossary to define the following terms:
a. Write-back cache   d. Burst cache
b. EIDE   e. Wavetable
c. NI   f. EDO RAM

3 In Explore, read the ads for the ZeePlus Multimedia Value Pak and the ZeePlus Multimedia Pro computers. The two systems differ substantially in price. If you purchase the more expensive system, what additional features do you get?

4 In Explore, read the ad for the ZeePlus Multimedia Pro Computer (233 MHz and the NP2 Super Systems Computer. What is the price difference between these two systems? What factors might account for this price difference?

5 In Explore, read the ads to find a notebook computer that's priced within $100 of the Nevada Tech Systems desktop computer. Make a list of the features the desktop computer has, that the notebook computer does not have. Which one would you buy? Why?

6 Photocopy a computer ad from a recent issue of a computer magazine. On a separate sheet of paper, write each specification (for example, Intel Pentium processor). For each specification, define each term (for example, Intel is a microprocessor manufacturer, Pentium is a type of microprocessor in the x86 family). Write out all acronyms (for example, RAM means random access memory). If you have difficulty with some of the terms and acronyms, click the Explore button and use the Shopping Glossary.

Local Area Networks and E-mail

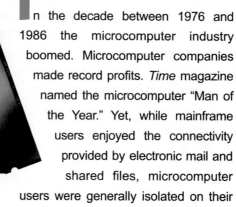

In the decade between 1976 and 1986 the microcomputer industry boomed. Microcomputer companies made record profits. *Time* magazine named the microcomputer "Man of the Year." Yet, while mainframe users enjoyed the connectivity provided by electronic mail and shared files, microcomputer users were generally isolated on their standalone computers. Communication between microcomputers was jokingly referred to as "the sneaker net"—meaning that to transfer a file from one computer to another, you put the file on a floppy disk, then walked with the disk to another computer. White Reeboks were popular corporate footwear at the time.

The idea that microcomputer users could benefit by connecting their computers into a network became feasible about 10 years ago with the introduction of reliable, reasonably priced software and hardware designed for microcomputer networks. The availability of this hardware and software ushered in a new era of computing, which increasingly provides ways for people to collaborate, communicate, and interact.

The purpose of this chapter is to help you understand the type of local area computer networks you would typically find in a college, university, or business. This chapter emphasizes the user perspective, beginning with a tour of network resources, then presenting practical information on network hardware and software including network applications such as groupware and electronic mail.

CHAPTER**PREVIEW**

In this chapter you will learn how to use microcomputer networks, such as those in your school labs or in a business where you work. You'll learn how to select a secure password and how to log into a network. You'll also learn how to share files with other users, and you'll pick up some tips for using electronic mail. When you have completed this chapter you should be able to:

- Describe the resources you would find on a typical local area network
- Explain how using a computer on a network is different from using a standalone computer
- List the advantages of using a local area network
- Explain the difference between sharing files on a network and using groupware
- Describe how processing differs on networks that use dedicated file servers, peer-to-peer capability, client/server architecture, and host-based time-sharing
- Describe the types of software you can use on a local area network
- Explain how software licenses for networks differ from those for stand-alone computers
- Explain how a network uses store-and-forward technology for e-mail

LABS

E-mail

A Local Area Networks

A computer network is a collection of computers and other devices that communicate to share data, hardware, and software. A network that is located within a relatively limited area such as a building or campus is referred to as a **local area network** or **LAN**. A network that covers a large geographical area is referred to as a **wide area network** or **WAN**. In this chapter you will learn about local area networks.

Local area networks are found in most medium-sized and large businesses, government offices, and educational institutions. Worldwide an estimated 25 million computers are connected to local area networks.

LANs
1

Not all LANs are the same. Different types of networks provide different services, use different technology, and require users to follow different procedures. The information in this section describes how a majority of microcomputer networks work. However, any specific network you use might work differently and require different user procedures. Don't hesitate to ask questions when you use an unfamiliar network.

Network Resources

What's the advantage of a computer network? A computer that is not connected to a network is referred to as a **standalone computer**. When you physically connect your computer to a local area network, using a cable or other communications channel, your computer becomes a **workstation** on the network and you become a "network user."

Your workstation has all its usual resources, referred to as **local resources**, such as your hard drive, software, data, and printer. You also have access to **network resources**, which typically include application software, storage space for data files, and printers other than those with your local workstation.

On a network, application software and storage space for data files are typically provided by a network server. A **network server** is a computer connected to the network that "serves," or distributes, resources to network users. A **network printer** provides output capabilities to all the network users. Each device on a network, including workstations, servers, and printers, is referred to as a **node** as shown in Figure 7-1.

Figure 7-1

Network nodes include workstations, printers, and servers.

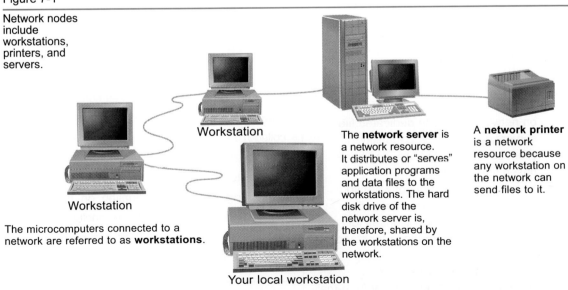

Workstation

Workstation

The microcomputers connected to a network are referred to as **workstations**.

The **network server** is a network resource. It distributes or "serves" application programs and data files to the workstations. The hard disk drive of the network server is, therefore, shared by the workstations on the network.

A **network printer** is a network resource because any workstation on the network can send files to it.

Your local workstation

The Login Process

Do I have to do anything special to access network resources? Even if your computer is physically connected to a network, you cannot use network resources until you log into the network. When you log in, you formally identify yourself to the network as a user.

During the login process you are prompted to enter your user ID and password. Your **user ID**, sometimes referred to as your **user name**, is a unique set of letters and numbers. Your **password**, a special set of symbols known only to you and the network administrator, gives you security clearance to use network resources. Your user ID and password are the basis for your user account. A **user account** provides access to network resources and accumulates information about your network use by tracking when you log in and log out. A **network administrator**, also called a **network supervisor**, is the person responsible for setting up user accounts and maintaining a network. The network administrator provides each new user with a user ID and a "starter" password.

On most networks, you can change your starter password to one of your own choosing. If you have this option, you should select a secure password so other people cannot log in as you and access your files. Your password should be unique, yet something you can remember. How do you select a secure password? Refer to the chart in Figure 7-2 for some password do's and don'ts.

Figure 7-2

Password do's and don'ts

Do	**Don't**
• Select a password that is at least five characters long.	• Select a password that is a word that can be found in the dictionary.
• Try to use numbers as well as letters in your password.	• Use your name, nickname, Social Security number, birth date, or name of a close relative.
• Select a password you can remember.	
• Consider making a password by combining two or more words.	• Write your password where it is easy to find—under the keyboard is the first place a password thief will look.
• Consider making a password by using the first letters of the words in a poem or phrase.	
• Change your password periodically.	

Entering a valid user ID and password is the beginning of the login process. As the login process continues, your workstation is connected to network drives, allowing you to use programs and data files stored on a server. The login process also connects your workstation to network resources such as a network printer. The next two sections explain how this works.

Drive Mapping

How does my computer access data files and application software from a network server?

Your workstation gains access to the file server and its hard drive when the server hard drive is *mapped* to a drive letter. **Mapping** is network terminology for assigning a drive letter to a network server disk drive. For example, on a typical workstation with a floppy drive A and a hard drive C, the login process maps the server hard drive as drive F.

Once a drive letter has been mapped, you can access data files and application software from that drive just as you would from your local hard disk drive. Essentially, you can then use the hard drive on the server just as if it was part of your workstation computer.

Drive mappings vary from one network to another, depending on the needs of the organization and its users. One organization might map the server drive as F, while another organization might map the server drive as J. In other organizations, multiple drives on more than one server might be mapped as F, I, J, and Z. As a network user, you will find it useful to know the drive mapping so you can more easily find programs and files. Figure 7-3 shows a typical drive mapping available to a workstation in a network with a single server.

Figure 7-3

A typical workstation drive map

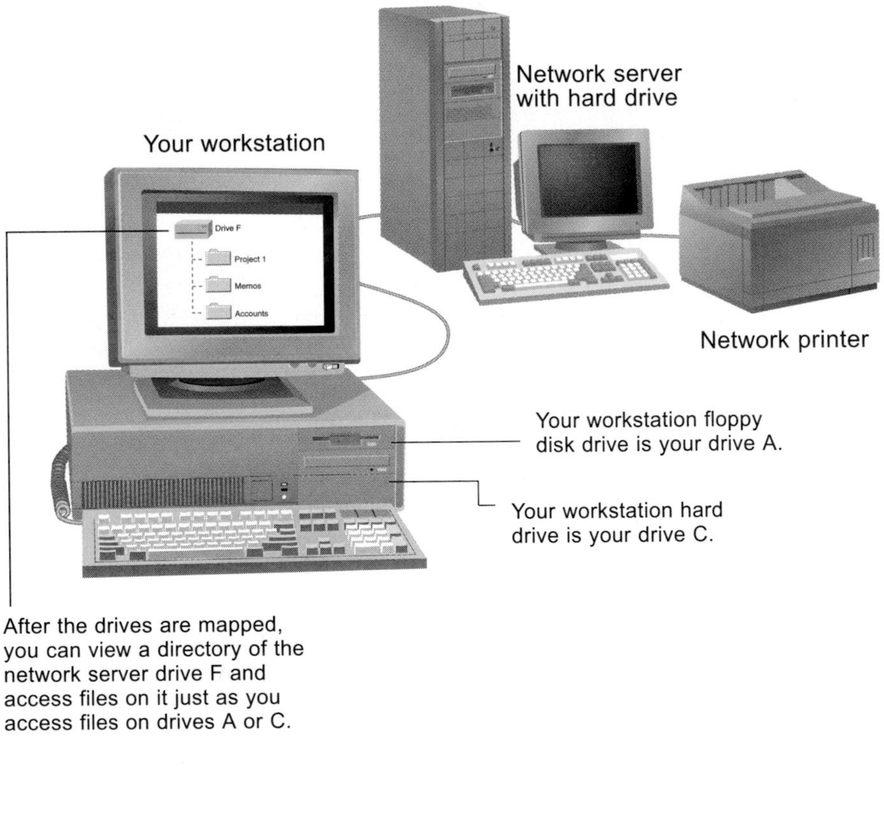

Your workstation

Network server with hard drive

Network printer

Drive F
Project 1
Memos
Accounts

Your workstation floppy disk drive is your drive A.

Your workstation hard drive is your drive C.

After the drives are mapped, you can view a directory of the network server drive F and access files on it just as you access files on drives A or C.

Using Programs on a Network

When I start a program supplied by a network server, is it the same as starting a program on a standalone computer? Remember from Chapter 5 that when you launch a program on a standalone computer, it is copied from your hard disk into RAM. Suppose you want to use a word-processing program that is stored on the hard disk of a network server. Will the program be loaded into the memory of the server or into the memory of your workstation?

When you start a program that is stored on a server, the program is copied to the RAM of your workstation. Once the program is in memory, it runs just as if you had started it from your workstation hard disk drive. Figure 7-4 shows how this works.

Figure 7-4

Starting a program that is stored on the file server

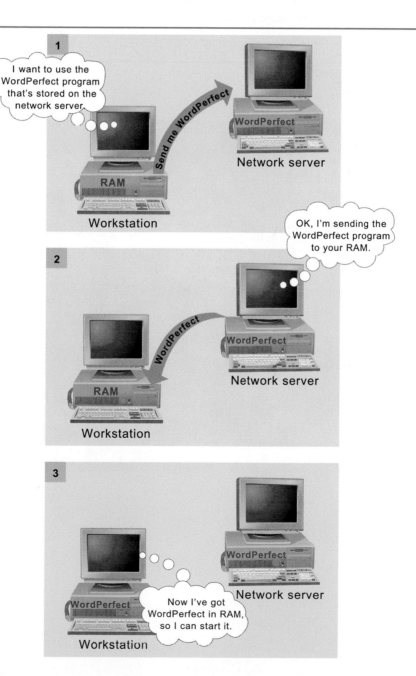

You might wonder if more than one user on a network can simultaneously use the same program. One advantage of a network is that with proper licensing many users can access a program at the same time. This is called **sharing** a program. For example, while CorelDraw is running on your workstation, other users can start the same program. The network server sends a copy of CorelDraw to the RAM of each user's workstation.

Sharing programs is effective for several reasons. First, less disk storage space is required because the program is stored only once on the server, instead of being stored on the hard disks of multiple standalone computers. Second, when a new version of the software is released, it is easier to update one copy of the program on the server than to update many copies stored on standalone computers. Third, purchasing a software license for a network can be less expensive than purchasing single-user licenses for each workstation on the network (Figure 7-5).

Figure 7-5

Sharing programs on a network saves disk space, reduces maintenance, and reduces licensing costs.

Using Data Files on a Network

Is there any advantage to storing data files on the server instead of my local hard disk?

Suppose that while connected to a network, you create a document using a word-processing program. You can store the document either on your local hard disk or on the server hard disk. If you store the file on your local hard disk, you can access the file only from your workstation. However, if you store the file on the hard disk of the server, you, or any other user, can access the file from any workstation on the network, as shown in Figure 7-6.

Figure 7-6

Network file access

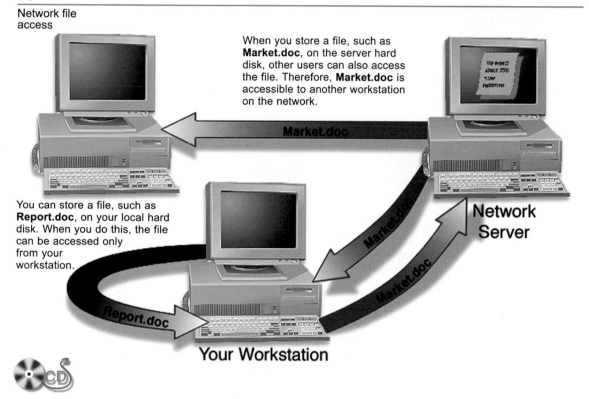

When you store a file, such as **Market.doc**, on the server hard disk, other users can also access the file. Therefore, **Market.doc** is accessible to another workstation on the network.

You can store a file, such as **Report.doc**, on your local hard disk. When you do this, the file can be accessed only from your workstation.

Network Server

Your Workstation

Although a *program file* from the file server can be used on more than one workstation at the same time, most of the *data files* on a network server can be opened by only one user at a time. When one user has a file open, it is **locked** to other users. File locking is a sensible precaution against losing valuable data. If the network allowed two users to open and edit the same data file, both users could make changes to the file; but one user's changes might contradict the other user's changes. Whose changes would be incorporated in the final version of the file?

Suppose two users were allowed to make changes to the same file at the same time. Each user would open a copy of the original file and make changes to it. The first user to finish making changes would save the file on the server. So far so good—the first user has replaced the original version of the file with an edited version. Remember, however, that the second user has been making revisions to the *original* file, but she has no idea of the first user's revisions. When the second user saves her revised version of the file, the changes made by the first user are overwritten by the second user's version, as shown in Figure 7-7.

Figure 7-7

Why networks lock files

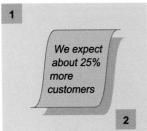
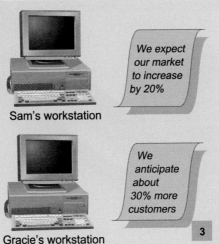

1 The original document is not well written and the percentage is wrong. Sam and Gracie both decide to fix it.

We expect about 25% more customers

2 If Sam and Gracie were allowed to open the document at the same time, they could edit the document in two different ways.

We expect our market to increase by 20%

Sam's workstation

We anticipate about 30% more customers

Gracie's workstation

3

We expect our market to increase by 20%

Network server

We anticipate about 30% more customers

Sam stores the edited document on the server, but when Gracie stores her version of the document on the server, it overwrites Sam's version, erasing all of his work.

Using a Network Printer

How does my word-processing software know it is supposed to send documents to the network printer instead of to my local printer? Most application software sends files you want to print to the printer that is connected to your computer's parallel port. But network workstations often do not have local printers. Instead, they need to access a network printer. Figure 7-8 shows how data sent to your workstation's parallel port is **captured** and **redirected** to the network printer.

Figure 7-8

Capturing your workstation printer port

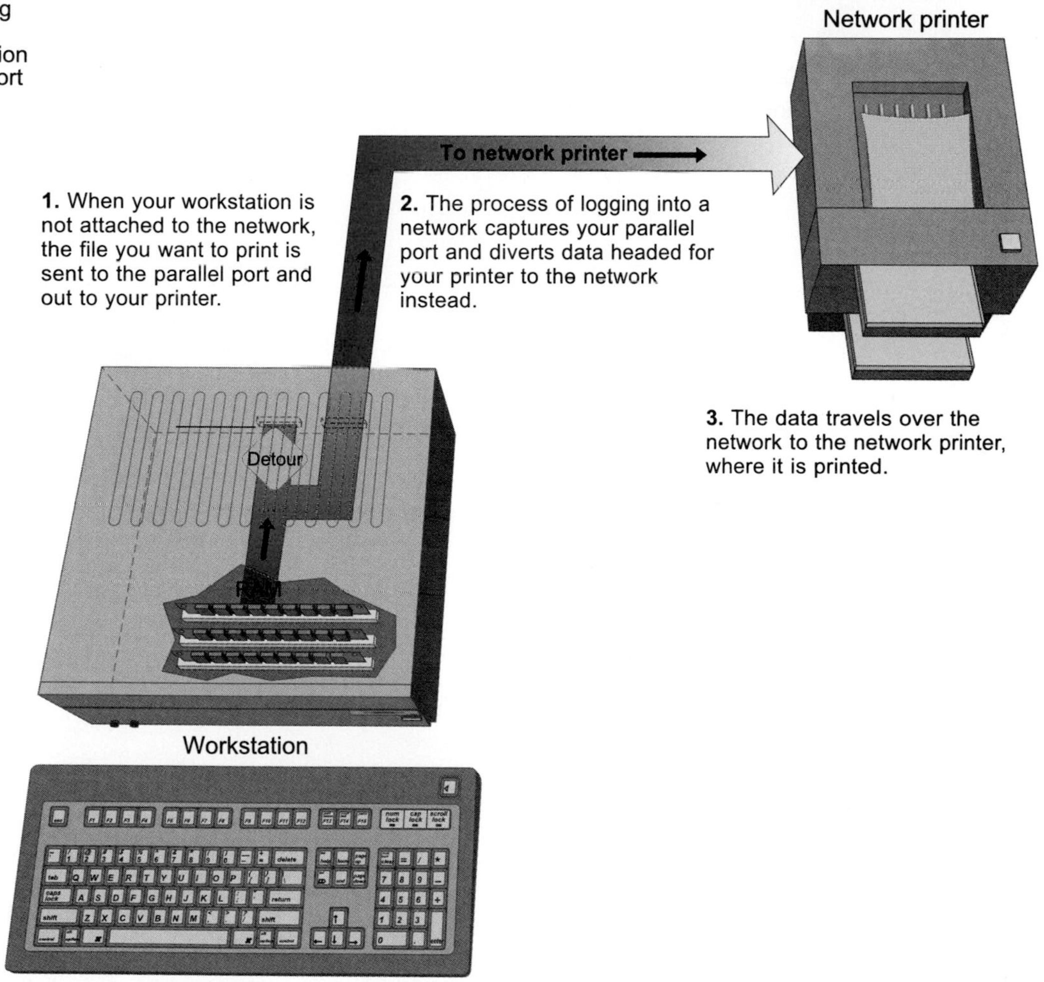

Network printer

To network printer ➞

1. When your workstation is not attached to the network, the file you want to print is sent to the parallel port and out to your printer.

2. The process of logging into a network captures your parallel port and diverts data headed for your printer to the network instead.

Detour

3. The data travels over the network to the network printer, where it is printed.

Workstation

What happens if a network printer receives more than one file to print? Most networks would not allow two files to travel simultaneously over the network. However, it is possible that before the printer has completed one printout, other files arrive to be printed. Files sent to a network printer are placed in a **print queue**. A print queue is a special holding area on a network server where files are stored until they are printed. When more than one user sends a file to the print queue, the files are added to the print queue and printed in the order in which they are received.

Figure 7-9 shows what happens when one user sends a document to the printer before another user's printout is completed.

Figure 7-9

The network print queue

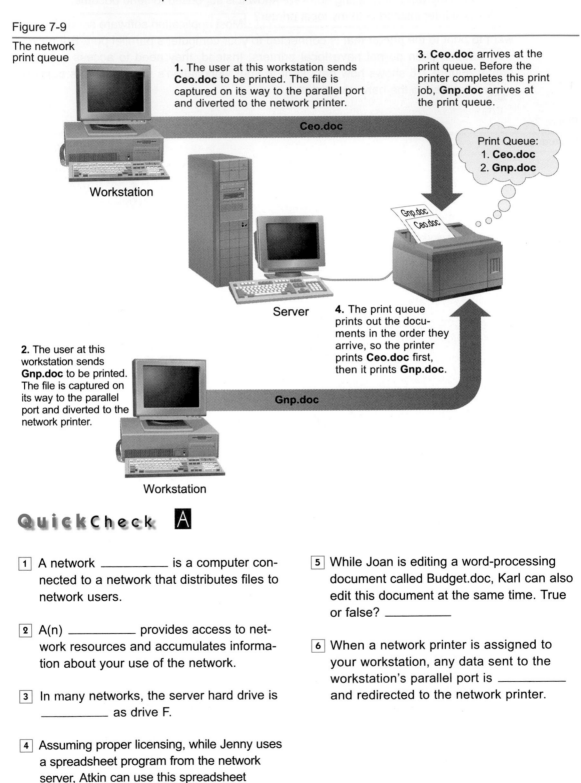

1. The user at this workstation sends **Ceo.doc** to be printed. The file is captured on its way to the parallel port and diverted to the network printer.

3. Ceo.doc arrives at the print queue. Before the printer completes this print job, **Gnp.doc** arrives at the print queue.

Ceo.doc

Print Queue:
1. **Ceo.doc**
2. **Gnp.doc**

Workstation

Server

2. The user at this workstation sends **Gnp.doc** to be printed. The file is captured on its way to the parallel port and diverted to the network printer.

4. The print queue prints out the documents in the order they arrive, so the printer prints **Ceo.doc** first, then it prints **Gnp.doc**.

Gnp.doc

Workstation

QuickCheck A

1 A network _____ is a computer connected to a network that distributes files to network users.

2 A(n) _____ provides access to network resources and accumulates information about your use of the network.

3 In many networks, the server hard drive is _____ as drive F.

4 Assuming proper licensing, while Jenny uses a spreadsheet program from the network server, Atkin can use this spreadsheet program at the same time. True or false?

_____

5 While Joan is editing a word-processing document called Budget.doc, Karl can also edit this document at the same time. True or false? _____

6 When a network printer is assigned to your workstation, any data sent to the workstation's parallel port is _____ and redirected to the network printer.

▣ Network Hardware

In the previous section, you looked at local area network resources and learned about the advantages of computer networks. Now let's look at the hardware components of a network.

Network Interface Cards

What establishes the physical connection for the computers in a network? A network interface card is the key hardware component for connecting a computer to a local area network. A **network interface card** or **NIC** (pronounced "nick") is a small circuit board that sends data from your workstation out over the network and collects incoming data for your workstation. A desktop computer NIC plugs into an expansion slot on the computer motherboard. A notebook computer NIC is usually a PCMCIA card. Figure 7-10 shows you NICs for desktop and notebook computers.

Figure 7-10

Desktop and notebook network interface cards

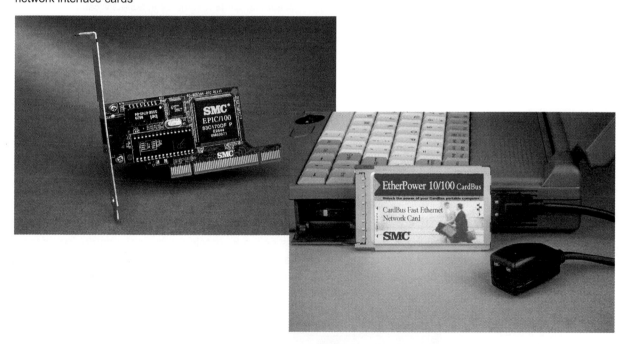

Ethernet
2

Each server, workstation, printer, or other device on a network must have an NIC. Different types of networks use different types of network interface cards. If you want to add a computer to a network, you need to know the network type so you can purchase the appropriate NIC. Popular network types include **Ethernet**, **Token Ring**, **ARCnet**, **FDDI**, and **ATM**.

Cable and Wireless Networks

The NICs have to be connected by a cable, right? Most networks use cables to connect servers, workstations, and printers. On a typical network, you would find one of the two cable types shown in Figure 7-11.

Figure 7-11

Network cables

A **twisted pair cable**, sometimes referred to as **UTP**, looks similar to a telephone cable with a square plastic **RJ-45 connector** on either end.

A **coaxial cable** resembles a cable-TV cable with a round, silver **BNC connector** on either end.

Wireless
Networks
3

Instead of using cables, **wireless networks** use radio or infrared signals to transmit data from one network device to another. Wireless networks are handy in environments where wiring is difficult to install, such as in historical buildings. In addition, wireless networks provide mobility. For example, a wireless network would make it possible to carry a notebook or hand-held computer throughout a large warehouse to take inventory. A third application for wireless networks is for temporary installations, when drilling holes to install wiring is not practical or economical.

The network interface cards for a wireless network contain the transmitting devices necessary to send data to other devices on the local area network. Signals can be sent by radio waves, microwave, or infrared. Figure 7-12 describes T.G.I. Fridays' wireless network.

Figure 7-12

Using a wireless network, the hostess at T.G.I. Fridays adds names to the waiting list for dinner. Note the antenna used to transmit data to the main dining room management database.

Network Servers

When I use a network, is my data processed locally or on the network server? You have already learned the general functions of a network server. However, there are different kinds of network servers. They are explained in this section. When you use a standalone computer, all your data is processed by your computer's microprocessor. The device that processes your data when you are connected to a network depends on the type of servers included on your network.

A **dedicated file server** is devoted only to the task of delivering programs and data files to workstations. As you can see in Figure 7-13, a dedicated file server does not process data or run programs for the workstations. Instead, programs run using the memory and processor of the workstation.

Figure 7-13

A dedicated file server

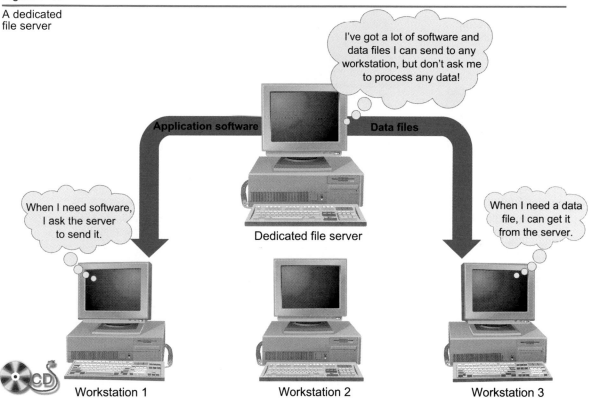

A typical local area network uses a microcomputer as a file server; but, a minicomputer or a mainframe computer can also be a file server. Many businesses with older minicomputer and mainframe systems have essentially recycled this equipment by adding microcomputer networking capabilities.

In some cases, a network computer performs a dual role as both file server and workstation. This is referred to as a **non-dedicated server** or **peer-to-peer** capability. When you use a non-dedicated server, your computer functions like a normal workstation, but other workstations can access programs and data files from the hard disk of your computer, as shown in Figure 7-14.

Figure 7-14

A non-dedicated file server

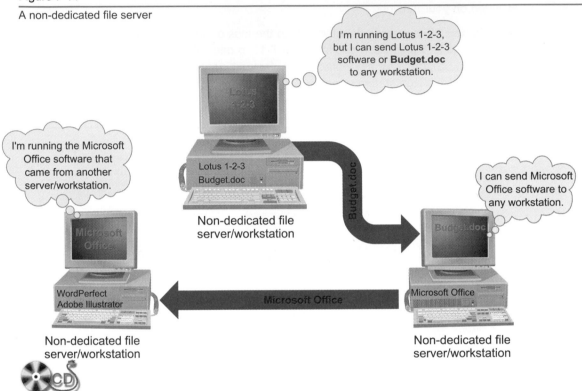

A **print server** stores files in a print queue and sends each queued file to the network printer. A **print job** is a file that has been sent to the printer. Print jobs are processed locally on workstations that have a local printer, but a print server controls the print jobs on a network server. A print server can be the same computer as the file server, or it can be another micro, mini, or mainframe computer connected to the network.

Client/
Server
4

An **application server** is a computer that runs application software and forwards the results of processing to workstations as requested. An application server makes it possible to use the processing power of both the server and the workstation. Also referred to as **client/server architecture**, use of an application server splits processing between the workstation *client* and the network *server*. Suppose you want to search for a particular record in a 50,000-record database stored on a network server. Study Figure 7-15 to see how client/server architecture makes use of the processing capacity of both the workstation and server.

Figure 7-15

Client/server
architecture

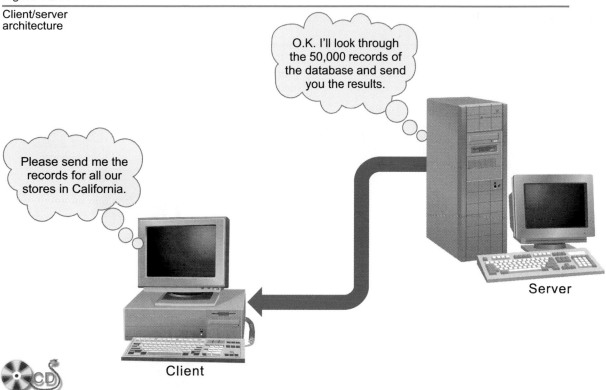

Some networks include a **host computer**, usually a minicomputer or a mainframe with attached terminals. When you use a host computer from a terminal, all the processing takes place on the host. Your **terminal** has a keyboard and a screen, but it does not have a local storage device, and it does little or no processing on its own. The host accepts commands from terminals and sends back a display of results. Because the terminals do not have processing power of their own, they cannot further process the results they receive. For example, if your terminal receives a list of 50 people sorted by address, you could not sort the list by last name on your terminal. You would have to ask the host to sort the list and send you the new results.

Although a system containing a host computer and terminals fits our general definition of a *network*, it is more customary to call it a **time-sharing system**. Because terminals can do little or no processing of their own, every terminal must wait for the host to process its request. The terminals essentially *share* the host's processor by being allocated a fraction of a second of processing time.

Before powerful microcomputer networks became available, connecting terminals to a host computer provided relatively low-cost computer access. For economic reasons, many organizations have not yet moved important data and programs from mainframe hosts to microcomputer networks.

It is possible to connect a microcomputer to a host using **terminal emulation software**, but your microcomputer will behave just like a terminal and will receive only a display of results, not data that you can process (Figure 7-16). If you want to process data you receive from a host, instead of using terminal emulation software you must use communications software to transfer the data to your computer.

Figure 7-16

Mainframe host

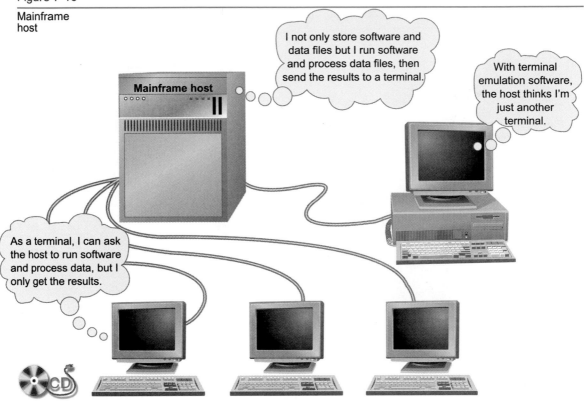

QuickCheck B

1. The circuit board that connects a computer to a local area network is called a(n) _____.

2. If a network computer functions both as a file server and as a workstation, it is referred to as a(n) _____ server.

3. A(n) _____ is devoted to the task of delivering programs and data files to workstations.

4. Client/server architecture takes advantage of the processing capabilities of both the workstation and the server. True or false? _____

5. On some networks, a(n) _____ computer processes data, then outputs the results on the screen of a terminal.

C Software for Networks

The software on a local area network typically includes specialized network software as well as many of the same applications you might use on a standalone computer.

Network Operating System

Does a network require any special software? A network requires a **network operating system** (NOS) to control the flow of data, maintain security, and keep track of user accounts.

InfoWeb

NOS
5

Network operating systems such as **Novell NetWare**, **Banyan Vines**, and **LANtastic** are software packages designed exclusively to control network data flow. Also, popular computer operating systems such as Windows 95, Windows 98, Windows NT, and UNIX include networking capability. What about Windows 3.1? This early version of Windows does not include networking capability. Therefore, if you want to network computers that use Windows 3.1 you must also install a network operating system such as Novell NetWare, shown in Figure 7-17.

Figure 7-17

A popular network operating system

A network operating system usually has two components: server software and client software. **Network server software** is installed on a file server and controls file access from the server hard drive, manages the print queue, and tracks user data such as IDs and passwords. **Network client software** is installed on the local hard drive of each workstation and is essentially a device driver for the network interface card. When your computer boots up, the network client software is activated and establishes the connection between your workstation and other devices on the network.

Standalone Applications

Do I need to buy a special version of my favorite application software to use it on a network? Most applications designed for standalone computers can be installed on a network server, which sends them to individual workstations as requested. Typically, your favorite word-processing, spreadsheet, graphics, and presentation software will work on a network just as they do on a standalone computer.

Some applications that you use on a standalone computer have built-in features for networking that appear only when the software is installed on a network. For example, when your word-processing software is installed on a network, it might show you a dialog box that lets you send files to another person on the network.

As you learned in the first section of this chapter, a network can supply an application to more than one person at a time by copying the program into the memory of the workstations. This capability applies to most standalone software. Therefore, software designed for standalone computers can usually be used on a network by more than one user at a time. However, most applications designed for standalone computers do not allow more than one person at a time to work on the same *data file*.

Installing Windows Software on a Network

How does my Windows menu know what's on the file server? Suppose the office is buzzing about a great new graphics package that has just been installed on the network server. You check out your Windows menu of programs, but can't find the new software. What's the problem? Before you can access a program on the file server, your local version of Windows needs to know that the software's been installed.

After a new Windows program has been installed on a network server, you or your network manager needs to also complete a workstation installation of the software. A **workstation installation** usually copies some, but not all, of the program files to your local hard disk, then it updates your Windows menu to include a listing for the new program. On some networks, the workstation installation can be done from a remote location such as the network manager's office. Sound complicated? Just remember that if you don't have a listing for a program that's on the network server, you probably need to complete a workstation installation.

Software Licenses for Networks

Can an organization buy just one copy of a software package and put it on the network for every one to use? It would be very inexpensive for an organization to purchase a single copy of a software package, then place it on the network for everyone to use. In an organization with 100 users, for example, word-processing capability might cost $295 for a single copy, instead of $29,500 for 100 copies. However, using a single-user license for multiple users violates copyright law.

Most single-user software licenses allow only one person to use the software at a time. However, many software publishers also offer a **network license** that permits use by multiple people on a network. Typically, such a network license will cost more than a single-user license, but less than purchasing single-user licenses for all of the users. For example, a word-processing software package that costs $295 for a single-user license might have a $5,000 network license that allows up to 100 people to use the software. Network licenses are available for most software packages by contacting the software publisher.

Workflow Software and Groupware

Is there a way for two or more people to work together on the same data file? When local area networks were first introduced, the concept of sharing files was limited because only one user at a time could work on a document. This concept of sharing does not, however, support many of the organizational activities that require collaboration and communication among employees. For example, in most organizations, people exchange information using memos, phone conversations, and face-to-face meetings. Employees collect, organize, and share information, which must be stored in a centralized repository. Documents and forms flow through organizations, picking up required signatures and approvals. Employees contribute sections of text that are compiled into a single report.

As the use of networks increased, organizations and businesses began to demand software that would facilitate the flow and sharing of documents. Software publishers responded to this demand by producing groupware and workflow software.

Groupware is application software that supports collaborative work by managing schedules, shared documents, and intra-group communications. Essentially, groupware manages a pool of documents and allows users to access those documents simultaneously as shown in Figure 7-18.

Groupware
6

Figure 7-18

Groupware provides simultaneous access to a pool of documents.

A key feature of groupware is *document version management*. When more than one group member revises a document, whose revisions should be accepted for the final version? The solution frequently implemented by groupware is to maintain all revisions within the document so the workgroup can accept or reject each revision as shown in Figure 7-19.

Figure 7-19

In this shared document, one user's revisions are shown in red, the other user's revisions are shown in blue.

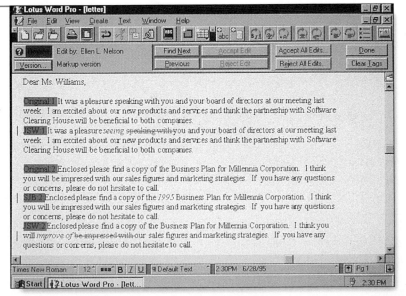

Workflow
Software
7

Workflow software, also referred to as **document routing software**, automates the process of electronically routing documents from one person to another in a specified sequence and time. Workflow software facilitates a process or a series of steps. For example, suppose you apply for a loan. The bank has a specific procedure for processing the loan application. First, a credit officer checks your credit rating and makes a recommendation whether to accept or reject your application. Next, the bank loan committee must approve the application. Finally, the approved application is processed by your loan officer. To facilitate this process, workflow software would route the loan application to the first bank officer, specify the due date for action, collect the necessary approval, then route the application to the next officer, and so on.

Workflow software is based on a "process-centered model" as opposed to groupware's "information-centered model." With workflow software the focus is on a series of steps. With groupware the documents are the focus. You can compare Figures 7-18 and 7-20 to see the difference between workflow software and groupware.

Figure 7-20

Workflow
software
facilitates a
process.

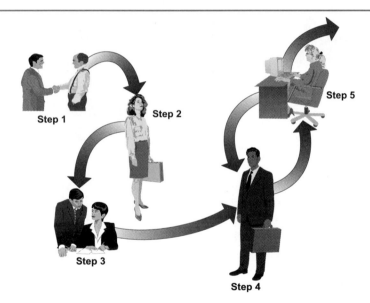

Step 1

Step 2

Step 3

Step 4

Step 5

QuickCheck C

1. Novell Netware would be classified as a(n) _____ system.

2. If your computer is connected to a network, you must install a special network version of your favorite application software. True or false? _____

3. If an organization is planning to use software on a network, it should purchase a(n) _____ so multiple users can legally use the software.

4. If you are a team leader and you want your team members to collaborate on a project using the network, you might try to find a(n) _____ product.

5. If you were the manager of a loan department in a bank, you might use _____ software to automatically send loan applications to each member of your department for processing and approval.

User Focus

D Electronic Mail

LAB

E-mail

Electronic mail, or **e-mail**, is correspondence conducted between one or more users on a network. E-mail is a more efficient means of communication than ground or air mail. Rather than waiting for a piece of paper to be physically transported by office mail or U.S. mail, you can send an electronic version of a message directly to someone's electronic "mail box." E-mail also helps you avoid frustrating "telephone tag."

How E-mail Works

InfoWeb

E-mail
8

When I send an e-mail message does it go directly to the recipient's workstation? What if the recipient's workstation is not turned on? An **e-mail message** is essentially a letter or memo sent electronically from one user to another. An **electronic mail system** is the hardware and software that collects and delivers e-mail messages. Typically, a local area network provides electronic mail services to its users. The software on the network server that controls the flow of e-mail is called **mail server software**. The software on a workstation that helps each user read, compose, send, and delete messages is called **mail client software**. Electronic mail systems are often classified as groupware because they facilitate communication among members of a workgroup.

E-mail messages are *stored* on a server. When you want to read this mail, the server *forwards* the messages to your workstation. Hence e-mail is called a **store-and-forward** technology. Because the server stores the messages, your workstation does not need to be on when someone sends you e-mail (Figure 7-21).

Figure 7-21

E-mail uses store and forward technology so your mail remains stored on a server until you are ready to read it.

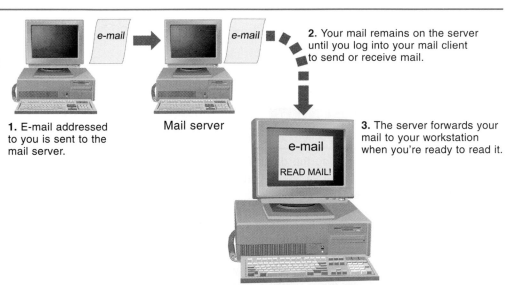

1. E-mail addressed to you is sent to the mail server.

Mail server

2. Your mail remains on the server until you log into your mail client to send or receive mail.

3. The server forwards your mail to your workstation when you're ready to read it.

Your workstation

What if you want to send e-mail to someone who is not connected to your computer network or host? Many e-mail systems are connected to other e-mail systems through electronic links called **gateways**. When you send an e-mail message to a user on another computer network, the message is transferred through the gateway to a larger e-mail system, which delivers the message to the recipient's network or host computer system.

Reading E-mail

How do I use e-mail? Your e-mail is transmitted through an electronic mail system and stored on a host or network server in an area you can think of as your **mailbox**. When you log into the electronic mail system and check your mail, unread messages are listed as new mail. You can choose to display and read the mail on your computer screen, print it, delete it, reply to it, forward it, or save it on disk, as shown in Figure 7-22.

Figure 7-22

Your e-mailbox lists new messages.

Buttons at the top of the mail window help you reply to, forward, send, and delete messages.

Your Inbox lists all the messages in your mailbox. An icon that looks like an unopened envelope indicates unread mail.

The text of the new message is displayed in the lower section of the window.

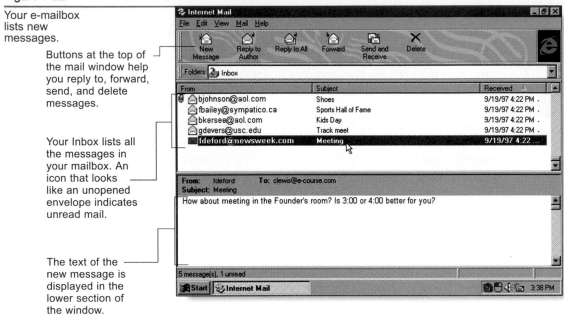

Replying to E-Mail

What are all those > symbols in my e-mail? Suppose you receive e-mail from your supervisor containing the dates for the next sales meeting. The sales meeting conflicts with your scheduled vacation. You decide to reply to the supervisor's e-mail to see if you need to reschedule your vacation. You click the Reply button on your e-mail software. The screen changes and now you see the supervisor's message, but each line has a > symbol in front of it. What's happened?

InfoWeb

Smileys
9

As part of your reply, most e-mail software includes the text of the message to which you are replying. This text is preceded with > symbols. Type the text of your reply before the text marked with the > symbols. When you send your reply, it will include your message and the message to which you are replying. In that way, your reply contains the text of the original e-mail to help remind the recipient.

Composing New Messages

How does my e-mail software help me compose and send messages? Your e-mail software has a button or menu option for New Mail that displays a message form. The first item for the form is the recipient's mail address. You can type this address or select it from an address book that contains a list of e-mail addresses for the people you correspond with frequently. You can even set up groups in your address book. For example, you could have a "CarPool" group containing the e-mail addresses of the people in your car pool. Then, you can easily e-mail everyone in the car pool by sending one e-mail addressed to "Car Pool."

The e-mail form usually contains a **cc: option** so that you can send a copy of an e-mail to someone other than the main recipient. The e-mail form also includes a **subject option** so you can specify the topic of the e-mail.

The e-mail form includes a space for you to type the text of your message. Like most word processors, the e-mail software takes care of word wrap. But, don't expect your e-mail to provide you with many formatting options. Standard e-mail is plain text—no bold, no underlines, no fancy fonts. If you want to send a formatted document, you'll have to use an attachment.

Most e-mail systems allow you to send an **attachment**, which is a file such as a word-processing document, worksheet, or graphic that travels through the e-mail system along with an electronic mail message. For example, suppose you've created a poster for a community beach cleanup day. You've stored the file on your disk as "Beach Cleanup.bmp". You want to send it to the head of the cleanup committee so she can have it printed. Figure 7-23 shows you how to attach this file to an e-mail message.

Figure 7-23

Sending
an e-mail
attachment

1. Create a new message and address it to the person to whom you are sending the attachment.

2. Use the menus provided by your e-mail software to attach the file containing the attachment.

3. An icon indicates the name of the file you attached. Send the mail following your usual procedures. The recipient of the message can click the icon to see the attachment.

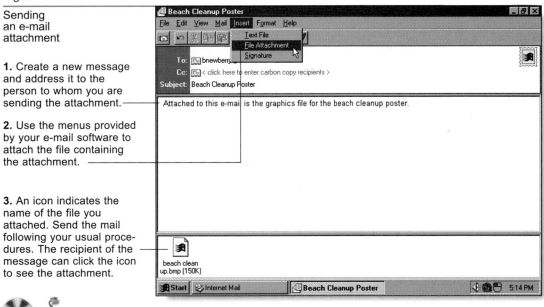

Managing Your E-mail

I know how to write letters and memos—is there anything special I need to know about writing e-mail messages? E-mail is not exactly the same as using the post office. With e-mail you can send messages right away—your letters don't sit around waiting for you to take them to the post office. You can send the same message to multiple people as easily as to a single person. It is easy to send replies automatically to messages you receive as well.

The advantages of e-mail can also create potential problems—for example, you might regret the contents of a message sent off in haste. Also, it's easy to accumulate an overwhelming number of messages in your mail box. Here are some tips to help you avoid e-mail problems:

Read your mail regularly. When you use electronic mail, your correspondents expect a quick response. You lose much of the advantage of e-mail if you check your mailbox only once every two weeks!

Delete messages after you read them. Your e-mail is stored, along with everyone else's, on a file server where storage space is valuable. Leaving old messages in your mailbox takes up space that could be used more productively.

You don't have to reply to every e-mail message. The purpose of some e-mail messages is to give you information. Don't reply unless you have a reason to respond, such as to answer a question. Sending a message to say "I got your message" just creates unnecessary mail traffic.

If you receive mail addressed to a group, it might be better to reply only to one person in the group. You might receive mail as a member of a mailing list; the same message will be sent to everyone on the list. If you use the automatic reply feature of your e-mail system, your message is likely to be sent to everyone on the list. Do this only if your reply is important for everyone to see.

Think before you send. It is easy to write a message in haste or in anger and send it off before you have time to think it through. If you're upset, write your message, but wait a day before you send it.

Don't write anything you want to remain confidential. Electronic mail is easily forwarded to other people. Suppose you write something unflattering about Rob in an e-mail message to Julie. Julie can easily forward your message to Rob.

Don't get sloppy. Your e-mail is a reflection of you, your school, and your employer. Use a spell checker if one is available; if not, proofread your message before you send it. Use standard grammar, punctuation, and capitalization. A message in all uppercase means you're shouting.

EndNote Local area networks have come a long way since the days of the sneaker net; they now provide connectivity for workgroups using groupware and for individuals exchanging e-mail. New technologies create opportunities, but they also create issues. Privacy is an important issue relevant to networks and e-mail.

InfoWeb

E-mail
Privacy
10

Be aware that your e-mail might be read by someone other than the recipient. Although the U.S. justice system has not yet made a clear ruling, current legal interpretations indicate that e-mail is not legally protected from snooping. You cannot assume that the e-mail you send is private. Therefore, you should not use e-mail to send any message that you want to keep confidential.

Why would an employer want to know the contents of employee e-mail? You might immediately jump to the conclusion that employers who read employee e-mail are snooping. This might be the case with some employers who, for example, want to discover what a union is planning. However, some employers read employee e-mail to discover if any illegal activities are taking place on the computer system. Many employers are genuinely concerned about such activities because they could, in some cases, be held responsible for the actions of their employees.

Also, the network administrator sometimes sees the contents of e-mail messages while performing system maintenance or when trying to recover from a system failure. Even if an employer does not intentionally read e-mail exchanges, technical difficulties might still expose the contents of e-mail messages to people other than the intended recipient.

Many businesses are now implementing policies and procedures to address e-mail privacy. Before you use a network at school or at work, make sure that you ask about network policies relating to privacy and security.

InfoWeb

InfoWeb

Chapter
Links

The InfoWeb is your guide to print, film, television, and electronic resources. Use it to obtain updates on quickly changing technical information and to locate information for research papers. If you're using the New Perspectives CD-ROM, click the InfoWeb icon on the left side of this paragraph to access the online InfoWeb links. Otherwise, use your Web browser and type in the address of the New Perspectives site: www.cciw.com/np3. At the New Perspectives site you'll find up-to-date links to the topics covered in this chapter.

1 LANs

For a more in-depth look at LANs, browse through the fine illustrations in **How Networks Work** by Derfler and Freed (Ziff-Davis Press, 1993). For answers to your technical questions about networks, refer to Novell's complete **Encyclopedia of Networking** by Werner Feibel (Novell Press, 1995). On the Web, connect to *LAN Times Online* at **www.wcmh.com** for updates on the latest LAN technologies. The British magazine *Network World* at **www.network-world.com** has excellent articles and links to a buyer's guide.

2 Ethernet

Today, most networks use the Ethernet standard, which was invented in 1976 by Robert Metcalfe. You can see Metcalfe's original sketch of an Ethernet at **wwwhost.ots.utexas.edu/ethernet**. For information on other network standards, connect to **www.webopaedia.com** and look up Token Ring, ARCnet, ATM, and FDDI.

3 Wireless Networks

Wireless networks are popping up everywhere. You'll find an excellent tutorial about wireless LANs at **www.wlana.com**. Lucent Technologies produces a popular wireless system called WaveLAN that you can check out at **www.wavelan.com**. To get a look at some wireless data collection devices, connect to IBM's Networking site at **www.networking.ibm.com**.

4 Client/Server

Client/server is now a somewhat tired buzzword in the computer industry, but it is still mentioned frequently in the press. You'll find a wealth of information on client/server computing at the Client Server Group Web site at **www.isa.co.uk/csg**.

5 NOS: Network Operating Systems

In the world of PCs, Novell NetWare is the best-selling network operating system. Visit Novell's Web site at **www.novell.com** for information about local area networks and Novell products. Is NetWare better than Windows NT? A *LAN Times* article sums up this debate at **www.wcmh.com/lantimes/ usetech/compare/pcNWvsNT.html**. Why fight two giants like Microsoft and Novell? Ask Artisoft, the publisher of the LANtastic network operating system. You'll find the Artisoft site at **www.artisoft.com**. A fourth NOS vendor, Banyan, maintains a Web site at **www.Banyan.com**.

6 Groupware

The July 1996 issue of *LAN Times*—on the Web at **www.lantimes.com/97/97jul/707a051a.html**—contains an excellent report on groupware, including case studies. Lotus Notes is one of the most popular groupware packages. Connect to the Lotus Notes site at **www2.lotus.com** to find out how the product works. For an insightful look at groupware from the perspective of management, look for the book **Groupware: Collaborative Strategies for Corporate LANs and Intranets** by David Coleman (Prentice Hall, 1997).

7 Workflow Software

On the Web, you can take a short tutorial on workflow systems at **cne.gmu.edu/modules/workflow**. For more information, check your library for **The Workflow Imperative** by Thomas Koulopolous (Van Nostrand Reinhold, 1995).

8 E-mail

For basic instruction on using e-mail, connect to the U-Wanna-What site at **www.uwannawhat.com/NetCourse/Internet/NetCH3PG2.html**. Unlike five years ago, today it is rare to receive e-mail THAT'S TYPED IN ALL CAPS TO FIT A 40 CHARACTER SCREEN. Instead, most people realize that e-mail messages should follow basic rules of grammar and basic guidelines for business letter format. For a discussion of e-mail context and contents, read *A Beginner's Guide to Effective Email* at **http://www.webfoot.com/advice/email.top.html**. At the Albion Cybercasting site, **www.albion.com/netiquette**, you'll find links to a Netiquette Quiz and excerpts from Virginia Shea's book, *The Core Rules of Netiquette*.

9 Smileys

Those > symbols aren't the only ones you'll find in e-mail messages. "Smileys" such as :-) (happy face) and =|:-] (Abraham Lincoln) add a little feeling and a little bit of whimsey into the otherwise stark world of electronic messaging. The book **Smileys** by D. Sanderson (O'Reilly, 1993) contains a collection of more

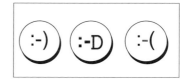

than 650 smileys and answers to your deepest questions such as "Why are smileys sideways?" You can find loads of information about smileys on the Web at sites such as the Geocities' Smiley House at **www.geocities.com/Heartland/6959/smiley.html**. To find other smiley sites, just enter the word "smiley" in any search engine.

10 E-mail Privacy

Concerned about the privacy of your e-mail? Many of your questions are answered at the E-Mail Privacy FAQ Web page at **www.well.com/user/abacard/email.html**. You can read an excellent article on e-mail privacy at the American Civil Liberties Union site, **www.aclu.org/issues/cyber/priv/privpap.html**.

An Amazon Book Store ad reads, "Reagan tried to destroy them, Bush tried to steal them, and Clinton tried to hide them—but the White House e-mail messages survived. Here are the highest-level communications on the most secret national security affairs of the US during the 1980s—shockingly candid electronic exchanges you were never meant to see!" It's all in the book, **White House E-Mail: The Top-Secret Messages the Reagan/Bush White House Tried to Destroy** by Thomas S. Blanton (New Press, 1995).

Review

1 Use your own words to answer the questions below each heading in this chapter.

2 List three reasons why sharing programs is effective for an organization.

3 Suppose Latisha Simms needs to select a password for herself. Rank the following, listing the most secure password first: BZ39A (a totally random selection of letters and numbers), LASIMMS (for Latisha Alexandra Simms), SSOSAPFOR (the first letters of "sing a song of sixpence, a pocket full of rye"), SMMIS (Latisha's last name spelled backwards), and Thomas (Latisha's husband's name).

4 Create a sentence outline of Section A that highlights the main concepts network users need to know.

5 Fill in the following table to summarize the characteristics of different network servers:

	File Server	Print Server	Non-dedicated Server	Client/server	Host
Are shared files stored locally?					
Are shared programs stored locally?					
Does some, all, or none of the processing take place on the server?					
Does some, all, or none of the processing take place on the terminals or workstations?					

6 Explain the difference between sharing files on a network and using a groupware product on a network.

7 Diagram the difference between groupware and workflow software.

8 Explain the purpose of network server software and network client software.

9 Explain the purpose of a workstation installion of Windows software.

10 Summarize the software licensing issues that pertain to local area networks.

11 Explain how store-and-forward technology applies to electronic mail systems.

12 Explain when you would use an e-mail attachment.

13 What is the purpose of the > symbol in the body of an e-mail reply?

14 Use the New Perspectives CD-ROM to take a practice test or to review the new terms presented in this chapter.

Projects

1 **Your School Network** Research your school network to answer the following questions:
   a. What is the network operating system?
   b. What drives are mapped to a student workstation?
   c. Is the file server a micro, mini, or main-frame computer?
   d. Is the print server a different device than the file server?

2 **Network Operating System Efficiency** Network operating systems are designed to optimize the process of sending program and data files to workstations. This means that the amount of time it takes multiple users to open the same file should not be much longer than it takes a single user to open the file. How efficient is the file server in your lab? To find out, form a team of three to five class members and do the following:

a. Using a stopwatch or the second hand of your watch, record the number of seconds it takes a word-processing software application to start on a workstation in your lab. For example, if your lab has Microsoft Word, click the Word icon to highlight it, then start timing when you press the Enter key to launch the program. Stop timing when the word processor is ready for you to start typing.

b. Exit the word-processing application to get ready for the second part of the test.

c. Position each member of your team at other workstations on the network. Each team member should click the word-processing icon so it is highlighted. One of the team members should give a signal so all the team members press the Enter key at the same time. Each team member should record how long it takes before the word-processing application is ready for typing.

d. Record each team member's results. Prepare a one-page document in which you summarize your experiment and results. Be sure you explain exactly how you carried out the experiment—how many members were on your team, which lab you used, and which software you used. Also, present your conclusions about the efficiency of your network server.

3 **Client/Server Architecture in Corporations**
Client/server architecture is becoming more and more popular in corporations. To find out more about client/server computing, use library and Internet resources to look for case studies and articles about corporations using client/server applications. Write a one- or two-page description of an effective use of client/server computing. Be sure to include a list of references.

4 **Networks in Action** Make an appointment to interview the network supervisor in an organization or business related to your career field. To prepare for the interview, make a list of questions you will ask about how the network works and how it is used. Use the topics in this chapter to help organize your questions about network hardware, network software, application software, and groupware. After the interview, write a two- to three-page summary of your findings. Include the name of the person you interviewed, the business or organization, and the date of the interview. In addition to the report summarizing your findings, submit a list of your questions.

5 **Network Careers** The companies that produce network operating systems encourage computer professionals to obtain professional certification to demonstrate their knowledge of networking. Such certification is often one of the qualifications listed in ads for network supervisor jobs. Novell offers certification as a CNE (Certified NetWare Engineer) or a CNA (Certified NetWare Administrator). Microsoft also offers a certification program for its Windows NT operating system. Write a one- to two-page paper that describes Microsoft's or Novell's certification process. Include the answers to the following questions: What is the process for certification? What is the cost? How would you prepare for the certification exam? What sort of jobs would you qualify for once you are certified?

6 **E-mail Smileys** E-mail has spawned a language of *emoticons*, or *smileys*, that are composed of keyboard characters. For example, the smiley ;-) looks like a person winking. You could use this smiley in an e-mail message to indicate that you are joking. Lists of smileys have been published on the Internet and in books, computer magazines, and newspapers. Find a list of smileys and select five that you would like to use. Make a list of your five smileys and describe what each means. Submit your list and indicate the source of your selection.

7 **Anonymous E-mail?** When you send e-mail, your user ID is automatically attached to your message. This return address indicates who sent the message (in case you forgot to include your name), lets your correspondents easily send you replies, and helps the mail system return messages that have incorrect addresses. Recently, some networks have offered a way to send anonymous e-mail. What are the pros and cons of anonymous mail? Under what circumstances would you want to send anonymous mail? Would you expect people to abuse this capability? Discuss this issue in a small group or research the issue individually. Write a one-page summary of your position on whether people should be allowed to send anonymous e-mail.

8 **E-mail Ethics** Assume that you are the network administrator at a small manufacturing company. While doing some maintenance work on the electronic mail system, you happen to view the contents of a mail message between two employees. The employees seem to be discussing a plan to steal equipment from the company. What would you do? Write a one-page essay explaining what you would do and describing the factors that affected your decision.

9 **E-mail Practice** Learn how to use the e-mail system available on your school network. Briefly describe how you do each of the following:

a. Compose and send a message.

b. Reply to a message you received.

c. Delete a message you received.

d. Forward a message you received to someone other than the person who sent the message.

e. Send a carbon copy of the message.

f. Send a message to a mailing list.

Lab Assignments

E-mail

E-mail that originates on a local area network with a mail gateway can travel all over the world. That's why it is so important to learn how to use it. In this Lab you use an e-mail simulator, so even if your school computers don't provide you with e-mail service, you will know the basics of reading, sending, and replying to electronic mail.

1 Click the Steps button to learn how to work with e-mail. As you proceed through the Steps, answer all of the Quick Check questions that appear. After you complete the Steps, you will see a Quick Check Summary Report. Follow the instructions on the screen to print this report.

2 Click the Explore button. Write a message to re@films.org. The subject of the message is "Picks and Pans." In the body of your message, describe a movie you have recently seen. Include the name of the movie, briefly summarize the plot, and give it a thumbs up or a thumbs down. Print the message before you send it.

3 In Explore, look in your In Box for a message from jb@music.org. Read the message, then compose a reply indicating that you will attend. Carbon copy mciccone@music.org. Print your reply, including the text of JB's original message before you send it.

4 In Explore, look in your In Box for a message from leo@sports.org. Reply to the message by adding your rating to the text of the original message as follows:

Equipment:	Your Rating:
Rollerblades	2
Skis	3
Bicycle	1
Scuba gear	4
Snowmobile	5

Print your reply before you send it.

THE INTERNET

The data jack slipped smoothly into the socket just behind Kyle's ear. He flipped the switch on his computer. The power light blinked green, and the universe shifted. A moment ago, Kyle was sitting at his desk in his apartment. Now, he seems to be standing in a landscape of sur-realistic terrain and fantastic buildings. Messages swirl and pulse down massive conduits, cre-ating data links between heavily guarded corporate computing centers. The World Health Organization cube spins lazily, tipped on one of its corners. In the distance—the towers of the Library of Congress. The golden pyramid of the Information Cartel dominates the landscape; its glowing forcefield a reminder that access requires security clearance.

InfoWeb

Cyberspace
1

This is a vision of **cyberspace**—a computer-generated mental image of a computer world. The term *cyberspace* was coined in 1984 by science-fiction writer William Gibson. Today, "cyberspace" has been popularized by journalists writing about worldwide information networks. No, you cannot plug your brain into a computer to prowl around in cyberspace. But your computer can provide you access to a digital "information highway" called the Internet that winds through a landscape of useful and fascinating information, on topics as diverse as hip hop music and military academies. In this chapter you will discover the astonishing potential of the Internet.

CHAPTER**PREVIEW**

In this chapter you will learn how the Internet works and you'll discover how your Web browser provides access to many different Internet services. You'll also find out how to publish your own Web pages. The *User Focus* section explains how to connect your own computer to the Internet. When you have completed this chapter, you should be able to:

- Describe how you can use a dial-up connection to access an ISP that in turn connects to an NSP on the Internet backbone
- Explain the difference between an IP address, domain name, URL, and e-mail address
- List the Internet services that you can access using a Web browser
- Explain the difference between downloading a file, viewing a Web page, and playing multimedia elements on a Web page
- Compare and contrast push and pull technologies
- Explain how synchronous and asynchronous interactions apply to chat groups, discussion groups, and interactive gaming
- Explain the purpose of HTML tags
- Evaluate the effectiveness of the design used for a Web page

LABS

The Internet:
World Wide Web

Web Pages
&
HTML

A   How It Works

The **Internet** is a collection of local, regional, and national computer networks that are linked together to exchange data and distribute processing tasks. The Internet evolved over the past 30 years from a fledgling experiment with four computers into a vast information network that connects millions of microcomputers, minicomputers, mainframes, and supercomputers. Why was the Internet created and how does it work? The answers to these questions will help you navigate cyberspace.

The Internet Then and Now

InfoWeb

Internet
History
2

How did the Internet get started? The history of the Internet begins in 1957 when the Soviet Union launched Sputnik, the first artificial satellite. In response to this display of Soviet superiority, the U.S. government resolved to improve its science and technical infrastructure. One of the resulting initiatives was the Advanced Research Projects Agency (ARPA).

ARPA swung into action with a project to help scientists communicate and share valuable computer resources. The **ARPANET**, created in 1969, connected computers at four universities. Using ARPANET technology, the National Science Foundation (NSF) created a similar, but larger network, linking not just a few large computers, but entire local area networks at each site. Connecting two or more networks creates an **internetwork** or **internet**. The NSF network was an internet (with a lowercase i). As this network grew, it became known as "The Internet" (with an uppercase I) as described in Figure 8-1.

Figure 8-1

The simple NSF network expanded to become today's Internet, providing access to information on every continent.

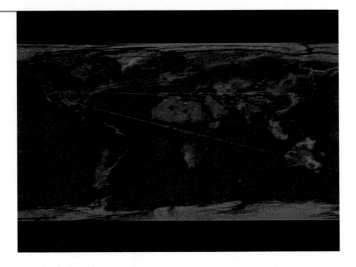

Early Internet pioneers—mostly educators and scientists—used primitive command-line user interfaces to send e-mail, transfer files, and run scientific calculations on Internet supercomputers. Finding information was not easy. Without search engines, Internet users relied on word of mouth and e-mail to tell colleagues "the data you need is on the Stanford computer in a file called Chrome.txt." In the early 1990s, software developers created new user-friendly Internet access tools, and Internet accounts became available to anyone willing to pay a moderate monthly fee. Today, the Internet connects computers all over the globe and supplies information to people of all ages and interests.

Internet Growth

How big is the Internet? To measure the size of the Internet, you can consider how many computers are connected, how many people use it, or how much data flows through it. Whatever measurement you use, the Internet is huge and continues to grow.

Internet Statistics 3

In 1969, the ARPANET consisted of four computers. In 1980, the Internet included 200 computers. By the beginning of 1997, the Internet had mushroomed to include 1.7 million computers worldwide, not counting computers making temporary connections. The graph in Figure 8-2 shows the incredible increase in the number of computers on the Internet over just the past 5 years.

Today, the Internet is the largest and most widely used network in the world, serving an estimated 57 million people in 194 countries. Over 15 million households in the U.S., 700,000 households in Canada, 700,000 households in the U.K., and 600,000 households in Australia have an Internet connection. Worldwide, more than 33,000 new users sign up for Internet accounts each day. About one third of all Internet users are females.

Figure 8-2

Internet growth

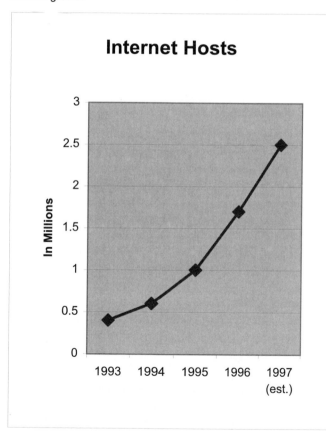

Although millions of people access the Internet, there is plenty of room for growth. The number of Internet users is less than two percent of the world population and less than 16 percent of the U.S. population age 15 and older.

Internet traffic is the number of bytes transmitted from one Internet host computer to another. By 1997, Internet traffic exceeded 100 terabytes a week. A **terabyte** is 1,000,000,000,000 bytes. One hundred terabytes is roughly equivalent to the amount of information printed on the paper made from 500,000 trees or the amount of information stored in books in the U.S. Library of Congress. Vast quantities of data are transmitted over the Internet, but how much data is actually stored on Internet computers? No one really knows. It is not currently possible to poll each computer to find out how many bytes of data are accessible.

Michael Dertouzos, director of the MIT Laboratory of Computer Science, estimates that the world has an exabyte of data to store. An **exabyte** is a quintillion (10^{18}) bytes. The Internet, as large as it is, probably has a long way to go before it contains an exabyte of data.

Internet Technology

How does data travel over the Internet? To understand how you can use the Internet to access information from a computer that is thousands of miles away, it is useful to have a little background on the Internet communications network. The cables, wires, and satellites that carry Internet data form an interlinked communications network. Data traveling from one Internet computer to another is transmitted from one link in the network to another, along the best possible route. If some links are overloaded or temporarily out of service, the data can be routed through different links. The major Internet communications links are called the **Internet backbone**. Figure 8-3 illustrates the Internet backbone in the continental United States and shows, for example, that data traveling from Seattle to Dallas could be routed through Chicago, Denver, or Los Angeles.

Figure 8-3

The Internet backbone in the continental U.S. provides many alternative pathways for data traveling from one computer to another.

In the U.S. nine **network service providers** (NSPs) each maintain a series of nationwide links. IBM, MCI, PSINet, and UUnet are the largest NSPs. The Internet backbone communications links are analogous to "pipes." Data flows through the pipes and large pipes can carry more data than smaller pipes. In Figure 8-3 the colors indicate the size of the data pipes. Blue OC3 links are the largest, with a capacity of about 155 million bits per second. If you had exclusive use of this line, you could transfer the contents of an entire 680 megabyte CD-ROM in 34.9 seconds. Green T3 and orange DS3 links have a capacity of about 44 million bits per second. Transferring the contents of a CD-ROM using one of these pipes would take about two hours. When Internet traffic is high, data takes longer to arrive at its destination. NSPs are continually adding new communications links to the backbone to accommodate increased Internet use.

Where does your computer fit into the scheme of things? When you connect your computer to the Internet, you do not connect directly to the backbone. Instead, you connect to an ISP that in turn connects to the backbone. An **Internet service provider** (ISP) is a company that provides Internet access to businesses, organizations, and individuals.

An ISP works in much the same way as your local phone company. You arrange for service, in this case for Internet access, and the ISP charges you a monthly fee. The ISP provides you with communications software and a user account. You supply a modem that connects your computer to your phone line. Your computer dials the ISP's computer and establishes a connection over the phone line. Once you are connected, the ISP routes data between your computer and the Internet backbone.

A connection that uses a phone line to establish a temporary Internet connection is referred to as a **dial-up connection**. Your dial-up connection is only temporary. When your computer hangs up, the connection is broken. A phone line provides a very narrow pipe for transmitting data. Its typical capacity is only 28.8 thousand bits per second. Using a phone line, the time to transfer the contents of a 680 megabyte CD-ROM would be over 53 hours. Figure 8-4 illustrates the layers of communication that make it possible for your home computer to access the Internet.

Figure 8-4

Your computer establishes a dial-up connection to an ISP. The ISP connects to the Internet backbone.

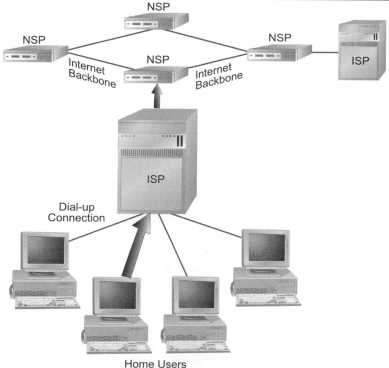

Home Users

The efficient flow of data over all the communications links on the Internet requires a standard mechanism for routing data to its destination. **TCP/IP** is the acronym for **Transport Control Protocol/Internet Protocol**, a standard set of communications rules used by every computer that connects to the Internet. By following the rules of TCP/IP, Internet computers can efficiently control and route data between your computer and the Internet computers maintained by ISPs and NSPs.

Hosts, Domains, and Sites

How does the Internet know where to send data? The Internet includes computers that perform different functions. Some computers on the Internet handle communications and route e-mail, but most publicity about the Internet focuses on computers that provide information such as stock quotes, movie reviews, and sports scores. Regardless of function, every computer connected to the Internet is referred to as a **host**. Each host has a unique identifying number called an **IP address**. An IP address is a set of four numbers between 0 and 255 that are separated by periods. For example, 204.146.144.253 is the IP address of the Coca Cola Company. When data travels over the Internet, it carries the IP address of its destination. At each intersection on the backbone, the data's IP address is examined by a device called a **router**, which forwards the data towards its destination.

InfoWeb

Domain
Names
4

Although an IP address works for inter-computer communications, humans find it difficult to remember long strings of numbers. Therefore, many host computers also have an easy-to-remember name such as cocacola.com. The official term for this name is **Fully Qualified Domain Name** (FQDN), but most people just refer to it as a **domain name**. By convention, you should type domain names using all lowercase letters. A domain name ends with a three-letter extension that indicates its top-level domain. A **top-level domain** groups the computers on the Internet into the categories shown in Figure 8-5.

Figure 8-5

Top-level domains

ORG	Professional and non-profit organization
COM	Commercial businesses
EDU	Four-year colleges and universities
NET	Internet administration
GOV	U.S. government agencies
MIL	U.S. military organizations
INT	Organizations established by international treaties

In the domain name cocacola.com, *com* indicates that the computer is maintained by a commercial business. In North America, an organization called **InterNIC** handles requests for IP addresses and domain names. By 1997, InterNIC had assigned over 16 million IP addresses.

Computers with domain names are popularly referred to as **sites**. A site is a metaphor for a virtual place that exists in cyberspace. For example, a Web site provides a virtual location that you can visit to view information in the form of Web pages.

URLs

What's the difference between a domain name and a URL? To access Web pages on the Internet, you use a **Uniform Resource Locator** (URL). A URL, like a domain name, is an Internet address. A URL is the address of a *document* on a computer, whereas a domain name represents the IP address of a *computer*. It is handy to understand how a URL is formed, in case you want to make an educated guess about the address to use to access a Web page.

Each Web page has a unique URL that begins with http://. The acronym HTTP stands for **HyperText Transfer Protocol**. Many of today's Web browsers assume that any address you type begins with http://. If you are using such a browser, you can omit http:// from the URL.

The next part of the URL is the server name. A **server** is a computer and software that make data available. A **Web server**, for example, is a computer that uses Web server software to transmit Web pages over the Internet. Most Web server names are domain names prefixed with www. The Web server name for your favorite Chinese restaurant might be something like www.fooyong.com.

Suppose you indicate to your Web browser that you want to access www.fooyong.com. By entering the Web server name, you'll access the site's home page. A **home page** is similar to the title page in a book. It identifies the site and contains links to other pages at the site.

A Web site usually contains more than one page. Each page is stored as a separate file and referred to by a unique URL. The URL of a Web page reflects the name of any folder or folders in which it is stored. For example, suppose the Chinese restaurant has a page listing its daily specials. The specials are stored in a file called specials.html in a folder called "information." The URL for this page would be www.fooyong.com/information/specials.html.

Some Internet computers are case sensitive. So although the domain name is always lower-case, parts of a URL might be uppercase. When you type URLs, you should be sure to use the correct case. Information/Specials.html is not the same as information/specials.html. Figure 8-6 illustrates the parts of a URL.

Figure 8-6

Components of a URL

http://www.fooyong.com/information/specials.html

Protocol   Web server name   Folder name   Document name and filename extension

Internet Mail

| How does Internet e-mail reach its destination? | As you learned in Chapter 7, sending e-mail on a local area network is simple. Each network user has a user ID such as wgibson. When you send an e-mail message to wgibson, the network stores it on the network mail server until Gibson logs in and checks his mail.

InfoWeb

Find It
5

Suppose that you want to send mail to wgibson; but you're in Baltimore and he is in Vancouver, British Columbia. You cannot simply address your e-mail to wgibson. How would it find its way over the Internet to Vancouver?

E-mail that travels over the Internet requires an **Internet mail address** that consists of a user ID and the user's mail server domain name. When Internet e-mail reaches an intersection on the Internet backbone, a router sends the e-mail on toward the mail server specified by the domain name. When the e-mail arrives at the mail server, it is held in a mailbox until the user next logs on to read mail. Figure 8-7 illustrates the parts of an Internet mail address.

Figure 8-7

Components
of an Internet
mail address

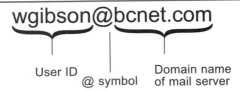

wgibson@bcnet.com

User ID   @ symbol   Domain name of mail server

Quick Check A

1. The term _____ was originally coined by science-fiction writer William Gibson to refer to a computer-generated reality that people could experience by connecting their brain to a computer network.

2. An internetwork, also referred to as a(n) _____ is created by connecting two or more networks.

3. Internet traffic is measured in _____.

4. Typically, you would connect your home computer directly to the Internet backbone using a T3 link. True or false? _____

5. All the computers on the Internet use a standard set of communications rules called _____.

6. The address **http://www.cyberspace.com** is a(n) _____.

⬚ The Versatile Web Browser

Internet host computers function as servers that locate information, transfer data from one computer to another, and handle electronic mail. If you want access to the services provided by a server, you need corresponding client software. For example, as you learned in Chapter 7, the purpose of an e-mail server is to store and forward electronic mail messages. To access e-mail services, you must have e-mail client software.

The Internet: World Wide Web

On the Internet, **FTP servers** maintain a collection of data that you can transfer to your own computer. **Web servers** maintain a collection of Web pages that you can view on your computer screen. A **Usenet server** handles the exchange of comments among members of Internet discussion groups.

InfoWeb

WWW 6

In the past, you needed a separate client software program to access each type of server. For e-mail, you needed an e-mail client. For FTP, you needed an FTP client. Archie, WAIS, TelNet, Gopher, and Newsreader clients were all part of the Internet user's software toolbox. Today, a single tool has replaced this awkward collection of client software. A **Web browser** provides Internet users with all-purpose client software for accessing many types of servers. You can use your Web browser to view Web pages, transfer files between computers, access commercial information services, send e-mail, and interact with other Internet users.

Web Pages

Sometimes my browser can't seem to get to a Web page. What's wrong? Back when disco music was popular, Ted Nelson was trying to devise a computer system that could store virtually every literary document, link them according to logical relationships, and allow readers to comment and annotate what they read (Figure 8-8). The establishment turned up its nose. Where would so much information come from and what computer would be powerful enough to handle it? Who would be interested in following hypertext links to find information? Who, except for scholars and scientists, would be interested in communicating online? Nelson's project Xanadu never became a reality, but his ideas resurfaced twenty-five years later as the World Wide Web.

The World Wide Web, created in 1990, is partially responsible for the explosion of interest in the Internet. As an easy-to-use, graphical source of information, the Web opened the Internet to millions of people interested in finding information rather than learning complex computer commands. Today, Web surfers (as Web users are sometimes called) can visit an estimated 80 million Web pages on over 1 million Web sites.

Figure 8-8

An early sketch of project Xanadu, a distant relative of the World Wide Web

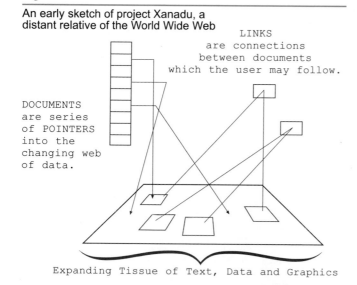

LINKS are connections between documents which the user may follow.

DOCUMENTS are series of POINTERS into the changing web of data.

Expanding Tissue of Text, Data and Graphics

The official description of the World Wide Web is a "wide-area hypermedia information retrieval initiative aiming to give universal access to a large universe of documents." The World Wide Web consists of documents, called Web pages, that contain information on a particular topic. A Web page might also include one or more **links** that point to other Web pages. Links make it easy to follow a thread of related information, even if the pages are stored on computers located in different countries. Figure 8-9 shows a conceptual model of linked Web pages.

Figure 8-9

How the
World Wide
Web works

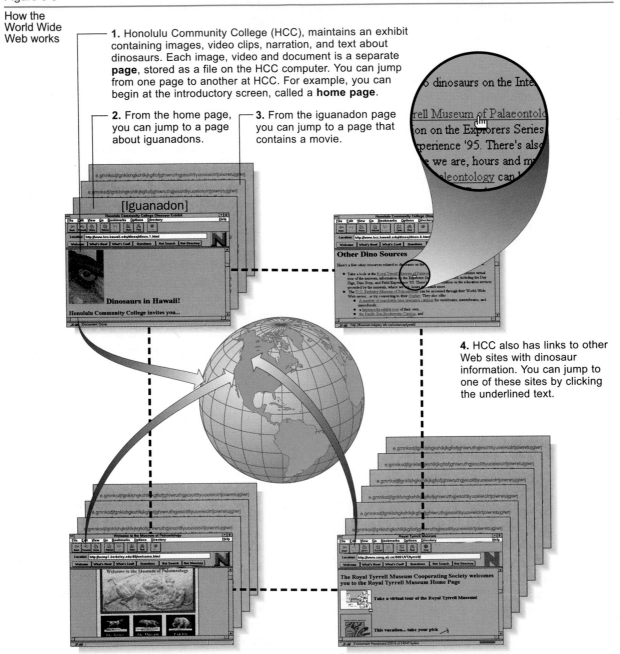

1. Honolulu Community College (HCC), maintains an exhibit containing images, video clips, narration, and text about dinosaurs. Each image, video and document is a separate **page**, stored as a file on the HCC computer. You can jump from one page to another at HCC. For example, you can begin at the introductory screen, called a **home page**.

2. From the home page, you can jump to a page about iguanadons.

3. From the iguanadon page you can jump to a page that contains a movie.

4. HCC also has links to other Web sites with dinosaur information. You can jump to one of these sites by clicking the underlined text.

6. Another jump and you are in California at the University of California Museum of Paleontology where more Web pages on dinosaurs are stored.

5. A quick jump from Hawaii and you are at the Royal Tyrrell Museum of Palaeontology in Alberta, Canada where additional Web pages on dinosaurs are stored.

You use a Web browser to request a Web page from a Web server. To request a page, you either type a URL or click a Web page link. The server sends the data for the Web page over the Internet to your computer. This data includes two things: the information you want to view and a set of instructions that tells your browser how to display it. The instructions include specifications for the color of the background, the size of the text, and the placement of graphics. Additional instructions tell your browser what to do when you click a link.

The Web is a constantly changing environment as new Web sites come online and old sites close. As a result, links are not always valid. Sometimes when you click a link nothing happens or you get an error message. If a Web server is off-line for maintenance or busy from heavy traffic, you won't be able to get the Web pages you requested, or you might get them slowly. If a Web page doesn't appear after fifteen to twenty seconds, you can click your browser's Stop button and try to access the page later. If you receive a message that the site no longer exists, you'll need to look for information elsewhere as shown in Figure 8-10.

Figure 8-10

If you have trouble connecting to a Web site, a message might indicate the site has closed or moved.

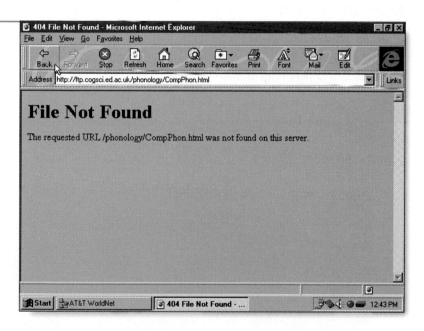

Your browser's **home page** is the first page you see displayed when your browser starts. You can always return to this page by clicking the browser's Home button. Most browsers let you pick any Web page as the home page, so select one that you use often, such as your favorite search engine.

Your browser's menu and tool bars help you navigate the Web as you follow links and then retrace your steps. You'll make frequent use of the Back and Forward buttons to retrace your path through the links you've followed from one Web page to another. Your browser stores a History list of the pages you visit during each session. It can display this list if you want to take big jumps to previously visited Web sites, instead of using the Back and Forward buttons. Your browser can also store a list of your favorite sites, often called **bookmarks**, so you can jump directly to them instead of entering a URL.

Internet Multimedia

Can I listen to music and play videos on the Web? It's hard to imagine that less than five years ago, Web pages contained only text. Now, Web pages include multimedia elements such as sound, animation, and video.

A media element is stored on the Web server in a file. When you click a Web page to play a media element, the Web server sends a copy of the media file to your computer. This can happen in one of two ways, depending on how the Web server has been set up. In one case, the Web server sends you the entire media file before starting to play it. For large video files, you might wait five minutes or more before the video begins to play.

A newer technology, sometimes referred to as **streaming media**, sends a small segment of the media file to your computer and begins to play it. While this first segment plays, the Web server sends the next part of the file to your computer, and so on until the media segment ends. With streaming media technology, your computer essentially plays a media file while receiving it.

As you browse the Web, you'll find multimedia that is displayed in place and multimedia that runs in a separate window. Of the two, in-place is technologically more sophisticated. **In-place multimedia technology** plays a media element as a seamless part of a Web page. For example, an animated GIF like the one in Figure 8-11, uses in-place technology so it appears to play right on the Web page.

Figure 8-11

An animated GIF runs in place as part of a Web page.

Multimedia overlay technology adds a separate window to your screen in which multi-media elements appear. With some overlay technologies, you must manually close the window when the multimedia segment is finished. Figure 8-12 illustrates a media window that overlays a Web page.

Figure 8-12

Some multimedia plays in a window that overlays the Web page.

InfoWeb

Plug-ins
7

A software program called a **media player**, provides you with controls to start, stop, and rewind media segments. Many media players play only one type of media file. For example, a media player might play only sound files with .wav extensions. Another media player might play only videos with .avi extensions. Before you can use a media element on the Web, your computer must have a corresponding media player. How does this work?

Your browser maintains a list of media players that have been installed on your computer. Suppose you're on the Financial News Network (FNN) site and you want to run a movie segment. FNN videos require a media player called Web Theater. You click the movie window. The Web server checks your browser to see if the Web Theater player has been installed on your computer. If not, the Web server usually gives you an opportunity to download and install it.

A software module that adds a specific feature to a system is called a **plug-in** or **viewer**. In the context of the Web, a plug-in adds a feature to your browser, such as the capability to play Web Theater videos. Popular plug-ins include Acrobat Reader, Shockwave, Real Audio, Real Video, VoxChat, and Cool Talk.

Push and Pull

InfoWeb

Push
8

With all this multimedia, isn't the Web becoming a lot like TV? The way most people use the Web is shaped by pull technology. With **pull technology** you use your browser to request Web pages and "pull" them into view on your computer screen. You only get those pages that you request and a Web server will not send you information unless you request it.

An alternative, called **push technology** sends you information that you didn't directly request. To receive pushed information from a Web site, you first register and then download the push plug-in software. There are several variations of push technology, and each requires its own plug-in. At most sites, the registration and the plug-in are free. Once you've registered, you receive pushed information whenever your computer is connected to the Internet. For example, suppose you register at a site that pushes stock information. Every time you connect to the Internet, your computer receives and displays current stock prices.

A growing number of Web sites provide "pushed" information. For example, many popular news sites, such as CNN and *The New York Times* allow you to set up a **personalized newspaper** by selecting the topics that interest you. You might, for example, request information about your local weather, stocks you own, your favorite sports team, or technology news. Whenever you visit the news site, you'll receive a personalized newspaper containing the latest information on the topics you selected when you first registered at the site. Figure 8-13 shows an example.

Figure 8-13

A personalized newspaper includes a pushed ticker-tape of headlines, temperatures, and sports scores.

Scrolling news and temperature ticker

A **webcast** uses push technology to broadcast a stream of continually changing information over the Web. Sometimes used for special event coverage, a webcast continues only as long as you remain connected to the Internet. If you are using a dial-up connection, you might not want to tie up your phone line for lengthy webcasts. Webcasts will be much more practical when everyone has a permanent high-speed connection to the Internet.

File Transfers

Can I get a copy of a picture, sound, or video that I find on the Web? When you're viewing a Web page, it is held temporarily in the RAM of your computer, but it is not stored as a file on disk. Suppose that a Web page contains a graphic, sound, or video that you would like to store on disk for later use. The process of transferring a copy of a file from a remote computer to your computer's disk drive is called **downloading**. Most Web browsers allow you to easily download Web page elements such as pictures, sounds, animations, and videos. Figure 8-14 explains how to do this.

Figure 8-14

Downloading a graphic from a Web page

1. To download a Web page element, point to it and click the right mouse button.

2. From the shortcut menu, select "Save Picture as..." to save a graphic. To save a sound or other media element, use the "Save Target As..." option.

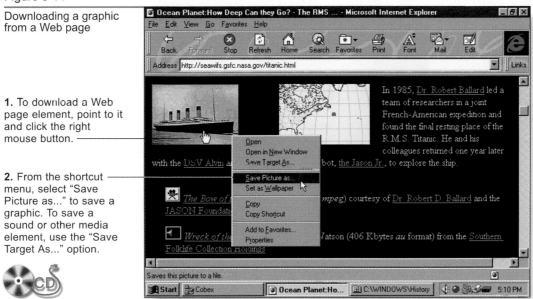

Uploading is the process of sending a copy of a file from your computer to a remote computer. Suppose, for example, that a writer living in British Columbia wants to send an 8 MB file containing the manuscript for a new novel to an editor in New York. What is the best way to deliver the manuscript to the editor? The writer could copy the file containing the manuscript to a Zip disk and send it via FedEx, but that would take at least 12 hours. Another possibility would be to attach the file to an e-mail, but some e-mail systems do not accept large attachments. A third option would be to upload the file to an Internet FTP server. The editor could then download the file from the server.

InfoWeb

FTP Software 9

Although most browsers allow you to download files, not all browsers allow you to upload. If your browser does not have upload capabilities, you can accomplish the task using **FTP client software**, such as WinFTP, published by Ipswitch, Inc.

Many FTP servers allow people to log in and obtain downloads using "anonymous" as the user ID and their e-mail address as the password. For security reasons, however, most FTP servers provide upload capabilities only to people who have valid user accounts. To upload a file using your browser or FTP client software, you'll need to know the domain name for an FTP server on which you have an account. You must log in using your user ID and password before you can initiate the upload.

Commercial Information Services

Why would I want to subscribe to a commercial information service? Your versatile

browser is the gateway to commercial information services as well as the free sites on the Internet. A **commercial information service** provides access to computer-based information for a fee. In 1997, approximately 17 million people subscribed to the top four commercial information services—America Online, CompuServe, Microsoft Network, and Prodigy. Most commercial information services are ISPs, offering dial-up Internet connections and e-mail, along with additional proprietary services described in Figure 8-15.

InfoWeb
Commercial
Services
10

Figure 8-15

Microsoft
Network
offers its
own chat
groups,
games, and
news
services that
are
accessible
only to
subscribers.

Commercial information services typically charge a $20 per month fee to access basic services, but the number of hours you can spend on the Internet might be limited. You might be charged additional fees, called **surcharges**, for additional Internet access or premium services. A **premium service** is information that has been designated as more valuable by the commercial information service. For example, many business-related services such as airline reservations, up-to-the-minute stock reports, and legal searches are often premium services.

If you have free access to the Internet provided by your school, you might not want to pay for a subscription to a commercial information service. However, many people do not have free Internet access, and would still like to send and receive e-mail, participate in online discussions, shop online, and have access to online information. For these people, a commercial information service might be the right choice.

Interactions

Chats &
Discussions
11

Can I interact directly with other people who are online? By far the most popular way to interact with other people on the Internet is with e-mail. It accounts for about one-third of all Internet activities. You can use your browser to send e-mail over the Internet. As an alternative, you can use standalone mail software such as Eudora or Pegasus.

Another way of interacting with people on the Internet is to join a **discussion group** in which participants share views on a specific issue or topic. On the Internet you'll find thousands of discussion groups on such diverse topics as snowboarding, urban policy, rave music, and William Gibson's cyberspace novels. Discussion groups take place **asynchronously**, meaning that the discussion participants are not online at the same time. For example, an English teacher might ask a question such as "Who has had the most impact on the development of cyberpunk novels?" Over the next few days other participants will post responses. When the English teacher next logs into the discussion group, he can read these responses, comment on them, or ask another question.

If you would rather interact synchronously with people who are online at the same time, you can join a **chat group**. To participate in a chat, you generally choose a nickname, then enter a chat room. As chat participants type, their messages appear on your screen. You'll see the messages from everyone in the chat room. Chat groups are often less focused than discussion groups as participants banter about the weather and themselves. That is not to say that serious chats never occur. On the contrary, chats can be an effective forum for professional interaction such as when physicians in different locations use the Internet to collaborate on a diagnosis.

Recently chat groups have come under fire because of potential dangers to personal safety and privacy. Use common sense in your chat room interactions. Don't represent yourself as something you're not. Don't provide personal information such as your name or address. Internet society, like society as a whole, has its share of deviants and rip-off experts. Most chats, however, are fairly civilized as shown in Figure 8-16.

Figure 8-16

A sample
chat session

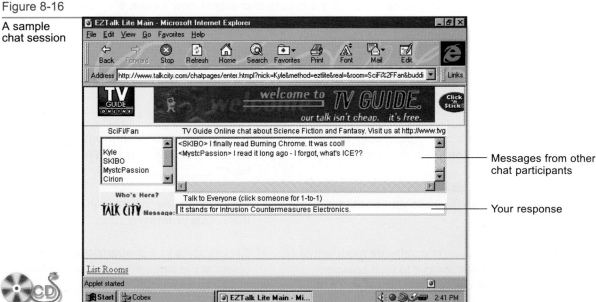

Messages from other chat participants

Your response

Games
12

Another aspect of Internet interaction is online **multi-player gaming**. From simple competitive word games to massive adventure games, the world of Internet gaming has it all. Imagine creating a cyber personna with the strength of a giant and the cunning of an elf. Arm yourself with your favorite weapon and venture into an imaginary world where you can defeat evil and accumulate treasure. Your fellow adventurers are people from all over the world (Figure 8-17).

Figure 8-17

Multi-player games give you an opportunity to play with, or play against, other players from all over the Internet.

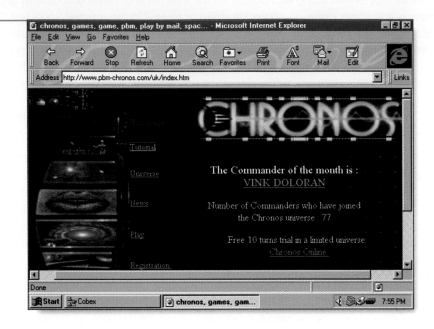

Some multi-player games are synchronous and others are asynchronous. As with chat groups, to participate in a synchronous game, you and the other players must be online at the same time. To participate in asynchronous games, you post each move to the game's referee, then you can pick up the results and submit new moves the next time you are online. Many multi-player games require a small fee to participate.

QuickCheck B

1 Your browser's _____ page is the first one you see when your browser starts.

2 A technology called _____ essentially plays a media file while your computer receives it.

3 A(n) _____ is a software module that adds a specific feature to your browser, such as the capability to play Web Theater videos.

4 Webcasting is pull technology that broadcasts information over the Web. True or false? _____

5 Most commercial information services are ISPs. True or false? _____

6 To participate in a chat group you must be online at the same time as other participants. True or false? _____

Web Authoring and Site Management

LAB

Web Pages HTML

Using the Web as a source for information and interaction is great, but at some time you might want to become a Web author and publish your own pages. You might become even more ambitious and decide to create and manage your own Web site. Using today's software tools, Web authoring and publishing is not much more difficult than word processing or desktop publishing.

Why would you want to publish on the Web? You might have information that you want to make available to the public, such as your resume or a calendar of events for your club. You might have services or products to offer that you would like people to easily obtain from any geographic location. You might want to collect information from people by using surveys or questionnaires. Web publishing will help you get your message out and collect data.

Web Publishing

What can I publish? The Web provides opportunities for publishing tasks ranging from a single page to an entire Web site.

A single Web page is simple to create and can publish useful information such as your resume or a publicity flyer for a small business. Another use for a single Web page is to provide a list of links to sites with information on a particular topic.

A series of interlinked Web pages is like a mini site, except that it does not have its own domain name. You might publish a series of Web pages as part of a corporate site to describe the products and services of your department. Freelance artists or programmers could use a series of Web pages to publish examples of their work. A university instructor might publish a series of Web pages containing the syllabus, study guide, and assignments for a course.

A Web site includes a series of Web pages and has its own domain name. Businesses and organizations of all sizes create Web sites to provide information to customers and to sell products. With the availability of security software to protect customers' credit card numbers, e-commerce is becoming popular. Having a recognizable domain name such as www.hilfinger.com is an asset that helps customers arrive at a site without a lengthy search.

Basic Web pages contain text, graphics, and links. More sophisticated Web pages include animation, sound, and video. Your pages can also include interactive elements such as questionnaires or surveys. To incorporate these sophisticated features in your Web pages, your Web server might require special server software, but you need only a few tools to publish basic pages that feature text, graphics, and links.

HTML

What's an HTML tag? Every Web page is stored as an HTML document. An **HTML document** contains special instructions that tell a Web browser how to display the text, graphics, and background of a Web page. These instructions, called **HTML tags**, are inserted into the text of the document. If you look at the text of a Web page before it is displayed by a browser, you'll see the HTML tags set off in angle brackets. For example, the HTML tag <B> means to begin boldfaced text. A companion tag </B> means to end the boldface. In Figure 8-18 you can examine an HTML document as it looks before and after it is displayed by a browser. See if you can figure out the purpose of the HTML tags <BR> and <IMG SRC>.

InfoWeb

HTML
13

Figure 8-18

An HTML document and
corresponding Web page

```
<HTML>
<HEAD><TITLE>Nichole F. Kase Home Page</TITLE></HEAD>
<BODY>a
<BODY BGCOLOR = "#ffffff">
<TR><IMG SRC="canyon.gif" ALIGN="LEFT">
<CENTER>
<FONT SIZE=+3><B>Nichole F. Kase</B><BR>
<B>Canyon Web Design</B></FONT><BR><BR>
<B>Email: </B>
<A HREF="MAILTO:Nichole.Kase@mail.state.edu">Nichole.Kase@state.edu</A>
<BR><BR><BR>
<IMG SRC="bluebar.gif">
</CENTER>
</BODY>
</HTML>
```

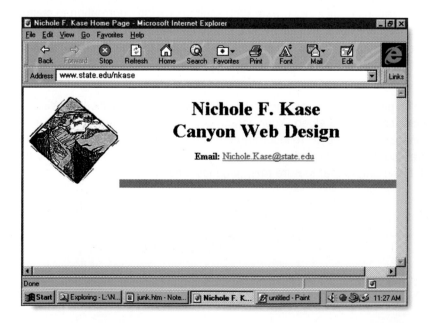

A basic HTML document has two parts. The **head** of the document specifies a title that appears on the title bar of the Web browser when the Web page is displayed. The **body** of the document contains informational text, graphics, and links.

Every HTML document should begin with the tag <HTML> and end with the tag </HTML>. This illustrates that some HTML tags work in pairs. The tag without the slash (/) is the opening tag. The tag with the slash is the ending tag. Some tags do not have a corresponding end tag. For example, you only need a single <BR> tag to create a line break. The table in Figure 8-19 contains a basic set of HTML tags that you can use to create HTML documents for Web pages.

The traditional way to create an HTML document is with a basic text editor such as the Notepad program included with Microsoft Windows. Simply type the HTML tags and the text for your Web page, then save the file with an .htm extension. You can also use a full-featured word processor such as Word, but saving the document is tricky because you don't want the word processor to insert its own non-HTML tags that confuse Web browsers. You'll learn more about using word-processing software to create Web pages in the next section.

Figure 8-19

Basic HTML tags

HTML Tags	Meaning and location
<HTML></HTML>	States that the file is an HTML document. Opening tag begins the page; closing tag ends the page (required).
<HEAD></HEAD>	States that the enclosed text is the header of the page. Appears immediately after the opening HTML tag (required).
<TITLE></TITLE>	States that the enclosed text is the title of the page. Must appear within the opening and closing HEAD tags (required).
<BODY></BODY>	States that the enclosed material (all the text, images, and tags in the rest of the document) is the body of the document (required).
<H1></H1>,	States that the enclosed text is a heading.
 	Inserts a line break. Can be used to control line spacing and breaks in lines.
<UL></UL>, <OL></OL>	Indicates an unordered list (list items are preceded by bullets) or an ordered list (list items are preceded by numbers or letters).
<LI>	Indicates a list item. Precedes all items in unordered or ordered lists.
<CENTER></CENTER>	Indicates that the enclosed text should be centered on the width of the page.
<B></B>	Indicates that the enclosed text should appear bold face.
<I></I>	Indicates that the enclosed text should appear italic.
<A HREF=""></A>	Indicates that the enclosed text is a hypertext link; the URL of the linked material must appear within the quote marks after the equal sign.
<IMG SCR=""	Inserts an in-line image into the document. The URL of the image appears within the quote marks following the SRC="" attribute.
<HR>	Inserts a horizontal rule.

HTML Authoring Tools

InfoWeb

Authoring
Tools
14

Do I have to use HTML? Remembering the purpose of each HTML tag, typing the tags into a document, and revising them is a fairly tedious task. New **HTML authoring tools** make it much easier to create Web pages using word processor-style interfaces, pre-designed templates, and Wizards. The tools you can use for Web authoring include familiar application software packages, Web browsers, and specialized Web authoring software.

If you have recent-generation word-processing software, it is likely to include Web authoring capabilities. You enter text and insert graphics just as you would for a standard document, then the software outputs that document in HTML format (Figure 8-20). Some spreadsheet, desktop publishing, and presentation software packages offer similar capabilities.

Figure 8-20

Your word-processing software might have a feature that converts your documents into HTML format.

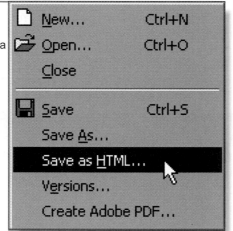

These familiar software tools create your Web page with a minimum of fuss, but they do not provide a high level of control over the final appearance of your Web page. For example, word-processing software is designed to create printed documents and includes features that are not available in HTML. Your word processor will do its best to translate your word-processing document into an HTML document. However, the exact formats and arrangement of elements that you see on your word processor's screen are not necessarily what will appear on the Web page.

Your browser might provide tools to create Web pages. For example, Netscape Communicator Professional Edition includes a module called Netscape Composer designed to make it easy to construct Web pages by selecting components from menus. The software automatically inserts HTML tags for each of the elements you've selected.

Web authoring software is designed specifically to create HTML documents that will be displayed as Web pages. Some of the top Web-authoring software titles include Microsoft FrontPage, Claris Home Page, Adobe Page Mill, and Corel Web Designer. Most of these packages provide a word processor-style interface, but allow you to implement only those features that are available in HTML. As you enter text, select type styles, and insert graphics, the Web authoring software automatically inserts appropriate HTML tags. Using this software, what you see is pretty much what you get, although slight format and placement variations might result depending on the browser used to view the page.

Many Web authoring software packages also provide tools to manage an entire Web site. In addition to helping you create individual Web pages, this software maintains a map of page links and automatically tests links to pages at other sites to make sure the links are still valid. Your Web authoring software might also include Web server software so you can turn any Internet host into a Web site accessible to Web surfers.

Compared to your familiar word-processing software, it takes a little longer to get up and running with Web authoring software because you are learning a new package. However, if you are planning to create more than an occasional Web page, you'll have more flexibility in Web page design, and you'll save time testing and maintaining your pages.

Page Design Tips

InfoWeb

Authoring
Tips
15

How do I make a really great Web page? It is not easy to find the right balance of art and functionality that makes a really great Web page. Your skills will improve as you gain experience designing pages and as you continue to use Web pages designed by others. To avoid some of the mistakes typically made by beginning Web page designers, use these tips:

Plan your Web page so it fulfills its purpose. Determine the function of your Web page. Is its purpose to entertain, to persuade, to inform, or to instruct? A clear idea of your page's goals and functions will guide all of your design decisions. In this way, the function of your Web page will determine the form that it takes. Designs are more effective when form follows function rather than when form is used for form's sake.

Design a template to unify your pages. A design template is a set of specifications for the location and format of all the elements that you want to include on your Web pages. The purpose of a design template is to visually tie together a series of Web pages and provide a consistent interface. Your template design might include any of the following elements: background, graphics, title, text, lists, headings, subheadings, video clips, music, animations, and navigation buttons. Get design ideas and develop a sense of style by looking at Web pages that are similar to those you plan to create.

Follow basic rules for good Web page design. Viewers will loose patience and move on to other Web sites if it takes too long for your pages to appear or if the text is illegible. Figure 8-21 summarizes basic design rules for the text, backgrounds, and graphics on your Web pages.

Figure 8-21

Basic Web design rules

Text:	■ For readability, use black type for large sections of text. ■ Maintain narrow line widths. Text that stretches across the entire width of the screen is more difficult to read than text in columns. ■ Make sure you proofread your document for spelling errors.
Background:	■ White or a very pale color makes a good background. ■ Avoid drab gray and don't let your background color or graphic make it difficult to read the text.
Graphics:	■ Try not to use graphics files that exceed 30 KB because larger files take too long to transfer, load, and appear on a Web page. ■ Use graphics with .gif, not .bmp extensions. ■ To include a large graphic, present it as a small "thumbnail" with a link to the larger version of the graphic.

If your Web site will have multiple pages, sketch a hierarchy chart that shows how the pages will link to each other. Avoid a link plan that looks like a spider web. Although it is acceptable to have many exit links going to other pages, if possible, each page on your site should have only one entry link as shown in Figure 8-22.

Figure 8-22

Sketch a plan that shows the structure of your Web site. Each box that represents a page has only one arrow pointing into the box, indicating a single entry point.

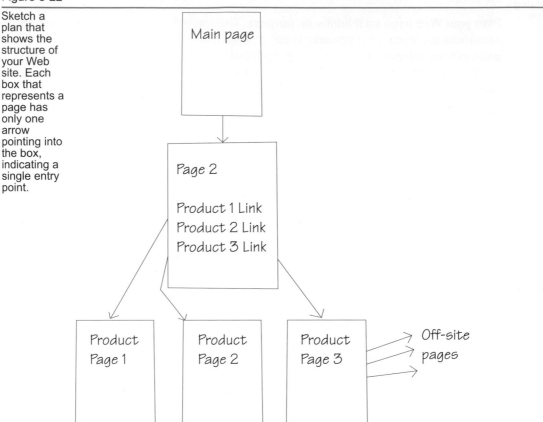

Include navigation elements. A carefully selected set of navigational buttons or links make it easy for people to jump from page to page in a logical order. Navigation elements should be clearly visible and easy to understand. If you have multiple pages, always include a navigation element that takes the viewer back to your home page. Use the same navigation system on every page of your site.

Respect copyright and intellectual property rights of other Web sites. If you use images and backgrounds that you have downloaded from the Web, make sure that you understand any copyright laws that apply to their reuse. Obtain permission before you use material from other Web sites and include a credit line on your page. For example, you could place a statement such as "Images courtesy of Paramount Pictures" at the bottom of your page.

Identify your pages. Make sure to use the <TITLE> tag on every page so it has a title. Also, include a way for people to contact you by including a link to your e-mail address. Place a copyright statement at the bottom of your page. The general format is the word "copyright," followed by the year or a range of years, followed by your name: Copyright 1998 Bobby Quine.

Publishing Your Pages

How do I get my pages on the Internet? Creating a Web page is not the end of the publishing process. You also need to test your pages, transfer them to a Web server, and test all your links. Figure 8-23 summarizes the process.

Figure 8-23

Four steps to publishing Web pages

1. Create each page

2. Test each page locally

3. Transfer the page to a Web server

4. Test all links

When you've completed the first draft of a Web page, you must test it to make sure every element is displayed correctly by a browser. You can do this without connecting to the Web by using your browser or Web authoring software. One caution: Your hard drive is much faster than a dial-up connection, so the text and graphics for your Web page appear more quickly during your test than they will for someone viewing your page over the Internet.

Whether you're publishing a single page, a series of pages, or an entire Web site, you must put your pages on a Web server. Although Web server software is available for your home computer, you'll probably not want to leave your computer on all the time with a live phone line link to the Internet. Instead, you should look for a site that will host your pages.

Many universities allocate space for student home pages and resumes. ISPs such as America Online and AT&T also offer space for individual home pages. If you are setting up a site for your business, consider a **Web hosting service** such as www.highway.com that provides space on its Internet servers for a monthly fee.

After you post your pages on a Web server, make sure you test the links between your pages and your links to pages on other sites. Then, sit back and watch as visitors flock to your site!

QuickCheck C

1. To create basic Web pages that contain only text, graphics, and _____, your Web server will not require additional software.

2. When HTML tags come in pairs, the first tag begins with a slash (/). True or false? _____

3. A basic HTML document has two parts— the head and the _____.

4. The traditional way to create HTML documents is with word-processing software. True or false? _____

5. _____ software is specifically designed to create HTML documents that will be displayed as Web pages.

6. A basic Web design rule is to avoid using graphic files larger than 30 KB on your Web pages. True or false? _____.

7. A careful selection of _____ buttons or links makes it easy for people to jump from page to page in a logical order.

8. When you test your pages locally, your Web pages appear more quickly than when viewed by a user with a dial-up Web connection. True or false? _____

U s e r F o c u s

D Connecting to the Internet

If your school has Internet access, your Academic Computing department has installed the hardware and software you need to access the Internet from your school lab, and possibly from your dorm room. But what if you want to access the Internet from your computer at home? To access the Internet from your home computer, you must set up the necessary computer equipment, locate an Internet service provider, install the appropriate software on your computer, then dial in.

Set Up Equipment

What special equipment do I need to access the Internet? The basic equipment for setting up online communications is a computer, a modem, and a telephone line. The equipment you use does not change the activities you can do online, but it can affect the speed at which you can accomplish these activities.

PCs and Macintosh computers can both connect to online services. A fast computer such as a 200 MHz Pentium speeds up some activities such as viewing graphics online. However, the overall speed of online activities is limited by the speed of the server, the speed of your modem, and the speed of your communications link.

InfoWeb

Modems
16

A **modem** converts the data from your computer into signals that can travel over telephone lines. It also translates arriving signals into data that your computer can store, manipulate, and display. A fast modem speeds the process of sending and receiving data. For example, a 33.6 Kbps (33,600 bits per second) modem provides you with faster online response than a 28.8 Kbps (28,800 bits per second) modem. Be careful when choosing a modem. Some require special phone lines. Follow the instructions included with your modem to set it up (Figure 8-24).

Figure 8-24

Connect your modem to your computer, then connect it to your phone line.

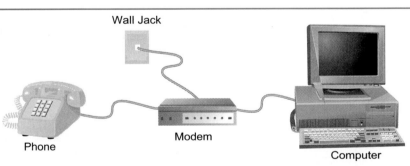

Wall Jack

Phone

Modem

Computer

The telephone line that you use for voice communications is suitable for most online activities. Corporations sometimes use faster communications links such as ISDN or T1. Your telephone line, though not the speediest communications link, is certainly the least expensive. When you are using your telephone line for online activities, you can't simultaneously use it for voice calls; while you are online, people who call you will get a busy signal. If you pick up the telephone receiver to make an outgoing call while you are online, your online connection will terminate.

Locate an Internet Service Provider

Who will provide me with an Internet connection, and how much will it cost? An Internet

InfoWeb

ISPs
17

service provider supplies you with a user account on a host computer that has access to the Internet. When you connect your personal computer to the host computer using a modem and the appropriate software, you gain access to the Internet. Your school might provide Internet access for students and faculty who want to use the Internet from off campus. An Internet connection provided by an educational institution is typically free.

Many commercial information services such as CompuServe, Prodigy, Microsoft Network, and America Online provide Internet access. Internet connections are also offered by some telephone companies, cable TV companies, and independent telecommunications firms. These firms charge between $20 and $30 per month for Internet access. Unlike commercial information services, they usually do not maintain their own online information, discussion groups, or downloadable software (Figure 8-25).

Figure 8-25

Internet service providers advertise in local newspapers and the Yellow Pages.

Internet Service Provider

SMALLTOWN TELEPHONE/INTERNET SERVICE

- FAST, RELIABLE SERVICE
- PROFESSIONAL TECHNICAL ASSISTANCE
- LOCAL ACCESS
- ENTER THE INTERNET THROUGH A FAMILIAR SOURCE

◇◇◇

SMALLTOWN TELEPHONE

SMALLTOWN TELEPHONE

297 Main St S   Wood 222-3201

Install Software

Where do I get the software I need? Many ISPs provide subscibers with a complete software package that includes a browser and Internet communications software. **Internet communications software** allows your computer to transmit and receive data using the Internet TCP/IP communications protocol. Standard TCP/IP software handles Internet communication between computers that are directly cabled to a network. **SLIP (Serial Line Internet Protocol)** and **PPP (Point to Point Protocol)** are versions of TCP/IP designed to handle Internet communications over dial-up connections. When you want to access the Internet from a computer using a modem, you must use PPP, SLIP, or other similar communications software.

In the past, luck played an important role in establishing successful computer communications. Today, the software supplied by most Internet service providers is self-configuring; in other words, the first time you run the software, it examines your computer system and automatically selects the appropriate software settings. You have to deal with technical specifications only if your computer equipment, modem, or telephone line are not standard.

Dial In

After my hardware is set up and my software is installed, how do I dial in to the Internet?

Most Internet communications software is represented by an icon on your computer's desktop or Start menu. You start the software by clicking this icon, and it automatically establishes a connection to the Internet. Figure 8-26 shows what happens when you dial in.

Figure 8-26

Dialing into the Internet

Click the Internet icon supplied by your Internet service provider.

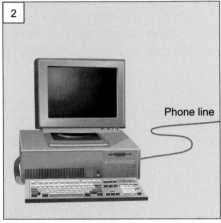

By clicking the Internet icon, you tell the computer to load your Internet communications client software. Your communications client will probably use SLIP or PPP to handle the TCP/IP protocols as your computer transmits and receives data through your modem.

Your communications client dials the Internet service provider. Usually, your communications client has stored the telephone number, so you do not need to enter it each time you want to connect.

If your communications client has stored your user ID and password, it will automatically log you in. Some people prefer to enter their password manually for better security.

End Note

The Internet has received much publicity. Many people agree that such a vast information network has potential to improve the quality of our lives. It provides us with an opportunity to interact with people of diverse backgrounds, engage in life-long education, and enrich our knowledge of the global community.

Information
Quality
18

Fifty years ago a new technology called television promised similar advantages. Today, many people believe that television has failed. They point to inane soap operas, an over-abundance of graphic violence, the commercialization of gratuitous sex, and popularity of talk shows featuring bizarre human experiences.

Will the information highway also fail to fulfill its potential? The answer to this question is difficult to predict. The amount of information available online is growing. Much of this data is useful, but other information is of questionable value. Online computer technical support helps thousands of people keep their computers operational, but who is helped by online instructions for manufacturing homemade bombs? Satellite photographs from NASA's online database contribute to our knowledge of the universe, but what is the contribution of graphical images of sexual exploitation?

Smart consumers know that they can't believe everything they read or hear. This holds true for information on the Internet as well as television, radio, newspapers, tabloids, and books. Don't be deceived by conspiracy theories, disinformation, pseudo-science, and wacky medicine. Check for the facts. The Internet has many reliable resources that make their best effort to validate the information they publish (Figure 8-27).

In many ways, the Internet is a reflection of the interests as well as the problems of our society. Its development is worth watching throughout your lifetime.

Figure 8-27

It is easy to spread conspiracy theories on the Internet, but several "watchdog" sites try to present the "facts" that dispute or confirm the theories.

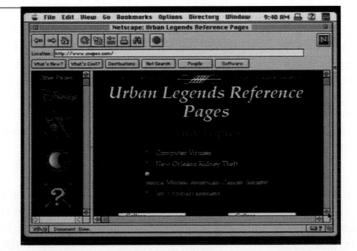

InfoWeb

InfoWeb

Chapter Links

The InfoWeb is your guide to print, film, television, and electronic resources. Use it to obtain updates on quickly changing technical information and to locate information for research papers. If you're using the New Perspectives CD-ROM, click the InfoWeb icon on the left side of this paragraph to access the online InfoWeb links. Otherwise, use your Web browser and type in the address of the New Perspectives site: www.cciw.com/np3. At the New Perspectives site you'll find up-to-date links to the topics covered in this chapter.

1 Cyberspace

According to *Forbes Magazine* (July 7, 1997 p. 348), "Science fiction is more than an inelegant prose for pencil-necked teenagers. Businesspeople and investors looking to discover where technology is taking us would do well to pay attention to it." The article describes how science fiction can sometimes become reality. For a serious analysis of the potential impact of cyberspace on society, check your library for the book **Cyberspace: First Steps**, edited by Michael Benedikt (MIT Press, 1993). William Gibson is generally recognized as the person who coined the term "cyberspace." His novel, **Neuromancer**, was the first of a literary genre now called cyberpunk. Visit William Gibson's Yardshow at **www.idoru.com/yardshow.html**. At The Electronic Freedom Foundation page, **www.eff.org/pub/Publications/William_Gibson**, you'll find some links to essays and interviews. You can scope out additional links by using the Yahoo! search engine and entering "William Gibson." On the lighter side of cyberspace literature, pick up the book **Dave Barry in Cyberspace** (Crown Publishers, 1966).

2 Internet History

Many reliable sources have reported that the Internet was built because the U.S. military wanted a computer network that would survive nuclear attack. Bob Taylor, father of the ARPANET refutes this myth in the book **Where Wizards Stay Up Late** by Hafner and Lyon (Simon & Schuster, 1996). A good video introduction to the Internet is **Understanding and Using the Internet** (PBS Home Video, 1996). Several of the people involved in the initial development and evolution of the Internet have written "A Brief History of the Internet" at **www.isoc.org/internet-history**. "The Roads and Crossroads of Internet's History" at **www.internetvalley.com/ intval.html** is an annotated timeline of events that contributed to cur-

rent Internet technology such as: the laying of transoceanic cable connecting the U.S. and Europe in 1866, the founding of the Advanced Research Projects Agency (ARPA) in 1957, and the invention of the Web at CERN in 1989. Also check out "NetHistory: The Discovery Channel: A History of the Internet: How Did We Get Here Anyway?" at **www.discovery.com/area/history/internet/inet1.html** for a timeline of the Internet illustrated with drawings and photographs and interspersed with other technological events of the time. For an on-going discussion of the history and evolution of the Internet, check out the Computer Professionals For Social Responsibility's Community Memory: Discussion List on the History of Cyberspace at **memex.org/community-memory.html**.

3 Internet Statistics: Amazing Growth

It's difficult to keep track of the wild growth of the Internet. Measuring the number of computers and users on the Internet seems to produce sometimes conflicting statistics. For a roundup of statistics from various sources, connect to the CyberAtlas site at **www.cyberatlas.com**. Twice a year, a company called Network Wizards counts the number of hosts on the Internet. You'll find a summary of their research at Matthew Gray's site. Find the site by searching for "mkgray" at **www.mit.edu**. Hop over to **www.genmagic.com/Internet/Trends** to see Tony Rutkowski's collection of slides about the Internet. You can have some fun and produce your own wild projections about the Internet using the Internet Statistic Generator at **www.anamorph.com/docs/stats/stats.html**.

4 **Domain Names**

If you set up your own Internet site, you'll want your own domain name. How will you know if the name you want is available? At the site **www.checkdomain.com** you can enter a domain name such as neuromancer.com to see if it has already been reserved. Could you select a generic domain name such as www.government.com? For information on restricted domain names, tips on creating a valid domain name, and instruction on how to register a domain name, connect to the InterNIC server at **www.internic.net**.

5 **Find It: Where to Find Internet Addresses**

Have you lost track of your high school friends and wonder if they're online? You don't have to wonder for long. Search services on the Internet can help you locate people's telephone numbers, addresses, and e-mail addresses. Yahoo! People Search at **www.yahoo.com/search/people** allows you to look up a telephone number if you know the person's first name, last name, city and state. This service also allows you to look up an e-mail address if you know the person's first name, last name, and Internet domain. An alternative source is C/NET Search.com at **www.search.com**, then select the link for Yellow Pages, Phone Numbers, or e-mail Addresses.

6 **WWW**

CERN (the European Particle Physical Laboratory) is the birthplace of the World Wide Web. You can visit its site at **www.cern.ch** and follow the link for World Wide Web to read a bit about its history. Official information about the Web is maintained by the World Wide Web Consortium (W3C) at **www.w3.org/History.html**. The same site contains a page of great links about everything Web at **www.w3.org/TheProject**.

7 **Plug-ins**

Plug-ins provide access to audio, video, graphics, and 3-D file formats. Netscape's Plug Ins page (access it from **home.netscape.com**) lists 154 Netscape plug-ins currently available. How do you know which plug-ins you really need? How do you know which plug-ins are worth trying? You can read reviews and download plug-ins from the Internet Plug-ins page at **www.download.com** (enter plug-in in the search box). BrowserWatch - Plug-In Plaza at **browserwatch.internet.com/plug-in.html** provides links to all of the plug-ins available on the Internet. Plug-ins are one of the most quickly changing aspects of the Web industry, and most computer magazines run one or two articles about plug-ins and browsers every six months. "Plunging into Plug-Ins" at **www.pcworld.com/software/internet_www/articles/apr97/1504p110m.html** from the April 1997 issue of *PC World*, gives a list of indispensable plug-ins with brief descriptions of each and a link to a Web page for downloading. This article also includes a good discussion of how to remove plug-ins that you no longer want to use—something that is not as easy to do as you would hope.

8 **Push**

A pioneer in push technology, PointCast hosts a site at **www.pointcast.com/tour** where you can take a quick tour of push technology. For an excellent article on push technology that includes links to some of the more popular push sites, connect to the Push Publishing page at the National Library of Canada at **www.nlc-bnc.ca/pubs/netnotes/notes41.htm**. Some experts would argue that there is no such thing as push technology, only variations of pull. Edmund DeJesus explains this viewpoint in **The Pull of Push** (*Byte*, August 1997). What do you use to wrap up a fish? A newspaper. That's the point of MIT's experimental personalized newspaper project, fishWrap at **fishwrap.mit.edu**. Where else can you sign up for a personalized newspaper? Head for the Newspage site at **pnp.individual.com** or CNN at **www.cnn.com** and follow the Custom News link.

9 **FTP Software**

FTP (file transfer protocol) software is probably one of the oldest, most useful, and easy to use Internet applications of them all. It allows you to upload and download files from computers throughout the world. Windows 95 includes a basic FTP utility, but it uses a command-line interface, so most users prefer other GUI-based FTP software such as WS_FTP Professional. You can download the shareware version from **www.ipswitch.com/Products/WS_FTP/index.html**. File Dog at **www.edgepub.com/fd** is a shareware FTP software for Windows that has been highly rated by *PC Magazine*. File Dog makes a free evaluation copy available to potential users. Fetch at **www.dartmouth.edu/pages/softdev/fetch.html** is FTP software for the Macintosh that is free for users affiliated with an educational institution or charitable non-profit organization. WinFTP at **www.winsite.com/info/pc/win3/programr/winftp.zip** is a popular Windows FTP program that also has Web functions.

10 **Commercial Information Services**

Commercial information services are generally considered to provide a good entry-level Internet experience for the novice. There are four major online services operating today. Each service offers some unique content and has a different personality. CompuServe at **www.compuserve.com** is one of the oldest online services and is often perceived as being strongest in technical content and its discussion forums are highly regarded. America Online at **www.aol.com** is the largest of the four online services in terms of members. It pioneered online interactive sessions with famous writers, politicians, sports figures, and rock stars. Prodigy Internet at **www.prodigy.com**, is often viewed as a family-friendly online service, and it has file libraries, chat rooms, and proprietary content, such as a Consumer Reports library. In February 1997, Prodigy re-launched itself as a full service Internet provider, while keeping its online service as a smaller part of its business. Finally, Microsoft Network at **www.msn.com** is the newest of the online services. It is generally regarded as having the coolest, most extravagant proprietary content. You can learn more about commercial information services through computer industry magazines. For example, *PC World's* **Best Routes to the Net**, in the February 1997, issue reviewed 12 Internet service providers, including the commercial information services. In addition, check out the Online Connection at **www.barkers.org/online/index.html**. This Web site provides news, comparisons of commercial information services and national ISPs, discusses pricing and features, and provides service profiles.

11 **Chats and Discussion Groups**

To participate in discussion groups using your browser, connect to **www.dejanews.com**. Make sure you read the rules before you begin posting comments. For interactive chats, the options seem limitless. If you log into Yahoo! chats at **www.yahoo.com** (and follow the Chat links) you'll see that typically over 5,000 "chatters" are logged on at any time. Chatweb at **www.chatweb.com** has an easy-to-use interface, making it a good place to get started. If you're a member of AOL, CompuServe, MSN, or Prodigy their members-only chat groups are also a good place to try out Internet Chat. At The WebChat Broadcasting System site, **wbs.net**, you can "just visit" or you can register (free) and participate. *Salon Magazine* sponsors chats that have a reputation for being more substantive than chats at other sites. Connect to the Salon site at **www.salonmagazine.com** and follow the Table Talk links.

12 **Games**

MOOs (MUD Object Oriented), MUDs (Multi User Dimension or Dungeon), and MUSHEs began as text-based role playing games. With the advent of graphical Web browsers and VRML, these games are evolving into graphical, 3-D interactive worlds. You can visit some of these interactive sites with a standard Web browser. To participate in other sites, you need to download their VRML browser. If you have a vivid imagination, text-based MOOs, MUDs, and MUSHEs still exist, and you can connect to them on the Web. The Sprawl at **sensemedia.net/sprawl** is one of the oldest running MOOs existing on the Internet. Two sites where you can find people to play traditional board games online are Gamer's Zone at **www.worldvillage.com/wv/gamezone/html/games.htm** and Microsoft's Internet Gaming Zone at **www.zone.com**. The Realm at **www.realmserver.com** is an interactive adventure game from Sierra online. You can carry out quests in a world of monsters, magic, and medieval society in the companionship of thousands of players from across the world. The Realm costs $49.95 a year for unlimited play. The Games Domain Games Information Pages at **www.gamesdomain.com/gdmain.html** is a good source of information about both off-line and online games, including hints, walk throughs, and reviews. Hot links to the Virtual World Industry at **www.ccon.org/hotlinks/hotlinks.html** has information about and links to most of the major virtual reality game sites and browsers. It is a good launching point if you want to explore the world of virtual reality on the Web.

13 HTML

According to Nicholas Negroponte of the Media Lab at MIT, the Web is doubling in size every 50 days, and people are publishing home pages at a rate of one every four seconds. How can you join the rush to the Web and publish your own home page? The key is HTML-hypertext markup language. For a basic introduction on how to use HTML to create a Web page, connect to NCSA's A Beginner's Guide to HTML at **www.ncsa.uiuc.edu/General/Internet/WWW/HTMLPrimer.html**. You can find additional instruction at Learning HTML by the Tags Tutorial at **wally.rit.edu/depts/via/HTML/Tutorial/tutorial.html**, which provides links to information about graphics for the Web and how to publicize your Web site, in addition to basic instruction. If you prefer to use a book, **Teach Yourself Web Publishing with HTML 3.2 in a Week**, Third Edition by Laura Lemay (Sams.net, 1996) will be a helpful reference. For clip art, connect to the Image Finder at **wuecon.wustl.edu/other_www/wuarchimage.html**. For more clip art and animations connect to Andy's Art Attack at **www.andyart.com/**.

14 Authoring Tools

Web authoring tools allow you to create and work on Web pages from within a graphical interface. They help you generate HTML documents and view the result in a browser window or page viewer. Three popular Web authoring applications are Microsoft's FrontPage (**www.microsoft.com/frontpage**), Claris's Home Page (**www.claris.com/smallbiz/products/claris/clarispage**), and Adobe's PageMill (**www.adobe.com/prodindex/pagemill/main.html**). For a comparative review of HTML authoring tools, check out "HTML Editors: find the right tool," at **www.cnet.com/Content/Reviews/Compare/Htmleditors/index.html**.

15 Authoring Tips

The Web contains many resources that provide suggestions, tips, and information on Web page design. Written in a highly entertaining style, Crafting A Nifty Personal Web Site at **www2.hawaii.edu/jay/styleguide** provides lots of great tips with illustrated examples. For a more serious presentation, connect to Yale's C/AIM Web Style Guide at **info.med.yale.edu/caim/manual**. You'll enjoy the Web page makeovers in the Ziff-Davis *Internet MegaSite Magazine*. Pick up a copy from your newsstand or visit online at **www.zdimag.com** and follow the Makeovers links. *Internet Magazine*, published by emap Business Communications in the U.K. contains excellent information for Web designers. As you gain experience in Web page design, you'll find critiques of real sites at the award-winning site, HTML Style Guide: Common Problems in Web Design at **www.cire.com/patrick/design**.

16 Modems

Modem technology is changing as fast as any other segment of the computer industry. In 1994, most people had 9.6 Kbps modems. Today, most computers come equipped with 28.8 Kbps or 33.6 Kbps voice/fax modems, but on the Internet faster is better. What's the next step up in modem speed? A 56 Kbps modem? ISDN connection? Cable modem? Your questions about modems and Internet connections are answered at Modem FAQ–Curt's High Speed Modem Page at **www.teleport.com/~curt/modems.html**. Modems, Modems, Modems at **www.rosenet.net/~costmo** has a section of links to the home pages of modem makers, tips and troubleshooting tips, and sources of FAQs and drivers. According to *PC World* in the summer of 1997, the top five modem makers were U.S. Robotics (**www.usr.com**), Diamond MultiMedia (**www.diamondmm.com**), Practical Peripherals (**www.practinet.com**), Zoom Telephonics (**www.zoomtel.com**), and Motorola Modems (**www.mot.com/modems**).

17 ISPs

To avoid long-distance charges when you connect to the Internet, you'll want an ISP with a dial-in number within your local calling area. How can you find a local ISP? CNET ISP Review at **www.cnet.com/Content/Reviews/Compare/ISP/highest.html** provides comparative reviews of ISPs and information about how to select an ISP. CNET conducts a national survey of ISPs in which national and local ISPs are rated by their subscribers. The List at **thelist.internet.com** includes over 3,006 Internet Service Providers from the U.S., Canada, and around the world. You can search for an ISP by area code or by country code. Finally, PC World ISP Finder at **www.pcworld.com/interactive/ isps/isps.html** is a database that you can search by area code.

18 Information Quality

Some conspiracies are now classics—the JFK assassination, Elvis sightings, and the Roswell UFO Incident. And new conspiracies keep popping up—the missile that shot down TWA flight 800, the spaceship hidden behind the Hale-Bopp comet. The Disinformation Web site at **www.disinfo.com** provides a database of information about the origins and credibility (or lack of it) of many conspiracy theories. The site includes 'dossiers,' which cover many sides of a given issue or topic, both pro and con. Worth reading is Lucian Floridi's thought-provoking article about the future direction of the Internet and disinformation. You'll find the article, "Brave.Net.World: The Internet as a Disinformation Superhighway?" at **www.well.com/user/hlr/texts/disinfo.html**. The National Fraud Information Center at **www.fraud.org** helps consumers report fraud and offers helpful advice on how to avoid becoming a victim.

R e v i e w

1 Below each heading in this chapter, there is a question. Look back through the chapter and answer each of these questions using your own words.

2 Draw a conceptual diagram that shows how the Internet connects computers. Include and label the following elements: backbone, dial-up connection, host computers, router, NSP computer, ISP computer, home computer.

3 Provide an example of an IP address, a domain name, a URL, and an e-mail address. Then in your own words, describe the elements each contains.

4 Make a list of the Internet services you can access using a Web browser.

5 Indicate the type of software you can use to do each of the following:

a. Download a file

b. View a Web page

c. Play a multimedia element

6 Describe what happens when you view a Web page and how it differs from downloading a file.

7 Describe the difference between a Web server and a Web site.

8 Use your own words to define the difference between push and pull technology.

9 On the Internet, you can interact with people in discussion groups, chat groups, and interactive games. Describe the difference between synchronous and asynchronous interactions and explain how each relates to chats, discussion groups, and games.

10 List four categories of tools that you can use to create HTML documents.

11 Make a list of the steps you would take to connect your computer at home to the Internet.

12 Use the New Perspectives CD-ROM to take a practice test or to review the new terms presented in this chapter.

Projects

1 The Great Internet Hunt
For several years Rick Gates hosted a monthly Internet scavenger hunt. The object of his hunt was to find information on the Internet. The hunt in this project is a little different from Gates' hunt. For this hunt, there are 10 questions. The questions are located at the CTI Web site, **www.cciw.com/np3/project8-1.html**. Go to this site and print out the questions. Each question carries a point value between 1 and 5. Use the Web to answer as many questions as you can. For each question, you must supply the answer, the URL of the site where you found the answer, and a one-page printout to verify that you actually visited the site.

2 Censored! Prodigy, which bills itself as a family information service, monitors the content of its services to remove X-rated and R-rated text and graphics. However, no such policing occurs at most other Internet services.

The Internet and commercial information services provide a growing forum for discussions on a wide range of topics. Recently, some online observers have begun to question the advisability of information exchanged over the Internet. Megabytes of Internet storage space are devoted to X-rated images. Several Usenet groups regularly discuss the details of making bombs and hollow point bullets. Other groups discuss methods of torture. In a well-publicized incident, a discussion group participant described in gory detail how he was going to murder a female college student.

Free speech laws protect the rights of Americans to express themselves, but should the Internet, which is supported with public taxes, provide a medium for transmitting pornographic or terrorist information?

For this project, research the issue of online censorship. Write a position paper arguing for or against censorship. Support your position with facts and examples. Be sure to include a bibliography. After you complete your research, your instructor might suggest that you discuss your ideas in a small group session.

3 Personalized News It's a good idea to keep informed of current events and keep up with issues and activities that interest you. Connect to one of the Personalized News Web sites described in the *InfoWeb* section and create a personalized newspaper of your own. As verification that you completed the assignment, indicate which site you used, describe the options you selected, and write a short summary of your opinions about the usefulness of your personalized newspaper.

4 No One Knows You're a Dog In a novel called *Ender's War*, two children are catapulted to national prominence because they have innovative ideas about how to solve critical social and economic issues. No one knows they are children, however, because they communicate their ideas on a public information service, which is the central political forum in their society. This brings up an interesting issue, humorously alluded to in the P. Steiner cartoon.

"On the Internet, nobody knows you're a dog."

Discuss this issue in a small group. In your discussion address questions a through e.

a. Does a communications medium that depends on the written word, rather than on videos, reduce cultural, class, ethnic, and gender bias?

b. According to pollsters, in 1980 many Americans voted for Ronald Reagan because they didn't like his opponent's southern accent. Do you think the election would have been different if campaigning was carried out over the Internet?

c. There is evidence that the younger generation does not like to read and write. Do you think this generation needs a communications medium that is more like television?

d. Do you believe that online communications have the potential to reduce biases in our society?

e. Can anyone in your group relate an experience when online communications would have been preferable to face-to-face communication?

5 **Compare ISPs** When you use a dial-up line to connect to the Internet, it is preferable to dial a local call, rather than long distance. Therefore, you should pick an ISP that offers a dial-up number in your local calling area. Use the Internet, your library, and other resources to find a list of ISPs in your area. Don't forget to check commercial information services such as Compu-Serve, Prodigy, MSN, and America Online. Discover all the information you can about rates, reliability, quality of technical support, and services. Now, suppose that you are a reporter for your local newspaper. Write an article (about two pages, double-spaced) for the paper that compares the ISPs that offer local dial-up connections to the Internet.

6 **Web Site Makeover** To some extent, good design is a matter of taste and when it comes to Web page design, there are usually many possible solutions that provide a pleasing look and efficient navigational tools. On the other hand, there are some designs that just don't seem to work because they make the text difficult to read or navigate.

For this project, select a Web page that you think could use improvement. You may find the page by browsing on the Web or by looking in magazines for screen shots of Web pages. Use colored pencils or markers to sketch your plan for the improved page. Annotate your sketch by pointing out the features you have changed and why you think your makeover will be more effective than the original Web page.

7  **Design Your Own Home Page** For this project, you'll design your own home page. Depending on the tools you have available, you might be able to create a real page and publish it on the Web. If these tools are not available, you will still be able to complete the initial design work. Your instructor will provide you with guidelines on which of the following steps to complete.

a. Write a brief description of the purpose of your home page and your expected audience. For example, you might plan to use your home page to showcase your resume to prospective employers.

b. Make a list of the elements you plan to include on your home page. Briefly describe any graphics or media elements you want to include.

c. Create a document that contains the information you want to include for your home page. If you have the tools, create this document in HTML format.

d. Make a sketch of your home page showing the colors you plan to use and the navigation elements you plan to include. Annotate this sketch to describe how these elements follow effective Web page design guidelines.

e. If you have the tools to create the entire HTML document for your home page, do so. Make sure that you test the page locally using your browser. Use the Print option on the File menu of your browser to print your page.

f. If you have permission to publish your Web page on a Web server, do so. Provide your instructor with the URL for your page.

8

Virtual Reality: Writer William Gibson envisioned a time when people would connect their brains directly to a computer to experience a virtual world in cyberspace. Technology and medical science have not found a way to make a direct connection between our brains and a computer, but today virtual reality takes other forms. On the Internet, interactive technologies provide virtual environments for games, meetings, and socializing. On microcomputers, the multi-player game Doom provides hours of virtual reality adventure. Using equipment, such as the stereo-optic goggles and sensor gloves, you can see and manipulate objects that do not exist.

Use your library and Internet resources to learn more about virtual reality. You might also try some virtual reality experiences. If you have Internet access, participate in an interactive 3-D game. Play a virtual reality computer game such as Doom or Myst. If available, try out virtual reality goggles.

Now suppose you are asked to produce a three-minute TV news segment on virtual reality. Based on the information you gathered from your library, the Internet, and your personal experiences, write the narrative and describe the images and video clips you would show.

9

Good Netiquette The Internet, like most societies has certain standards for behavior. What's generally acceptable online behavior in cyberspace culture? Use the Internet or your library resources to research this topic, then design a poster of netiquette rules. You can decide what audience your poster targets: children, high school students, college students, business people—you could even select a specific business. Try to use words and images that will appeal to your target audience.

Lab Assignments

The Internet: World Wide Web

One of the most popular services on the Internet is the World Wide Web. This Lab is a Web simulator that teaches you how to use Web browser software to find information. You can use this Lab whether or not your school provides you with Internet access.

1 Click the Steps button to learn how to use Web browser software. As you proceed through the Steps, answer all of the Quick Check questions that appear. After you complete the Steps, you will see a Quick Check Summary Report. Follow the instructions on the screen to print this report.

2 Click the Explore button on the Welcome screen. Use the Web browser to locate a weather map of the Caribbean Virgin Islands. What is its URL?

3 A SCUBA diver named Wadson Lachouffe has been searching for the fabled treasure of Greybeard the pirate. A link from the Adventure Travel Web site **www.atour.com** leads to Wadson's Web page called

"Hidden Treasure." In Explore, locate the Hidden Treasure page and answer the following questions:

a. What was the name of Greybeard's ship?

b. What was Greybeard's favorite food?

c. What does Wadson think happened to Greybeard's ship?

4 In the Steps, you found a graphic of Jupiter from the photo archives of the Jet Propulsion Laboratory. In the Explore section of the Lab, you can also find a graphic of Saturn. Suppose one of your friends wanted a picture of Saturn for an astronomy report. Make a list of the blue, underlined links your friend must click in the correct order to find the Saturn graphic. Assume that your friend will begin at the Web Trainer home page.

5 Enter the URL **http://www.atour.com** to jump to the Adventure Travel Web site. Write a one-page description of this site. In your paper include a description of the information at the site, the number of pages the site contains, and a diagram of the links it contains.

6 Chris Thomson is a student at UVI and has his own Web pages. In Explore, look at the information Chris has included on his pages. Suppose you could create your own Web page. What would you include? Use word-processing software to design your own Web pages. Make sure you indicate the graphics and links you would use.

Web Pages & HTML

It's easy to create your own Web pages. As you learned in this chapter, there are many software tools to help you become a Web author. In this Lab you'll experiment with a Web authoring wizard that automates the process of creating a Web page. You'll also try your hand at working directly with HTML code.

1 Click the Steps button to activate the Web authoring wizard and learn how to create a basic Web page. As you proceed through the Steps, answer all of the Quick Check questions. After you complete the Steps, you will see a Quick Check summary Report. Follow the instructions on the screen to print this report.

2 In Explore, click the File menu, then click New to start working on a new Web page. Use the wizard to create a Home page for a veterinarian who offers dog day-care and boarding services. After you create the page, save it on drive A or C, and print the HTML code. Your site must have the following characteristics:

a. Title: Dr. Dave's Dog Domain

b. Background color: Gold

c. Graphic: Dog.jpg

d. Body text: Your dog will have the best care day and night at Dr. Dave's Dog Domain. Fine accommodations, good food, play time, and snacks are all provided. You can board your pet by the day or week. Grooming services also available.

e. Text link: "Reasonable rates" links to www.cciw.com/np3/rates.htm

f. E-mail link: "For more information:" links to **daveassist@drdave.com**

3 In Explore, use the File menu to open the HTML document called Politics.htm. After you use the HTML window (not the wizard) to make the following changes, save the revised page on Drive A or C, and print the HTML code. Refer to Figure 8-19 of your textbook for a list of HTML tags you can use.

a. Change the title to Politics 2000

b. Center the page heading

c. Change the background color to FFE7C6 and the text color to 000000

d. Add a line break before the sentence "What's next?"

e. Add a bold tag to "Additional links on this topic:"

f. Add one more link to the "Additional links" list. The link should go to the site **http://www.elections.ca** and the clickable link should read "Elections Canada".

g. Change the last graphic to display the image "next.gif"

4 In Explore use the Web authoring wizard and the HTML window to create a Home page about yourself. You should include at least a screenful of text, a graphic, an external link, and an e-mail link. Save the page on drive A, then print the HTML code. Turn in your disk and printout.

DATASECURITY and CONTROL

According to legend, the war between the Trojans and the Greeks continued for more than nine years, until one of the Greek leaders conceived a brilliant plan. He ordered his men to create a huge wooden horse. When it was completed, a few soldiers hid inside and the Greek army pretended to sail away. The Trojans believed that the horse was a gift, pulled it into the city, and spent the day celebrating what they thought was a great victory. Late that night, the soldiers hidden inside the horse crept out and opened the city gates for the waiting Greek army.

What does the Trojan War have to do with computers? Like the city of Troy, modern computer users are under siege. They are battling computer criminals, pranksters, viruses, equipment failures, and human errors. There is even a modern software version of the Trojan horse that might erase your data after you unknowingly bring it into your computer system.

This chapter begins by describing mistakes and equipment failures that inadvertently cause lost or inaccurate data. Next, the focus moves to intentional acts of vandalism and computer crime in which data is tampered with or stolen. The section on risk management explains the steps you can take to protect your data. This chapter concludes with an in-depth look at a most important computing activity—data backup.

CHAPTERPREVIEW

In this chapter you learn about threats to the data stored on computer systems. You will find out why data backup is one of the most effective security measures for protecting your data. On a practical level, you will learn how to disinfect disks that contain viruses, make backups, and design an effective backup plan for your data. After you have completed this chapter you should be able to:

- List some of the causes for lost or inaccurate data
- Describe how you can protect your computer data from damage caused by power problems and hardware failures
- List at least five symptoms that might indicate your computer is infected by a virus
- Differentiate between the terms virus, Trojan horse, worm, logic bomb, and time bomb
- Describe techniques for avoiding, detecting, and eradicating a computer virus
- Explain why special computer crime laws are necessary
- Describe the process of risk management
- List the advantages and disadvantages of the most popular data security techniques

LABS

Data
Backup

A What Can Go Wrong

Today's computer users battle to avoid lost, stolen, and inaccurate data. **Lost data**, also referred to as **missing data**, is data that is inaccessible, usually because it was accidentally removed. **Stolen data** is not necessarily missing, but it has been accessed or copied without authorization. **Inaccurate data** is data that is not accurate because it was entered incorrectly, was deliberately or accidentally altered, or was not edited to reflect current facts.

Despite all the sensational press coverage of computer criminals and viruses, the cause of many data problems is simply operator error, power abnormalities, or hardware failure.

Operator Error

What's the most likely cause of lost or inaccurate data? **Operator error** refers to a mistake made by a computer user. At one time or another, everyone who has used a computer has made a mistake. A few examples will illustrate that it is not an exclusive club.

- Working late at night the President's press secretary finished the final revisions for the next day's speech. Intending to make a copy of the speech as a backup, he mistakenly copied the old version of the speech over the new version.

- The head of personnel grabbed a disk without a label and thinking it was unformatted, shoved it in the disk drive and started the formatting process. Unfortunately, the disk contained her only copy of a report that had been mailed from the Houston office.

- A hospital clerk makes a typing error and bills a patient for 555 aspirins instead of 5.

It might seem that nothing can prevent operator error. After all, mistakes do happen. However, the number of operator errors can be reduced if users pay attention to what they're doing and establish habits that help them avoid mistakes.

Computer software designers can help prevent mistakes by designing products that anticipate mistakes that users are likely to make. For example, Microsoft Windows users can activate a feature that requests confirmation before the computer carries out any activity that might destroy data. Figure 9-1 shows a Windows dialog box that asks for confirmation before a file is deleted.

Figure 9-1

A confirmation dialog box helps reduce operator error

1. The user selects the file Sales Summary. Pressing the Delete key initiates an operation that will, in effect, destroy the data in the selected file.

2. The Microsoft Windows operating system displays a prompt asking the user to confirm the delete. The file is deleted only if the user clicks the Yes button.

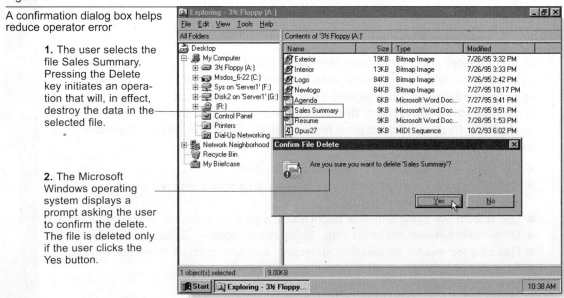

Power Failures, Spikes, and Surges

If the power goes out, will I lose all my data? A **power failure** is a complete loss of power to the computer system. Although you can lose power by accidentally bumping the computer on/off switch, a power failure is usually caused by something over which you have no control, such as a downed power line or a malfunction at the local power plant.

Data stored in RAM is lost if power is not continuously supplied to the computer system. Even a brief power interruption, noticeable only as a flicker of the room lights, can force your computer to reboot and lose all the data in RAM.

InfoWeb

UPS
1

An uninterruptible power supply is the best protection against power problems. An **uninterruptible power supply**, or **UPS**, is a device containing a battery and other circuitry that provides a continuous supply of power. A UPS is designed to provide enough power to keep your computer working through momentary power interruptions and to give you time to save your files and exit your programs in the event of a longer power outage. A UPS for a microcomputer costs from $100 to $600, depending on the power requirements of the computer and the features of the UPS. Most computer dealers can help you determine your computer's power requirements and recommend the appropriate size and features for a UPS that meets your needs. Figure 9-2 shows a typical UPS.

Figure 9-2

A UPS contains a battery that keeps your computer going for several minutes during a power failure. The battery does not supply indefinite power, so in the event of a power failure that lasts more than two or three minutes you should save your work and turn off your computer.

A light on the case lets you know that the UPS is charged and ready.

To connect a UPS, plug it into a wall outlet, then plug your computer and monitor cables into the outlets on the UPS.

Lightning and malfunctions at the electric company can cause spikes and surges that can damage sensitive computer components. A **power spike** is an increase in power that lasts only a short time—less than a millionth of a second. A **power surge** lasts a little longer—a few millionths of a second. Power surges and spikes are potentially more damaging than power failures. A surge or spike can damage your computer's motherboard and the circuit boards on your disk drives, putting your computer out of action until the boards are replaced.

Many experts recommend that you unplug your computer equipment, including your modem, during electrical storms. Unfortunately, there is not much you can do to increase the reliability of the local power system. However, the same UPS you use to provide a few minutes of power in the event of a power loss will also filter out power surges and spikes. As a low-cost alternative, you can plug your computer into an inexpensive device called a **surge strip** (also called a **surge suppressor** or **surge protector**) shown in Figure 9-3.

Figure 9-3

A surge strip is a small device that contains electrical outlets, so you can plug in your computer, monitor, and printer. It protects your equipment from electrical spikes and surges. It does not have a battery and cannot keep your computer running if the power goes off.

Hardware Failure

How reliable are the components of my computer system? The reliability of computer components is measured as **mean time between failures**, or **MTBF**. This measurement is somewhat misleading to most consumers. For example, you might read that your hard disk drive has an MTBF of 125,000 hours, which is about 14 years. Does this mean your hard drive will work for 125,000 hours before it fails? Unfortunately, the answer is no.

A 125,000 hour MTBF means that, *on average*, a hard disk drive like yours is likely to function for 125,000 hours without failing. The fact remains, however, that your hard disk drive might work for only 10 hours before it fails. With this in mind, you should plan for hardware failures, rather than hope they won't happen.

The effect of a hardware failure depends on the component that fails. Most hardware failures are simply an inconvenience. For example, if your monitor fails, you can obtain a replacement monitor, plug it in, and get back to work. If a RAM chip fails, you must obtain and install a replacement chip before you can boot your computer again. Even if your computer's microprocessor chip fails, it can easily be replaced. Unless you were in the middle of a long project that you had not saved, problems with the monitor, RAM chips, or processor would not cause any data loss.

On the other hand, a hard disk drive failure can be a disaster because you might lose all the data stored on the hard disk. The impact of a hard disk drive failure is considerably reduced if you have complete, up-to-date backup copies of the programs and data files on your hard disk.

Fires, Floods, and Other Disasters

Should I buy insurance for my computer? Computers are not immune to unexpected damage from smoke, fire, water, and breakage. However, it is not practical to barricade your computer from every potential disaster. Many insurance policies provide coverage for computers. Under the terms of many standard household and business policies, a computer is treated like any other appliance. You should make sure, however, that your insurance policy covers the full cost of purchasing a new computer at current market prices.

InfoWeb

Computer
Insurance
2

Replacing your damaged computer equipment will not replace your data. Some insurance companies provide extra coverage for the data on your computer. This coverage would provide you a sum of money to cover the time it takes to reload your data on a replacement computer. However, being able to reload your data assumes that you have a computer-readable backup copy of your data. Without a backup, much of your data cannot be reconstructed. For a business, the situation is even more critical. Customer accounts, inventory, daily transactions, and financial information are difficult, if not impossible, to reconstruct.

To summarize, a good insurance policy provides funds to replace computer equipment, but the only insurance for your data is an up-to-date backup copy on tape or disk.

QuickCheck A

1. Inadvertently deleting a file is an example of _____ error.

2. As a result of a power failure your computer will lose all the data stored in RAM and the hard disk. True or false?_____

3. A(n) _____ contains a battery that provides a continuous supply of power to your computer during a brief power failure.

4. A(n) _____ protects your computer from electrical spikes and surges, but it does not keep your computer operating if the power fails.

5. The circuitry on your computer circuit boards can be damaged by accidentally turning off your computer. True or false? _____

6. MTBF tells you how often an electronic device needs to be serviced. True or false? _____

7. The best insurance for your data is _____.

B Viruses, Vandalism, and Computer Crime

Computer data can be damaged, destroyed, or altered by vandals called **hackers**, **crackers**, or **cyberpunks**. The programs these hackers create are colorfully referred to by various sources as *malware*, *pest programs*, *vandalware*, or *punkware*. More typically, these programs are referred to as *viruses*. What would you do if you saw the message in Figure 9-4 on your computer screen?

Figure 9-4

A virus alert:
real or fake?

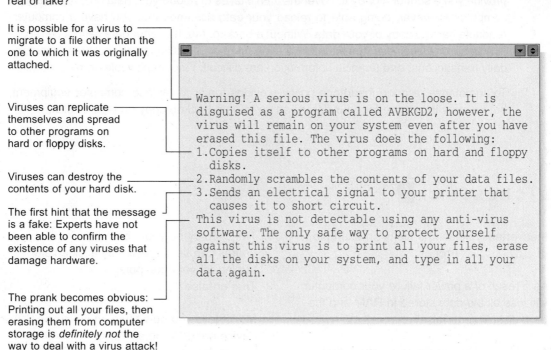

It is possible for a virus to migrate to a file other than the one to which it was originally attached.

Viruses can replicate themselves and spread to other programs on hard or floppy disks.

Viruses can destroy the contents of your hard disk.

The first hint that the message is a fake: Experts have not been able to confirm the existence of any viruses that damage hardware.

The prank becomes obvious: Printing out all your files, then erasing them from computer storage is *definitely not* the way to deal with a virus attack! If you see a message like this, ignore it.

> Warning! A serious virus is on the loose. It is disguised as a program called AVBKGD2, however, the virus will remain on your system even after you have erased this file. The virus does the following:
> 1. Copies itself to other programs on hard and floppy disks.
> 2. Randomly scrambles the contents of your data files.
> 3. Sends an electrical signal to your printer that causes it to short circuit.
> This virus is not detectable using any anti-virus software. The only safe way to protect yourself against this virus is to print all your files, erase all the disks on your system, and type in all your data again.

InfoWeb

Virus
Alert
3

The term *virus* technically refers to only one category of troublesome program. Additional categories include Trojan horses, time bombs, logic bombs, and worms. As you'll learn in this chapter, the programs in each of these categories behave differently when attacking a computer system.

Viruses, Trojan horses, time bombs, logic bombs, and worms lurk on disks and on the Internet waiting to destroy data and cause mischief to your computer system. Understanding how these programs work is the first line of defense against attacks.

Computer Viruses

Exactly what is a computer virus? A **computer virus** is a program that attaches itself to a file, reproduces, and spreads from one file to another. A virus can destroy data, display an irritating message, or otherwise disrupt computer operations. The jargon that describes a computer virus sounds similar to medical jargon. Your computer is a "host," and it can become "infected" with a virus. A virus can spread from one computer to another. You can "inoculate" your computer against many viruses. If your computer has not been inoculated and becomes infected, you can use anti-viral software to "disinfect" it.

A computer virus generally infects the executable files on your computer system, not the data files. When you run an infected program, your computer also runs the attached virus instructions to replicate or deliver its payload. The term **payload** refers to the ultimate mission of a virus. For example, the payload of the "Stoned" virus is the message, "Your PC is now stoned." Figure 9-5 illustrates how a computer virus spreads and delivers its payload.

Figure 9-5

How a computer
virus works

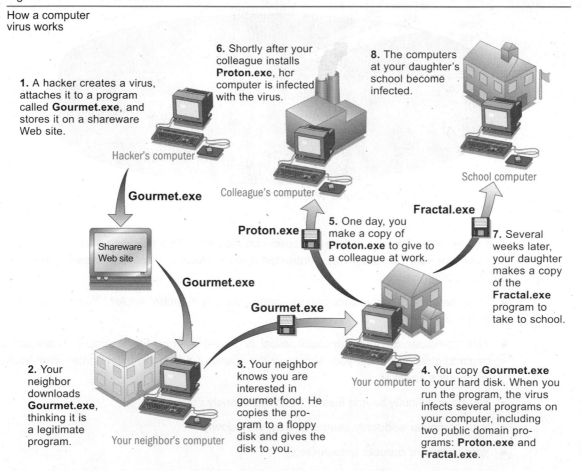

1. A hacker creates a virus, attaches it to a program called **Gourmet.exe**, and stores it on a shareware Web site.

6. Shortly after your colleague installs **Proton.exe**, her computer is infected with the virus.

8. The computers at your daughter's school become infected.

Hacker's computer

Gourmet.exe

Shareware Web site

School computer

Fractal.exe

Proton.exe

5. One day, you make a copy of **Proton.exe** to give to a colleague at work.

7. Several weeks later, your daughter makes a copy of the **Fractal.exe** program to take to school.

Colleague's computer

Gourmet.exe

Gourmet.exe

2. Your neighbor downloads **Gourmet.exe**, thinking it is a legitimate program.

Your neighbor's computer

3. Your neighbor knows you are interested in gourmet food. He copies the program to a floppy disk and gives the disk to you.

Your computer

4. You copy **Gourmet.exe** to your hard disk. When you run the program, the virus infects several programs on your computer, including two public domain programs: **Proton.exe** and **Fractal.exe**.

Most viruses attach themselves to executable files because these are the files that your computer runs. If a virus attaches to an executable file that you rarely use, it might not have an opportunity to spread and do much damage. On the other hand, **boot sector viruses**, which infect the system files your computer uses every time you turn it on, can cause widespread damage and persistent problems.

InfoWeb

Macro
Viruses
4

A **macro virus** infects documents such as those created with a word processor. Infected documents are stored with a list of instructions called a macro. A **macro** is essentially a miniature program that usually contains legitimate instructions to automate document production. However, a hacker can create a destructive macro, attach it to a document, and then distribute it over the Internet or on disk. When anyone views the document, the macro virus duplicates itself into the general macro pool where it is picked up by other documents. The two most common macro viruses are the Concept virus that attaches to Microsoft Word documents, and Laroux that attaches to Microsoft Excel spreadsheets.

Experts say there are over 2,000 viruses. However, 90 percent of virus damage is caused by fewer than 10 viruses. Of the top ten viruses, macro viruses account for about 75 percent of the virus attacks as shown in Figure 9-6.

Figure 9-6

Of the top ten viruses, macro viruses are the most prolific.

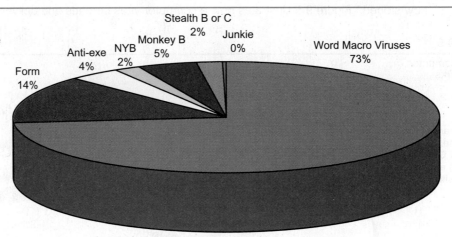

Data source: NCSA 1997 Virus Prevalence Survey

The symptoms of a virus infection depend on the virus. The following symptoms *might* indicate that your computer has contracted a virus. However, some of these symptoms can have other causes.

- Your computer displays annoying messages such as "Gotcha! Arf Arf," "You're stoned!," or "I want a cookie."

- Your computer develops unusual visual or sound effects. For example, characters begin to disappear from your screen or the sound of a flushing toilet comes from your computer's speaker.

- You have difficulty saving files or files mysteriously disappear.

- Your computer suddenly seems to work very slowly.

- Your computer reboots unexpectedly.

- Your executable files unaccountably increase in size.

Viruses are just one category of software designed by hackers to disrupt or damage the data on computers. After looking at other categories, you'll find out how to avoid and minimize the damage they cause.

A Modern Trojan Horse

How can I avoid being fooled by a Trojan horse? At the beginning of this chapter, you learned about the legendary Trojan horse. A modern **Trojan horse** is a computer program that appears to perform one function while actually doing something else. A Trojan horse might carry a virus that replicates itself once it reaches your computer system. Hackers also design Trojan horses that don't carry replicating viruses, but that do other damage. For example, suppose a hacker writes a program to format hard disks and embeds this program in a file called **Sched.exe.** The hacker then distributes disks containing this Trojan horse and posts it on the Internet where other users are likely to assume it is a free scheduling program. Users who download and run **Sched.exe** will discover that the program has erased all the files on their hard disk. This Trojan horse does not harbor a virus because it does not replicate itself. Figure 9-7 shows how this type of Trojan horse program works.

Figure 9-7

How a Trojan horse works

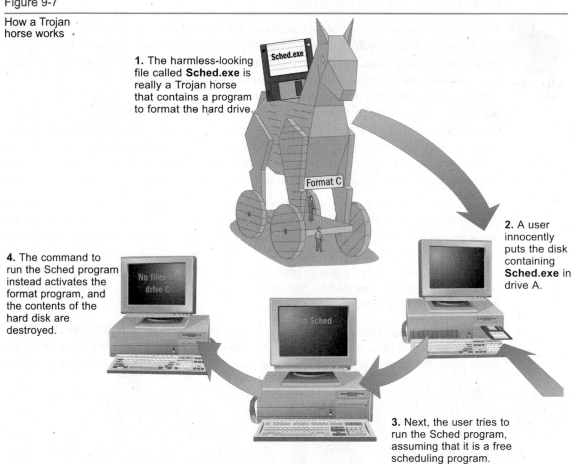

1. The harmless-looking file called **Sched.exe** is really a Trojan horse that contains a program to format the hard drive.

2. A user innocently puts the disk containing **Sched.exe** in drive A.

3. Next, the user tries to run the Sched program, assuming that it is a free scheduling program.

4. The command to run the Sched program instead activates the format program, and the contents of the hard disk are destroyed.

Another popular Trojan horse looks just like the login screen on a network. However, as a user logs in, the Trojan horse collects the user's ID and password. These are stored in a file that a hacker can access later. Armed with a valid user ID and password, the hacker can access the data stored on the network. As with the earlier example, this Trojan horse does not harbor a virus. The hacker's program, designed to defeat network security measures, does not replicate itself.

Time Bombs and Logic Bombs

Can a virus lurk in my computer system without my knowledge? Although a virus usually begins to replicate itself immediately when it enters your computer system, it will not necessarily deliver its payload right away. A virus or other unwelcome surprise can lurk in your computer system for days or months without discovery. A **time bomb** is a computer program that stays in your system undetected until it is triggered by a certain event in time, such as when the computer system clock reaches a certain date. A time bomb is usually carried by a virus or Trojan horse. For example, the Michelangelo virus contains a time bomb designed to damage files on your hard disk on March 6, the birthday of artist Michelangelo. The Olivia virus activates on April 10th and December 23rd, automatically opens the CD-ROM drive, and displays a message instructing the user to insert a music CD. After the CD begins, the virus overwrites the FAT on the hard disk and displays a message in Taiwanese. Many other time bomb attacks are keyed to dates such as Halloween, Friday the 13th, and April Fool's day.

InfoWeb

Year 2000
5

A surprising number of computers contain a time bomb that was unintentionally designed into software. The **year 2000 time bomb** refers to a problem with software that does not require a four-digit date field. The programmers who wrote this software decided that dates entered as 89 instead of 1989 would save disk space and processing time. As it turns out, this decision has the potential to cause havoc when the year 2000 arrives. Why? Suppose a person born in 1984 applies for a driver's license in 1999. The computer uses the last two digits of the dates, subtracts 84 from 99, and determines that the applicant is 15 years old. Now suppose the same person applies for a license in the year 2000. The computer subtracts 84 from 00 and gets -84 years old! Many banks and government organizations, such as the Internal Revenue Service are currently wrestling with this problem.

A **logic bomb** is a computer program that is triggered by the appearance or disappearance of specific data. For example, suppose a programmer in a large corporation believes that she is on the list of employees to be terminated during the next cost-cutting campaign. Her hostility overcomes her ethical judgment, and she creates a logic bomb program that checks the payroll file every day to make sure her employment status is still active. If the programmer's status changes to "terminated," her logic bomb activates a program that destroys data on the computer.

A time bomb or logic bomb might do mischief in your computer long before the timer goes off. If the bomb contains a virus, it could replicate and spread to other files. Meanwhile, you might send files from your computer to other computers, not knowing that they are infected.

Worms

Is a worm some type of virus?

InfoWeb

Internet
Worm
6

"At 2:28 a.m. a besieged Berkeley scientist—like a front-line soldier engulfed by the enemy—sent a bulletin around the nation: *We are currently under attack...* Thus began one of the most harrowing days of the computer age." This lead story in *The Wall Street Journal* reported the now famous Internet worm that spread to more than 6,000 Internet host computers. A software **worm** is a program designed to enter a computer system—usually a network—through security "holes." Like a virus, a worm reproduces itself. Unlike a virus, a worm does not need to be attached to a document or executable program to reproduce.

The software worm that attacked the Internet entered each computer through security holes in the electronic mail system, then used data stored on the computer to, in effect, mail itself to other computers. The worm spread rapidly, as shown in Figure 9-8.

The Internet worm was not designed to destroy data. Instead, it filled up storage space and dramatically slowed computer performance. The only way to eradicate the Internet worm was to shut down the electronic mail system on the Internet hosts, then comb through hundreds of programs to find and destroy the worm, a process that took up to eight hours for each host.

Figure 9-8

A worm attacks
the Internet.

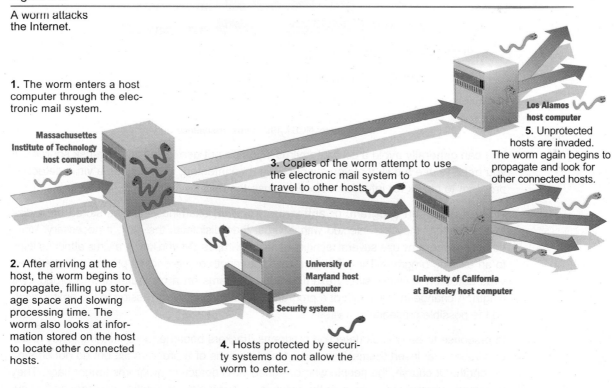

1. The worm enters a host computer through the electronic mail system.

Massachusettes Institute of Technology host computer

2. After arriving at the host, the worm begins to propagate, filling up storage space and slowing processing time. The worm also looks at information stored on the host to locate other connected hosts.

3. Copies of the worm attempt to use the electronic mail system to travel to other hosts.

University of Maryland host computer

Security system

4. Hosts protected by security systems do not allow the worm to enter.

University of California at Berkeley host computer

Los Alamos host computer

5. Unprotected hosts are invaded. The worm again begins to propagate and look for other connected hosts.

Avoidance and Detection

Can I protect my computer from viruses and other types of attacks? Computer viruses and other types of malicious software typically lurk on disks containing shareware or pirated software, in files downloaded from the Internet, and in e-mail attachments. A virus cannot, however, hitch a ride in a plain e-mail message. The graph in Figure 9-9 illustrates the sources of most infected files.

Figure 9-9

Sources of infected files

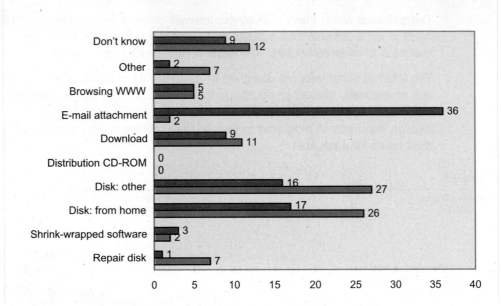

Data source: NCSA 1997 Virus Prevalence Survey

You can generally avoid a computer virus if you do not use files from high-risk sources. If you need to use a disk that you suspect might be infected, you can use a virus detection program to check for infection before you use the files.

A **virus detection program**, or **anti-virus program**, examines the files stored on a disk to determine if they are infected with a virus, then disinfects the disk, if necessary. Virus detection programs use several techniques to find viruses. As you know, a virus attaches itself to an existing program. This often increases the length of the original program. The earliest virus detection software simply examined the programs on a computer and recorded their length. A change in the length of a program from one computing session to the next indicated the possible presence of a virus.

In response to early virus detection programs, hackers became more cunning. They created viruses that insert themselves into unused portions of a program file but do not change its length. Of course, the people who designed virus detection programs fought back. They designed programs that examine the bytes in an uninfected application program and calculate a checksum. A **checksum** is a value that is calculated by combining all the bytes in a file. Each time you run the application program, the virus detection program recalculates the checksum and compares it to the original. If any byte in the application program has been changed, the checksum will be different, and the virus detection program assumes that a virus is present. The checksum approach requires that you start with a copy of the program that is not infected with a virus. If you start with an infected copy, the virus is included in the original checksum, and the virus detection program never detects it.

Another technique used by virus detection programs is to search for a signature. A **virus signature** is a unique series of bytes that can be used to identify a known virus, much as a fingerprint is used to identify an individual. A signature is usually a section of the virus program, such as a unique series of instructions. Most of today's virus detection software scans for virus signatures; for this reason, virus detection software is sometimes referred to as a "scanner."

The signature search technique is fairly quick, but it can identify only those viruses with a known signature. To detect new viruses—and new viruses seem to appear every week— you must obtain regular updates for your virus detection program that include new virus signatures.

Some viruses are specifically designed to avoid detection by one or more of these virus detection methods. For this reason, the most sophisticated virus protection schemes combine elements from each of these methods.

A common misconception is that write protecting your disks prevents virus infection. Although a virus cannot jump onto your disk when it is write protected, you have to remove the write protection each time you save a file on the disk. With the write protection removed, your disk is open to virus attack.

What to Do If You Detect a Computer Virus

What should I do if my computer gets a virus? If you detect a virus on your computer system, you should immediately take steps to stop the virus from spreading. If you are connected to a network, alert the network administrator that you found a virus on your workstation. The network administrator can then take action to prevent the virus from spreading throughout the network.

If you are using your own computer system and you detect a virus, you should remove it to prevent any further damage. There are two methods for removing a virus. First, you can attempt to restore the infected program to its original condition by deleting the virus with the disinfect function of virus detection software. However, depending on how the virus attached itself to the program, it might not be possible to remove the virus without destroying the program. If the virus cannot be removed successfully, you must use the second method: erase the infected program, test the system again to make sure the virus has been eliminated, then reinstall the program from the original disks. In cases where the virus has infected most of the programs on the system, it's often best to make a backup of your data files (which are unlikely to have been infected), reformat the hard disk, and install all the programs again from the original disks or CD-ROM.

If your computer is attacked by a macro virus, you might have to manually extract the macros from each infected document. You'll find information on combating macro viruses at Microsoft's Web site and in recent editions of computer magazines.

When your computer contracts a virus, you must check and, if necessary, remove the virus from every floppy disk and backup used on your computer system. If you don't remove every copy of the virus, your system will become infected again the next time you use an infected disk or restore data from an infected backup. You should also alert your colleagues, and anyone with whom you shared disks, that a virus might have traveled on those disks and infected their computer systems.

Computer Crime

Is it a crime to spread a computer virus? The accounting firm Ernst & Young estimates that computer crime costs individuals and organizations in the United States between $3 billion and $5 billion a year. "Old-fashioned" crimes that take a high-tech twist because they involve a computer are often prosecuted using traditional laws. For example, a person who attempts to destroy computer data by setting fire to a computer might be prosecuted under traditional arson laws.

InfoWeb

Computer
Crime
7

Traditional laws do not, however, cover the range of possibilities for computer crimes. Suppose a person unlawfully enters a computer facility. That person might be prosecuted for breaking and entering. But would breaking and entering laws apply to a person who uses an off-site terminal to "enter" a computer system without authorization? And what about the situation in which a person steals a file by copying it without authorization? Is the file really "stolen" if the original remains on the computer?

Most U.S. states have computer crime laws that specifically define computer data and software as personal property. These laws also define as a crime the unauthorized access, use, modification, or disabling of a computer system or data.

In early 1995, cybersleuth Tsutomu Shimomura tracked down a hacker who broke into dozens of corporate, university, government, and personal computers. Before his arrest, the hacker stole thousands of data files and more than 20,000 credit card numbers. "He was clearly the most wanted computer hacker in the world," commented assistant U.S. attorney Kent Walker. The hacker's unauthorized access and use of computer data are explicitly defined as criminal acts by computer crime laws.

Under most U.S. state laws, intentionally circulating a destructive virus is a crime. Study the excerpt from a typical computer crime law in Figure 9-10 to see what is specifically defined as illegal.

Figure 9-10

Excerpt
from a state
computer
crime law

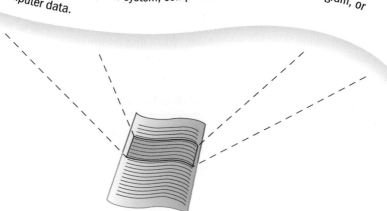

No person shall intentionally access any computer system or computer network for the purpose of devising or executing any scheme or artifice; to defraud, or extort, or obtain money, property, or services with false or fraudulent intent, representations, or promises; or to maliciously access, alter, delete, damage, or destroy any computer system, computer network, computer program, or computer data.

In the U.S., State authorities have jurisdiction over computer crimes committed in one state, but crimes that occur in more than one state or across state boundaries are under federal jurisdiction. The Computer Fraud and Abuse Act of 1986 makes it a federal crime to access a computer across state lines for fraudulent purposes. This act also specifically outlaws the sale of entry pass codes, passwords, and access codes that belong to others.

In a well-publicized espionage case, dramatized in a documentary called *Computers, the KGB, and Me*, hackers used an unclassified military network and the Internet to piece together details on current military research in the United States, which they then sold to the KGB. The hackers, based in Germany, used stolen passwords and telephone access codes to set up communications links from Europe to Virginia, and on to California. The communications crossed state lines, so under the Computer Fraud and Abuse Act the case was placed under federal jurisdiction. With FBI assistance, the case was ultimately cracked by Cliff Stoll, a computer operator of an Internet host computer at the Lawrence Berkeley Laboratory in California.

Laws are made to deter criminals, bring them to trial if they are caught, and punish them if they are convicted. But laws don't actually protect your data. That is something you need to do by making frequent backup copies and taking steps to prevent unauthorized access to data.

QuickCheck B

1 A(n) _____ is a program that reproduces itself when the computer executes the file to which it is attached.

2 A(n) _____ virus attaches itself to documents, rather than to an executable file.

3 A(n) _____ is a software container that might contain a virus or time bomb.

4 A(n) _____ is a program that reproduces itself without being attached to an executable file.

5 Suppose that your computer displays a weird message every time you type in the word "digital." You might suspect that your computer has contracted a(n) _____.

6 Three sources of files that should be considered a high risk virus infection are , disks brought from home, downloads, and _____.

7 Many virus detection programs identify viruses by looking for a unique series of bytes called a(n) _____.

8 Computer crime laws define computer software and _____ as personal property.

☾ Data Security and Risk Management

Data security is the collection of techniques that provide protection for data. Sometimes computer users cite Jeff Richards' Laws of Data Security as tongue-in-cheek advice on how to attain foolproof security:

1. Don't buy a computer.

2. If you buy a computer, don't turn it on.

InfoWeb

Risks
8

Richards' Laws emphasize the point that it is not practical to totally protect computer data from theft, viruses, and natural disasters. In most situations, providing total security is too time-consuming, too expensive, or too complex. For example, if you are using your computer primarily for word processing, it is too time-consuming to make daily backups, too expensive to keep your data in a fire-proof vault, and too complex to implement password security. On the other hand, if you take no precautions, one day you will be sorry.

In the context of computers, **risk management** is the process of weighing threats to computer data against the amount of data that is expendable and the cost of protecting crucial data. The steps in risk management are listed in Figure 9-11.

Figure 9-11

Planning a risk management strategy

1. Determine the likely threats to computer data. In the case of individual computer users, the major threats are hardware failure, operator error, and data vandalism.

2. Assess the amount of data that is expendable. For this assessment you must ask yourself how much data you would *have* to re-enter if your hard drive was erased and how much of your data would be forever lost because it could not be reconstructed.

3. Determine the cost of protecting all of your data versus protecting some of your data. Costs include time as well as money.

4. Select the protective measures that are affordable, effective against the identified threats, and easy to implement.

Data security techniques evolve quickly to meet the challenges offered by new technology and by clever hackers. You'll notice that many of these techniques apply to organizations. This information is also important for you as an individual for three reasons. First, it is likely that you will work with computers within an organization as part of your career, so you will share the responsibility with your coworkers for that organization's data. Second, many organizations maintain data about you such as your credit rating, educational record, and health records. You have a vested interest in the accuracy and the confidentiality of this data. Finally, you currently have data stored on disks that might be time-consuming to reconstruct. You should consider using two of the techniques discussed in this section—backup and virus detection—to secure your own data.

Establish Policies and Procedures

How can an organization educate its employees on the rules for acceptable computer use?

In a computing environment, **policies** are the rules and regulations that specify how a computer system should be used. Policies are most often determined by management and used by large organizations to stipulate who can access computer data. Policies also help an organization define appropriate uses for its computers and data.

InfoWeb

Acceptable
Use
9

For example, an organization might have a policy that provides e-mail accounts, but does not guarantee the privacy of e-mail messages, especially if there is reason to believe that those messages might be used for illegal or unethical transmission of data. Many employers have specific policies prohibiting software piracy and limiting the use of company computers to company business.

The advantages of policies are that they define how a computer system should be used, make users aware of limits and penalties, and provide a framework for legal or job action for individuals who do not follow policies. Policies are an inexpensive building block in the overall structure of data security. Policies do not require any special hardware or software. The cost of policies is the time it takes to compose, update, and publicize them. The disadvantage of policies for data security is that some users disregard policies.

Policies do not typically prevent operator errors that lead to lost or corrupted data. However, many mistakes can be prevented. Successful computer users develop habits that significantly reduce their chances of making mistakes. These habits, when formalized and adopted by an organization, are referred to as **procedures**. Procedures, such as those listed in Figure 9-12 can help you avoid lost or corrupted data.

Figure 9-12

Following procedures can help you avoid lost or corrupted data.

Save your files frequently as you work so you don't lose too much data if the power fails.
When you format a disk, always view a directory of its contents first to make sure the disk in the drive is the one you want to format.
Use virus detection software immediately to scan any files that you have downloaded from a commercial information service or the Internet.
When entering long columns of data, check off each number as it is entered.

By now you might have already figured out how policies and procedures differ. Policies are rules and regulations that apply to computer use in a general way. Procedures describe steps or activities that are performed in conjunction with a specific task. Because procedures are more specific, they generally take longer to write than policies, making them somewhat more costly for an organization to create and document.

The major advantage of procedures is reducing operator error. However, procedures have two disadvantages. First, they must be kept up to date as equipment and software change. Second, there is no way to make sure that people follow them.

Restrict Physical Access to the Computer System

If it is so easy for hackers to access data from networked computers or terminals, or over phone lines, is there any point to keeping computers locked up? In 1970, during the Vietnam War, anti-war activists bombed the Army Mathematics Research Center at the University of Wisconsin. A graduate student was killed, the building was damaged, and the computer, along with 20 years of accumulated research data, was destroyed (Figure 9-13).

One of the best ways to prevent people from damaging equipment is to restrict physical access to the computer system. If potential criminals cannot get to a computer or a terminal, stealing or damaging data becomes more difficult. Here are some ways to physically protect computer equipment and data:

- Restrict access to the area surrounding the computer to prevent physical damage to the equipment.

- Keep floppy disks and data backups in a locked vault to prevent theft and to protect against fire or water damage.

- Keep offices containing computers locked to prevent theft and to deter unauthorized users.

- Lock the computer case to prevent theft of components such as RAM and processors.

Figure 9-13

In 1970, anti-war activists bombed the Army Mathematics Research Center at the University of Wisconsin.

Restricting physical access to computers has disadvantages. Locks and other screening measures can make it more difficult for authorized users to access the computer system. Also, restricting physical access will not prevent a determined criminal from stealing data. Access from a remote location is more difficult, but it might not be impossible. Finally, although restricting access might deter intentional acts of destruction, it will not prevent accidents.

Restrict Online Access to Data

Can people be prevented from accessing data so they can't steal it or tamper with it?

Obviously everyone should not have access to the data stored in military computers, banks, or businesses. And yet, the communications infrastructure makes it technically possible for anyone with an Internet connection to interact with these systems. In today's web of interlaced computer technologies, it has become critical to restrict data access to authorized users. The question is, how do you identify authorized users, especially those who are logging in from remote sites thousands of miles away?

There are three methods of personal identification: something a person carries, something a person knows, or some unique physical trait. Any one of these methods has the potential to positively identify a person, and each has a unique set of advantages and disadvantages.

An identity badge featuring a photo and, perhaps a fingerprint or bar code, is still a popular form of personal identification in hospitals and government agencies. Designers have created high-tech identity card readers, like the one in Figure 9-14, that can be used from any off-site PC.

Figure 9-14

A disk-shaped carrier allows a floppy disk drive to read an identity card.

Because an identity badge can be easily lost, stolen, or duplicated, it works best on-site where a security guard checks the face on the badge with the face of the person wearing the badge. Without visual verification, the use of identity badges from a remote site is not secure, unless combined with a password or PIN (personal identification number).

The most common way to restrict access to a computer system is with user IDs and passwords. These fall into the "something you know" category of personal identification. When you work on a multiuser system or network, you generally must have a user ID and password. Data security on a computer system that is guarded by user IDs and passwords depends on password secrecy. If users give out their passwords, choose obvious passwords, or write them down in obvious places, hackers can break in.

How easy is it, really, to discover someone's password? It is easier to find a password written on the bottom of a keyboard than to try to guess it from nicknames and birthdates as they always do in the movies. There is also the brute force method of trying every word in an electronic dictionary, but the success of the method decreases if a password is based on two words, a word and number, or a nonsense word that does not appear in a dictionary. Figure 9-15 shows how the composition of passwords affects the chance of unauthorized access.

Figure 9-15

How password length and composition affect the chances of unauthorized access

Password Strategy	Example	Number of Possibilities	Average Time to Discover
Any short or long name	Ed, Christine	2,000 (a name dictionary)	5 hours
Any short or long word	It, electrocardiogram	60,000 (in a spell checker)	7 days
Two words together	Whiteknight	3,600,000,000	1,140 years
Mix of initials and numbers	JP2C2TP307	3,700,000,000,000,000	1,200,000,000 years
First line of a poem	Onceuponamidnightdreary	10,000,000,000,000,000, 000,000,000,000	3,000,000,000,000,000, 000,000 years

InfoWeb

Biometrics
10

A third method of personal identification called **biometrics** bases identification on some unique physical characteristic, such as a fingerprint or the pattern of blood vessels in the retina of the eye. Unlike passwords, biometric data can't be forgotten, lost, or borrowed. Once the technological fiction of spy thrillers such as *Goldfinger* and *Man from U.N.C.L.E*, biometric devices are today becoming affordable technologies that could be built into personal computer systems. Biometric technologies include hand-geometry scanners, voice recognition, face recognition, and fingerprint scanners (Figure 9-16).

Figure 9-16

Fingerprint scanners cost less than $500 and can confirm your identity in less than two seconds, even from a pool of thousands of employees.

User Rights: A Second Line of Defense

What if a hacker slips past the security screening? One way to limit the amount of damage from a break-in is to assign user rights. **User rights** are rules that limit the directories and files that each user can access. When you receive an account on a computer system, the system administrator gives you rights that allow you to access only particular directories and files. For example, in your computer lab, you might have only read rights to the directories that contain software. This would prevent you from deleting or changing the programs on lab computers. Most networks and host computers allow the system administrator to assign user rights such as those in Figure 9-17.

Figure 9-17

User rights

Rights	Description
Erase rights	Allow you to erase files
Create rights	Allow you to create new files
Write rights	Allow you to save information in existing files
Read rights	Allow you to open files and read information
File find rights	Allow you to list files with a directory command

Granting users only the rights they need helps prevent both accidental and deliberate damage to data. If users are granted limited rights, a hacker who steals someone's password has only those rights granted to the person from whom the password was stolen.

Hackers occasionally gain unauthorized access to computer systems through something called a trap door. A **trap door** is a special set of instructions that allows a user to bypass the normal security precautions and enter the system. Trap doors are often created during development and testing; they should be removed before the system becomes operational.

InfoWeb

War
Games
11

In the 1983 film *WarGames*, a trap door was the key to preventing widespread nuclear destruction. A young hacker breaks into a secret military computer that has been programmed to deal with enemy nuclear attacks. The hacker begins to play what he thinks is a detailed computer game. The computer, however, thinks it is an actual attack. Soon the computer passes the stage at which it can be stopped from launching nuclear missiles, except by a trap door designed by the reclusive programmer who created the original program. The trap door provides a way for the programmer to bypass official military channels and access the computer's fail-safe program. A special password is required to enter the trap door, and in the exciting climax of the film, the hacker races against time to get the password and gain access to the computer deep within the military installation in Cheyenne Mountain. In this fictional example, a trap door helped save the world. In general, however, if a trap door is not removed, it becomes a possible means of entry for any hacker who discovers it.

Encrypt Data

| Is there any way to prevent criminals from using stolen data? | When an unauthorized person reads data, the data is no longer confidential. Although password protection and physical security measures are taken to limit access to computer data, hackers and criminals still manage to access data.

InfoWeb

Encryption
12

Encryption is the process of scrambling or hiding information so it cannot be understood until it is decrypted, or deciphered, to change it back to its original form. Encryption provides a last line of defense against the unauthorized use of data. If data is encrypted, unauthorized users obtain only scrambled gibberish instead of meaningful information. Edgar Allan Poe, the American writer famous for his tales of horror, was quite interested in secret codes. He was convinced that it was impossible to design an unbreakable method of encryption. You might be familiar with simple encryption and decryption techniques, such as the one shown in Figure 9-18.

Figure 9-18

Encryption
by simple
substitution

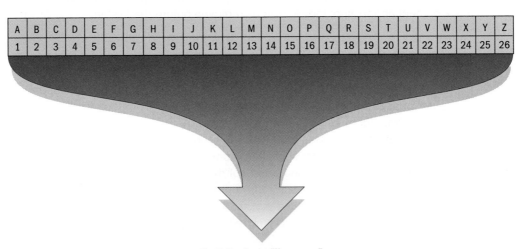

17 21 15 20 8 20 8 5 18 1 22 5 14 14 5 22 5 18 13 15 18 5

1. This is a message encrypted using a simple substitution technique in which the number of each letter's position in the alphabet represents the letter.

2. The key to this encryption looks like this. The 17 in the encrypted message is the "Q," the 21 is the letter "U," and so forth. This is a very simple encryption technique.

A	B	C	D	E	F	G	H	I	J	K	L	M	N	O	P	Q	R	S	T	U	V	W	X	Y	Z
1	2	3	4	5	6	7	8	9	10	11	12	13	14	15	16	17	18	19	20	21	22	23	24	25	26

Quoth the Raven "Nevermore"

3. Once you know the key, you can then decipher the message to see that it is the famous quote from Edgar Allan Poe's poem "The Raven."

Important data such as credit card accounts, bank records, and medical information should be stored in encrypted format to foil hackers who break into computers. In addition, when this sort of data is transmitted over the Internet, it should also be encrypted.

When a computer encrypts data for storage, the program that encrypts the data also decrypts it. The encryption method or key needs only to be known by the encrypting computer. Encrypting transmitted data presents a different problem because the sender's computer that encrypts the data is not the same computer that decrypts the data on the recipients end of the transmission. Somehow, transmitted data must use an encryption key that is shared by everyone, but that cannot be decrypted by everyone. Impossible as it might seem, such an encryption method exists.

Public key encryption (PKE) is an encryption method that uses a pair of keys, a public key known to everyone and a private key known only to the message recipient. The public key encrypts a message. The private key decrypts a message. Suppose you want to send an encrypted message to CitiBank. You would use the CitiBank public key to encrypt the message. Once a message is encrypted, no one can use the public key to decrypt it. To decrypt the message, Citibank uses its private key. Because CitiBank does not publish its private key, no one else can decrypt it. Figure 9-19 explains more about public key encryption.

Figure 9-19

Public key encryption

Software is available to encrypt data on micro, mini, and mainframe computers. The cost of this software varies with its sophistication. Regardless of its cost, encryption software is virtually a necessity for some businesses—such as financial institutions that transmit and store funds electronically. Several public key encryption systems are currently available, including the popular and easy-to-use **Pretty Good Privacy** (PGP).

Install and Use Virus Detection Software

Antivirus
Software
13

How effective is virus detection software? Virus detection software is an important weapon in your security arsenal, but it is not 100 percent reliable. It might fail to detect viruses without a known signature, **polymorphic viruses** that change after they infect your computer, and viruses that use **stealth technology** to hide from virus detection programs. Virus detection software generally does not detect Trojan horses unless they carry a virus. When virus detection software does not detect a virus in an infected computer, it is called a "false negative report." Sometimes virus detection software tells you that your computer is infected, but a virus is *not* actually present. This is a "false positive report." False negative and false positive reports are infrequent. Virus detection software generally succeeds in detecting and eradicating most widespread viruses, so you should include it in your software collection.

There are many virus detection programs, produced by different software publishers. You can purchase these programs from your local computer dealer, by mail order, or you can download a trial version from the Web. The cost of a virus detection program for microcomputers is generally less than $100.

Virus detection software can both detect viruses and eradicate them. But this software works only if you use it. You should run your virus detection program periodically to check if any viruses have found their way into your computer system. If viruses are a recurring problem in your computing environment, you might want to configure your virus detection software to continually monitor the behavior of your computer files and alert you if it spots signs of virus-like activity.

There is no "magic pill" that will protect your computer from hackers, crackers, and cyberpunks. However, you can reduce the risk of infection if you follow the checklist in Figure 9-20.

Figure 9-20

Reduce the risk of infection

Install and use virus detection software.
Keep your virus detection software up to date.
Make frequent backups *after* you use virus detection software to scan your files for viruses.
Download software only from virus free sources. Use a virus detection program to scan downloaded software before you use it.
Exercise care with disks that contain shareware or pirated software. Scan them before you run or copy any of the files they contain.

Internet Security

Internet
Security
14

Should I have special security concerns when I'm using the Internet? When you download a file from the Internet, you can use virus detection software to make sure the file is virus free before you run it. But some Web sites automatically send a program to your computer and run it before you have a chance to check it for viruses. Can you just trust that this program is harmless? Unfortunately, the answer to this question is "no." While you're connected to the Internet, you could be unaware of a program that is reformatting your hard drive, getting ready to shut down your computer, making your browser hang, or scanning your hard disk for your IP address, user ID, and password. Many security problems on the Internet are the result of two technologies: Java applets and ActiveX controls.

Java applets are small programs that are intended to add processing and interactive capabilities to Web pages. For example, a Java applet might total the cost of the merchandise you are purchasing online. When you access a Web page containing a Java applet, it is downloaded automatically to your computer, and executed in a supposedly secure area of your computer known as a **sandbox**. In theory, the sandbox limits Java applets from running amok and damaging files in your computer's regular RAM and disk areas. However, some hackers have been able to breach sandbox security and create hostile Java applets that damage or steal data.

ActiveX controls provide another way to add processing capabilities and interaction to Web pages. Programs that use ActiveX controls are downloaded automatically to your computer. Unlike Java applets, ActiveX controls are not limited by a sandbox, so they have full access to your entire computer system. It is possible for hackers to use ActiveX controls to cause havoc. A partial solution to this problem is the use of a **digital certificate** that identifies the author of an ActiveX control. A programmer in effect "signs" a program by attaching his or her digital certificate. Theoretically, a programmer would not sign a hostile program, so all programs with a digital certificate should be "safe." Your browser will warn you about programs that do not have a digital certificate so you can decide whether or not to accept them, as shown in Figure 9-21.

Figure 9-21

Your browser will warn you before it accepts an unsigned Java applet or ActiveX control.

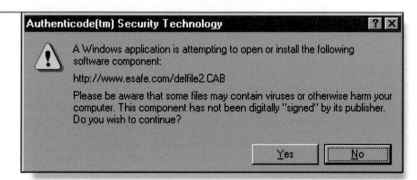

The only way to entirely avoid dangerous Java applets and ActiveX controls is to tell your browser not to accept any of them. However, many Web pages include legitimate applets and controls. If your browser doesn't accept them, you might miss some valuable features and interactions. As an alternative, you could consider installing **personal firewall software** that protects your computer from hostile Java applets and ActiveX controls.

Secure e-Commerce

Is it safe to use the Internet for shopping and banking? The increasing popularity of on-line shopping has created some nervousness about the security of on-line transactions. Publicity about intercepted credit card numbers and high-tech crimes make most consumers think twice before providing credit card numbers or other personal information over the Internet. The security of an Internet transaction is about the same as when you purchase merchandise by mail or by phone. However, as with mail and phone transactions, current Internet security technology does not guarantee a secure transaction. Therefore, caution is justified.

Want to purchase sunglasses from www.niemanmarcus.com? Before you send your credit card number over the Internet, make sure the Neiman Marcus Web server encrypts your transmission with a security protocol such as SSL or S-HTTP. **SSL**, short for **Secure Sockets Layer**, uses encryption to establish a secure connection between your computer and a Web server. When you use an SSL page, the URL will begin with https: instead of http:, and you will generally receive a message that transactions are secured. **S-HTTP (Secure HTTP)** also encrypts data sent between your computer and a Web server, but does so one message at a time rather than by setting up an entire secure connection.

Encrypted transactions ensure that your credit card number cannot be intercepted as it travels from your computer, through Internet routers, and to a Web server. As shown in Figure 9-22 your browser shows you if you are using a secure transaction.

Figure 9-22

During secure transactions, Internet Explorer displays a lock icon and Netscape Navigator displays a key icon.

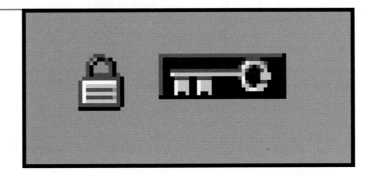

Some Web sites keep track of your visits. These sites use a "cookie" to remember the date of your last visit, your e-mail address, your last purchase, and the links you followed at the site. A **cookie** is a message sent from a Web server to your browser and stored on your hard disk. When you use a Web site that distributes cookies, it collects information such as your name, e-mail address, and the pages you visit. This information is incorporated into the cookie that the Web server stores on to your computer. The next time you connect to that Web site, your browser sends the cookie to the Web server.

Cookies are usually harmless, but some Web sites might ask for information that you would not want to make public. Try to use good sense when responding to requests for personal information. Supply information about your address, credit cards, bank accounts, and social security number only to sources that you're certain are reputable and that use adequate security measures to protect personal data—that includes encrypting the data stored in cookies. Even though the cookies are on your computer, they can be accessed by other cookie-like programs from disreputable sources.

Provide Redundancy

Can anything be done to minimize the damage from accidents? Accidents can destroy data and equipment. The result is **downtime**, computer jargon for the time a computer system is not functioning. The most dependable way to minimize downtime is to duplicate data and equipment. You will learn about duplicating data in the *User Focus* section of this chapter. Duplicating equipment simply means maintaining equipment that duplicates the functions critical to computing activities. This is sometimes referred to as **hardware redundancy**.

Hardware redundancy reduces an organization's dependency on outside repair technicians. If it maintains a stock of duplicate parts, an organization can swap parts and be up and running before the manufacturer's repair technician arrives. Duplicate parts are expensive, however, and these costs must be weighed against lost revenue or productivity while repairs are underway. Figure 9-23 shows some of the equipment that can be used to provide hardware redundancy.

Figure 9-23

Hardware redundancy

An extra printer in case the main printer breaks down.

A duplicate file server to maintain network communications in case of a breakdown in the server disk drive or main board.

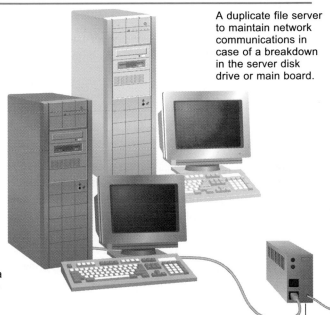

RAID storage to keep copies of data on several platters in case one platter is damaged.

A UPS or generator to provide electricity in case of a power failure.

Make Backups

If I implement only one security measure, should it be a backup? A **backup** is a duplicate copy of a file or the contents of a disk drive. If the original file is lost or damaged, you can use the backup copy to restore the data to its original working condition. Back-up probably provides the best all-round security for your data. It protects your data from hardware failures, vandalism, operator error, and natural disasters, as long as you do the following:

- Make frequent backups. You can't restore data that you haven't backed up; so if you wait a month between backups, you could lose a month's worth of data.

- Scan for viruses before you backup. If your computer is infected with a virus when you back up, your backup will also be infected.

- Store your backup away from your computer. If your backup is next to your computer, a fire or flood could also damage your backup.

- Test your backup. Before you depend on your backups, make sure that you can restore data from your backup to your hard disk. You would not want to discover that your back-up files were blank because you didn't correctly carry out the backup procedure.

The major disadvantage of backups is user forgetfulness and procrastination. You will learn more about backups in the next section of this chapter.

QuickCheck C

1. _____ is the process of weighing threats to computer data against the amount of data that is expendable and the cost of protecting crucial data.

2. A(n) _____ is a rule designed to prohibit employees from installing software that has not been pre-approved by the information systems department.

3. Procedures help reduce human errors that can erase or damage data.
True or false? _____

4. If a network administrator assigns _____, users can access only certain programs and files.

5. Hackers sometimes gain unauthorized entry to computer systems through a(n) _____ that is not removed when development and testing are complete.

6. A(n) _____ is a digital message that a Web server uses to store information about your visits to its Web site.

7. _____ is computer jargon that refers to the time a computer system is not functioning.

8. If your virus detection software tells you that your computer is infected when it really is not, the software has given you a false _____ report.

User Focus

D Backup

LAB

Data
Backup

osing all your data is one of the most distressing computing experiences. It might be the result of a hardware failure or a virus. Whatever the cause, most users experience only a moment of surprise and disbelief before reaching the depressing realization that they might have to recreate all their data and reinstall all their programs (Figure 9-24). A backup can pull you through such trying times, making the data loss a minor inconvenience, rather than a major disaster.

Figure 9-24

A hard drive failure might happen at any time.

Industry experts recommend that all computer users make backups. Sounds simple, right? Unfortunately, this advice tells you what to do, not how to do it. It fails to address some key questions: How often should I make a backup?, What should I back up?, and What should I do with the backups? To keep your data safe, you need a data backup plan, one tailored to your computing needs. To devise your data backup plan, you should consider factors such as the value of your data, the amount of data stored on your computer, the frequency with which your data changes, and the type of backup equipment you have. As these factors change, you need to revise your plan. For example, the backup plan you use while in college is likely to change as you pursue your career. In this section of the chapter you will learn about the advantages and disadvantages of various backup tools and techniques, so you can select those appropriate for your own data backup plan.

Backup Equipment

Does my computer need a tape drive so I can make backups? Tape backups are the most popular microcomputer backup solution for small businesses, and they are gaining popularity with individuals as the price of tape drives decreases. When you make a tape backup, data from the hard disk is copied to a magnetic tape. If the data on the hard disk is lost, the backup data is restored by copying it from the tape to a functional hard disk drive. Tape backup requires tapes and a tape drive, costing less than $300. However, you can back up your data without a tape drive.

Many microcomputer users back up their data onto floppy disks. This method is unrealistic for backing up the entire contents of today's high-capacity disk drives—a drive with a 4 GB capacity would require at least 2,800 floppy disks for a complete backup! However, backing up every file is not necessary. Many users back up only those directories that contain data files. In the event of a hard disk failure, these users would need to reinstall all their software from original disks or CD-ROMs, then copy their data files from the backups (Figure 9-25).

Figure 9-25

You can backup selected files, instead of backing up an entire disk.

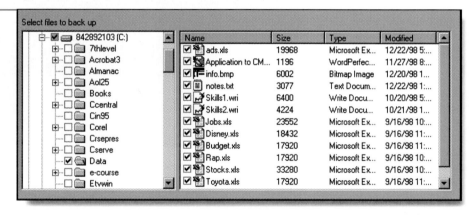

If you use the computers in a college computer lab, your situation is somewhat unique because you might store your data on a floppy disk instead of the hard disk. An effective way to back up if you're in this situation is to make a copy of your disk using the Copy Disk utility, described in the next subsection, "Backup Software."

Usually, backups are stored on magnetic media such as disk or tape. However, you can also use a printout of your data for backup purposes. To restore the data from a printout, you can use a scanner or you can retype it. With either restoration method, you can easily introduce errors, so paper backups should be considered only as a last resort.

Backup Software

Do I need special software to make backups? A backup is essentially a copy of data. You must use software to tell the computer what to copy. There are three types of software you might use: backup software, a copy utility, or a disk copy program.

Backup software is designed to manage hard disk backup to tapes or disks. When you use backup software you can select the files you want to back up. Most operating systems include backup software. However, if your tape drive requires special proprietary backup software, you should use it. Most backup software offers automated features that allow you to schedule automatic backups and back up only those files that have changed since the last backup.

A **copy utility** is a program that copies one or more files. You can use a copy utility to copy files between a hard disk and a floppy disk, between two floppy disks of any size, from a CD-ROM to a hard disk, or from a CD-ROM to a floppy disk. A copy utility is usually included with a computer operating system.

The **Copy Disk** utility is a program that duplicates the contents of an entire floppy disk. You can use a Copy Disk utility only to copy all the files from one floppy disk to another floppy disk of the same size. You cannot use the Copy Disk utility for files on a hard disk drive. Figure 9-26 shows how to duplicate a floppy disk.

Figure 9-26

Using Copy Disk to back up a floppy

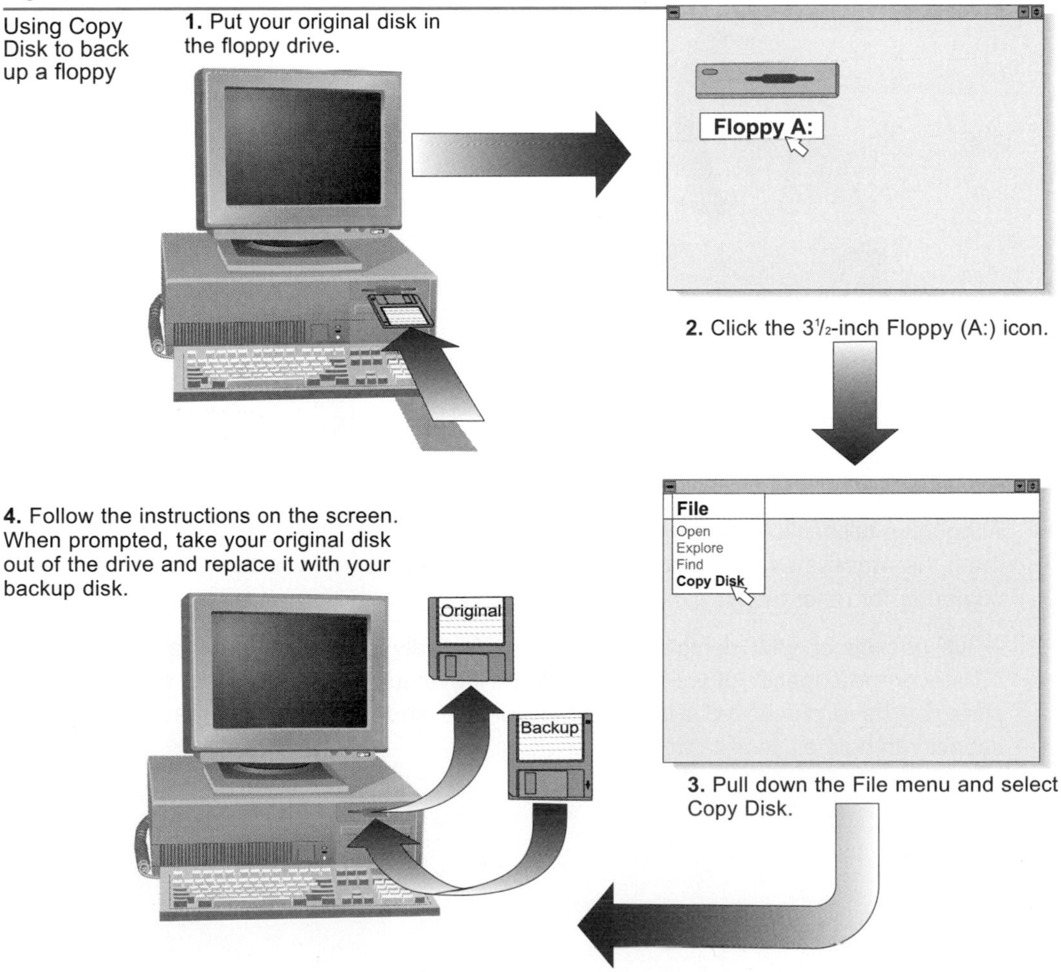
1. Put your original disk in the floppy drive.
Floppy A:
2. Click the 3½-inch Floppy (A:) icon.
File
Open
Explore
Find
Copy Disk
3. Pull down the File menu and select Copy Disk.
4. Follow the instructions on the screen. When prompted, take your original disk out of the drive and replace it with your backup disk.
Original
Backup

Types of Backups

Should I back up everything on my disk? | A **full backup** is a copy of all the files on a disk. A full backup is very safe because it ensures that you have a copy of every file on the disk—every program and every data file. Because a full backup includes a copy of every file on a disk, it can take a long time to complete. While the backup is in progress, the computer cannot generally be used for other tasks. Some users consider it worth the time because this type of backup is easy to restore. You simply have the computer copy the files from your backup to the hard disk, as shown in Figure 9-27.

Figure 9-27

Full backup

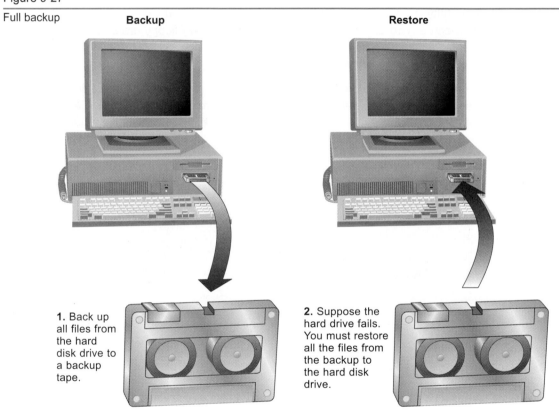

Backup

Restore

1. Back up all files from the hard disk drive to a backup tape.

2. Suppose the hard drive fails. You must restore all the files from the backup to the hard disk drive.

Although a full backup takes a long time to complete, many backup programs let you automate the process so the backup takes place overnight when you don't want to use your computer for other tasks.

A full backup of your computer's hard disk is likely to be many megabytes of data. Whatever the capacity of your hard disk, you'll eventually fill it almost to capacity. Make sure you have purchased a tape backup device and backup tapes that have enough capacity to hold all your data.

A **differential backup** is a copy of all the files that have changed since the last full backup. You'll use a differential backup in conjunction with a full back up. First, you'll make a full backup of all the files on your system. Then, at regular intervals you will make a differential backup. It takes less time to make a differential backup than to make a full backup; however, restoring data from a differential backup is a little more complex. To restore your data after a differential backup, you first restore data from the last full backup, then restore the data from the latest differential backup, as shown in Figure 9-28.

Figure 9-28

Differential backup

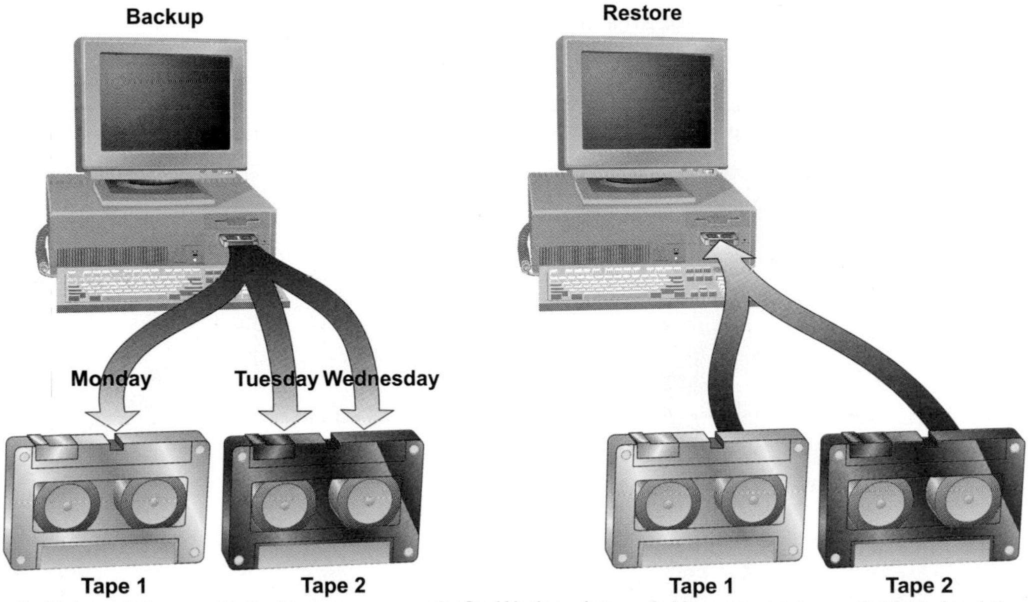

Backup

Restore

Monday

Tuesday Wednesday

Tape 1

Tape 2

Tape 1

Tape 2

1. Make a full backup on Monday evening.

2. On Tuesday evening use a different tape to back up only the files that have been changed since the full backup.

3. On Wednesday evening, back up only the files that have been changed since the full backup. These are the files you changed or created on Tuesday and Wednesday. Put these files on the same tape you used for Tuesday's backup.

4. Now, suppose the hard disk fails. To restore, first load the full backup onto the hard disk. This step restores the files as they were on Monday evening.

5. Next, load the data from the differential backup tape. This step restores the files you changed on Tuesday and Wednesday.

Differential backups are probably the most popular type of backups because they are easy to create. If you are using tapes for your backup, you need only two tapes, one for the full backup and one for the differential. Take care to label your tapes so you know which one contains the full backup and which one contains the differential files.

An **incremental backup** is a copy of the files that have changed since the last backup. When you use incremental backups, you must have a full backup and you must maintain a series of incremental backups. The incremental backup procedure is similar to the differential backup procedure, but there's a subtle difference. With a differential backup, you maintain one full backup and one differential backup. The differential backup contains any files that were changed since the last full backup. With an incremental backup procedure, you maintain a full backup and a series of incremental backups. Each incremental backup contains only those files that changed since the last incremental backup.

To restore the data from a series of incremental backups, you restore the last full backup, then sequentially restore each incremental backup. Figure 9-29 illustrates the backup and restore process for an incremental backup.

Figure 9-29

Incremental backup

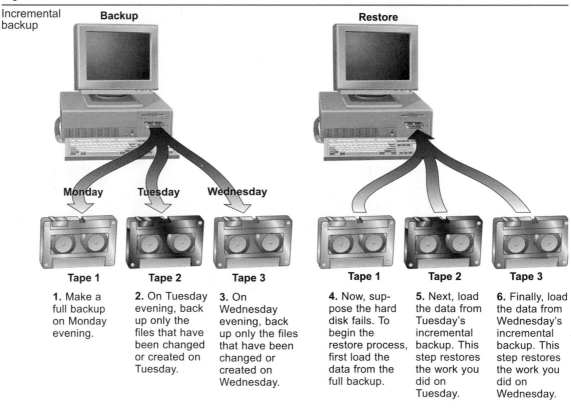

Backup   **Restore**

Monday   Tuesday   Wednesday

Tape 1   Tape 2   Tape 3   Tape 1   Tape 2   Tape 3

1. Make a full backup on Monday evening.

2. On Tuesday evening, back up only the files that have been changed or created on Tuesday.

3. On Wednesday evening, back up only the files that have been changed or created on Wednesday.

4. Now, suppose the hard disk fails. To begin the restore process, first load the data from the full backup.

5. Next, load the data from Tuesday's incremental backup. This step restores the work you did on Tuesday.

6. Finally, load the data from Wednesday's incremental backup. This step restores the work you did on Wednesday.

Incremental backups take the least time to make and provide a little better protection from viruses than other backup methods because your backup contains a series of copies of your files. However, incremental backups are the most complex type of backup and require good record keeping. You must make sure you accurately label the tape you use for each incremental backup. Otherwise, you might not be able to restore the tapes in the correct order.

Backup Schedule

How frequently should I make a backup? Any data backup plan is a compromise between the level of protection and the amount of time devoted to backup. To be absolutely safe, you would need to back up your data every time you change the contents of a file, which would seriously reduce the amount of work you could complete in a day. Realistically, however, you should make backups at regular intervals. The interval between backups will depend on the value of your data—what that data is worth to you or your employer in terms of time and money.

An individual using a personal computer might not be particularly worried about the consequences of data loss. Data backup for such an individual should be quick and easy to complete and should reduce some of the inconvenience of data loss. However, it would not necessarily restore all data or programs. A backup schedule that offers this minimal amount of protection would require a once-a-week backup of those data files that have changed since the last backup, as shown in Figure 9-30.

Figure 9-30

A basic
backup plan

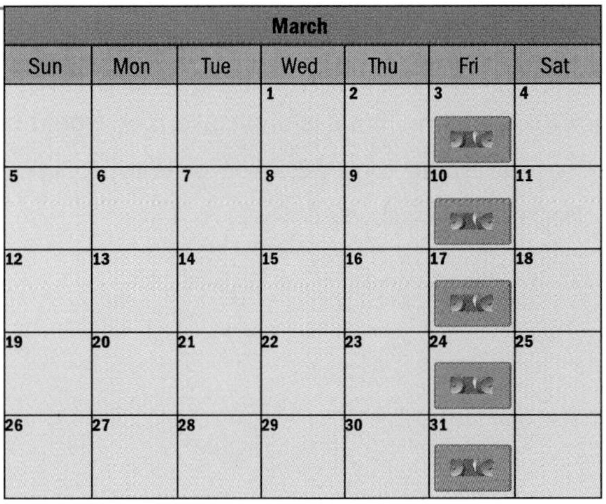

In the event of a hard disk drive failure, an individual who uses this backup plan would have to reinstall all software from original disks and restore all the data from the backup disks. The data entered or changed since the last backup would be lost. If the last backup was made at the end of the day on Monday and the hard disk failed on Thursday, the data from Tuesday, Wednesday, and Thursday would be lost.

A more rigorous backup plan would be required for more valuable data, particularly if the data was produced by an application, such as an accounting system or payroll program, that operates on a weekly or monthly cycle. Every time you use an accounting system, for example, you do not use all the files that contain your data. Therefore, a file could be damaged by a virus or disk error, but you might not know it for several days or weeks until you try to access the file. In the meantime you might have made backups that contain the damaged file. A more sophisticated backup procedure—one that you might use with an accounting system—would typically combine daily, weekly, and monthly backups to allow you to reconstruct data at any point before file damage occurred.

End Note

The amount of data stored on computer systems, combined with the vulnerability of those systems, creates a potentially risky situation. A surprising amount of personal data about you is stored on computers. All of it might not be accurate. It can be accessed and altered by criminals. It can be destroyed by hardware failure, human sabotage, or natural disaster. The same can be said for national security data or the data that keeps the world financial market running smoothly. One of the main issues of the computer age concerns the security and ethical use of computer data. Risk management has, therefore, become a necessity in most organizations.

In the story of the Trojan War, the Trojans seem so naive. Who would be so foolish as to pull such a suspicious horse into the city? But you have learned that today's computer users are often just as naive about modern technology. They install programs on their computers without checking for viruses, they store massive amounts of data without back-ups, and they transmit sensitive data without first encrypting it. The Trojans fell for the wooden horse trick the first time, but it is a mistake they would be unlikely to repeat. Will modern computer users repeat their mistakes or learn to take precautions? Now that you've read this chapter, what will you do?

InfoWeb

Chapter Links

The InfoWeb is your guide to print, film, television, and electronic resources. Use it to obtain updates on quickly changing technical information and to locate information for research papers. If you're using the New Perspectives CD-ROM, click the InfoWeb icon on the left side of this paragraph to access the online InfoWeb links. Otherwise, use your Web browser and type in the address of the New Perspectives site: www.cciw.com/np3. At the New Perspectives site you'll find up-to-date links to the topics covered in this chapter.

1 UPS: Uninterruptible Power Supplies

Buying and using an uninterruptible power supply (UPS) is the best way to avoid the problems that power outages cause. Periodically, computer magazines feature articles about the latest UPS technology. For example, *PC Computing*, "Usability Test: Call for Backup" by David Gerding at **www4.zdnet.com/pccomp/features/excl0897/zap/zap.html** is where you can read about several of the latest UPS devices and the companies that make them. *Information Week's* "Keep The Power On" by Logan Harbaugh at **www.techweb.com/se/directlink.cgi?IWK19970414S0050** will fill you in on why you need a UPS and how to evaluate various models. The major UPS vendors are American Power Conversion (**www.apcc.com**), Best Power Technology, Inc. (**www.bestpower.com**), Deltec Electronics Corp. (**www.deltecpower.com**), MGE UPS Systems (**www.mgeups.com**), and Tripp Lite (**www.tripplite.com**).

2 Computer Insurance

Does your homeowner's insurance policy cover your desktop computer? Your notebook computer? You might want to check with your insurance agent. Before you do, learn more about computer insurance in an article from *Computer Shopper*, "Sure, My PC's Insured: you may think so, but check your policy carefully" by Tami D. Peterson at **www5.zdnet.com/cshopper/filters/9610/buyper.html**. You can learn about laptop theft and insurance in another *Computer Shopper* article, "Laptop Theft Largely Overestimated" by Erik Sherman at **www5.zdnet.com/cshopper/content/9705/cshp0077.html**. A few insurance companies offer special insurance on computer equipment, and Safeware at **www.safeware-ins.com/** is one of them. Safeware publishes an annual report on computer theft losses, "Theft Losses 95-96: $2.3 Billion in Computers Lost During 1996," that you can read at their Web site, **www.safeware-ins.com/losses96.html**. You can also learn about techniques for preventing computer theft from Business Protection Products at **www.pc-security.com/**. "Crime Statistics That Will Surprise You" at the PC Guardian site, **www.pcguardian.com/facts-crst.html**, is interesting reading about hardware and information theft.

3 Viruses Alert!

To learn more about viruses, what they are, and how they work, read "Frequently Asked Questions" on Virus-L/comp.virus at **www.bocklabs.wisc.edu/~janda/virl_faq.html**. You can also find information about the latest viruses including descriptions of what specific viruses do at Symantec's AntiVirus Research Center at **www.symantec.com/avcenter/index.html** and at McAfee's Virus Info & Technical Documentation Library at **www.mcafee.com/support/techdocs/vinfo/index.html**. Would you like to see the screens of some computers with viruses? Connect to Data Fellows at **www.datafellows.com/usa.htm**. Some virus reports are hoaxes. Before you panic and spread information about a fake virus, check it out at the site, "Don't spread that hoax!" at **www.nonprofit.net/hoax/hoax.html**.

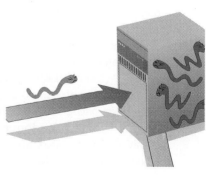

4 Macro Viruses

Macro viruses are some of the most prolific. By attaching themselves to macros in documents or spreadsheets, these viruses are transmitted over networks and with e-mail attachments by users who are not aware that their documents are infected. For up-to-date information on combatting macro viruses, your first stop should be Microsoft's site. Use the Search button to locate their list of articles for "macro virus." A good explanation of the Word Concept virus is at **www.microsoft.com/ msword/freestuff/mvtool/mvtool2.htm**. TechWeb at **www.techweb.com** is another good source of information if you search for "macro virus." Look for information on the ShareFun virus that automatically creates and mails infected e-mail attachments. While at the TechWeb site, you might want to read about how macro viruses work in the April 1, 1997 article, "Anatomy of a Macro Virus".

5 Year 2000

Can we really expect a rash of computer glitches when the year 2000 arrives? The "year 2000 problem," sometimes called the "year 2000 time bomb" or "Y2K" is real and programmers are feverishly working to correct hardware and software. An excellent site with links to articles, press releases, user groups, vendors, and FAQs is **www.year2000.com**. At that site you should find a link to Peter de Jager's chatty, but informative article "You've got to be Kidding!" at **www.year2000.com/y2kkidding.html**. An older, but still relevant article at **http://www.cnn.com/TECH/9601/2000/index.html** explains why "The year 2000 does not compute." Is your PC Year 2000 compliant? You'll find instructions for testing your PC at **www.tyler.net/tyr7020/y2kinput.htm**.

6 The Internet Worm

In November 2, 1988 Robert Morris, a computer science graduate student at Cornell and the son of the chief scientist at the National Computer Security Center, launched a worm that invaded thousands of Internet computers. A *Tour of the Worm* at **www.mmt.bme.hu/~kiss/docs/opsys/worm.html**, written by Donn Seeley of the Department of Computer Science at the University of Utah, presents a chronology and a detailed description of the internal workings of the Internet Worm. The Internet Worm at **www2.ncsu.edu/eos/info/computer_ethics/www/worm/index.html** is part of an instructional site on computer ethics at North Carolina State University. The site includes links to various articles that analyze the worm attack, the ethics of computer hacking, chronological reports on the worm and its aftermath, and the ethics of computer hacking.

7 Computer Crime

Computer crime law is a double edged sword. We need laws that protect us from computer crimes, yet we also need to make sure that computer crime laws are not so broad and sweeping that they infringe on our civil liberties and constitutional rights. In "Civil Liberties in Cyberspace: When does hacking turn from an exercise of civil liberties into crime" at **www.eff.org/pub/Legal/cyberliberties_kapor.article** Mitchell Kapor discusses government's response to computer crimes. The Electronic Frontier Foundation at **www.eff.org** was founded by Kapor and others to protect civil liberties as technology changes the way we work and do business. At the EFF Web site you can find of articles about computer crime, civil liberties, computer searches and seizures, and other topics related to computers and the law. At the Laws and Crime site, **www.blkbox.com/~guillory/comp4.html**, you can find a directory that includes links to U.S. state and federal computer crime laws, computer crime sentencing guidelines, and computer crime categories. At the National Security Institute (**nsi.org/**), you can read "Computer Security and the Law" (**nsi.org/Library/Compsec/cslaw.txt**), an article that provides information for lawyers on the legal aspects of computer security. For an international perspective, read *International Security: Issues involving Computers* at **stuweb.ee.mtu.edu/~jdhansen/320.html**. **Computer Crime: A Crime Fighter's Handbook** by David Icove, Karl Seger, and William VonStorch (O'Reilley, 1995) is a highly regarded book about computer crime. You can read a synopsis and review of this book at **www.ora.com/catalog/crime/desc.html**.

8 Risk Management

To learn more about data security and the dangers to which your data can be exposed, read "RIMS Report; Risk Management; Don't Overlook Data Security: Technology A Powerful Tool, But Exposure to Hackers Can Prove Costly" *Business Insurance*, May 6, 1996 at **rmisweb.com/rmisartc/050696a.htm**. One of the best ways to protect yourself from data loss is to always keep a backup of important data. The Internet offers new ways to provide data backup and data warehousing. Panorama Software Corporation at **www.pansoft.com/index.html** is one of many companies that offer products that allow corporations to back up their large computer systems over the Internet. To learn more about risk management analysis, services, and products, check out IBM's Risk Management Web pages at **www.brs.ibm.com/rmdescr.html**. If you would like to read about some of the latest computer incidents, connect to the *Risks Digest* at **http://www.csl.sri.com/~risko/risks.txt**.

9 Acceptable Use Policy

Have you ever thought about starting a word-processing business using the computers in one of your school's computer labs? Could you operate such a business from your dorm room using your own computer? Can you use your company's e-mail for personal business? You can find the answers to these questions in your school's or company's acceptable use policy. For an example of an acceptable use policy, check out "Acceptable Use Policy for Computer Facilities at Nassau Community College" at **www.sunynassau.edu/policies/labpol.htm**. Nassau's policy specifies who can use the college's computer equipment, what that computer equipment consists of, and who is responsible for activity on an assigned computer account. It also specifies what activities are unethical, unacceptable, and in violation of state or federal law. Mountainview Computer Technology, Inc. (MCT)—Acceptable Use Policy at **www.new-hampshire.net/aup.htm** list rules for MCT's Internet customers. "Developing a School or District 'Acceptable Use Policy' for Student and Staff Access to the Internet," **www.etdc.wednet.edu/aup/index.html**, discusses guidelines and a philosophy for developing an acceptable use policy for K-12 school districts. This Web site also includes links to a PowerPoint slide presentation; samples of policies, consent forms, and letters to parents; an article that reviews Internet case law; and other resources on legal aspects of acceptable use and the Internet.

10 Biometrics

The New York Times article, "Use of Recognition Technology Grows in Everyday Transactions" at **www.nytimes.com/library/cyber/week/082097biometrics.html** gives you a good introduction to new computer technology that is making computer use more secure. To learn about the latest biometric technology, check out Automatic Data Collection at Purdue University at **www.tech.purdue.edu/it/adc/**. Another great basic article is **"The Body as a Password"** by Ann Davis (*Wired* magazine, July 1997).

What about commercial products? Mr. Payroll Corporation, at **www.mrpayroll.com/** makes an automatic check cashing machine that compares a picture of your face with a picture it has on file. The Mr. Payroll automated check cashing system uses face recognition software developed by Miros, Incorporated at **www.miros.com**. International Automated Systems at **www.iaus.com/** has developed equipment for grocery stores that allows customers to check out their own groceries without waiting in long lines. You can check out their new grocery stores at **www.iaus.com/ucheck.htm**. Biometrics Identification Inc. is one of several companies that make fingerprint verification equipment. You can learn more about Biometrics' products at **www.biometricid.com**.

11 WarGames

In the 1983 film *WarGames* a young boy with an amazing grasp of computers accidentally engages a secret government supercomputer in what he thinks is a game. Unfortunately, the supercomputer, which controls the U.S. nuclear armaments, believes it is engaged in a real World War 3-type engagement with Russia. To learn more about this film, check out its page at the Internet Movie Database at **us.imdb.com/M/title-exact?WarGames+(1983)** where you can find a plot summary, cast list, trivia information, and more. For a Web-based Java-enabled taste of what the film is like, check out WarGames Logon at **www-public.rz.uni-duesseldorf.de/~ritterd/wargames/logon.htm**. At this Web site, you can view pictures from the film, listen to sound clips, play some games, take a tour of a decommissioned missile silo, and engage in some nostalgia for the 1980s.

12 Encryption Methods

You can learn about encryption at Netsurfer Focus on Cryptography and Privacy at **www.netsurf.com/nsf/v01/03/nsf.01.03.html**. This Web site presents an introduction to cryptography, information about key certification, a discussion of e-mail issues, information on the current status of the Clipper Chip, and other resources. One of the most popular and well-publicized encryption methods is Pretty Good Privacy (PGP). You can learn all about PGP at "Getting Started with encryption: An Introduction to PGP" at **www.cs.uchicago.edu/~cbarnard/pgptalk/index.html**. This Web site is an online PGP tutorial that was presented at the Computer Professionals for Social Responsibility conference in October 1995. The MIT distribution site for PGP at **web.mit.edu/network/pgp.html** includes information on how to integrate PGP with mail programs, a link to frequently asked questions, and links to Internet information on PGP, in addition to a link through which you can download a copy of the program. There are also several recent books on encryption, including **Building in Big Brother: The Cryptographic Policy Debate** by Lance J. Hoffman (Springer Verlag, 1995), **The Computer Privacy Handbook: A Practical Guide to E-Mail Encryption, Data Protection, and PGP Privacy Software** by Andre Bacard (Peachpit Press, 1995), and **Internet Cryptography** by Richard E. Smith (Addison-Wesley, 1997).

The Spartans of ancient Greece might have been the first to use military cryptography perhaps as early as the fifth century B.C. Since then cryptography has been used to keep secrets, provide mental exercise, and amuse those who appreciate mathematics and analysis, as well as to preserve and protect military secrets. Are there coded messages in the works of Francis Bacon and Shakespeare? Find out at "Setting.Forth." at **fly.hiwaay.net/~paul/cc.html**. Was Edgar Allan Poe also a dabbler in cryptography? You can learn the answer at "The Legend of Poe the Cryptographer" by Daniel W. Dukes at **www.nadn.navy.mil/EnglishDept/poeperplex/cryptop.htm**. If you're interested in trying your hand at cryptograms, check out Today's Cryptogram and Contest at **www.mindspring.com/~fmnshare/today.html**, and the Magic Decoder Game at **raphael.math.uic.edu/~jeremy/crypt/cgi-bin/magic-gateway.cgi**.

13 Anti-virus software

Many anti-virus software packages are available—some commercial, some shareware, and some even freeware. The two most highly rated companies that make antivirus software are Symantec (**www.symantec.com**) and McAfee (**www.mcafee.com**). Their products will protect your computer from virus attacks of all sorts. If you purchase and use their software, make sure you download the updates regularly so that new viruses don't slip by.

14 Internet Security

A great introduction to Web security issues is the Web Security Primer at **http://www.entrust.com/ primer.htm**. You might also check **www.techweb.com** for the August 1, 1996 article "Safety on the Net" by David Methvin. A good set of FAQs and links to a variety of security issues is **http://www.consensus.com/security/ssl-talk-sec02.html**. Many of the digital certificates you'll see on the Web have been registered with VeriSign. You can read more about the certification process at **www.verisign.com**. Cylink, a network security firm, provides an excellent summary of digital certificates at **http://www.cylink.com/products/security/x509.htm**. Find out if your browser maintains the security of your Internet mail address at **http://www.helie.com/BrowserCheck/**. Want to find out more about cookies? Marc Slayton's HotWired Geek Talk column at **www.hotwired.com/webmonkey/ webmonkey/geektalk/96/45/index3a.html** explains how cookies work and how to read the cookie file on your computer. A new Internet security standard called SET is currently in the testing phase. For updates, check VISA's Website at **www.VISA.com**.

Personal firewall software provides some protection against Web-borne vandalism. Cybermedia's firewall named Guard Dog is designed to protect your computer from Internet intruders that can damage your hard drive or steal private files, such as viruses, cookies and Trojan Horses. Read all about Guard Dog at **www.cybermedia.com**. eSafe Protect creates a secure SandBox for Internet files that you can download. The eSafe Web site at **www.esafe.com** is really great. You can take a quick tour of the eSafe Protect software, then download it. You can view simulations of vandal software that might be transmitted over the Internet and you can take a "test" to find out how your computer security rates. A third product, SurfinShield is published by Finjan Software. You can download a product demo at **www.finjan.com** and link to some excellent articles on the dangers of the Internet at **www.finjan.com/educate/news.html**.

Review

1. Use your own words to answer the questions that appear under each section heading in this chapter.

2. List each of the boldface terms used in this chapter, then use your own words to write a short definition of each term.

3. Complete the following chart to review the factors that cause data loss or misuse. List the factors you learned about in this chapter in the first column. Then place an X in the appropriate column to indicate if the factor causes data loss, inaccurate data, stolen data, or intentionally damaged data. Some factors might have more than one X.

Factor	Unintentional data loss	Inaccurate data	Stolen or misused data	Intentional data loss or damage
Operator error				
[You fill in the rest of the factors]				

4 Complete the following chart to summarize what you have learned about viruses, macro viruses, Trojan horses, time bombs, logic bombs, and software worms.

Type	Spreads by	Triggered by
Virus		
Trojan horse		
Worm		
Time bomb		
Logic bomb		
Macro virus		

5 Make a check list of steps to take if you suspect that your computer is infected with a virus.

6 List the four steps in the risk management process.

7 Make a list of the data security techniques discussed in the *Data Security and Risk Management* section. Then indicate the advantages and disadvantages of each technique.

8 Use your own words to write descriptions of full, incremental, and differential backup procedures. Make sure your descriptions clearly explain the difference between incremental and differential backups.

9 Thinking back over the entire chapter, what was the most useful concept you learned? What questions do you have about data security that still remain unanswered?

10 On a sheet of paper, list all the reasons you can think of for making a backup of computer data.

11 Use the New Perspectives CD-ROM to take a practice test or to review the new terms presented in this chapter.

Projects

1 **Lost Data: What's Your Experience?** Describe a situation in which you or someone you know lost data stored on a computer. What caused the data loss? What steps could have been taken to prevent the loss? What steps could you or the other person have taken to recover the lost data?

2 **Risk Management: A Personal Perspective** Assess the risk to the programs and data files stored on the hard disk of your computer by answering the following questions:

a. What threats are likely to cause your data to be lost, stolen, or damaged?

b. How many files of data do you have?

c. If you add up the size of all your files, how many megabytes of data do you have?

d. How many of these files are critical and would need to be replaced if you lost all your data?

e. What would you need to do to reconstruct the critical files if the hard disk drive failed and you did not have any backups?

f. What measures could you use to protect your data from the threats you identified in the first question? What is the cost of each of these measures?

g. Balancing the threats to your data, the importance of your data, and the cost of protective measures, what do you think is the best plan for the security of your data?

3 **Lost Weekend: Full, Incremental, and Differential Backups** Assume that your hard disk drive fails on a Friday afternoon. Explain how you would restore your data over the weekend if you had been using each of the following backup systems:

a. A full backup every Friday evening

b. A full backup every Friday evening with a differential backup on Wednesday evening

c. A full backup every Friday evening with an incremental backup Monday through Thursday evenings

4
INTERNET
Optional

Word Macro Viruses In this chapter you learned that Word documents can harbor a macro virus. Using library or Internet resources, find a list of symptoms for the Word macro viruses that are currently circulating. Check your disks to see if you have the virus.

Write a one-page report describing what you learned about the Word macro virus and its presence on, or absence from, the documents you have on your disks.

5
INTERNET
Optional

The Internet Worm The Internet worm created concern about the security of data on military and research computer systems, and it raised ethical questions about the rights and responsibilities of computer users. Select one of the following statements and write a two-page paper that argues for or against the statement. You might want to use the Internet or library resources to learn more about each viewpoint. Be sure you include the resources you used in a bibliography.

a. People have the "right" to hone their computing skills by breaking into computers. As a computer scientist once said, "The right to hack is held higher than the right of someone to tell you not to. It's an inalienable right."

b. If problems exist, it is acceptable to use any means to point them out. The computer science student who created the Internet virus was perfectly justified in claiming that he should not be convicted because he was just trying to point out that security holes exist in large computer networks.

c. Computer crimes are no different from other crimes, and computer criminals should be held responsible for the damage they cause by paying for the time and cost of replacing or restoring data.

6 **Understanding an Acceptable Use Policy** Obtain a copy of your school's student code or computer use policy, then answer the following questions. If your school does not have such a policy, create one that addresses these questions.

a. To whom does the policy apply—students, faculty, staff, community members, others?

b. What types of activities does the policy specifically prohibit?

c. If a computer crime is committed, would the crime be dealt with by campus authorities or by state law enforcement agents?

d. Does the policy state the penalties for computer crimes? If so, what are they?

7
INTERNET
Required

Hoax! Most Internet users have received panicked e-mail about the GoodTimes virus. It turns out that this virus does not exist—it is a hoax. How can you tell the difference between a real virus alert and a hoax? The best policy is to check a reliable site. You can easily locate sites that list hoaxes by entering "hoax" in any Internet search engine such as Yahoo! Sites with reliable reports include **www.nonprofit.net/ hoax/hoax.html**, **www.goodfellows.com**, **www.urbanlegends.com**, and **ciac.llnl.gov/ciac/CIACHoaxes.html**.

Visit at least one of these sites and find the descriptions of five hoaxes. Write a one-page summary that includes the name and description of each hoax, how the hoax is spread, and why you think people believe the hoax.

8 **Virus Detection Software** If you suspect your computer has become infected, it is prudent to immediately activate virus detection software to scan your files for a virus. With the continued spread of viruses, virus detection software has become an essential utility in today's computing environment. Many virus detection software packages are available in computer stores, on computer bulletin boards, and on the Internet. Find information about three virus detection software packages and fill out the following comparison chart.

	Software 1	Software 2	Software 3
Product name			
Publisher			
Price			
Current version			
Update frequency			
Special features			

Lab Assignments

Data Backup

The Data Backup Lab gives you an opportunity to make tape backups on a simulated computer system. Periodically, the hard disk on the simulated computer will fail, which gives you a chance to assess the convenience and efficiency of different backup procedures.

1 Click the Steps button to learn how to use the simulation. As you work through the Steps, answer all of the Quick Check questions that appear. After you complete the Steps, you will see a Summary Report of your Quick Check answers. Follow the directions on the screen to print this report.

2 Click the Explore button. Create a full backup every Friday using only Tape 1. At some point in the simulation, an event will cause data loss on the simulated computer system. Use the simulation to restore as much data as you can. After you restore the data, print the Backup Audit Report.

3 In Explore, create a full backup every Friday on Tape 1 and a differential backup every Wednesday on Tape 2. At some point in the simulation, an event will cause data loss on the simulated computer system. Use the simulation to restore as much data as you can. Print the Backup Audit Report.

4 In Explore, create a full backup on Tape 1 every Monday. Make incremental backups on Tapes 2, 3, 4, and 5 each day for the rest of the week. Continue this cycle, reusing the same tapes each week. At some point in the simulation an event will cause data loss on the simulated computer system. Use the simulation to restore as much data as you can. Print the Backup Audit Report.

5 Photocopy a calendar for next month. On the calendar indicate your best plan for backing up data. In Explore, implement your plan. Print out the Backup Audit Report. Write a paragraph or two discussing the effectiveness of your plan.

DATA REPRESENTATION

CHAPTER**PREVIEW**

The information in this chapter will help you understand why your files are stored in different formats and the significance of file extensions such as .pcx, .tif, .wmf, .mid, and .wav. You will learn how to use compression software to shrink the size of files and save storage space on your disks. When you have completed this chapter, you should be able to:

- Explain how information theory applies to the data representation codes used by computers
- Determine how many bits are needed to represent a given number of messages
- Define the key characteristics of ASCII, ANSI, EBCDIC, and Unicode
- Explain the difference between bitmap and vector graphics
- Calculate the storage space required for a monochrome, grayscale, or color bitmap graphic
- Explain the difference between waveform audio and MIDI music
- List the advantages and disadvantages of data compression
- Use the file extension to identify the format used to compress file data

It was April 18, 1775, the eve of the American Revolution. The Massachusetts Minutemen were huddled around a plank table planning a defense strategy against well-armed and professionally trained British troops. If the Minutemen sent a scout to collect information on the British route of attack, how would he communicate what he learned? The Minutemen solved this problem by using the plan recounted in Longfellow's poem about Paul Revere's famous ride:

One if by land, and two if by sea;
And I on the opposite shore will be,
Ready to ride and spread the alarm
Through every Middlesex village and farm.

The Old North Church tower was visible for miles. As a signal for Paul Revere, either one or two lanterns would be lit in the church tower. One lantern meant the British were coming by land. Two lanterns meant the British were coming by sea. But what if some of the British troops arrived on land and others arrived by sea? Would the Minutemen need another lantern for this third possibility? The answer to this question is clear when you understand data representation and information theory, the topics of this chapter.

In Chapter 5 you were introduced to the use of binary numbers and ASCII and EBCDIC codes to represent data. In this chapter, you will pursue the subject of data representation in more depth and discover how computers store graphical, video, and sound data.

InfoWeb

Paul Revere
1

LABS

Data
Representation

A Information Theory

The Minutemen could have positioned 20 or 30 lanterns on a hillside to spell out the words "LAND" or "SEA." Instead, if we accept Longfellow's account of the historical evening in 1775, the Minutemen used a simple code in which one light meant "by land" and two lights meant "by sea." It seems that the Minutemen selected a fairly efficient way to convey information. Was there an even more efficient way? You can answer this question using **information theory**, the study of the most efficient way to represent or encode information. Information theory is an important concept for computer and software design. If information is represented efficiently, it can be stored in a small amount of space and it can be transmitted quickly.

Using information theory, computer scientists have designed various ways of encoding and storing information. The way information is encoded and stored in a computer is referred to as a **file format**. A computer stores the data for your word-processing documents in a file format different from the file format it uses to store your graphics data or audio data. In this chapter you'll learn about different ways of encoding data and the file formats this encoding produces.

Efficiently Storing and Transmitting Information

Could the Minutemen have sent their message with fewer than two lanterns? Some methods for storing and transmitting information are more efficient than others. Using information theory, you can evaluate the efficiency of the Minutemen's code. Then you can apply what you learn to understanding the efficiency with which computers store and transmit information.

The Minutemen had two possible messages to convey. We'll refer to these possible messages as "units of information." One of these units of information was "by land." The other unit of information was "by sea," as shown in Figure 10-1.

Figure 10-1

Paul
Revere's
code

One lantern in the church tower signaled that the British were coming by land.

Two lanterns signaled that the British were coming by sea.

Information theory tells us that the Minutemen could have used a more efficient code, using one lantern instead of two. Figure 10-2 shows that with one lantern, it is possible to convey up to two units of information; the lantern can be on or off, representing "yes" or "no," "land" or "sea," "true" or "false," and so forth.

Figure 10-2

One lantern can convey up to two units of information

In the on state, the lantern indicates the British are coming by land.

or

In the off state, the lantern indicates the British are coming by sea.

How does this apply to computers? As you learned in Chapter 4, a computer is an electronic device that stores and manipulates electrical currents that represent bits—0s and 1s. Think of a bit as the equivalent of one lantern. A bit can be a 1 or a 0, just as a lantern can be on or off. The on state of the lantern corresponds to a 1 bit, and the off state of the lantern corresponds to a 0 bit. A computer can use a single bit (one lantern) to store and convey up to two units of information; a 1 bit might correspond to "yes" and a 0 bit might correspond to "no;" a 1 bit might correspond to "land" and a 0 bit might correspond to "sea," and so forth.

You might think that it is not a good idea to use an unlit lantern to convey the message "by sea." A dark church tower could mean many things. For example, the church might have been locked, so no one could get to the tower to place the lantern. Or, maybe the lantern burned out. In either of these cases, the church tower would be dark, but the British might still be arriving by sea.

The point is that information theory tells you that it is *theoretically* possible for the Minutemen to convey either "by land" or "by sea" using only one lantern. However, it might not have been *practical* to do so. As you will see in Chapter 11, information theory can be extended to account for potential problems that might occur when data is actually transmitted.

LAB

Data
Representation

Representing Information

How can we code more complex messages? A computer uses a bit as the building block for more complex messages, constructed with a series of bits. One bit can convey two messages. If a computer uses two bits (two lanterns) or three bits (three lanterns) how many different units of information can it convey? Figure 10-3 shows that two bits can convey four units of information.

Figure 10-3

Representing information using two bits

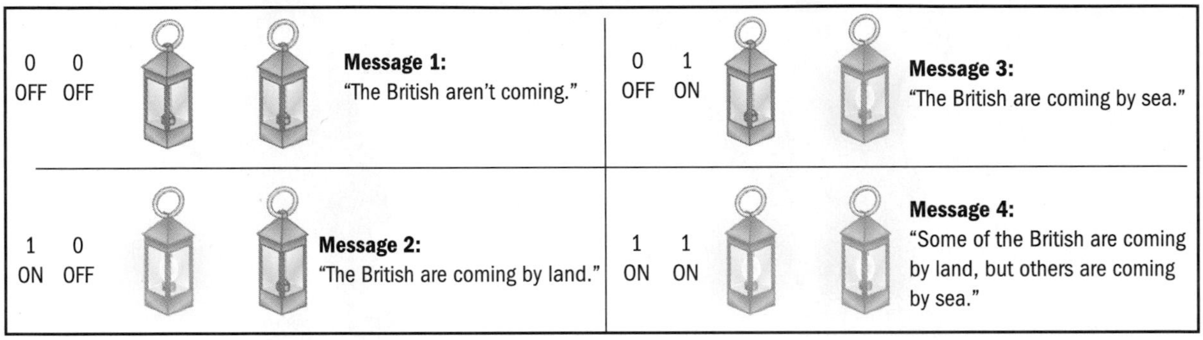

| 0   0
 OFF OFF | **Message 1:**
 "The British aren't coming." | 0   1
 OFF ON | **Message 3:**
 "The British are coming by sea." |
| 1   0
 ON OFF | **Message 2:**
 "The British are coming by land." | 1   1
 ON ON | **Message 4:**
 "Some of the British are coming by land, but others are coming by sea." |

The number of units of information that you can convey is simply the number of different combinations you can make with a given number of bits. There is a pattern to this. With one bit, you can convey two units of information. With two bits, you can convey four units of information. With three bits, you can convey eight units. The pattern is 2, 4, 8; these numbers are all powers of 2, as shown in Figure 10-4.

Figure 10-4

Powers of 2

$$2^0 = 1$$

$$2^1 = 2$$

$$2^2 = 2 \times 2 = 4$$

$$2^3 = 2 \times 2 \times 2 = 8$$

$$2^4 = 2 \times 2 \times 2 \times 2 = 16$$

$$2^5 = 2 \times 2 \times 2 \times 2 \times 2 = 32$$

$$2^6 = 2 \times 2 \times 2 \times 2 \times 2 \times 2 = 64$$

$$2^7 = 2 \times 2 \times 2 \times 2 \times 2 \times 2 \times 2 = 128$$

$$2^8 = 2 \times 2 \times 2 \times 2 \times 2 \times 2 \times 2 \times 2 = 256$$

We now have a rule about conveying information: The maximum number of different units of information you can convey with n bits is 2^n. For example, if you use four bits (or four lanterns), the exponent n is 4. The maximum number of units you can convey is 2^4 or $2\times2\times2\times2$, which is 16. So, if you use four bits, you can convey a maximum of 16 different units of information. Figure 10-5 summarizes this rule.

Figure 10-5

The maximum number of different units of information you can convey with n bits is 2^n.

When you use one bit (one lantern)...		...you can convey up to two (2^1) messages.	Message one: 0 Message two: 1
When you use two bits (two lanterns)...		...you can convey up to four (2^2) messages.	00 01 10 11
When you use three bits (three lanterns)...		...you can convey up to eight (2^3) messages.	000 100 001 101 010 110 011 111
When you use four bits (four lanterns)...		...you can convey up to sixteen (2^4) messages.	0000 0100 1000 1100 0001 0101 1001 1101 0010 0110 1010 1110 0011 0111 1011 1111

If you have a certain number of bits (or lanterns), you can use the rule in Figure 10-5 to determine how many different messages you can send. Now turn the rule around. If you know how many messages you might want to convey, how can you determine the minimum number of bits you need? Suppose that Paul Revere knew a spy in the British army that was going to signal information about the month when British reinforcements would arrive. How many bits (lanterns) would the spy need to convey any month between January (month 1) and December (month 12)? You can determine this by figuring out what power of 2 provides an adequate number of messages. What power of 2—what exponent—would provide at least 12 different messages?

Suppose the spy uses three lanterns. The exponent would be 3, so the spy could send 2^3 messages (8 messages)—not enough to report 12 months. Four lanterns provide 2^4 messages (16 messages). So the spy would need at least four lanterns to send 12 different messages.

Representing Numbers

What if the Minutemen wanted to send a message about the number of British troops in the advance force? Suppose the person in the church tower knew that the British advance force had 50 troops. You know that this information could be sent using fewer than 50 lanterns! Information theory tells us that the Minutemen could use only six lanterns to convey the message that 50 British troops would attack. Which of the lanterns would be off and which would be on to send this message?

Although the Minutemen, like the rest of us, are accustomed to working with the decimal number system (base 10), the binary number system (base 2) would provide a more efficient way for the Minutemen to transmit numbers to Paul Revere. The binary number system uses only two digits, 0 and 1, which correspond to the off and on states of a lantern.

The decimal number 50 is 110010 in binary. To convey the number 50, the Minutemen would arrange six lanterns as follows: on-on-off-off-on-off, as shown in Figure 10-6.

Figure 10-6

Six lanterns represent the number 50.

Binary digits	1	1	0	0	1	0
Place value	2^5 thirty-twos	2^4 sixteens	2^3 eights	2^2 fours	2^1 twos	2^0 ones
Binary to decimal conversion	1×32 +	1×16 +	0×8 +	0×4 +	1×2 +	0×1 = 50 (decimal)

Computers can use on and off bits to store decimal numbers in binary format. Information theory tells us, however, that the binary number system has limitations. For example, many early microcomputers had only an 8-bit word size. What is the largest decimal number that one of these computers could store in binary format? If your answer is 255, you are correct. If you assign 1s to all eight bits, you have the binary number 11111111, which is equivalent to the decimal number 255.

Binary Numbers 3

Using the binary number system, an 8-bit computer could not work with numbers greater than 255 or less than 0. Such a computer would not be very useful, so computer scientists devised alternative ways to use on and off bits to represent large numbers. Because these alternatives use the binary digits 0 and 1, they are referred to as **binary codes**. If computing is your major, you will learn about these other binary codes in your more advanced courses.

You have now seen how the Minutemen could use lanterns to represent numbers and how a computer can use a series of 1s and 0s to represent a number. Next, you'll learn how computers store letters and punctuation symbols.

Representing Characters

How many lanterns would the Minutemen need to send messages composed of words?

Character representation refers to the way non-numeric data, such as a letter of the alphabet or a punctuation mark, is represented by a series of bits. A **character representation code**, also referred to simply as a *code*, is a series of bits that represents a letter, symbol, or numeral. Don't confuse these "codes" with encryption and secret codes. The codes used to represent data on computers are public and must remain that way so computers can share data.

Suppose that you want to represent each of the 26 characters in the alphabet. How many lanterns or bits would you need? Although it might seem that five bits are enough to represent the 26 characters in the alphabet, written English uses uppercase and lowercase versions of each letter of the alphabet and a variety of symbols for punctuation and abbreviations, such as $ # @ & +. If you count these letters, symbols, and the numerals 0 through 9, 95 different characters must be represented. More than five bits are required.

As computers evolved from the primitive number crunchers of the 1940s and 1950s, several character representation codes emerged. Today, the three character representation codes most widely used are ASCII, ANSI, and EBCDIC. A fourth code, Unicode, has been proposed for future worldwide use.

ASCII (American Standard Code for Information Interchange) is the most widely used coding scheme for character data. A file of data encoded using ASCII is referred to as an **ASCII file** or as "a file in ASCII format." The standard ASCII code uses seven bits to represent 2^7 symbols (128 symbols), including uppercase and lowercase letters, special control codes, numerals, and punctuation symbols. A table or matrix is often used to provide a compact reference to the ASCII code. Figure 10-7 shows you how to use a matrix to find the ASCII code for the lowercase letter "a."

Figure 10-7

An ASCII matrix

1. Locate the lowercase letter "a" in the matrix.

2. The three binary digits at the top of the column show you the values of the leftmost bits.

3. The four binary digits at the beginning of the row show you the values of the rightmost bits.

4. The ASCII code for the lowercase letter "a" is 1100001.

1100001

	000	001	010	011	100	101	110	111
0000	NUL	DLE	SP	0	@	P		p
0001	SOH	DC1	!	1	A	Q	a	q
0010	STX	DC2	"	2	B	R	b	r
0011	ETX	DC3	#	3	C	S	c	s
0100	EOT	DC4	$	4	D	T	d	t
0101	ENQ	NAK	%	5	E	U	e	u
0110	ACK	SYN	&	6	F	V	f	v
0111	BEL	ETB	'	7	G	W	g	w
1000	BS	CAN	(	8	H	X	h	x
1001	HT	EM	)	9	I	Y	i	y
1010	LF	SUB	*	:	J	Z	j	z
1011	VT	ESC	+	;	K	[	k	{
1100	FF	FS	,	<	L	\	l		
1101	CR	GS	-	=	M	]	m	}
1110	SO	RS	.	>	N	^	n	~
1111	SI	US	/	?	O	_	o	DEL

The **ANSI** (American National Standards Institute) code uses eight bits to represent each character. The 8-bit ANSI code can convey up to 2^8, that is, 256 units of information, so it can be used to code 256 letters and symbols. The first 128 of the characters of the ANSI code are the same as those defined by the ASCII code, but with an additional zero as the leftmost bit. For example, the letter "a" is represented by the ASCII code 1100001 and by the ANSI code 01100001. In addition to the 128 characters represented by the ASCII code, the ANSI code represents 128 other characters such as the copyright symbol ©, the pound sterling symbol £, and foreign language characters such as á, ê, and æ.

EBCDIC (Extended Binary Coded Decimal Interchange Code) is an 8-bit character representation code developed by IBM for its mainframe computers. EBCDIC does not use the same code as ASCII or ANSI for the initial 128 characters. For example, in EBCDIC the letter "a" is represented by 10000001.

Standard ASCII defines 128 characters, which is sufficient for the numbers, letters, and punctuation marks used in English. ANSI represents all these characters plus many of the characters used in European languages. EBCDIC represents the standard alphabet and an assortment of control codes. However, none of these coding schemes supports alternate character sets such as Hebrew, Cyrillic, or Arabic. These coding schemes also do not support languages such as Japanese or Chinese, which require thousands of different symbols.

Unicode
4

Unicode is a 16-bit code that can represent over 65,000 different characters. Theoretically, Unicode can represent characters in every language used today, as well as characters from languages that are no longer used. Such a code would be very helpful in international business and communications, where a document might need to contain sections of text in Japanese, English, and Chinese. Unicode also facilitates the **localization** of software, that is, the modification of software for use in specific countries. With Unicode, a software developer can modify a computer program to display on-screen prompts, menus, and error messages in different languages for use in specific countries or regions. Both Microsoft and Apple have announced plans to add Unicode support to their operating systems.

QuickCheck A

1 _____ is an area of research that describes how the amount of information you can convey depends on the way you encode the information.

2 To convey nine units of information, you need a minimum of _____ lanterns.

3 If you code data using the _____ number system, 255 is the largest number that an 8-bit computer can work with.

4 The _____ code uses seven bits to represent 128 symbols, including uppercase letters, lowercase letters, control codes, and punctuation symbols.

5 _____ is a 16-bit code used to represent characters in every language used today.

6 When a software developer modifies a computer program to display prompts, menus, and error messages in different languages, it is referred to as _____ of software.

B Representing Graphics and Video

InfoWeb

Graphics Formats 5

Graphics, such as photographs and drawings, are quite different from documents that contain numbers and text. Obviously, computers cannot store and transmit graphics using character representation codes such as ASCII. However, computers must somehow encode graphics as 1s and 0s to store and transmit them electronically. How does this work?

There are two very different approaches to encoding graphics for computer systems: bitmap and vector. The differences between these two graphical coding schemes affect the image quality, the amount of space required to store the image, the amount of time required to transmit the image, and the ease with which you can modify the image.

Bitmap Graphics

How does a computer store graphical data? Computers store **bitmap graphics** using a code that indicates the state of each individual dot, or pixel, displayed on the screen. The simplest bitmap graphics are monochrome. A **monochrome graphic** contains only the colors white and black. To understand how a computer codes monochrome bitmap graphics, think of a grid superimposed on a picture. The grid divides the picture into cells, each equivalent to a pixel on the computer screen. With monochrome graphics, each cell, or pixel, can be colored either black or white. If the section of the photo in a cell is black, the computer represents it with a 0 bit. If the section of the photo in a cell is white, the computer represents it with a 1 bit. Each row of the grid is represented by a series of 0s and 1s, as shown in Figure 10-8.

Figure 10-8

Storing a monochrome bitmap graphic

The original picture

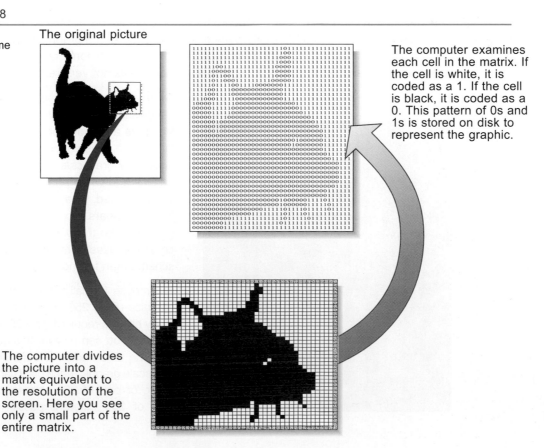

The computer examines each cell in the matrix. If the cell is white, it is coded as a 1. If the cell is black, it is coded as a 0. This pattern of 0s and 1s is stored on disk to represent the graphic.

The computer divides the picture into a matrix equivalent to the resolution of the screen. Here you see only a small part of the entire matrix.

With monochrome graphics, the number of bits required to represent a full-screen picture is the same as the number of pixels on the screen. The number of *bytes* required to store the image is the number of bits divided by eight. To see how this works, study the calculation in Figure 10-9.

Figure 10-9

Calculating the size of a monochrome bitmap graphic

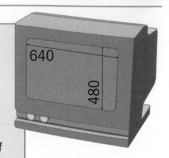

1. Multiply the horizontal by the vertical resolution of the screen:

640 × 480 = 307,200 pixels

This calculates the number of pixels on the screen. Because a monochrome graphic uses only one bit to represent each pixel, this also calculates the number of *bits* needed to store the graphic.

2. It is more conventional to measure storage requirements in bytes rather than bits. Because there are eight bits in a byte, divide the total number of bits by eight to calculate the number of *bytes* required for the graphic:

307,200 ÷ 8 = 38,400 bytes

As you saw in Figure 10-9, a monochrome graphic displayed at 640 × 480 resolution requires 640 × 480 or 307,200 bits. With eight bits per byte, the graphic requires 38,400 bytes, a relatively small amount of storage space. However, monochrome graphics are seldom used because their two-dimensional appearance is not very realistic.

Figure 10-10

A 256-grayscale bitmap graphic

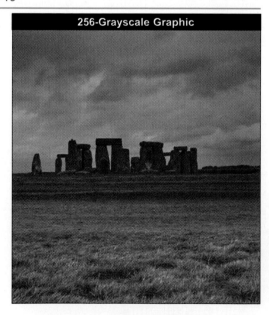

256-Grayscale Graphic

Grayscale graphics display an image using shades of gray or "gray scales." Whereas a monochrome graphic is similar to an old-fashioned paper cut-out silhouette, a grayscale graphic is similar to a black and white photo. The more gray shades used, the more realistic the image appears. To represent grayscale graphics, like the one in Figure 10-10, a computer uses a more complex coding scheme than for monochrome graphics.

A computer typically represents grayscale graphics using 256 shades of gray. How many bits are required for a 256-grayscale picture? You can answer this question by applying information theory. In a 256-grayscale graphic, each pixel can be white, black, or one of 254 shades of gray—a total of 256 different possibilities. How many bits are needed to convey 256 units of information? The answer is eight: 2^8 is 256. Therefore, a 256-grayscale graphic requires eight bits (one byte) for each pixel. A full-screen 256-grayscale graphic at 640 × 480 resolution requires 307,200 bytes, as shown by the calculation in Figure 10-11.

Figure 10-11

Calculating the size of a 256-grayscale graphic

Multiply the horizontal by the vertical resolution of the screen:

640 × 480 = 307,200

This calculates the number of pixels on the screen. A 256-grayscale graphic uses one byte to represent each pixel, so this is also the number of *bytes* needed to store the graphic.

For more realism, computers can display color images. A computer represents color graphics using either 16, 256, or 16.7 million colors. For a **16-color graphic**, each pixel can have one of 16 colors. To represent these 16 different units of information, you need only four bits of storage space for each pixel. A full-screen 16-color graphic requires 153,600 bytes of storage space.

A **256-color graphic** requires eight bits (one byte) for each pixel. A full-screen image requires 307,200 bytes—twice as much storage space as a 16-color image, but the same amount as a 256-grayscale graphic.

A photographic-quality graphic displays up to 16.7 million colors and is called a **24-bit** or **true-color graphic**. To represent 16.7 million colors requires 24 bits (3 bytes) for each pixel. Is there a difference in the image quality of 16-, 256-, and true-color graphics? You can judge for yourself by comparing the appearance of the graphics in Figure 10-12.

Figure 10-12

A comparison of color graphics

Files that contain graphics can be quite large, as you have seen. Such large files also require lengthy transmission or download times. For example, it would take at least a minute to download a 256-color, 640 × 480 bitmap image from an Internet site to your computer at home. A 16-color graphic would take only half as long to download.

Two techniques are used to decrease graphics storage space and transmission time. First, the size of graphics files can be reduced by a technique known as compression, which is discussed later in this chapter. Second, a technique called dithering reduces file size by reducing the number of colors in a graphic. **Dithering** uses patterns composed of two or more colors to produce the illusion of additional colors and shading, relying on the human eye to blend colors and shapes. For example, an area of solid amber on a 256-color image can be dithered into a pattern of yellow and red dots in a 16-color image.

Dithering is a popular technique for reducing the size of graphics on Internet World Wide Web pages. Suppose you have a 256-color graphic of Stonehenge that you want to use on a Web page. You would like to reduce the time a Web browser requires to display the image, so you need to reduce the number of bytes used to represent the image. If you simply convert the file to a 16-color graphic, the colors of the resulting graphic are quite different from the original. However, if you dither the 256-color graphic, the result is a graphic composed of 16 colors that appear much more similar to the original. You can see the difference in Figure 10-13.

Figure 10-13

A dithered image simulates colors. The amber sky is simulated by a pattern of yellow and red dots.

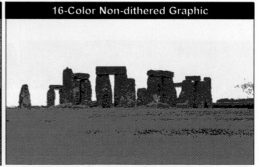

Bitmap graphics are used for realistic images such as scanned photos. The filename extensions .bmp, .pcx, .tif, .jpg, and .gif typically indicate files that contain bitmap images. File extensions are often used as the name of the file format; a file with a .gif extension (pronounced "Jiff" or sometimes "Giff") is usually called a "GIF file."

Because bitmap graphics are coded as a series of bits that represent pixels, you can modify or edit this type of graphic by changing individual pixels. To modify a bitmap graphic, you use **bitmap graphics software**, sometimes referred to as **photo editing software** or **paint software**. Software packages such as Microsoft Paint, PC Paintbrush, Adobe Photoshop, or Micrografx Picture Publisher let you zoom in on a section of a picture so you can modify individual pixels more easily. Because making large-scale changes pixel by pixel can be a tedious process, bitmap graphics software provides additional tools to cut, copy, paste, and change the color of sections of a picture.

Bitmap graphics software gives you the capability to modify photographic-quality images. For example, you can retouch or repair old photographs and design eye-catching new pictures using images you cut and paste from several photos (Figure 10-14).

Figure 10-14

Using bitmap graphics software, you can edit images bit-by-bit. For example, you could erase the pixels for the woman in this photo, then replace her with a different person.

Vector Graphics

What's the difference between vector graphics and bitmap graphics? **Vector graphics** consist of a set of instructions that recreates a picture. When you create a vector graphic, you draw lines and shapes in various colors. The computer then translates these lines and shapes into a set of instructions that can recreate your graphic. The computer stores the instructions instead of the actual picture. Vector graphics do not look as realistic as pictures created with bitmap graphics, as you can see by comparing the images in Figure 10-15.

Figure 10-15

Vector graphics generally look less realistic than bitmap graphics.

Vector graphics, however, have several important advantages. First, a vector graphic image is likely to require much less storage space than a bitmap image. The storage space required for a vector graphic picture depends on its complexity. Each instruction requires storage space, so the more lines, shapes, and fill patterns the picture contains, the more storage space it requires. The vector graphic picture shown in Figure 10-15 requires only 4,894 bytes of storage.

A second advantage of vector graphics is that you can easily modify the pictures you create using vector graphic software. You can think of the parts of a vector graphic picture as separate objects that you can individually stretch, shrink, distort, color, move, or delete. For example, your vector graphic picture might contain a sun that you created with a yellow circle. You could easily move the sun to a different location in the picture, enlarge it, or change its color.

Files that contain a vector graphic typically have file extensions such as .wmf, .dxf, .mgx, and .cgm. Vector graphic software is referred to as **drawing software**, and it is often packaged separately from the paint software used to produce bitmap graphics. Popular vector graphic software packages include Micrographx Designer and CorelDRAW.

When you use vector graphic software to draw a picture, you use drawing tools to create shapes or objects. For example, you can use the filled circle tool to draw a circle that is filled with a solid color. The data for creating the circle is recorded as an instruction such as CIRCLE 40 Y 200 150, which means create a circle with a 40-pixel radius, color it yellow, and place the center of the circle 200 pixels from the left of the screen and 150 pixels from the top of the screen.

Using drawing tools, you can create geometric objects such as filled rectangles or circles. You can also create irregular shapes by connecting points to create the outline of a shape. Objects you create with the drawing tools can be assembled into a picture by changing the position, size, and color of the objects. The drawing software adjusts the instructions accordingly. For example, if you move the circle to the right side of the image, the instruction that the computer stores for the circle changes to CIRCLE 40 Y 500 200. Figure 10-16 shows how to use drawing tools to create a vector graphic.

Figure 10-16

To draw a circle, select the filled circle tool, then drag the mouse pointer to indicate the location and size of the circle. A color palette at the bottom of the window allows you to select the circle color.
Once you've created the circle object, you can move it, change its size, or color.
You can draw irregular shaped objects, such as clouds by connecting short line segments.

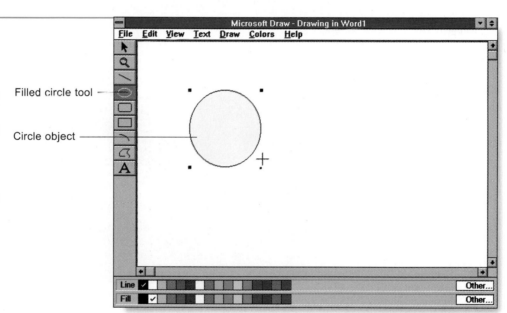

Filled circle tool

Circle object

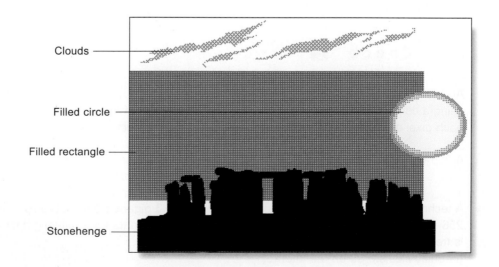

Clouds

Filled circle

Filled rectangle

Stonehenge

Digital Video

How do computers store video data? A video is composed of a series of frames. Each frame is essentially a still picture, which could be represented using the same techniques as bitmap graphics. However, video displays 30 frames per second, which means that digital video recording requires tremendous storage capacity.

As you have seen, a full-screen 256-color image at 640 × 480 resolution requires 307,200 pixels. Multiply this number by 30 to calculate how many bytes are needed for each second of video—that's 9,216,000 bytes, or about nine megabytes, for one second of video (Figure 10-17). A two-hour movie would require 66,355,200,000 bytes, more than 66 gigabytes! It would be only marginally possible to play back such a digitally recorded video, even using the most powerful supercomputer. As you will learn later in this chapter, video data requires some special coding techniques to produce a video file of manageable size.

Figure 10-17

If this four-second video was as large as a 640 × 480 screen it would require about 36 megabytes of storage space.

QuickCheck B

1. A(n) _____ graphic is represented using a code that indicates the state of each pixel displayed on the screen.

2. A 256-grayscale graphic requires _____ bit(s) for each pixel.

3. A technique called _____ reduces a 256-color graphic to a 16-color graphic and is frequently used to reduce the size of graphics files stored on the Internet.

4. _____ graphics are stored as a series of instructions on how to recreate the objects in the picture.

5. Bmp, .wmf, .dxf, and .tif are bitmap file extensions. True or false? _____

6. A 3-gigabyte hard drive can easily store the digital data for a full-length movie. True or false? _____

C Representing Sound

Computers can record, store, and play back sounds such as voices and music. Sound or audio data can be represented in two very different ways: as a waveform or as MIDI music. The difference between the two is much like the difference between a tape recording and a player-piano roll.

Waveform Audio

InfoWeb

Digital Audio 6

How do computers store music? **Waveform audio** is a digital representation of sound. To digitally record sound, samples of the sound waveform are collected at periodic intervals and stored as numeric data. Music, voice, and sounds can all be recorded as waveforms. Figure 10-18 shows how a computer digitally samples a waveform.

Figure 10-18

Sampling a sound wave

The distance between peaks is called the frequency. The frequency indicates the tone or note. When the peaks are far apart, the sound is low. When the peaks are close together, the sound is high.

The height of the wave is recorded for each sample. Eight bits are used to record each sample, so the height of a wave is measured on a scale of 0 to 255.

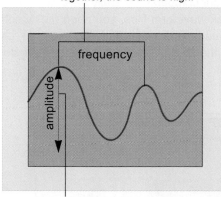

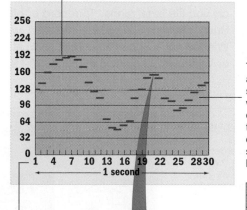

The samples approximate the shape of the wave, but the details of what the sound wave does between samples are lost.

The height of a sound wave is called the amplitude. The amplitude indicates the loudness of the sound.

To sample the wave, each second of the wave's duration is divided into thousands of segments. It is too difficult to show all such samples here, so only 30 samples are shown for this wave.

The height of this wave is 155 so this sample is coded as binary 10011011.

If you assume the height does not change between each sample, you can draw a vertical line between the height of each. The result is a digitized representation of a sound wave, known as a "stepped wave form."

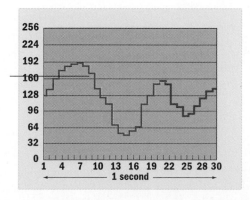

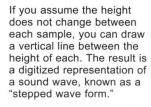

```
10000010
10011100
10000000
10101111
10111001
10111011
10111110
10111001
10101010
10001100
01111101
01110011
01000110
00110111
00110100
00111100
01000110
01110011
10010110
10011011
10010110
01110011
01101110
01011010
01011111
01101110
01111101
10001100
10010001
```

Sampling rate refers to the number of times per second the sound is measured during the recording process. The sampling rate is expressed in hertz (Hz). One thousand samples per second is expressed as 1,000 Hz or 1 KHz (kilohertz). Higher sampling rates increase the quality of the sound recording but require more storage space than lower sampling rates.

The audio CDs you buy at your favorite music store are recorded at a sampling rate of 44.1 KHz, which means a sample of the sound is taken 44,100 times per second. Each sample requires two bytes of storage space. At a sampling rate of 44.1 KHz, one second of music requires 88,200 bytes. A stereo recording requires twice as much storage space because you are essentially making two recordings to achieve the stereo effect. When you sample music at 44.1 KHz, you can store only eight seconds of stereo music on a 1.44 megabyte floppy disk. Forty-five minutes of music, the length of a typical rock album, requires about 475 megabytes.

To conserve space, applications that do not require such high-quality sound use much lower sampling rates. Voice is often recorded with a sampling rate of 11 KHz or 11,000 samples per second. This results in lower-quality sound, but the file is about one-fourth the size of a file for the same sound recorded at 44.1 KHz.

The waveform files you record and store on your computer generally have .wav, .mod, .au, or .voc file extensions. To record or play back waveform files, you need music software. Such software is usually included with sound cards. Alternatively, you can use the Windows 3.1 Sound Recorder application or the Media Player application in Windows 95 or Windows 98, shown in Figure 10-19.

Figure 10-19

Using music software such as the Windows Sound Recorder, you can see the sound wave as you listen to the sound.

MIDI Music

Can I use MIDI to store voice and music data? **MIDI** (Musical Instrument Digital Interface) files contain the instructions that MIDI instruments and MIDI sound cards use to recreate sounds. MIDI files store and recreate musical instrument sounds, but not voice. MIDI files are much more compact than waveform files. Three minutes of MIDI music requires only 10 KB of storage space, whereas three minutes of waveform music requires 15 MB.

MIDI is a music notation system that allows computers to communicate with music synthesizers. The computer encodes the music as a sequence and stores it as a file with a .mid, .cmf, or .rol extension. A **sequence** is analogous to a player-piano roll that contains punched information indicating which musical notes to play. A MIDI sequence contains instructions including the pitch of a note, when a note begins, what instrument plays the note, the volume of the note, and the duration of the note as shown in Figure 10-20.

Figure 10-20

A MIDI sequence is stored as a series of tracks. Each track represents an instrument. When you compose MIDI music, you can assign an instrument to each track, write the notes the instrument should play, and indicate the volume and sound quality.

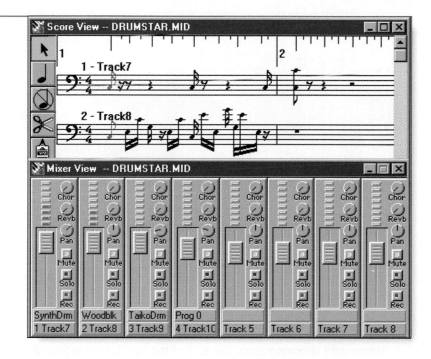

QuickCheck C

1. _____ audio is analogous to bitmap graphics, whereas _____ music is analogous to vector graphic.

2. The _____ rate refers to the number of times per second a sound is measured during the recording process.

3. A MIDI sequence is a digital recording of human speech. True or false? _____

4. Human speech should be recorded at a higher sampling rate than music. True or false? _____

5. Ten minutes of music stored in WAV format would require more storage space than ten minutes of music stored in a MIDI file. True or false? _____

Ⅾ Data Compression

Ⅾespite the use of information theory to design effective coding schemes for representing characters, graphics, and sounds, the files that contain such data can be quite large. As you learned earlier in this chapter, one second of video requires nine megabytes, a full-screen bitmap graphic requires 307,200 bytes, and a 45 minute waveform sound file might be as large as 475 megabytes. Large files require lots of storage space, easily become fragmented thereby reducing the efficiency of your computer's hard disk drive, and require lengthy transmission times. If you could reduce the size of a file without losing any of the data it contains, you would be able to avoid these problems.

Data compression is the general term used for recoding data so it requires fewer bytes of storage space. Data compression is reversible, so the data can be returned to its original form. The process of reversing data compression is sometimes referred to as **uncompressing**, **decompressing**, **extracting**, or **expanding** a file. Figure 10-21 will help you visualize how compression affects the number of bytes required to represent the data in a file.

Figure 10-21

Data
compression

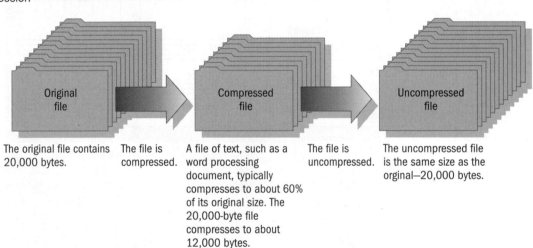

The original file contains 20,000 bytes.

The file is compressed.

A file of text, such as a word processing document, typically compresses to about 60% of its original size. The 20,000-byte file compresses to about 12,000 bytes.

The file is uncompressed.

The uncompressed file is the same size as the orginal—20,000 bytes.

When data is compressed, the size of the file that holds the data shrinks. The amount of shrinkage is referred to as the **compression ratio**. A compression ratio of 20:1, for example, means that a compressed file is 20 times smaller than the original file.

Data compression techniques can be applied to text, graphics, sound, and video data. Some compression techniques require specialized computer hardware, whereas other techniques are implemented entirely by software. The hardware or software routine that compresses and uncompresses digital graphics, sound, and video files is referred to as a **codec** (COmpressor/DECompressor).

There are two types of data compression: disk compression and file compression. **Disk compression** shrinks your files and places them in a special volume on your hard disk. A **disk volume** is a disk or an area of a disk that has a unique name and is treated as a separate disk. Disk compression creates a **compressed volume** containing data that has been recoded to use storage space more efficiently. When you want to use a file from the compressed volume of the disk, the computer automatically expands the file to its regular size. When you store a file on the compressed volume, the computer automatically shrinks it.

The advantage of disk compression is gaining storage space without purchasing additional hardware. Under optimal circumstances, you can effectively double the capacity of a hard disk, but usually the gains from disk compression are somewhat less (Figure 10-22).

Figure 10-22

To compress a disk, you must use a disk compression utility. Popular disk compression utilities include DoubleSpace, DriveSpace, Stacker, SuperStor, and AddStor. Windows 95 (shown) and Windows 98 operating systems also include a disk compression utility.

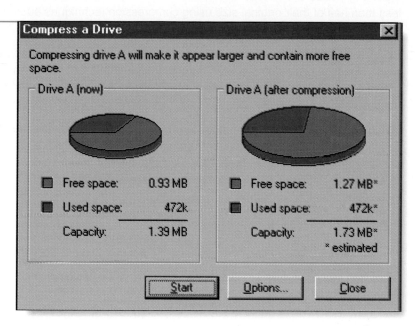

Disk compression has two potential drawbacks. First, if you decide that you no longer want a compressed volume on your drive you must have enough drive space for all the files in their uncompressed size. Many users, taking advantage of the extra storage space provided by disk compression, would not have this space available. The second drawback is that a file error in the compressed volume could mean the loss of all the data in that volume. Regular backups are important for compressed disks.

File compression shrinks one or more files into a single smaller file. Unlike disk compression, which creates a disk volume, file compression creates a compressed file. You cannot use this compressed file until it has been uncompressed. PKZIP and WinZip are popular shareware programs that compress and uncompress files. In computer jargon, compressing a file is sometimes called **zipping**; uncompressing a file is called **unzipping**. The advantage of file compression is that you can zip selected files and fit them on a single floppy disk, upload them, or e-mail them. The disadvantage is that you must manually unzip the files before you use them.

An additional twist to file compression is a **self-extracting executable file**, which contains compressed data and the software necessary to uncompress it. These files have an .exe extension, so you can run them. When you run a self-extracting executable file, it automatically uncompresses the data it contains. This saves you the time of firing up your compression utility, locating the file you want to uncompress, and running the uncompression routine.

Using a file compression utility, you can shrink text and .bmp files up to 70%. However, some other types of files hardly shrink at all because they are already stored in a compressed format. In the next sections you will learn why compression utilities shrink text and .bmp files, but do not have much effect on .tif and .pcx files.

Text File Compression

How does a compression utility shrink my document files? Text files contain many repeating patterns of words and spaces, so compression utilities can shrink text files to less than half of their original size using compression techniques such as adaptive pattern substitution and pointers.

Adaptive pattern substitution is a compression technique designed specifically to compress text files. This compression technique scans the entire text and looks for patterns of two or more bytes. When it finds such a pattern, it substitutes a byte pattern that is not used elsewhere in the file and makes a "dictionary" entry. Let's look at a simple example.

Using adaptive pattern substitution, how much can you compress the phrase, "the rain in Spain stays mainly on the plain, but the rain in Maine falls again and again"? The uncompressed phrase is 88 bytes long, including spaces and punctuation. Look at Figure 10-23 to see how adaptive pattern substitution compresses this phrase.

Figure 10-23

Text compression: adaptive pattern substitution

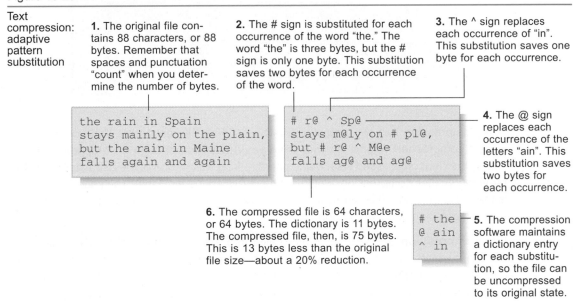

1. The original file contains 88 characters, or 88 bytes. Remember that spaces and punctuation "count" when you determine the number of bytes.

2. The # sign is substituted for each occurrence of the word "the." The word "the" is three bytes, but the # sign is only one byte. This substitution saves two bytes for each occurrence of the word.

3. The ^ sign replaces each occurrence of "in". This substitution saves one byte for each occurrence.

4. The @ sign replaces each occurrence of the letters "ain". This substitution saves two bytes for each occurrence.

6. The compressed file is 64 characters, or 64 bytes. The dictionary is 11 bytes. The compressed file, then, is 75 bytes. This is 13 bytes less than the original file size—about a 20% reduction.

5. The compression software maintains a dictionary entry for each substitution, so the file can be uncompressed to its original state.

```
the rain in Spain
stays mainly on the plain,
but the rain in Maine
falls again and again
```

```
# r@ ^ Sp@
stays m@ly on # pl@,
but # r@ ^ M@e
falls ag@ and ag@
```

```
# the
@ ain
^ in
```

The symbols used for the substitution in Figure 10-23, are actual characters and used only for the purpose of an example. Obviously, in a real document, these characters could not be used because they might occur in the document. You would not want the computer to replace the e-mail address coco@canine.com with cocoaincanine.com!

The effectiveness of adaptive pattern substitution depends on the content of the document. Compression will be best in documents that contain large chunks of repeating information. Longer documents are more likely to contain repetitions, so they usually compress at a better ratio than documents shorter than one page.

Another text compression technique scans a file and looks for repeated words. When a word occurs more than once, the second and all subsequent occurrences of the word are replaced with a number. The number acts as a "pointer" to the original occurrence of the word. Figure 10-24 shows how this works.

Figure 10-24

Text compression: using pointers to compress a file

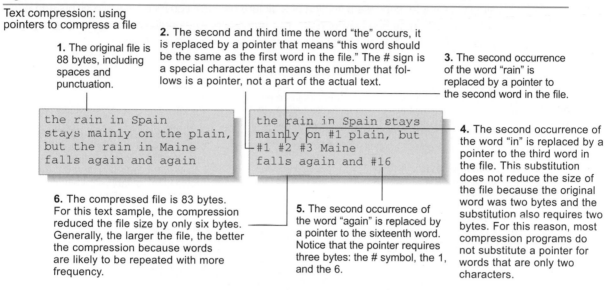

1. The original file is 88 bytes, including spaces and punctuation.

2. The second and third time the word "the" occurs, it is replaced by a pointer that means "this word should be the same as the first word in the file." The # sign is a special character that means the number that follows is a pointer, not a part of the actual text.

3. The second occurrence of the word "rain" is replaced by a pointer to the second word in the file.

```
the rain in Spain
stays mainly on the plain,
but the rain in Maine
falls again and again
```

```
the rain in Spain stays
mainly on #1 plain, but
#1 #2 #3 Maine
falls again and #16
```

4. The second occurrence of the word "in" is replaced by a pointer to the third word in the file. This substitution does not reduce the size of the file because the original word was two bytes and the substitution also requires two bytes. For this reason, most compression programs do not substitute a pointer for words that are only two characters.

6. The compressed file is 83 bytes. For this text sample, the compression reduced the file size by only six bytes. Generally, the larger the file, the better the compression because words are likely to be repeated with more frequency.

5. The second occurrence of the word "again" is replaced by a pointer to the sixteenth word. Notice that the pointer requires three bytes: the # symbol, the 1, and the 6.

Remember that you have to uncompress a file before you can use it. If you try to open a compressed file using your word-processing software, the document will be unreadable. The compressed bytes no longer translate into letters and words. Instead they produce an illegible scramble of letters and symbols as shown in Figure 10-25.

Figure 10-25

If you try to open a compressed document before uncompressing it, the text will be unreadable.

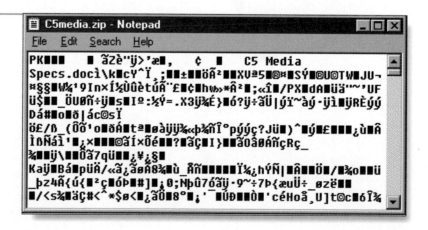

Graphics File Compression

Can I use a compression utility to shrink a graphics file? Uncompressed bitmap graphics files are very large; however, they often contain repetitious data, such as large blocks of the same color, that can be compressed. **Run length encoding** is a compression technique that looks for patterns of bytes and replaces them with a message that describes the pattern. As a simple example, suppose a section of a picture has 167 consecutive white pixels and each pixel is described by one byte of data. The process of run length encoding compresses this series of 167 bytes into as few as two bytes, as shown in Figure 10-26.

Figure 10-26

Run length encoding of graphics

1. This bitmap graphic has been enlarged to show individual pixels, such as this white pixel. Each pixel is represented by eight bits (one byte). This white pixel is coded as 11111111.

2. The first five rows and the first seven pixels of row six are white. In the uncompressed file for this graphic, these pixels require 167 bytes. This can be compressed using the code "10100111 11111111." The first byte is the binary representation of 167. The second byte is the code for white.

3. The next five pixels are black. The binary representation for black is 00000000. This section of the graphic is coded "00000101 00000000." The first byte is the binary representation of 5. The second byte is the code for black.

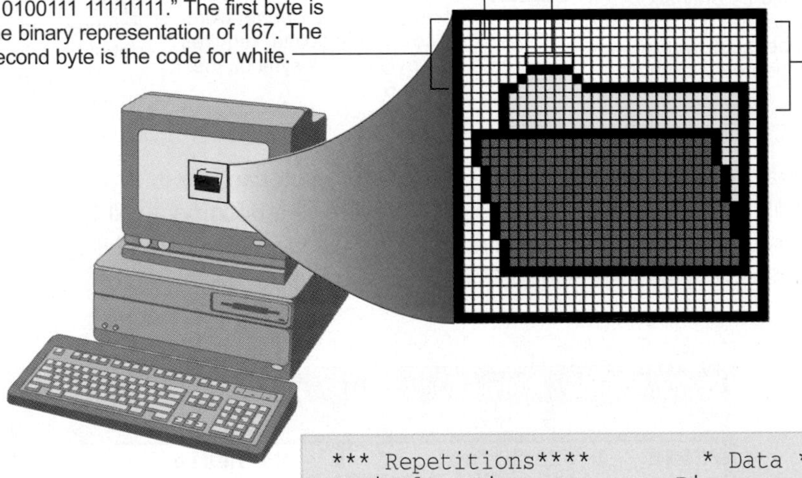

4. Without compression, the first nine rows of the graphic require 288 bytes of file space because there are 288 pixels. Using run length encoding to compress this section of the graphic, only 30 bytes are required.

5. Binary representations of the number of repetitions

6. Binary representation of the colors

*** Repetitions****		* Data *
Decimal	Binary	Binary
=============	=============	=============
167	01010011	11111111
5	00000101	00000000
26	00011010	11111111
1	00000001	00000000
5	00000101	10100000
1	00000001	00000000
23	00010111	11111111
2	00000010	00000000
7	00000111	10100000
18	00010010	00000000
5	00000101	11111111
1	00000001	00000000
25	00011001	10100000
1	00000001	11111111
1	00000001	00000000
=============	=============	=============

Files with .bmp extensions usually contain bitmap images that have not been compressed. Files with .tif, .pcx, and .jpg extensions contain bitmap images that have been compressed. A .tif extension refers to files that have been compressed using **TIFF** or Tag Image File Format. Files stored in PCX format use a different compression technique.

Files with a .jpg extension have been compressed into **JPEG** (Joint Photographic Experts Group) format using lossy compression. **Lossy compression** loses some of the original data for the graphic; in theory, the human eye won't miss the lost information. When you save a graphic, most graphics software lets you select whether you want the image stored in BMP, TIFF, PCX, or JPEG file format. Once you have stored a file in compressed format, you generally cannot make it much smaller by using a file compression utility such as PKZIP. Therefore, you can use PKZIP to significantly shrink .bmp files, but .pcx, .tif, or .jpg files will not shrink significantly.

Video File Compression

Is there a way to compress large video files? You learned earlier in this chapter that video is composed of a series of frames, each of which is essentially a bitmap image. You also learned that non-compressed video requires huge amounts of storage space. The feature-length movie, *Toy Story*, was generated entirely by computers (Figure 10-27).

Figure 10-27

The full-length film *Toy Story* was generated entirely by computer and requires the equivalent of 1,200 CD-ROMs of storage space.

Toy Story
8

Clearly, storing and playing a feature-length film is beyond the capacity of today's personal computer systems. It is possible, however, to display video on your personal computer by reducing the number of frames displayed per second, reducing the size of the video window, or coding only the changes that take place from one frame to the next.

Digital Video
9

Video for Windows, **QuickTime**, and **MPEG** are popular formats used to encode, compress, store, and play back digitized video. You can recognize Video for Windows files by their .avi filename extension. QuickTime files have a .mov extension. MPEG (Moving Picture Experts Group) is technically a compression technique, rather than a file format, although it creates files with an .mpg extension. Originally, MPEG required specialized hardware for compression and uncompression. With today's fast computers it is possible to play MPEG videos without such special hardware. However, specialized hardware is still required for the compression process. MPEG can compress a two-hour video into a few gigabytes. Figure 10-28 compares features of today's three major video formats.

Figure 10-28

Video formats

Format	File extension	Frames/ second	Resolution	Color palette	Sound
Video for Windows	.avi	30	320 × 240	8-bit	8-bit mono
QuickTime	.mov	10–12	320 × 240	8-bit	8-bit mono
MPEG-1	.mpg	30	352 × 240	24-bit	CD-quality stereo
MPEG-2	.mpg	60	720 × 480 or 1280 × 720	24-bit	CD-quality stereo

The number of frames per second directly affects the perceived smoothness of the video. High-quality video displays 30 frames per second. Lower-quality video displays only 15 frames per second; that video might appear jerky but is acceptable for some computer applications, such as training videos or animated product catalogs.

Another technique that makes video display possible on a microcomputer is reducing the image size. Displaying an image on one-quarter of your screen requires only a fourth of the data required to display a full-screen image, so most computer video applications use only a small window on your computer screen.

Video files shrink if you compress each frame using a standard graphics compression technique such as JPEG. Called **intraframe compression**, this technique produces compression ratios between 20:1 and 40:1, depending on the data in the frame.

Yet another technique requires the computer to evaluate the difference between two frames and only store that data that has changed. Suppose you have a video segment that doesn't change very much from one frame to the next. A "talking head" is a good example; the mouth and eyes change from frame to frame, but the background remains fairly stable. Instead of recording all the data for each frame, a technique called **motion compensation** stores only the data that changes between one frame and the next. Depending on the data, motion compensation compression can produce compression ratios of 200:1. Figure 10-29 illustrates how combining several compression techniques reduces the size of a video file.

Figure 10-29

This four-second video has been compressed to a 689 KB file using intraframe compression and motion compensation. When you play the video it is easy to tell that it is not the quality you would expect from an original non-compressed video.

QuickCheck D

1 _____ is a technique for recoding data so it requires fewer bytes of storage space.

2 Disk compression creates a compressed _____ on your hard disk.

3 The advantage of _____ is that you can compress selected files and fit them on a single floppy disk.

4 A technique called _____ compresses text files by substituting a small byte pattern for reoccurring sequence of characters.

5 JPEG files have been compressed with a technique called _____ compression that loses some of the data from the original image.

6 One technique for reducing the size of video files is to reduce the number of frames displayed per second. True or false? _____

E Using a Compression Utility

WinZip is a popular file compression utility that you can obtain by mail from a shareware distributor, download from the Internet, or purchase from a local computer store. This software is effective for reducing the size of text and .bmp files. Let's take a specific example to see how you might use this software. Suppose you have a 1.8 megabyte file called Clients.doc on your hard disk (drive C) in a folder called REPORTS. The file contains information about the customers for a mail-order business that you want to give to your coworker. You want to put this file on a single 1.44 megabyte floppy disk that you inserted in drive A. Because Clients.doc requires 1.8 megabytes, it will not fit on a single floppy disk in its uncompressed state.

InfoWeb

Compression
Utilities
10

Compressing a File with WinZip

How do I use WinZip to compress a file? To compress the file for your coworker, you'd first need to be sure you have the WinZip software installed on your computer. You should be able to locate it on the Programs menu after you click the Windows Start button. To compress the **Clients.doc** file, you would first create a name for the compressed file—Clients.zip, for example. Next you tell WinZip which file you would like to compress.

As a result, WinZip would compress **Clients.doc** to make a smaller file on drive A called **Clients.zip** as shown in Figure 10-30.

Figure 10-30

After you compress a file, your compression software will display information about the size of the compressed file.

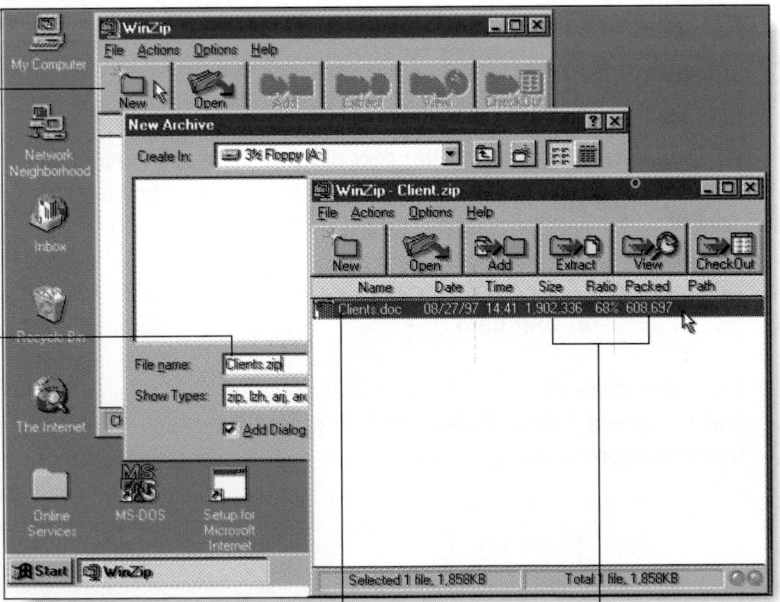

1. Use the New button.

2. Enter a name for the compressed file.

3. Select the file you want to compress.

4. Original and compressed file sizes

Unzipping a File

Does my coworker need to uncompress the file before using it? Because it is not possible to use a compressed file directly, your coworker must uncompress the **Clients.zip** file. To do this, your coworker must start the WinZip program, then indicate which file to uncompress. WinZip will also want to know where to put the uncompressed file. Figure 10-31 shows WinZip uncompressing the Clients.zip file and storing the uncompressed file on drive C as Clients.doc.

Figure 10-31

WinZip uncompresses Clients.zip from drive A and places the uncompressed file Clients.doc on drive C.

1. Use the Extract button.

2. Select the file you want to uncompress.

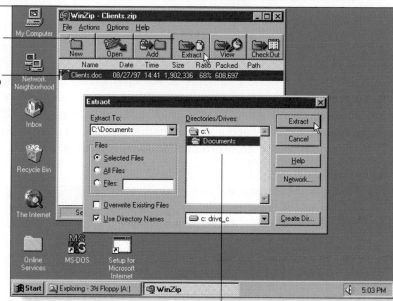

3. Indicate the destination for the uncompressed file.

EndNote
On the evening of April 18, 1775, Paul Revere saw the lantern signal in the tower of the Old North Church, mounted his horse, and sped off on his famous ride. Did the British come by land or by sea? It is interesting that most people remember the code, "one if by land, and two if by sea," but have forgotten (or never knew) if the British actually came by land or by sea. Perhaps this reflects a genuine fascination with codes and the impact of information theory in an age when computers have become an indispensable aspect of everyday life. On the other hand, it may reflect the enduring value of poetry and remind us that technology, though indispensable, is only one aspect of our complex culture.

InfoWeb

Chapter
Links

The InfoWeb is your guide to print, film, television, and electronic resources. Use it to obtain updates on quickly changing technical information and to locate information for research papers. If you're using the New Perspectives CD-ROM, click the InfoWeb icon on the left side of this paragraph to access the online InfoWeb links. Otherwise, use your Web browser and type in the address of the New Perspectives site: www.cciw.com/np3. At the New Perspectives site you'll find up-to-date links to the topics covered in this chapter.

1 Paul Revere

If you want to know whether the British came by land or by sea, you can read Longfellow's poem, *Paul Revere's Ride*. But reader beware, Longfellow used poetic license and played a bit with the facts. To learn the real story, read the poem, and listen to an interpretive reading, visit the River Cities site created by Ross School students at **ross.pvt.k12.ny.us/boston/revere.htm**. For more facts about the events of April 18, 1775 check the Discovery Channel feature "From Here to Obscurity" at **www.discovery.com/DCO/doc/1012/world/obscurity/obscurity081296/obscurity1.1.htm**. And if you'd like to read a parody about the real hero that night, read *The Midnight Ride of William Dawes* written by Helen Moore at **colorpro.com/wmdawes/theride.html**.

2 Information Theory

How is it that you can scratch a CD-ROM and yet it still plays without error? Chalk it up to Claude Shannon's Information Theory. An easy-to-understand introduction to information theory is Warren Weaver's introduction to Claude Shannon's 1949 classic, *The Mathematical Theory of Communication*. You can find excerpts at **darkwing.uoregon.edu/~felsing/virtual_asia/info.html**.

If your major is math or computer science, you might be interested in a technical tutorial on information theory written by Thomas Schneider at **www-lmmb.ncifcrf.gov/~toms/paper/primer/primer.ps.1.html**.

3 Binary Numbers

John Selvia has a great site on binary numbers. He says "I learned how to interpret binary from reading Michael Crichton's *Andromeda Strain* in college. Now, you gotta understand that for an artistic, creative-type like myself, suddenly understanding how binary works was a big deal, worthy of running out of the bathroom stall where I was reading the book and yelling Eureka!" Selvia's site at **www.dnaco.net/~ivanjs/binary.html** includes a clear explanation of binary numbers and instructions on binary finger counting. Learn how cavepeople could have counted up to 103 on their fingers, instead of only counting to 10! Another good source of information on binary numbers is PC Webopaedia at **www.webopaedia.com/binary.htm**. For a more complete presentation, visit the Department of Electrical Engineering site at the Univeristy of Hawaii at Manoa at **spectra.eng.hawaii.edu/Courses/EE150/Book/chap1/subsection2.1.2.1.html**. For an alternative explanation of how computers use binary numbers, refer to Chapter 3 of *The Electronic Cottage* by J. Denkin (New York: Bantam Books, 1981). In this chapter, the author uses a unique bucket-and-hose analogy to explain how computers communicate.

4 Unicode

The Unicode standard is of special interest to countries and ethnic groups with written languages that use characters other than the Latin alphabet. The Arabic Scientific Alliance hosts a Web page (**www.asca.com/unicode.html**) where you can learn all about the Unicode standard and the languages it supports. You'll find another interesting article at the Chinese Software Digest site, **www.gy.com/www/ww1/ww2/unne.htm**. The Unicode consortium Web page is at **www.unicode.org**.

5 Graphics Formats

With the increasing popularity of digital art and Web-based graphics, it is useful to understand the advantages and disadvantages of the many graphics formats, such as TIFF, GIF, JPEG, BMP, and PCX. A good source of links to pages and FAQs about graphics formats is the Graphics File Formats Page at **www.dcs.ed.ac.uk/~mxr/gfx/utils-hi.html**. Bryan Chamberlain has written an excellent article, "Understanding image file formats," that you can read at **www.cobb.com/tma/9508/tma89501.htm**. Chamberlain's article is packed with practical advice, comparative tables, and descriptions of the most popular graphics formats. Check your library for the definitive reference on file formats, **Encyclopedia of Graphics File Formats**, 2nd ed. by James Murray and William VanRyper (O'Reilly, 1996).

A really fine introduction to Web graphic issues is the Wide Area Communications site at **www.widearea.co.uk/designer/compress.html**. At the Bandwidth Conservation Society page, **www.infohiway.com/way/faster/**, you'll find links to lots of useful information on graphics formats, such as a quick tutorial on color palettes and how to reduce the size of GIF files without degrading image quality. *PC Magazine* has a great article about Web graphics at **www.zdnet.com/pcmag/issues/1512/pcmg0015.htm**. The Web version of the Louvre Art Museum is so popular that special Internet sites called "mirror sites" have been set up all over the world to accomodate the more than 200,000 weekly cyber visitors. Check out this site for art of all types at **www.sunsite.unc.edu/wm**.

6 Digital Audio

One of the most comprehensive sound links on the Web is sponsored by Oxford University at **www.comlab.ox.ac.uk/archive/audio.html**. Another extensive site, called Sound-Ring, has links to hundreds of music sites and a good set of basic FAQs on sound file formats at **sound-ring.com/faq.html**. You'll find a good discussion of audio formats in Zap's MUSIC-ON-THE-NET Tutorial at **www.lysator.liu.se/~zap/tutorial/formats.html**.

You can take a comprehensive tutorial on MIDI music and file formats by Jim Heckroth at **datura.cerl.uiuc.edu/netstuff/midi/MMA/tutorial.html**. You'll find lots of links to MIDI information and sample MIDI files and products at the MidiWeb™ site, **www.midiweb.com**. Can your sound card make a difference in sound quality? Compare sound quality at the Wavetable sound card test drive site, **pubweb.nwu.edu/~jll544/sndsmpl.html**. MP3 files are compressed WAV files using MPEG layer 3 audio compression. Find out more about these svelte files at **ds.dial.pipex.com/beast/mp3/index.htm#whatisit**.

7 Data Compression

You can find everything you wanted to know (and more!) about data compression in a series of FAQs at **www.cis.ohio-state.edu/hypertext/faq/usenet/compression-faq/top.html**. Dave Kristula maintains "The Compression Site" at **www.davesite.com/computers/compress.shtml** where he has tested several different compression programs and graphed the results. Wavelet compression is a relatively new technique for compressing graphics and videos. The Compression Engines site at **www.cengines.com** includes details about wavelet compressing, downloads for wavelet compression software, and compares graphics compressed with wavelet technology to graphics compressed with other technologies.

8 Toy Story

The film *Toy Story*, a co-production of Walt Disney Pictures and Pixar, is the first completely computer-animated feature film in the history of motion pictures. It took more than 800,000 machine hours to render the final frames. You'll find more about the film at the Disney Web site, **www.disney.com/DisneyVideos/ToyStory/about/_abfilm.htm**.

9 Digital Video

To learn more about digital video, start at the Internet Video Services site, **www.netvideo.com/technology/guidelines.html**, for a comparison of digital video formats. You can also connect to New Frontiers in Learning at **ibis.nott.ac.uk/guidelines/ch62/chap6-2-6.2.4.2.html** for an excellent overview of digital video formats. These formats are categorized as (1) those formats that require

additional computer hardware and (2) formats that are software only. For in-depth information on Video for Windows AVI format, link to John McGowan's site at **www.rahul.net/jfm/avi.html**. McGowan's site gets top honors for its wealth of information on file formats and data compression—don't miss this site! MPEG appears to be the up-and-coming video standard. Read more about it at **www.mpeg.org/index.html/starting-points.html**. Apple Computers hosts the definitive site for QuickTime video information, samples, links, and plug-ins at **www.quicktime.apple.com**. For example, you'll find a clear description of the QuickTime format at **quicktime.apple.com/qt30/specsheet**. For updates on video codecs, check the FAQs at the Cinepak site, **scitsc.wlv.ac.uk/~le1812/tech/cinepak.htm**.

10 Compression Utilities

The two most popular compression utilities for Windows are PKZIP and WinZip. You can visit the PKWARE site at **www.pkware.com** and download a trial copy of PKZIP. If you would like to download an evaluation version of WinZip, visit **www.winzip.com**.

Review

1 Use your own words to answer the questions under each of the section headings.

2 List each of the boldface terms used in this chapter, then use your own words to write a short definition.

3 Complete the following chart to show how many units of information you can convey with a given number of bits:

Number of Bits	1	2	3	4	5	6	7	8
Number of Units of Information	2	4	8					

4 Perform the calculations necessary to complete the following table:

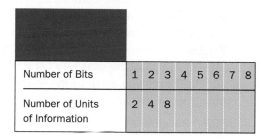

Screen Width in Pixels	640	640	640	640
Screen Height in Pixels	480	480	480	480
Graphics Type	Monochrome	16-color	256-color	True-color
Number of Bytes Required	38,400			

5 List the characteristics of the ASCII, ANSI, EBCDIC, and Unicode character representation codes.

6 A monochrome graphic with two colors per pixel requires one bit to represent each pixel. A color graphic with 16 colors per pixel requires four bits to represent each pixel. How many bits per pixel are required for a color graphic with four colors per pixel?

7 Describe the difference between bitmap graphics and vector graphic.

8 Describe the difference between waveform audio and MIDI music.

9 Define the terms "codec" and "compression ratio."

10 Describe the difference between disk compression and file compression.

11 Make a list of the file extensions mentioned in this chapter, then for each extension on your list indicate the type of data it contains (text, graphics, sound) and whether the data in the file is stored in a compressed format.

12 Use the New Perspectives CD-ROM to take a practice test or to review the new terms presented in this chapter.

Projects

1 **Your Own Bitmap Graphics** Make two photocopies of the grid below or make two 8 × 8 grids on graph paper. Using the first grid, fill in the pixels on the grid to reconstruct an 8-pixel × 8-pixel one-bit monochrome graphic from the following binary codes: 00100000, 01010000, 10001010, 10001111, 11111010, 10001000, 10001000, 10001000. Using the second grid, create your own graphic, then convert it into binary format.

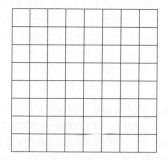

2 Try Your Hand at Text Compression One way to compress text is to replace repeated occurrences of words with a pointer to the first occurrence of that word. Using a vertical bar and a number as your pointer, write out the compressed form of the following paragraph:

A computer system is composed of a computer and peripheral devices, such as a printer. The components of a computer system that you can see and touch are referred to as hardware. Software refers to the nonphysical components of a computer system, particularly the programs, or lists of instructions, that are needed to make the computer perform a specific task.

3 Modern, Classical, and Rock Use your library and Internet resources to find more information about MIDI music and write a two- to three-page report. You might want to address questions such as: To what extent do musicians use computer-generated music today? Which modern, classical, and rock composers or performers make extensive use of computer-generated music? How has computer-generated music enhanced the sound quality, creativity, or appeal of modern music?

4 Dithering on the Internet Surf the Internet, looking at the graphics used by various World Wide Web sites. See if you can determine by the appearance of the graphic or by the file size whether a graphic is 16-color, dithered, or 256-color. You might find it useful to do the Bitmap Graphics section of the Data Representation Lab before you tackle this project. Write a one-page report summarizing your findings. Include the sites you visited, your conclusions about the type of graphics used, and printouts of one or two graphics.

5 Graphics Software Software publishers produce a variety of graphics software packages that differ based on the type of graphics supported and the tools they provide to manipulate graphics. Use current computer magazines to research graphics software packages. Write a paper describing three of the software packages you read about. Indicate the key features, the graphics formats supported, and the price of each package. Finally, indicate which package you would purchase and why.

6 Unzip It You learned that PKZIP and WinZip are popular compression utilities. The *User Focus* section of this chapter describes how to use WinZip. Using PKZIP is similar. For this project, you must download and unzip the file Surprize.zip from **www.cciw.com/np3/project10-6.html**. If your computer does not have PKZIP or WinZip, you'll need to download this software from one of the sites listed in InfoWeb 10. Make sure you abide by the license agreement when you use this software.

After you download and unzip the Surprize.zip file, follow the instructions in the Readme.txt file to complete the project.

7 Globalization, Localization, and Unicode Current trends in the globalization of communications and business require the use of computers. Much of the data, such as financial transactions, is usable regardless of local language. However, the programs that manipulate that data are generally most effective if they are localized so users do not have to translate screen prompts and error messages. Using your library resources, write a two- to three-page paper on software localization and how it contributes to globalized communications and business.

8 Converting Binary to Decimal to Hexadecimal Although today's computer users rarely need to deal with binary, octal, or hexadecimal numbers, the Windows calculator provides a quick and easy way to convert numbers if you need to do so. For this project, complete a through e, then fill out the table in f.

a. On a computer with the Microsoft Windows operating system, look for the Windows Calculator program. In Windows 3.1 it is in the Applications program group. In Windows 95 use the

Start button, select Programs, then select Accessories. If you can't find the Calculator program, ask your technical support person for help.

b. Start the Windows Calculator.

c. Click the View menu, then click Scientific.

d. To convert from decimal to binary, make sure the Decimal button is selected. Then enter a decimal number such as 255. Click the Binary button and the calculator will show the binary equivalent, in this case 11111111.

e. To convert from binary to decimal, make sure the Binary button is selected, then enter a binary number such as 101. Click the Decimal button to show the decimal equivalent, in this case 5.

f. Fill in the following table:

Decimal	Binary (Base 2)	Octal (Base 8)	Hexa-decimal (Base 16)
10			
	10		
		10	
			10
32			
	111011		
		77	
			B
255			
	1101101		
		33	
			FE

9 **Another Picasso?** You learned that bitmap graphics require quite a lot of storage space. You can create your own bitmap image and see for yourself. Use Microsoft Paintbrush (Windows 3.1), Microsoft Paint (Windows 95), or any available paint software to create a simple graphic. Store the graphic on a floppy disk in BMP format. Print your graphic and don't forget to sign your original work of art! To find the size of your graphic file, you will probably need to use File Manager or Windows Explorer. Write the file size on your printout.

Lab Assignments

Data Representation

A computer stores many types of data—text, graphics, sound, animation, and video. Digital computers, such as the micro-computers you use, store all these different types of data as the electronic equivalent of 1s and 0s. How is it possible to reduce a long document or complex graphic to a series of 1s and 0s? In this Lab you'll find out how this is done.

1 Click the Steps button to learn how text, monochrome graphics, color graphics, and vector graphic are stored. As you proceed through the Steps, answer all of the Quick Check questions that appear. After you complete the Steps, you will see a Quick Check Summary Report. Follow the instructions on the screen to print this report.

2 Click the Explore button, then click the Text button. Suppose you are a computer and you need to sort a list containing words, numbers, and symbols. Look up the ANSI representation for the first character of each item on the list. Then, sort the list according to this ANSI code. The item with the lowest ANSI code should be first in the list. The list is as follows:

broom

3

Tree

]

Bottle

03

10

3 Using Explore's Text button find the ANSI code for your first and last name. Write this on paper. Then write the decimal equivalent to the ANSI code for your first and last name.

4 Suppose you are a computer, and you receive the following 1s and 0s from your modem. Using Explore's Text button, convert these 1s and 0s into the letters, numerals, and symbols you would display on the screen.

01010100	01101000	01100101
00100000	00110100	00100000
01101111	01100110	00100000
01001000	01100101	01100001
01110010	01110100	01110011

5 Suppose you are a computer, and you receive a monochrome graphics file containing a string of 1s and 0s. Using Explore's Monochrome graphics button, create this graphic, then print it.

```
00010000
00111000
01111100
11111110
11101110
01000100
00000000
```

6 Using Explore's Monochrome graphics button, convert the following decimal numbers into a monochrome graphic, then print it.

8, 12, 254, 255, 254, 12, 8, 0

7 Suppose you are a computer, and you must send a monochrome graphic to another computer over a local area network. Using Explore's Monochrome graphics button, convert the following graphic into 1s and 0s, then print it.

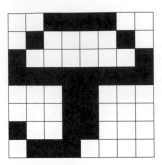

8 Suppose you are a computer, and you receive a 16-color graphics file containing a string of 1s and 0s. Using Explore's Color graphics button, recreate this graphic, then print it.

11111111	11001111	11001111	11001111
00000000	11000100	01000100	11001111
11111111	11001100	01001100	11001111
00000000	11111100	11001100	11111111
11111111	11111111	00101111	10101111
00000000	11111111	00101010	10101111
11111111	11111111	00101010	11111111
00000000	11111111	00101111	11111111

9 Using Explore's Vector graphics button, recreate a vector graphic from the following set of instructions. Print your completed graphic.

Shape	Color	Top	Left	Width	Height
Circle	red	73	212	50	50
Circle	yellow	137	212	50	50
Circle	green	202	212	50	50
Rounded rectangle	black	39	200	73	241

COMMUNICATIONS
SYSTEMS INFRASTRUCTURE

Communications means getting information from point A to point B. Communications technology can be simple or sophisticated. Link two cans together with string and you have a simple "telephone." Link two computers using modems, telephone lines, satellites, and fiber-optic cables and you have a sophisticated communications system.

We are surrounded by data, transmitted over a communications infrastructure made up of telephone lines, cable television lines, satellites, computer networks, and transmitters for microwave, radio, and television signals. Although most of the systems in this communications infrastructure were originally designed for other purposes (such as carrying voice communications), they are being pressed into service to transport computer data. Today, individuals and organizations are taking advantage of this vast communications infrastructure to gather, transmit, and locate computer-based information.

The purpose of this chapter is to show how the communications infrastructure provides many pathways for transporting computer-generated information. This chapter begins with an overview of important data communications terminology. The focus then shifts to ways that current telephone, cellular phone, Internet, cable TV, and local networks provide an infrastructure for computer data communications. This chapter ends with how to build a low-cost computer network—it's easier than you think!.

CHAPTER **PREVIEW**

In this chapter you will learn the basic terminology of data communications and some technical details about how modems and LANs transport data. You will learn how to access Internet data using the telephone system, the cellular phone system, the cable TV system, and satellites. You will also learn how to set up a simple local area network for data communications. When you have completed this chapter, you should be able to:

- Explain Shannon's communications system model
- Define bandwidth and discuss how it affects data communications
- Explain the differences in simplex, half duplex, full duplex, and echoplex protocols
- Explain how a computer uses odd or even parity
- Differentiate between synchronous and asynchronous communications protocols
- Discuss the advantages and disadvantages of Internet access over telephone, cellular phone, cable TV, and satellite systems
- Describe how packet switching differs from circuit switching
- Describe today's popular LAN standards and LAN communications protocols
- Explain the differences between collision handling on Ethernet and Token Ring networks
- Understand how to set up a simple Ethernet network

LABS

Building a Network

Ⓐ Data Communications

Data **communications** is the process of transmitting and receiving data in an orderly way so the data that arrives at its destination is an accurate duplication of the data that was sent. When data travels a short distance, such as when you send data from your computer to your printer, it is referred to as **local communications**. When data travels a long distance, the communication is referred to as **telecommunications**; the prefix "tele" is derived from a Greek word that means "far" or "far off."

InfoWeb

Communications
Terminology
1

The difference between a short distance and a long distance is somewhat arbitrary. For example, if your computer sends data to a printer in the next room, it is regarded as local communications. However, if you phone the person in the next room, you are transmitting data over a telecommunications device. Because the same basic communications concepts apply to both local communications and telecommunications, in this chapter we will not further distinguish between the two.

Basic data communications concepts are the building blocks for understanding how data travels on a communications system. These concepts come in handy when you install, configure, or upgrade a local area network. In addition, these concepts help you set up modems, fax machines, and cellular data transfers.

A **communications system** is the combination of hardware, software, and connecting links that transport data. In 1949, Claude Shannon, an engineer at the prestigious Bell Labs, published an article that described a communications system model. In this model, data from a source is encoded and sent over a communications channel where it is decoded by a receiver. According to Shannon, the effectiveness of communication depends on the efficiency of the coding process and the channel's resistance to interference called "noise." Study Figure 11-1 to get an overview of Shannon's communications system model.

Figure 11-1

Shannon's communications system model

5. Noise, such as electrical interference, sometimes disrupts a transmission. The message can become garbled unless the communications system has the capability to check for errors and correct them.

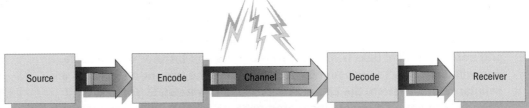

Noise

1. The **source** originates or initiates the communication. The source might be a person or a computer.

2. The **message**, represented here by a folder, is the information that the source wants to communicate to the receiver. The message might be a document, picture, sound, or numeric data.

3. The message is **encoded** by changing its format into one that can be transmitted. In a modern communications system, a message typically is encoded into an electronic signal that can be sent over telephone lines, broadcast by radio waves, or transmitted as microwaves.

4. The encoded message travels by means of a **channel** or **communications link**. A communications link might include telephone wiring, fiber-optic cable, microwaves, or satellites.

6. The message is decoded at the end of the transmission. **Decoding** usually means reversing the coding process that occurred before the message was sent.

7. The **receiver** is the destination for the message. The receiver can be a person, a computer, or another communications device.

Communications Signals

Exactly what is transmitted when I send a message? When you use a modem to send a document from your computer to another computer or fax machine, symbols such as "A" and "!" don't somehow squirt through the phone cables. Instead, most of today's communications systems transmit messages and data in the form of electromagnetic signals. You can think of these signals as waves that ripple through cables or through the air.

Like ocean waves, electromagnetic waves are characterized by their spacing and their height. The spacing between waves is referred to as the **frequency**. Waves that are spaced close together have a higher frequency than waves spaced far apart. The size of an electromagnetic wave is referred to as its **amplitude** (Figure 11-2). Waves with higher amplitudes are more powerful, louder in the case of sound waves, than waves with low amplitudes.

Figure 11-2

Wave frequency
and amplitude

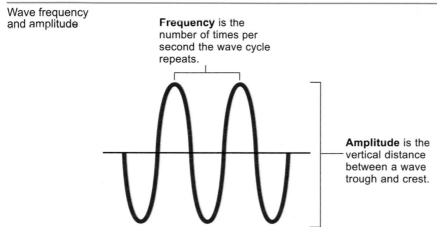

Frequency is the number of times per second the wave cycle repeats.

Amplitude is the vertical distance between a wave trough and crest.

Signal frequency is measured in Hertz (Hz), kiloHertz (KHz), megaHertz (MHz), or gigaHertz (GHz). One Hertz is equal to one "wave" or oscillation per second. So, for example, a radio broadcast at 101 MHz means the radio wave is oscillating 101,000 times per second.

The sound signals that travel over phone lines have frequencies between 300 Hz and 3,000 Hz. Computer communications carried out using telephone company equipment use the same frequencies allocated to voice transmissions. For example, when sending a string of 1s and 0s for an ASCII code, a 0 is transmitted as a 1,070 Hz wave and a 1 is transmitted at 1,279 Hz.

Although we usually think of a wave as a smooth curve, waves can have different shapes. These shapes are referred to as **wave forms** or **wave patterns**. Analog signals may represent an unlimited range of values and, therefore, have a smooth, curved wave form. Digital signals, on the other hand, represent discrete values within a limited range and, therefore, have a square wave pattern. Compare the analog and digital wave patterns shown in Figure 11-3.

Figure 11-3

Analog and digital
wave patterns

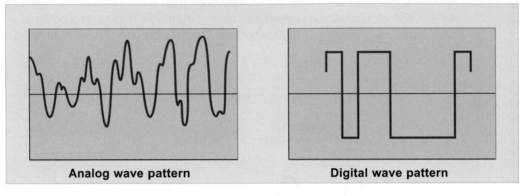

| **Analog wave pattern** | **Digital wave pattern** |

It is possible to convert analog signals into digital signals and vice versa. For example, as you learned in an earlier chapter, the process of sampling a sound wave creates a digital version of an analog sound. Also, your computer modem converts the digital signal from your computer into an analog signal that can be sent over phone lines. What is the advantage of a digital signal? Compared to analog, digital transmissions are usually less susceptible to noise, are easier to "clean" before boosting, and require simpler circuitry. Remember that a digital transmission is in the form of 1s and 0s, whereas an analog transmission is composed of a range of values.

Suppose a part of a digital transmission uses different voltages to transmit 0s and 1s. A "perfect" 0 is sent as 0 volts. A "perfect" 1 is sent as +5 volts. Now, what if during transmission the frequency of a "perfect" 1 changes slightly to +4 volts. When the signal is received, the receiving device recognizes the +4 volt signal as a 1 and can "clean" it up by reestablishing its voltage to +5.

Compare this with an analog transmission in which a 1,200 Hz wave changes to a 1,233 Hz wave. The receiving device cannot determine if the 1,233 Hz signal is an error or if it is just one of the many analog values that was originally sent. Determining whether this signal needs to be cleaned and determining how it should be cleaned becomes more difficult because it is analog.

Channels and Communications Media

What technology options are available for carrying communications signals? A **communications channel** is a physical path or frequency for a signal transmission. For example, telephone cables provide a physical path for analog audio signals. Another example points out that a communications channel might be a frequency or range of frequencies, rather than a physical cable. A television channel, such as Channel 12, is a specific frequency used to broadcast audio-visual data for a television station.

A **communications medium** carries one or more communications channels and provides a link between transmitting and receiving devices. The media most frequently used in today's communications systems include twisted-pair cable, coaxial cable, and fiber-optic cable.

Bandwidth

Why do some communications systems have a higher capacity than others? The capacity of a communications system depends on the bandwidth of the channels it uses. **Bandwidth** is the range of frequencies that a channel can carry. The bandwidth of a digital signal is usually measured in bits per second (bps). The bandwidth of an analog signal is expressed in Hertz (Hz) and is calculated by subtracting the lowest channel frequency from the highest one, as shown in Figure 11-4.

InfoWeb

Bandwidth
2

Figure 11-4

Calculating bandwidth

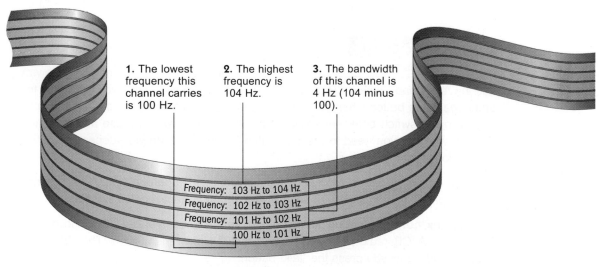

1. The lowest frequency this channel carries is 100 Hz.

2. The highest frequency is 104 Hz.

3. The bandwidth of this channel is 4 Hz (104 minus 100).

Frequency: 103 Hz to 104 Hz
Frequency: 102 Hz to 103 Hz
Frequency: 101 Hz to 102 Hz
100 Hz to 101 Hz

Transmission Speed

How fast can computer data travel over a communications channel? Although bandwidth is a measure of the capacity of a communications channel, it does not necessarily coincide with the speed at which you can transmit your data. Many communications channels work something like an airport conveyor belt. The conveyor belt moves at a constant speed. If you have three pieces of luggage and you are the only person on the plane, your bags will arrive one right after another. However, if you have just arrived on a full 747, your bags will be inter-mixed with those of hundreds of passengers, and it will take longer for you to get them. The packets of data you send over a communications channel are like pieces of luggage. When a communications channel is busy, it takes longer to send and receive data.

Communications engineers have developed many ways to speed up communications. Speed has been a key area of research for computer communications, which are not limited (as are human communications) by the pace of human speech.

Most communications take place serially: one piece of information follows another. For a computer, **serial transmission** means that a byte is broken down into individual bits that are transmitted one after another over the communications medium. Faster data transfer can be achieved by **parallel transmission**, in which all the bits for an entire byte are sent at the same time. Parallel transmission requires a communications media that can carry simultaneous units of data. In computer systems, this is usually achieved using a parallel cable that contains one wire for each bit.

Serial transmission is typically used for modem and network communications. Parallel transmission is typically used for sending data to a printer.

Signal Direction

Do all channels send and receive data? You use a CB radio differently from the way you use the telephone—with a CB radio, you must press a button when you are ready to send and release the button when you want to receive; with a telephone you don't have to take any action to switch between talking and listening. The way you use a communications device—whether you need to press a button to talk, for example—depends on the communications mode.

Simplex communication allows communication in only one direction. A radio transmitter uses simplex communication—it can transmit, but it cannot receive signals.

Half-duplex communication allows you to send or receive, but not to do both at the same time. A CB radio is an example of half-duplex transmission. The CB radio is in receive mode until you press the "talk" button.

Duplex or **full-duplex communication** allows you to send and receive at the same time. A telephone line is an example of full-duplex communication; most computer communications take place in this mode.

Some communications are sent and then echoed back to the sender as a means of check-ing accuracy. This type of communication is referred to as **echoplex**, or simply as an **echo**. Echoplex is useful in situations when it is important to be absolutely certain that data was transmitted accurately.

Parity Protocols

How does a communications channel deal with interference? In Shannon's communications system model, noise sometimes interferes with transmissions. Suppose that you send a message to a business colleague, "Let's meet at the exhibition hall at 5:00 p.m." As the sequence of bits for the word "hall" travels across the communications channel, some interference changes a single bit. The "a" in the word "hall," which was transmitted as 01100001, arrives at its destination as 01101001, which is the ASCII code for the letter "i." When "hall" is changed to "hill," the meaning of your message has been altered.

To ensure that the data you transmit is not altered by noise or interference, both the sending and the receiving computers must follow a set of communications protocols. **Communications protocols** are rules that ensure the orderly and accurate transmission and reception of data. When two devices communicate they must agree on protocols for starting and ending a transmission, recognizing transmission errors, sending data at the right speed, and formatting or packaging the data.

Computers use error-checking protocols to ensure accurate delivery of data. One error-checking protocol uses a **parity bit** to describe the number of 0s or 1s in a sequence of data. The transmitting computer attaches a parity bit to the transmitted data. The parity bit is either a 0 or a 1, depending on the protocol. With **even parity**, the number of 1 bits in a data block is an even number. With **odd parity**, the number of 1 bits in the data block is an odd number. Study Figure 11-5 to see how parity works.

Figure 11-5

Parity

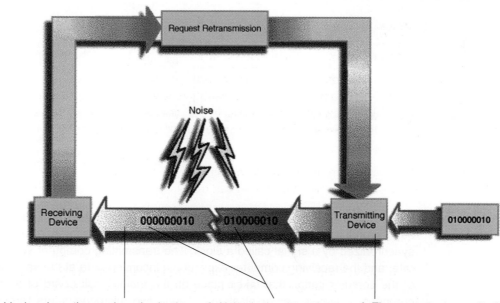

3. When the data block arrives, the receiver checks the total number of 1 bits. There is an odd number of 1 bits, which is not correct under even parity. The receiver transmits a message back to the sender requesting that the data block be transmitted again.

2. Noise in the channel changes the second bit from 1 to 0.

1. The computer transmits the data block that contains the ANSI code for the letter "A" including the 0 parity bit.

Synchronous and Asynchronous Protocols

How does the receiving computer know when the transmission begins and ends?

A major challenge with serial communications is coordinating the transmission and the reception. The transmitting computer sends a series of bits, but if the receiving computer misses the first three bits of a serial transmission, the message would be hopelessly garbled, as shown in Figure 11-6.

Figure 11-6

A garbled data transmission

1. The word "Hello" is encoded, then transmitted. Each set of 8 bits represents one character. In a successful transmission, "Hello" arrives at its destination.

2. If the receiving device misses the first 3 bits of data, the message becomes garbled.

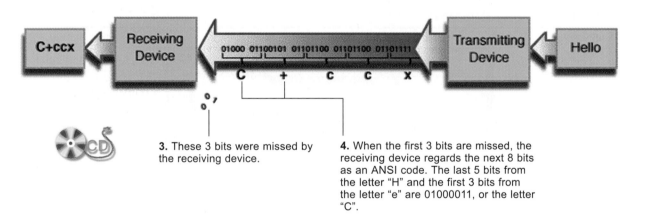

3. These 3 bits were missed by the receiving device.

4. When the first 3 bits are missed, the receiving device regards the next 8 bits as an ANSI code. The last 5 bits from the letter "H" and the first 3 bits from the letter "e" are 01000011, or the letter "C".

There are two ways to coordinate serial communication, referred to as synchronous and asynchronous protocols. Using **synchronous protocol**, the sender and the receiver are synchronized by a signal called a clock. The transmitting computer sends data at a fixed rate, and the receiving computer expects the incoming data at the same fixed rate. Much of the communication that takes place on the main circuit board of a computer is synchronous; however, communication between two microcomputers rarely uses the synchronous protocol.

Computers typically use asynchronous protocol when they communicate using modems. Using **asynchronous protocol**, the sending computer transmits a start bit to indicate the beginning of the data. Next, the sending computer transmits the data as a series of bits, called a block. The end of each block is indicated by transmitting one or more stop bits, as shown in Figure 11-7.

Figure 11-7

Asynchronous protocol

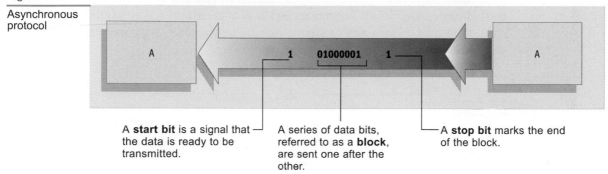

A **start bit** is a signal that the data is ready to be transmitted.

A series of data bits, referred to as a **block**, are sent one after the other.

A **stop bit** marks the end of the block.

QuickCheck A

1. _____, such as electrical interference, can disrupt data communications.

2. _____ is the range of frequencies that a channel can carry.

3. A telephone line is an example of a(n) _____ channel, whereas a radio is an example of a simplex channel.

4. Communications _____ are rules that ensure the orderly and accurate transmission and reception of data.

5. A computer using _____ parity would need to add a 1 bit to 11011100 before sending it.

6. Most data communications are asynchronous. True or false? _____

B Communications Links

A **communications link** is a path for data transmission between two points. These links are provided by cables, transmitters, and satellites. When you connect your computer and any device, you'll use a communications link.

Twisted-Pair Cable

What's the most typical communications link? Throughout the world, miles and miles of twisted-pair cable connect telephones and local area networks. A **twisted-pair cable** consists of pairs of copper wire twisted together. The wires are bundled together to form a cable, as shown in Figure 11-8.

Figure 11-8

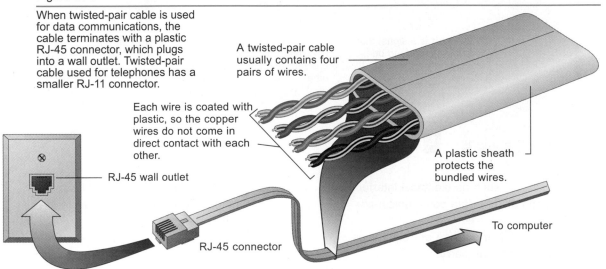

When twisted-pair cable is used for data communications, the cable terminates with a plastic RJ-45 connector, which plugs into a wall outlet. Twisted-pair cable used for telephones has a smaller RJ-11 connector.

A twisted-pair cable usually contains four pairs of wires.

Each wire is coated with plastic, so the copper wires do not come in direct contact with each other.

A plastic sheath protects the bundled wires.

RJ-45 wall outlet

RJ-45 connector

To computer

There are two main types of twisted-pair cable. In a **shielded twisted pair** (STP) cable, the wire pairs are coated with a foil shield that reduces signal noise that might interfere with data transmission. **Unshielded twisted pair** (UTP) cable contains no shielding. It is less expensive than shielded cable, but more susceptible to signal noise.

Twisted-pair cable is divided into five categories based on transmission capacity. Category 1 cable is UTP recommended only for analog voice communications. Category 2 is a better grade of UTP suitable for digital voice and data communications at rates up to one Mbps (one megabit per second). Categories 3, 4, and 5 are high-grade UTP and STP cables suitable for communications at 16 Mbps, 20 Mbps, and 100 Mbps, respectively. Category 1 cable is considered **voice-grade cable**, which means that it is recommended for transmitting voice, but not data signals. In contrast, **data-grade cables** are considered suitable for data transmission. Today, most new network installations use Category 5 UTP or STP cable.

Coaxial Cable

Any other popular cable options? **Coaxial cable**, often called **coax cable**, (pronounced "co-ax") is a high-capacity communications cable consisting of a copper wire conductor, a non-conducting insulator, a foil shield, a woven metal outer shielding, and a plastic outer coating, as shown in Figure 11-9.

Figure 11-9

Coaxial cable

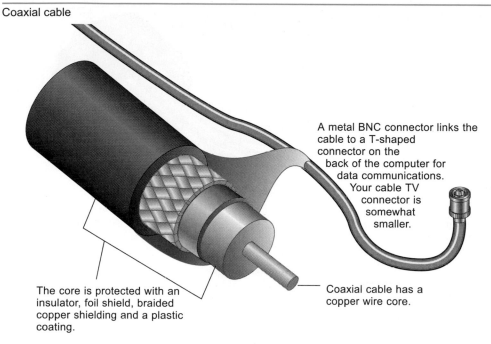

A metal BNC connector links the cable to a T-shaped connector on the back of the computer for data communications. Your cable TV connector is somewhat smaller.

The core is protected with an insulator, foil shield, braided copper shielding and a plastic coating.

Coaxial cable has a copper wire core.

Coaxial cable is used for cable television where its high capacity allows it to carry signals for more than 100 television channels simultaneously. It also provides good capacity for data communications and is used in situations where twisted-pair cable is not adequate to carry the required amount of data.

Coaxial cable is sometimes called a **Category 6 cable** and has a bandwidth that exceeds 100 Mbps. Of the two types of coax cable, **thin coax** is $^3/_{16}$-inch in diameter and typically found in local area network installations and home cable TV wiring. Thick coax cable is $^3/_8$-inch thick and is found in older local area networks and in cable TV trunk lines.

Although it has excellent bandwidth, coaxial cable is less durable, more expensive, and more difficult to work with than twisted-pair cable. Coaxial cable used to be one of the most widely used cables for connecting computers in local area networks; however, today it is being replaced by twisted-pair cable. But for situations where high bandwidth is required, both coaxial cable and twisted-pair cable are being replaced by fiber-optic cable.

InfoWeb

Fiber Optics
3

Fiber-Optic Cable

What's so special about fiber-optic cable? **Fiber-optic cable** is a bundle of extremely thin tubes of glass. Each tube, called an **optical fiber**, is much thinner than a human hair. A fiber-optic cable usually consists of a strong inner support wire; multiple strands of optical fiber each covered by a plastic insulator; and a tough outer covering, as shown in Figure 11-10.

Figure 11-10

Fiber-optic cable

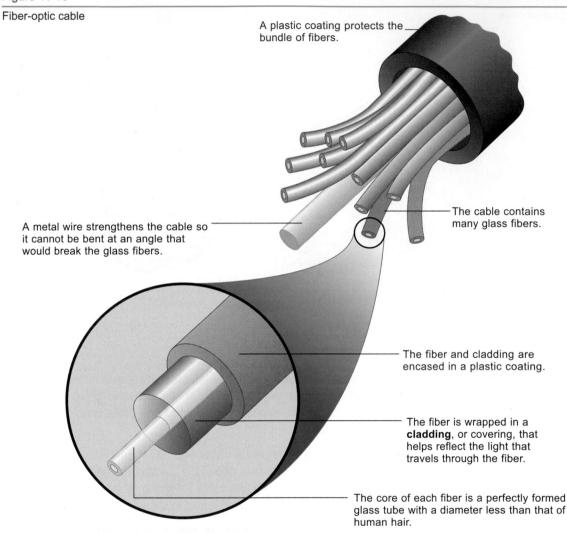

A plastic coating protects the bundle of fibers.

A metal wire strengthens the cable so it cannot be bent at an angle that would break the glass fibers.

The cable contains many glass fibers.

The fiber and cladding are encased in a plastic coating.

The fiber is wrapped in a **cladding**, or covering, that helps reflect the light that travels through the fiber.

The core of each fiber is a perfectly formed glass tube with a diameter less than that of human hair.

The use of optical fibers for communications is a relatively new development. It was not until the 1970s that glassmakers were able to manufacture fibers of acceptable purity. Early researchers had determined that optical-fiber transmissions would be severely limited if the glass contained traces of water and metals. By the 1980s glassmakers had developed a process to create glass of such purity that if the ocean was as pure, you would be able to see through it to the floor of the 32,000 foot deep Marianas Trench.

Unlike twisted-pair and coaxial cables, fiber-optic cables do not conduct or transmit electrical signals. Instead, miniature lasers or **LEDs** (light emitting diodes) send pulses of light through the fibers. Electronics at the receiving end of the fiber convert the light pulses back into electrical signals. Each fiber is a one-way communications channel, which means that at least two fibers are required to provide a two-way communications link. Figure 11-11 shows you how signals travel through fiber-optic cable.

Figure 11-11

A laser sends up to 1.7 billion pulses of light per second down the hollow core of a glass tube. The cladding reflects the light to keep it in the tube.

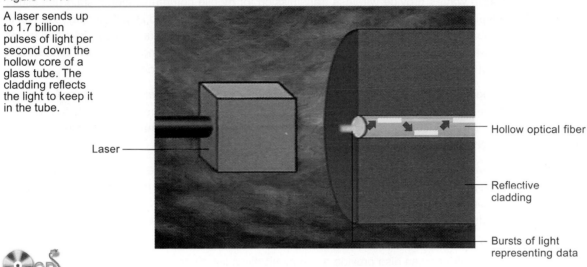

Laser

Hollow optical fiber

Reflective cladding

Bursts of light representing data

One advantage of fiber optics is that light signals encounter very little resistance when moving through the glass cable. Whereas twisted-pair and coaxial cable signals need an electrical "boost" after traveling less than a mile, light signals can travel very long distances over optical fiber. Researchers have been able to send signals as far as 5,000 miles without a boost.

Fiber-optic cable is sometimes referred to as Category 7 cable. There are two types of fiber-optic cable. **Single-mode cable** has a very narrow core, usually less than 10 microns. Light can take only a single path through this cable, which results in transmission speeds that can exceed 50 gigabytes per second. **Multi-mode cable** has a relatively wide 50 to 100 micron core. This width gives a light beam room to bounce around, causing signal distortion and reducing bandwidth. However, multi-mode cable is easier to install, making it the optical cable of choice for most computer networks.

Radio and Infrared Links

Some data communications use wireless links, right? It is possible to communicate without using wires. We do this when we speak to each other face to face, but what about data communications? Data communications can take to the airwaves using radio, infrared, or microwave signals. In this section you'll find out about radio and infrared communications. You'll find out about microwaves in the next section.

Radio waves provide wireless transmission for mobile communications, such as cellular telephones, and in situations where it is difficult or impossible to install cabling, such as in remote, geographically rugged regions. Radio wave networks operate in frequencies between 1 MHz and 3 GHz, but before you can use a frequency for communications, it must be licensed from the Federal Communications Commission (FCC).

A radio communications link uses a **transmitter** to send a signal at a particular frequency or group of frequencies. A **receiver** at the other end of the transmission picks up the signal. Wireless communications channels are generally slower than cables. They are also susceptible to signal interference, eavesdropping, and jamming.

Infrared transmissions use a frequency range just below the visible light spectrum to transport data. An FCC license is not required for infrared transmission. Infrared transmission is an example of **line-of-sight communication**, in which the transmitter that sends the signal must have an unobstructed path to the receiver for it to work.

You're probably familiar with infrared devices, such as hand-held remote controls for televisions. Infrared can also provide a communications link for transferring data between a computer and peripheral devices. In Figure 11-12, for example, you can see the infrared sensor in the lower-left corner of the printer; the notebook computer has an infrared port built into the back of the case.

Figure 11-12

By pointing the infrared port of the computer at the printer's infrared sensor, you can send data to the printer without using cable.

Microwave and Satellite Links

How do communications satellites fit into the picture? A **microwave** is an electromagnetic wave with a frequency of at least one gigahertz (GHz). Data converted into microwaves can be sent over a microwave link. **Microwave transmission** sends a high-frequency radio signal from a ground or satellite microwave transmitting station to a microwave receiving station. Microwave stations cannot be more than 25 or 30 miles apart because at farther distances, the curve of the earth blocks transmission. To avoid this problem, many communications systems use communications satellites as a link between geographically disbersed transmitting and receiving stations called **earth stations** or **ground stations**.

InfoWeb

Satellites
4

First-generation communications satellites were placed in geosynchronous orbits 22,282 miles above the earth. A satellite in a **geosynchronous orbit** (GEO) stays above the same part of the earth by orbiting around the earth at the same speed as the earth rotates. A GEO satellite provides continuous coverage over a particular area, but because of the distance between the satellite and earth it requires about 24 seconds to transmit data. Many of the most recent communications satellites have been launched into **low-earth orbit** (LEO) about 1,000 miles above the earth. Because they are closer to earth, LEO satellite transmission times decrease to only a few hundredths of a second. However, an LEO satellite does not remain above the same earth location as it orbits, so an LEO communications system requires a web of satellites, like the one shown in Figure 11-13.

Figure 11-13

A low-earth orbit communications system requires a web of satellites to provide continual coverage over an area such as North America.

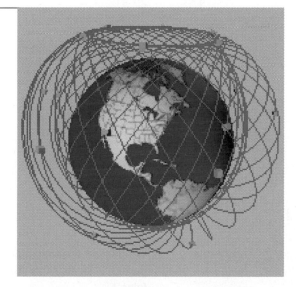

A telecommunications satellite contains a **transponder** that receives a signal on one frequency, amplifies the signal, then retransmits the signal on a different frequency. The transponders in today's satellites typically transmit at one of seven frequency ranges, referred to as "bands." Of these seven, three are typically used for data communications: C-band with frequencies between 3.7 and 6.4 GHz, Ku-band with frequencies between 11.7 and 17.8 GHz, and Ka-band with frequencies between 18 and 31 GHz.

Transmissions from a satellite transponder are sent to satellite dishes. A familiar site in most communities throughout the United States and Canada, a **satellite dish** "catches" satellite transmissions on its parabolic surface, then reflects these signals to a feed. The **feed** contains a small metal probe that is a microwave antenna. The feed funnels signals to a device called a low noise block downconverter (LNB) that converts the microwave signal into an electrical current, amplifies it, and lowers its frequency. The downconverted signal is conveyed by cable to the indoor receiver. Figure 11-14 illustrates the major parts of a satellite dish.

Figure 11-14

A satellite dish

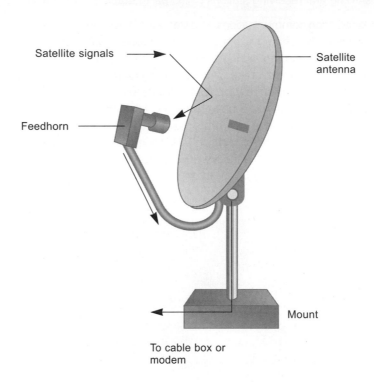

Satellite signals

Satellite antenna

Feedhorn

Mount

To cable box or modem

QuickCheck B

1 UTP has the highest bandwidth of any cable you can buy. True or false? _____

2 _____ cable is typically used for local area networks and cable television.

3 Twisted-pair and coaxial cables transmit _____ signals, whereas fiber-optic cables transmit _____.

4 The highest capacity fiber-optic cable is called _____ cable.

5 Wireless communications channels are generally slower than using cables. True or false? _____

6 Satellites send a high-frequency _____ signal to a ground station or satellite dish.

C Communications Systems

Cables, satellites, transmitters, and receivers are the building blocks of communications systems. Today's communications systems evolved from early courier services such as the Pony Express and Wells Fargo. Technology began to shrink the globe, so to speak, in 1844 when Samuel Morse sent the first telegraph message. By the turn of the century, more than one million miles of telegraph lines linked cities and continents. The telegraph was soon upstaged by a new communications system based on the telephone. Riding on the coattails of the telephone system came the cellular phone system. At the same time, cable television companies began stringing thousands of miles of cable to deliver "pay TV." In addition to these commercial communications systems, many businesses established local area networks (LANs) and a decentralized communications structure called the Internet grew rapidly into a world-wide link for computer communications. The rest of this section explains how individuals and organizations use these communications systems to send and receive computer data.

The Telephone System

What are the advantages and disadvantages of using the telephone system to communicate computer data? Looking back, a marriage between telephones and computers seemed inevitable. Computers provide lightning fast data processing and tremendous capacity for storing data. The telephone network provides a pipeline for sending that data throughout the world.

InfoWeb

Bell
5

In 1876 Alexander Graham Bell transmitted the first telephone message (Figure 11-15), and over the next century his company, now known as AT&T, built a communications empire that established much of the communications technology the telephone network uses today.

Figure 11-15

A re-enactment of the first telephone message; Alexander Graham Bell spilled acid on his trousers while testing a new liquid transmitter. When he called to his assistant, "Mr Watson, come here—I want you!" his voice was transmitted to the receiver in the next room.

The telephone network uses **circuit switching**, which temporarily connects one telephone to another for the duration of a call. This type of switching provides callers with a direct pipeline over which streams of voice data can flow. You can also use this pipeline to access your Internet service provider. As you'll see later in this chapter, other communications systems use different types of switching when carrying information that is not formatted as a constant stream.

Phone
System
6

Telephone companies use a five-tier network to transmit calls. At each level of the network, a switch creates a connection so your call eventually has a continuous circuit to its destination. The first tier of this network physically connects each telephone in a city to a local switch in what's called a **central office** (CO). The second tier links several local offices to toll switches. Connections then fan out to primary switches, sectional offices, and regional offices. Figure 11-16 shows how you use the telephone network to make a voice call or to access Internet data.

Figure 11-16

Using the telephone system for voice
communication and Internet access.

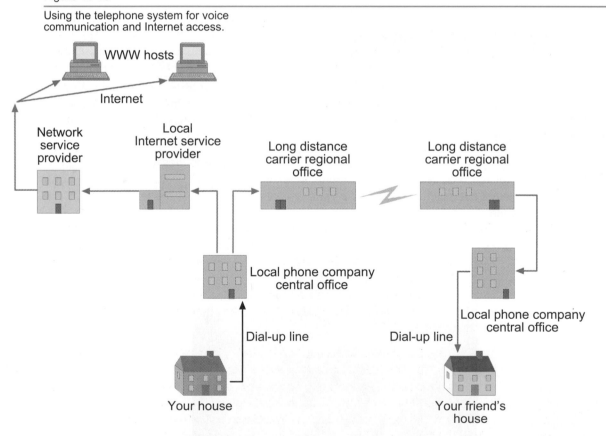

The telephone network offers a variety of services for voice and data communications. Originally, telephones communicated using analog audio signals and that is the type of service that today connects most homes and many businesses to the central office. This type of service, sometimes referred to as **POTS** for "plain old telephone service," is characterized by a dial-up connection that is created when you dial, then destroyed when you hang up. When you want to send digital computer data over a POTS line, you must use a **modem** to convert digital pulses into analog audio tones.

The term "modem" is derived from the words "modulate" and "demodulate." In communications terminology, **modulation** means changing the characteristics of a signal, as when a modem changes a digital pulse into an analog signal. **Demodulation** means changing a signal back to its original state, as when a modem changes an audio signal back to a digital pulse. Modulating a digital signal allows computers, fax machines, and other digital devices to use POTS lines for data transport.

Inexpensive access is the primary advantage of the telephone system for computer communications. Most people have telephone service, so an inexpensive modem is all that's required to set up communications. Computer communications are virtually indistinguishable from voice communications, and so service charges are the same as for voice calls.

Using the latest modem technology, POTS lines have a maximum data transport capacity of about 56 kilobits per second. Some applications, such as videoconferencing, require more capacity than provided by these lines. Telephone companies are scrambling to offer higher capacity digital services. Digital services transport voice and computer data using a digital sampling technique similar to the way a computer digitizes music in WAV format. When you send computer data over a digital line, your computer must have a device called a **DSU** (data service unit) that places the data in the proper format for transmission. A DSU is similar to a modem in some respects, but instead of converting analog to digital, a DSU simply changes data from the digital format used in your computer to a digital format that is suitable for transport over the digital line. In North America, the telephone network offers digital services including ISDN, T1, and T3. European and Asian telephone networks offer a slightly different variety of digital services.

An **ISDN (Integrated Services Digital Network)** service transports data digitally over dial-up or dedicated lines. A **dedicated line**, also called a **leased line**, is a permanent connection between two locations. Phone companies offer two grades of ISDN service: a basic service with 64 kilobits per second capacity and an enhanced service with 2 megabits per second capacity. **T1 service** provides 1.5 megabits per second capacity over a dedicated line. **T3 service** uses fiber-optic cables to provide dedicated service with a capacity of 45 megabits per second.

Many businesses pay higher rates to access high-capacity lines, but these services are not available in all areas. For data communications applications, the telecommunications infrastructure is only as good as its weakest link. For example, suppose a law firm wants to have a videoconference between its home office in Washington, D.C., and a Nashville hotel, where one of the firm's lawyers is staying. If the Washington office has ISDN service but the hotel has only POTS lines, the POTS line would limit the speed of data transmission. At both sites the video images would appear as a series of still images instead of full-motion video.

The Cellular Phone System

Can I use a computer with a cellular phone? The cellular phone system is based on wireless technology and provides mobile communications facilities that you can carry with you. As with the telephone system, the cellular phone system was originally designed to carry voice communications, but has been pressed into service for data communications as well.

InfoWeb

Mobile Computing 7

The advantage of data communications on the cellular phone system is mobility. Police can access local and national law enforcement computer databases while on patrol. Sales representatives can check their computerized scheduler and read e-mail while traveling. Investors can access stock quotes over the Internet while at lunch.

The disadvantages of cellular communications include cost, reliability problems, and lack of security. Communications charges are considerably higher than the regular telephone system. You pay for **air time**, the number of minutes you are connected, whether you dial a call or answer an incoming call. Add to this any long distance charges you incur and surcharges for **roaming** calls placed outside of your local calling area.

Cellular transmissions are susceptible to more interference than communications that travel over regular telephone lines. Overloaded cellular channels are noisy with transmissions that sometimes spill over from other calls and with static caused by electrical equipment and other transmitting devices. Channel noise is especially troublesome for transmitting data. If there's too much channel noise, a data transmission becomes unreliable.

Communications over the cellular system are literally floating in the air and easy to intercept with the right equipment. When transmitting sensitive or confidential data over a cellular phone system, it is advisable to encrypt it.

A cellular phone uses FM radio waves to send voice and data communications to a base station tower. Towers are spaced in the middle of a limited geographical area called a **cell**. Each cell provides 50 to 70 radio channels, one for each simultaneous call within the cell. To see how this works, study Figure 11-17, which depicts each cell as a hexagon and represents groups of channels by a color.

Figure 11-17

The towers in adjacent cells of a cellular phone network cannot use the same radio channels.

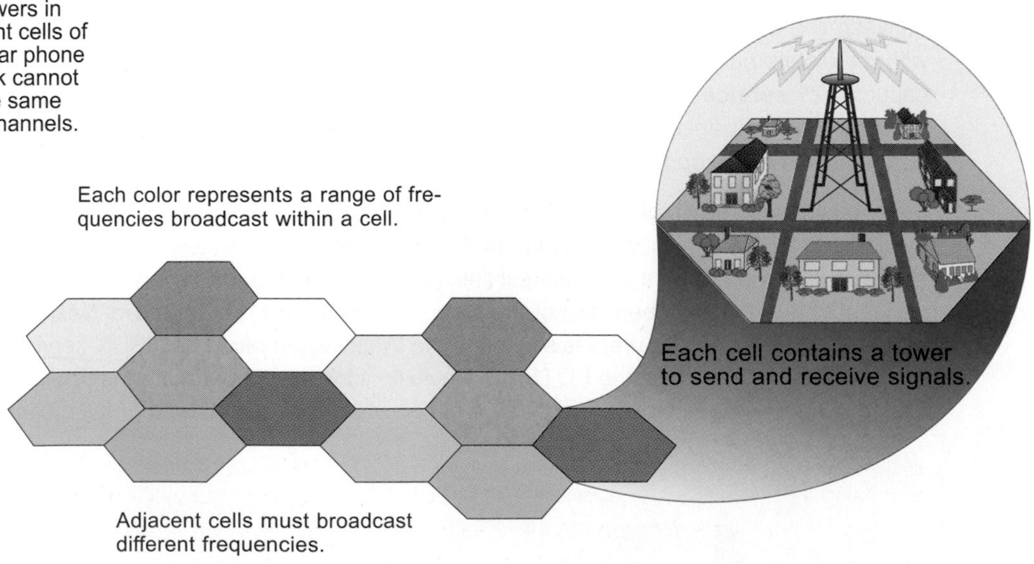

Each color represents a range of frequencies broadcast within a cell.

Each cell contains a tower to send and receive signals.

Adjacent cells must broadcast different frequencies.

From the tower, calls are routed to lines provided by the telephone system; calls to other cellular phones are routed to the tower currently serving that phone. When a call is in progress and you move from one cell to another, your call is switched from one tower to another. Figure 11-18 traces the path of cellular Internet access.

Figure 11-18

When you use your cellular phone to call your Internet service provider, your call is routed to the nearest cell tower. From the tower, you are connected to your ISP by land lines. Your ISP then provides you access to the Internet, just as if you were using your home phone.

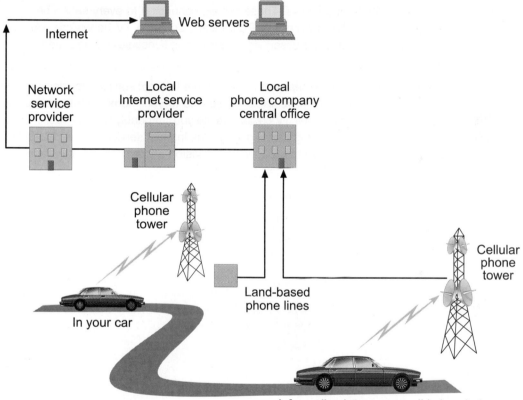

Most cellular phone companies offer digital and analog service, but typically data communications take place using analog service because of the widespread use and availability of modems for analog transmission. If you are using analog service, you can theoretically use a standard modem. However, a cellular phone has no dial tone, so you need some way to fool your modem into hearing a dial tone. Cellular phone companies provide an inexpensive converter box, called a **data module**, that you can use to connect your standard modem to your cellular phone. Some modem manufacturers market **cellular-ready modems** that you can connect to either the telephone system or the cellular phone system.

Cellular-ready modems are available as PCMCIA cards for notebook computers and in external or internal configurations for desktop computers. To install a cellular-ready modem, you just plug it into the appropriate expansion slot or port of your computer. Plugging the other end into your cellular phone might not be so simple. Unfortunately, the cellular phone industry has not yet settled on standard data plugs. Before you buy a cellular-ready modem, make sure it works with the brand and model of your cellular phone.

The Cable Television System

Does the cable television system offer any facilities for computer communications?

In the past 20 years, cable television has become available to an estimated 90 percent of the homes in the United States. Cable TV stations receive broadcasts via satellite, then rebroadcast them to homes via cables. Users pay a fee for this service, depending on the number and type of channels to which they subscribe.

Cable TV companies have installed miles and miles of high bandwidth (400 MHz) coaxial cables and are currently in the process of adding additional miles of even higher-bandwidth (700 MHz) fiber-optical cable. These cables, connected to every subscriber's home, have a carrying capacity far in excess of POTS lines, so cable TV bandwidth could provide quick transmission for computer-based video, audio, and teleconferencing in addition to a variety of television programs.

Today, many cable TV companies have become Internet service providers. To subscribe to a cable TV ISP, you must have cable TV service to your home. Most cable companies offer Internet service only to their TV customers, so you'll probably have to subscribe to a package that includes television programming as well as Internet service. Figure 11-19 illustrates how the cable television system broadcasts television shows and provides Internet access.

Figure 11-19

Your local cable TV office receives television programs from a satellite, then transmits them over a cable to all its subscribers. To provide Internet access, your cable company must also have a connection to the Internet and make some provision for you to send data, as well as receive it.

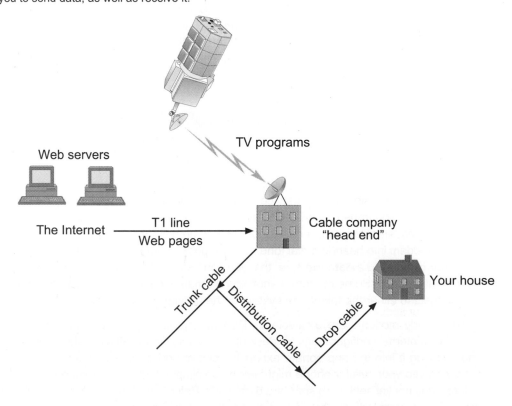

Cable
Modems
8

To access the Internet your computer needs a cable modem and an Ethernet card—the same network interface card you would use to connect your computer to a local area network. A **cable modem** is a device designed to demodulate a signal from the cable and translate it back into Internet data. Your cable company will provide you with the type of cable modem that works with its equipment. Figure 11-20 illustrates how you connect your computer and your TV to the cable TV communications infrastructure.

Figure 11-20

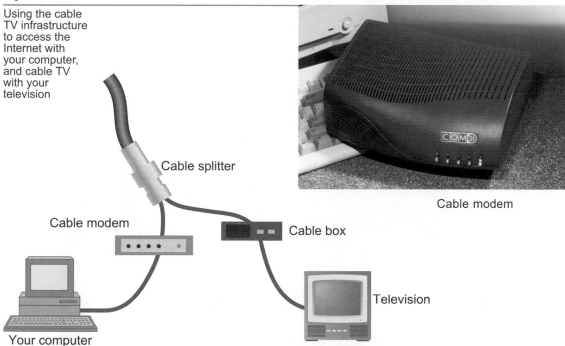

Using the cable TV infrastructure to access the Internet with your computer, and cable TV with your television

Cable splitter

Cable modem

Cable modem

Cable box

Television

Your computer

A cable modem has a capacity of 30 mbps (megabits per second)—100 times as fast as today's standard 33.6 kbps (kilobits per second) phone modems. What's everyone waiting for? As it turns out, 30 mbps is not the entire story. Although the capacity of a cable modem is 30 mbps, the rate at which you can send and receive data is only as fast as the slowest link in the communications circuit. For example, the Ethernet card that receives data from the cable modem might have a capacity of only 10 mbps.

Another potential data bottleneck is the size of the connection between the cable office and the Internet. Most cable companies use a T1 line, which provides maximum speeds of 1.55 mbps, considerably slower than the maximum capacity of a cable modem. You'll notice access speeds slowing down when many cable modem users are online through your cable company. Most cable systems were constructed only for broadcasting, so one-way communications were sufficient. When you send data using the cable system, you, and all the other cable modem users, must share a narrow band of frequencies.

U.S. and Canadian cable companies first offered Internet access in 1997 and attracted about 25,000 subscribers. Some experts project that this service will be available to 4.5 million customers in 1998. How many of these customers are Internet users and how many will abandon their POTS modems is anyone's guess. Stay tuned to see if cable TV can challenge the telephone company's dominant role in computer communications.

Direct Satellite Service

Can I use a satellite to access the Internet? **Direct satellite service** (DSS) uses a geo-synchronous or low-earth orbit satellite to send television, voice, or computer data directly to a satellite dish owned by an individual. Initially pioneered for broadcasting television programs, in 1997 this technology was first used commercially to transmit Internet data directly to homes and offices.

InfoWeb

DSS
9

One of the first Internet DSS services, DirecPC, transmits Internet data directly to your private 21-inch satellite dish. Up to 400 kbps of bandwidth provide lightning fast display of Web pages and streaming videos.

DirecPC satellites transmit in only one direction, referred to as **downstream**, meaning from the satellite to you. How, then, can you transmit information upstream? For example, suppose you click a Web page link or type in a URL. Somehow that information must be transmitted from your computer to the Web, so the page you've requested can be located and sent via satellite. DirecPC uses a standard modem and phone line for upstream transmission. The entire system is illustrated in Figure 11-21.

Figure 11-21

DirecPC sends Internet data downstream, but uses a conventional phone line for upstream requests.

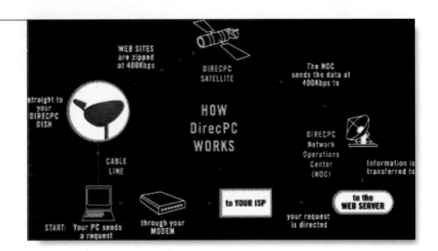

The Internet and Intranets

How do data networks differ from phone, cellular, and cable TV networks? The Internet has become the hub of data communications. As you have discovered, most communications systems provide some way to access the Internet and use it to transport data. The Internet is rapidly replacing other data communications technology such as private WANs (wide area networks) and dial-in computer bulletin boards.

InfoWeb

Intranets
10

Some organizations have employed Internet technology for smaller networks. An **intranet** uses TCP/IP protocols and Internet software to handle the data communications within an organization. In a sense it is a mini-Internet with Internet services such as Web pages and Internet mail. An Intranet, however, is designed for access primarily from local users, not Internet surfers.

A LAN is a network that serves users in a limited local area. The distinction between a LAN and an Intranet is somewhat fuzzy. A LAN might use TCP/IP protocols, but will also use other protocols such as Novell Netware's IPX or Digital's LAT. The characteristics of the Internet, intranets, and LANs are summarized in Figure 11-22.

Figure 11-22

Internet, Intranets, and LANs

	Internet	Intranet	LAN
Coverage area	World-wide	Local	Local
Operated by	Consortium	Private company	Private company
Protocol	TCP/IP	TCP/IP	TCP/IP, IPX, NetBUI, Lat, AFP
Services	Web, Internet e-mail	Web, Internet e-mail	File server, print server, file sharing
Number of servers	+2 million	Typically 1–5	Typically 1–5

The Internet, intranets, and LANs were all specifically invented and designed for efficient data transmission. Contrast this goal with the telephone and cellular phone systems, which were originally optimized for voice communications, or the cable TV system, which was originally optimized for visual data. Basic differences between these systems results from the nature of the "stuff" that is transmitted. Phone conversations and television broadcasts are continuous and sequential events that seem, intuitively, to require some sort of continual circuit. Therefore, it is logical that these communications systems use circuit switching technology to create a continuous connection for communications.

It would seem unlikely that chopping a phone conversation into little chunks and then reassembling it, could somehow make the communication more efficient. Data communications, on the other hand, are not necessarily continuous. More like a letter than a phone conversation, it is conceivable that you might chop up a data message then send the pieces to their destination where they would be reassembled into the original message.

Unlike the telephone network that uses circuit switching technology, the Internet employs **packet switching** technology that divides a message into smaller units called **packets**. Each packet is addressed to its destination, but it might travel a different route over the network than other packets. At the receiving end of the transmission, all the packets are gathered and reassembled. Packets can be routed to avoid congested or inoperable communications links, as shown in Figure 11-23.

Figure 11-23

Sending data as packets

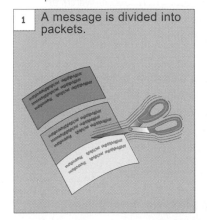
1 A message is divided into packets.

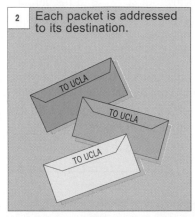
2 Each packet is addressed to its destination.

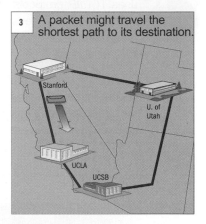
3 A packet might travel the shortest path to its destination.

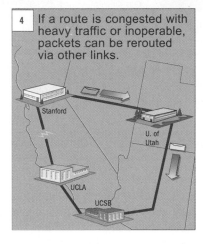
4 If a route is congested with heavy traffic or inoperable, packets can be rerouted via other links.

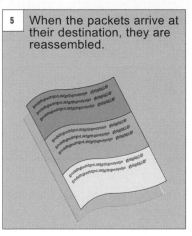
5 When the packets arrive at their destination, they are reassembled.

Packet Switching 11

InfoWeb

The advantage of packet switching is its efficient use of available bandwidth. Packets from many different messages can share a single communications circuit. Packets are shipped down the circuit on a "first come, first served" basis. If some packets from a message are not available, the system does not need to wait for them. Instead, the system sends whatever packets are ready, regardless of the message that they belong to. Contrast this with a circuit switched network such as the telephone system. Suppose someone is "on hold." No communication is taking place, yet the circuit is reserved and cannot be used for other communications.

Even though packet switching provides an efficient and dependable protocol for data communications, most experts agree that the Internet in its current form will not meet the data transport needs of a growing population of users, especially for graphics, audio, video, or teleconferencing applications. Network service providers are continually adding bandwidth to the Internet backbone by increasing the number and capacity of its communications links.

Ethernet and Token Ring LANs

How do local area networks handle data communications? LANs are a popular type of small communications system. Most local area networks use packet-switching technology, as does the Internet. Think of a LAN as a railroad system that transports cargo (data) between destinations (workstations). Like railroad tracks, network cables provide physical connections between workstations. Network software does the work of shipping companies, "packing" each shipment (message) into acceptable containers, making sure each container is addressed to the correct destination, and verifying that each container arrives at its final destination. Network hardware directs the flow of data over network cables, in much the same way that railroad dispatchers direct the movement of trains on the railroad tracks to prevent collisions and to make sure that each train arrives at its assigned destination.

The physical arrangement of devices and cables in a network is referred to as its **topology**. LANs typically use one of three topologies. Cables can branch out in a **star** pattern to each network node from a central device called a **concentrator** or **hub**. As a second option, cables form a **ring** that connects **MAUs (multistation access units)**, which in turn connect to each network node. Alternatively, the cable can run directly from one network node to another, connecting them in a series called a **bus**, as shown in Figure 11-24.

Figure 11-24

Network
topology

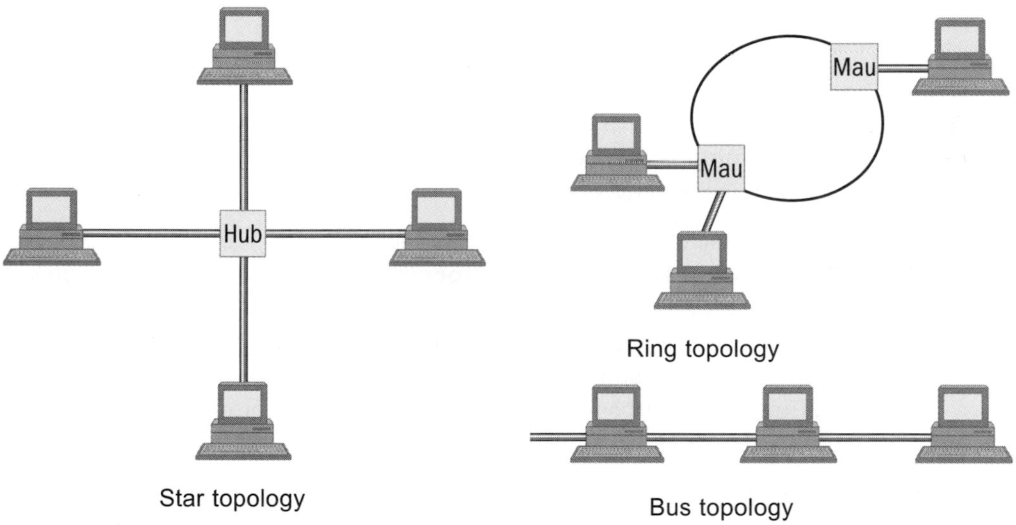

Star topology

Ring topology

Bus topology

Network
Standards
12

Each device on a network requires a network interface card to establish a data pathway between a computer and the network communications channel. A network interface card plugs into an expansion slot in the computer main board or into a PCMCIA slot. A cable plugged into the interface card connects the computer to the rest of the network. A network interface card supports a particular network standard. A **network standard** is a set of communications protocols for orderly transmission of data. Every device on a network must use the same network standard or else it cannot communicate and share the network resources. Today's most popular network standards include Ethernet and Token Ring.

Ethernet, the most popular network standard, typically transmits data at 10 megabits per second. There are several variations of Ethernet, characterized by the type of cable that connects the workstations. Figure 11-25 summarizes Ethernet communications technology.

Figure 11-25

Ethernet technologies

Ethernet Type	Cable Type	Max. Length	Topology	Speed
10Base5 "Thick Ethernet"	Thick coax	1,640 ft.	bus	10 Mbps
10Base2 "Thin Ethernet"	Thin coax	607 ft.	bus	10 Mbps
10BaseT	Twisted-pair	328 ft.	star	10 Mbps
10BaseF	Fiber optic	1.2 mi.	star	10 Mbps
100BaseT	Twisted-pair	328 ft.	star	100 Mbps

Token Ring, the second most popular network standard, transmits data at either 4 megabits or 16 megabits per second over twisted-pair wire. As its name suggests, a Token Ring network connects a ring of MAUs. Cables from the MAUs connect to network computers and printers.

InfoWeb

TCP/IP
13

The flow of data over a network is controlled at two levels: software and hardware. Regardless of whether a network is an Ethernet or Token Ring, it requires some sort of **network communications protocol**, which specifies the structure of the packets. This protocol is controlled by software.

The most widely used network communication protocols are TCP/IP, IPX, LAT, and AFP. **TCP/IP (transmission control protocol/Internet protocol)** is used on Ethernet and Token Ring networks, as well as on the Internet. **IPX (internetwork packet exchange)** is the protocol used by Novell NetWare, the most popular microcomputer network software. **LAT (local area transport**, also known as **DECnet)** is a network protocol developed by Digital Equipment Corporation (DEC) for use with its minicomputers. **AFP** was developed by Apple Computer, Inc. for AppleTalk networks and Apple Macintosh computers.

At the hardware level, network interface cards and switching devices also control the flow of data. They perform functions similar to those of a railroad dispatcher—directing data to the appropriate workstation and trying to prevent collisions.

The way a network distributes packets to workstations depends on the network standard. An Ethernet network distributes packets quite differently from a Token Ring network. On an Ethernet network, before a network interface card sends a packet, it checks to see if the network is busy. If another network interface card is sending a packet, it waits and tries again later. If the network is not busy, the network interface card broadcasts the packet to every device on the network. Every device receives the packet, but it is accepted only by the device to which it is addressed.

Sometimes, two devices on an Ethernet network simultaneously check the network and see that it's not busy. These two devices then send packets at the same instant. When two packets are sent at the same time, it's called a **collision**. Ethernet networks use a method called **carrier sense multiple access with collision detection (CSMA/CD)** to deal with collisions.

When messages collide, both devices stop sending and wait for a random period of time before attempting to send again. You can probably see why it is essential that both devices wait a random period of time. If the devices were designed to wait for a specific period of time, both would wait and try again at the same time, resulting in another collision. They would continue to wait and collide, wait and collide, and never send the message. Figure 11-26 shows how packets are transmitted on an Ethernet network.

Figure 11-26

How Ethernet works

1. One of the workstations checks the network to make sure it is not busy, then broadcasts a packet. The packet is addressed to workstation #21, but all the workstations receive it. Every workstation examines the address of the packet, but only the workstation to which it is addressed reads it.

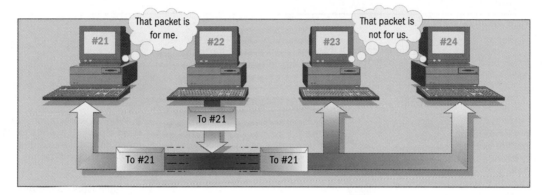

2. If two workstations simultaneously check the network, find it is not busy, and send packets at the same time, a collision occurs.

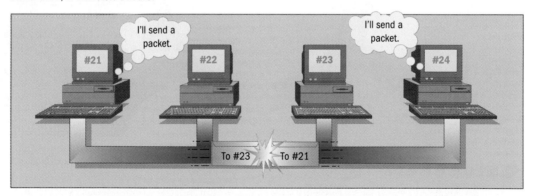

3. When a collision occurs, a special signal travels over the network to indicate that it is "jammed." This signal lasts a fraction of a second, then the network is again ready for traffic. The two workstations that had sent simultaneous packets each wait for a random length of time before trying to send their packets again.

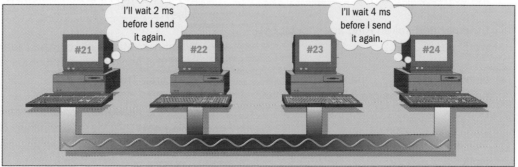

In a Token Ring network, a special message called a **token** continuously travels around the network. The token carries a signal to indicate whether the token is busy or available to carry a packet. If a device wants to send a packet, it waits for the token. If the token is busy, the device must wait. If the token is available, the device attaches the packet to the token, sets a signal to indicate the token is busy, and sends the token on its way. As the token passes each device, a network interface card checks the address and accepts the packet if it is addressed to that device. The token and message continue traveling around the network until they return to the sending device. The sending device then removes the packet, sets the signal to indicate the token is available, and sends the token on down the cable. The token prevents collisions. Figure 11-27 shows how packets are transmitted on token-passing networks.

Figure 11-27

How token passing works

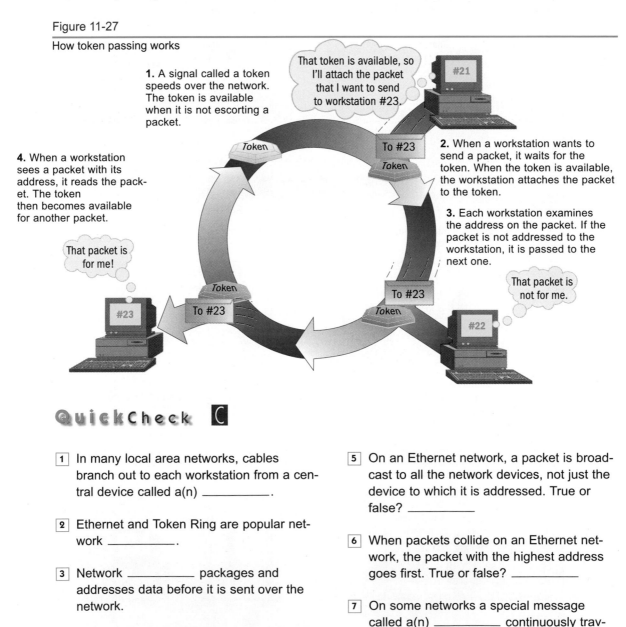

1. A signal called a token speeds over the network. The token is available when it is not escorting a packet.

That token is available, so I'll attach the packet that I want to send to workstation #23.

2. When a workstation wants to send a packet, it waits for the token. When the token is available, the workstation attaches the packet to the token.

3. Each workstation examines the address on the packet. If the packet is not addressed to the workstation, it is passed to the next one.

4. When a workstation sees a packet with its address, it reads the packet. The token then becomes available for another packet.

That packet is for me!

That packet is not for me.

QuickCheck C

1 In many local area networks, cables branch out to each workstation from a central device called a(n) _____.

2 Ethernet and Token Ring are popular network _____.

3 Network _____ packages and addresses data before it is sent over the network.

4 TCP/IP, IPX, and LAT are examples of network _____.

5 On an Ethernet network, a packet is broadcast to all the network devices, not just the device to which it is addressed. True or false? _____

6 When packets collide on an Ethernet network, the packet with the highest address goes first. True or false? _____

7 On some networks a special message called a(n) _____ continuously travels around the network carrying packets.

Ⅾ Building a Low-Cost LAN

Data communications networks are not the exclusive property of large corporations, huge government agencies, and giant telecommunications companies. You can have your own computer network, and if you already have two or three computers (counting your friends' or coworkers' computers), your network will cost less than $200!

When you've built your network, you can use it to share data, collaborate on computer projects, and try out some multi-player games.

LAB

Building a
Network

What You'll Need

What do I need to set up my network?   First, you'll need some computers—at least two. To make it easy, all the computers you'll connect to your network should run Windows 95, WindowsNT, or Windows 98. These versions of Windows include built-in networking software that will handle the network protocols.

You'll need one network interface card for each computer. For the simplest and least expensive network, look for 10BaseT Ethernet cards. These cards cost between $20 and $100. You can get a dependable basic card for about $25.

The next item on your shopping list is a 10BaseT hub. Look for a hub with eight ports so you can connect up to eight devices to your network. Even if you don't have eight computers that you want to connect, an 8-port hub provides room for expansion. Eight-port hubs range in price from $60 to $200. For a basic network, one of the low cost hubs should suffice (Figure 11-28).

Figure 11-28

An inexpensive
8-port 10BaseT
hub

You'll also need 10BaseT cables. These cables are sold in various lengths with RJ-45 plugs at each end. These cables are often referred to as **patch cables**. They're suitable for distances up to 100 feet. For each computer you'll need a cable long enough to reach the hub. Look for category 5 UTP (unshielded twisted-pair) cables. A 20-foot cable costs about $15.

Finally, make sure you have a Philips-head screw driver handy.

Install Network Cards

What do I do with all this stuff? Your first step is to put a network card in each computer. To do this, follow the manufacturer's instructions for opening the computer's system unit. Usually, you'll need to unscrew a few screws on the back of the case.

Before you touch any components inside the case, it is a good idea to "ground" yourself to release static electricity that might damage components on the motherboard. "Real" technicians use special grounding straps that attach to their wrists. If you don't have a grounding strap, touch some metal before you reach into the computer case.

Locate an unused expansion slot on the main board of your computer and carefully plug in the network card, as shown in Figure 11-29.

Figure 11-29

Installing a
network card

If you're a gambler, you can refasten the system unit case now. However, if things don't go exactly right, you might have to access the network card to troubleshoot the problem. It's probably prudent to reassemble the system unit after your network is up and running smoothly.

Install the Cables and Hub

What do I do with all these cables? The cables are meant to connect each computer to the hub. So, plug one end of a cable into the network card that you just installed in the computer. Plug the other end into any one of the ports in the hub. You'll see why 10BaseT topology is referred to as a star—the cables branch out from the hub sort of like the points of a star.

Your hub needs electrical power. Follow the manufacturer's directions for plugging your hub into a wall outlet or UPS (uninterruptible power supply). In case of a power failure, you'd like your network connections to remain intact until you can save your files and shut down the system gracefully.

Activate Network Software

How will the computers on my network know how to communicate? Now, you can turn on the computers. Windows should automatically detect the network cards you have just installed. A Windows wizard will display a series of dialog boxes to guide you through the rest of the installation process. For your first network, you should select the Client for Microsoft Networks protocol and indicate to the wizard that you want to share files and printers, as shown in Figure 11-30.

Figure 11-30

Use the Windows Network dialog box to select Client for Microsoft Networks, then select File and Print Sharing.

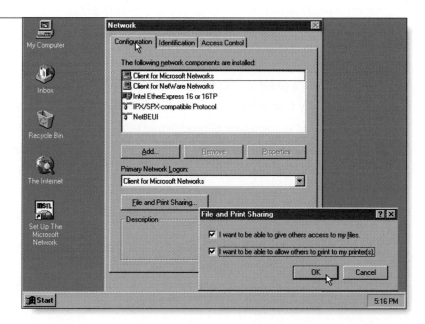

EndNote

Computers are no longer isolated devices, thanks to a communications infrastructure that integrates telephone lines, satellites, and radio transmitters. This evolving communications infrastructure is also having a profound effect on the way people work and socialize. Here's one person's account:

"I guess you could call me a telecommuter because I work at home, but I like to think of myself as a virtual employee. To my coworkers it seems like I'm right next door. Actually, I live and work in a different city. I have two phone lines at home—one for voice communications and one for my computer and my fax machine. I also have a voice mail system at "corporate" that takes calls from my customers. Many of them don't know I'm virtual.

InfoWeb

Telecommuting
14

"My desktop videoconference system lets me attend meetings without leaving home. I can instantly fax documents to my customers and coworkers. FedEx drives up to my door to collect documents that cannot be transmitted electronically because they require signatures. I don't need to trek to the library to do market research. Instead, I fire up my computer and surf the Internet. I avoid telephone tag by sending e-mail. If the person I need to contact doesn't have an e-mail account, I use AT&T's message delivery system—they place the call and deliver the message.

"Entertainment? Of course I have cable TV, but I spend more time answering e-mail from my friends. It's a great way to keep in touch and it's nice to know that I can just fire off a message to my friends in Germany or India and it will be in their mailbox within minutes. OK, I admit that I spend time playing virtual reality games on the Internet. I also hang out with other people in my profession through Internet Usenet groups and chat rooms on commercial information services. That's where I heard about this graduate course at Colorado State University. I registered and took the course. Never went to campus. I watched televised lectures and submitted all my coursework using the Internet. It was actually fun."

This is today. Imagine the future!

InfoWeb

Chapter
Links

The InfoWeb is your guide to print, film, television, and electronic resources. Use it to obtain updates on quickly changing technical information and to locate information for research papers. If you're using the New Perspectives CD-ROM, click the InfoWeb icon on the left side of this paragraph to access the online InfoWeb links. Otherwise, use your Web browser and type in the address of the New Perspectives site: www.cciw.com/np3. At the New Perspectives site you'll find up-to-date links to the topics covered in this chapter.

1 Communications Terminology

Although communications has become an integral part of computing, many computer dictionaries do not yet include many communications terms. On the Internet you'll find several good sources that explain communications terminology. For basic definitions, connect to the General Communications Glossary at **www.mendonet.com/telecom/glossary/index.html**. You'll find another basic glossary at the Sprint Web site, **www.sprint.com/sprint/annual/is_96/GLOSS/p_42main.html**, and an interactive quiz you can use to test your familiarity of communications terms at **www.sprint.com/cool/recroom/ quiz/quiz.html**.You'll find a great set of links to many technical glossaries and dictionaries in Alex's Giant Glossary Listing at **www.iserv.net/~alexx/glossary.htm**. A good glossary of cable TV terms is at **videotron.ab.ca/Technology/glossary.html**, the Web site hosted by Videotron Communications Ltd. Finally, for those difficult-to-find definitions of satellite communications terms check out **ilab.com/list9/definit.txt**.

2 Bandwidth

The number of devices transmitting data over cables and the airways is multiplying at an astounding rate. Is there enough bandwidth for all these transmissions? A chronic problem on the Internet is lack of bandwidth that causes delays in data transmission and translates to slow response from a Web site. Read about the evolution of Internet bandwidth in the article "Internet Pipe Schemes" by connecting to **www.internet.com** and searching for the author's name, Glen Banta. Another good source of information on bandwidth is the High Bandwidth Web Page at **www.specialty.com/hiband/**.

3 Fiber Optics

An important part of the telecommunications infrastructure that supports voice and data transmission is fiber-optic cable. With fiber-optic cable, data travels as light wave transmissions, rather than digital or analog electrical transmissions. What exactly is fiber-optic cable, and how does it work? Lascomm Fiber Optic Data and Video Communications at **www.lascomm.com/toc.htm** has tutorials on fiber-optic cables, articles on a variety of fiber-optic topics, a glossary of industry terms, and case stories of innovative uses of fiber optics. AT&T Labs has an excellent overview of fiber optics at **www.att.com/attlabs/brainspin/fiberoptics/** that discusses how sound is transmitted over fiber-optic cables, provides some history about fiber-optics in telecommunications, and describes why fiber-optic cables work the way they do. The Corning Optical Fiber Information Center at **www.corningfiber.com** presents an

online course on fiber optics called Fiber 101. Topics include how fiber was invented, how fiber works, and facts about fiber. To learn about the fiber-optic industry and fiber-optic manufacturers, check out The Fiber Optic Marketplace at **fiberoptic.com/**.

4 Satellites

How Do Satellites Work? at **www.atek.com/satellite/work.html** provides an easy to understand discussion of the basics, including geosynchronous, medium, and low-earth orbiting satellites. More information on satellite orbits can be found at **www.np.ac.sg/~chw/orbits.html**. The November 1997 issue of *BYTE* (**www.byte.com/art/9711/Sec5/art1.htm**) contains an excellent overview of satellite technology. You can view some interesting satellite images at Dundee Satellite Receiving Station, **www.sat.dundee.ac.uk/**, a satellite receiving installation in the United Kingdom. You can interact with satellite simulations at **www.cea.berkeley.edu/Education/lessons/indiv/dataflow/animation.html**, a wonderful set of Web pages designed by Eric Olson.

5 Alexander Graham Bell

Perhaps more than any other invention, the telephone has changed the fabric and texture of our society. In fact without the telephone, the Internet probably would not exist. Alexander Graham Bell was a young 29 years old when he invented the telephone and the telephone was only one of many inventions and contributions that he made to our society. In addition to the telephone, Bell invented a type of telegraph that could transmit more than one message at a time and a device called a photophone, which transmitted sound on a beam of light. He also worked on the phonograph, aerial vehicles, hydroairplanes, and the selenium cell; and he founded the National Geographic Society. Several excellent books about Bell have been written, including *Bell: Alexander Graham Bell and the Conquest of Solitude* by Robert Bruce (Boston: Little, Brown, 1973) and the more recent biography *Alexander Graham Bell: Making Connections* by Naomi Pasachoff (Oxford University Press, 1996).

The Web site, Alexander Graham Bell's Path to the Telephone, at **cti.itc.virginia.edu/~meg3c/albell/homepage.html** reconstructs the path Bell took when he invented the telephone. It includes a detailed cognitive map that shows the inspiration for Bell's work and discusses some of the sources of his ideas in the work of other scientists and inventors. You can also view excerpts from Bell's original notebooks.

At The Telephone History Web Site, **www.cybercomm.net/~chuck/phones.html**, you can find links to telephone history, photographs of antique telephones, histories of U.S. and international telephone companies, telephone history articles, and more.

At AT&T's Alexander Graham Bell's Happy 150th Birthday! site, **www.att.com/agbell/**, you can watch a Quick Time movie of Bell and Watson, take an interactive quiz about Bell, write predictions about the next 150 years of telephony, or read others' predictions. You can also find links here to other interesting Bell sites on the Web.

6 The Phone System

You probably use it at least once a day, but have you ever wondered how the plain old telephone system works? How does your voice get from your kitchen telephone to your Aunt Belinda's living room 2,000 miles away? At Inside AT&T Labs, **www.att.com/attlabs/**, you can find answers to some of your questions about how the telephone system works. The section called "Brain Spin, Routing Calls Through the Network" outlines the basics of how local and long distance calls are routed. An interactive exercise gives some insight into the tasks that switching computers perform. If learning some of the basics sparks your interest, the TELECOM Digest's Frequently Asked Questions file at **mirror.lcs.mit.edu/telecom-archives/archives/new-readers/frequent-ask-questions-97** contains detailed information about how telecommunications systems work and about current issues in the telecommunications field. POTS (plain old telephone system) is just one facet of today's telephone network. Pacific Bell provides a user's guide to ISDN at **gw2.pacbell.com/products/business/fastrak/networking/isdn/info/isdn-guide/index.html** that can help you learn more about this type of high speed telephone line. How fast is your Internet connection? You can find out at test your connection to Utopia!, **www.onlive.com/cgi-bin/nettest.cgi**, a Web site that lets you test the speed of your Internet connection.

7 Mobile Computing

Mobile computing makes use of the latest technology in portable computers, cellular, and other wireless telecommunications technologies. Lucent.context at **www.lucent.com/context/wireless/** has a lot of information about wireless communications, products, and technology through a Web-based multimedia presentation. For an excellent technical introduction to this area, read "Mobile Computing & Disconnected Operation: A Survey of Recent Advances" at **www.cis.ohio-state.edu/~jain/cis788/ mobile_comp/index.html**. For more general articles, ranging from reviews of new products to advice about choosing a cellular telephone, avoiding injury while traveling, or protecting your equipment from theft, read *Mobile Computing Online* (magazine) at **www.mobilecomputing.com/**. Using the cellular phone network for Internet access can be a bit tricky. For a general introduction to cellular technology, read "What is Cellular?" at **www.internet-connections.net/web2/cellrone/whatiscelular.html**.

Xircom, a company that manufactures cellular modems, has a good set of FAQs at **www.xircom.com/Products/cel/ celqa.html**. Another modem manufacturer, U.S. Robotics, provides a helpful overview at **www.usr.com/intransit/ briefs/wpcell5.html**. Suppliers of mobile computing products and services include Bell Atlantic Mobile (**www.bam.com/**), Cellular One (**www.cellularone.com/**), Aironet Wireless Communications, Inc. (**www.aironet.com/**), Philips Mobile Computing Group (Velo) (**www.velo1.com/**), and Fujitsu Personal Systems (**www.fpsi.com/**).

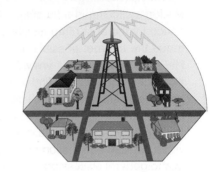

8 Cable Modems

During 1997, people started referring to something called the World Wide Wait, previously known as the World Wide Web. Why change "Web" to "Wait"? Increases in the number of online users and in the use of graphics and multimedia on Web sites have created a traffic jam on the Information Highway. Cable modems are one possible solution to the Internet traffic jam. Make sure you read the C/NET article "cable modems burn up the wires" at **zuni.cnet.com/Content/Features/Techno/Cablemodems/index.html**. CableLabs, a Colorado cable television provider, has a collection of articles and newsletters at **www.cablelabs.com/Publications.html**, which provides information about cable data modems, cable data modem performance, and the role of cable television in the National Information Infrastructure. CATV CyberLab at **www.catv.org/index.html** is an encyclopedia of information on the current cable industry. Of particular interest is the section called "Cable Classroom," which includes information about integrated digital services over cable networks and links to FAQs on cable modems. For a general introduction to how the entire cable TV system works, connect to How a Cable System Works at **www.geocities.com/SiliconValley/Park/3254/cabletv.htm**.

9 DSS

Several new companies are poised to bring satellite powered telecommunications to consumers and businesses. Among them are Teledesic, Hughes Network Systems, Voice Span, CyberStar, Odyssey, and M-Star. The Satellite Broadcasting & Communications Association Web site at **www.sbca.com/** includes information for consumers on direct-to-home satellite, including its history, a timeline, and a glossary of terms. You can also find information here on how to locate a satellite specialist in your area. Telesat DirecPC (Canada) has a good explanation of how DirecPC works, how fast it is, and success stories about DirecPC. The main Web site for DirecPC is at **www.direcpc.com**. The article, "How Satellites from Outer Space Will Save the Web," at **www5.zdnet.com/anchordesk/ story/story_914.html** is from ZDNet's Anchordesk, and provides an overview of the anticipated impact of satellite telecommunications on the Web as well as links to several articles about the satellite telecommunications industry. For a look at what the future has in store, tune into "Satellite Communications in the 21st Century," a speech by Steven D. Dorfman. Dbs-Online's satellite industry news at **www.dbs-online.com/DBS/index.html** can help keep you current on what is happening in the home satellite industry.

10 Intranets

By 1997, "intranet" was a popular buzz word in corporate America and had spawned a several billion dollar industry. At the complete intranet resource, **www.intrack.com/intranet/**, you can learn about the basics of intranets, calculate the cost of implementing an intranet, view intranet demos, read articles about timely intranet topics, and read intranet case studies. *The Intranet Journal* at **www.intranetjournal.com** presents interviews with experts, advice on building intranets, special reports about the use of intranets in the banking and health industries, and many other resources. Netscape and Microsoft are two of the biggest providers of intranet software solutions. You can read case studies of intranets at Netscape's Enterprise Solutions site, **www.netscape.com/comprod/ at_work/index.html**, and at Microsoft's Intranet Solutions Center site, **www.microsoft.com/intranet/**.

11 Packet Switching

Packet switching is a technique that divides a message into smaller units, sends them to their destination by the best route available, and reassembles the packets at the receiving end. This technology made the Internet possible. In "Economic FAQs about the Internet" by Jeffrey K. MacKie-Mason and Hal R. Varian at **www.ipps.lsa.umich.edu/ipps/papers/info-nets/Economic_FAQs/FAQs/ node19.html** you can find a section on Internet Technology that explains how packet switching works, how it is different from circuit switching, and why data networks use packet switching. Introduction to Networks-Class Handouts for Spring 1996 at **www.cis.ohio-state.edu/~jain/cis6779604/** provides detailed information on packet switching and routing in addition to general discussions of many aspects of networking and data transmission. Packet Switching at **www.erg.abdn.ac.uk/users/ gorry/eg3561/intro-pages/ps.html** includes diagrams that make the packet switching process easy to understand, along with a discussion of the details. If you find it easier to understand and retain information that you listen to, as opposed to read, Circuit Switching versus Packet Switching at **www.seas.upenn.edu/~ross/lectures/ over/cs_vs_ps.htm** includes an audio file of a 15 minute lecture.

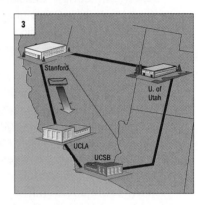

12 Network Standards

The major network standards include Ethernet, Token Ring, ARCnet, FDDI, and ATM. Bay Networks has provided Networking: A Primer at **www.baynetworks.com/Products/Papers/wp-primer.html** that begins with background information on LANs, reviews all of the major network protocols, and discusses hubs, bridges, routers and switches. To learn more about Ethernet check out Lantronix's Ethernet Tutorial at **www.lantronix.com/htmfiles/mrktg/catalog/et.htm**. Lantronix has produced Ethernet and Fast Ethernet connectivity products since 1989. Charles Spurgeon's Ethernet Web Site at **wwwhost.ots.utexas.edu/ethernet/** displays a drawing of the first Ethernet systems and includes links to technical papers, a list of vendors, configuration guides, frequently asked questions, and Ethernet Usenet groups. The Alliance for Strategic Token Ring Advancement and Leadership presents "An Educational Guide to Token Ring" at **www.astral.org/astrlwp1.html**. The guide discusses cost of network ownership, the need for bandwidth, and what to expect in the future in addition to the basics of the Token Ring standard. You can find ARCNet features and benefits, a resource guide, and a list of companies with example applications at the ARCNET Trade Association at **www.arcnet.com/**. Cisco Systems presents a thorough discussion of Fiber Distributed Data Interface (FDDI) at **www.cisco.com/univercd/data/doc/cintrnet/ito/55773.htm**. Another good source of information about FDDI is the FDDI Web page at **jmazza.shillsdata.com/tech/fddi/**. To learn about the ATM standard, connect to the Aynchronous Transfer Mode Tutorial at **www.npac.syr.edu/users/mahesh/ homepage/atm_tutorial/**. The Cell Relay Retreat at **cell-relay.indiana.edu/cell-relay/** has links to documents that will help you get started with ATM, including a FAQ, dictionary, acronyms list, and tutorials, among many other resources.

13 TCP/IP

A good, but detailed overview of TCP/IP by Gary Kessler is on the Web at **www.hill.com/library/tcpip.html**. When you use a dial-up line to access the Internet, you need a special version of TCP/IP, such as SLIP or PPP. For an introduction to TCP/IP, PPP, and SLIP, including what they are and how to use them, read "Chapter 11: WinSock, PPP, and SLIP" at **ss2.mcp.com/resources/geninternet/frame_iskm.html** from the book *Internet Starter Kit* by Adam Engst (Hayden Books, 1996). The Windows 95 Page: Configuring Dial-Up Internet Access at **www.halcyon.com/cerelli/dialup.htm** provides step-by-step directions on how to add a dial-up networking adapter to the Windows 95 control panel and how to add and configure the TCP/IP protocol. Windows95.com: Internet Connection Set Up at **www.windows95.com/connect/tcp.html** sets out to make dial-up networking easy. It includes detailed, step-by-step, illustrated instructions on establishing PPP, SLIP, and PPP Dial-back connections. The SLIP/PPP Homepage at **sunsite.nus.sg/pub/slip-ppp/** discusses accessing the Internet, what is SLIP/PPP, the differences between SLIP and PPP, what hardware and software you need, what kind of SLIP/PPP account to get, and how to find an Internet Service Provider.

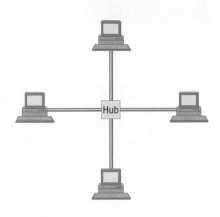

14 Telecommuting

Do network protocols, high speed telecommunications lines, video conferencing, and mobile computing have any practical relevance for most of us? The answer is a resounding yes! According to the most recent surveys, 11 million Americans were telecommuting—working from their homes—in 1997; by 2000 about 14 million people are expected to be telecommuting. Network protocols, high speed telecommunications, and new applications are making this shift from office work to home work possible. The benefits of telecommuting are legion. Experts claim that telecommuting can decrease traffic congestion and air pollution; reduce stress and help promote a balance between work and personal life; and increase productivity and reduce overhead costs. Telecommute America! at **www.att.com/Telecommute_America/index.html** is the Web site of a public-private initiative developed to educate people about telecommuting. At this Web site you can find information about telecommuting, view visual examples of telecommuting jobs, and find links to other telecommuting resources on the Internet. The Advocates for Remote Employment and the Virtual Office Web site at **www.globaldialog.com/~morse/arevo/index.htm** lists the many benefits of telecommuting, provides some advice on how to set up an office for remote employment, and provides links to additional resources on the Internet. There are two professional organizations for people interested in telecommuting, The International Telework Association at **www.telecommute.org/** and The American Telecommuting Association at **www.knowledgetree.com/ata.html**. At Extreme Telecommuting, **www.officeodyssey.com./**, you can follow the odyssey of Sid and Kristanne, who telecommuted across North America in 1997.

Review

1 Arrange the boldface terms in this chapter into one of the following categories: communications services, communications protocols, communications devices, communications channels, and miscellaneous.

2 Without looking back in this chapter, try to sketch out Shannon's communications system model and add appropriate labels. When your sketch is complete, compare it to Figure 11-1 and make any necessary corrections.

3 List and describe some of the different services offered by telephone companies for data communications.

4 Describe how you could use the cellular phone system to access the Internet.

5 List the advantages and disadvantages of cable modems for Internet access.

6 Design a poster illustrating how packet switching works.

7 This chapter provided an example of simplex (radio), half-duplex (CB radio), and full-duplex (telephone) communications. Can you think of at least one more example of each?

8 Suppose you are a computer packaging data for transmission and you must assign a parity bit. Given each of the following bytes and the required parity, fill in the table to indicate if you would add a 1 or a 0 as the parity bit:

Byte	Parity	Parity bit (1 or 0)
10000011	even	
11100100	even	
00000000	even	
10011001	odd	
10000111	odd	
11111110	odd	

9 Make a list of the communications links in the *Communications Links* section and note the advantages and/or disadvantages of each.

10 Associate the following terms with either a network standard, network communications protocol, or network topology:

Star	Ethernet	CSMA/CD
Token	Token Ring	Bus
IPX	TCP/IP	Ring

11 Use the New Perspectives CD-ROM to take a practice test or to review the new terms presented in this chapter.

Projects

1
INTERNET Optional

Communications Archeologist Using information from this chapter, from your library, and the Internet, make a list of important artifacts (objects) in the evolution of communications systems. Make sure you can associate a date with each of these artifacts. Now suppose it is the year 2500 and you are an archeologist newly arrived from another planet. You see these artifacts in a museum. How would you use them to explain the evolution of communications systems on planet Earth? Write a report detailing your theories about the evolution of Earth communications systems, using diagrams, timelines, and other visual elements.

2 **Phone, Cable, or Satellite?** You can access the Internet using the telephone, cable, or satellite systems. Which one would be best for you? Research the Internet access options that are available in your area, then, answer the following questions:

a. If available, what is the cost of ISDN service from your local phone company?

b. Does your cable company offer Internet access? If so, what is the cost of the equipment you'll need? What are the charges for Internet access?

c. Is direct satellite service available in your area for Internet access? If so, what is the cost of equipment and access?

d. Which system would you prefer for accessing the Internet? Why?

3 **2001 Today** In 1945 a young British engineer and aspiring writer (who later wrote the science fiction classic, *2001: A Space Odyssey*) conceived the idea of artificial satellites that would orbit the earth in geosynchronous orbit. It was not until 1960 that the United States launched an inflatable satellite called Echo I, which transmitted and received voice, music, and data from Earth. Satellite technology opened up new horizons in communications, now incorporated in telephone and cable TV systems. Use your library and Internet resources to learn more about satellite technology. Then create a brief information brochure describing satellite technology. You can select your target audience (elementary school children, college students, seniors, science club members, etc.). Your instructor might specify that you should use word processing or desktop publishing software to produce your brochure.

4 **The Scoop on Data Communications** Suppose you are a news reporter for your student newspaper. What do you think other students would like to know about using their computers for data communications? Write a two-page article targeted at student use of the communications infrastructure available at your school.

5 **Communications in the Workplace** Your career field probably makes extensive use of communications technologies. To prepare for your career you should understand which communications technologies are used and how to use them. Research and write a paper describing how communications technologies are used in your career field. At the end of the paper, include a list of these technologies. Check off those that you currently know how to use.

6 **Communications Tour** Arrange to tour an office at your school or a local business. As part of the tour, interview your tour guide about technologies used for internal and external communications. Don't forget low-tech options such as U.S. mail. Create a diagram to illustrate what you learned about the flow of communications into and out of the office you toured.

7 **Alexander Graham Bell** Many of today's communications technologies are based on Bell's research and inventions. Born in Scotland, Bell emigrated to the United States, but lived much of his life in Canada. When he married, his wedding present to his wife was all but ten of his shares in his newly-formed company, Bell Telephone. Use the Internet and the library to find out more about Bell's life and research, then write a brief biographical sketch describing his impact on today's communications systems.

8  **The Worldwide Wait** As more and more people use the Internet for communications, the more difficult it becomes to provide the necessary bandwidth for fast access. Use the Internet and your library to find information on the Internet bandwidth problem. Make sure that you use references less than 12 months old because Internet technology is changing very rapidly. Write a summary of the current Internet bandwidth, and recent proposals to increase it. Your instructor will provide guidelines on the length and format for your paper.

9 **Is It Shrinking?** We've all heard people exclaim that communications are shrinking the globe. It's an understandable image for a world in which you can pick up a telephone and call someone in Singapore or watch television images of events taking place right now in virtually any country in the world. But how does this technology affect people? What are the advantages and the disadvantages of instant access and worldwide communications? Make a list of at least 10 advantages and disadvantages. Then do a little research to find out what the experts think. Write an essay that presents your opinion about how society can best deal with the impact of new and planned communications technologies. Your instructor will give you guidelines for the essay's length and format.

10 **Distance Learning and the Virtual Classroom** In this chapter's *End Note* section you heard from someone who had taken a university course without going to campus. Referred to as "distance education," such courses are being taken by an increasing number of students who complete them at home with the use of computer and communications technology. Suppose you were enrolled in a distance

education program this semester. How would you receive and submit your assignments, do research, and communicate with your instructors and with other students? Imagine that you had access to any computer and communications technologies that exist today, and suppose that money is no object—what would be your ideal distance education environment? Write a paper describing a typical "school day" with your ideal distance education environment and explain the technologies you would use for the courses you are taking this semester.

Lab Assignments

Building a Network

 How many times have you waited in line to use the computers in your school labs? Here's your chance to become a computer lab manager and see if you can please all the students who use your labs. In the Building a Network Lab, you control a simulated computer network that provides services to student computer labs and to students dialing in from home. By monitoring usage and installing new equipment, see if you can make all your students happy!

1 Click the Steps button to learn how to use the simulation to monitor and configure the network. As you work through the Steps, answer all of the Quick Check questions that appear. After you complete the Steps, you will see a Quick Check Summary Report of your answers. Follow the directions on the screen to print this report.

2 In Explore, use File/Open to set up the network configuration stored as **msu.net**. Record the statistics for one day in Figure 11-31 provided, then answer questions a through e.

Figure 11-31

Time	Lab users without work-stations	Remote users without access	File server load	Printer load
8:00				
9:00				
10:00				
11:00				
Noon				
1:00				
2:00				
3:00				
4:00				
5:00				
6:00				
7:00				
8:00				
9:00				
10:00				
11:00				

a. How many hours during the day are more than 25 percent of the lab users without computer access?

b. Are remote users satisfied with the level of dial-in service?

c. Would you characterize the printer load as high or low?

d. Does the current demand exceed the capacity of the file server?

e. What should you do to improve the network to meet demand?

3 In Explore, install a network hub and a file server in the Tech Room. Install a print server with an attached printer in Lab 1. Install another print server and attach a printer in Lab 2. Install three workstations in Lab 1 and five workstations in Lab 2. Record the statistics for one day in Figure 11-32, then answer questions a through e.

a. How many hours during the day are more than 25 percent of the lab users without computer access?

b. Are remote users satisfied with the level of dial-in service?

c. Would you characterize the printer load as high or low?

d. Is the current demand exceeding the capacity of the file server?

e. What should you do to improve the network to meet demand?

4 In Explore, use File/Open to set up the network configuration stored as **wfcc.net**. Use no more than 30 devices to construct what you think is an optimal network for the students in the simulation. (Hint: Don't forget to save your network frequently on your floppy disk as you are working on it.) Make sure you test your network for at least five days. The percentage of students unable to access workstations and modems should rarely go above 25 percent. Server and printer loads should never reach 100 percent. After you are satisfied with your network, print out your network configuration report.

Figure 11-32

Time	Lab users without work- stations	Remote users with- out access	File server load	Printer load
8:00				
9:00				
10:00				
11:00				
Noon				
1:00				
2:00				
3:00				
4:00				
5:00				
6:00				
7:00				
8:00				
9:00				
10:00				
11:00				

In J.R.R. Tolkien's classic adventure novel, *The Hobbit*, an eccentric wizard sends a hobbit named Bilbo Baggins on a dangerous expedition in search of a fabulous treasure guarded by a cranky old dragon. Bilbo bustles off without a hat, walking stick, money, or (as he suddenly realizes) any handkerchiefs! "Don't worry," says one of his fellow adventurers, "you will have to manage without pocket-handkerchiefs, and a good many other things, before you get to the journey's end."

In contrast to Bilbo's pitifully-equipped departure, modern expeditions are carefully orchestrated events requiring high-tech gear, ranging from deep-water submersible vessels to freeze-dried ice cream.

Abercrombie & Livingston Outfitters, Ltd, has provisioned hundreds of expeditions that challenge human skill, knowledge, and endurance. In addition to supplies, A&L provides highly respected expertise on appropriate gear for any terrain or climate. A&L's main offices are located in London. Branch outlets are spread across the globe in Telluride, Katmandu, Geneva, Lima, Guatemala City, and Dar es Salaam.

A&L relies on a computerized information system to conduct business efficiently and effectively. An **information system** collects, maintains, and provides information to people. Today, many information systems are computerized. These computerized information systems can be defined as the computers, peripheral devices, programs, data, people, and procedures that work together to record, store, process, and distribute information. In this chapter, the terms "information system" and "computer information system" are used interchangeably to refer to information systems that are computerized. This chapter describes how computer systems like the one at A&L Outfitters—a fictitious company—help businesses and organizations function effectively.

CHAPTERPREVIEW

As you read this chapter, you should think about the relationship between people, organizations, and information. Consider the ways you interact with organizations: You make purchases from sales organizations, you are a student in an educational organization, you will probably have a career as an employee of an organization—you might even create your own organization. The information you learn in this chapter will help you interact with organizations as a client, customer, employee, or founder. After you have completed this chapter you should be able to:

- Provide examples of mission statements from for-profit and non-profit organizations
- Classify the activities that take place in a typical business
- Discuss some trends that affect the way organizations operate
- Describe the information needs of executives, managers, and workers
- Provide examples of office automation that make significant improvements in the way an organization operates
- Describe the transaction processing systems typically used in businesses
- Differentiate between an MIS and a DSS
- Explain how an expert system works

A Organizational Structure

Drucker
2

According to Peter Drucker, one of today's most influential writers about business and management, "the purpose of an organization is to enable ordinary people to do extraordinary things." Organizations have accomplished amazing feats such as sending astronauts into space, building a huge communications network, and inventing freeze-dried ice cream.

An **organization** is a group of people working together to accomplish a goal. You are probably a member of an organization, such as a student club, a fraternity or sorority, a sports team, or a political party. You also deal with many organizations every day: your school, stores, banks, and government agencies. Many organizations use computers to operate more effectively, gather information, and accomplish tasks. In this section, you'll review some basic concepts about organizations and businesses. These concepts give you a foundation for understanding how computers and related technologies enhance organizational activities.

Business
3

Types of Organizations

What's the difference between an organization and a business? You have learned that an organization is a group of people working together toward a goal. Any organization that seeks profit by providing goods and services is called a **business**. A&L Outfitters is an example of a business that was formed to make a profit selling expedition equipment. Some organizations are formed to accomplish political or charitable goals that do not include amassing personal profit. These organizations are known as non-profit organizations.

Mission
Statements
4

Every organization has a **mission**—a goal or plan. All the activities that take place in an organization, including those activities that involve computers, should contribute to this mission. The written expression of an organization's mission is called a **mission statement**. A mission statement describes not only an organization's goals, but also how those goals will be accomplished. For example, the mission of A&L Outfitters is to make a profit by providing high-quality equipment and services for professional expeditions in mountain, jungle, and polar environments. Companies publish their mission statements in corporate reports and on the Web, as shown in Figure 12-1.

Figure 12-1

At Course Technology's corporate Web site, you can find the company's mission statement.

Organizational Activities

Are there activities that all organizations have in common? Computer and communications technologies help organizations carry out many activities. It is useful to look at some of the broad categories of organizational activities where information systems are applied. Most organizational activities fall into the four functional groups shown in Figure 12-2.

Figure 12-2

Four functional groups common to most organizations

Operations	Financial Management
Sales and Marketing	Human Resources Management

The primary activities of an organization are called **production** or **operations**. Different organizations carry out different production activities. For example, a university educates students. An automobile manufacturer makes cars. A hospital provides health care. A&L Outfitters sells expedition equipment and provides expedition support services.

In addition to production, every organization must manage its money. A university tracks tuition payments, payroll, and maintenance expenses. An automobile maker tracks manufacturing costs, payroll expenses, and income from sales. A hospital tracks patient bills, insurance payments, staff wages, and supply expenses. A&L Outfitters tracks the cost of the equipment it sells, customer payments, and expenses for salaries, rents, and business taxes. Tracking the flow of money through an organization is referred to as **accounting** or **financial management**.

Most organizations need to promote their activities. A university needs to let prospective students know what educational services it provides. An automobile manufacturer must advertise its products. A hospital needs to convince patients that it can best serve their health care needs. A&L Outfitters advertises its products and services in specialized mountaineering and expedition magazines. Advertising and promoting an organization is called **sales and marketing**, or **public relations**.

Organizations are made up of people. University faculty, staff, and administrators; automotive workers and managers; and health care workers in a hospital must be hired, evaluated, and supervised. A&L Outfitters hires sales associates, experienced expedition consultants, purchasing agents, shippers, maintenance workers, and managers. It must keep track of these employees' salaries and benefits, evaluate how well they perform their jobs, and plan how to best use each employee's skills and talents. Keeping track of employees in an organization is referred to as **human resource management**.

Computers are increasingly being deployed to assist the tasks in all four of these functional groups. You'll read about some specific examples later in this chapter.

Trends and Challenges

Today's organizations can't function without computers, right? Computers are certainly an important aspect of organizational activities. Organizations exist in a rapidly changing and competitive environment where opportunities and threats abound. A well-known business analyst, Michael Porter, created the Five Forces model, shown in Figure 12-3, to illustrate the interaction between these opportunities and threats.

Figure 12-3

Five Forces model

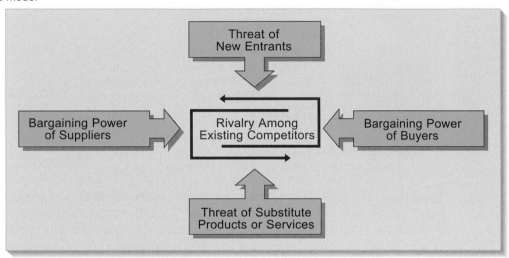

Competition
5

To be successful in its mission, an organization must respond effectively to opportunities and threats. But what is an effective response? An organization has a choice of three fundamental strategies. First, it can become better at what it does, for example, by lowering costs and prices, by improving its products or services, or by offering better customer service. A second response is to change the structure of an industry. For example, the film industry previously generated income only from movie theater ticket sales. Video rental stores significantly redefined this industry by providing an alternative way to view films. As a third response, an organization can create a new product or service. The music industry responded to pirated music tapes by promoting difficult-to-copy audio CD technology.

Business analysts continuously devise variations of these three fundamental strategies. Popular strategies include use of technology, downsizing, total quality management, re-engineering, benchmarking, "just in time" inventory, and employee empowerment. Let's look at how A&L has responded to some of the challenges it faced throughout the years.

A&L was founded in 1892. At first it had only one office, located in the heart of London. Business was conducted in person and by mail until A&L installed a revolutionary technology, the telephone. The telephone enhanced communications between A&L, its customers, and its suppliers. However, the telephone did nothing to change the basic way employees processed and shipped customer orders—everything was done manually.

In the 1950s, "automation" was fashionable. A&L installed a system of pneumatic tubes to transport order forms quickly from the salesroom to the warehouse. **Automation** is the use of electrical or mechanical devices to improve manufacturing or other processes.

The company added branch outlets in the 1970s and took a big step into **computerization**. A&L purchased a minicomputer and hired information system staff to write programs to process orders and track inventory. The computer system was a success—A&L managers always knew what was in stock and could place timely orders to restock the warehouse.

InfoWeb

TQM
6

In the 1980s, despite the computerized inventory system, customers were defecting to competitors who promised faster delivery. A&L employed a technique called TQM to increase customer satisfaction by decreasing shipping times. **TQM (total quality management)** is a strategy in which an organization makes a commitment to analyzing and implementing ways to improve the quality of its products or services. A&L used computers to track the entire shipping process. Managers analyzed this data and then devised a plan to streamline shipping operations.

Shipping operations were further streamlined by distributing some of the warehousing operations to the outlets. Each outlet now kept its own stock of frequently ordered products, ready for immediate delivery. Employees in the outlets were empowered to make more decisions, such as what to stock for their local markets. **Employee empowerment** means giving employees the authority to make business decisions.

A&L's centralized minicomputer system was not designed for this distributed inventory structure, so in 1992 A&L managers decided to move to a completely new computerized inventory system. They decided to "rightsize" by moving inventory management from the minicomputer to networked microcomputers. **Rightsize** means to find the most effective configuration for computer resources. It often means moving operations from a mainframe computer system to a network of smaller computers.

InfoWeb

BPR
7

To further improve the company, A&L's managers considered **business process redesign** (BPR), sometimes referred to as **business process re-engineering**, which requires radical changes to existing business practices to achieve improvements in performance. They also considered **benchmarking**, in which a business measures its products, services, and practices against those of its toughest competitors.

Techniques for improving organizations fade in and out of popularity. What's important is that organizations continually strive to improve their products, services, and employees.

QuickCheck A

1. A(n) _____ system collects, maintains, and provides information to people.

2. All the activities that take place in an organization should contribute to the organizational _____.

3. Most organizations include four functional groups of organizational activities. True or false? _____

4. Organizations must successfully respond to opportunities and _____, or they will cease to exist.

5. _____ is the use of electrical or mechanical devices to improve manufacturing and other business processes.

6. _____ is a strategy in which an organization makes a commitment to analyzing and implementing ways to improve the quality of its products and services.

7. Many companies _____ by moving operations from a mainframe computer to a microcomputer network.

▣ People, Decisions, and Information

Every organization requires people. To coordinate the activities of its employees, most organizations have an organizational structure that arranges employees in ascending order of authority and pay. An organizational chart, such as the one in Figure 12-4, depicts the pyramid-shaped hierarchy of employees in an organization such as A&L Outfitters.

Figure 12-4

At the top of most organizations is a single individual. As you progress down the organizational chart, each level fans out to encompass more employees.

InfoWeb

Organizational Charts 8

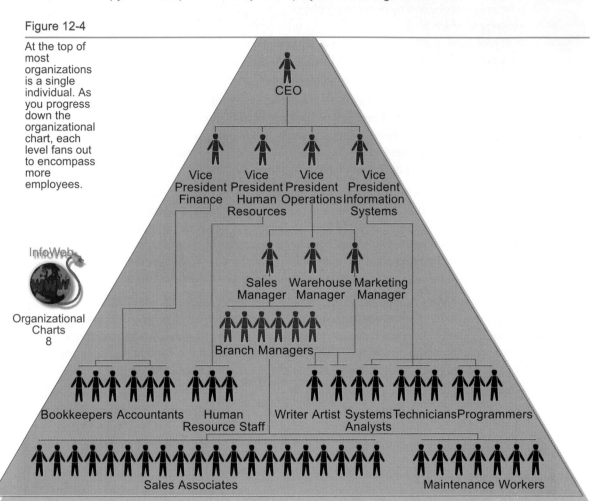

People in the organization pyramid can be classified as either workers or managers. **Workers** are the people who carry out the organization's mission. For example, they assemble cars, write newspaper articles, sell merchandise, answer telephones, lay bricks, cut trees, or fix engines. Workers are usually supervised by managers.

Managers make decisions about how an organization carries out its activities. They decide organizational goals and plan what steps to take to achieve those goals. Managers approve new products, authorize new construction, and supervise workers.

Workers and managers all perform activities that contribute to the success of an organization. Their activities frequently require decisions. To appreciate the significance of an information system, it's useful to understand the types of decisions made by people at each level of the organization pyramid.

Workers

Do workers use information systems? In today's workplace, a high percentage of workers use information systems and other computer or communications technologies. The technology available to a worker depends on what the organization provides and what is needed to do the job. Every worker's situation is unique, but it is possible to make some generalizations about the technology that workers use by looking at worker classifications. Some business experts classify workers as information workers, service workers, or goods workers. These workers are the foundation of the organization pyramid, as shown in Figure 12-5.

Figure 12-5

Worker classification in the organization pyramid

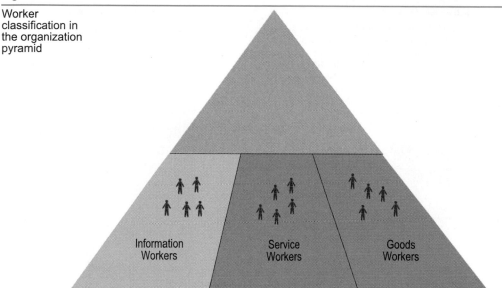

Information Workers

Service Workers

Goods Workers

Information workers produce and manipulate information. Examples of information workers include architects, writers, computer programmers, secretaries, and accountants. These workers often make extensive use of information systems. A computer is one of the information worker's most important tools.

Service workers are employees whose primary activity is delivering services to customers. Examples of service workers include waiters, sales associates, taxi drivers, nurses, and receptionists. Service workers often use information systems, but their main focus is person-to-person interaction.

Goods workers create and manipulate physical objects. Examples of goods workers include farmers, construction workers, assembly line workers, miners, mechanics, and plumbers. Goods workers sometimes use computerized equipment and robots to manipulate and analyze physical objects.

A&L employees include information workers and service workers. Like many of today's businesses, A&L does not have goods workers because it does not manufacture any products. According to the Department of Labor, less than 20% of the labor force in the United States is employed as goods workers. England, Canada, France, and Germany have workforces with similar compositions. Figure 12-6 on the next page, describes the jobs of A&L service and information workers.

Figure 12-6

A&L workers

Accountants and bookkeepers are information workers. They keep track of cash flowing in and out of the business. Some bookkeepers are responsible for sending customer bills and recording customer payments. Others make sure that A&L promptly pays its expenses for inventory, phone, electricity, and so on.

The human resource staff consists of secretarial and clerical information workers. They continually monitor employee contracts, insurance policies, and other benefit programs.

Sales associates are service workers. They help customers by taking orders and recommending products.

Systems analysts and programmers are information workers. They use computers to plan and implement changes to A&L's information system.

A&L's technicians are service workers who install, move, and repair in-house computers.

A&L's in-house writer and artist are information workers. The writer produces advertising copy and product descriptions, assisted by the artist, who supplies graphics. Both use computers to produce their work, and they make extensive use of online information services for ideas.

Managers

What managerial tasks are enhanced by information systems? Just as there are different types of workers, there are also different types of managers, with different responsibilities in an organization. Managers are classified as executive managers, middle managers, or supervisors, as shown in Figure 12-7.

Figure 12-7

Managerial levels of the organization pyramid

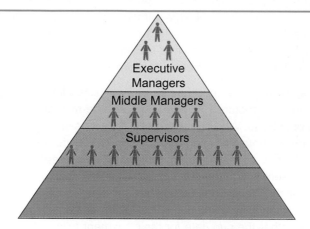

Executive managers, sometimes referred to as **senior managers**, make long-range plans and goals for the organization. Executives are the entrepreneurs who create new businesses under the expectation that they will be a long-range success. They select the mission statement for an organization. They also cultivate business relationships with bankers, politicians, and other industry leaders in case their influence is needed in the future. This emphasis on long-range and future goals is referred to as **strategic planning**.

A&L's founder stated the company's mission as "providing the highest quality expedition equipment and exceptional customer service." Today, A&L's chief executive officer, is trying to anticipate market changes in the next five to ten years. He is using A&L's information system to assist with this planning effort.

Middle managers are responsible for designing ways to achieve the plans laid out by executive managers. In general, middle managers decide how to deploy human, financial, and natural resources to achieve organizational goals. This type of action planning is referred to as **tactical planning**.

At A&L, middle managers are responsible for figuring out how to achieve the founder's goals of providing the highest quality equipment and exceptional customer service. Several years ago, a group of managers made plans to create a quality assurance lab to test new products. The managers used data from A&L's information system to identify financial resources for the new test lab. Using these financial resources, they found a suitable location and hired employees to staff the lab. The managers now use the information system to monitor the ongoing expenses of the lab.

Supervisors are managers who deal primarily with day-to-day operations. They schedule and monitor workers and processes. Scheduling and monitoring are sometimes referred to as **operational planning**. At A&L, the quality assurance lab supervisor receives a list of new products. Using computerized scheduling capabilities provided by A&L's information system, the supervisor assigns each product to a tester and schedules the test date. After testing a product, test results are stored in the information system so they can be accessed by sales associates who are consulting with customers.

Problems and Decisions

For what purpose do workers and managers use information systems? One of the major functions of an information system is to help people make decisions in response to problems. Problems occur at all levels of an organization and require strategic, tactical, or operational solutions and decisions. According to Herbert Simon, who is well-known for his insights into organizational behavior and for his pioneering role in artificial intelligence, the decision-making process has three phases. First, a person must recognize a problem or a need to make a decision. Next, a person has to devise and analyze possible solutions or actions to solve the problem. Finally, a person selects an action or solution. Sometimes, the decision-making phases are clear-cut, objective, standardized, and based on factual data. At other times, decision-making is more intuitive.

All problems are not alike, but they can be classified into three types: structured, semi-structured, and unstructured. Everyday, run-of-the-mill, and routine problems are called **structured problems**. When people make decisions in response to structured problems, the procedure for obtaining the best solution is known, the objective is clearly defined, and the information necessary to make the decision is easy to identify. An example of a structured problem is figuring out which customers should receive overdue notices. The information for this decision is usually stored in a file cabinet or in a computer system. The method for reaching a solution is to look for customers with an outstanding balance, then check whether the due date for their payment falls before today's date.

Semi-structured problems are less routine than structured problems. When solving a semi-structured problem, the procedure for arriving at a solution is usually known; however, it might involve some degree of subjective judgment. Also, some of the information regarding the problem might not be available, might lack precision, or might be uncertain. An example of a semi-structured problem at A&L is how to respond to last year's increase in the number of rain forest expeditions. Should A&L stock more warm-weather gear? Should it increase advertising in ecology publications? Managers at A&L can use data on last year's sales, last year's advertising, and projected advertising budgets to make the decision. However, there is no firm data about how many rain forest expeditions will actually take place. Therefore, the decision involves a degree of uncertainty.

Unstructured problems require human intuition as the basis for decision making. Information relevant to the problem might be missing, and few, if any, parts of the decision can be tackled using concrete models. An example of an unstructured problem at A&L would be whether to decrease inventory levels of cold-weather equipment in response to global warming trends. Inventory and sales information on cold-weather equipment exists for past years. However, information on global warming, though it exists, is not definitive. To determine future inventory levels of cold-weather equipment, someone at A&L will have to make an educated guess based on historical inventory data and inconclusive information on climactic changes.

Computer information systems help people solve structured, semi-structured, and even unstructured problems. However, the degree of assistance an information system provides will vary with the problem. Traditionally, computers have contributed most to solving structured, routine, and repetitive problems. Although some computer tools can be applied to unstructured problems, these problems are still often resolved based on someone's "gut feeling."

Information and Information Analysis Tools

Where do computers get the information that they supply to the workers and managers who make decisions? Information systems are designed to collect information that workers and managers need to make decisions. This information comes from both internal and external sources. Organizations generate **internal information** about inventory levels, cash flow, personnel, customers, orders, sales, and so on. Today, this internal information is increasingly generated with the help of computerized input devices such as terminals, bar-code readers, and personal computers. Once it is generated, the information is stored in an information system.

Organizations collect **external information** from outside sources. External information, unlike internal information, is typically not stored permanently in an organization's information system. Instead, it is collected when needed for a specific purpose, then erased later when it is no longer needed.

Using Internet resources and other communications capabilities, it is becoming increasingly easy to collect external information about competitors' products, pricing, finances, and plans. Such information is often available from a company's Web site or from sites housing business publications or analyses. Organizations can also collect external information, such as mailing lists and credit reports, about potential customers. Other readily available external information includes patent information, demographics, labor statistics, maps, and government documents. Figure 12-8 illustrates one popular Web site for gathering external information on business competitors.

Figure 12-8

The Zacks Web site provides competitive information and news about businesses.

Information systems supply workers and managers with reports and information analysis software tools to manipulate information. Most information systems periodically produce a fixed set of reports, such as daily cash receipts or monthly sales summaries. In addition, some information systems allow users to customize their own reports to provide the right information in the right format for making a decision.

Information analysis tools help people model problems, then find a logical path to a solution or decision. Information analysis tools include spreadsheets, flow charts, and special-purpose analysis software, such as the package shown in Figure 12-9.

Figure 12-9

Using Criterium DecisionPlus to select a college, you define criteria such as cost and academic program. After you provide weights for each criterion, the software displays a graph ranking each school.

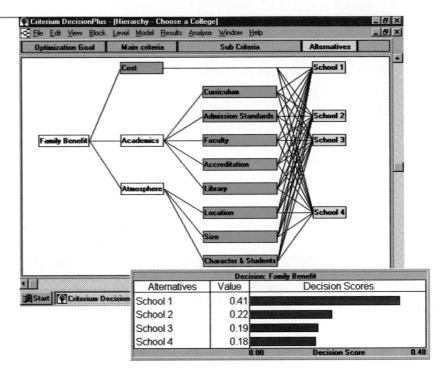

QuickCheck B

1 _____ is the highest level of management in the organizational pyramid.

2 Less than 20% of the U.S. labor force is _____ workers.

3 The managerial activity that emphasizes long-range and future goals is called _____ planning.

4 Middle managers are typically responsible for _____ planning.

5 _____ problems require human intuition as the basis for decision making.

6 _____ information is generated by the organization itself, whereas _____ information is collected from sources outside the organization.

C Information Systems

The purpose of an information system is to improve the effectiveness of an organization by providing useful, accurate, and timely information. For example, a computerized information system helps A&L Outfitters improve the effectiveness of its operations by providing data communications among outlets, tracking orders from customers, scheduling shipments to expedition base camps, and tracking inventory at each branch outlet.

An information system might have one or more of the following components or subsystems: an office automation system, a transaction processing system, a management information system, a decision support system, and an expert system. Let's take a closer look at each of these systems.

Office Automation

Does an information system automate routine office tasks? As its name suggests, an **office automation system** "automates," or computerizes, routine office tasks such as producing documents, tracking schedules, making calculations, and facilitating interoffice voice and written communication. Word processing, spreadsheet, scheduling, and electronic mail software are integral parts of most office automation systems. The table in Figure 12-10 lists some of the ways computers have automated offices.

Figure 12-10

Office automation

Document distribution	LANs, intranets, and the Internet make it easy to electronically store, distribute, and access memos, reports, and other data
Schedules	Scheduling software tracks appointments for numerous employees and automatically determines workable times for group meetings
Communications	Voice mail and e-mail have made telephone tag virtually obsolete
Form letters	Word-processing and database software save secretaries the effort of typing and retyping form letters
Forms	Now displayed on a computer screen so that as data is entered it is automatically incorporated into a database and can be routed for necessary approvals
Presentations	Presentation graphics software helps design and display a computer-generated slide show
Calculations	Spreadsheet software replaces pencil, paper, and calculators

InfoWeb

Office Automation
9

The office automation system at A&L uses electronic mail to overcome the problem of communicating between outlets in seven time zones. Word-processing software helps with routine correspondence, such as responses to inquiries from potential customers, congratulatory messages to successful expeditions, and letters to suppliers. In the London office, scheduling software maintains appointment calendars for A&L sales agents and executives.

Transaction Processing

How does an organization collect information on production or operations? In an information system context, a **transaction** is an event that requires a manual or computer-based activity. When you order a product by mail or when you buy merchandise in a store, you are involved in a transaction. When you make a phone call or when you pay your phone bill, you are also involved in a transaction. Most transactions require a sequence of steps. For example, to pay your phone bill, you must receive the bill, write a check for the amount, and place the check in the mail. Then, the post office must deliver your payment to the phone company, and the phone company must record the payment. For the transaction to be successful, all the steps of the transaction must be completed. If even one step fails, the entire transaction has failed.

InfoWeb

Transaction
Processing
10

Production or operations activities usually involve one or more transactions. A **transaction processing system** (TPS) keeps track of all the transactions for an organization by providing a way to collect, display, modify, or cancel transactions. The transaction data is stored in files or databases. Usually, a transaction processing system uses the data it has collected about transactions to produce a regularly-scheduled set of reports, such as monthly bills, weekly paychecks, annual inventory summary, daily manufacturing schedules, or periodic check registers. Figure 12-11 diagrams the processes that take place in a typical transaction processing system.

Figure 12-11

Characteristics of a
transaction processing
system

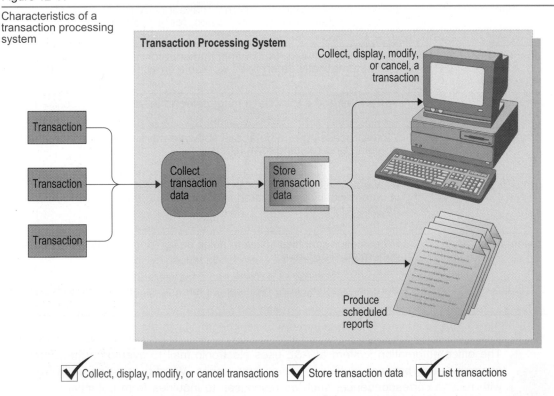

Transaction Processing System

Collect, display, modify, or cancel, a transaction

Transaction

Transaction

Transaction

Collect transaction data

Store transaction data

Produce scheduled reports

✓ Collect, display, modify, or cancel transactions   ✓ Store transaction data   ✓ List transactions

Some examples of transaction processing systems that are found in businesses today include:

- An **order-entry/invoice system** provides a way to input, view, modify, and delete customer orders. It helps track the status of each order, and it creates invoices.

- A **point-of-sale (POS) system** records items purchased at each cash register and calculates the total amount due for each sale. Some POS systems automatically verify credit cards, calculate change, and identify customers who have previously written bad checks.

- A **general accounting system** records the financial status of a business by keeping track of income, expenses, and assets.

Transaction processing systems at A&L Outfitters computerize order entry, invoicing, inventory control, and general accounting. Study Figure 12-12 to learn how A&L's order entry system processes transactions for customer orders.

Figure 12-12

A&L Outfitter's transaction processing system

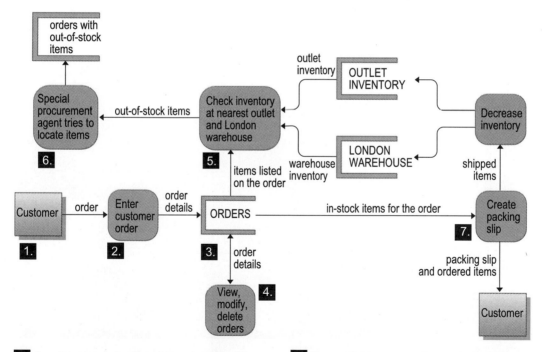

1. A customer wants to order equipment and supplies.

2. A sales representative takes an order from a customer by entering the customer's selections on a microcomputer connected to A&L's network. Occasionally, A&L agents are dispatched to remote locations, where they take orders on a notebook computer, then send the completed order to the London office using a modem.

3. The order is stored on the network file server.

4. Sales associates can modify an order if a customer wants to add or change items. If an expedition is canceled, the order can be deleted.

5. Each item on the order is checked against the existing inventory. If it is not in stock at the local outlet, a telecommunications link to London checks to see if the item is available from the central warehouse.

6. Ordered items that are not in stock locally or in the central warehouse are tracked down by a special procurement agent.

7. A list of available items becomes the packing slip that accompanies the shipment to the customer.

Management Information Systems

How can the data collected by a transaction processing system be presented in a format more conducive to decision making? A transaction processing system is designed mainly for use by clerical personnel to record transactions. Most transaction processing systems generate a limited number of reports that provide a basic record of completed transactions. However, managers need more sophisticated reports to help them understand and analyze data. These reports are usually created by a management information system.

The term **management information system**, or **MIS**, is used in two different contexts. It can be a synonym for the term "information system," or it can refer to a specific category or type of information system. We'll use it in this second context to refer to a type of information system that uses the data collected by a transaction processing system but manipulates that data to create reports that managers can use to make routine business decisions in response to structured problems. As Figure 12-13 shows, an MIS is characterized by the production of routine reports that managers use for structured and routine tasks.

Figure 12-13

Characteristics of a
management
information system

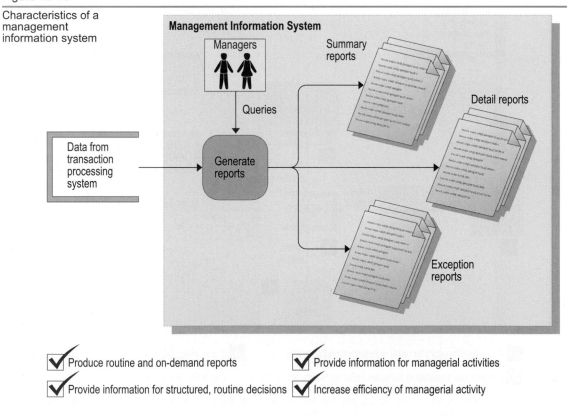

✔ Produce routine and on-demand reports   ✔ Provide information for managerial activities

✔ Provide information for structured, routine decisions   ✔ Increase efficiency of managerial activity

One of the major goals of an MIS is to increase the efficiency of managerial activity. As you learned earlier in this chapter, different levels of management have different information needs. In response to these different needs, a management information system produces several types of reports. A **detail report** is an organized list, for example, a report of inventory items alphabetized by product name. Such reports are suitable for some supervisory activities, but they are rarely used for tactical or strategic planning. A **summary report** combines or groups data and often shows totals. For example, a summary report might show the total annual sales for the past five years. Summary reports are useful in tactical and strategic planning. An **exception report** like the one in Figure 12-14 contains information that is outside of normal or acceptable ranges, such as a reorder report showing low-stock items in inventory.

Figure 12-14

Exception reports help managers take action, such as reordering inventory. Managers also use exception reports to analyze potential problems, such as continued inventory shortages or large numbers of customers making late payments.

Low Stock Inventory - London			
Item#	**Description**	**QOH**	**Vendor**
00876543	Qualo-fil Sleeping bag	3	REI
00887654	Sm. Alum. Back pack - red	10	Sierra
01456788	Waterproof matches	23	Striker

The A&L management information system supplies managers of branch outlets with many reports, produced on a daily, weekly, or monthly basis. Once a day, the managers at each branch outlet receive a summary report showing the number of orders filled, the total amount due for the orders, the number of payments received, and the total amount of all the payments. On a weekly basis, the inventory manager of each branch outlet receives a report that lists inventory items that need to be reordered. Every month each branch outlet manager receives a summary report of total income and expenses for the branch. Also on a monthly basis, the Vice President of Sales in the London office receives a summary report showing income and expenses for all the branches, along with the total profit for the entire company.

To create these reports, the MIS sorts, extracts, and totals the data from the transaction processing system. The specifications for most of these reports were created by A&L's information systems department when the MIS was designed. Managers at A&L can also request additional customized reports if the current reports do not meet their needs. However, managers can request reports based only on the data collected by the TPS and MIS systems. To incorporate data from external information systems or to create data models of "what-if" scenarios, A&L's managers would need to use a decision support system.

Decision Support Systems

Can managers and workers get information relevant to problems that weren't anticipated when the information system was designed? A **decision support system**, or **DSS**, allows

InfoWeb

DSS
11

users to manipulate data directly, to incorporate data from external sources, and to create data models of "what-if" scenarios. A DSS is designed to help managers and workers make non-routine decisions, such as solving semi-structured problems in which the decision might be based on imprecise data or might require "guesstimates." Decision makers use a DSS to design decision models and make queries. A **decision model** is a numerical representation of a realistic situation, such as a cash flow model of a business that shows how income adds to cash accounts and expenses deplete those accounts. A **decision query** is a question or set of instructions that describes the data that needs to be gathered to make a decision.

A decision support system derives its name from the fact that it "supports" the decision maker, that is, it provides the tools the decision maker needs to examine the data. However, a DSS does not make decisions—that remains the role of the human decision maker.

A DSS typically includes modeling tools, such as spreadsheets, so managers can create a numerical representation of a situation and explore "what-if" alternatives. A DSS also typically includes statistical tools so managers can study trends before making a decision. A DSS usually includes data from the organization's transaction processing system, but it might also include or access external data such as stock market reports, as shown in Figure 12-15.

Figure 12-15

Characteristics of a decision
support system

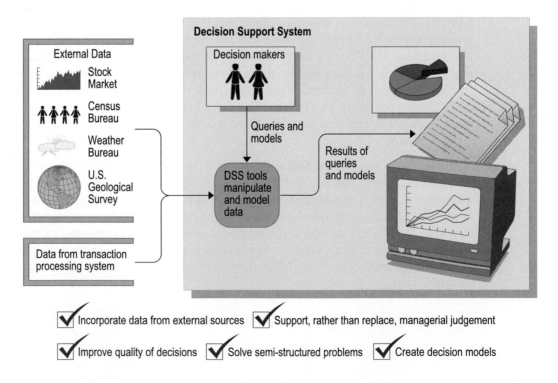

The managers at A&L Outfitters use their DSS to tackle diverse problems because it contains a good selection of decision support tools. For example, one A&L branch outlet manager is using the DSS to project next year's sales of cold-weather camping equipment. To make this projection, he first retrieves from the A&L transaction processing system the data on the past two years' sales of each item of cold-weather camping equipment. He then transfers the data into a spreadsheet so he can manipulate it and examine several "what-if" scenarios. He uses the DSS link to a commercial information service to filter through articles about camping, recreation, and weather. For example, the manager discovers that weather systems last year were especially intense. Because of the bad weather, expeditions to cold climates were not advisable and sales of cold-weather equipment declined.

Next, the manager uses the DSS to search through an A&L database that contains information on all the expeditions of the past five years. The DSS helps him create a graph showing that expeditions to cold regions declined last year after a steady increase for the previous three years. Should he gamble and assume that last year was an unusual deviation in a steadily increasing cold-weather equipment market? By manipulating the data in the spreadsheet, the manager looks at best- and worse-case scenarios and decides that it is not too risky to order 5% more cold-weather camping equipment.

Expert Systems and Neural Networks

InfoWeb

Expert Systems 12

Do information systems ever make decisions? You've just seen how a DSS helps a manager manipulate the data necessary to make a decision. However, the DSS does not make a decision. The manager must analyze the data and reach a decision. The DSS does not substitute for the judgment of the manager, which is appropriate in situations where trained professionals are making decisions. However, in many organizations, it would be useful if every decision did not need to be made by a highly paid expert.

An **expert system**, or **knowledge-based system**, is a computer system designed to analyze data and produce a recommendation or decision. An expert system is a computerized expert, as shown in Figure 12-16.

Figure 12-16

An expert system encapsulates the knowledge of a human expert within a narrowly defined area, such as spectral analysis, medical diagnosis, or geological formations.

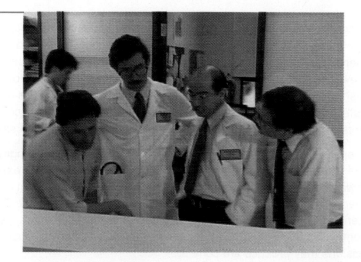

To create an expert system, the knowledge of an expert about a particular type of decision is captured in a set of facts and rules called a **knowledge base**. A knowledge base is stored in a computer file and then manipulated by software called an **inference engine**. When it is time to make a decision, the inference engine begins analyzing the available data by following the rules in the knowledge base. If the expert system needs additional data, it checks external databases, looks for the data in a transaction processing system, or asks the user to answer questions, as shown in Figure 12-17.

Figure 12-17

Characteristics of
an expert system

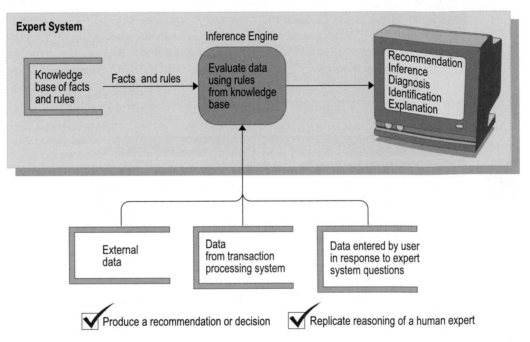

An expert system is not a general-purpose problem solver or decision maker. Each expert system is designed to make decisions in a particular area or "domain." For example, an expert system created for use at the Campbell Soup Company captured the knowledge of an expert cooking-vat operator to help less experienced employees troubleshoot problems that might arise as the soup cooks. Other expert systems have been developed to locate mineral deposits, diagnose blood diseases, evaluate corporate financial statements, underwrite complex insurance policies, and recommend stock purchases.

Expert systems are sometimes created using a computer programming language, but more often they are created using an expert system shell. An **expert system shell** is a software tool used for developing expert system applications. An expert system shell is an expert system without any rules. The shell contains the inference engine and a method for entering the rules for the knowledge base. To create the expert system, you use the shell to enter the rules, then use the inference engine to test the rules and make certain the decisions they produce are correct.

Expert systems are often designed to deal with data that is imprecise or with problems that have more than one solution. Using a technique called **fuzzy logic**, an expert system can deal with imprecise data by asking for a level of confidence. For example, suppose an expert system is helping you identify a whale you spotted off the coast of Hawaii. The expert system asks, "Did you see a dorsal fin?" You're not sure. You think you saw one, but it could have been a wave. If the expert system is using fuzzy logic, it will let you respond with something like "I'm 85% certain I saw a dorsal fin." Based on the confidence level of your answers to this and to other questions, the expert system might be able to tell you that it is "pretty sure," maybe 98% confident that you saw a grey whale.

InfoWeb

Neural Networks 13

An expert system begins with a set of facts and rules. What if the rules are unknown? Can a computer "learn" how to make decisions based on hundreds or thousands of lightning-fast attempts at trial and error? A **neural network** uses computer circuitry to simulate the way a brain processes information, learns, and remembers. For example, a neural network might be connected to a digital projector that displays photos of people's faces. Which faces are males and which are females? The neural network begins with a list of criteria with no values attached. "Hair length" might be one criteria, but the neural net is not programmed to expect that females usually have longer hair than men. Based on the evidence, the neural network begins to establish its own criteria—its own rules—about the data. Neural networks have been successfully implemented in many business and financial applications where identification and trend analysis are important.

QuickCheck C

1. Word-processing software is likely to be part of a(n) _____ system.

2. An information system that collects information when customers purchase merchandise is a point-of-sale system that would be classified as a(n) _____ processing system.

3. A(n) _____ system is characterized by the production of regularly scheduled reports that managers use for structured and routine tasks.

4. A(n) _____ report contains information that is outside of normal, or acceptable, ranges, such as a reorder report showing inventory items that need to be restocked.

5. A(n) _____ system provides users the ability to manipulate data directly, create data models, and incorporate external data.

6. A(n) _____ system is designed to capture the knowledge of a specialist in the form of rules. These rules are the basis for the computer to make a decision in response to a problem.

7. A(n) _____ contains an inference engine and a method for analyzing data, but it does not contain any rules.

8. A(n) _____ uses computer circuitry to simulate the way the brain processes, learns, and remembers information.

D Creating Expert System Facts and Rules

What's really fascinating about an expert system is its ability to make inferences based on the rules and data in a knowledge base. This ability essentially means that an expert system can "think for itself" to draw conclusions from a set of facts.

You might have read J.R.R. Tolkien's fantasy novels about the adventures of Frodo and Bilbo Baggins. Tolkien's books are populated with an extensive cast of characters from several generations of hobbits. A genealogy chart would be useful to understand the family tree. For example, read through the facts in Figure 12-18 about the Baggins family and see if you can determine how Linda and Bungo are related.

Figure 12-18

Baggins family
knowledge base

> Linda is a female, her mother is Laura, her father is Mungo, and she is married to Bodo.
>
> Bilbo is a male, his mother is Belladonna, his father is Bungo, and he is single.
>
> Belba is a female, her mother is Laura, her father is Mungo, and she is married to Rudigar.
>
> Bungo is a male, his mother is Laura, his father is Mungo, and he is married to Belladonna.

InfoWeb

Rules
14

You were probably able to infer from these facts that Linda and Bungo are siblings—sister and brother, actually. What could a computer do with these facts? Computers, as you have probably heard, know only the facts they have been given. If you want a computer to know that Linda and Bungo are siblings, you have to explicitly enter this fact. This was true until expert systems and logic programming were developed. Now, however, we can give an expert system the set of facts in Figure 12-18 and a general rule about siblings, such as "If two people have the same mother or father, they are siblings." The expert system can then use this rule to infer that Linda and Bungo are siblings.

Because the sibling rule is generic—because it doesn't mention any specific people—the expert system can also use it to make inferences about other people in the knowledge base who are siblings. Suppose for a moment that you are the expert system's inference engine. Using the sibling rule, can you find any other siblings in the knowledge base shown in Figure 12-18? Knowing that the purpose of an expert system is to use rules to make inferences based on a series of facts, you can see that the core activity for creating an expert system is writing facts and rules for the knowledge base. Let's take a closer look at the characteristics of facts and rules.

Facts

How do I write the facts for a knowledge base? A fact is a basic building block of a knowledge base. You can think of a fact as a statement or simple sentence. For example, here is a knowledge base with three simple facts:

> Belladonna is a female.
> Bilbo is a male.
> Belladonna is Bilbo's mother.

Once the facts are in a knowledge base, you can ask questions, and the expert system will search through the facts to produce an answer. For example, you might ask, "Is Bilbo a male?" and the expert system would respond with the answer "Yes." Or, you might ask, "Who is Bilbo's mother?" and the expert system would answer, "Belladonna." These answers seem obvious to you because you have seen the relevant rules in the knowledge base. However, in a realistic situation, the knowledge base might contain hundreds of facts about the Baggins family. You could ask "Who was Balbo's wife?" The expert system could tell you that Balbo Baggins, Bilbo's great grandfather, was married to Berylla.

The way you write the facts for a knowledge base depends on the development tool you use. When you use an expert system shell, you might be able to type the facts as simple sentences, such as "Belladonna is a female." If you use a programming language, such as Prolog, to construct your expert system, you might use a shorthand notation called **predicate logic**. Suppose you want to enter a fact about Bilbo's parents. Instead of entering a rule like "Bilbo's mother is Belladonna and his father is Bungo," you can use the predicate logic shorthand, parents('Bilbo', 'Belladonna', 'Bungo'). Using predicate logic, you put facts into the framework described in Figure 12-19.

Figure 12-19

Expressing facts using predicate logic

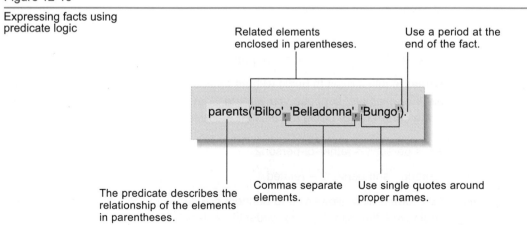

Related elements enclosed in parentheses.

Use a period at the end of the fact.

parents('Bilbo', 'Belladonna', 'Bungo').

The predicate describes the relationship of the elements in parentheses.

Commas separate elements.

Use single quotes around proper names.

At the beginning of this *User Focus* section, you looked at a series of facts that described the Baggins family. Figure 12-20 shows these facts written in predicate logic.

Figure 12-20

Baggins facts in predicate logic format

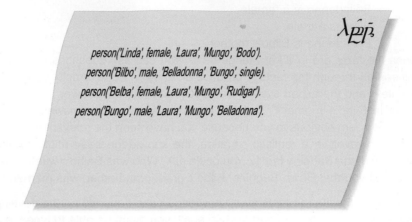

```
person('Linda', female, 'Laura', 'Mungo', 'Bodo').
person('Bilbo', male, 'Belladonna', 'Bungo', single).
person('Belba', female, 'Laura', 'Mungo', 'Rudigar').
person('Bungo', male, 'Laura', 'Mungo', 'Belladonna').
```

Rules

Can I use predicate logic for rules, too? As with facts, the way you enter the rules for an expert system depends on the development tool you use. You'll be disappointed to learn that most development tools do not allow you to enter rules in free-form English. Even though you might think of the siblings rule as "Any two people who have the same mother or father are siblings," you will not be able to use this wording when you enter the rule. The reason most expert system development tools do not accept free-form English rules is that such rules are often too ambiguous for the computer to use in making inferences. Therefore, a more structured format for writing rules is required. In general a development tool requires you to use IF...THEN format or predicate logic to write rules.

IF...THEN format requires rules to begin with an IF clause. The IF clause is followed by a THEN clause. For example, suppose you want to write a rule that if two people have the same father they are related. Using the IF...THEN format, your rule would be:

IF father-of-person1 = father-of-person2

THEN person1 and person2 = related

The IF...THEN format also allows you to connect clauses with the words AND, OR, and NOT. You could write the following rule to identify sisters:

IF father-of-person1 = father-of-person2

AND mother-of-person1 = mother-of-person2

AND person1=female

AND person2=female

THEN person1 and person2 = sisters

The format for predicate logic rules is a little more abstract, but it's fun to figure out how this shorthand works. First, think of the rule as the *outcome* followed by a series of facts that would make the outcome true. For example, you would think about the siblings rule as "Person A and Person B are siblings *if* Person A has a mother and father *and* Person B has the same mother and the same father."

Now take each clause, beginning with "Person A and Person B are siblings." How would you express this in predicate logic? You would write siblings(PersonA, PersonB). You make PersonA one word to show that it is one thing. If you wrote it "Person A" (with a space) the computer might think it was two things: one Person and some other thing called A. It is important to capitalize PersonA. That way the computer knows that you're not referring to someone named "PersonA," such as a man named "Mr. PersonA." Instead, PersonA means any person, and the computer needs to figure out that person's name.

Next, how would you express "Person A has a mother and father" in predicate logic format? You would write person(PersonA, Mother, Father). Again, you capitalize Mother and Father to tell the computer that it needs to substitute some real mother and father names here. Can you guess how to express the clause, "Person B has a mother and father?"

When you write the clause person(PersonB, Mother, Father) how does this imply that Person B has *the same* mother and father as Person A? In the rule for Person B you used "Mother" and "Father," the same as you did in the rule for Person A. If you had written person(PersonB, Ma, Pa), you would be implying that Person A has different parents from Person B.

Now you need to join these clauses together. You use the symbols :– for "if". You use a comma to represent the word "and." Your completed rule is shown in Figure 12-21.

Figure 12-21

The sibling rule expressed in predicate logic

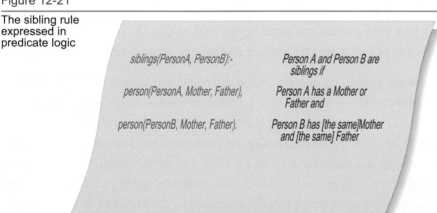

siblings(PersonA, PersonB):-	Person A and Person B are siblings if
person(PersonA, Mother, Father),	Person A has a Mother or Father and
person(PersonB, Mother, Father).	Person B has [the same]Mother and [the same] Father

As you can see, creating the facts and rules for an expert system exercises your mind. In everyday activities, you probably don't think about how you think. How did you look at the facts about the Baggins family and infer which were siblings? You "just did it," right? But when you write facts and rules for an expert system, you have to become aware of your own mental processes—how you analyze information and make decisions. The people who create expert systems have a job that is sometimes complex and often introspective. Their goal, however, is to create an expert system in which all the details of a decision are hidden from the user. Therefore, using an expert system is much easier than creating one.

EndNote

In Tolkien's book, *The Hobbit*, Bilbo Baggins alone and lost in the dark tunnel under a mountain gropes about in the dark, finds a small ring, and drops it in his pocket. That seemingly insignificant incident set in motion events that would plunge the Hobbits' world into the evil grip of chaos.

According to some scientists, our world—the real world—is already chaotic. **Chaos theory**, more formally known as the **theory of complex dynamical non-linear systems**, is the qualitative study of unstable behavior in complex systems. Basically, the theory attempts to explain and measure the effect of seemingly random events. Maybe you've played the popular computer game SimCity. This game simulates a complex system—a city populated with little "simmies" or simulated people who go to work, have kids, build houses, pile up garbage, and grumble when the electric company builds a nuclear power plant next door. In the game, you become the city planner and try to keep the simmies happy. What you soon discover is that a seemingly insignificant event might set in motion other events that can turn your once thriving city into a ghost town. That insignificant event is an element of chaos.

InfoWeb

Chaos
15

What does chaos have to do with organizations? Organizations are complex systems that must function within the larger complex system of planet earth. Most organizations depend on some form of strategic planning to improve and evolve. However, current methods of strategic planning use linear tools and models that do not account for the possible effects of chaotic events. Researchers are just beginning to study the limitations of the linear tools provided in today's decision support systems. In the meantime, intuition tells us that despite powerful computer information systems, it is difficult to accurately predict the future. The stock market, the weather, the next hit CD—all seem to depend on a complex interaction of events and a variety of unknown or chaotic elements.

Chaos theory is an attempt to quantify these unknown elements or at least insert a mathematical representation of them into a computer model. Some experiments are already yielding useful results. At the accounting firm Coopers & Lybrand, a computer program predicts whether a new music CD will become a hit. The program contains 50,000 simmies who are fad-following music fans and whose record buying habits have been determined from market research. For example, some of the simmies are programmed to run right out and buy any CD produced by their favorite musician, while others wait until they've heard the song a few times on the radio. After requesting some background information on the current popularity of the musician, the program sets the simulated music fans in action to see how many purchase the CD. Managers can use the simulation to make decisions about which new CDs to include in their product line.

Chaos theory is still in its infancy, but it promises to provide useful tools and techniques for understanding the complex world around us.

InfoWeb

InfoWeb

Chapter Links

The InfoWeb is your guide to print, film, television, and electronic resources. Use it to obtain updates on quickly changing technical information and to locate information for research papers. If you're using the New Perspectives CD-ROM, click the InfoWeb icon on the left side of this paragraph to access the online InfoWeb links. Otherwise, use your Web browser and type in the address of the New Perspectives site: www.cciw.com/np3. At the New Perspectives site you'll find up-to-date links to the topics covered in this chapter.

1 Hobbits

If you haven't read J.R.R. Tolkien's books, you've missed out on a really great adventure. Start with *The Hobbit* and then move directly to the trilogy *Lord of the Rings*. Tolkien has a dedicated following on the Web. Try the Grey Havens site at **tolkien.cro.net** where you'll find maps of Middle Earth, original art, songs, and discussion groups. At **www.geocities.com/Area51/Vault/7882/tolkiennav.html** you'll find more hobbit information and lots of links to other sites. By the way "hobbit" is also a somewhat obscure computer term that refers to the high-order bit—that's the leftmost bit in a sequence of 1s and 0s.

2 Peter Drucker

Peter Drucker is known as a somewhat unorthodox analyst of business, economics, politics, and society. He is extensively quoted and has written 28 books that have been translated into more than 20 languages. One of his most recent books, *Managing in a Time of Great Change*, includes some insights on how information systems can help a business succeed in the emerging global market. You'll find a short biography of Drucker at **www.cgs.edu/drucker/pfdbio.html** hosted by the Peter F. Drucker Graduate School of Management at Claremont Graduate University. You can read a quick synopsis of Drucker's achievements at the Digital Drucker Web site, **www.dgsys.com/~tristan/technodrucker.html**. And don't miss the somewhat bizarre *Wired* magazine interview with the "arch-guru of capitalism" at **www.wired.com/wired/1.3/features/drucker.html**.

3 Business: Terminology and Magazines

Information systems are one of the building blocks of modern businesses and organizations. If you're thinking about a career in computer information systems, it will pay to be familiar with current terms and trends in the corporate world. The *Management and Technology Dictionary* at **www.euro.net/innovation/Management_Base/Mantec.Dictionary.html** bills itself as the "largest Internet dictionary on management and technology. Colorful icons classify terms as technology, management, books or articles, database, magazine, conference/exhibition, or CD-ROM. Yogesh Malhotra's award-winning site at **www.brint.com** contains a superb collection of information on many aspects of business and technology. *Outlook* (**www.ac.com/outlook/o_frintro_1.html**) is an electronic magazine on "changing for success," from Andersen Consulting. The popular print magazine, *Upside*, has an electronic counterpart at **www.upside.com** where you can read about the latest trends in business technology. And for a more academic perspective, connect to the *Technology Review* from MIT at **web.mit.edu/techreview/www/tr.html**.

4 **Mission Statements**

You can read the mission statements for a variety of businesses by entering "mission statement" in any Web search engine. You'll find information on how to develop a mission statement in the online SOHO Guidebook at **www.toolkit.cch.com/Text/P03_4001.htm**. It's not a new idea, but many business consultants suggest that in addition to a mission statement, a business should have a "story." Read about the benefits of a business story in Edward O. Welles article, "Why Every Company Needs a Story" at **www.inc.com/incmagazine/archives/05960691.html**.

5 **Competition**

Business and competition go hand-in-hand in today's marketplace. Michael Porter's Five Forces model illustrates how competitive forces shape a business. You'll find a summary of the Five Forces model that has been excerpted from the *Harvard Business Review* at **iir1.uwaterloo.ca/MOTW96/readings96/Porter79.html**. Porter's book, *Competitive Advantage: Creating and Sustaining Superior Performance* (Free Press, 1985) contains a full discussion of competitive theory. Strategic information systems help companies compete in an increasingly competitive market. Roger Clarke has written a superb summary of classic business theory relating to strategic information systems. You'll find his article, "The Path of Development of Strategic Information Systems Theory," at **www.anu.edu.au/people/Roger.Clarke/SOS/StratISTh**.

6 **TQM**

The American Society for Quality promotes quality concepts, principles, and techniques. Its Web site at **www.asq.org** includes FAQs and a glossary. A good book on the topic is *Route to Quality and Productivity: Road Maps and Roadblocks*, by William W. Scherkenbach (Mercury Press, 1991). In the United States, something of a national frenzy erupted over "quality" and as a result, the U.S. congress created a 1988 law establishing the Malcolm Baldrige National Quality Award. Read about it at **www.quality.nist.gov/law.htm**.

A derivative of quality management is benchmarking. The American Productivity & Quality Center hosts a Web site at **www.apqc.org/b1/B1.HTM** that includes a brief description of benchmarking and links to articles and other resources. You'll find a good executive summary of benchmarking by Peter Griffin at **www.quality.co.uk/quality/benchadv.htm**. Japanese corporations are widely envied for their exacting quality control. The NASA Web pages at **mijuno.larc.nasa.gov/dfc/kai.html** provide information about a Japanese quality technique called "Kaizen."

7 **BPR**

The classic definition of BPR is a six-step approach to radical redesign of business processes. For a summary of the six-step approach, visit **www.abs.uci.edu/depts/facil/renovate/bpi_what.html**. At **www.brint.com/papers/bpr.htm** you'll find an excellent overview of business process redesign written by Yogesh Malhotra. The U.S. Department of Defense has an online course about BPR at **www.dtic.dla.mil/c3i/bprcd/0113.htm**.

8 **Organizational Charts**

It's interesting to look at the organizational charts for a variety of businesses. You can do this easily by entering "organizational chart" as the search term in any search engine. For a quick tutorial on creating organizational charts, connect to **web.miep.org/bus_plan/organ_chart.html**. In recent years, organizational charts have been a somewhat controversial tool in a manager's toolbox. One analyst claims "the only reason to draw an organizational chart is to help you decide which layers to eliminate." Ethan Winning, author of *Labor Pains: Employee Rights and Obligations*, discusses this controversy in an online article, "The Org Chart—Whither thou Goest?" at **www.all-biz.com/org.htm**.

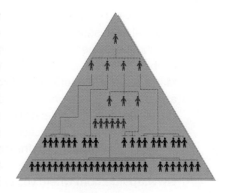

9 Office Automation

For a good overview of how to incorporate office automation into a business, connect to Bill's Corner at **www.banking.com/article1.htm**. To get an idea of how organizations implement basic office automation technologies read about the Coastal Engineering Research Center's office automation system at **zule.cerc.wes.army.mil/oa/oa_description/**. The FCSI site at **www.dbcams.com/case1.htm** uses colorful charts to show how "John" spends his time before and after office automation comes to his rescue. For additional references, check out the Groupware links in the Chapter 7 *InfoWeb* section.

10 Transaction Processing

Transaction processing seems like old technology. Most information systems have gone beyond simply tracking transactions to offering more flexible reporting and information management capabilities. Is there anything new in transaction processing? You'll find some insights on this in Christopher Avram's article on "New paradigms for transaction processing" at **www.ct.monash.edu.au/~cavram/papers/tp/tr94-02h.html**. For additional information on transaction processing, connect to the site of the granddaddy of all transaction processing systems, IBM. At the CICS site, **www.hursley.ibm.com/cics**, you'll find links to articles about transaction processing technology and industry solutions.

11 DSS

Daniel Power provides a good overview of decision support systems at **power.cba.uni.edu/isworld/dsshistory.html**. You'll find an extensive list of links to DSS Web sites maintained by Clyde Holsapple and Andrew Whinston, authors of the excellent textbook, *Decision Support Systems: A Knowledge-based Approach* at **www.uky.edu/BusinessEconomics/dssakba/periodcl.html**. IBM has an extensive Web site devoted to DSS information, technology, and industry solutions at **direct.boulder.ibm.com/bi/**. Many Web sites are decision support systems that you can use to make real-life decisions. Trying to make a career decision? Check out *Computerworld's* CareerAgent site at **careeragent.computerworld.com**. Trying to figure out a low-cost, yet healthy diet? Connect to The Diet Problem at **www.mcs.anl.gov/home/otc/Guide/CaseStudies/diet**. How about making decisions about investing for retirement? The Web site hosted by Americans for Tax Reform helps you fill out a simple questionnaire, then explains your investment options. Thinking of moving? The Homebuyer's Fair at **www.homefair.com** helps you compute equivalent salaries, calculate the cost of your move, and rates cities based on crime, schools, environment, and so on. For travel decisions, connect to Microsoft's online "travel agent" at **www.expedia.com**.

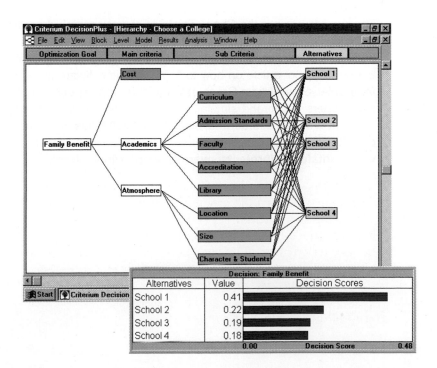

12 Expert Systems

For a quick overview of expert systems, connect to the CLIPS site at **www.ghgcorp.com/clips/ExpertSystems.html** or to MultiLogic's site at **www.exsys.com/Info/whatisit.html**. For additional information and links jump to the site maintained by *PC AI* magazine at **www.primenet.com/pcai**. Don't miss the Knowledge Box feature! MultiLogic's expert system shell EXSYS, runs over the Web. You can try some neat demos at **www.exsys.com/Wren/menu.html**. Acquired Intelligence, Inc. also has Web-based demos—an expert system that helps you identify whales at **vvv.com/ai/demos/whale.html**, and an expert system that will rate your qualifications for graduate school at **vvv.com/ai/demos/gradorig.html**.

13 Neural Networks

Bernard Widrow carried out the pioneering research for neural networks at Stanford University in the 1950s. It is a technology that requires massive computer capacity and, therefore, practical applications using this technology have been limited. However, it is a fascinating technology—imagine computers that function the way scientists think the brain functions! *An Introduction to Neural Networks* by Leslie Smith at **www.cs.stir.ac.uk/~lss/NNIntro/InvSlides.html** is a good place to begin exploring this technology. Next, check out the Neural Network Tutorial at **ourworld.compuserve.com/homepages/ltechnologies/tutorial.htm**. For more information and lots of links to other neural network sites, connect to the Pacific Northwest National Laboratory site at **www.pnl.gov**, click the Science link, then look for the Neural Network link.

14 Rules

In the *User Focus* section, you learned how to create predicate-logic rules for a knowledge base. The syntax for those rules are modeled on Prolog, a programming language popular for developing expert systems. For more information on the syntax of these rules, use your favorite Web search engine to search for "Prolog." A good source of information is the Amzi! site at **www.amzi.com**. At this site you can click the Automated Site Guide link to use an expert system that asks you questions to determine which articles about Prolog it should recommend. You'll especially like two of the articles at this site. The first, "White Paper on Rules, Prolog, and Logic Server Technology" (**www.amzi.com/prolog.htm**) provides a quick overview and examples of how to use rules. A second article, "Exploring Prolog" (**www.amzi.com/profun.htm**) describes how to use Prolog to write an adventure game. The classic book on Prolog is *Programming in Prolog*, 3rd. ed. by Clocksin and Mellish (Springer-Verlag, 1987).

15 Chaos

The place to begin is the Chaos ThinkSite at **www.orgmind.com/chaos/whatis.shtml**. Here you'll find a quick introduction to chaos theory and a set of interesting FAQs. Next, check out the chapter, "Thinking Past the Obvious" by Joseph O'Connor at **www.radix.net/~crbnblu/assoc/oconnor/chapt1.htm**.

For a really cool article on how to apply chaotic software to manufacturing processes, read *The Man from CHAOS* by William Green at **www.fastcompany.com/01/chaos.html**. You'll find more details on the Coopers & Lybrand simulation in the Forbes article, "Playing the game of life," which is posted online at **www.forbes.com/forbes/97/0407/5907100a.htm**. The Santa Fe Institute is the "mecca" for computational approaches to complex systems. Don't miss the online demos of chaos simulations at **www.santafe.edu/projects/swarm/examples/index.html**.

Review

1. Divide a sheet of paper into four quadrants labeled Operations, Sales and Marketing, Human Resource, and Financial Management. In each quadrant list at least five examples of a specific organization's activities. For example, in the Operations quadrant you might list "A computer manufacturer assembles microcomputers."

2. Complete the following table, indicating if each activity is part of operations, financial management, sales and marketing, or human resource management.

Activity	Activity Type
A worker assembles cars at an automobile plant	
A restaurant owner plans newspaper ads for the restaurant	
A store manager trains new employees in a clothing store	
A manager calculates total monthly sales	
A member of a recycling group speaks to a service organization to explain how the group encourages home owners to recycle bottles and cans	

3. Complete the following table, indicating the type of computer system represented by each example. The first one is filled in for you.

Example	Type of Computer System
System used to write reports and schedule meetings in a law office	Office automation
System used to sell airline tickets at a travel agency	
System used to analyze automobile problems and determine the most likely cause and solution to the problem	
System used by an executive who wants to find out how many toasters the Wichita store sold in October	

4. Refer to Michael Porter's Five Forces model in Figure 12-3. For each of the following events, indicate if it would be classified as bargaining power of suppliers, threat of new entrants, bargaining power of buyers, threat of substitute products or services, or rivalry among existing competitors.

   a. The value of the dollar falls in world markets, making Japanese car imports very expensive.

   b. Luxury-car makers move into the utility vehicle market, offering upscale competition to the once popular Jeep Cherokee.

   c. 3½-inch disk drives become popular with computer users.

   d. The Mideast war results in serious oil shortages.

   e. Cable TV companies offer two-way communications links for sending computer data.

5   Without looking back in this chapter, draw an organization pyramid showing the three levels of management and the three categories of workers.

6   Classify the following as information workers, goods workers, or service workers:

secretaries	construction	workers miners
electricians	dock workers	cashiers
beauticians	actors	writers
scientists	welders	chefs

7   Shades Inc. manufactures sunglasses. The senior management of the firm includes the President, the Vice President for Operations, the Vice President for Finance, and the Vice President for Sales and Marketing. Each vice president is in charge of one or more departments, as described below.

The Vice President for Operations is responsible for three departments: Shipping, Warehousing, and Human Resources. The Vice President for Finance is in charge of the Finance department. The Sales department and the Marketing department are the responsibility of the Vice President for Sales and Marketing.

Draw an organizational chart showing how Shades Inc. is structured.

8   List the three fundamental strategies that an organization can use to respond to threats or take advantage of opportunities.

9   Create a summary table or grid to illustrate the differences between structured, semi-structured, and unstructured problems.

10   List three examples of transaction processing systems. For each system, explain the type of data that is entered into the system and describe one or two reports that the system might produce.

11   Explain the difference between a detail report, a summary report, and an exception report.

12   Create a chart or table that summarizes the characteristics of transaction processing systems, management information systems, decision support systems, and expert systems.

13   Look at the following knowledge base expressed in predicate logic format. Does the rule at the end identify brothers, sisters, friends, or cousins? If an expert system uses this knowledge base, what will it infer? (Careful, it's tricky!)

male(sam).
male(charlie).
male(linus).
male(pat).
male(george).
female(lucy).
female(lynn).
female(amanda).
female(gretchen).
parents(linus, amanda, sam).
parents(lynn, amanda, sam).
parents(pat, gretchen, george).
brothers(X,Y):–
    male(X),
    parents(X, Mother, Father),
    male (Y),
    parents(Y, Mother, Father).

14   Use the New Perspectives CD to take a practice test or to review the key terms presented in this chapter.

Projects

INTERNET Optional

1 Mission, Threats, and Opportunities Suppose you are a management consultant for one of the following well-known companies. The company needs to produce a mission statement, and it is your job to help. The company also wants to know what factors might influence its business in the future. Pick one of the companies. Do some library or Internet research to get some background information on the company. Write a mission statement for your company, then use Michael Porter's Five Forces model as the basis for listing five factors that you think are likely to affect your company's business in the next year or two.

Netscape
NIKE
Black & Decker
Harley-Davidson
Mattel
Intel
Royal Caribbean Cruise Line

2 Charting an Organization Interview someone from an organization or business. Draw an organizational chart showing the structure of the organization.

3 Organizational Activities Think of any real or hypothetical business or non-profit organization. Assume that the organization is divided into four departments— operations, financial management, sales and marketing, and human resource management. Write a one-paragraph summary of the types of activities that would be handled by each of the four departments.

4 Responding to a Threat Assume that you are the manager of a movie theater. Local video rental businesses have boomed, and attendance at movies has declined. Write a short paper explaining how you would deal with this threat and keep the movie theater profitable.

5 Taking Advantage of Opportunities Assume you are the manager of a medium-sized snowmobile company. Jet skis are just becoming popular. Write a short paper explaining why you think your company should or should not get into the jet ski business.

6 Evaluating Strategies Assume that you are the president of a national fast-food chain. The board of directors has proposed that you empower the employees at the local outlets by allowing them to make decisions about menu items, restaurant decor, and general operations. List three possible advantages to this approach. List three possible disadvantages to this approach.

7

Researching Decision Support Systems Assume you are the Information Systems Director for a manufacturer of office furniture. The president of the company has asked you to learn more about decision support systems. Use the library or the World Wide Web to search for more information about current decision support systems. Make a list of ten DSS resources and write a one-sentence description of each.

8

The Russian Royal Family Your organization is preparing a Web site containing genealogical information on royal families from around the world. You have been asked to collect information on the Russian czars. Use your library or the Internet to find the full name, mother's name, father's name, spouse's name, and siblings for each of the last three Russian czars. Record this information as if you were going to use it in a knowledge base. Use the predicate logic syntax you learned in the *User Focus* section.

DEVELOPING EFFECTIVE INFORMATION SYSTEMS

T hree men sat around a kitchen table in Oslo, Norway. "So we'll try it!" one said, and the rest agreed. It was the beginning of a daring attempt to cross 413 nautical miles of shifting ice, snow drifts, and frigid water between Canada and the North Pole without assistance from sled dogs, snowmobiles, or resupply flights. Each man would pull a specially designed Kevlar and fiberglass sled containing food, water, and fuel. Each sled would weigh 265 pounds fully loaded.

The expedition members knew that their success depended on having the right gear and provisions, so they immediately contacted Abercrombie & Livingston Outfitters, Ltd. of London. The expedition's order was routed to the A&L branch in Telluride, Colorado—the closest A&L location to the expedition's staging area in Resolute, Canada.

Expeditions
1

Unfortunately, several items needed by the expedition were not in stock in the Telluride branch. The team couldn't wait for the back-ordered items to arrive with the next scheduled inventory shipment, so a helpful store manager called other A&L outlets, found the items at the Geneva outlet, and had the items shipped to the Telluride branch. The team received the necessary equipment in time, but the process required significant effort on the part of a motivated store manager.

To provide better service to its customers, A&L management decided to upgrade its information system. One of the objectives of the upgrade was to help managers check other outlets to find out-of-stock items. This chapter describes the process A&L used to plan and implement the upgrade to its information system.

CHAPTER PREVIEW

In this chapter you'll find out how to create or upgrade an information system—how to determine what needs to be done, how to design and construct the system, how to test the system to make sure it works correctly, and how to maintain the system. The *User Focus* section introduces you to an important development tool, data flow diagrams. When you have completed this chapter, you should be able to:

- Explain the system development life cycle
- Understand the difference between a systems analyst and a programmer
- Understand the difference between a problem statement and a solution
- Use the PIECES framework to identify problems in an information system
- Explain how data flow diagrams, data dictionaries, and process specifications document the way an information system works
- Understand the difference between system requirements and application specifications
- Differentiate between a request for proposal and a request for quotation
- Explain the difference between unit testing, integration testing, system testing, and acceptance testing
- Explain the advantages and disadvantages of direct conversion, parallel conversion, phased conversion, and pilot conversion when switching to a new system

LABS

System Testing

A Systems Analysis

Mythical
Man-Month
2

The computer industry abounds with tales of information systems, developed at great expense, that didn't meet expectations because they didn't work correctly, were too complex to use, or weren't flexible enough to meet changing business needs. As Frederick Brooks observes in his book *The Mythical Man-Month*, "One can expect the human race to continue attempting systems just within or just beyond our reach, and software systems are perhaps the most intricate and complex of all man's handiwork."

Creating an information system can be compared to building a house. You don't just grab a hammer and start nailing pieces of wood together. It is important to have a plan. The process of planning and building an information system is referred to as **systems analysis and design**.

Methodologies
3

Whether you are part of a team to develop a complex corporate information system, or whether you are developing a small information system for your own use, you will be more likely to succeed if you analyze the purpose of the information system, carefully design the system, test it thoroughly, and document its features. The methodology you use to develop an information system depends on the type of system and the company you work for. **Systems analysis methodologies** include structured analysis, joint application development (JAD), rapid application development (RAD), and object-oriented development.

A **system development life cycle** (SDLC), is an outline of a process that helps develop successful information systems. The SDLC is divided into phases, and each phase includes a number of tasks. Although several variations of the SDLC exist, most of them include phases similar to those shown in Figure 13-1.

Figure 13-1

System development
life cycle

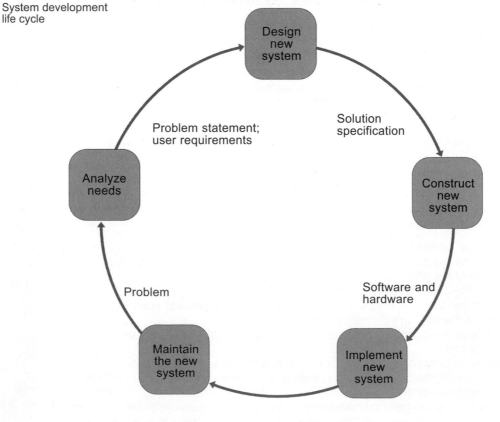

Working system

Analyze Needs

What's the beginning of the life cycle?

Figure 13-2

Analysis activities

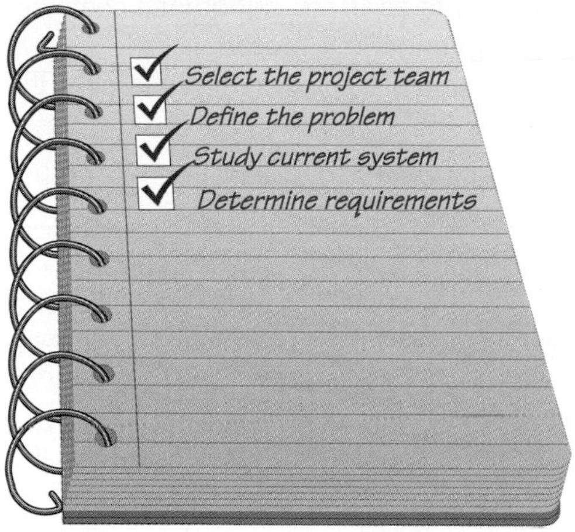

- ☑ Select the project team
- ☑ Define the problem
- ☑ Study current system
- ☑ Determine requirements

The motivation for a new information system usually emerges from a serious problem with the current system. If the current system is manual, it might not be cost effective or competitive. Computerized systems can become obsolete when, for example, the hardware is out of date or when the software no longer meets the needs of the business mission.

The first phase of the SDLC is to **analyze needs**. This phase requires several activities, listed in Figure 13-2.

Select the Project Team

InfoWeb

IS Departments 4

Who participates in the process of building an information system?

An **information systems department**, or IS department for short, is the wing of a business or organization responsible for developing and maintaining the computers, data, and programs for an information system. Historically, computers were deployed in businesses for accounting and inventory management functions, so IS departments were initially part of the finance component.

As computers spread to assist with more and different business tasks, some organizations changed their organizational charts to place IS as a separate entity reporting directly to the chief executive officer or president. This reorganization provided IS with more autonomy to make budget and project decisions. In addition, it improved lines of communication with end users by providing access to IS from departments other than Finance. Most IS departments acknowledge, however, that there is still room for improvement in user support.

InfoWeb

Systems Analysts 5

Most IS departments are headed by a **chief information officer** (CIO). Managers and team leaders report to the CIO and manage the technicians and computer professionals who develop new systems and operate the computer equipment.

Computer professionals called **systems analysts** are often responsible for analyzing information requirements, designing a new information system, and supervising the new system implementation. Systems analysts also create specifications for application software for the new system, then give those specifications to computer programmers, who create computer programs to meet those specifications.

Increasingly, managerial and clerical employees initiate and participate in the development of information systems. That's why no one was surprised when the special procurement agent at A&L suggested that it was time to automate part of her job. The special procurement agent and a systems analyst from A&L's information systems department formed a project team to work on the new system.

InfoWeb

Project
Teams
6

A **system development project team**, or **project team** for short, is a group of people who are assigned to analyze and develop an information system. The composition of the project team depends on the scope of the project. Larger and more complex projects have large project teams, and a majority of the people on the team are systems analysts or other computer professionals. Smaller projects have fewer members on the project team and a higher percentage of the team members are likely to be users, rather than computer professionals. Figure 13-3 contains some excerpts from the first meeting of the special procurement project team as the special procurement agent explains what she calls the "cross-shipping problem."

Figure 13-3

Excerpts from
the first
special
procurement
project team
meeting

Systems Analyst (SA): I'm not very familiar with your job. Would you fill me in?

Special Procurement Agent (SPA): As you probably know, when a customer places an order, it is usually filled with items from the local outlet's inventory. However, if that outlet is out of stock on an ordered item, the computer checks to see if it is available in the London warehouse.

SA: Yes, I know how that works. And if the item is in stock in London, we ship it from London to the outlet.

SPA: Right. But if the item is not in the outlet or the London warehouse, the order comes to me. I try to locate the item by using the MIS system. If I find the item at another outlet, I usually ask them to "cross-ship" the item to the outlet where it was ordered.

SA: By cross-ship, do you mean that one outlet ships the item to another outlet?

SPA: Exactly.

SA: That sounds like you're making effective use of the system. So what's the problem?

SPA: The problem is that it takes time for me to check the inventories, check shipping rates, and decide which outlet can supply the item fastest and least expensively. I usually don't receive notification for 24 hours; then, with my workload, it might be another day or two before I can tackle it.

SA: I see.

SPA: It's costing the company a lot of money to deliver some of these items, considering the time I spend and the possible delay to the customer.

SA: So I assume you would like to automate the cross-shipping decision, if possible?

SPA: Yes, I think it would be cost-effective.

Define the Problem

How do I begin to analyze an information system? The first activities in the analysis phase are to define the problem and create one or more problem statements. A **problem statement** is a sentence that identifies what needs to be improved or fixed. Here are some examples of well-defined problem statements for information systems:

- In a garden supply store: The price tags frequently fall off items—especially the plants—so customers have to wait at the registers while an employee checks the price.

- In a police car: Officers do not have access to out-of-state arrest warrants, so they might stop a motorist for a minor violation but fail to make an arrest on a more serious charge.

A common pitfall in the analysis phase is to state a solution, rather than a problem. Solutions are not appropriate at this stage of the SDLC because you should not consider solutions until you understand more about the problem with the current system. Although the following statements might sound reasonable, they are solutions, not problems:

- The garden supply store needs a bar-code reader so cashiers can determine the price of an item even if it doesn't have a price tag.

- The police car should be equipped with a computer that can access a national database of outstanding arrest warrants.

James Wetherbe's **PIECES framework** helps identify problems in an information system. Each letter of PIECES stands for a potential problem, as shown in Figure 13-4.

Figure 13-4

PIECES helps identify problems.

Performance
The system has a performance problem if it does not respond fast enough to users or it takes too long to complete processing tasks.

Information
There is an information problem if users don't receive the right information at the right time, in a usable format.

Economics
There is an economics problem if the system costs too much to use.

Control
There is a control problem if information is available to unauthorized users or if authorized users are not given the authority to make decisions based on the information they have.

Efficiency
There is an efficiency problem if too many resources are used to collect, process, store, and distribute information.

Service
There is a service problem if the system is too difficult or inconvenient to use.

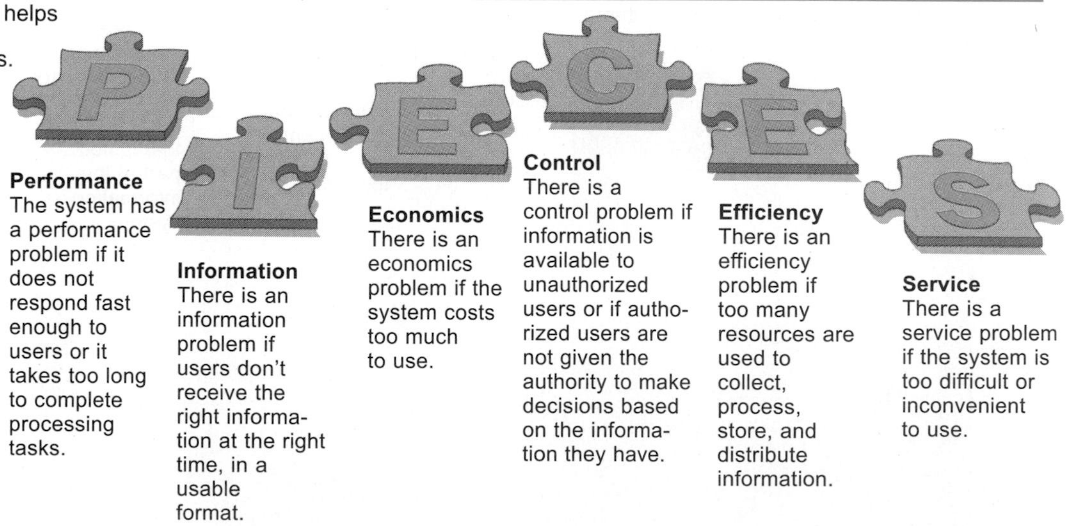

At A&L Outfitters the special procurement agent classified the procurement problem as an efficiency problem. Too many resources, that is, too many hours of her time, are devoted to choosing the best location from which to cross-ship items. The special procurement agent and systems analyst at A&L Outfitters created the following problem statement:

> **If a customer orders an item that is out of stock, the current procedures are not efficient for determining whether other outlets have the item in stock, and from which outlet the item could be cross-shipped cost-effectively.**

Study the Current System

Is it important to understand the current system before planning a new system?

Typically, a new information system is designed to replace a system or process that is already in place. It is essential to study the current system carefully and understand its strengths and weaknesses before planning the new system. Systems analysts create *data flow diagrams*, *data dictionaries*, and *process specifications* to document the way a system works.

A **data flow diagram**, sometimes called a **DFD**, graphically illustrates how data moves through an information system. You can think of a DFD as a map that traces the possible paths for data traveling from entities (such as customers) to processes (such as printing), or to storage areas. Figure 13-5 uses a DFD to document how an order is processed by A&L's information system.

Figure 13-5

On this DFD, the data moving through an information system is represented by arrows. The rounded rectangles are processes that affect the data. Inventory is a data storage area. The Customer box represents a data destination.

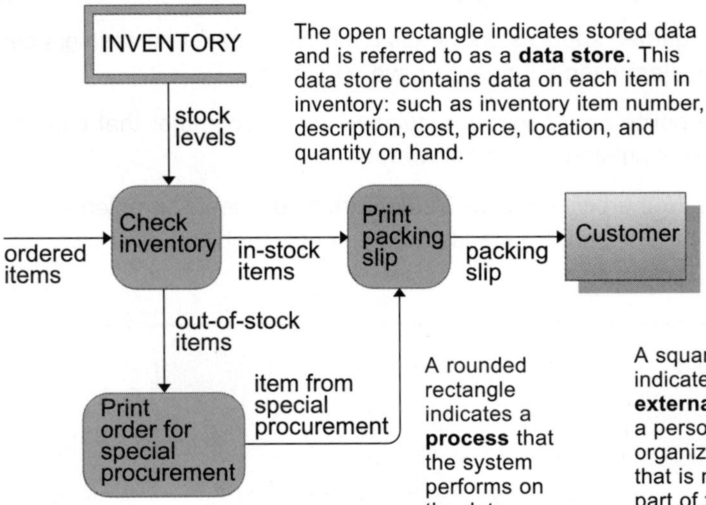

INVENTORY

The open rectangle indicates stored data and is referred to as a **data store**. This data store contains data on each item in inventory: such as inventory item number, description, cost, price, location, and quantity on hand.

stock levels

Check inventory

ordered items

in-stock items

Print packing slip

packing slip

Customer

out-of-stock items

Print order for special procurement

item from special procurement

A rounded rectangle indicates a **process** that the system performs on the data.

A square indicates an **external entity:** a person or organization that is not part of the information system.

A DFD illustrates an overview of a system, but how does the analyst describe the details? For example, one of the arrows on the DFD is labeled "ordered items." Does the data for "ordered items" include the retail price of the item? Analysts use a **data dictionary** to document detailed descriptions of the data that flows through an information system and data that is stored by that system. Read the data dictionary description for "ordered items" in Figure 13-6.

Figure 13-6

Data dictionary description of the "ordered items" data from the DFD in Figure 13-5

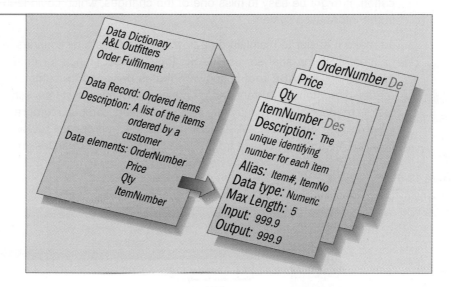

A **process specification** explains what happens to data within a process. For example, the A&L DFD includes a process called "Check inventory." What exactly does this mean? What is the information system supposed to do when it checks the inventory? A process specification would describe in detail exactly what the information system accomplishes in this process.

Analysts often use **structured English** to concisely and unambiguously explain the logic of a process. Structured English differs from standard English because it limits the words you can use to those defined in the data dictionary and to specific logical terms such as "if...then." Figure 13-7 provides you an example of process specifications written in structured English.

Figure 13-7

This process specification, written in structured English, describes the Check inventory process shown on the DFD in Figure 13-5.

```
Check inventory

If the QuantityOnHand at the nearest Outlet>=Qty

    then print item information on packing slip

    otherwise, if QuantityOnHand at the London warehouse>=Qty

        then print item information on packing slip

        otherwise, print the order for the special

        procurement agent.
```

Data flow diagrams, data dictionaries, and process specifications are valuable tools for analyzing information systems. These tools help analysts produce documentation that is also useful in the design and maintenance phases. However, it can be difficult to keep the diagrams, dictionaries, and specifications for an information system up to date. For example, if the information systems department at A&L decided to rename Qty to QtyOrdered, several revisions would need to be made in the data dictionary and the process specification. It might be easy to miss one of the changes, which could lead to errors and bugs in the information system.

InfoWeb

CASE Tools
7

To make it easier to maintain data flow diagrams, data dictionaries, and process specifications, systems analysts use CASE tools. CASE stands for computer aided software engineering. A **CASE tool** is software that is designed for summarizing system requirements, diagramming current and proposed information systems, scheduling development tasks, preparing documentation, and developing computer programs. If you change a label in one place, the CASE tool makes the appropriate revisions everywhere else. Figure 13-8 shows a screen from a CASE tool called PowerDesigner®.

Figure 13-8

PowerDesigner®
CASE tool

A collection of special shape and connector tools makes it easy to draw data flow diagrams.

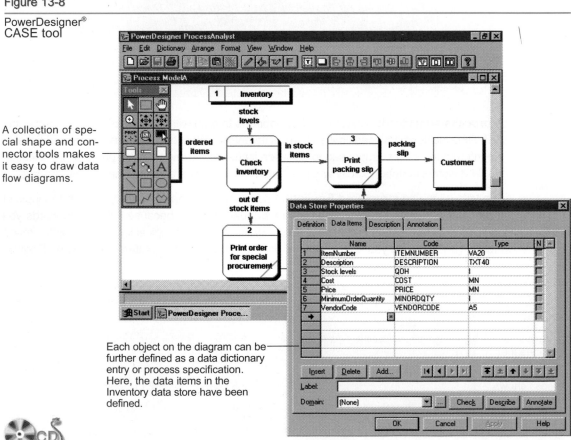

Each object on the diagram can be further defined as a data dictionary entry or process specification. Here, the data items in the Inventory data store have been defined.

Determine System Requirements

How do you determine what the new system should do? **System requirements** are the criteria for successfully solving the problem or problems you have identified. These requirements will guide you as you design and plan a new information system. Requirements also serve as an evaluation checklist at the end of the development project, so they are sometimes called **success factors**. The information system you create should meet the requirements you defined.

An analyst determines requirements by interviewing users and studying successful information systems that solve problems similar to those found in the earlier stages of analysis.

The special procurement agent at A&L Outfitters created the following list of requirements:

- **When the current information system fills an order, it should check stock in all the outlets, then correctly determine the best outlet from which to ship each item.**

- **The system should be able to determine the best outlet from which to ship without any human intervention.**

- **The system should be easy to maintain. When shipping rates or shipping times between outlets change, it should be easy to change that information in the system.**

Another way to determine requirements is to construct a prototype. A **prototype** is an experimental or trial version of an information system. Often the prototype is not a fully functioning system because it is designed only to demonstrate selected features that might be incorporated into a new information system. An analyst demonstrates the prototype to users who evaluate which features of the prototype are important for the new information system.

QuickCheck A

1. The _____ is an outline of a process that helps develop effective information systems.

2. _____ are often responsible for analyzing information requirements, designing a new information system, and supervising the new system implementation.

3. A(n) _____ is a sentence that identifies what needs to be improved or fixed in an information system.

4. A(n) _____ tool is software that is designed for drawing diagrams of information systems, writing process specifications, and maintaining data dictionaries.

5. _____ are the criteria for successfully solving a problem or problems.

6. A(n) _____ is an experimental or trial version of an information system that is under development.

Ⓑ Design the New System

In the design phase, alternate solutions are identified and evaluated, hardware and software are selected, and the specifications for constructing the system are developed, as noted in Figure 13-9.

Figure 13-9

Design activities

Identify Potential Solutions

What if there seem to be multiple ways to solve the problem?

There might be more than one way to solve the problem you have identified and meet the requirements you specified in the analysis phase of the SDLC. Some potential solutions might be better than others: more effective, less costly, or less complex. Therefore, it is not a good idea to proceed with the first solution that comes to mind. You should, instead, identify several potential solutions, then compare the advantages and disadvantages of each. Finally, select the solution that provides the most benefits for the least cost.

Remember that information systems include people, procedures, data, hardware, and software. When you identify potential solutions, consider whether there are alternatives in any of these areas. For example, you might consider if there are software alternatives such as using an application development tool, writing custom software, or purchasing a commercial program. Let's see how A&L might look at alternative software solutions for its upgraded information system.

An **application development tool**, is essentially a type of software construction kit that contains building blocks you can assemble into a software product. Application development tools include expert system shells, 4GLs, and component objects. A **4GL**, or fourth-generation language, is a programming language that contains built-in commands for complex tasks such as sorting data or creating columnar reports. A component object is a pre-programmed module such as a menu bar that a programmer can insert into a program written in a programming language such as VisualBasic. The term "application development tool" sometimes also refers to CASE software.

Application development tools usually produce applications faster than traditional programming languages. As an analogy, consider baking a cake. You can sift the flour with the salt, mix the sugar, eggs, shortening, and milk, then combine the dry and wet ingredients, and so forth to create a cake "from scratch." This is analogous to creating a software application using a programming language. Another way to bake a cake is with a cake mix. You just add water and eggs, mix, and bake. An application development tool is the programmer's "cake mix" and provides a quicker, easier way to construct an application.

Creating an information system using a programming language takes many months or years and is very costly. Using an application development tool reduces the time and cost somewhat, but application development is still a major effort. Another possibility is to purchase a commercial software application and customize it where possible to fit with the way the organization works. In summary, there are often three alternative software solutions: (1) build the application using an application development tool; (2) create the application using a programming language; or (3) buy a commercial software application.

Evaluate Solutions and Select the Best

How do you choose the best solution? After you list alternative solutions, you can evaluate each solution based on its advantages and disadvantages. The project team at A&L Outfitters is considering three software options. They could use a programming language or other software development tool to write a custom module to determine when and where to cross-ship. The advantage of this solution is that a custom program can be designed to meet the procurement agent's requirements exactly. The disadvantage of this solution is that it requires the services of one or more programmers. Considering the backlog of upgrade requests in the information systems department, the module would probably not be available for 18 months.

InfoWeb

Solutions
8

Another potential solution for A&L is to purchase a commercial software application that already includes the ability to determine when and where to cross-ship. The advantage of this solution is that commercial applications have already been well tested and could be installed very quickly. But it might be difficult to locate a commercial application that would work with the current transaction processing system. Many commercial applications are designed to interact only with other modules purchased from the same vendor. Aside from the cross-shipping problem, A&L is happy with the current transaction processing system and doesn't intend to switch to an entirely new system just to add cross-shipping capability.

Another possible solution is to use an application development tool such as an expert system shell. An advantage of this solution is that the special procurement agent can play an active role in the development process. Disadvantages of this solution include the time the special procurement agent will have to spend developing the system and the possible trouble she and the systems analyst might have integrating the expert system with the rest of the transaction processing system.

To evaluate the three potential solutions, the special procurement agent creates a list of evaluation criteria:

- **The solution must run on A&L's current hardware.**

- **The software application for the solution must integrate with the current transaction processing system.**

- **The solution must be in place within six months.**

- **The solution must meet the requirements delineated in the analysis phase.**

- **Support for the solution must be available from a vendor, software publisher, manufacturer, or the A&L information systems department.**

After evaluating the alternatives, the project team decides that the best solution is to use an expert system shell to create an expert system that would work with the current transaction processing system. Custom programming would take too long, and the team was unable to locate an appropriate commercial application that would work with A&L's current system.

The project team takes its proposal to management. In most organizations, management approval is necessary for modifications or additions to the current information system. Management approval is also necessary for equipment purchases, software purchases, and time commitments for personnel resources, such as the time it takes to design, create, test, and maintain an information system.

Purchase Hardware and Software

Once you've decided what you want to do and have selected a solution, how do you get started? Once you select a solution and management has cleared the project to proceed, the next activity is to purchase the hardware and software needed to implement the solution. Typically, more than one vendor sells the hardware and software necessary for the new system, so an organization often has a choice of vendors.

InfoWeb

RFPs & RFQs
9

The method for selecting the hardware, software, and vendor depends on the project team's understanding of what is required for the solution. If the team members do not know exactly what hardware and software are needed, they can describe the problem and ask vendors how they would resolve it. If the project team members know exactly what they want, they just need to find a reputable vendor who sells the equipment at a reasonable price.

A **request for proposal**, or RFP, is a document you send to vendors that describes the problem you are trying to solve and the requirements for the solution. The RFP essentially asks the vendors to recommend a solution and describe their qualifications to implement the solution. You usually use an RFP when you have not yet selected the equipment or software that meets your needs. Look at the sample RFP in Figure 13-10.

Figure 13-10

An RFP describes the problem and asks the vendor to suggest a solution.

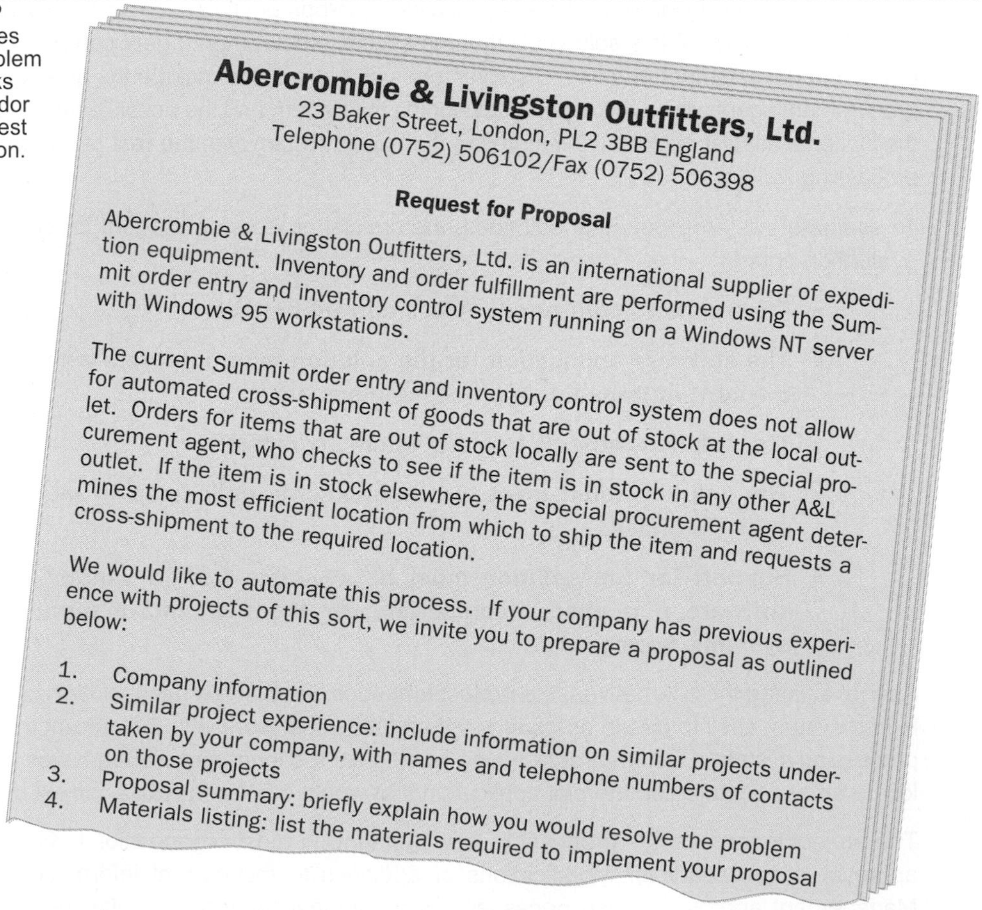

Abercrombie & Livingston Outfitters, Ltd.
23 Baker Street, London, PL2 3BB England
Telephone (0752) 506102/Fax (0752) 506398

Request for Proposal

Abercrombie & Livingston Outfitters, Ltd. is an international supplier of expedition equipment. Inventory and order fulfillment are performed using the Summit order entry and inventory control system running on a Windows NT server with Windows 95 workstations.

The current Summit order entry and inventory control system does not allow for automated cross-shipment of goods that are out of stock at the local outlet. Orders for items that are out of stock locally are sent to the special procurement agent, who checks to see if the item is in stock in any other A&L outlet. If the item is in stock elsewhere, the special procurement agent determines the most efficient location from which to ship the item and requests a cross-shipment to the required location.

We would like to automate this process. If your company has previous experience with projects of this sort, we invite you to prepare a proposal as outlined below:

1. Company information
2. Similar project experience: include information on similar projects undertaken by your company, with names and telephone numbers of contacts on those projects
3. Proposal summary: briefly explain how you would resolve the problem
4. Materials listing: list the materials required to implement your proposal

A **request for quotation**, or RFQ, is a request for a formal price quotation on a list of hardware and software. You submit an RFQ when you know the make and model of the equipment and the titles of the software packages you need, but you want to compare prices. Compare the RFQ in Figure 13-10 with the RFP in Figure 13-11.

Figure 13-11

An RFQ asks the vendor for a price on specific hardware or software items.

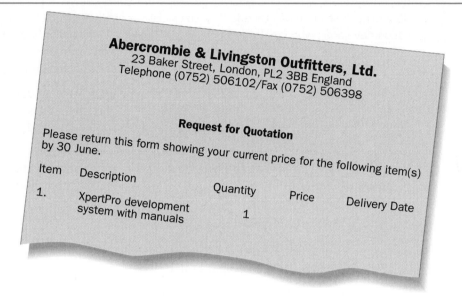

Abercrombie & Livingston Outfitters, Ltd.
23 Baker Street, London, PL2 3BB England
Telephone (0752) 506102/Fax (0752) 506398

Request for Quotation

Please return this form showing your current price for the following item(s) by 30 June.

Item	Description	Quantity	Price	Delivery Date
1.	XpertPro development system with manuals	1		

The special procurement agent and systems analyst at A&L Outfitters explore a variety of expert system development tools. Eventually they select a product called XpertPro. It is an expert system shell that has been used successfully in many companies in Europe and North America. They selected XpertPro because it runs on their current hardware, it is compatible with Windows operating systems, it will integrate with their current transaction processing system, and it appears to provide the capabilities they need. Because the special procurement agent knows exactly what she wants, she asks the A&L purchasing department to send RFQs to vendors who sell XpertPro. When the vendors return the RFQs, the purchasing agent at A&L looks for the vendor that offers the most competitive price and then orders XpertPro from that vendor.

Develop Application Specifications

How do you make sure that the information system that is finally created will meet your needs? **Application specifications** describe the way an application should interface with the user, store data, process data, and format reports. The specifications are similar to an architectural blueprint that shows the detailed plan for constructing a building. For large information systems, a systems analyst develops the specifications after interviewing users to determine their information needs. The specifications are then given to a programmer or application developer, who creates the application. In a small information systems project, you as the user might develop your own specifications. Then you might give the specifications to a programmer, or if you have the expertise, you might create the application yourself.

Whether a large or small system is under development, it requires detailed specifications so that the final system solves the problem defined during the analysis phase. At A&L, the specifications for the expert system define the rules for the knowledge base. The project team develops the following rules for the cross-ship expert system:

- **If the ordered item is in stock at the outlet nearest the destination of the order, then deliver the item from that outlet.**

- **If the ordered item is not in stock in any outlet, then send the order to the special procurement agent.**

- **If the ordered item is in stock at only one outlet, then cross-ship the item from that outlet.**

- **If the ordered item is in stock in more than one outlet, then cross-ship it from the outlet with the lowest shipping cost and fastest delivery time.**

QuickCheck B

1. In the _____ phase, a systems analyst identifies several potential solutions, evaluates these solutions, and then selects the one that offers the most benefits at the lowest cost.

2. A(n) _____ is essentially a software construction kit that contains building blocks you can assemble into a software product.

3. A(n) _____ is a document sent to vendors that describes the problem and the requirements for the solution.

4. You would send out a(n) _____ if you know exactly what hardware and software you want to purchase.

5. _____ describe the way an application should interface with the user, store data, process data, and format reports.

C Construct the System

In the construction phase, new hardware and software are installed, applications are created to meet the specifications developed during the design phase, and the new system is tested, as noted in Figure 13-12.

Figure 13-12

Construction activities

Install Hardware and Software

What's the first step in the construction phase?

Installing hardware and software is the first step in the construction phase. The expert system for A&L Outfitters does not require any new hardware. However, in many development projects, new hardware is required and is installed during the construction phase. New hardware can either replace old equipment or be connected to existing equipment. In either case, new hardware must be tested to make sure it operates correctly. As shown in Figure 13-13, problems with the hardware or connections to other equipment must be corrected during the construction phase so they do not disrupt the implementation phase.

Figure 13-13

Whether you're installing a micro, mini, or mainframe computer, make sure you refer to the manufacturer's manuals.

Many new information systems require new software such as a commercial application, a programming language, an application development tool, or an expert system shell. Before it is used, software must be installed and tested to make sure it works correctly. Software testing can reveal problems that result from incompatibilities with the existing hardware or an incorrect installation of the software. These problems must be corrected before continuing with system construction activities. Other problems might result from bugs, or errors, in the software and must be corrected by the organization that originally wrote the software.

The A&L project team installs and tests the expert system development shell, XpertPro. At this stage, the project team is only testing the *development tool* to make sure it runs on the computer without generating error messages—the rules for the expert system have not yet been entered, so the team is not testing the cross-shipping rules yet. When the team members are sure that the expert system shell operates correctly, they continue with the construction of the cross-shipping system.

Create Applications

So, you've got the new hardware, new software tools, and complete application specifications. Are you ready to begin? So far, you have seen that information systems can be constructed using tools such as a programming language, an application development tool, commercial software, or an expert system shell. As Figure 13-14 shows, the construction technique depends on the construction tool.

Figure 13-14

Construction techniques depend on the tool.

Construction Tool	Construction Techniques
Programming language	Install programming language. Write application modules using programming language. Test application modules separately and as a whole to make sure there are no errors.
Application development tool	Install the application development tool. Use the tool's building blocks to construct application. Test application modules separately and as a whole to make sure there are no errors.
Commercial software	Install the commercial software. Customize software to meet specifications, if possible. Test the software to make sure the customization reflects the specifications.
Expert system shell	Install the expert system shell. Enter facts and rules in the knowledge base. Test the expert system to make sure the rules are correct.

When the applications or programs for an information system are created using a programming language or application development tool, the process is referred to as **programming** or **software engineering**.

When an information system is constructed using a commercial application, the application has been written and tested by the software publisher. However, the application sometimes needs to be customized. **Software customization** is the process of modifying a commercial application to reflect the needs of the users. Customization might include changing the appearance of the user interface, enabling or disabling the mouse, selecting the menus that appear, and designing forms or reports. The extent to which a commercial application can be customized depends on the options available in the application. For example, some commercial applications provide options for customizing report formats while other commercial applications do not.

When an information system requires the construction of an expert system, the facts and rules for the knowledge base must be entered and tested. The process of designing, entering, and testing the rules in an expert system is referred to as **knowledge engineering**. Because the members of the A&L project team have decided to use an expert system shell to construct the cross-ship application, their major construction activities are to enter and test the facts and rules for the expert system. As with any application, the A&L expert system must meet the design specifications and go through a rigorous testing process to ensure that the facts and rules produce the expected results.

Test Applications

How can you make sure that a new information system works? A rigorous testing process is the only way to make sure a new information system works. Different types of testing during the construction phase help identify and fix problems before the information system is incorporated into day-to-day business activities.

System Testing 10

Application testing is the process of trying out various sequences of input values and checking the results to make sure the application works correctly. Application testing is performed in three ways: unit testing, integration testing, and system testing.

As each application unit is completed, it undergoes **unit testing** to make sure that it operates reliably and correctly. When all units are complete and tested, **integration testing** is performed to ensure that the units operate correctly together. Unit testing and integration testing are usually performed in a test area. A **test area** is a place where software testing can occur without disrupting the organization's regular information system. A test area might be an isolated section of storage on the computer system that runs the organization's regular information system, or it might be on an entirely separate computer system. When problems are discovered during unit testing or integration testing, the cause of the problem is determined and the problem is corrected. Unit testing and integration testing are then repeated to make sure that the problem is corrected and to make sure that no new problems were introduced when the original problem was fixed (Figure 13-15).

System Testing

Figure 13-15

The results of unit and integration testing must be carefully examined to make sure the application processes data reliably and accurately.

After the unit and integration testing are completed, **system testing** ensures that all the hardware and software components work together. If an existing information system is modified, system testing is performed when the new or modified units are combined with the rest of the existing system. In a completely new information system, system testing is performed to simulate daily work loads and make sure that processing speed and accuracy meet the specifications. System testing is ideally performed in a test area; however, an organization might not have the hardware resources to duplicate its existing information system for testing purposes. In this case, system testing must be performed on the "live," or production, system; this can cause some disruption in the normal functions of the organization.

The A&L project team has one application unit to test: the expert system. To perform the test, the project team places a series of sample orders. The results of the test are examined to see if the expert system completes the orders as expected. In most cases, the expert system works, but the team discovers that two orders do not go through correctly. On examining these two orders, the A&L team notices that in both cases, the item was in stock in two locations that had the same shipping cost and the same shipping time. No rule had been entered that told the system which location to select when an item is available in more than one location that has the same shipping time and the same shipping cost. The A&L team added the following rule and retested the system.

- **If more than one outlet has the item in stock and the shipping cost and the shipping time are the same, then ship from the outlet that has more of the items in stock.**

After adding this rule, the team tests the expert system again. This time all the test orders are processed correctly.

The A&L project has only one module, so integration testing is not necessary. For system testing, the project team loads the expert system and a copy of the order system into a test area. The purpose of this testing session is to make sure the order data is correctly communicated between the existing order entry system and the new expert system. The system test goes smoothly, and so it is time for the project team to schedule implementation of the new system.

QuickCheck C

1 _____ is the process used to create a program using a programming language or application development tool.

2 The process of designing, entering, and testing the rules in an expert system is referred to as _____.

3 _____ testing verifies correct operation of a particular component.

4 _____ testing verifies correct operation of multiple components working together.

5 A(n) _____ is a place where software testing can occur without disrupting the existing information system.

6 _____ testing ensures that all hardware and software components work correctly together.

D Implement the New System

In the implementation phase, the information system is placed into operation. This phase requires careful planning and preparation. The activities that occur in the implementation phase are shown in Figure 13-16.

Figure 13-16

Implementation activities

Training
11

Train Users

How do people find out how to use the new information system? The expert system for A&L Outfitters works behind the scenes, so it doesn't require any user interaction or training. However, for many new information systems, the users need extensive training on system operation, data entry, and additional procedures. If user training is required, the organization schedules training sessions.

Training sessions are sometimes conducted by systems analysts, but might also be conducted by professional trainers or by users from the project team. During the training sessions, users learn how to interact with the interface, how to perform their tasks using the new system, and how to find additional information in user manuals or procedure handbooks. **Procedure handbooks** contain step-by-step instructions for performing a specific job task. A procedure manual takes the place of a complete user manual because in large organizations, employees in a particular department usually perform specific tasks and do not need to know how all the features of the system work.

Convert Data

What happens to the data from the old system? The data used by the A&L expert system is taken directly from the transaction processing system, so it is not necessary to convert any data before implementing the new system. However, implementation of many new information systems requires data to be converted from a manual or previous computer system to the new system. For example, suppose a local building inspector's office has a manual system for issuing and renewing construction permits. It has more than 8,000 permits on record. If this office computerizes, it will need to convert these 8,000 records into electronic format that can be accessed by the new computerized system.

When converting data from a manual system to a computer system, the data can either be typed or scanned electronically into the appropriate storage media. Some organizations have a lot of data that must be converted, and the conversion process can take a long time, require extra personnel, and be quite costly. When converting data from a previous computer system to a new system, a programmer writes **conversion software** to read the old data and convert it into a format that is usable by the new system.

Convert to New System

How does a business go about switching from the old system to the new system?

System conversion refers to the process of deactivating the old system and activating the new one. System conversion is also referred to as "cutover" or "go live." There are several strategies for converting to a new system.

A **direct conversion** means that the old system is completely deactivated and the new system is immediately activated. Direct conversion usually takes place during non-peak hours to minimize disruption to normal business routines. Direct conversion is risky, however, because if the new system does not work correctly, it might need to be deactivated and tested further. In the meantime, the old system must be reactivated and the transactions that were entered into the new system need to be reentered into the old system so business can continue.

A **parallel conversion** avoids some of the risk of direct conversion because the old system remains in service as some or all of the new system is activated. Both the old and the new systems operate in parallel until it can be determined whether the new system is performing correctly. Parallel conversion often requires that all entries are made in both the new and old systems, which is costly in terms of time, computer resources, and personnel. Parallel conversion is fairly safe, but often not practical because of the cost and duplication of effort.

Phased conversion works well with larger information systems that are modularized. In a **phased conversion**, one module of the new information system is activated at a time. After it has been determined that the module is working correctly, the next module is activated, until the entire new system is operating. In a phased conversion, each module of the new system has to work with both the old system and the new system, greatly increasing the complexity and cost of the conversion.

A **pilot conversion** works well in organizations with several branches that have independent information processing systems. The new information system is activated at one branch. After it has been determined that the system works correctly at one branch, it is activated at the next branch. During a pilot conversion, some method must be developed to integrate information from branches using the new system with information from branches still using the old system.

A&L Outfitters has decided on a direct conversion for the following reasons:

- **The added expense of a parallel conversion is probably unnecessary because the expert system has been extensively tested and is likely to work correctly.**

- **A pilot conversion is not possible because all the branch outlets access the same information system.**

- **Phased conversion would not be feasible because there is only one module.**

Acceptance Testing

What about the people who are buying or will be using the system? Do they get a chance to make sure it is working correctly? An information system undergoes a final test called acceptance testing. **Acceptance testing** is designed to assure the purchaser or user of the new system that the system does what it is supposed to do. The procedures for acceptance testing are usually designed by the users and system analysts, and they often include the use of real data to make sure that the system operates correctly under normal and peak data loads. Acceptance testing might occur at the end of the construction phase or during the implementation phase, depending on the organization's implementation plan.

At A&L Outfitters, the special procurement agent has allotted a week's time to observe the expert system in operation to make sure it is working acceptably. If the week passes and no major problems appear with the system, the project team will consider the implementation phase complete.

QuickCheck D

1 A(n) _____ contains step-by-step instructions for performing a specific task.

2 _____ is often used to convert data from an old information system into a format that is usable by the new system.

3 Data conversion refers to the process of converting data, while _____ refers to the process of switching from the old system to the new system.

4 _____ conversion means the old system is completely deactivated and the new system is immediately activated.

5 In a(n) _____ conversion, both the new system and the old system remain operational—entries are made in both systems until it is determined that the new system is performing correctly.

6 In a(n) _____ conversion, one module of the new system is activated at a time.

7 In a(n) _____ conversion, the new system is activated in a single branch or location, where it is thoroughly tested before being activated in the rest of the organization.

8 _____ testing is designed to assure the purchaser or user of the new system that the system does what it is supposed to do.

E Maintain the System

After a system is implemented, it remains in operation for a period of time. During this time, maintenance activities ensure that the system functions as well as possible. Figure 13-17 shows the major maintenance activities for a typical information system.

Figure 13-17

Maintenance activities

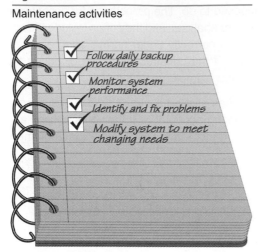

- ✓ Follow daily backup procedures
- ✓ Monitor system performance
- ✓ Identify and fix problems
- ✓ Modify system to meet changing needs

InfoWeb

Maintenance
12

The task of operating the computer on a day-to-day basis is the responsibility of the **system operator**, also called the **computer operator**. The system operator performs system backups and data recovery, monitors system utilization loads, and troubleshoots operational problems. Additional responsibilities might include installing new versions of the operating system and software applications, but in some organizations these responsibilities are delegated to a systems programmer. A **systems programmer** is the operating system guru, usually for a mainframe or mini-computer information system. Responsibilities include installing new versions of the operating system and modifying operating system settings to maximize performance.

Maintaining the hardware and operating system are only a small part of the overall maintenance activities. Modifications to the application software require significantly more of the IS department's resources to fix bugs, add new features, and deal with new versions of commercial applications. Some organizations spend as much as 80% of their information systems budget on software maintenance. As shown in Figure 13-18, maintenance tasks follow a U-shaped curve—an information system requires the most maintenance at the beginning and at the end of its life cycle.

Figure 13-18

Factors that require
system maintenance

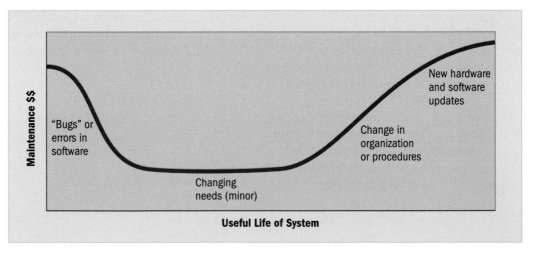

Another maintenance activity that requires extensive IS department resources is end-user support. Even after in-depth training, employees sometimes forget procedures or have difficulty when they encounter a new set of circumstances. These employees turn to the IS department for help. Many organizations have established a **help desk** to handle end-user problems. The help desk is staffed by a support technician who is familiar with the application software. The support technician keeps records of problems and solutions, and routes bug reports to the appropriate programming group.

The maintenance phase continues until the information system is no longer cost-effective or until changes in the organization make the information system obsolete. It is not unusual for an information system to remain in operation for 20 years, but eventually its useful or cost-effective life nears a close. Then it is time to begin the systems development life cycle again.

The A&L expert system will be maintained along with the rest of the transaction processing system. Information systems personnel will make sure that it is backed up regularly. They will also monitor system performance to make sure the expert system does not create a bottleneck and slow down the rest of the system. The special procurement agent has a copy of the expert system that she can use to make modifications in response to changing conditions, for example, if FedEx changes its shipping rates.

QuickCheck E

1 _____ activities include backing up the system, monitoring the system for correct performance, and modifying the system in response to changing conditions.

2 Some organizations spend as much as _____% of their information systems budget on software maintenance.

3 In the early stages of a new information system, much of the maintenance effort deals with _____.

4 An information system is typically used until it is no longer _____ or until it is made obsolete by changes in the organization.

5 When an information system becomes obsolete, it is time to begin the _____ once again.

F Using Data Flow Diagrams

DFDs
13

It is much easier to get an overview of an information system by studying a DFD than by reading a lengthy description. Therefore, DFDs are one of the most important tools in a systems analyst's toolbox. Before you learn about DFD details, look at the DFD in Figure 13-19 and see if you can figure out whether it represents A&L's transaction processing system, MIS, DSS, or expert system.

Figure 13-19

Does this DFD represent A&L's transaction processing system, MIS, DSS, or expert system?

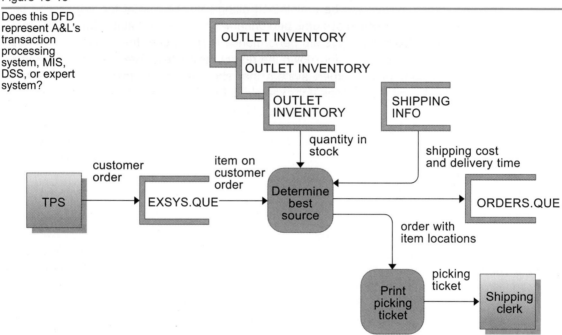

As you have probably recognized, the DFD in Figure 13-19 depicts A&L's new expert system. The purpose of this system is to figure out the best source for the items ordered by a customer. Obviously, if the item is in stock at the local warehouse, that is the best source. However, if the item is not in stock locally, the expert system will search the inventory of warehouses at other A&L locations. When it finds the item at one or more other warehouses, the expert system will analyze shipping prices and times to select the best source. The system then prints a picking ticket at the appropriate warehouse, so a shipping clerk can pack the item and send it.

DFD Symbols

What's the significance of the different symbols on a DFD?   The symbols shown in Figure 13-20 are the basic building blocks for a DFD.

Figure 13-20

Data flow
diagram symbols

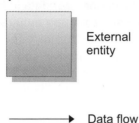
External
entity

Data flow

Process

Data store

An **external entity** is typically a square box that represents an outside source or destination for data. An external entity might be a customer who places an order, a supplier from which you receive inventory items, or another computer system that provides data. You should label external entities with a singular noun such as "Customer" or "Supplier." The A&L system in Figure 13-19 shows two external entities: TPS (transaction processing system) and Shipping clerk. This system receives data from the A&L transaction processing system and sends data to a shipping clerk.

A **data flow** is a line that represents data as it flows through an information system. Arrows at the end of a data flow indicate the direction in which data moves. A double-ended arrow indicates that data moves in both directions. You should label data flow lines with the name of a record, such as "order form," or with a field name, such as "Lastname." The DFD for the A&L system in Figure 13-19 shows that the data in this system is a customer order. A customer order contains the customer name and address, as well as the items the customer ordered.

A **process box** is typically a rounded rectangle that contains the name of a process or procedure. A process box might represent an activity such as "Print picking ticket," "Remove duplicates," or "Sort by last name." When you draw a DFD, you label each process box. The label usually begins with a verb such as "Print" or "Sort" to show that a process does something to the data. The DFD for the A&L system in Figure 13-19 contains two processes. You can see from the labels on these processes that this system determines which outlet is the best source for an item that a customer ordered. It also prints a "picking ticket," which is a list of inventory items and their locations that shipping clerks use to find the items they must pack in an order.

A **data store** is depicted as an open-ended rectangle. A data store shows data at rest, such as when data is stored in a file on a hard disk. You can label data stores with the name of the file that contains the data. The A&L system in Figure 13-19 contains four data stores. EXSYS.QUE holds customer orders while they are waiting to be processed. A series of data stores labeled OUTLET INVENTORY each contain a file of inventory items, their prices, and the quantity of each currently in stock. Each OUTLET INVENTORY represents the data stored at one of A&L's branch outlets. The SHIPPING INFO data store contains the rates and shipping times for shipping companies such as FedEx, UPS, and U.S. mail. ORDERS.QUE is a file that contains customer orders and, importantly, the nearest A&L outlet that has the item in stock.

Interpreting a DFD

How do I read a DFD so I can understand the information system it represents?

To understand a DFD, you should first look at the external entities to find out where the data originates and where it is ultimately headed. Next, you begin to trace the path of the data by following the arrows. To find out how the data gets processed, you read the labels on the process boxes.

It is important to recognize that the data you are tracing is not the only data in the system. To process the data you are tracing, the information system often requires other data. For example, to determine which outlet is the best source for items on a customer order, the information system needs to look at data stored in the OUTLET INVENTORY and SHIPPING INFO. The annotated DFD in Figure 13-21 highlights some of the important points you can discover from the DFD of A&L's expert system.

Figure 13-21

Annotated A&L DFD

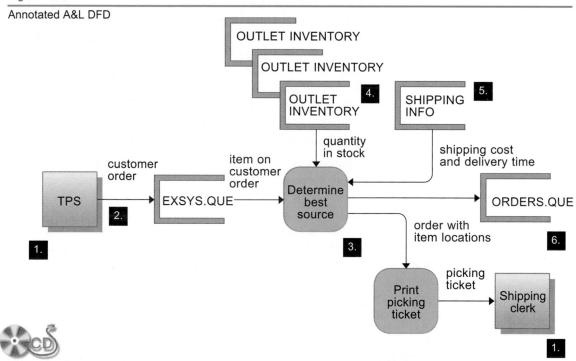

1. Data originates from the A&L transaction processing system and ends up in the hands of a shipping clerk and in the ORDERS.QUE data store.

2. The data originates as a record called "customer order."

3. The system carries out two processes: It determines the best source for an ordered item, and it prints a picking ticket.

4. To determine the best source for an inventory item, the system checks inventory using data from a series of data stores called OUTLET INVENTORY. Each data store contains the inventory for one A&L warehouse.

5. The system needs to use data from the SHIPPING INFO data store if the item is not in stock at the local warehouse.

6. After the system determines the best source, it now has a customer order that contains a list of ordered items and the warehouse from which each item can be shipped. This data is stored in ORDERS.QUE, where it can be accessed by A&L's other information systems. The order data is further processed by being printed as a picking ticket.

Accuracy and Completeness

How can I tell if a DFD is accurate? If someone shows you a DFD, it is likely that your feedback is needed on the completeness and accuracy of the data flows and processes. After you have interpreted the DFD and have an overview of the system it depicts, think carefully about each process. Examine the data that enters the process and the data that it produces. Is the data that enters the process sufficient to produce the data that leaves the process? For example, suppose the OUTLET INVENTORY data store was missing from A&L's expert system DFD. Without this data, how could the "Determine best source" process take an order item and produce the name of the outlet that has the item in stock? If OUTLET INVENTORY was omitted, the DFD would not be accurate.

Figure 13-22

Black holes and miracles

serial numbers → Sort serial numbers

Black hole

Print airline ticket → ticket

Miracle

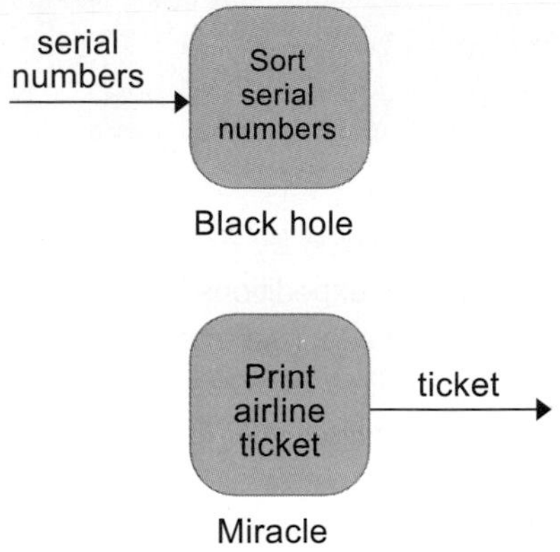

You can also check the DFD for black holes and miracles. A **black hole** is a process that has no output. A process that just "does something" to data, but doesn't put that data anywhere is useless. A **miracle** is a process that has no input. This is an aptly named mistake—like a wizard trying to conjure a bouquet of flowers from thin air, it is impossible for an information system to process data it doesn't have. The black holes and miracles you see in Figure 13-22 would be errors if you found them on a DFD.

EndNote The Norwegian expedition members carefully checked their gear in Resolute, Canada before their departure. Everything had arrived, including the ski poles that the A&L expert system ordered cross-shipped from the Geneva outlet. "You're the best prepared expedition I've ever seen!" exclaimed the pilot, who flew the Norwegians to their departure point on Ellesmere Island.

The trek was not uneventful. Just six days out, one expedition member injured his back when his sled slipped into a crevasse. They radioed for help and a rescue plane ferried him back to Resolute. Weeks later, a hungry polar bear attack proved almost fatal, but the two remaining expedition members trudged northward and, finally, reached the North Pole on May 4. The next day, a U.S. Navy research plane established contact with the expedition. "Who are you?" the pilot radioed. "Is there an emergency?"

"No," was the reply. "We are just two Norwegians who skied here from Canada."

InfoWeb

InfoWeb

Chapter Links

The InfoWeb is your guide to print, film, television, and electronic resources. Use it to obtain updates on quickly changing technical information and to locate information for research papers. If you're using the New Perspectives CD-ROM, click the InfoWeb icon on the left side of this paragraph to access the online InfoWeb links. Otherwise, use your Web browser and type in the address of the New Perspectives site: www.cciw.com/np3. At the New Perspectives site you'll find up-to-date links to the topics covered in this chapter.

1 Expeditions

The Norwegian expedition to the North Pole is based on a true story chronicled by Borge Ousland in a March 1991 *National Geographic* article, "The Hard Way to the North Pole." If expeditions interest you, you can connect to **www.nationalgeographic.com/features/97/andes/** to read a journal of an October 1997 National Geographic Society expedition to the Andes in search of Inca religious sites. At the Web site you can find maps, pictures of Inca tombs, and a discussion forum. In addition, you can view a virtual autopsy of a teenage Inca girl who was sacrificed in an ancient Inca ritual. At another Web site, you can read "Outside Online: Kilimanjaro Climb for <u>CARE</u>" (**outside.starwave.com/places/africa/**) and listen to RealAudio broadcasts that were made during the climb. At the University of California Research Expeditions Program at **shanana.berkeley.edu/urep/** you can learn about field research expeditions that are open to public participation. The range of expeditions is broad, from studies of biodiversity to studies of archaeological sites. Expedition sites are located in Yosemite National Park, Ireland, Costa Rica, Kenya, Brazil, Hawaii, Ecuador, and other places around the world.

2 Mythical Man-Month

Frederick P. Brooks' book, *The Mythical Man-Month* is one of the classics of information systems literature. The book describes why information systems are so difficult to develop. First published in 1975, the book was revised in 1995 and several new chapters were added. You can read reviews of this new edition at **daffy.robelle.com/smugbook/manmonth.html**. Another source of reviews is the Amazon online bookstore at **www.amazon.com**. After you connect to the site, enter "Mythical Man-Month." Brooks received the Bower award and Prize in Science (**sln.fi.edu/inquirer/brooks.html**).

3 Methodologies

Different systems analysis and design methodologies offer a variety of approaches to the process of creating an information system. The classic methodology, structured analysis, was pioneered by Gane, Sarson, and Yourdon. Yourdon's book, *Modern Structured Analysis* (Yourdon Press, 1989) summarizes this approach. The University of Missouri at St. Louis has as excellent systems analysis site with links to many related topics at **www.umsl.edu/~sauter/analysis/analysis_links.html**. Andersen consulting has spent many years refining a systems analysis methodology referred to as METHOD/1. Because Andersen is one of the largest single-source employers of IS personnel, it pays to become familiar with their methodology. Connect to their Web site at **www.ac.com/aboutus/tech/method/au_frmpstart1_0.html**. Joint application development (JAD) emphasizes the requirements of the new information system, rather than an extensive analysis of the old one. Users provide input to analysts during JAD sessions. The book, *Joint Application Development 2nd Edition* by Jane Wood and Denise Silver (John Wiley, 1995) provides a good overview of JAD. For a quick introduction to JAD connect to **www2.computerworld.com/home/print9497.nsf/All/SL47jad**. Another popular methodology is rapid application development (RAD) which uses extensive prototyping to churn out software within a compressed timeframe. The book to read on this topic is *Rapid Development: Taming Wild Software Schedules* by Steve McConnell (Microsoft Press, 1996). You'll find excerpts on the Web at **www.construx.com/stevemcc/rdexcrpt.htm**. Finally, you can learn about object-oriented analysis and design methodologies in *Object-oriented Analysis* by Peter Coad and Edward Yourdon (Yourdon Press, 1991). The Web site **quepasa.cs.tu-berlin.de/ ~bg/diplom/section1_6_0_1.html**, has a nice discussion and diagrams of how object-oriented analysis fits into the SDLC.

4 IS Departments

Information system departments are relatively new arrivals on the corporate organizational chart. In some organizations, IS is a separate organizational branch, but in others it is under the organizational umbrella of the finance department. Within the IS department, employees were traditionally arranged in a hierarchy that included high-level managers, middle managers, and technicians. You can see examples of some IS department organizational charts if you enter "IS department organizational chart" in any Web search engine. Recently, the trend is to flatten this hierarchy. You can read about this trend in "Dotted lines and crooked arrows" by Mitch Betts at **www2.computerworld.com/home/print9497.nsf/All/Slorg214AD6** and in "Rebuilding the IS organization" by Robert Zawacki at **www.computerworld.com/search/ AT-html/9511/951101SL9511lead.asc.html**. What's it like to work in an IS department? Connect to **www2.computerworld.com/home/online9697.nsf/All/971006path** to read "Choosing your Career Path" by Lina Fafard.

5 Systems Analysts

What are the career prospects for systems analysts? You can find out at the Jobquest site, **www.jobquest.com/ooh1996/ooh/ooh04101.htm**. At *ComputerWorld's* Online careers site, **www.computerworld.com/car/index.html**, you can find current and archived articles on important career issues, a salary survey, a special report on IS education, a skills survey, and a list of the 100 best places to work. The Computer Museum's Careers in Computing section at **www.tcm.org/resources/ cmp-careers/cnc-sysanalyst.html** has a detailed description of what systems analysts do, where they are likely to work, and the career outlook for this profession. In addition, this Web page provides links to other Internet resources for systems analysts, including the Institute of Electronic and Electrical Engineers, The Computer Society, and the International Programmers Guild.

6 Project Teams

The trend in most organizations is toward teamwork, and IS departments are no exceptions. What makes a successful team? *Managing Complexity* at **www.as400.ibm.com/ complex/mancom.htm** is a newsletter that IBM publishes for its AS/400 customers. Topics include tips on making teams work from management consultants such as Peter Drucker, team success stories, avoiding the pitfalls of teams, how Lotus Notes can be used to support teamwork, and how workgroup computing can support teamwork. The Academy of Human Resource Development has links to Internet resources on team building at **www.ahrd.org/hrdteams.htm**. Resources include a bibliography on self-directed work teams, a discussion of methods for building and maintaining work teams, a presentation on the traits of successful work teams, and more. NASA Headquarters Library has an extensive reading list on teams and teamwork at **www.hq.nasa.gov/office/ hqlibrary/ppm/ppm5.htm**. Items on the list range from articles in *Fortune* magazine to books from the late 1980s and early 1990s, when corporations first began to recognize the importance of teamwork for successful project development.

7 CASE Tools

CASE software automates, manages, and simplifies the development of information systems by providing tools to summarize system requirements, diagram old and proposed systems, schedule development tasks, prepare documentation, and develop program code. You'll find a good, though lengthy discussion of CASE tools and applications in "The Effective use of Automated Application Development Tools" by P. J. Guinan, J. G. Cooprider, and S. Sawyer at **eagle.almaden.ibm.com/journal/sj/361/guinan.html**. The University of California Administrative Computing & Telecommunications department hosts a site with reviews of

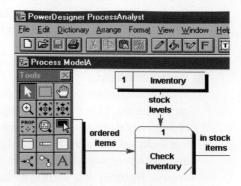

CASE software at **teller.ucsd.edu/spt/case.html**. A really terrific CASE site is hosted by Applied Information Science at **www.aisintl.com**. At the AIS site you'll find non-biased product reviews of CASE tools, and a detailed bibliography (**www.aisintl.com/case/biblio.html**) of CASE book and articles. In addition, you'll find links to the major CASE software vendors such as CASEwise (**www.casewise.com**), Designer/2000 (**www.oracle.com**), WinA&D (**excelsoftware.com**), PowerDesigner (**www.powersoft.com**), and System Architect (**www.popkin.com**).

8 Solutions

One way to come up with solutions is to look at how other organizations have solved similar problems. Microsoft Solution Product Guides at **www.microsoft.com/industry/sguides/** presents articles that describe how Microsoft's information technology products provide business solutions in industries as diverse as accounting, education, engineering, healthcare, manufacturing, retail, and public safety. IBM Business Solutions at **www.ibm.com/Solutions/** has descriptions of how IBM products provide solutions to both small businesses and multinational corporations. Some of the industries include banking, finance, and securities; insurance; telecommunications and media; travel and transportation; and utility and energy services. You can find similar discussions of information technology solutions for businesses at Digital Products and Solutions, **www.digital.com/products.html**, and Sun Products & Solutions at **www.sun.com/products-n-solutions/**.

9 RFPs & RFQs

RFPs and RFQs can become fairly lengthy documents because organizations like to "cover all the bases" to make sure that a vendor is legitimate and will supply an accurate price quote. Before you create your own RFP or RFQ, it pays to look at those created by other organizations. Use the Lycos search engine (**www.lycos.com**) and enter "RFP" or "RFQ" as the search term. The Nova Scotia Department of Finance site at **www.gov.ns.ca/fina/ptns/guideto.htm** illustrates in great detail all of the steps and documents that can be used in a request for proposal process. Looking over this document should give you a good idea of the steps in the RFP process in a government agency and the various documents that need to be prepared. Requests for Quotation generally come from vendors and suppliers and ask clients to provide the necessary information that would allow a salesperson to assess the client's needs and suggest a price for product or services. Some companies make their RFQ forms available on the Internet and World Wide Web, which helps streamline the RFQ process. Some examples include ASIC Semiconductor International Corp. Request for Quotation at **www.asicasic.com/rfq_from_feedbac.htm**; DFS International, Inc. Request for Quotation at **www.dfsintl.com/rfiquote.html**; and Mission Electronics Corporation Request for Quotation at **www.dram.com/ss-6.html**.

10 System Testing

A good set of testing FAQs is at **www.faqs.org/faqs/software-eng/testing-faq/**. You'll find an excellent overview of system testing In Petri Kuusela's master's thesis at **www.to.icl.fi/~kuusela/mt/dip_2p.html**. A good set of links to testing information is the STORM site at **www.mtsu.edu/~storm/** hosted by Middle Tennessee State University.

11 Training

Training employees to use a new information system can become a logistical nightmare. Imagine training thousands of employees on a system they have to begin using tomorrow. *Datamation* and *Computerworld* magazines frequently have articles about employee training. For example, "The Right Formula for Training" by Lauren Gibbons Paul provides an overview of training options, including computer-based and Web-based training (**www.datamation.com/PlugIn/issues/1997/september/09jit.html**). Another article, "Choose the Right Training Strategy" by Peter Katz and Cynthia Katz provides a framework for evaluating various training methods (**www.datamation.com.PlugIn/issues/1995/dec15/ChoosetheRight.html**). One analyst maintains that "Eighty of every $100 of IS training is a complete waste." Read why training often fails in Joseph Maglitta's article "Train in vain?" at **www2.computerworld.com/home/print9497.nsf/All/SL0825jm**.

12 Maintenance

Two approaches to the high cost of maintaining an information system include outsourcing and restructuring. The *Datamation* article, "Outsource your maintenance migraines" by Deborah Ashbrand (**www.datamation.com/PlugIn/issues/1997/june/06out.html**) explains why and how it can be cost effective to outsource information system maintenance tasks. Another *Datamation* article, "Death by Development" by Peter Vogel (**www.datamation.com/PlugIn/issues/1996/march15/Thinkwrap.html**) explains why it might be advantageous to re-think the division between development and maintenance IS personnel. Many maintenance responsibilities fall on the shoulders of the systems operator, also called the systems programmer. To find out if you might like this job, connect to **stats.bls.gov/oco/ocos128.htm** or **www.tcm.org/resources/cmp-careers/cnc-operator.html**. For an overview of how maintenance activities fit into the overall IS department, connect to **www.blackmagic.com/ses/bruceg/sysadm.html** and read *Sample System Administrator Manual* by Bruce C. Gabrielson.

13 DFDs

A data flow diagram (DFD) is one of the many diagramming tools in the systems analyst's toolbox. For a quick overview of DFDs connect to the Applied Information Science site at **www.aisintl.com/case/dfd.html**. You'll find a sample set of DFDs at Professor Sauter's site, **www.umsl.edu/~sauter/analysis/dfd/dfd.htm**. DFDs were suggested by Gane and Sarson in the now classic text, *Structured Systems Analysis* (Prentice-Hall, 1979). An alternative approach using a slightly different symbol set was proposed by Tom De Marco in *Structured Analysis and Systems Specifications* (Yourdon Inc., 1978).

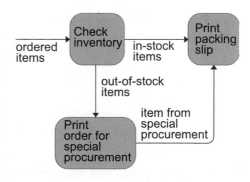

Review

1. Arrange each of the boldface terms in this chapter into one of the following categories: analyzing needs, designing the system, constructing the system, implementing the system, maintaining the system, miscellaneous.

2. Write a short explanation of the types of activities that occur in each of the five phases of the system development life cycle.

3. Some of the following statements describe a problem, and others describe a solution. Indicate if each statement is a problem or a solution.

   a. The desk clerks at a hotel need access to the central reservations database so they can find out if rooms are available due to cancellations.

   b. Notebook computers should be purchased for the salespeople so they can prepare quotations without returning to the main office.

   c. When a customer calls and orders an item that is not in stock, the order clerks cannot find out when the item is expected to be back in stock.

   d. The clerk in accounting needs a Zip drive.

   e. It takes too long to print the current daily reports.

   f. The IS department is not providing end-users with the technical support they need.

4. Create a table that shows the differences between unit testing, integration testing, system testing, and acceptance testing. Your table should show the purpose of the test, what is tested, and the phase of the SDLC in which it is tested.

5. For each of the problem descriptions, use the PIECES framework to indicate if each should be classified as a Performance, Information, Economics, Control, Efficiency, or Service problem.

   a. When an employee quits, sometimes the network manager is not notified and the ex-employee continues to have access to company data by using the Internet.

   b. Customers at the Department of Motor Vehicles must wait while sales clerks walk to computer terminals located in the back of the office, check records, then return.

   c. When order entry clerks complete an order, they must wait 10 seconds while the computer stores the order. During this time, they cannot enter other orders.

   d. When patients are admitted to a hospital, the admitting clerk writes information on a paper form. This information is then sent to data entry, where it is entered into the hospital computer system. The data entry clerks are backlogged, so patient data is not available in the computer system for at least 12 hours.

6. Suppose you want to diagram the data flowing into a mail room. The data comes from the post office and ends up in employee mailboxes. There is one process in which each item is sorted according to its address. Draw a DFD of the mail-sorting system. Make sure you label each symbol on the diagram.

7. Suppose you are a teacher and you want to compute student grades. The data comes from student tests and goes into your grade book. You will take a numeric score such as 76 and convert it into a letter grade A, B, C, D, or F. It is the letter grade that you want in your grade book. Draw a DFD of the grading system. Make sure you label each symbol on the diagram.

8. Use the New Perspectives CD-ROM to take a practice test or to review the new terms presented in this chapter.

Projects

1 Evaluating Possible Solutions Rodney Watson is a systems analyst for U-Fix-It hardware stores. U-Fix-It installed bar-code readers at each register to speed checkouts and improve inventory control. Unfortunately, the clerks are complaining that the bar-code labels are falling off many of the items. When this happens, the clerk must call for someone to go back and check the price of the item. Rodney has identified four possible solutions.

a. Switch to a bar-code label that has better adhesive on the back so the labels are less likely to fall off.

b. Modify the system so clerks can check the current price of an item on a computer price list from their terminals.

c. Print weekly price lists and place them at each register so the clerks can check the price at any item.

d. Hire additional workers to check prices so customers don't have to wait so long for a price check.

Explain which of these solutions you would select and why you would select that solution. If you need additional information before making a decision, describe the information that you need.

2 Problems and Solutions Jennifer Aho works in the circulation department of *Cycle*, a magazine dedicated to bicycle and triathlon enthusiasts. The IS department prints a monthly report showing the current number of *Cycle* subscribers in each zip code. Jennifer calculates the total number of subscribers for the current month and enters this total in a worksheet. She then creates a line chart showing the increase or decrease in total subscribers for the current year. It takes Jennifer four hours each month to calculate the total number of subscribers, enter the total on her worksheet, and print the latest copy of the chart.

a. Define the problem.

b. Think of two possible solutions to this problem. Describe each solution.

c. Which solution would you select? Why?

3  **Request for Proposal** Use your Web browser to search the Web for an actual request for proposal. You can use the search function at **www.lycos.com** or any of the other Internet search engines. Try the phrase "request for proposal" as the search string.

Select a request for proposal from the list and write a brief summary of the proposal that includes the following:

a. The URL of the proposal

b. The organization or business that submitted the proposal

c. A brief summary of the problem the organization is trying solve

4 Cool CeeDees, Inc. Assume you are the manager of a music store called Cool CeeDees. You have defined the following problem: "The current cash register and checkout system does not keep track of the titles of the CDs we sell. It takes too much time to manually count the number of copies of each CD remaining in stock in order to determine which CDs must be reordered." Write a one-page request for proposal, asking vendors to recommend a solution to this problem.

5

CASE Tools CASE tools are one of the most important items in a systems analyst's tool kit. Suppose you have been recently hired as a systems analyst and your supervisor asks you to find and evaluate three CASE tools. Browse the Web and look in computer trade journals to find three CASE tools. Write a memo to your supervisor to report your progress. In the memo include the name of each CASE tool, the company that produces it, its price, and a short description of its purpose and features.

6 **Purchase Process** Most businesses purchase equipment, supplies, or inventory from various vendors. For example, the publisher of Barnett newspapers purchases supplies and equipment for its staff of reporters, editors, advertising agents, and production crew. Suppose a reporter needed a new notebook computer to take on field assignments. Use the data flow diagram below to discover how Barnett would track this reporter's purchase order. Write a one-page description of this process.

Lab Assignments

System Testing

In the System Testing Lab, you are responsible for testing the expert system designed for A&L Outfitters. You will discover if the expert system correctly determines how to cross-ship orders from one A&L outlet to another. If you do all the Lab Assignments in order, you will thoroughly test the system. Your instructor might select only one or two of these assignments, however; in that case you'll get just a flavor of the system testing process.

1 Click the Steps button to learn how to place test data in A&L's inventory, and how to place test orders. As you proceed through the Steps, answer the Quick Check questions. After you complete the Steps, you will see a Quick Check Summary Report summarizing your answers. Follow the instructions on the screen to print this report.

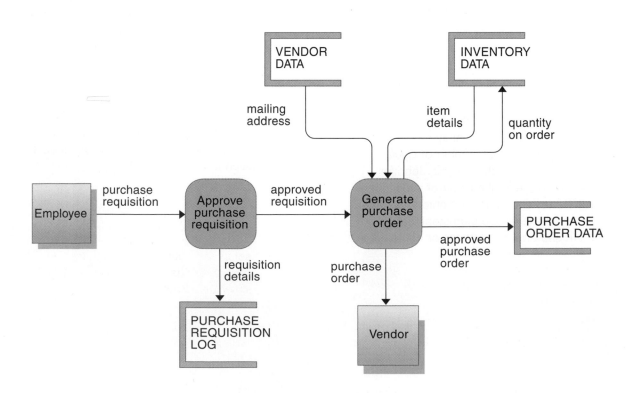

2 When an item is not in stock at the destination outlet, but is in stock at *one* other outlet, the system should find the outlet that has the item in stock. In Explore, test A&L's system to see if it processes such orders correctly. To do this:

a. Use the **View/Edit Inventory** dialog box to make sure that only the Geneva outlet has item 3002 in stock.

b. Place an order on the queue for item 3002 with Katmandu as the destination outlet.

c. Process the order. The item is not in stock at the destination outlet, Katmandu, so the expert system should search the inventory of other outlets and find the item in Geneva. The picking ticket should show Ship From: Genv and Ship to: Katm.

d. Design a test plan that tests at least one order from each outlet and that tests at least one order for each of the five inventory items. Carry out your test plan and record the results. Does the system correctly process orders for an item that is not in stock at the destination outlet, but is in stock at one of the other A&L outlets? If not, explain what the system does wrong, and how it should work.

3 When an item is not in stock at the destination outlet, but is in stock at *two or more* other outlets, the system should find the outlet with the lowest shipping cost. In Explore, conduct the following tests to see if such orders are processed correctly:

a. Use the **View/Edit Inventory** dialog box to make sure that only the Geneva and Telluride outlets have item 3002 in stock.

b. Place an order for item 3002 with Katmandu as the destination outlet.

c. Process the order. The item is not in stock at the destination outlet, Katmandu, but it is available in Geneva and Telluride. The expert system should select the outlet with the lowest shipping cost.

d. Click the **View Shipping Info** button to check the shipping information. Click **Katmandu**, the destination outlet, to view the cost per pound and the time in days to ship an item to that outlet from each of the other outlets. Of the two outlets where this item is available (Geneva and Telluride), Geneva's shipping cost is lowest. The picking ticket should show Ship From: Genv.

e. Design a test plan of five tests to further test how the system handles orders that are in stock at two or more outlets other than the destination outlet. Carry out your test plan and record the results. Did the system correctly process the orders in your test plan? If not, explain what the system did wrong, and how it should work.

4 When an item is in stock at two outlets with the same shipping cost, the system should find the outlet with the fastest shipping time. In Explore, conduct the following tests to see if such situations are processed correctly.

a. Click the **View Shipping Info** button, then click **Guatemala City** as the destination outlet. Notice that items shipped to Guatemala City from Lima and Geneva have the same shipping cost—$26 per pound. Also notice that items shipped from Lima will arrive faster—shipping takes 2 days from Lima, but 3 days from Geneva. Therefore, if an item is needed in Guatemala City, but it is in stock in Geneva and Lima, the expert system should select Lima. Let's test this.

b. Make sure item 3004 is in stock *only* in Lima and Geneva, then order item 3004 with Guatemala City as the destination.

c. Process the order. Because the shipping cost is the same from Lima and Geneva, the expert system should select the outlet with the fastest shipping time. The picking ticket should show Ship From: Lima.

d. Shipping rates are also the same from Telluride and Guatemala City to Geneva. Set up a test in which item 3005 needs to be shipped to Geneva, but is in stock only in Telluride and Guatemala City.

e. Does the system correctly process an order for an item that is in stock at two outlets with the same shipping cost? If not, explain what the system does wrong, and how it should work.

5 In Explore, test the following scenario: if an item is not in stock in the destination outlet, but is in stock at two other outlets with the same shipping cost and the same shipping time, the system should find the outlet that has the highest quantity of the item in stock.

a. There is one situation in which an item can be in stock in two outlets with the same shipping cost and the same shipping time. This situation arises if an item is in stock in Telluride and Guatemala City and is to be shipped to Katmandu. Make sure Telluride has two of item 3005 in stock, and Guatemala City has five of item 3005 in stock. Also make sure item 3005 is not in stock in any other outlets.

b. Place an order on the queue for item 3005 with Katmandu as the destination outlet.

c. Process the order. Because there are more of item 3005 in stock in Guatemala City, the picking ticket should show Ship From: Guatemala City.

d. Does the system correctly process an order for an item that is in stock in two outlets with the same shipping cost and the same shipping time? If not, explain what the system does wrong, and how it should work.

MANAGINGTHEDATA
INFILESANDDATABASES

M*A*S*H, a "two thumbs up" film made in 1970, depicted the hijinks of doctors and nurses in a Mobile Army Surgical Hospital (M.A.S.H.) during the Korean War. The film quickly was recast for television and became a hit series. Millions of viewers tuned in to catch the exploits of two irreverent doctors, John McIntyre and Hawkeye Pierce; a clever procurement officer named Radar O'Reilly; and an officious head nurse, Margaret "Hot Lips" Houlihan.

It was during the Korean War that the first commercial electronic computer predicted the outcome of the 1952 presidential election and some experts predicted that five or six of these machines would be sufficient to satisfy the world's data processing needs. Using computers to maintain data in a M.A.S.H. unit was unthinkable back then. Today, however, computers are deployed with U.S. troops all over the world. Computers are also standard equipment in virtually every hospital and medical clinic.

Our society is becoming increasingly dependent on information stored in financial, medical, law enforcement, and government databases. This chapter will help you understand how to plumb these databases for information—a valuable skill in today's information age.

M*A*S*H
1

CHAPTERPREVIEW

In this chapter you will learn the terminology associated with files and databases. You will discover the advantages and disadvantages of different types of data management software. You will learn about typical data management tasks such as creating files, entering data, searching, sorting, updating, and reporting. And you will learn how to use a query language to search for information. When you have finished this chapter you should be able to:

- Explain the difference between a database and a file
- Define the term "data independence" and explain how it applies to file management systems and database management systems
- Differentiate between a record type and a record occurrence
- Describe the distinguishing characteristics of the four major database models
- Recommend whether to use custom software, file management software, database management software, or object-oriented tools to best solve a data management problem
- Demonstrate how to reduce data redundancy in a file
- List six major database management activities
- Describe the difference between sorting and indexing
- Select an appropriate output format for your data
- Use Boolean logic to construct SQL and Internet search engine queries

LABS

?

SQL Queries

A File and Database Concepts

The term *data file* has several different meanings within the context of computing. You might think of a data file as any file that contains data—word-processing documents, graphics, sounds, and so on. You might think of a data file as any file that is not an executable or program file. These are valid definitions, but the term *data file* might also refer to a file that contains information organized in a uniform format. An example of this type of file is a telephone directory. All the information is in a uniform format: last name, first name, address, and phone number. Other examples include an inventory list, a library card catalog, and a schedule of university courses.

InfoWeb

Database
Concepts
2

A file that is organized in a uniform format is formally referred to as a **structured data file** or a **database file**; more commonly, it is referred to as a "data file" or just a "file." Unfortunately, the terms "data file" and "file" do not distinguish files that are organized in a uniform format from those that are in a more free-form format, such as word processor, spreadsheet, graphics, and sound files. Therefore, when you see the term "data file" or "file" in a computer magazine or documentation, you might have to use clues from the context of the article to decide whether "file" means a structured data file or a free-form file. In this chapter, "data file" refers to a file organized in a uniform format, and the concepts you learn in this chapter apply specifically to this type of data file.

The tasks associated with maintaining and accessing the data stored in a data file are often referred to as **data management**. In this chapter, you will learn about data management concepts using data about the employees who work at Midtown General Hospital. The people who work in the Midtown human resource department use some of this data to maintain basic information about each employee, track absenteeism, examine gender equity, and make staffing projections. The payroll department also uses some of the data to generate employee paychecks. The Midtown data is stored in a series of data files. Each of these data files has a **file structure** that describes the way the data is stored in the file. Figure 14-1 shows some of the data in Midtown's Employee file and provides a conceptual overview of data file terminology.

Figure 14-1

Data file terminology

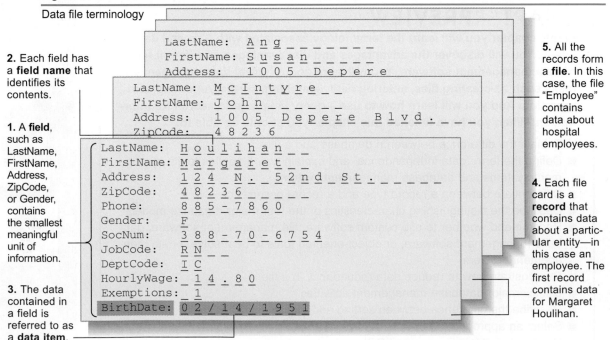

2. Each field has a **field name** that identifies its contents.

1. A **field**, such as LastName, FirstName, Address, ZipCode, or Gender, contains the smallest meaningful unit of information.

3. The data contained in a field is referred to as a **data item**.

5. All the records form a **file**. In this case, the file "Employee" contains data about hospital employees.

4. Each file card is a **record** that contains data about a particular entity—in this case an employee. The first record contains data for Margaret Houlihan.

Fields

What is the basic building block for a data file? As you saw in Figure 14-1, a **field** contains the smallest unit of meaningful data, so you might call it the basic building block for a data file. Each field has a **field name** that describes the contents of the field. For example, the field name BirthDate might describe a field containing an employee birth date.

A field can be either variable-length or fixed-length. A **variable-length field** is like an accordion—it expands to fit the data you enter, up to a maximum limit. A **fixed-length field** has a predetermined number of characters (bytes) it must contain. The data that you enter in a fixed-length field cannot exceed the allocated field length. Moreover, if the data you enter in a field is shorter than the allocated length, blank spaces are automatically added to fill the field. All the fields in Figure 14-1 are fixed length. The underscores indicate the maximum number of characters that each field can contain.

Data Types

Are there any special rules about the data I can enter in a field? The data you can enter into a field depends on the field's data type. From a technical perspective the **data type** specifies the way the data is represented on the disk and in RAM. From a user perspective, the data type determines the way you can manipulate the data. Every field in a file is assigned a data type.

The two most common data types are character and numeric. A **numeric data type** is assigned to fields containing numbers that you might want to manipulate mathematically by adding, averaging, multiplying, and so forth. As an example, the HourlyWage field in Figure 14-1 is a numeric field, so the data in this field can be multiplied by the number of hours worked to calculate pay. There are two main numeric data types: real and integer. The data in the HourlyWage field is a **real number** because it contains a decimal point. The data in the Exemptions field is a whole number or **integer**.

The **character data type**, also referred to as the **string data type**, is assigned to fields containing data that does not need to be mathematically manipulated. Examples of character data include names, descriptions, cities, and state abbreviations.

Some of the data we call "numbers" does not require a numeric data type. A Social Security "number" is an example of data that looks numeric but would not be mathematically manipulated. Social Security numbers, therefore, are usually stored as character data. Other examples of "numbers" that are generally stored as character data include phone numbers and zip codes.

Some file and database management systems provide additional data types such as date, logical, and memo. The **date data type** would be used when you want to manipulate dates, such as when you want to store 10/15/99, but manipulate it to display "October 15, 1999." The **logical data type** is used to store true/false or yes/no data using minimal storage space. For example, you might want to store data in a field to indicate if an employee has a CPR certificate. You could use a logical field called CPRCert in which you would enter either Y or N. A **memo data type** is also called a **memo field** and usually provides a variable-length text field into which you can enter comments. For example, a manager might use a memo field to make notes about an employee's outstanding job performance.

Records

What is the relationship between an entity and a record? An **entity** is a person, place, thing, or event about which you want to store data. A **record** contains fields of data about one entity. For example, one of the records for Midtown employees contains data about the entity Houlihan, Margaret. In a medical office, a patient record contains data such as name, address, and insurance carrier for one patient. In a retail business an inventory record contains data such as part number, cost, and quantity in stock for one inventory item.

A data file with fixed-length fields will have fixed-length records; therefore, the storage space required for each record is the same. For example, every record in the Midtown Employee file contains the same number of characters. You might wonder how this is possible if the data in the fields is different for each record. What if an employee has a very long last name—shouldn't that record be longer than one for an employee with a short last name? The answer is no. Recall that blanks are added to fields that contain data with less than the maximum allocated bytes, so including the blanks, each of the records contains the same number of bytes.

Calculating the record length is important because it helps determine storage needs. Suppose you want to store a data file on a high-density 3¹/₂-inch floppy disk. You have approximately 1,440,000 bytes of storage space available. Could you fit 10,000 of the Midtown employee records on this disk? To answer this question, you need to calculate the size of one employee record by summing the field sizes. Figure 14-2 shows you how to calculate the size of one employee record and then, from that calculation, determine the number of records that will fit on a disk.

Figure 14-2

Calculating record size and storage requirements

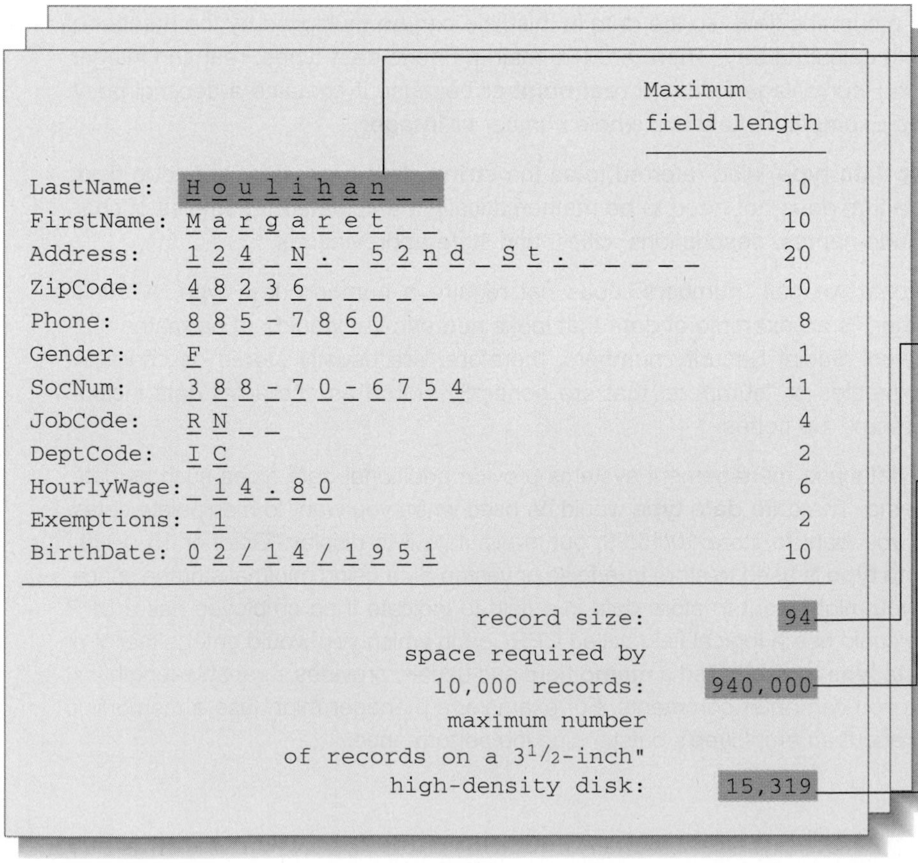

1. Each field has a fixed length. For example, the LastName field can hold up to ten characters, so it has a maximum length of ten. In this case the employee's last name is eight characters, so two blanks are added at the end. If the last name was "Stephanopolous" the field would only hold "Stephanopo."

2. To calculate the record size, list the maximum length of each field. Then, sum the field lengths.

3. To calculate the storage space required for 10,000 records, multiply the record size by 10,000.

4. To calculate how many of these records would fit on a 3¹/₂-inch floppy disk, divide the total disk capacity (1,440,000 bytes) by the size of one record (94 bytes). The result, 15,319, is the number of records that will fit on a 3¹/₂-inch floppy disk.

Record Occurrences and Record Types

Who specifies the fields a record contains? The person who creates the file structure for a data file defines the fields it will contain. This is similar to designing a blank form for a manual record-keeping system or card file. This record structure is referred to as a **record type**.

Once you've entered data into a record, it is referred to as a **record occurrence**. Midtown has record occurrences for Margaret Houlihan and other employees. It is important to understand the difference between a record type and a record occurrence.

The number and names of the fields in a record depends on the data that the records will contain. Different record types are needed for different data. A business or organization will typically need a number of different record types for storing data. For example, Midtown has defined four different record types for storing human resources data:

- **Employee information is stored in a record type called Employee.**

- **Job classifications are stored using a record type called Job.**

- **Department descriptions are stored using a record type called Department.**

- **Payroll history is stored using a record type called Timecard.**

Look at Figure 14-3 to get a general idea of the data that Midtown stores.

Figure 14-3

Midtown maintains data for employees, payroll, department descriptions, and job classifications in four record types.

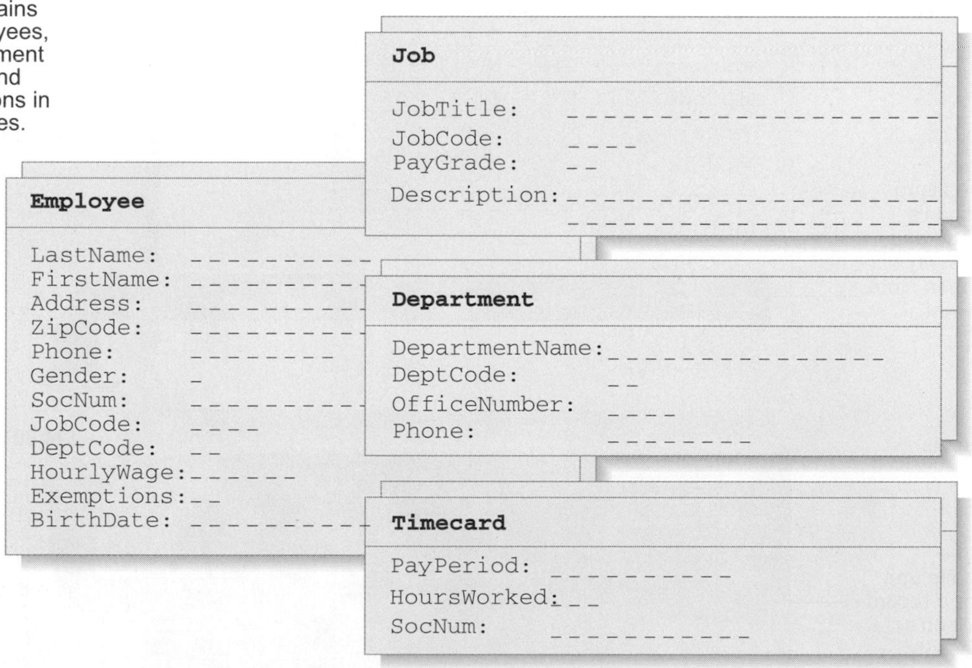

```
Job

  JobTitle:      _ _ _ _ _ _ _ _ _ _ _ _ _ _ _ _ _
  JobCode:       _ _ _ _
  PayGrade:      _ _
  Description: _ _ _ _ _ _ _ _ _ _ _ _ _ _ _ _ _ _
               _ _ _ _ _ _ _ _ _ _ _ _ _ _ _ _ _ _
```

```
Employee

  LastName:      _ _ _ _ _ _ _ _ _ _
  FirstName:     _ _ _ _ _ _ _ _ _ _
  Address:       _ _ _ _ _ _ _ _ _ _
  ZipCode:       _ _ _ _ _ _ _ _ _ _
  Phone:         _ _ _ _ _ _ _ _
  Gender:        _
  SocNum:        _ _ _ _ _ _ _ _ _
  JobCode:       _ _ _ _
  DeptCode:      _ _
  HourlyWage:_ _ _ _ _ _
  Exemptions:_ _
  BirthDate:     _ _ _ _ _ _ _ _ _
```

```
Department

  DepartmentName:_ _ _ _ _ _ _ _ _ _ _ _ _
  DeptCode:        _ _
  OfficeNumber:    _ _ _ _
  Phone:           _ _ _ _ _ _ _ _
```

```
Timecard

  PayPeriod:     _ _ _ _ _ _ _ _ _ _
  HoursWorked:_ _
  SocNum:        _ _ _ _ _ _ _ _ _ _
```

Flat Files

Do all the records in a data file contain the same fields? The term **flat file** is sometimes used to refer to a data file in which all the records have the same **record format**, that is, the same field names, field lengths, and data types. You could also say that a flat file is a single *record type*.

People use the term flat file primarily when they want to distinguish between a single file and a database. The Employee data file you saw in Figure 14-1 is a flat file because all the records have the same record format—the same fields, field lengths, and data types.

Flat files are not particularly efficient for complex data management tasks. Suppose, for example, that Midtown stored employee data in one file and timecards in another file. Margaret Houlihan's hourly wage is stored in the Employee file, but the number of hours she worked is stored in the Timecard file. To calculate Houlihan's paycheck, the computer has to first open the Employee file to get the hourly wage, then close this file. Next it must open the Timecard file, find Houlihan's time card, find the hours she worked, and finally perform the multiplication, as shown in Figure 14-4.

Figure 14-4

Using two flat files to calculate pay

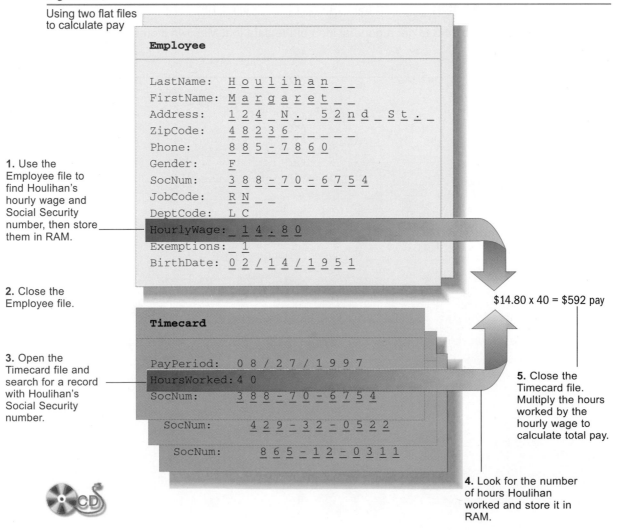

1. Use the Employee file to find Houlihan's hourly wage and Social Security number, then store them in RAM.

2. Close the Employee file.

3. Open the Timecard file and search for a record with Houlihan's Social Security number.

$14.80 x 40 = $592 pay

5. Close the Timecard file. Multiply the hours worked by the hourly wage to calculate total pay.

4. Look for the number of hours Houlihan worked and store it in RAM.

Databases

Does a database offer flexibility for using more than one file? "Database" is one of those terms that has no single definition. It is sometimes loosely used to describe any data file made up of records and fields. This usage, however, does not distinguish between a flat file and a database, so it is not completely accurate from a technical perspective. It is more accurate to define a **database** as a variety of different record types that are treated as a single unit. This definition implies that several flat files or record types can be consolidated or related in such a way that they can be used as essentially one unit—a database.

To use Midtown's four record types as essentially one unit, they must be consolidated into a database. After you create this database, you can combine the data from more than one record type. For example, you could combine the Employee and Timecard record types so you could access the HourlyWage data and the HoursWorked data without opening and closing multiple files. As you examine the process for calculating employee pay in Figure 14-5, contrast it to the more complex process required if the data is stored in flat files (Figure 14-4).

Figure 14-5

Using related record types to calculate pay

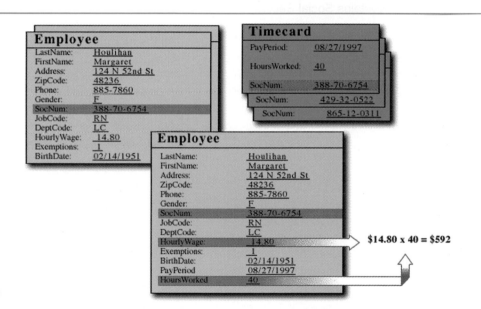

InfoWeb

Database
Administrator
3

Although a database provides more flexibility than a flat file, a database is typically more difficult to design and maintain. In businesses and organizations with substantial data management needs, a **database administrator** generally supervises database design, development, testing, and maintenance. In many respects the database administrator performs tasks similar to those of a systems analyst, but the emphasis is on data collection, manipulation, and reporting. As a career, database administration provides opportunities to work with many aspects of a business and interact with employees, managers, and executives.

QuickCheck A

1 A(n) _____ field expands as you enter data.

2 You should use a(n) _____ data type for a field that contains Social Security numbers.

3 Real numbers and integers can be entered into fields that have been defined as a(n) _____ data type.

4 The abstract or general description of the Midtown employee file is called a record _____, whereas a record that contains the data for John McIntyre is called a record _____.

5 All the records have the same format in a(n) _____ file.

6 A database would be better than a flat file for data that requires different record types, but has relationships between the different record types. True or false? _____

B Data Models

A **data model** is a description of the way data is stored in a database. An efficient data model is important so that data can be entered, located, and manipulated in ways that provide useful information for a business or organization. When you design the structure for a database, a data model helps you understand the relationships between entities and helps you create the most efficient structure for your data.

Entity Relationships

How does a data model describe data? In the previous section of this chapter, you learned that a record represents an entity and is structured into a series of fields. A **relationship** is an association between entities. For example, at Midtown there is a relationship between an employee entity and a time card. You could describe this relationship by saying "an employee has a time card." A data model lets you describe relationships between entities and define these as relationships between record types when you create the structure for a database.

Data Modeling 4

Database designers graphically model data using diagramming techniques such as entity-relationship diagrams, Bachman diagrams, and data structure diagrams. These diagrams provide a graphical representation of relationships and cardinality. For example, the data diagram in Figure 14-6 shows the relationship between an employee and a department.

Figure 14-6

Diagramming relationships

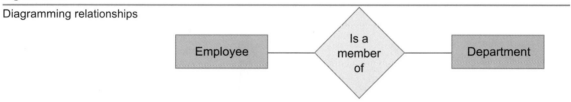

A data diagram can also show **cardinality**, the number of occurrences that can exist between two record types. There are three possible types of cardinality: one-to-one, one-to-many, and many-to-many as shown in Figure 14-7.

Figure 14-7

Diagramming cardinality

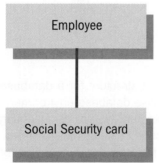
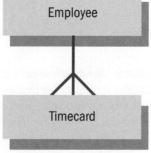
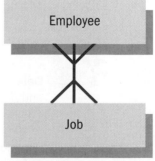

A **one-to-one** relationship is shown by using a single line to connect the boxes that represent record types.

A **one-to-many** relationship is shown by adding a "crow's foot" to the end of the line next to the record type with many occurrences.

A **many-to-many** relationship is shown by adding a "crow's foot" to both ends of the line that connects the record type boxes.

A **one-to-one relationship** means that one record in a particular record type is related to only one record of another record type. For example, each employee has one Social Security card. Also, a particular Social Security card is assigned to only one person.

A **one-to-many relationship** means that one record in a particular record type may be related to more than one record of another record type; for example, one employee has many time cards, one job title can be held by many employees, or one department can have many employees.

A **many-to-many relationship** means that one record in a particular record type can be related to many records in another record type and vice versa. For example, a department might require personnel with many job descriptions such as nurses, technicians, and physicians. At the same time, a particular job might be required in more than one department; for example, nurses might be required in the intensive care department and in obstetrics. The data diagram in Figure 14-8 shows the relationships between Midtown record types.

Figure 14-8

Data diagram for Midtown General Hospital

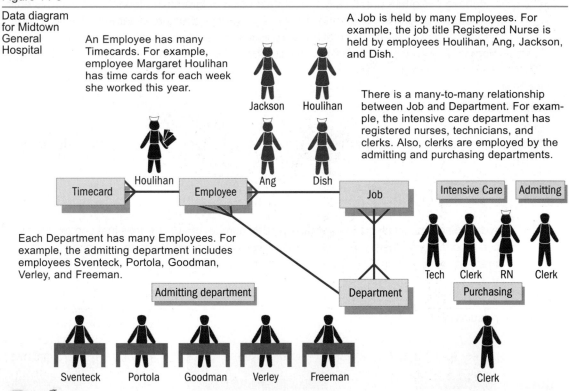

An Employee has many Timecards. For example, employee Margaret Houlihan has time cards for each week she worked this year.

A Job is held by many Employees. For example, the job title Registered Nurse is held by employees Houlihan, Ang, Jackson, and Dish.

There is a many-to-many relationship between Job and Department. For example, the intensive care department has registered nurses, technicians, and clerks. Also, clerks are employed by the admitting and purchasing departments.

Each Department has many Employees. For example, the admitting department includes employees Sventeck, Portola, Goodman, Verley, and Freeman.

Data models help database designers create the most efficient structure for a database and decide which database model will provide the most effective database environment. There are four major **database models**, and each has a different way of representing relationships between entities. Each database model is described using slightly different terminology, but the concepts of record types, fields, and relationships are useful for understanding all of the models.

Hierarchical Database Model

What is the simplest database model? The simplest database model arranges record types as a hierarchy. In a **hierarchical database**, a "parent" record type can be linked to one or more "child" record types, but a child record type can have only one parent. The relationships between records are established by creating physical links between the stored records. A **physical link** means that each record is stored on the disk medium with a set of pre-defined access paths to other records.

A hierarchical database is effective for data that has fairly simple relationships and when data access is routine and predictable. Hierarchical databases are less effective for data with complex relationships and in situations that require flexible or "on the fly" data access because the relationships are physical links defined at the time the database is created. If you want to add a record type or define a new relationship, you need to redefine the database and then store it in its new form. Study Figure 14-9 for an overview of the hierarchical database model.

Figure 14-9

Hierarchical database model

In a hierarchical database, a record type is referred to as a **segment** or **node**. Department, Job, Employee, and Timecard are nodes. The top node of the hierarchy is referred to as the **root**.

Nodes are arranged in a hierarchical structure as a sort of upside-down tree. A **parent** node can have more than one child node. However, a **child** node can have only one parent node. For example, Department has two children: Employee and Job. Timecard has only one parent: Employee.

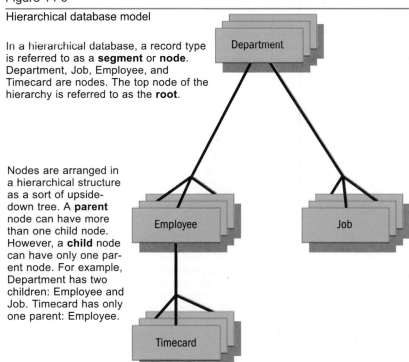

The relationship between a parent node and a child node must be **one-to-many**. Notice that the one-to-many relationship between Job and Department is different from the many-to-many relationship shown between these two record types in Figure 14-8. Using the hierarchical model, you do not have the ability to define many-to-many relationships and, therefore, it is difficult to define some databases so they reflect the actual relationships that exist between entities.

Network Database Model

What if some record types have more than one parent? The model for a **network data-base** resembles the hierarchical model in many respects, but it allows additional types of relationships. As with the hierarchical model, the network model is a collection of physically linked records in a one-to-many relationship. The physical link is created when the data is stored on tape or disk. There are differences between the two models, however. In a network database, related record types are referred to as a **set**. A set contains an **owner**, which is similar to a parent record in a hierarchical database. A set also includes one or more **members**, roughly equivalent to child records in a hierarchical database.

A network database provides more flexibility than a hierarchical database because it allows member records to have more than one owner. However, as shown in Figure 14-10, many-to-many relationships are not allowed in a set; therefore, the network model does not allow you to define some real-world data relationships.

Figure 14-10

Network database model

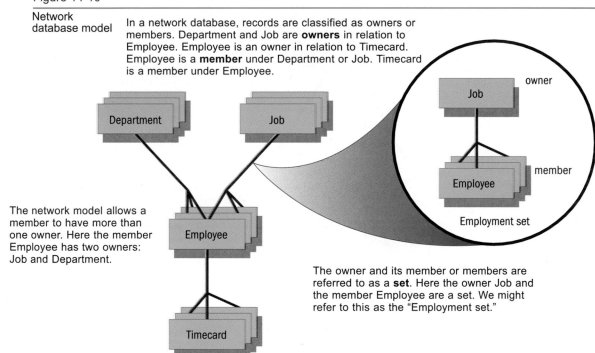

In a network database, records are classified as owners or members. Department and Job are **owners** in relation to Employee. Employee is an owner in relation to Timecard. Employee is a **member** under Department or Job. Timecard is a member under Employee.

The network model allows a member to have more than one owner. Here the member Employee has two owners: Job and Department.

The owner and its member or members are referred to as a **set**. Here the owner Job and the member Employee are a set. We might refer to this as the "Employment set."

Relational Database Model

Suppose I need even more flexibility to define relationships? A **relational database** is perceived by its users to be a collection of **tables** roughly equivalent to a collection of record types. Today's microcomputer databases most frequently use the relational database model because it offers great flexibility for defining relationships.

The strategy for defining relationships in the relational model is fundamentally different from that of the hierarchical or network models. In the relational model, records are related by the data stored jointly in fields of the records in two files. For example, Margaret Houlihan's Employee record is related to her Timecard records because the data in the SocNum fields is the same. The significance of the relational database model is that the tables seem to be essentially independent, but they can be related in many flexible ways. Further, because the tables are a conceptual aid, the user does not need to deal with a physical storage plan for the data on disk. Figure 14-11 provides an overview of relational database structure and terminology.

Figure 14-11

Relational database model

The data for each record type is stored in a **table**, also called a **relation**. A relational database for the Midtown General Hospital would have four tables: Employee, Timecard, Job, and Department.

Data from the two tables can be combined by matching the data in two fields. For example, the data in the Employee and the Timecard tables can be joined by matching the data in the SocNum field.

Table: Employee

LastName	FirstName	Address	SocNum
Ang	Susan	99 Lake Shore Dr.	453-78-2311
Houlihan	Margaret	124 N. 52nd St.	388-70-6754
McIntyre	John	1005 Depere Blvd.	475-66-6245

Table: Timecard

PayPeriod	HoursWorked	SocNum
05/26/1997	45	453-78-2311
05/26/1997	40	388-70-6754
05/26/1997	49	475-66-6245
06/02/1997	40	453-78-2311
06/02/1997	40	388-70-6754
06/02/1997	43	475-66-6245

Table: Job

JobTitle	JobCode	PayGrade	Description
Registered Nurse	RN	5	A registered...
Staff Physician	SMD	9	A Staff...

Table: Department

DepartmentName	DeptCode	OfficeNumber	Phone
Intensive Care	IC	S0502	885-7070
Emergency Room	ER	B100	885-1222
Obstetrics	OB	S0301	885-1344
Accounting	AC	AD230	885-4536
Human Resources	HR	AD260	885-1908

A row of the table is called a **tuple** and is equivalent to a record. The columns in the table are called **attributes** and are equivalent to fields.

Object-Oriented Database Model

Is the relational database model the most effective?   An **object-oriented database** (OODB) organizes data into a hierarchical class of objects defined by **attributes**. An **object** can be manipulated using **methods**. An analogy will explain the meaning of class, object, attribute, and method.

Suppose you have a class of things called "fasteners" that includes objects such as screws and nails. Each object has attributes. A nail has a point, and it has a flat head. A screw has a point, it has a grooved head, and it has spiral ridges on its shaft. What method do you apply to a nail? You pound it with a hammer. What method do you use with a screw? You twist it with a screwdriver.

OODB
6

How does this apply to the data at Midtown? A Midtown employee can be described as an *object* with *attributes* such as a last name, first name, and Social Security number. Employee objects are grouped by *class*: registered nurse, clerk, staff physician, and so on. The *method* for paying an employee depends on the class to which an employee object belongs. Registered nurses and clerks are paid by the hour. Staff physicians are paid a salary. Figure 14-12 shows an object-oriented approach to Midtown data.

Figure 14-12

Object-oriented
database model

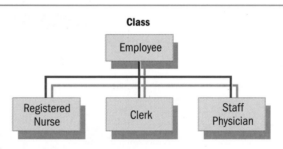

Objects that share common characteristics are grouped into a **class**. The class Employee includes the objects Employee, Registered Nurse, Clerk, and Staff Physician. The Timecard object is a separate class.

Objects

	RN		MD		Clerk
	LastName:_____		LastName:_____		LastName:_____
	FirstName:_____		FirstName:_____		FirstName:_____
	Address:_____		Address:_____		Address:_____
	SocNum:_____		SocNum:_____		SocNum:_____
	HourlyWage:_____		Salary:_____		HourlyWage:_____

All the objects in a class share certain **attributes**, so all have fields for LastName, FirstName, Address, and so on. Unique attributes can also be assigned to some objects. In this case, staff physicians have a Salary field, whereas RNs and Clerks have an HourlyWage field

Methods to calculate weekly pay

Find hours worked on Timecard   Divide annual
and multiply by HourlyWage   salary by 52

The method CalculateWeeklyPay calculates the weekly pay for registered nurses, clerks, and staff physicians. To find the hours worked by each clerk or nurse, the method looks in the HoursWorked field of the Timecard object. Staff physicians are paid based on salary. Therefore, the method CalculateWeeklyPay is different for staff physicians than for registered nurses or clerks.

Using an object-oriented database for Midtown data provides a structure capable of defining complex data relationships. It also provides the flexibility to create variations of a single record type. For example, in the hierarchical, network, and relational models, all the employee records have the same structure, which includes a field for hourly wage. To use these models for salaried employees you would need to design a new record type such as SalaryEmployee. With the object-oriented database, the record type for salaried employees would be only a variation of Employee and would not require a separate series of commands.

In the past, mainframe databases often followed the hierarchical or network model. During the 1980s the relational model gained popularity. Databases that companies and individuals maintained on microcomputers typically followed the relational model, primarily because most database management software for microcomputers supported the relational database model. The trend over the last five years has been toward the object-oriented model on both mainframe and microcomputer platforms.

QuickCheck B

1. A database designer creates a(n) _____ to describe the way data is stored in a database.

2. In addition to relationships, a data diagram can also show _____, the number of occurrences that can exist between two record types.

3. For the Midtown data, the Employee and Timecard record types would be diagrammed as a(n) _____-to-many relationship.

4. The simplest database model is a(n) _____ model.

5. If member records have more than one owner, it is best to use a hierarchical database model. True or false? _____

6. The _____ database model is structured as a collection of tables.

7. If you want to assign methods to your data, you should use an object-oriented database. True or false? _____

⊂ **File and Database Software**

File and database software helps you create an efficient hierarchical, networked, relational, or object-oriented collection of data. It helps you enter and manipulate data, format data into reports, and interact with data on the Web. The software you select for these tasks depends on your data model, the flexibility you require for manipulating your data, and the resources you can devote to maintaining your data. In this section you will learn the advantages and disadvantages of custom software, file management software, database management systems, object-oriented tools, and Web-enabled database tools.

Custom Software

Because every database is unique, do I need to write my own custom file management software? Historically, file management tasks were often accomplished using **custom software** designed to hold data, such as time cards, and to manipulate that data. To manipulate other data, such as employee records, additional custom software was required. An organization with many different data files would require many custom programs to manipulate the data in those files, as shown in Figure 14-13.

Figure 14-13

In the custom program approach, each file requires its own set of programs. Notice that many of the programs for the Employee file are similar in function to programs for the Timecard file.

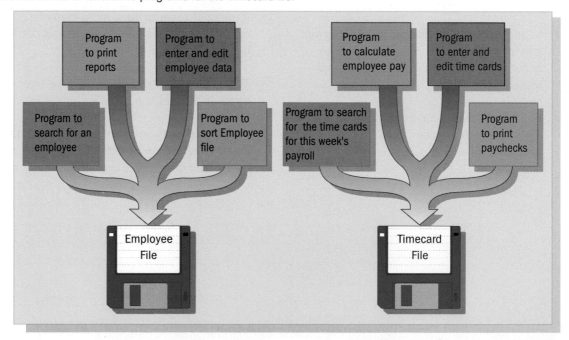

It is possible to create custom software to accommodate hierarchical, network, relational, and object-oriented models. Custom data management software has the advantage of being tailored to the exact needs of a business or organization.

In the past, custom software was built "from scratch" using a programming language, but today this is seldom the case. Instead, custom software is assembled using programming languages and specially designed database components. This combination maximizes flexibility and minimizes development time.

File Management Software

Can commercial file management software adapt to my data management needs?

File management software adapts to your data management needs by allowing you to specify field names, select data types, and designate field lengths for each file you create. You then use standard features provided by the software for basic data management tasks such as entering, changing, organizing, displaying, locating, and printing data. Figure 14-14 illustrates how file management software handles the data management tasks common to a number of data files.

Figure 14-14

File management software provides a standard set of programs that handle basic data management functions for any file. If needed, custom programs, such as one to calculate employee pay, can supplement the standard set of file management programs.

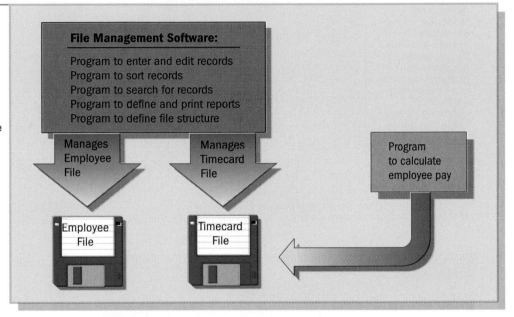

File management software adapts to different files as a result of a concept called data independence. **Data independence** refers to the separation of data and the programs that manipulate that data. For example, if you change the file structure by adding a field, the programs that manipulate the data still function. File management software promotes data independence because the file management software is not tied to a particular data file.

File management software is not part of a data file; therefore, you might say that it is **external** to the data. In fact, if you found that you didn't like the file management software you used to create your data files, you could change to different file management software and use it with your existing data files.

In some situations, the basic file management features provided by commercial file management software are not sufficient for the needs of an organization—perhaps the software does not allow enough flexibility in designing reports, or perhaps it does not provide a way to graph the data. If the file management software's basic features are not sufficient, you might require a customized program, but you would typically use it in addition to the commercial file management software.

File management software, generally considered the easiest and least expensive data manipulation tool, does have limitations. File management software creates and manipulates only flat files, opens only one file at a time, and does not allow you to specify relationships between entities.

Database Management System

Can I buy commercial software that will let me work with data in more than one file at a time? A **database management system** (DBMS) is application software that helps you manage the data in more than one file at a time. A DBMS performs the same functions as a file management system, but in addition a DBMS allows you to work with more than one file by defining relationships among record types, as shown in Figure 14-15.

Figure 14-15

A single generalized database management system provides the programs necessary to manage the data in all the record types of a database. It also helps you define relationships between record types and allows you to write custom programs to handle additional data.

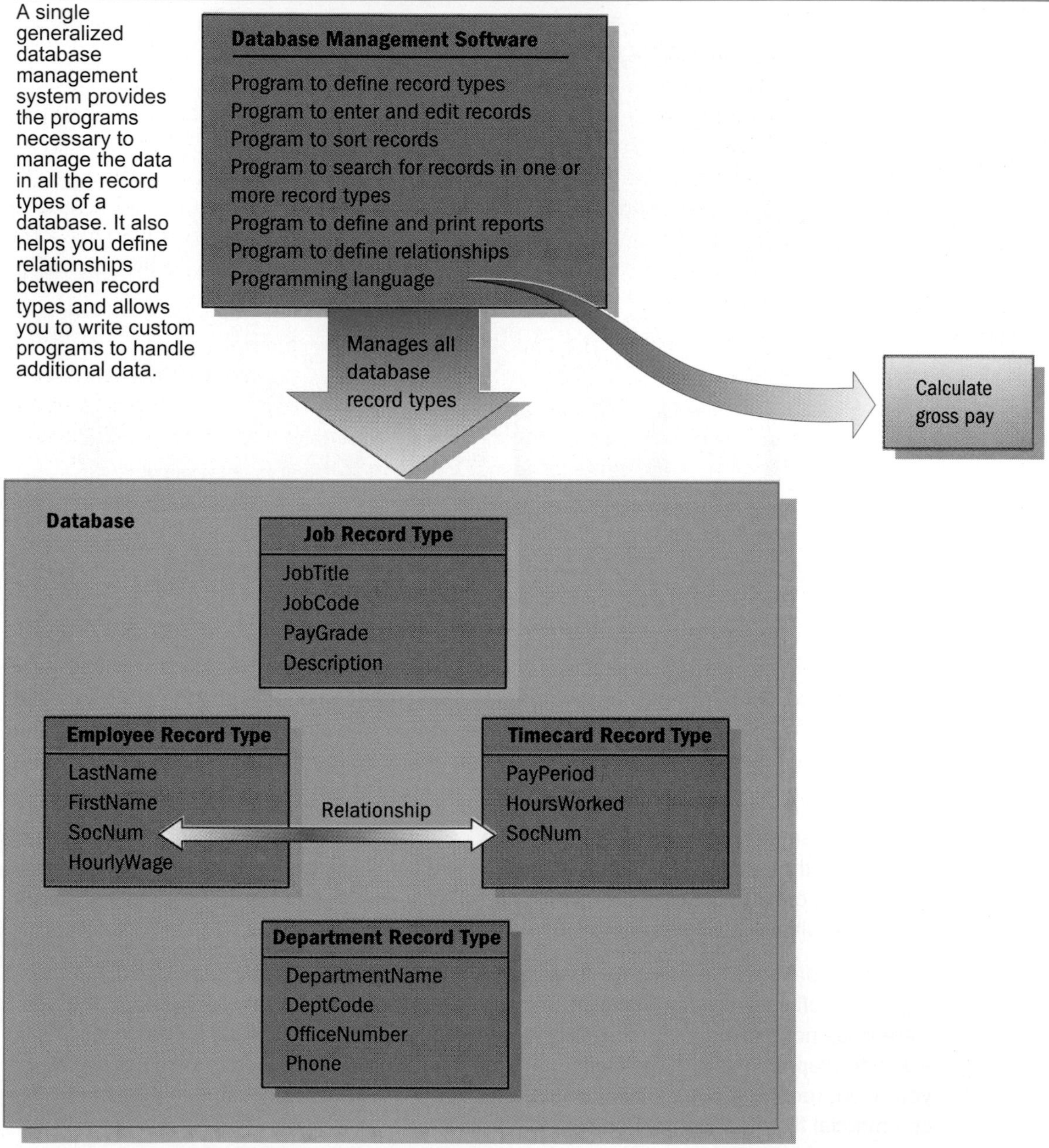

Database Management Software

Program to define record types
Program to enter and edit records
Program to sort records
Program to search for records in one or more record types
Program to define and print reports
Program to define relationships
Programming language

Manages all database record types

Calculate gross pay

Database

Job Record Type

JobTitle
JobCode
PayGrade
Description

Employee Record Type

LastName
FirstName
SocNum
HourlyWage

Relationship

Timecard Record Type

PayPeriod
HoursWorked
SocNum

Department Record Type

DepartmentName
DeptCode
OfficeNumber
Phone

A DBMS typically provides a way to create customized programs for tasks you frequently perform. For example, every two weeks you might want to find all the time cards for the current pay period, then find the hourly wage from each employee's Employee record, and finally calculate total pay. You could use the built-in functions of the database software to do each of these operations, one by one. However, by creating a custom program to do this, you could tell the DBMS to "do payroll" and it would automatically perform all the necessary operations.

InfoWeb

DBMS Software 7

Many of today's database management systems provide an option for **client/server** operation. Using a client/server DBMS on a network, **DBMS server software** runs on the network server. This server software processes requests for data searches, sorts, and reports that originate from the **DBMS client software** running on individual workstations. For example, you might want to search an aircraft database for a list of the aircraft used by commercial airlines worldwide. Your DBMS client refers this request to the DBMS server. The server searches for the information and sends it over the network to your workstation. Once at your workstation, you can sort the list and create your own customized report. Client/server operations distribute data processing tasks. If your DBMS did not have client/server capability, the entire database would be copied to your workstation and your software would search for the requested data—a process that would typically take much longer than if the data was processed with the help of the server.

It would be possible to create a database management system using a programming language. However, because a DBMS is quite complex, most users elect to purchase a commercial DBMS package. The cost of a database management system can be a worthwhile investment, especially for an organization with many record types and databases to maintain. Figure 14-16 shows popular DBMS software.

Figure 14-16

Popular DBMS software

Object-Oriented Tools

Can I use a DBMS to create an object-oriented database? File management systems and database management systems operate on a **passive data set** in which the data simply waits for a program to process it. However, an object-oriented database often includes **methods** that perform actions on the data. To construct an object-oriented database you should use an **object-oriented database management system** (OODBMS) or a programming language, such as **Smalltalk**, that is designed to manipulate objects and define methods.

OODBMS
Tools
8

With the object-oriented approach, the only programs that operate external to the database are those you use to define the objects, methods, and classes for the database. These programs are usually included in the object-oriented database software, although they do not become part of the database itself. Figure 14-17 illustrates the object-oriented approach.

Figure 14-17

An OODBMS provides a way to define objects, methods, and classes. Most other data management activities, such as sorting, searching, and calculating, are performed by methods incorporated in the database.

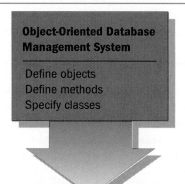

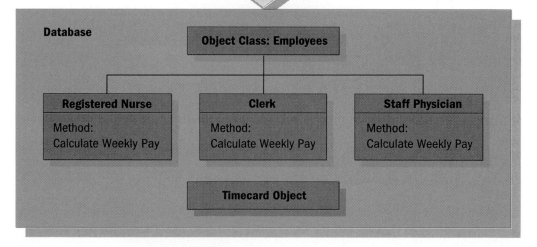

Web-Enabled Database Tools

Is it difficult to design a database that can be accessed over the Web? **Web-enabled databases** allow you to access a database over the Internet using a standard Web browser. As an example, suppose you're designing a Web-based bookstore. You want customers to connect to your Web site and type in an author name or book title. You then want to display a list of matching books that you have in stock, along with information on each book such as title, author, publisher, publication date, and price. The results of a customer's search depend on what the customer is looking for and what you have in stock. Since HTML pages are static, it would seem impossible to create a series of Web pages that would provide results for any customer's search. Also, because you have all this data already stored in a database, it would be very inefficient to re-enter it as HTML-formatted Web pages. Instead, you would like your database to automatically generate a Web page of books in response to a customer's search.

InfoWeb

DB Web
Tools
9

To interact with a Web-based database, it is necessary to pass requests from the browser to the database, then pass the results back to the browser. Programs written to the Common Gateway Interface (**CGI**) provide this capability. These programs can be written in programming languages such as Perl, C, and Visual Basic. High-performance alternatives to CGI include proprietary interfaces such as **ISAPI** (Internet Server Application Program Interface) and **NSAPI** (Netscape Server Application Program Interface) provided by Web servers. Specialized **Web application development tools** such as Cold Fusion and Corel WEB.DATA provide a way to link HTML pages to a database without programming. Web-enabled database tools are included with many popular database packages such as Microsoft Access and IBM DB2.

Using any of these tools you can set up a bookstore site, for example, where a customer enters a book title or author name such as "John Grisham." The customer's search is sent to your Web server where your database software searches for any books by John Grisham. Your Web server then generates a Web page listing all of Grisham's books available from your bookstore and sends the page back to the customer's browser.

QuickCheck C

1. Historically, file management tasks were often accomplished by _____ software designed to hold data and to manipulate that data.

2. File management software adapts to different files as a result of a concept called _____.

3. File management software is external to a data file, but the methods that manipulate data are internal in a(n) _____ database.

4. File management software works with only one file at a time, but if you want to define relationships between data in two or more files you must use _____ software.

5. A(n) _____ DBMS distributes data processing tasks between the workstation and a network server.

6. You can create a Web-enabled database using standard HTML tags. True or false? _____

D File and Database Management Tasks

A **data management environment** refers to the software or program you use to design and manage data, whether you use custom software, file management software, database management systems, object-oriented, or Web-enabled tools. Regardless of the data management environment you use, many data management tasks remain the same. In this section you will learn more about specific data management tasks.

Designing the File Structure

Where do I begin? The key to an effective file or database is the initial design of its structure. With a good structure, the data can be flexibly manipulated to provide meaningful, accurate, and timely information for decision making. Suppose that you are a database administrator faced with the task of designing an effective way to store and manage your organization's data. How do you proceed?

The first step is to determine what data needs to be collected and stored. In other words, you must decide what fields to include. To do this, you might begin by listing the information that is available, as well as any additional information that is necessary to produce the screen output or printed reports that your organization requires. Each piece of information on your list is a candidate for a data field. If you are designing a file or database for the human resource department, for example, you would probably recognize the need for information such as employee name, address, phone number, job code, and birth date. Each of these might become a data field.

The next step in the design process is to decide how to organize the information into fields so it can be used flexibly. For example, would it be better to store an employee name as one field or would it be better to have separate fields for the first name and the last name? If you would like to print mailing labels with the name in the format "Margaret Houlihan" and also print an employee list with the names in the format "Houlihan, Margaret" you would need to have separate fields for the first and the last names. If you did not use separate fields for the first and last names, "Margaret Houlihan" would be entered into a single field. It would then be very difficult to devise a way to separate the first name from the last name and reverse them if you wanted to output the name as "Houlihan, Margaret."

Next, you must decide on the data type for each field. As you learned earlier in this chapter, most data management environments let you select from character, numeric, date, logical, and memo data types. Remember that data you want to use for calculations should be defined as numeric.

After you select data types, you should decide on the format and valid range for each field. The **field format** provides a template for the way data is displayed on the screen and printed. For example, if you specify a field format of XX/XX/XXXX, when you enter 10151999 it appears as 10/15/1999. On the other hand, if you specify the format XX-XX-XXXX, the entry 10151999 appears as 10-15-1999. In addition to dates, other commonly use field formats are shown in Figure 14-18.

Figure 14-18

A series of 9s indicates the field type is numeric. A series of Xs indicates the field type is character.

Currency	$9,999.99
Social Security number	XXX-XX-XXXX
Telephone number	(XXX)XXX-XXXX
Zip code	XXXXX-XXXX

Many data management environments allow you to use a **range check** to specify what constitutes the range of valid entries in each field and, thereby, decrease errors. For example, you might specify that the HourlyWage field can contain values from $0.00 to $20.00. Then if a user enters $150 instead of $15, the database will not accept the entry.

Your ability to define field formats and range checks depends on the particular data management environment you use. The programming languages used to create custom software generally provide you with the commands necessary to create a section of your program that will display and print fields as you specify. With the object-oriented approach, you would define formats and range checks as methods. Not all file and database management systems provide a way to define field formats and range checks. You would need to refer to the documentation to find out if a particular environment supports these two features.

The next consideration in database design is how to group the fields. Each group you create becomes a record type; or if you are using an object-oriented model, each group becomes an object and the objects may further be grouped into classes. You should structure the groups to reduce storage space requirements and provide the level of access-flexibility required by the people who use the data.

In an object-oriented environment you can also define methods that process the data in each object. A careful consideration of which objects inherit each method will help you produce an efficient object-oriented database.

When you group fields into record types, you essentially make the choice between using a flat file and a database. If you arrange all the fields in a single record type, you are using a flat file structure. If you arrange the fields into more than one record type, you are using a database structure. Let's look at an example.

Suppose the information systems manager of Midtown wants to keep track of computer equipment in case it needs to be replaced or repaired. Should he maintain a flat file or a database? Figure 14-19 shows a flat file, which would keep track of computer equipment and provide the information necessary to send it to a repair center.

Figure 14-19

Equipment flat file

Item	Serial Number	Date Purchased	Repair Center	Repair Center Phone	Repair Center Address
Computer	458876	02/12/1995	Epson	415-786-9988	93 Torrance Blvd.
Computer	433877	03/03/1996	IBM	913-559-5877	2 Bradhook Ave.
Printer	6855200	03/03/1996	Epson	415-786-9988	93 Torrance Blvd.
Computer	884411	01/21/1995	Epson	415-786-9988	93 Torrance Blvd.
Modem	B7654D	01/21/1995	High Tech	509-776-7865	4109 Highway 56
Computer	5544998	01/21/1995	IBM	913-559-5877	2 Bradhook Ave.

Using a flat file for the equipment data is not very efficient. The problem with this flat file structure becomes evident when you look at the repair center data. The Epson repair center name, address, and phone number are repeated on many records. If the repair center moves to a different location, a data entry clerk will have to change the address in many records.

Repetition of data is referred to as **data redundancy** and is very undesirable because it makes inefficient use of storage space and makes updating cumbersome. In a well-structured database, the data is stored non-redundantly.

InfoWeb

The process of analyzing data to create the most efficient database structure is referred to as **normalization**. There are five normalization procedures, the first of which is to eliminate data redundancy. The remaining normalization procedures are somewhat technical and are best left to more advanced students of database management. To eliminate data redundancy, you remove the repeating fields and group them as a new record type, as shown in Figure 14-20.

Normalization
10

Figure 14-20

Eliminating data
redundancy

Record type: Equipment

Item	Serial Number	Date Purchased	Repair Center
Computer	458876	02/12/1995	Epson
Computer	433877	03/03/1996	IBM
Printer	6855200	03/30/1996	Epson
Computer	884411	01/21/1995	Epson
Modem	B7654D	01/21/1995	High Tech
Computer	5544998	01/21/1995	IBM

Record type: RepairCenter

Repair Center	Repair Center Phone	Repair Center Adress
Epson	415-786-9988	93 Torrance Blvd.
IBM	913-559-5877	2 Bradhook Ave.
High Tech	509-776-7865	4109 Highway 56

You might wonder why you couldn't have the computer search for each of the records you want to change and automatically make the update. This, of course, is possible. However, everytime data is entered, the possibility of an error creeps in. If an entry clerk enters "Epsom" instead of "Epson," the software will not find this record as part of the search and will not make the update. Errors such as this have a way of increasing over time, eventually leaving the database with many inaccuracies.

Entering Records

When can I enter my data? When you specify the database structure, you essentially design a blank form that will hold data. After the form is complete, you can begin to enter data. As you enter each record, it is assigned a **record number**. The first record you enter becomes record #1. The second record you enter becomes record #2, and so forth. In an object-oriented database, each object receives a unique **object ID number**, which is similar to a record number. The computer uses record numbers and object IDs to keep track of the data you enter.

Consistency is important for data entry because it affects the efficiency of your searches. Suppose you're entering employee data for registered nurses and you enter "RN" as the job code for some employees, but you enter "NURS" for other employees who hold the same position. If you later want the database software to print a list of all nurses and you ask for all the RNs, the employees you identified as NURS will not be included on the list.

Another issue related to entering consistent data is case sensitivity. **Case sensitivity** means that uppercase letters are not equivalent to their lowercase counterparts. In a case-sensitive database, the state abbreviation MI is not the same as the abbreviation Mi. Not all data management environments are case sensitive. You must read the documentation to determine whether a particular data management environment is case sensitive.

Database designers try to minimize inconsistent input by using input lists whenever possible. An **input list** contains all the valid choices for a field. Instead of typing data into a field, a user selects one of the items from the list (Figure 14-21) and avoids the possibility of a typographical error.

Figure 14-21

Using an input list reduces typographical errors and data inconsistencies.

Instead of typing a state name or abbreviation, clicking the field displays an input list.

When you select a state, the database software enters the state abbreviation in the field so that you avoid typing the wrong abbreviation or making a typographical error.

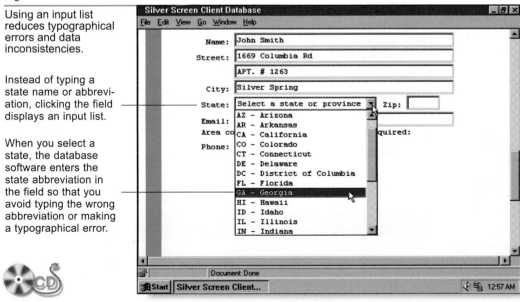

Searching

How do I find a particular record once it is entered? A realistic file or database contains hundreds or thousands of records. If you want to find a particular record or a particular group of records, scrolling through every record is too cumbersome. Instead, you enter search specifications called a **query**, and the computer will quickly locate the records you seek.

Queries can be simple or complex. An example of a simple query would be if you want a list of everyone who has "Jones" as a last name. A more complex query might be to find anyone in the database with a last name of "Jones" who works as a "LPN" and was hired after "01/01/97" but before "01/01/98."

Most database management systems have a special query language that you use to state search criteria. A **query language** provides a set of commands you can use to locate and manipulate data. A popular query language for both mainframes and microcomputers is **Structured Query Language**, more commonly called **SQL**.

SQL
11

As an alternative to a query language, many data management environments allow you to query by example. **Query by example** provides you with a blank record into which you enter examples or specifications of the records you want to find. Figure 14-22 shows how you might use query by example on a form for the Midtown employee records.

Figure 14-22

Query by example

When you begin a query by example, the software displays the field names on a blank form.

You specify the query by typing in examples of the records you want to find. Here, the query specifies all female RNs who make more than $10 an hour.

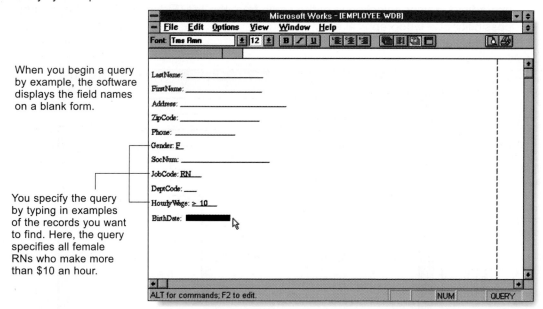

In many respects a database is like a vast warehouse of data from which you can locate information that provides you with insights about the status of a business or the success of an organization. The similarity between databases and warehouses has given rise to the terms data warehousing and data mining. **Data warehousing** means collecting vast amounts of data—usually at least 10 gigabytes. **Data mining** means combing through that data to discover patterns and relationships important to decision making.

Data
Warehouses
12

Updating Information

What if I want to change some of the data? Often the reason you search for a particular record is to **update** it, that is, to change it or delete it. The typical process is to enter a query so the computer finds and displays the record you wanted to update. Next, you make the changes and, if necessary, indicate that you want to save the record in its changed format.

Different data management environments have different ways of saving updated records. With many environments, changes are automatically saved as soon as you move to the next record. With other environments, you must issue a command to save the changes you make. To learn the specific procedures for the data management environment you use, you should refer to the software documentation or online help.

In addition to individual changes, computers make it easy to perform **global updates** to change the data in more than one record at a time. Consider the Employee file in the Midtown General Hospital database. A number of employees are working at $5.15 per hour, the minimum wage set by the government. Suppose that the minimum wage increases to $5.65 per hour. Instead of searching for each employee with an hourly wage of $5.15 and manually changing the numbers to $5.65, you could enter a command such as:

UPDATE EMPWAGE SET HourlyWage = 5.65 WHERE HourlyWage <5.65

Let's see how this command performs a global update. The UPDATE command means you want to change the data in some or all of the records. EMPWAGE is the name of the file that contains the data you want to change. SET HourlyWage = 5.65 tells the DBMS to change the data in the HourlyWage field to 5.65. WHERE HourlyWage <5.65 tells the DBMS to change only those records in which the current hourly wage is less than $5.65.

Organizing Records

Can I organize my data in different ways? It is easier to use information if it is presented in a sequence related to how the information is going to be used. For example, if you want to view a list of employees and you are looking for a specific employee by name, it is handy to have the employee records alphabetized by last name. If, on the other hand, you want to view a list of employees to compare hourly wages, it is useful to have the records in numeric order according to the number in the HourlyWage field.

A **sort key** is the field used to arrange records in order. Suppose Midtown managers want employee records arranged alphabetically by last name. The sort key would be LastName. Alternatively, if they want the records arranged by hourly wage, the sort key would be HourlyWage.

There are two ways to organize records in a file; you can sort them or you can index them. If you change the order of the file itself, by essentially rearranging the sequence of the records on the disk, you are **sorting**. Because the records are rearranged, each record receives a new record number to indicate its new position in the file. For example, in a file sorted by last name, the record with the last name that appears first in the alphabet would become record #1.

Sorting is an acceptable procedure for smaller files in which the time to sort the records is minimal. Sorting is also acceptable for files that you don't want sorted multiple ways. However, if you sometimes need to view a file in alphabetical order by last name, but at other times you need to view the file in order by salary, sorting is not very efficient.

An alternative way to organize records is indexing. **Indexing** leaves the records in their original order and retains the original record numbers but creates additional files, called **index files**. Think of an index file as being similar to the index of a book. The index of a book contains topics in alphabetical order, which allows you to find a topic in the index list easily. Next to the topic is a page number that points to the location of the actual information about the topic. Figure 14-23 shows how an index file lists the contents of the LastName field in alphabetical order, then uses the record number as a pointer to the corresponding record number in the original file.

Figure 14-23

Indexing

1. Records are typically numbered in the order in which they are entered, so the employee record with the earliest start date is record 1.

2. To index the records by last name, the computer creates an index file containing the data in the LastName field.

3. The only other field in the index file contains the original record numbers. In the original table, Susan Ang is record 3. In the index file, Susan's record is listed first because her name is first in the alphabet.

4. To display the first and last names in alphabetical order, the computer looks at the first item in the index file and displays the contents of the LastName field, Ang. To find Ang's first name, the computer looks at record 3 in the table. It finds Susan in the FirstName field and displays it.

Record #	LastName	FirstName	Gender	StartDate	JobCode
1	Houlihan	Margaret	F	10/05/1985	RN
2	McIntyre	John	M	04/14/1986	SMD
3	Ang	Susan	F	08/10/1988	RN
4	Jackson	Tony	F	12/04/1989	SMD
5	Burns	Frank	M	05/04/1990	SMD
6	Dish	Betty	F	01/16/1992	RN
7	Bailey	Rick	M	02/03/1992	RN

Database table

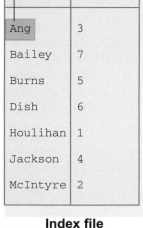

LastName	Record #
Ang	3
Bailey	7
Burns	5
Dish	6
Houlihan	1
Jackson	4
McIntyre	2

Index file

Ang   Susan

What makes indexing so flexible is that you can have multiple index files for each of your data files. For example, Midtown could have three index files for the employee data file—one index file to arrange employees by last name, one to arrange employees by hourly wage, and one to arrange employees by job category.

In some database management systems, the distinction between sorting and indexing will help you more effectively utilize the DBMS to organize your data. However, you should be aware that not all data management environments differentiate between the terms "sort" and "index." For example, Microsoft Access uses the term "sort" for procedures that organize data *without* rearranging records.

Generate Reports

How can I produce a professional-looking report based on the data in a file or database?

The output from a data file presents information in a format that facilitates making a decision, preparing an analysis, or taking some action. Traditionally, output is presented as words and numbers in reports, but output can assume other formats such as Web pages, graphs, graphics, and sound.

In response to a query, your data management environment might display a list of records that match your search criteria. This simple list displays the information you need, but it might not provide it in the optimal format. The list might include some unnecessary fields, it might not include a title or page numbers, it might not display subtotals or totals, and the column headings might not be as descriptive as you would like. If a list is not adequate, you can design a screen-based or printed report that conveys information more effectively. A **database report** is the formatted output of some or all of the data from a database.

The part of a data management environment that provides you with the ability to design reports is called a **report generator**. Usually a report generator helps you create a report template. A **report template** does not contain any data. Instead it contains the outline or general specifications for a report including such things as what to title the report, which fields to include, which fields you want to subtotal or total, and how the report should be formatted. For example, you might create a report template called Midtown Employees, which specifies the following:

- **The title of the report is Midtown General Hospital Employees.**
- **The report contains six columns with data from the LastName, FirstName, SocNum, Gender, StartDate, and JobCode fields.**
- **The headings for the columns are: Last Name, First Name, Social Security #, Gender, Start Date, and Job Code.**
- **The report is arranged alphabetically by last name.**

This template would produce a report similar to the one shown in Figure 14-24.

Figure 14-24

Columnar report

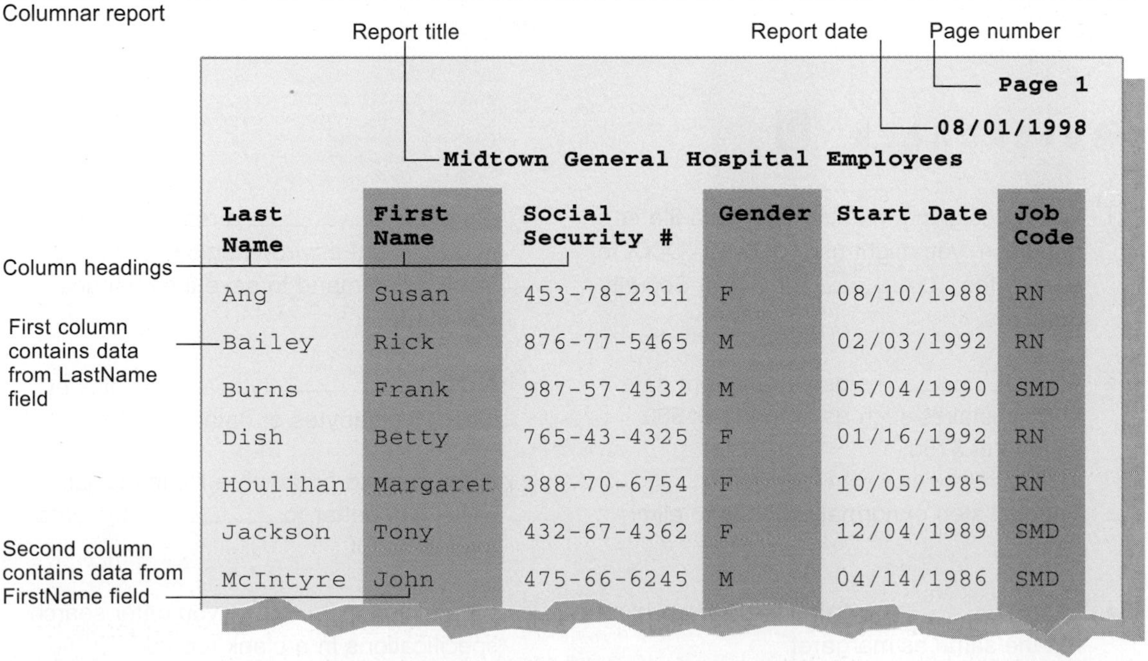

Last Name	First Name	Social Security #	Gender	Start Date	Job Code
Ang	Susan	453-78-2311	F	08/10/1988	RN
Bailey	Rick	876-77-5465	M	02/03/1992	RN
Burns	Frank	987-57-4532	M	05/04/1990	SMD
Dish	Betty	765-43-4325	F	01/16/1992	RN
Houlihan	Margaret	388-70-6754	F	10/05/1985	RN
Jackson	Tony	432-67-4362	F	12/04/1989	SMD
McIntyre	John	475-66-6245	M	04/14/1986	SMD

Report title — Midtown General Hospital Employees

Report date — 08/01/1998

Page number — Page 1

Column headings

First column contains data from LastName field

Second column contains data from FirstName field

After you use a report generator to design a template for a report, you can produce the report at any time. When you produce the actual report, it is based on the data currently contained in the file. For example, the report in Figure 14-24 was produced on August 1, 1998. This report includes employees who are listed in the database as of August 1. Now suppose that on September 1 your organization hires several new employees who are added to the database. You then use the Midtown Employee report template to print a report on September 2. This report will follow the same format as the previous report, but the new employees will be included.

The reports you generate using a report generator can be displayed, printed, saved as a file, or output as Web pages. Some data management software also provides tools to output data as a graph, as sound, or as graphics. Whatever format you select for your output, you can effectively present information by observing the guidelines in Figure 14-25.

Figure 14-25

Guidelines for effective output

Present only the amount of information necessary to make a decision and to take appropriate action. Too much information makes it difficult to identify and interpret the essential information.

Present information in a usable format. If subtotals and totals are necessary for making a decision, present them. Your readers should not need to make additional manual calculations.

Information should be timely. Reports must arrive in time to be used for effective decision making. Some decisions require information periodically, for example, monthly sales reports. Other decisions require ongoing information that will be best satisfied by a continuous display, for example, changing stock prices.

Information should be presented in a clear and unambiguous format. Make sure you include necessary titles, page numbers, dates, labels, and column headings to help decision makers identify the information.

Present the information in the format most appropriate for the decision and the decision maker. In many cases a traditional report, organized in rows and columns, is most appropriate. In other cases, graphs might be more effective.

QuickCheck D

1. When designing the structure for a file or database, you might use XXX-XX-XXXX to specify the _____ for Social Security numbers.

2. A(n) _____ helps you prevent data entry mistakes such as entering $1500 instead of $150.

3. The first step of normalization is to eliminate _____ .

4. In a(n) _____ database, Margaret is not the same as margaret.

5. After you _____ a record, some data management environments require you to issue a command to save the changes you made.

6. A data _____ typically contains at least 10 gigabytes of data.

7. If you want to organize a file in multiple ways, it is better to _____ the data than to sort it.

8. When you _____ , you enter search specifications in a blank record.

E Using Boolean Logic in Queries

The mathematician George Boole (Figure 14-26) is responsible for defining a system of logic now called Boolean logic or Boolean algebra. Boolean logic uses three main operations: NOT, AND, and OR. Elements of Boole's system of logic have been universally adopted by database query languages such as SQL and are used to enter queries into search engines that help you find information on the Internet.

According to experts such as Alan Cooper, who claims, "Users don't understand Boolean," some people have difficulty using Boolean logic for search specifications. It is easy to confuse the meaning of Boolean AND and OR because in casual speech we often use these words exactly opposite from the way that Boole defined them. However, the use of Boolean in query languages for databases and Internet searches is so pervasive that it is important for computer users to understand Boole's meanings for AND and OR.

Figure 14-26

George Boole

InfoWeb

Boolean
13

Set Theory

So what is the difference between AND and OR? To understand the difference between AND and OR, it is useful to think about set theory. **Set theory** is a simple way of depicting what happens when you combine, select, or exclude elements from a group. Imagine a group of things. In set theory, all the things in your group are called "the universe." Graphically, you represent this universe with a rectangle. Now suppose that some of the things in your universe are electronic gizmos. You represent these gizmos with a circle, as shown in Figure 14-27.

Figure 14-27

A circle represents the electronic gizmos in your universe.

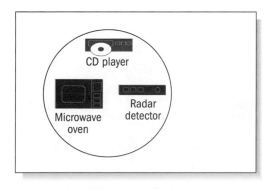
CD player

Microwave oven

Radar detector

Your universe might also contain car parts, such as tires, hood ornaments, steering wheels, CD players, and radar detectors. As you expect, you would draw another circle in the universe to represent car parts. The catch is that some car parts are also electronic gizmos (CD players and radar detectors, for example). You show this by overlapping the circles in your universe. Study Figure 14-28 and make sure you understand the four different categories of things in your universe.

Figure 14-28

Adding car parts to your universe

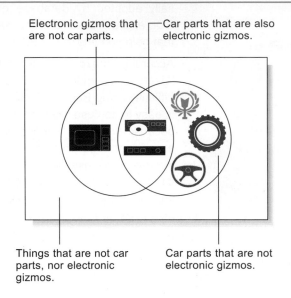

Electronic gizmos that are not car parts.

Car parts that are also electronic gizmos.

Things that are not car parts, nor electronic gizmos.

Car parts that are not electronic gizmos.

Now, here's the part that many people find tricky. Which things in your universe are **electronic gizmos AND car parts**? According to Boole, they are CD players and radar detectors. AND means a thing must fit *both* criteria: It must be both an electronic gizmo and also a car part.

To show this on your diagram, color in only the overlapping part of the circles, as shown in Figure 14-29.

Figure 14-29

Electronic gizmos AND car parts

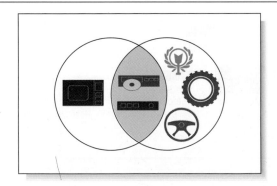

Now, what about the things that are **electronic gizmos OR car parts**? OR means a thing fits *either* criterion. So tires, radar detectors, CD players, hood ornaments, steering wheels, and microwave ovens fit the bill. To show this in your universe, color in both circles, as shown in Figure 14-30.

Figure 14-30

Electronic
gizmos OR
car parts

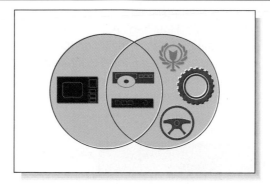

NOT means to select the opposite. For example, what things in your universe are **NOT car parts**? Everything not in the car parts circle. What things are **NOT(car parts or electronic gizmos)**? To figure this out, first do the OR in parentheses. What in your universe is car parts OR electronic gizmos? All the things in the circles. The NOT is what's left—everything outside the circles, as shown in Figure 14-31.

Figure 14-31

NOT (car
parts OR
electronic
gizmos)

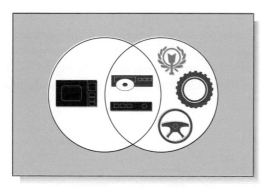

To summarize: AND means a thing must meet both criteria. It is restrictive—it only includes the overlapping area of the two circles. OR means a thing must fit either criterion. It is more inclusive—it includes anything in either circle. NOT means "the other things."

Boolean Queries

How does set theory apply to database queries? When you use a query to locate data in a database, it tells the DBMS what you want to find. Most popular query languages, such as SQL, use command words, expressions, relational operators, and Boolean operators to formulate a query.

Simple queries are usually accomplished using a command word such as FIND and an expression such as LastName = 'Houlihan'. A simple **expression** usually has a field name on the left and the specific thing you want to find on the right. The query you use to locate the record for an employee with the last name Houlihan is *FIND LastName = 'Houlihan'*. You can create expressions using any of the **relational operators**: =, >, <, >=, <=, and <>. You can review the meanings of these operators in Figure 14-32.

Figure 14-32

Relational operators

Operator	Description
=	equal to
>	greater than
<	less than
>=	greater than or equal to
<=	less than or equal to
<>	not equal to

A complex query, such as one to find only those employees who are registered nurses and have Houlihan for their last name and are female, requires the use of Boolean operators. Let's use the sample set of employees, shown in Figure 14-33, to visualize the results from queries of the Midtown General Hospital Employee database.

Figure 14-33

Midtown employees

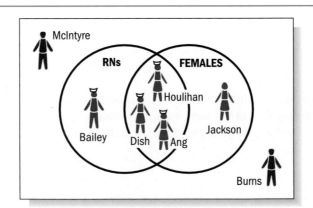

Figure 14-34

JobCode = 'RN' AND Gender = 'F'

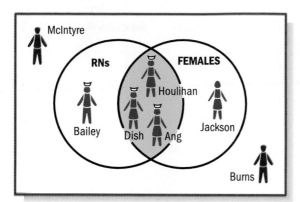

When used in a query, the logical operator AND connects two expressions, both of which must be true to match the search criteria. For example, the search criteria **JobCode = 'RN' AND Gender = 'F'** requests only those records for female registered nurses. If Margaret Houlihan is a female and a registered nurse, her record would match the search criteria. Figure 14-34 shows the results of such a search.

The logical operator OR connects two expressions, but only one of them must be true to match the search criteria. The search criteria **JobCode = 'RN' OR Gender = 'F'** would produce all the records for females, regardless of their job code. The search would also produce all the records for registered nurses of either gender.

The logical operator NOT precedes a simple or complex expression and, in a search specification, produces the records that do not match the expression. For example, the expression **NOT JobCode = 'RN'** would produce records for any employee who is not a registered nurse. What about the search criteria **NOT(JobCode = 'RN' AND Gender = 'F')**? Think of it this way: The computer will locate the records for all employees who are registered nurses and female (like Margaret Houlihan, who is a female registered nurse), but it will not produce these records. Instead it will produce all the other records. So, will the search **NOT(JobCode = 'RN' AND Gender = 'F')** produce Rick Bailey? Yes, it will and Figure 14-35 shows why.

Figure 14-35

NOT (JobCode = 'RN' AND Gender = 'F')

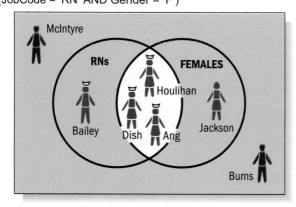

What about using NOT and OR, as in the search criteria **NOT(JobCode = 'RN' OR Gender = 'F')**? This time, the computer essentially eliminates any records for registered nurses. It also eliminates any records for female employees. Figure 14-36 shows a conceptual diagram for this query.

Figure 14-36

Not (JobCode = 'RN' OR Gender = 'F')

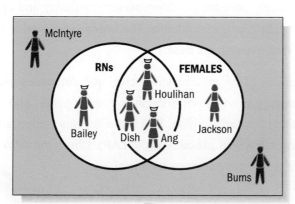

Search criteria can become quite complex. Look at the employee table in Figure 14-37; let's use it to learn how to use a complex query to locate data in the table.

Figure 14-37

Midtown employee table

LastName	FirstName	Gender	StartDate	JobCode
Ang	Susan	F	08/10/1988	RN
Bailey	Rick	M	02/03/1992	RN
Burns	Frank	M	05/04/1990	SMD
Dish	Betty	F	01/16/1992	RN
Houlihan	Margaret	F	10/05/1985	RN
Jackson	Tony	F	12/04/1989	SMD
McIntyre	John	M	04/14/1986	SMD

You might, for example, want to find the salaries of only those female employees who started working after August 1, 1988, but before August 1, 1990, as registered nurses or staff physicians (SMD). The search criteria would be *Gender = 'F' AND (StartDate > 08/01/1988 AND StartDate < 08/01/1990) AND (JobCode = 'RN' OR JobCode = 'SMD')*. You can use parentheses to specify the order in which the expressions should be evaluated by the DBMS. The expressions in parentheses should be evaluated first.

SQL Queries

When you need to do a complex search, you might want to experiment with parts of the search first, to be certain the parts produce what you expect. For example, in the complex search above, you might first test the expression *(StartDate > 08/01/1988 AND StartDate < 08/01/1990)* to be certain it retrieves records with start dates during the correct time period. Once you have tested parts of your query, you can combine them to create your complete query. To try some SQL queries, use the New Perspectives CD-ROM to connect to the SQL Lab.

EndNote
The final episode of *M*A*S*H* aired on September 19, 1983. On that date, a typical hospital was likely to be using separate minicomputer systems to automate billing, maintain patient records, and track lab results. Microcomputers were just then appearing on the business scene after the launch of the IBM PC in 1982. Microcomputer networking was virtually unheard of. Client/server computing and object-oriented databases were just ideas batted around academia. The Internet consisted of fewer than 1,000 computers; the World Wide Web did not exist.

InfoWeb

OLAP 14

Today, computers are an integral part of our information society and databases are the cornerstone of information technology. But it is not enough to merely gather and store data; that data must provide us with useful information. This is the impetus behind current interest in data mining and **online analytical processing** (OLAP). Check the InfoWebs for the latest information on these and other database technologies.

InfoWeb

InfoWeb

Chapter
Links

The InfoWeb is your guide to print, film, television, and electronic resources. Use it to obtain updates on quickly changing technical information and to locate information for research papers. If you're using the New Perspectives CD-ROM, click the InfoWeb icon on the left side of this paragraph to access the online InfoWeb links. Otherwise, use your Web browser and type in the address of the New Perspectives site: www.cciw.com/np3. At the New Perspectives site you'll find up-to-date links to the topics covered in this chapter.

1 MASH

M*A*S*H was both a movie and a television series that captured the attention and hearts of Americans from 1970, when the movie was released, through 1983, when the last television episode was broadcast. *M*A*S*H* was written by Richard Hooker (NY: Pocket Books, 1968). The movie was directed by Robert Altman and distributed by 20th Century Fox. At the M*A*S*H 4077th home page at **www.netlink.co.uk/users/mash/** you can read profiles of the characters and actors, learn where the cast members are now, take a tour of the camp, take a trivia challenge, and more. Mobile Army Surgical Hospitals did not go away with the end of the Korean War. At the 807th MASH Operations Desert Shield and Operation Desert Storm site, **www.iglou.com/law/mash.htm**, you can read a diary that runs from December 8, 1990 to June 29, 1991, detailing the experiences of the Army medical corps during the most recent war fought by U.S. troops.

1952 was an election year. The Korean War contributed to a close race between Eisenhower and Stevenson. As a promotional gimmick, CBS used the new UNIVAC computer to predict the election results. Did CBS trust the results of that first computer prediction of election outcomes? Read *The IEEE Computer Society Events in the History of Computing* at **www.computer.org/50/history/1952.htm** to find out. The photographs and descriptions of the UNIVAC and all of its components at the Pictures and Analysis of UNIVAC site, **www.eagle.ca/~harry/harry/computer/univaci/index.htm**, will give you a good idea of how this early computer differed from today's PCs and mainframes.

2 Database Concepts

Database Design for Mere Mortals: A Hands-On Guide to Relational Database Design by Michael J. Hernandez (Addison-Wesley, January 1997) provides an introduction to relational database design concepts that's easy to understand and apply. On the Web, a good place to begin is the Los Alamos National Laboratory site at **www.acl.lanl.gov/sunrise/dbms/index.html**. You'll find a glossary of database terms at **ftn.net/cc/CanadaComputes/Sept95/Terms.html**. At the University of Massachusetts Database Systems Laboratory Database site, **www-ccs.cs.umass.edu/db/databasesites.html**, you can find links to database textbooks, research journals and bulletins, bibliographies and technical reports, professional books and magazines, and database-related discussion groups.

Popular database magazines include *Database Programming and Design* at **www.dbpd.com/**, *Datamation* at **www.datamation.com**, and *DBMS* at **www.dbmsmag.com**. In addition, you can find links to articles on database technology and software at the ZDNet's AnchorDesk: Database site, **www.zdnet.com/anchordesk/topics/topics_9.html**.

The Data Management Association International (DAMA) at **www.dama.org** is the key professional organization for professionals in database management. Three other professional associations include the Information Resources Management Association at **www.hbg.psu.edu/Faculty/m1k/IRMA.html**

The International Data Warehousing Association at **www.idwa.org**, and the Society for Information Management at **www.simnet.org**.

3 Database Administrator

What does a database administrator do? How is a database administrator's job different from a systems analyst's job or a database manager's job? A good place to start looking for answers to these career questions is the *Bureau of Labor Statistics Occupational Outlook Handbook* section on the Computer Scientists and Systems Analysts site, **stats.bls.gov/oco/ocos042.htm**. At The Boston Computer Museum's Careers in Computing, you can find more information about the basic job duties and what you can expect from a database-oriented career path on the Database Specialists Web page at **www.tcm.org/resources/cmp-careers/cnc-data.html**.

In April 1997, *ComputerWorld* spoke with several information systems managers and recruiters about careers and jobs in the database profession. The resulting article "DB Dandies" at **careers.computerworld.com/cwnews/archives/0367.html** will give you an idea of the current demand for database skills, which database skills are the most highly valued, and some of the qualities that managers look for in job candidates.

When considering any career, it is worthwhile to consider what your starting salary will be and what salary increases will be like over the course of your career path. DataMaster's 1997 Computer Industry Salary Survey at **www.datamasters.com/dm/survey.html** provides a list of IS/IT positions with salary information (median low, region median, median high) organized by region of the country. "Are your pay scales right?" at **www.datamation.com/PlugIn/execjob/stories/scales.html** discusses the idea of establishing pay scales based on benchmark information. This article includes a list of IT jobs with brief descriptions, including database manager, and includes links to *Datamation's* very extensive salary survey. In Computerworld's 11th Annual Salary Survey at **www2.computerworld.com/home/online9697.nsf/All/970901survey** you can get an idea of the kind of salary increases you can expect from a career path in database management.

4 Data Modeling

One of the most highly recommended books on data modeling is *Data Modeling Essentials* by Graeme Simsion (Van Nostrand Reinhold, 1994). For a quick online introduction to data modeling techniques, connect to the Applied Information Science site at **www.aisintl.com/case/method.html**. Another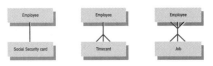
online article, "Building a Logical Data Model" at **www.dbmsmag.com/9506d16.html** from *DBMS Online*, by George Tillman, provides a basic definition of data modeling, discusses the various elements of a data model (for example, objects, entities, relationships, and attributes) and describes how they relate to each other. The article is based on his book *A Practical Guide to Logical Data Modeling* (McGraw-Hill, 1993) and uses the entity-relationship approach to data modeling. The Canadian Ministry of Forests provides an online tutorial on data modeling at **www.for.gov.bc.ca/isb/datadmin/s7_mdl12.htm**. Another excellent data modeling site is hosted by CERN at **www.cern.ch/Adamo/guide/Chapter-2.html**. Data modeling tools such as Embarcadero Technologies ER/Studio (**www.embarcadero.com**) and Logic Works' ERwin (**www.logicworks.com**) help database designers build easy-to-manipulate graphical data models, then turn them into production databases.

5 Relational Databases

The Association for Computing Machinery site at **www.acm.org** includes "A Relational Model of Data for Large Shared Data Banks" by Edgar F. Codd, which first appeared in *Communications of the ACM*, Vol. 13, No. 6, June 1970. Codd invented the relational database, and in this article he describes the 12 characteristics of a relational database system. Codd's classic reference book, *The Relational Model for Database Management* (Addison-Wesley, 1990) expands on his earlier work and defines 333 characteristics of a "pure" relational database system.

In "Overview of the Relational Model" at **www.utexas.edu/cc/dbms/utinfo/relmod/index.html** from the University of Texas at Austin's Database Management Services, you can find a simple explanation of the relational model and why you might need to understand it. The Web-based document discusses the relational data structure, including notation, properties of relational tables, relational keys, and data integrity; manipulating relational data; and normalization. There is also a brief reading list and links to other database resources on the Internet.

C. J. Date is one of the most prolific writers on the topic of databases. Through his extensive teaching, training, and writing activities, Date has explained the relational model to thousands of software engineers, software designers, educators, students, journalists, and end users. In a 1994 interview, Date talked about the future of the database industry and integrating object-oriented database concepts with relational concepts. Date's Classic book on databases is now in its sixth edition: *An Introduction to Database Systems* (Addison-Wesley, 1995).

6 OODB

According to "So what the hell is OODBMS?" at **www2.computerworld.com/home/print9497.nsf/All/SL1106rev** from *ComputerWorld*, the key difference between a relational database and an object-oriented database lies in the way an object-oriented database stores data and manages the relationships among data elements. Is an object-oriented database best suited for use with complex data? Can it describe simple relationships or complex relationships? Are object-oriented databases particularly good at handling certain kinds of data? Are object-oriented databases beginning to replace other kinds of databases in the business world? This article will give you insight into the answers to these questions and help you understand the key differences between OODBs and relational databases.

The book, *Object Databases—The Essentials*, by Dr. Mary E.S. Loomis (Addison-Wesley, 1995) can help you understand the differences between object-oriented databases and relational databases. It explains the basic concepts of OODBs, compares OODB features with relational database management system features, and illustrates how to use an OODBMS on a project. The end of the book has a more technical emphasis because it describes using object-oriented languages such as Smalltalk and C++ to program an OODBMS.

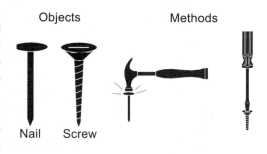

You can read a *DBMS Online* interview with Dr. Mary Loomis at **www.dbmsmag.com/int9412.html**. In the interview, Dr. Loomis explains what an object database is, discusses the differences in philosophy between traditional database systems and object databases, and describes some of the differences between relational database models and object-oriented models.

"Object DBMSs: Now or Never" at **www.dbmsmag.com/9707d13.html** from *DBMS Online*, can give you a less technical view of the differences between traditional databases and object-oriented databases. It very vividly describes an example of a database that contains image, audio, and animation data and contrasts these with the typical transaction data found in traditional databases. The article goes on to discuss the nature of complex data and complex relations among data, how object-oriented database models are better able to handle this level of complexity, and differences in how relational databases and object-oriented databases handle data.

7 DBMS Software

DatabaseUser from ZDNet at **www.zdnet.com/products/databaseuser.html** presents reviews of the latest database application software. Some recently reviewed products include Sybase PowerBuilder, Lotus Approach 97, Microsoft Access 97, Claris FileMaker Pro 3.0, and Easybase. At this site you can also find database software tips and download database related software. "Application Suites: Databases" at **www.zdnet.com/pcmag/features/suites/ft-db.htm** from ZDNet's *PC Magazine*, presents a table that summarizes and compares significant features of Paradox, Microsoft Access 97, and Lotus Approach 97. This Web page includes links to reviews of these products and to "suitability to task" test results.

Check out the Web sites for these database software publishers: Sybase PowerBuilder at **www.powersoft.com/products/panther/**, Lotus Approach at **www.lotus.com**, Microsoft Access at **www.microsoft.com/access/**, Claris FileMaker Pro at **www.claris.com**, Oracle at **www.oracle.com**, Corel Paradox at **www.corel.com/products/wordperfect/paradox8/index.htm**, and IBM DB2 at **www.software.ibm.com/data/db2/udb**.

8 OODBMS Tools

A *Datamation* article, "Does your OO app need an OO database?" (**www.datamation.com/PlugIn/issues/1996/dec/oops1.html**) features object-oriented projects at Sprint, Access Systems Research, and Lockheed Martin, along with a reference list of object-oriented database vendors. For more information on OODBMS products visit vendor sites. Computer Associates, the world's third-largest software publisher produces an OODBMS called Jasmine (**www.cai.com/products/jasmine.htm**). Objectivity publishes the Objectivity OODBMS (**www.objectivity.com**). The popular Versant OODBMS is published by Versant Object Technology (**www.versant.com/products/rel5/index.html**).

Object-oriented databases are still struggling to gain a foothold in the corporate data picture. One of the problems has been reconciling the object model with the relational model. David Linthicum discusses this problem in the *DBMS Online* article, "Objects Meet Data" (**www.dbmsmag.com/9609d16.html**) and includes a list of object-to-relational products and vendors. A comprehensive list of object-oriented CASE tools from the July 1997 issue of DBMS Online can be found at **www.dbsmag.com/9707d161.html**.

9 DB Web Tools

"Web Database Development: From the Ground Up" at **www.zdnet.com/pcmag/features/webdatabase/_open.htm**, discusses products that help make traditional corporate databases accessible to the Internet and intranets through Web browsers. The article provides a brief outline of the basic strategy: create specialized applications that enable corporate LAN-based databases to have Web-based functionality. Then, it reviews six products: Oracle Web Developer Suite, Borland Intrabuilder, Microsoft Visual InterDev, Netscape Visual JavaScript, PowerBuilder Enterprise, and WebObjects Enterprise. The article also previews several products that are currently under development and lists information about 21 other products that are available. You can find another review of tools designed to integrate traditional DBMS's with the Web at "DBMS Tools for Web Intergration: Pour it On!," **techweb.cmp.com/nc/817/817f1.html**.

At WWW Database Tools, **picture.gov.nb.ca/hotlist/wwwdbase.htm**, you can find an extensive list of annotated links to the Web sites of companies who are producing products designed to link databases with the Web. Some of the popular Web database tools include: Oracle Web Developer Suite at **www.oracle.com**, Borland Intrabuilder at **www.borland.com**, Microsoft Visual InterDev, Active Server Pages technology, and Web Assistant at **www.microsoft.com**, Netscape Visual JavaScript at **www.netscape.com**, Sybase's PowerBuilder Enterprise and NetImpact Dynamo at **www.sybase.com**, Allaire Cold Fusion at **www.allaire.com**, Bluestone Software's Sapphire/Web 4.0 at **www.bluestone.com**, EveryWare Development Corp.'s Tango Enterprise at **www.everyware.com**, and IBM's Net.Data at **www.ibm.com**.

10 Normalization

You can find a basic definition of the concept of normalization at PCWebopedia's normalization page at **www.pcwebopedia.com/normalization.htm**. For more information with detailed examples and tips, read "Normalization" at **www.troubleshooters.com/littstip/ltnorm.html**. At The Software Developer's Handbook, you can read a discussion of normalization in an article on database design at **www.mtjeff.com/~calvin/devhbook/databasedesign.html**. The discussion includes the rules of normalization with a detailed example illustrating how the rules are used. At the end of the article you can find information on other database resources including a list of books and links to other normalization resources on the Web. In "Database Normalization and Design - Part 1" at **www.inetspace.com/ database.html** Phil Dobranski, Senior Software Engineer at iNetSpace, describes the five steps of normalization. He begins with the point that normalization yields "efficient access and storage of data in a relational database."

11 SQL

In exploring the area of query languages, PCWebopedia's basic definition of query languages, particularly SQL at **www.pcwebopedia.com/SQL.htm** is a good starting place. At the end of the definition, you can find links to SQL resources on the Web.

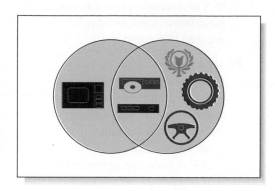

The SQL Tutorial at **w3.one.net/~jhoffman/ sqltut.htm** begins with a basic definition of SQL and then provides a detailed description of how to use SQL queries. There is also a helpful section of commonly asked questions, such as "Why can't I just ask for the first three rows in a table?" and "Aren't database tables just files?" Allen Taylor's series of three articles, "What is SQL, and why should I care?" at **www.computerbits.com/archive/19960500/sql1.htm** is as entertaining as it is informative.

12 Data Warehouses

The basic definition of data warehouse at **www.cait.wustl.edu/cait/papers/prism/vol1_no1/** introduces the concept and provides a concise explanation of why it is important to organizations. "Data Warehousing Fundamentals: What You Need to Know To Succeed" at **www.data-warehouse.com/ resource/articles/lamb8.htm** argues that data warehousing isn't just a way of storing historical data about an enterprise—it is a unifying and coherent method for organizing information systems. This article discusses five factors that underlie the data warehouse concept and that have an impact on its successful implementation: operational versus decision support applications; primitive versus derived data; time series data; data administration; and systems architecture. In "The wiser, gentler data warehouse" at **www.sun.com/sunworldonline/swol-05-1997/swol-05-datawarehouse.html** SunWorld presents a step-by-step guide to developing a successful data warehouse; the main steps include pre-engineering, engineering, and implementation. *CIO* magazine argues that data warehouses provide organizations with a competitive advantage by providing access to their inherent knowledge and intelligence about their business. At the Data Warehouse Research Center site, **www.cio.com/CIO/rc_dw.html**, CIO provides general resources on data warehousing that range from articles, case studies, a glossary, and white papers to a list of vendors that sell data warehousing applications.

Once you have an organization's data stored and accessible in a data warehouse, how do you extract information from it? The answer is data mining. FAQs about Data Mining at **www.rpi.edu/ ~vanepa2/faq.html** provides a brief introduction to the key concepts of data mining, including a basic definition, a list of data mining techniques with definitions, a short reading list, and links to other Web resources. You'll find additional information in "Digging into Data Mining" at **www.dbmsmag.com/ 9710d05.html** from *DBMS Online's* column "Data Warehouse Architect." Ralph Kimball, the author, answers some data mining questions and more. The article "Data Mining Today" at **www.dbmsmag.com/ 9702d16.html** reviews the most current data mining technologies, and you can find information about tools vendors at the Data Warehousing Information Center site, **pwp.starnetinc.com/larryg/index.html**.

13 Boolean

George Boole is a luminary of mathematics and logic whose work shows the practicality of these fields. Using his basic definitions of AND, OR, and NOT, individuals can wade through piles of irrelevant data in minutes to find the one piece of information they need. To learn more about Boole, read the brief essay "George Boole" at **www.advbool.com/Misc/boole.html**. At the end of the essay, you can find a short reading list that points to sources of further material on George Boole's life. For a longer biographical sketch and to see a portrait of Boole, see the George Boole site at **www-groups.dcs.st-andrews.ac.uk/~history/Mathematicians/Boole.html**. At "The Calculus of Logic," **www.maths.tcd.ie/pub/HistMath/People/Boole/CalcLogic/CalcLogic.html**, you can read an essay that Boole wrote to describe his "application of a new and peculiar form of Mathematics to the expression of the operations of the mind in reasoning." Computer Logic at **www.ort.org/edu/itweb/itcourse.htm** hosted by ORTnet, presents a tutorial on basic Boolean logic as it is implemented in computers.

14 OLAP

OLAP—online analytical processing—is a method that allows users to extract data from a database and turn it into information that can be used for making business decisions. The OLAP process is an interactive one, and it allows organizations to view their data strategically so that they can make predictions about the future in addition to understanding their history. The OLAP Council provides a technical introduction to OLAP at **www.olapcouncil.org/research/whtpaply.htm**. This white paper on OLAP defines the concept, outlines who uses it and why, and reviews the key features required for OLAP software. You can also find OLAP and OLAP server definitions at the OLAP Council Web site, **www.olapcouncil.org/**. In "Three Routes to OLAP" at **www.datamation.com/PlugIn/issues/1995/august15/08bcom10.html** *Datamation* reports on its performance test of the three main OLAP software tools: Arbor Software's Essbase, Pilot Software's Lightship, and IRI Software's Express. This article should give you a good idea of what OLAP tools can and cannot do. *Datamation* also has a special section on OLAP at **www.datamation.com/PlugIn/workbench/olap/olap.htm** that features articles on the latest developments in OLAP, how companies are using it, who makes OLAP tools, white papers, and more. The OLAP Report at **www.olapreport.com/** provides market analyses, product reviews, and case studies.

Review

1 Look back through this chapter and make sure you can answer the questions under each heading.

2 Complete the following chart to summarize the terminology used as synonyms for the terms "record type," "record," and "field" in hierarchical, network, relational, and object-oriented databases:

	Relational	Hierarchical	Network	Object-oriented
Record Type				
Record				
Field				

3 List the steps you should follow to design a file or database.

4 Create a topic outline for the material presented in the section "File and Database Concepts."

5 Draw a hierarchy diagram showing the relationship among the following terms: file, program file, data file, free-form data file, structured data file, flat file, database, relational database, hierarchical database, network database, object-oriented database.

6 Complete the following chart to summarize the characteristics of the four types of file and database management software:

7 Describe the difference between a record occurrence and a record type.

8 For each of these pairs of record types, draw a data structure diagram showing whether the relationship is one-to-one, one-to-many, or many-to-many.

Author	Book
Musician	CD
Person	Social Security number
House	Mailbox
Lawyer	Client
Truck	Tire

9 Suppose you have a universe that contains overlapping circles for pilots and CIOs (chief information officers). Draw diagrams showing each of the following:
a. Pilots OR CIOs
b. Pilots AND CIOs
c. NOT(Pilots AND CIOs)
d. NOT(Pilots)
e. (NOT Pilots) AND (NOT CIOs)
f. NOT(Pilots OR CIOs)

10 Use the New Perspectives CD-ROM to take a practice test or to review the new terms presented in this chapter.

	Custom Software	File Management	Database Management	Object-Oriented
Files manipulated with:	a custom program	file management software		
Promotes data independence:	No			
File support:	one at a time			
Manipulates relationships:		No		

Projects

1 **Gourmet Gallery** Suppose you are the database administrator for a large gourmet supply store. You're working with the inventory manager to define an effective record format for your inventory file. The inventory manager gives you a sample of the index cards now being used to keep track of the inventory.

Use this card to design an effective record format for the inventory data file. To do this:

a. List each field the inventory record should contain. Your field names should be descriptive, contain no more than 10 characters, and be only one word. For example, use "PARTNUMBER", not "PN." Remember to think about how the data might be used for output—the fields you define might not be exactly the same as the fields on the index card.

b. Assign a data type to each field. You may use the following data types: character, numeric, date, and logical.

c. Define the length of each field. You might have to make some intelligent guesses about the field length because you do not know what all the data looks like. For example, you can see from the example that some part numbers are at least 10 characters long, but you might guess that some part numbers will be longer—use your judgment. Be careful about the length of fields that contain dollar values. Do not leave a space for the $ sign, but you should leave a space for the decimal point.

d. Where appropriate, indicate the input or output format for a field, for example, you would use 9999.99 for currency fields.

2 **Central State University** Suppose that you work on the staff at Central State University and you have the following data:

The Management Department (phone: 455-9800) has three graduate faculty: Professor Sharon Smith (office: BA 502, phone: 455-9897), Associate Professor Rico Gomez (office: BA 510, phone: 455-9888), and Associate Professor Ariel Headly (office: BA 402, phone: 455-9776). S. Smith teaches Quantitative Analysis (course ID: MM525) on Tuesday and Thursday, 7-9 p.m., in room BA 10. She also teaches the Graduate Seminar (course ID: MM698) on Monday, 7-10 p.m., in room BA 21. R. Gomez teaches Personnel Management (course ID: MM560) on Monday and Wednesday, 7-9 p.m., in room BA 20. A. Headly teaches Leadership in Organizations (course ID: MM610) on Thursday, 6-9 p.m., in room BA 20.

a. Draw a data structure diagram showing how you would arrange this data in a hierarchical database, then draw the specific occurrence of the data that was described above.

b. R. Gomez decides to help A. Headly teach the Leadership in Organizations course. Now this course has two instructors. Redraw your data structure diagram using a network model to show this relationship. Also redraw your diagram showing an occurrence of the data.

c. Diagram the tables you would use if you were to structure this data as a relational database.

3 **Toy Store** Use the printout of a small toy store inventory below to determine the result of the queries in a through f.

a. Quantity < 50

b. Wholesale > 2.50 AND Wholesale < 4.00

c. Ordered < '7/1/89'

d. Brand = "Nature's Kids" OR Brand = "Plastic Pets"

e. Brand = "Galaxy Toys" AND Brand = "Flying Fun"

f. (Brand = "Flying Fun" OR Brand = "Nature's Kids") AND Retail < 5.00

4 **Toy Store II** Using the fields in the toy store database, write out the query you would use to find:

a. All the toys ordered between July 1 and July 7

b. Any toys with a wholesale cost more than $4.99 that were not ordered by J. Mathers

c. All the Brown toys that retail for more than $10.00

d. Any toys that were ordered by T. Livingston or A. Hayes before 7/1/89

e. Any purple toys that retail for less than $5.00 or any green toys that the store has fewer than 10 in stock

Toy store inventory

Toy	Brand	Color	Ordered	Ordered By	Quantity	Wholesale	Retail	Stock
Fortran Learner	Computer Fun	Yellow	7/1/89	A. Hayes	50	$3.99	$5.39	32
Rocket Racer	Flying Fun	Red/Blue	7/14/89	A. Hayes	50	$2.50	$3.38	32
Day-Glo Frisbees	Flying Fun	Lime/Pink	7/1/89	A. Hayes	50	$2.50	$3.38	45
Model Cessna	Flying Fun	Black	7/1/89	A. Hayes	50	$8.99	$12.14	0
Model Satellite	Flying Fun	Red/White	6/25/89	A. Hayes	50	$5.50	$7.43	12
Satellite Launcher	Flying Fun	Silver/Taupe	6/24/89	A. Hayes	50	$12.50	$16.88	10
Kaleidoscope	Galaxy Toys	Purple	7/14/89	T. Livingston	50	$3.99	$5.39	10
Warp 10 U.F.O.	Galaxy Toys	Silver/Blue	7/1/89	T. Livingston	50	$2.50	$3.38	40
Space Station	Galaxy Toys	N/A	7/1/89	T. Livingston	25	$12.50	$16.88	50
Orbitron	Galaxy Toys	Magenta	6/23/89	T. Livingston	25	$13.99	$18.89	3
Brontosaurus Bruce	Nature's Kids	Olive	7/14/89	T. Livingston	25	$4.99	$6.74	6
Ferdie Frog	Nature's Kids	Green	7/1/89	T. Livingston	25	$2.50	$3.38	70
Stegosaurus Sam	Nature's Kids	Brown/Olive	7/1/89	T. Livingston	25	$2.50	$3.38	84
Agatha Alligator	Nature's Kids	Green	7/1/89	T. Livingston	25	$4.99	$6.74	54
Eight-color Paintset	Non-Toxic Toys	N/A	7/14/89	J. Mathers	25	$2.99	$4.04	75
Wooden Tugboat	Non-Toxic Toys	Brown	6/25/89	J. Mathers	50	$6.50	$8.78	23
Wooden Train Set	Non-Toxic Toys	Brown	6/25/89	J. Mathers	25	$8.50	$11.48	1
Inflatable Crab	Plastic Pets	Red	7/5/89	J. Mathers	50	$4.99	$6.74	1
Inflatable Lobster	Plastic Pets	Pink	7/5/89	J. Mathers	50	$4.99	$6.74	18
Inflatable Snails	Plastic Pets	Green/Olive	7/5/89	J. Mathers	50	$4.99	$6.74	20
Plastic Penguin	Plastic Pets	Black/White	7/5/89	J. Mathers	50	$4.99	$6.74	20
Micro Mice	Plastic Pets	White	7/5/89	J. Mathers	50	$4.99	$6.74	21
Vampire Fangs	Plastic Pets	Pink	7/5/89	J. Mathers	50	$4.99	$6.74	22
Thinking Trees	Plastic Pets	Brown	7/5/89	J. Mathers	50	$4.99	$6.74	13
Model Mercedes	Rich Folks	Blue/Tan	7/5/89	J. Mathers	50	$4.99	$6.74	4
Model Ferrari	Rich Folks	Red/Blue	7/5/89	J. Mathers	50	$4.99	$6.74	25
Plastic Sushi	Rich Folks	Yellow/Green	7/5/89	J. Mathers	50	$4.99	$6.74	33
Expanding Espresso	Rich Folks	Brown	7/5/89	J. Mathers	50	$4.99	$6.74	27
Rock'n'Roll Ron	Zap Toys	Magenta/Red	7/5/89	J. Mathers	50	$4.99	$6.74	28
Singing Slugs	Zap Toys	Green/Olive	7/5/89	J. Mathers	50	$4.99	$6.74	2

5 Indexing Suppose you have a small file with the following records about computer books:

Record Number	Author	Title	Publication Date
1	Norton, Peter	Programmer's Guide to the IBM PC	1985
2	Craig, John Clark	Visual Basic Workshop	1991
3	Minsky, Marvin	Society of Mind	1986
4	Nelson, Theodore	Literary Machines	1987
5	Wodasky, Ron	Multimedia Madness	1992
6	Waite, Mitchell	Unix Primer Plus	1983

a. Complete the following table to create an index that will organize the records in alphabetical order according to author last name:

Author Name	Record Number
Craig, John Clark	2
Minsky, Marvin	3

b. Create an index table similar to the table in (a) to organize the records by publication date.

6 INTERNET Required

The Boolean Web Most Web search engines allow you to formulate "advanced" searches using Boolean operators. By using these operators, you can specify a very precise search that, in many cases, will help you pinpoint the information you need without having to wade through thousands of potential site links. To complete this project, find the answers to questions a through e below using the boolean search capabilities of a Web browser, such as **www.lycos.com**, **www.altavista.com**, or **www.infoseek.com**. In addition to writing out the answers, indicate the boolean search you used to find the answer.

a. What did Albert Einstein think about socialism?

b. Where can you find information about the dogs that the Soviets launched into space?

c. Where can you find a quote from Confucius about learning?

d. How many sites contain information about the Magna Carta or about netserfs?

e. Where would you find information about what netserfs think of the Magna Carta?

7 Normalization Take the first step in the normalization process by eliminating the data redundancy in the Invoice file below. If necessary, create new record types. Assume you are working with a relational database model.

Invoice File

Invoice Number	Customer Name	Address	Date	Item Number	Item	Price	Number Purchased
0010	Jack Wei	503 S. HWY 7	09/01/1994	56887	B&D Hammer	17.69	1
0010	Jack Wei	503 S. HWY 7	09/01/1994	67433	Sand Paper–Fine	4.98	2
0010	Jack Wei	503 S. HWY 7	09/01/1994	2230B	CTR Sink	2.49	1
0011	Sally Zachman	834 N. Front St.	09/01/1994	56887	B&D Hammer	17.69	1
0012	Brad Koski	2910 52nd St.	09/02/1994	56887	B&D Hammer	17.69	2
0012	Brad Koski	2910 52nd St.	09/02/1994	4311A	9-inch Brush	7.89	1

Lab Assignments

SQL Queries Lab

To query many relational databases, you use SQL (usually pronounced by saying the letters of the acronym, "S Q L"). IBM developed SQL in the mid 1970s for use in mainframe relational database products such as DB2. In 1986 the American National Standards Institute (ANSI) adopted SQL as the standard relational database language and it is now used extensively on microcomputer databases as well. Understanding how to use SQL is an important skill for many data management jobs. In this Lab, you will get a taste of this powerful and flexible database language. To gain further expertise, you should refer to the course offerings at your school.

1. Click the Steps button to learn how to formulate SQL queries. As you proceed through the steps, answer the Quick Check questions. After you complete the Steps, you will see a Quick Check Summary Report. Follow the instructions on the screen to print this report.

2. In Explore, use the scroll bar to browse through the database to find the answers to the following questions:
   a. What are the names of the staff physicians? (Hint: The JobCode for staff physicians is SMD.)
   b. How many LPNs are in the database?
   c. Who makes more than $20 an hour?
   d. What is Ralph Smith's job?
   e. When was Tony Jackson hired?

3. In Explore, try the following queries and indicate if each accomplishes the result listed:
   a. **QUERY:** SELECT * FROM Employee order by Hourlywage

   RESULT: Displays employees beginning with the person who is the lowest paid
   b. **QUERY:** SELECT * FROM Employee where Gender = 'F' AND Jobcode = 'SMD'

   RESULT: Displays all the female staff physicians
   c. **QUERY:** SELECT * FROM Employee where LastName between 'C' and 'M'

   RESULT: Displays all the employees with last names that begin with a C, D, E, F, G, or H
   d. **QUERY:** SELECT * FROM Employee where Gender = 'M' or Hourlywage > 20.00

   RESULT: Displays only the men who make more than $20 an hour
   e. **QUERY:** SELECT * FROM Employee where DeptCode <> 'OB' order by BirthDate

   RESULT: Displays all the obstetricians' birthdays

4. In Explore, suppose that the database contains thousands of records and it is not practical to browse through all of the records using the scroll bar. Write down the queries you use to do the following:
   a. Find the record for Angela Peterson.
   b. Find the records for all the RNs.
   c. Find all the employees who work in Intensive Care (IC).
   d. Find all the employees who make less than $15 an hour.
   e. Find all the employees who do not work in obstetrics (OB).

5   In Explore, suppose that the database contains thousands of records and it is not practical to browse through all of the records using the scroll bar. Write down the queries you use to do the following:

   a. Find the name of the oldest employee.

   b. Find the departments that have female employees.

   c. Find out how many employees work in Intensive Care.

   d. Find the last names of the female employees who make between $10 and $15 per hour.

   e. Get an alphabetized list of male employees who work as Rns or LPNs.

6   Circle the errors in the following SQL queries:

   a. SELECT * FROM Employee where DeptCode <> OB order by BirthDate

   b. SELECT * FROM Employee where Wages between 10 and 50

   c. SELECT * FROM Employee where order = LastName

   d. SELECT * FROM Employee where DeptCode <> 'OB' and Hourly Wage > '$10.00' order by LastName

   e. SELECT * FROM Employee where FirstName like T*

It's Tuesday night. You and a group of friends are studying late when the munchies strike. Pizza sounds really good, but when you and your friends pool all your money, you have a grand total of $24.63—not much to feed eight hungry students. You all agree to call several pizza places to compare prices. One of your friends, looking up from her financial management text, says, "Maximize pizza, minimize cost!"

You call VanGo's Pizzeria first and find out that they have an 8" round pizza with two toppings for $8.99. Next, you call a pizza place named The Venice and discover that they have a 10" square pizza for $11.99. Which one is the better deal? You search for a calculator but can't find one. Your friend with the pocket protector offers to let you use his notebook computer so you can write a program to compare pizza prices. Now what?

This chapter is an introduction to **computer programming**, the process of writing instructions that direct the computer to carry out a specific task. Basic concepts of computer programming include problem statements, algorithms, coding, control structures, testing, and documentation. Additional chapter topics include characteristics of computer programming languages and brief descriptions of today's most popular programming languages. This chapter is a steppingstone for programming activities, such as the Visual Programming Lab.

CHAPTER**PREVIEW**

In this chapter, you'll learn about computer programming and find out how to write a program that compares pizza prices. You can apply what you learn about the pizza program to many different problems that a computer can help you solve. You will also learn about the methodology programmers use to specify, code, and test computer programs. Understanding this methodology will be useful if you become involved in software development as a programmer or as a computer user. When you have completed this chapter, you should be able to:

- Describe the difference between a systems analyst and software engineer
- List today's most popular computer programming languages
- Describe the difference between a "small" program and a "large" program using the Department of Defense standards
- Identify the assumptions and known information in a problem statement
- Describe the relationship between an algorithm, pseudocode, and program code
- List at least four ways to express an algorithm
- Identify control structures in a simple BASIC program
- Describe the difference between syntax and logic errors
- Explain the purpose of program documentation, remarks, and user reference
- List the major characteristics that differentiate programming languages

LABS

Visual
Programming

Ⓐ Software Engineering

Software engineering is the systematic approach to the development, operation, maintenance, and retirement of software. Software engineers are responsible for designing software that is used in an information system. The jobs of the systems analyst and the software engineer overlap, but they are not the same. A systems analyst plans an entire information system, including hardware, software, procedures, personnel, and data. A software engineer focuses on the software component of an information system: on software design, programming, and testing.

InfoWeb

Software
Engineering
1

What is the point of learning about software engineering and computer programming if you do not plan to become a programmer? There are several reasons. First, you are likely to use many computer programs during your career, and when you realize that your word-processing program contains 750,000 lines of code, you will understand how a few bugs might exist. You will also understand that you, individually, would not want to undertake the task of writing a word-processing program; that is a project best left to professional programming teams. Finally, although you would not typically write the productivity software you use, it is possible that you might have the opportunity to develop or participate in the development of software applications that are specific to your needs. Your understanding of computer programming and software engineering will help you plan constructively and participate productively in the development process.

Computer Programs

Is it difficult to write a computer program? Compared to the commercial applications you use, the programs you'll work with in this chapter are relatively "tiny." By the Department of Defense standards, a "small" program is one with fewer than 100,000 lines of instructions. A "medium-sized" program is one with 100,000 to one million lines. A "large" program is one with more than one million lines. Research has shown that on average, one programmer completes only 20 lines of code per day. It is not surprising, then, that most commercial programs are written by a team of programmers and take many months, or years, to complete.

In Chapter 2, you learned that a **computer program** is a set of detailed, step-by-step instructions that tell a computer how to solve a problem or carry out a task. Although we speak of "writing a computer program," it is not exactly the same process as writing a letter. When you write a letter you are not particularly concerned about its structure or efficiency, as long as you communicate your message.

People can tolerate some degree of ambiguity when they communicate. Suppose you write your friend a letter that includes the following statement: "Remember to water my plants and lock the doors. Oh, and don't forget to feed the fish." You assume your friend knows which plants to water and how much water to use, you hope your friend remembers what to feed the fish, and you assume your friend will feed the fish before leaving the house and locking the door. Computers don't deal with ambiguity as well as people. So, when you give the computer a set of instructions, you need to be more explicit than you would be with a person. Consequently, you must think of computer programming as a process that is more structured than writing a casual letter to a friend. You must be more precise and less ambiguous.

Writing a computer program is more complex than writing a letter. However, the software engineering process offers guidelines that help you achieve a successful outcome to this complex task. Computer programming begins with a problem statement, which is the basis for an algorithm. An algorithm, in turn, is the basis for program instructions. Let's take a closer look at what we mean by problem statement, algorithm, and program instructions.

The Problem Statement

What's a good problem statement for the pizza program? Problems that you might try to solve using a computer often begin as questions. For example: "Which pizza place has the best deal?" But this question is not stated in a way that helps you devise a way for the computer to arrive at an answer. The question is vague. It doesn't tell you what information is available for determining the best deal. Do you know the price of several pizzas at different pizza places? Do you know the size of the pizzas? Do you know how many toppings are included in the price? The question "Which pizza place has the best deal?" does not explain what "best deal" means: Is it merely the cheapest pizza? Is it the pizza that gives you the most toppings for the dollar? Is it the biggest pizza you can get for the $24.63 that you and your friends managed to scrape together? Study Figure 15-1 and see if you can pose a problem statement that is better than the initial vague question, "Which pizza place has the best deal?"

Figure 15-1

What's the best deal on a pizza?

A **problem statement** defines certain elements that must be manipulated to achieve a result or goal. A well-posed problem statement has three characteristics:

- It specifies any assumptions that define the scope of the problem.
- It clearly specifies the known information.
- It specifies when the problem has been solved.

In a problem statement, an **assumption** is something that you accept as true in order to proceed with the program design. For example, in the pizza problem, you can make the assumption that you want to compare two pizzas. Further, you can assume that some pizzas are round and others are square. To simplify the problem, you might make the additional assumption that none of the pizzas are rectangular, that is, none will have one side longer than the other. This simplifies the problem because you need to deal only with the "size" of a pizza, rather than the "length" and "width" of a pizza. A fourth assumption for the pizza problem is that the pizzas you compare have the same toppings. Finally, you assume that the pizza with the lowest cost per square inch is the best buy.

The **known information** in a problem statement is the information you supply the computer to help solve a problem. For the pizza problem, the known information includes the prices, the shapes, and the sizes of pizzas from two pizza places. The known information is often included in the problem statement as "givens." For example, a problem statement might include the phrase, "given the prices, the shapes, and the sizes of two pizzas... ."

After you specify the known information in a problem statement, you specify how you will determine when the problem has been solved. Usually this means specifying the output you expect. Of course, you cannot specify the answer in the problem statement—you won't know, for example, whether VanGo's Pizzeria or The Venice has the better deal before you run the program. But you can specify that the computer should output which pizza is the better deal.

Suppose you and your friends decide that the best deal means getting the biggest pizza at the lowest price; in other words, the best deal is the pizza that has the cheapest price per square inch. In this case, pizza that costs 5¢ per square inch is a better deal than pizza that costs 7¢ per square inch. The problem is solved, therefore, when the computer has calculated the price per square inch for both pizzas, compared the prices, and printed a message indicating which one has the lower price per square inch. You could write this part of the problem statement as "The computer will calculate the price per square inch of each pizza, then print a message indicating whether Pizza 1 or Pizza 2 has the lower price per square inch."

After thinking carefully about the problem, you have a list of assumptions, a list of known information, and a description of what you expect as output. The complete problem statement for the pizza program is:

Assuming that there are two pizzas to compare, that both pizzas contain the same toppings, and that the pizzas could be round or square; and given the prices, the shapes, and the sizes of the two pizzas; the computer will calculate the price per square inch of each pizza, then print a message indicating which pizza has the lower price per square inch.

This problem statement is rather lengthy. The following format for the problem statement is easier to understand:

ASSUMPTIONS:
There are two pizzas to compare, Pizza 1 and Pizza 2
The pizzas have the same toppings
A pizza is either round or square
Neither of the pizzas is rectangular
The pizza with the lower cost per square inch is the "best buy"
GIVEN:
The prices of two pizzas in dollars
The shape of each pizza (round or square)
The size of each pizza in inches
COMPUTE:
The price per square inch of each pizza
DISPLAY:
"Pizza 1 is the best deal" if Pizza 1 has the lower price per square inch
"Pizza 2 is the best deal" if Pizza 2 has the lower price per square inch
"Neither is the best deal" if both pizzas have the same price per square inch

Now that you have learned how to write a problem statement, we can move to the next step in the programming process—creating an algorithm.

Algorithms

How do I formulate an algorithm for the pizza problem? An **algorithm** is a set of steps for carrying out a task. An algorithm is an abstract idea, but it can be written down and it can be implemented. For example, the algorithm for cooking a batch of macaroni and cheese is a set of steps that includes boiling water, cooking the macaroni in the water, and adding cheese. The algorithm is written down, or expressed, as instructions in a recipe. You can implement the algorithm by following the instructions.

InfoWeb

Algorithms
2

An important characteristic of a correctly formulated algorithm is that by carefully following the steps, you are guaranteed to accomplish the task for which the algorithm was designed. So, if you carefully follow the recipe on the macaroni package, you should be guaranteed a successful batch of macaroni and cheese.

An algorithm for a computer program is the set of steps that explains how to begin with the known information specified in a problem statement and manipulate that information to arrive at a solution. An algorithm for a computer program is typically first written in a format that is not specific to a particular computer or programming language. This way, the software engineer focuses on formulating a correct algorithm, rather than on expressing the algorithm using the commands of a computer programming language. In a later phase of the software development process, the algorithm is translated into instructions written in a computer programming language so the algorithm can be implemented by a computer.

When you are just beginning to work with computer programming, determining the amount of detail required to express an algorithm might seem difficult. For example, you might wonder if your algorithm needs to specify the steps necessary to do addition—do you need to explain how to "carry"? The detail necessary for the algorithm depends on the computer language you intend to use to write the program. As you become familiar with the commands that a language contains and what each command does, you will gain an understanding of the level of detail required. For the pizza problem, let's suppose that you will use the BASIC computer language. Study Figure 15-2 to understand the level of instructions that are appropriate for algorithms that are the basis for BASIC programs.

Figure 15-2

A sample of the kinds of tasks an algorithm for a BASIC program can specify

Algorithm Task	Example
Assign a value to a variable	Size = 10
Evaluate an expression or "solve an equation"	SquareInchPrice = Price / SquareInches
Ask for information (input) from the user	Enter the Price of a pizza
Display or print the results of calculations	Display the SquareInchPrice
Make decisions	If the pizza is square, calculate SquareInches by multiplying the Size * Size
Repeat some instructions	Repeat the price calculations for as many pizzas as the user wants

To design an algorithm, you might begin by solving the problem yourself and recording the steps you take. If you take this route, remember that to solve the pizza problem you have to obtain initial information on the cost, the size, and the shape of the pizzas. The computer also needs this initial information, so part of your algorithm must specify how the computer gets it. When the pizza program runs, it should request the user to enter the initial information needed to solve the problem. Your algorithm might begin like this:

Ask the user for the shape of the first pizza and hold it in RAM as Shape1.
Ask the user for the price of the first pizza and hold it in RAM as Price1.
Ask the user for the size of the first pizza and hold it in RAM as Size1.

Next, your algorithm should specify how to manipulate this information. You want to calculate the price per square inch, but an instruction like "Calculate the price per square inch" neither specifies how to do the calculation nor deals with the fact that you must perform different calculations for square and round pizzas. A more appropriate set of instructions is shown in Figure 15-3.

Figure 15-3

Algorithm for calculating the
price per square inch

1. To calculate the area of a square pizza, multiply the length of one side by the length of the other side. The sides are the same size in a square, so you can use the formula Size1 * Size1.

2. To calculate the area of a round pizza, use the formula for the area of a circle: πr^2. π is approximately 3.142. r^2 is the square of the radius of the circle. The size of a pizza is its diameter, so you need to divide the diameter by 2 to get the radius, using Size1 /2. Then you need to square the radius. ^2 is the notation you use on a computer to indicate the exponent 2.

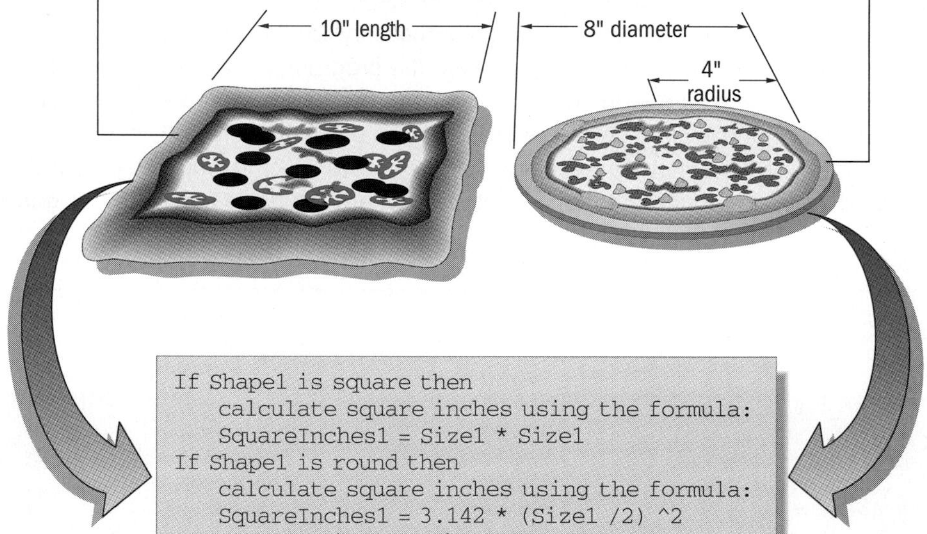

← 10" length →   ← 8" diameter →

4"
radius

```
If Shape1 is square then
    calculate square inches using the formula:
    SquareInches1 = Size1 * Size1
If Shape1 is round then
    calculate square inches using the formula:
    SquareInches1 = 3.142 * (Size1 /2) ^2
SquareInchPrice1 = Price1 / SquareInches1
```

3. After you know the area of a pizza, you can calculate the price per square inch.

The algorithm you have designed so far calculates the price per square inch of one pizza. The algorithm should specify a similar process for calculating the price per square inch of the second pizza:

Ask the user for the shape of the second pizza and hold it in RAM as Shape2
Ask the user for the price of the second pizza and hold it in RAM as Price2
Ask the user for the size of the second pizza and hold it in RAM as Size2
If Shape2 is square then calculate the square inches using the formula:
   SquareInches2 = Size2 * Size2
If Shape2 is round then calculate the square inches using the formula:
   SquareInches2 = 3.142 * (Size2 / 2) ^2
SquareInchPrice2 = Price2 / SquareInches2

Finally, the algorithm should specify how the computer decides what to display as the solution. You want the computer to display a message telling you which pizza has the lowest square-inch cost, so your algorithm should include something like this:

If SquareInchPrice1< SquareInchPrice2 then display the message "Pizza 1 is the best deal."
If SquareInchPrice2 < SquareInchPrice1 then display the message "Pizza 2 is the best deal."

But don't forget to indicate what you want the program to do if the price per square inch of both pizzas is the same:

If SquareInchPrice1 = SquareInchPrice2 then display the message "Both pizzas are the same deal."

The complete algorithm for the pizza problem is shown in Figure 15-4.

Figure 15-4

Algorithm for pizza problems

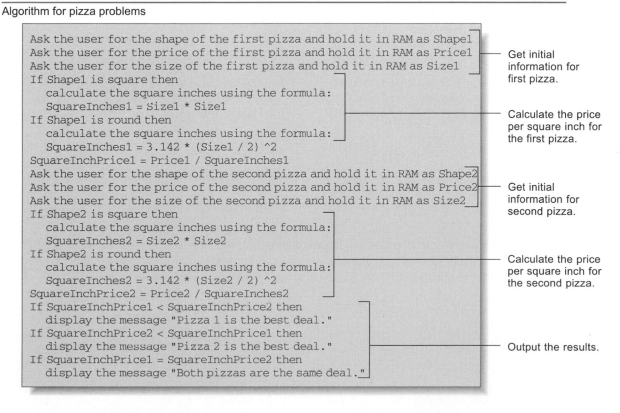

Expressing an Algorithm

| What's the best way to express an algorithm? | You can express an algorithm in several different ways, including structured English, pseudocode, flow charts, and object definitions. These tools are not programming languages and they cannot be processed by a computer. Their purpose is to provide a way for you to document your ideas for program design.

InfoWeb

Pseudocode
&
Flow Charts
3

Structured English is a subset of the English language with a limited selection of sentence structures that reflect processing activities. Look back at Figure 15-4 to see how you can use structured English to express the algorithm for the pizza problem.

Another way to express an algorithm is with pseudocode. **Pseudocode** is a notational system for algorithms that has been described as "a mixture of English and your favorite programming language." Pseudocode is less formalized than structured English, so the structure and wording are left up to you. Also, when you write pseudocode, you are allowed to incorporate command words and syntax from the computer you intend to use for the actual program. Compare Figure 15-4 with Figure 15-5 and see if you can pick out some of the differences between Structured English and pseudocode.

Figure 15-5

Pseudocode for
pizza program

```
display prompts for entering shape, price, and size
input Shape1, Price1, Size1
if Shape1 = square then
    SquareInches   ← Size1 * Size1
if Shape1 = round then
    SquareInches1  ← 3.142 * (Size1 / 2) ^2
SquareInchPrice1 ← Price1 / SquareInches1

display prompts for entering shape, price, and size
input Shape2, Price2, Size2
if Shape2 = square then
    SquareInches2  ← Size2 * Size2
if Shape2 = round then
    SquareInches2  ← 3.142 * (Size2 / 2) ^2
SquareInchPrice2 ← Price2 / SquareInches2

if SquareInchPrice1 < SquareInchPrice2 then
    output "Pizza 1 is the best deal."
if SquareInchPrice2 < SquareInchPrice1 then
    output "Pizza 2 is the best deal."
if SquareInchPrice1 = SquareInchPrice2 then
    output "Both pizzas are the same deal."
```

A third way to express an algorithm is to use a flow chart. A **flow chart** is a graphical representation of the way a computer should progress from one instruction to the next when it performs a task. The flow chart for the pizza problem is shown in Figure 15-6.

Figure 15-6

Flow chart for pizza program

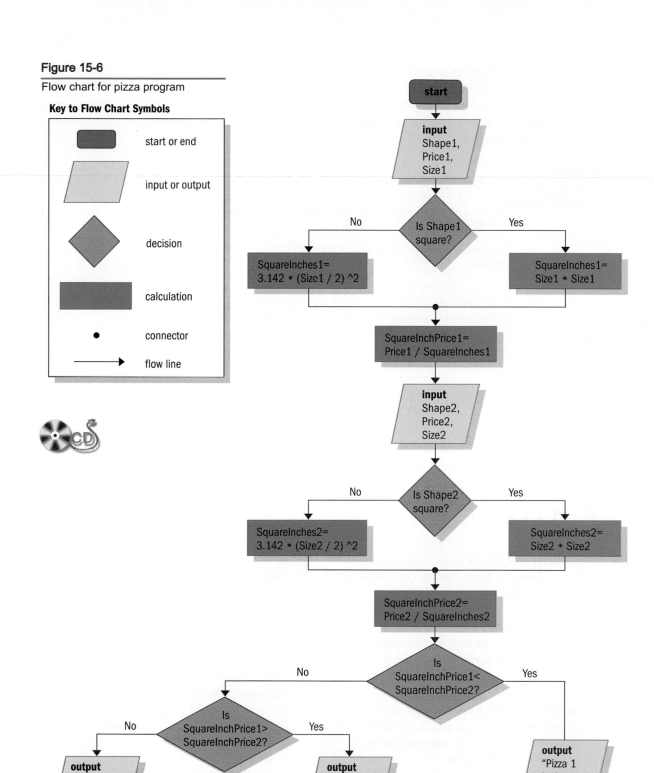

Key to Flow Chart Symbols

- start or end
- input or output
- decision
- calculation
- connector
- flow line

start

input Shape1, Price1, Size1

Is Shape1 square?
- No → SquareInches1= 3.142 * (Size1 / 2) ^2
- Yes → SquareInches1= Size1 * Size1

SquareInchPrice1= Price1 / SquareInches1

input Shape2, Price2, Size2

Is Shape2 square?
- No → SquareInches2= 3.142 * (Size2 / 2) ^2
- Yes → SquareInches2= Size2 * Size2

SquareInchPrice2= Price2 / SquareInches2

Is SquareInchPrice1< SquareInchPrice2?
- Yes → **output** "Pizza 1 is the best deal."
- No → Is SquareInchPrice1> SquareInchPrice2?
  - No → **output** "Both pizzas are the same deal."
  - Yes → **output** "Pizza 2 is the best deal."

end

Another way to express an algorithm is to **define the objects** that the computer must manipulate, then specify the method for manipulating each object. This way of expressing an algorithm is useful for designing object-oriented programs, which you will learn more about later in this chapter. Figure 15-7 shows a description of one of the objects for the pizza program.

Figure 15-7

An object description
for the pizza program

```
Object: Calculate Best Deal
Type: Button
Appearance:   [ Calculate Best Deal ]
Method:
if Shape1 = "square" THEN SquareInches1 = Size1 * Size1
if Shape1 = "round" THEN SquareInches1 = 3.142 * (Size1 / 2) ^2
SquareInchPrice1 = Price1 / SquareInches1
if Shape2 = "square" THEN SquareInches2 = Size2 * Size2
if Shape2 = "round" THEN SquareInches2 = 3.142 * (Size2 / 2) ^2
SquareInchPrice2 = Price2 / SquareInches2
if SquareInchPrice1 < SquareInchPrice2 then BestDeal = "Pizza 1 is the
best deal."
if SquareInchPrice2 < SquareInchPrice1 then BestDeal = "Pizza 2 is the
best deal."
if SquareInchPrice1 = SquareInchPrice2 then BestDeal = "Both pizzas are
the same deal."
```

QuickCheck   A

1. If you have a job as a(n) _____ you would focus on the software component of an information system.

2. The U.S. Department of Defense defines a "large" program as one that has about 100,000 line of code. True or false? _____

3. Before you write a computer program, you should write a(n) _____ to define the elements that must be manipulated to achieve a result or goal.

4. A(n) _____ is a set of steps for carrying out a task or solving a problem.

5. "A mixture of English and your favorite programming language" is the description of _____.

6. A(n) _____ is a graphical representation of the way a computer should progress from one instruction to the next when it performs a task.

B Coding Computer Programs

InfoWeb

Programming Careers 4

A problem statement and an algorithm are often combined into a document called the **program specification**, which is essentially a blueprint for a computer program. When the program specification is complete, it is time to begin coding the program. **Coding** is the process of using a computer language to express an algorithm. A person who codes or writes computer programs is called a **computer programmer**.

With many computer programming languages, the coding process means entering commands. With other computer programming languages, you enter or select the characteristics of objects, or you enter descriptive statements about the objects.

To code the pizza algorithm using the BASIC computer language, you type a list of commands. Look at the completed program in Figure 15-8 and study the callouts to get a general understanding of the elements of a computer program.

Figure 15-8

BASIC code for the pizza program

Command words are shown in boldface.

The program is written as a list of steps. The computer executes the steps starting at the top of the list.

```
REM   The Pizza Program
REM   This program tells you which of two pizzas is the best deal
REM   by calculating the price per square inch of each pizza.

REM   Collect initial information for first pizza.
INPUT   "Enter the shape of pizza one:", Shape1$
INPUT   "Enter the price of pizza one:", Price1
INPUT   "Enter the size of pizza one:", Size1

REM   Calculate price per square inch for first pizza.

REM   If the first pizza is square, calculate the square inches by multiplying
one side by the other.
If Shape1$ = "square" THEN SquareInches1 = Size1 * Size1

REM   If the first pizza is round, calculate the number of square inches where
REM   pi = 3.142, size / 2 = radius, and (size / 2) ^2 = radius squared:
If Shape1$ = "round" THEN SquareInches1 = 3.142 * (Size1 / 2) ^2
SquareInchPrice1 = Price1 / SquareInches1

REM   Collect initial information for second pizza.
INPUT   "Enter the shape of pizza two:", Shape2$
INPUT   "Enter the price of pizza two:", Price2
INPUT   "Enter the size of pizza two:", Size2

REM   Calculate price per square inch for second pizza.
If Shape2$ = "square" THEN SquareInches2 = Size2 * Size2
If Shape2$ = "round" THEN SquareInches2 = 3.142 * (Size2 / 2) ^2
SquareInchPrice2 = Price2 / SquareInches2

REM   Decide which pizza is the best deal and display results.
If SquareInchPrice1 < SquareInchPrice2 THEN Message$ = "Pizza 1 is the best deal."
If SquareInchPrice2 < SquareInchPrice1 THEN Message$ = "Pizza 2 is the best deal."
If SquareInchPrice1 = SquareInchPrice2 THEN Message$ = "Both pizzas are the
same deal."
Print Message$
END
```

Remarks that begin with REM explain each section of the program.

Data is stored in variables, or memory locations, in RAM. The variable Shape1$ stores text, such as the word "round." The $ indicates a text variable. Other variables, such as Price1, store numbers, and the variable name does not include a $.

Program Sequence

How do I tell the computer the sequence in which it should perform instructions?

Called **sequential execution**, the normal pattern of program execution is for a computer to perform each instruction in the sequence established by the programmer. The first instruction in the program is executed first, then the second instruction, and so on through the rest of the instructions in the program. Here is a simple program written in the QBASIC computer language that outputs "This is the first line." then outputs "This is the second line."

Visual Programming
```
PRINT "This is the first line."
PRINT "This is the second line."
```

Although most modern programming languages do not use line numbers, older programming languages, such as the original version of BASIC, required programmers to number each instruction like this:

```
100 PRINT "This is the first line."
200 PRINT "This is the second line."
```

If the lines in a program are numbered, a computer begins executing the instruction with the lowest number, then proceeds to the instruction with the next highest number, and so on. The flowchart in Figure 15-9 represents a simple sequential execution of commands.

Figure 15-9

Sequential program execution

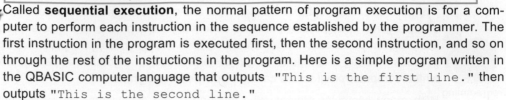

Some algorithms specify that a program execute instructions in an order different from the sequence in which they are listed, skip some instructions under certain circumstances, or repeat instructions. **Control structures** are instructions that specify the sequence in which a program is executed. There are three types of control structures: sequence controls, selection controls, and repetition controls.

Sequence Controls

Is there any way to have the computer follow a different sequence? A **sequence control structure** changes the sequence, or order, in which instructions are executed by directing the computer to execute an instruction elsewhere in the program. In the following simple QBASIC program, the GOTO command tells the computer to jump directly to the instruction labeled "Widget." The program will never execute the command PRINT "This is the second line."

InfoWeb

GOTO
5

```
PRINT "This is the first line."
GOTO Widget
PRINT "This is the second line."
Widget: PRINT "All Done!"
END
```

The flowchart in Figure 15-10 represents how the computer follows a series of sequential commands, then "jumps" past other commands as the result of a GOTO command.

Figure 15-10

Executing a GOTO

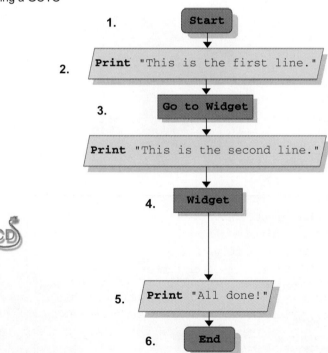

Although it is the simplest control structure, the GOTO command is rarely used by skilled programmers because it can lead to programs that are difficult to understand and maintain. In 1968, the journal, *Communications of the ACM*, published a now famous letter from Edsger Dijkstra, called "Go To Statement Considered Harmful." In his letter, Dijkstra explained that injudicious use of the GOTO statement in programs makes it difficult for other programmers to understand the underlying algorithm, which in turn means that such programs are difficult to correct, improve, or revise.

Experienced programmers prefer to use sequence controls other than GOTO to transfer program execution to a subroutine, procedure, module, or function. **Subroutines**, **procedures**, **modules**, and **functions** are sections of code that are part of a program, but are not included in the main sequential execution path. Figure 15-11 shows the execution path of a program that uses the GOSUB command to transfer execution to a subroutine.

Figure 15-11

Executing a
GOSUB command

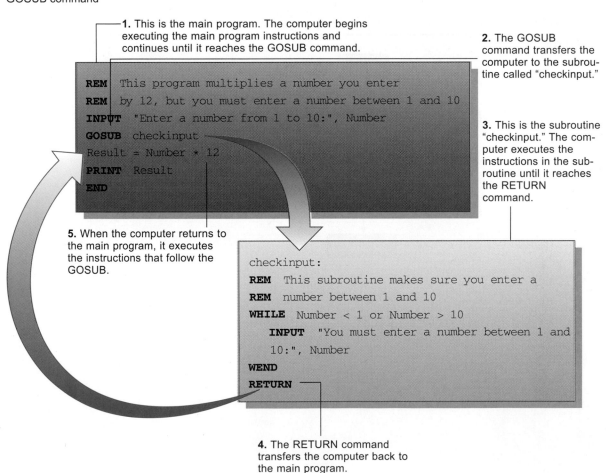

1. This is the main program. The computer begins executing the main program instructions and continues until it reaches the GOSUB command.

2. The GOSUB command transfers the computer to the subroutine called "checkinput."

```
REM   This program multiplies a number you enter
REM   by 12, but you must enter a number between 1 and 10
INPUT  "Enter a number from 1 to 10:", Number
GOSUB  checkinput
Result = Number * 12
PRINT  Result
END
```

3. This is the subroutine "checkinput." The computer executes the instructions in the subroutine until it reaches the RETURN command.

5. When the computer returns to the main program, it executes the instructions that follow the GOSUB.

```
checkinput:
REM   This subroutine makes sure you enter a
REM   number between 1 and 10
WHILE  Number < 1 or Number > 10
   INPUT  "You must enter a number between 1 and
   10:", Number
WEND
RETURN
```

4. The RETURN command transfers the computer back to the main program.

Selection Controls

Can the computer make decisions as it executes a program? A **selection control structure**, also referred to as a **decision structure** or **branch**, tells a computer what to do based on whether a condition is true or false. A simple example of a selection control structure is the IF..THEN..ELSE command. The following program uses the IF..THEN..ELSE command to decide whether a number entered is greater than 10. If the number is greater than 10, the computer prints "That number is greater than 10!" If the number is not greater than 10, the program does not print this message.

```
INPUT "Enter a number from 1 to 10:", Number
IF Number > 10 THEN PRINT "That number is greater than 10!"
ELSE PRINT "That number is 10 or less."
END
```

Figure 15-12 uses a flow chart to illustrate how a computer follows commands in a decision structure.

Figure 15-12

The computer executes a selection

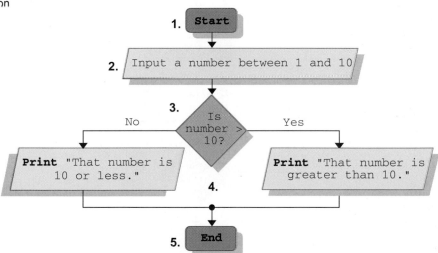

Repetition Controls

Can a computer perform a series of instructions more than once? A **repetition control structure**, also referred to as a **loop** or **iteration**, repeats one or more instructions until a certain condition is met. In QBASIC, the most frequently used loop commands are FOR..NEXT and WHILE..WEND. The following simple QBASIC program uses the FOR..NEXT command to print a message three times.

```
FOR N = 1 TO 3
   PRINT "There's no place like home."
NEXT N
END
```

Follow the path of program execution in Figure 15-13 to see how a computer executes a series of commands in a repetition structure.

Figure 15-13

The computer
executes a loop

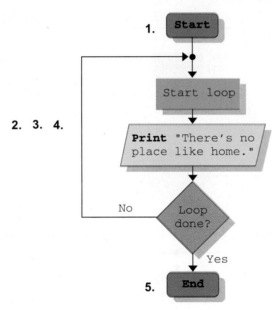

To get a better idea of how a FOR..NEXT loop works, pretend that you're the computer executing the FOR..NEXT loop below. You can use the box labeled N in the margin as a RAM location. As the computer, you would also have a screen on which to display output. Use the Screen Output box. Now, let's walk through the loop.

```
FOR N = 1 TO 3
   PRINT "There's no place like home."
NEXT N
END
```

N

Screen Output

1. As the computer, the first time you see the instruction FOR N = 1 TO 3, you set N equal to 1. To do this, write the number 1 in the N box in the margin.

2. You would then execute the next instruction, PRINT "There's no place like home." To do this, write the phrase "There's no place like home" in the Screen Output box.

3. The instruction NEXT sends you back to the command FOR N = 1 TO 3. Because this is the second time you have executed this statement, put a 2 in the N box in the margin (you can erase the 1 that was there previously).

4. You need to check if the value in box N is greater than 3. Why do this? Because the command FOR N = 1 TO 3 means you can continue to loop only if N is 3 or less. Well, N is only 2, so you can proceed.

5. Go to the next instruction, which is PRINT "There's no place like home." So, write this again in the Screen Output box.

6. Moving on, you reach the NEXT statement again, and this sends you back to the FOR statement.

7. Continue by changing the value in the N box to 3. Check the N box to make sure it does not contain a value greater than 3. It doesn't, so continue.

8. The next line instructs you to PRINT "There's no place like home," so write this again in the Screen Output box. The NEXT statement sends you back to the FOR statement. Increase the value in the N box to 4. This time when you check if the value in N is greater than 3, it is. That means the loop is complete and you should jump to the statement past the end of the loop.

9. The next statement is END, so you've completed the program.

QuickCheck B

1. _____ is the process of using a computer language to express an algorithm.

2. A(n) _____ control changes the order in which instructions are executed by transferring program execution to instructions elsewhere in the program.

3. A(n) _____ structure tells a computer what to do, depending on whether a condition is true or false.

4. A(n) _____ structure repeats one or more instructions until a certain condition is met.

C Debugging and Documenting

As you are coding a program, you must test each section of your code to make sure it works correctly. This process is referred to as **debugging** because the process "gets the bugs out" so they don't cause errors when you use the program. As you are coding, you should also write **documentation** as a permanent record that explains how your program works.

Testing a Program

How do I know if my program will function correctly? A computer program must be tested to ensure that it works correctly. Testing often consists of entering test data to see if the program produces correct results. If the program does not produce correct results, the programmer must examine the program for errors, correct the errors, and test the program again. The process can get a bit frustrating at times, as shown in Figure 15-14. However, testing is a crucial step in the programming process.

Figure 15-14

A video created by Stanford students in 1967 depicts a programmer's frustration with the coding, testing, and debugging process.

For example, to test the pizza program, you could run the program and enter data for which you have already calculated the results. Suppose you use a calculator to determine that the price per square inch of an $18.50, 15" square pizza is about $.08. One way to test the program is to run it and enter $18.50 for the price, 15 for the size, and square for the shape. The program should produce the result $.08 for the price per square inch of this pizza. If it doesn't, you know that you made an error when you wrote the program and that you must correct the error.

But testing a single set of values is not enough. At minimum, you should test every statement at least once, and you should test every decision branch. The pizza program has two possible decision branches for calculating the price per square inch. One branch is for square pizzas; the other branch is for round pizzas. Even if you enter a set of test data for a square pizza and the program provides the correct result, you cannot assume the program is working correctly until you also test it with data for a round pizza.

When you find an error, or bug, in a program, it might be a syntax error or it might be a run-time error. A **syntax error** is caused when an instruction does not follow the syntax rules, or grammar, of the programming language. For example, when you want to print a message, you need to use the PRINT command. The command `IF AGE = 16 THEN "You can drive."` will produce a syntax error because the command word PRINT is missing. The correct version of the command is `IF AGE = 16 THEN PRINT "You can drive."`

Syntax errors are very common, but they are easy to detect and correct. Syntax errors can be caused by omitting a command word, misspelling a command word, or using incorrect punctuation, such as a colon (:) where a semicolon (;) is required. Many of today's programming languages detect and point out syntax errors when you are in the process of coding each instruction. Because these languages show you syntax errors when you type each line of code, you typically will have few syntax errors when you test programs written with these languages.

The other type of program bug is a run-time error. A **run-time error** is an error that shows up when you run a program. Run-time errors can be caused by a typing error that results in the correct syntax but does not produce the intended result. For example, suppose you erroneously use the < symbol in the following command for the pizza problem:

```
IF SquareInchPrice1 < SquareInchPrice2 THEN PRINT "Pizza 2 is a
better deal than Pizza 1."
```

The command produces the wrong output as a result of the error you introduced when you used the < sign instead of the > sign.

Other run-time errors are classified as logic errors. A **logic error** is an error in the logic or design of the program. Logic errors can be caused by an inadequate definition of the problem or by an incorrect or incomplete solution specified by the flowchart or pseudocode. Logic errors are usually more difficult and time-consuming to identify than syntax errors.

Program Documentation

Why do I need to document my programs? A computer program inevitably must be modified because needs change. Modifying a program is much easier if the program has been well documented. For example, suppose VanGo's Pizzeria and The Venice have both added a new rectangular pizza to their menu. In that case, you and your friends would want to modify the pizza program so you can enter the dimensions of a rectangular pizza. First, you need to understand how the current program works. Although this might seem like a fairly easy task for the short pizza program, imagine trying to understand a 50,000-line program that calculates income tax, especially if you weren't the person who wrote the original program. You might want some additional information to explain the logic behind the program and the formulas that the programmer devised to perform calculations.

Program documentation explains how a program works and how to use it. The documentation you create should be useful to other programmers who need to modify your code and to people who use your program. Typically, program documentation takes two forms: remarks inserted into the program code and "written" documentation.

Remarks are explanatory comments inserted into the lines of code of a computer program. To revise a computer program, a programmer reads through the original program to find out how it works, then makes revisions to the appropriate sections of code. It is easier to understand the original program if the person who writes it places remarks in the program.

Remarks are ignored by the computer when it executes the program, but for programmers who must modify the program, these remarks are very handy. A well-documented program contains initial remarks that explain the purpose of the program. These remarks contain essentially the same information as the problem statement. For example, the pizza program contains the following initial remarks:

```
REM    The Pizza Program
REM    This program tells you which of two pizzas is the better deal
REM    by calculating the price per square inch of each pizza.
```

Remarks should also be added to the sections of a program in which the purpose of the code is not immediately clear. For example, in the pizza program, the purpose of the expression 3.142*(size/2)^2 might not be immediately obvious to a programmer reading the code. Therefore, it would be helpful to have a remark preceding the expression, like this:

```
REM The program calculates the number of square inches
REM in a round pizza where
REM pi = 3.142, size/2 = radius, and (size/2)^2 = radius squared:
SquareInches = 3.142*(size/2)^2
```

There is no hard and fast rule about when you should include a remark in a program. However, if you were to work with a group of other programmers on a project, your group might develop guidelines to ensure that remarks are used consistently throughout the code for the project. As you gain experience writing programs, you will develop a sense for using remarks appropriately.

Written documentation is external to a program and contains information about the program that is useful to programmers and the people who use the program. Written documentation can be paper-based or in electronic format. Because documentation serves two audiences—the programmers and the users—there are two broad categories of written documentation for computer programs: program manuals and user references.

A **program manual** contains any information about the program that might be useful to programmers, including the problem statement and algorithm. Because a program manual is a software development and maintenance tool, it is used by programmers, not users. The **user reference**, or **reference manual**, contains information that helps users learn to use a computer program. A computerized version of the user reference is usually supplied as online help. Figure 15-15 compares the types of information that might be included in a program manual and a user reference.

Figure 15-15

Program documentation

Program Manual	User Reference
Problem statement	Description of what the program does

Algorithm expressed as:
    Structured English
    Pseudocode
    Flow chart
	Instructions on how to install the program
	Instructions on how to start the program
	Description of how to use each feature
	Diagrams of screen and menus

Printout of program code	Troubleshooting tips

InfoWeb

Technical
Writing
6

Programmers are generally responsible for documenting their code and contributing to the program manual, but the trend is to hire professional technical writers to author user reference manuals. A **technical writer** specializes in explaining technical concepts and procedures, often by simplifying complex concepts for a non-technical audience. Many colleges and universities offer technical writing courses and some also offer technical writing degrees. Experienced technical writers are in demand as contract, part-time, and full-time employees in the computer industry.

QuickCheck C

1. Entering known data to see if a program produces the correct results is part of the _____ process.

2. If you ignore the rules or grammar of a programming language, you are likely to get a(n) _____ error.

3. Suppose you run the pizza program and the output indicates Pizza 2 is the best deal. However, your test data shows that Pizza 1 is the best deal. Because this error appeared when you ran the program, it would be classified as a(n) _____ error.

4. _____ errors are usually the most difficult and time-consuming errors to identify.

5. _____ explains how a program works and how to use it.

6. Programmers insert _____ into programs to explain how the program works and to make it easier for other programmers to modify the program.

7. A(n) _____ is documentation used by programmers, whereas a(n) _____ is documentation designed for the people who use the program.

D Programming Language Characteristics

Hundreds of programming languages have been developed over the last 35 years. Some languages were developed to make the programming process more efficient and less error-prone. Some languages were developed to provide an effective command set for specific types of programs, such as business programs or scientific programs. Other languages were created specifically as teaching tools.

Programming languages have characteristics that describe how they work and provide information about the types of computing tasks for which they are appropriate. For example, Pascal can be described as a high-level, procedural, compiled language. When you need to select a language to use for a program, it is useful to understand some of the general characteristics of programming languages and the advantages or disadvantages of these characteristics.

Procedural

Was the pizza program written using a procedural language? Languages with procedural characteristics create programs composed of a series of statements that tell the computer how to perform the processes for a specific task. Languages with procedural characteristics are called **procedural languages**. BASIC, the language that you used for the pizza program, has procedural characteristics. The instructions tell the computer exactly what to do: display a message on the screen asking the user to enter the shape of the pizza; display a message asking for the size of the pizza; display a message asking for the price of the pizza; if the shape is square, calculate the square-inch price with the formula SquareInchPrice = Price/Square Inches, and so forth.

As you might guess, procedural languages are well suited for programs that follow a step-by-step algorithm. Programs created with procedural languages have a starting point and an ending point. The flow of execution from the start to the end is essentially linear; that is, the computer begins at the beginning and executes the prescribed series of instructions until it reaches the end, as shown in Figure 15-16.

Figure 15-16

Execution of procedural languages

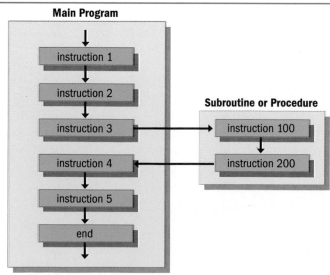

Declarative

Do all languages require the programmer to specify the exact procedure for the solution?

A **declarative language** lets a programmer write a program by specifying a set of statements and rules that define the conditions for resolving a problem. The language has a built-in method for considering the rules and determining a solution. Describing a problem and the rules that lead to a solution places an emphasis on words rather than on mathematical formulas. For this reason, declarative languages are useful for programs that manipulate ideas and concepts, rather than numbers.

Unlike programs that are created using a procedural language, programs created with a declarative language do not tell the computer how to solve a problem. Instead, a program created with a declarative language describes what the problem is. For example, Figure 15-17 contains a short program written in the Prolog language that describes several people and determines which of these people have a sister in the list.

Figure 15-17

A Prolog program

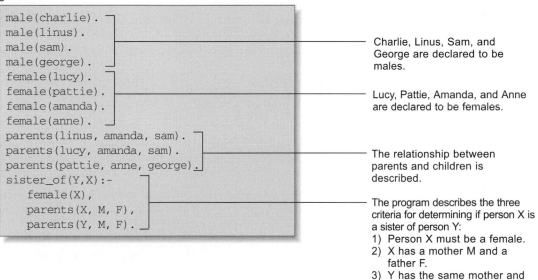

```
male(charlie).
male(linus).
male(sam).
male(george).
female(lucy).
female(pattie).
female(amanda).
female(anne).
parents(linus, amanda, sam).
parents(lucy, amanda, sam).
parents(pattie, anne, george).
sister_of(Y,X):-
    female(X),
    parents(X, M, F),
    parents(Y, M, F).
```

Charlie, Linus, Sam, and George are declared to be males.

Lucy, Pattie, Amanda, and Anne are declared to be females.

The relationship between parents and children is described.

The program describes the three criteria for determining if person X is a sister of person Y:
1) Person X must be a female.
2) X has a mother M and a father F.
3) Y has the same mother and father as X.

Scripting Languages

Is HTML a language? HTML is generally classified as a scripting language. A **scripting language** defines a task in the form of a script. Scripts require a host application to run, and cannot be run as a standalone application. For example, you use HTML tags to specify a script for how to display a Web page. This script is interpreted by a Web browser. The Web browser is the host application—without it, the HTML script cannot run.

Scripting languages are included with many applications such as word processor and spreadsheet software. You can use such scripting languages to automate tasks within the applications. These automated routines are often referred to as **macros**.

Scripting languages are typically easier to use than other types of programming languages, but have fewer features and control options. They are a good choice for non-programmers who want to automate and customize the tasks performed by their application software.

Low-Level

Our pizza program used commands like PRINT and END. Don't computers understand only ones and zeros? A **low-level language** requires a programmer to write instructions for the lowest level of the computer system, that is, for specific hardware elements such as the processor, registers, and RAM locations. A low-level language is useful when a programmer needs to directly manipulate what happens at the hardware level. Programmers typically use low-level languages to write system software such as compilers, operating systems, and device drivers.

Each instruction in a low-level language usually corresponds to a single instruction for the processor. Recall that in Chapter 5 you saw how an instruction, such as MMR M1 REG1, tells a computer to move a number from a RAM location into a register. Using a low-level language, several instructions are necessary to tell the computer how to do even simple operations, such as add two numbers together. Figure 15-18 shows a section of a program, written in a low-level language, that adds two numbers together.

Figure 15-18

Low-level
instructions

Assembly Language Instructions	Explanation of Instructions
LDA 5	Load 5 in the accumulator
STA Num1	Store the 5 in a memory location called Num1
LDA 4	Load 4 in the accumulator
ADD Num1	Add the contents of memory loation Num1 to the number in the accumulator
STA Total	Store sum in a memory location called Total
END	Stop program execution

A **machine language** is a low-level language in binary code that the computer can execute directly. Machine languages are very difficult for humans to understand and manipulate. They were primarily used in the earliest days of computer development when other programming languages were not available.

High-Level

What's the alternative to using a low-level language? A **high-level language** allows a programmer to use instructions that are more like human language, such as the BASIC command, PRINT "Please wait..." When high-level languages were originally conceived in the 1950s, computer scientists thought they would eliminate programming errors. This was not to be the case—syntax and logical errors are possible even with high-level languages. However, high-level languages significantly reduce programming errors and make it possible to write programs in less time than when using low-level languages. Programs written in high-level languages must be translated into instructions the computer can execute. Therefore, a high-level language must be compiled or interpreted.

Compiled

How does a high-level language produce machine-executable instructions? A **compiler** translates a program written in a high-level language into low-level instructions before the program is executed. The commands you write in a high-level language are referred to as **source code**. The low-level instructions that result from compiling the source code are referred to as **object code**. Figure 15-19 explains more about the compiling process.

When you use a **compiled language**, you must compile your program to produce executable program code. Therefore, if you write, compile, and run a program, but then discover that it contains a bug, you must fix your program, then recompile it before you test it again. Once you've compiled your bug-free final version, you can run the program without recompiling it.

Figure 15-19

A programming language compiler

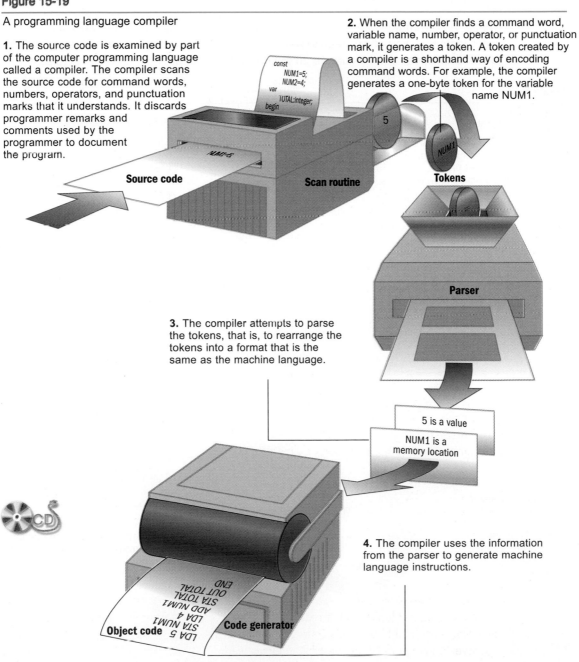

1. The source code is examined by part of the computer programming language called a compiler. The compiler scans the source code for command words, numbers, operators, and punctuation marks that it understands. It discards programmer remarks and comments used by the programmer to document the program.

2. When the compiler finds a command word, variable name, number, operator, or punctuation mark, it generates a token. A token created by a compiler is a shorthand way of encoding command words. For example, the compiler generates a one-byte token for the variable name NUM1.

```
const
  NUM1=5;
  NUM2=4;
var
  TOTAL:integer;
begin
```

Source code

Scan routine

Tokens

Parser

3. The compiler attempts to parse the tokens, that is, to rearrange the tokens into a format that is the same as the machine language.

5 is a value

NUM1 is a memory location

4. The compiler uses the information from the parser to generate machine language instructions.

Object code   **Code generator**

```
LDA 5
STA NUM1
LDA 4
ADD NUM1
STA TOTAL
OUT TOTAL
END
```

Interpreted

How is an interpreter different from a compiler? An interpreted language uses an interpreter instead of a compiler to create code that the computer can execute. When you run a program that is written in an interpreted language, the language's interpreter reads one instruction and converts it into a machine language instruction, which the computer executes. After the instruction is executed, the interpreter reads the next instruction, converts it into machine language, and so forth. Programs written in interpreted languages take longer to execute because the computer must translate every instruction as it is executed. A program with many loops is especially inefficient in an interpreted language because the instructions contained in the loop are translated multiple times, once for each time the loop is executed.

What is the advantage of an interpreted language over a compiled language? With an interpreted language, you do not need to wait for your program to compile, so the testing process seems to take less time. Figure 15-20 illustrates the concept of a language interpreter.

Figure 15-20

A programming language interpreter

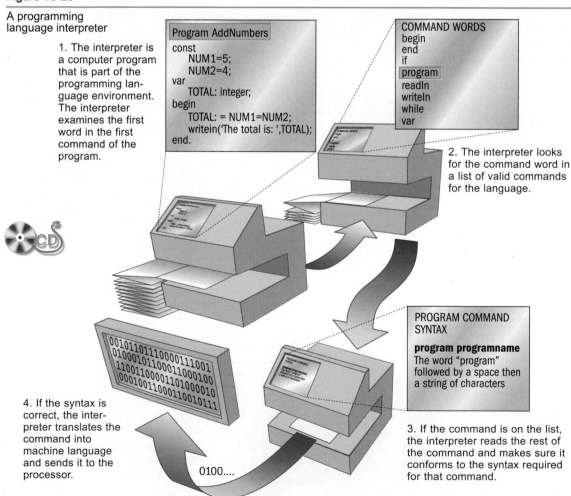

1. The interpreter is a computer program that is part of the programming language environment. The interpreter examines the first word in the first command of the program.

Program AddNumbers
```
const
    NUM1=5;
    NUM2=4;
var
    TOTAL: integer;
begin
    TOTAL: = NUM1=NUM2;
    writein('The total is: ',TOTAL);
end.
```

COMMAND WORDS
begin
end
if
program
readln
writeln
while
var

2. The interpreter looks for the command word in a list of valid commands for the language.

PROGRAM COMMAND SYNTAX

program programname
The word "program" followed by a space then a string of characters

4. If the syntax is correct, the interpreter translates the command into machine language and sends it to the processor.

```
00101101110000111001
01000101100011000100
11001100001100010100
00010011000110010111
```
0100....

3. If the command is on the list, the interpreter reads the rest of the command and makes sure it conforms to the syntax required for that command.

Object-Oriented

How do objects figure into computer programming? Object-oriented languages are based on an approach to programming that uses objects. An object is an entity or "thing" that a program manipulates. For example, a button—a rectangular icon on the screen—is an object. You are familiar with the way you can click a button using the mouse. A programmer can use an object-oriented language to define a button object in a program and display the button when the program runs.

InfoWeb

OOP
7

An object belongs to a class, or group, that has specific characteristics. A common example is the object class called *window*. All window objects, including application windows, belong to the class called *window* and share certain characteristics, such as a title bar and a close button. When a programmer creates a new window object, it acquires, or inherits, the characteristics and capabilities of the *window* class. Each specific instance of a window object may also have its own unique characteristics, such as its title, size, or location on the screen. Figure 15-21 shows several objects from an object class.

Figure 15-21

Two objects on the screen are in the class "window": the Document - WordPad window and the Save As window. All windows are rectangular and have a title bar. You can open and close windows, and you can move them around on the screen.

1. The Document - WordPad window is a subclass of "window" object generally referred to as an application window. Windows in this class have a maximize button, a minimize button, and a menu bar.

2. The Save As window is a subclass of "window" called a "dialog box window." It has a title bar, but it does not have a menu bar, a minimize button, or a maximize button.

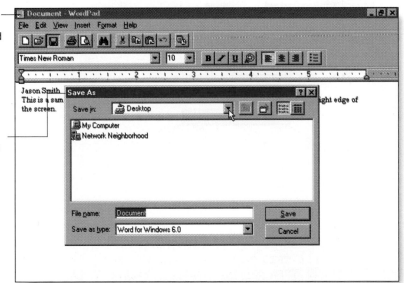

The same object can be used in many different programs, thus significantly enhancing programmer productivity. For example, many software applications provide users with a way to save a file, save a file under a new name, open a file, and print a file. If you were programming such applications, it would be handy to have an object to perform these tasks. Anytime you wrote a program that needed to do these tasks, you could simply use this object and avoid "recreating the wheel."

In fact, this object is such an obviously good idea that it already exists. Version 3.1 of Microsoft Windows includes a file called Comdlg.dll (for COMMon DiaLoG) that contains the menu and dialog box objects for opening, saving, and printing files.

Event-Driven

Do all programs follow a set sequence of activities? A **program event** is an action or occurrence, such as a key press or mouse click, to which a program might respond. An **event-driven language** helps programmers easily create programs that constantly check for and respond to a set of events. Most programs that use graphical user interfaces are event-driven—they display controls, such as menus, on the screen and take action when the user activates one of the controls. To create an event-driven program, code segments are attached to graphical objects, such as command buttons and icons. Users manipulate an object to generate an event, for example, clicking a button labeled "Continue." The event causes the instructions attached to that object to be executed. Figure 15-22 shows a screen from an event-driven program and the program code attached to one of the events.

Figure 15-22

An event-driven program

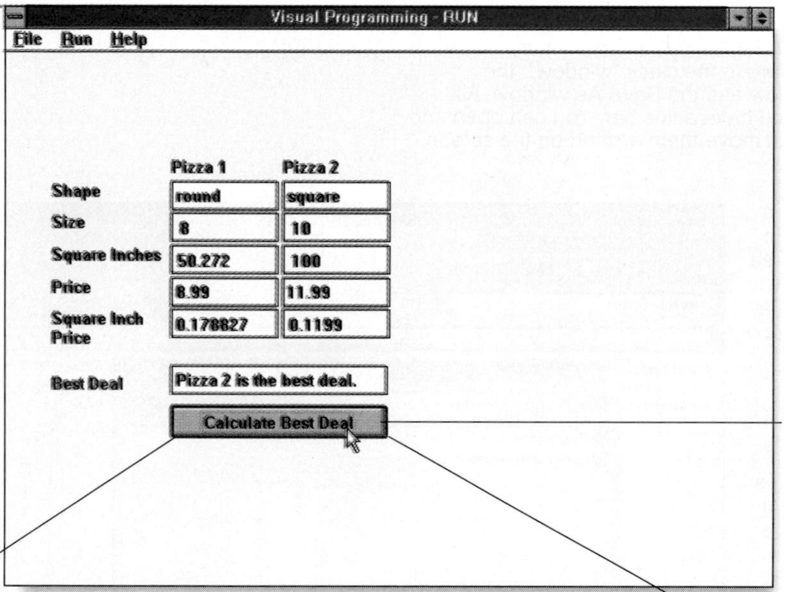

Clicking this button generates an event.

The event causes the computer to execute these instructions to calculate the best pizza deal.

```
[PROGRAM]
IF Shape1 = "square" THEN SquareInches1 = Size1 * Size1
IF Shape1 = "round" THEN SquareInches1 = 3.142 * (Size1/ 2)^2
SquareInchPrice1 = Price1/SquareInches1
IF Shape2 = "square" THEN SquareInches2 = Size2 * Size2
IF Shape2 = "round" THEN SquareInches2 = 3.142 * (Size2/ 2)^2
SquareInchPrice2 = Price2/SquareInches2
IF SquareInchPrice1 < SquareInchPrice2 THEN BestDeal = "Pizza
1 is the best deal."
IF SquareInchPrice2 < SquareInchPrice1 THEN BestDeal = "Pizza
2 is the best deal."
IF SquareInchPrice1 = SquareInchPrice2 THEN BestDeal = "Both
pizzas are the same deal."
```

Components

Who creates the objects I use in my programs? In practice, object-oriented programs contain objects that were created by the program designer. However, programmers can also purchase objects called components or libraries. **Components** are prewritten objects that programmers can customize and add to their own programs. Components are available commercially for a few of today's most popular programming languages. Using components is referred to as **component programming**.

For example, suppose you have been hired by a city government to write software to track recyclables. The engineers want to generate graphs periodically to compare amounts of glass, paper, aluminum, and other recyclable materials. A graphing component will help you provide this function in your software. You simply attach the graphing component to the rest of your program code. The engineers also need to fill in government forms. You can purchase a forms component, customize it for the government forms, and attach it to your recycling software.

Programmers can select from a wide array of components that add functions such as spreadsheet-like rows and columns, database management, expert systems, report generation, on-line help, data acquisition, text editing, scientific imaging, and 3-D graphics. Components are advertised in programming language magazines, such as *Visual Basic Programmer's Journal*.

QuickCheck D

1. A(n) _____ language creates programs that are composed of a series of statements that tell a computer how to perform the processes for a specific task.

2. A(n) _____ language lets a programmer construct a program by specifying a set of rules that define the conditions for resolving a problem.

3. A(n) _____ language requires a programmer to write instructions for the lowest level of the computer system, that is, for the specific hardware elements, such as the processor, registers, and RAM locations.

4. In a compiled language, _____ code is compiled, or translated, into object code, which the computer can execute.

5. Some computer programming languages use a(n) _____ to convert instructions to machine language one line at a time when the program is executed.

6. In a(n) _____ language, program code is attached to objects and executed when something happens to that object.

7. _____ are prewritten objects designed to be customized and added to programs.

8. A(n) _____ is an action, such as a key press or mouse click, to which a program might respond.

User Focus

E Selecting a Programming Language

Usually, more than one programming language is suitable for a task. So, when you select a language for a project, keep in mind the following questions:

- Do the characteristics of the programming language fit the task at hand?

- Is the language currently used for other applications in the organization?

- Does the organization have expertise using the language?

If the answers to all these questions are "yes," the language you are considering should be a good choice for the project. The descriptions of popular programming languages in this section will help you answer the first question.

InfoWeb

Visual
Basic
8

BASIC (Beginner's All-purpose Symbolic Instruction Code) was designed as a language for beginning programmers. Since its introduction in 1964, many popular versions of BASIC have been created, including GW-BASIC, shipped with the original IBM PCs, and Microsoft's QBASIC. BASIC has become one of the most popular and widely used programming languages because it is easy to use and available for almost every type of computer system. BASIC is a high-level, procedural language. Most versions of BASIC are interpreted languages, although some versions provide compiling capabilities.

Early versions of BASIC were too limited for the development of sophisticated commercial programs, but newer versions, such as Microsoft's **Visual Basic** (VB), are comprehensive and powerful programming languages suitable for use in professional programming projects. Visual Basic is especially useful for creating event-driven programs that have a graphical user interface.

COBOL (COmmon Business-Oriented Language) is the language most typically used for transaction processing on mainframe computer systems. Developed in 1960, COBOL is a high-level, procedural, compiled language used by thousands of professional programmers to develop and maintain complex programs in large organizations and businesses. COBOL programs tend to be rather long, but they are easy to understand, debug, and maintain. This functionality is particularly important in large organizations where critical programs must be maintained and modified by many different programmers over a period of years.

FORTRAN (FORmula TRANslator), developed in 1954, is the oldest high-level computer language still in use, although it has undergone several revisions since its creation. FORTRAN was designed by scientists and is often used to create scientific, mathematical, and engineering programs on mainframes and minicomputers.

Pascal was designed in 1971 to help students learn how to program computers. Pascal is a high-level, procedural, compiled language. The design of the language encourages a structured approach to programming. Despite its structured design, Pascal is not typically used as a programming language for professional and commercial applications.

C is a compiled procedural language that provides both high-level commands and low-level access to hardware. This duality gives the programmer significant flexibility in writing programs. Because of this flexibility, experienced C programmers can make their programs very fast and efficient. However, this flexibility can make C programs difficult to understand, debug, and maintain.

C++
9

C++ is an object-oriented version of C. Many people believe that the object-oriented nature of C++ can make programmers more productive. However, object-oriented programming requires a significantly different mental perspective from that of procedural programming. Therefore, many programmers experience difficulty using the object-oriented features of C++.

LISP (LISt Processor) and **Prolog** are declarative languages, often used to develop expert systems. These languages, developed in 1960 and 1971, respectively, have not gained as much popularity as procedural languages, probably because early computer applications were designed to handle tasks that required simple and repetitious calculations—tasks that procedural languages could handle effectively. Tasks that require a computer to perform complex logical operations on character data are better handled by declarative languages.

SQL (Structured Query Language) was developed to provide a standard language for defining and manipulating a database. SQL is a high-level declarative language that allows programmers and users to describe the relationship between the data elements in a database and the type of information they want to derive from the database. Although a database can also be manipulated by a procedural language such as COBOL, SQL is generally regarded as more effective because SQL commands are tailored to database activities.

Java, etc.
10

Java and **J++** are high-level, object-oriented programming languages based on C++ but optimized for Web applications. Java and J++ programs are typically used to create animated graphics on a Web page, or to create applications, called **applets**, that contain customized Web page controls such as buttons, check boxes, or text input boxes. When a browser connects to a Web page that has an associated Java or J++ program, the program code is downloaded and runs on your computer. Because the program runs on your computer instead of the Web server, you'll avoid the transfer time for sending your input and receiving a response.

Java and J++ differ in one significant respect. Java is a platform-independent language, which means that Java programs will run on a Macintosh or UNIX computer as well as on a PC. J++ provides programmers with tools to call upon specific Windows features. By using these tools a programmer can produce faster, more efficient applications. However, if a programmer uses these tools, the program will only run on a computer that uses the Windows operating system.

Not to be confused with Java, **JavaScript** is a scripting language that provides a subset of Java features. JavaScript code is embedded in a Web page just like HTML tags. The JavaScript is interpreted by your Web browser when it receives a Web page. The primary use of Java script is to create Web pages with interactive forms.

8086 assembly language is a low-level language consisting of short mnemonic commands that the computer can easily translate into machine language. The 8086 assembly language instruction set is specific to the Intel 8086 microprocessor. Programs written in this language can execute only on computers with microprocessors from the x86 family. Today, 8086 assembly language is used primarily for programs, or segments of programs, that must be made as short as possible or that must run as quickly as possible. Professional programmers use 8086 assembly language for the sections of application programs that need to execute quickly and for system software that controls computer hardware.

EndNote Like human languages, computer languages change and evolve. New words and expressions enter common usage. Other words fade into disuse. With human languages, change is a slow but continual process. With computer languages, on the other hand, changes are mandated and structured by the companies that publish computer languages and by special organizations that set standards.

COBOL, created in 1959, was standardized in 1968 and revised in 1974. Since that time, it has remained essentially the same. FORTRAN was standardized in 1966, revised in 1977, and revised again in 1990. With revisions occurring at an average of ten-year intervals, programmers could expect to learn a language in college, for example, and then use that language for many years into their careers. Programmers had time to become fluent in a computer language and accumulate a collection of "tricks" that they could apply to subsequent programming projects. Things are different today. The window of stability for a language is very small—in some cases less than two years—as publishers change the language syntax, the programmer's interface, and even the underlying paradigm of the language. The development of BASIC is a case in point.

In the late 1960s Kemeny and Kurtz developed BASIC. It became the "people's programming language" in the 1980s when it was shipped with virtually every PC. A few "new and improved" versions of BASIC allowed programmers to apply structured programming principles to the development of BASIC programs, but the syntax and programmer interface of the language remained essentially the same.

Suddenly, in 1991 Microsoft introduced Visual Basic, a major departure from previous versions of the Basic language. Then, in the next six years, Microsoft produced four substantial revisions of the Visual Basic language. Programmers were barely able to finish one programming project before they had to scrap a large part of their knowledge about VB and learn it all again. Forget about fluency. Programmers were often forced to hack together code with only a rudimentary understanding of the language. It is a tribute to the power of these languages that viable products were produced at all.

Changes in Visual Basic reflect new technologies and methodologies, such as the shift from 16-bit to 32-bit processors, the introduction of Windows 95, requirements for Internet programming, and the move toward object-oriented programming. Can the cost of these changes outweigh their benefits? Some signs indicate that programmers and information systems managers are becoming more resistant to the demands of industry marketers and their promises of new features. Perhaps consumers will demand more stability in the computer marketplace. Watch and see.

InfoWeb

InfoWeb

Chapter
Links

The InfoWeb is your guide to print, film, television, and electronic resources. Use it to obtain updates on quickly changing technical information and to locate information for research papers. If you're using the New Perspectives CD-ROM, click the InfoWeb icon on the left side of this paragraph to access the online InfoWeb links. Otherwise, use your Web browser and type in the address of the New Perspectives site: www.cciw.com/np3. At the New Perspectives site you'll find up-to-date links to the topics covered in this chapter.

1 Software Engineering

Mickey Williamson provides an in-depth overview of software engineering in the *CIO* magazine article, "Software Development" (**www.cio.com/archive/041596_devenpor_content.html**). You might pay particular attention to the last page, which lists the habits of highly effective developers. The Software Engineering Institute (SEI) at Carnegie Mellon University publishes research results and guidelines about effective software development. The SEI Web site at **www.sei.cmu.edu** is definitely worth a visit. Similar activities take place at the NASA/Goddard Space Flight Center Software Engineering Laboratory (SEL) at **fdd.gsfc.nasa.gov/seltext.html**.

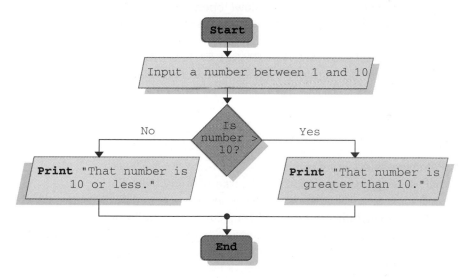

You'll find CERN's software engineering glossary at **dxsting.cern.ch/sting/glossary-intro.html**. One of the best books about programming is Steve McConnell's *Code Complete* (Microsoft Press, 1993). It is full of practical tips that will help you complete your programming projects on time, within budget, and with minimal bugs. You'll find a series of software development checklists excerpted from Steve's book at the Construx Software Builder's site at **www.construx.com/chk.htm**. Are you curious about the books that famous programmers have on their bookshelves? If so, check out Gregory Wilson's article, "Great Books," published in the fall 1997 issue of *Dr. Dobb's Journal* (**www.ddj.com/ddj/1997/1997.careers2/wils.htm**).

Many programmers subscribe to *Dr. Dobb's Journal*, which has got to be one of the first computer magazines ever published (**www.ddj.com**). Another favorite is *American Programmer*, edited by the renowned Ed Yourdon (**www.cutter.com/amprog/**). For Windows application development, a good source is the *Microsoft Systems Journal* (**www.microsoft.com/msj**). Programmers' professional organizations include the National Association of Programmers (**www.naponnet.org**) and the International Programmer's Guild (**www.ipgnet.com/ipghome.htm**).

2 Algorithms

To learn more about algorithms, start at the PC Webopaedia page at **www.pcwebopaedia.com/ algorithm.htm** where you'll find a clear definition and some links to sites with more in-depth information. Want to amaze your friends with your ability to predict the day of the week for any date? You can read about John Horton Conway's "Doomsday" algorithm at Rudy Limeback's Web site, **www.interlog.com/ ~r937/doomsday.html**. Computer algorithms are frequently employed for sorting and searching. Thomas Niemann provides an intuitive approach to these algorithms in his sorting and searching algorithm "cookbook" at **www.geocities.com/SoHo/2167.book.html**. A computer can also use an algorithm to solve Rubik's Cube. Find out how at **www.sunyit.edu/~millerd1/RUBIK.HTM**. You might want to visit the Stony Brook Algorithm Repository at **www.cs.sunysb.edu/~algorith/index.html** where you will find a collection of algorithms for more than 70 fundamental problems. The classic text on algorithms is Donald Knuth's *Art of Computer Programming* (Addison-Wesley, 1997), now in its third edition (originally published in the 1970s). So far there are three volumes in this set, but Knuth is working on volumes four and five. For a progress update, connect to Knuth's home page at **www-cs-staff.stanford.edu/~knuth/taocp.html**.

3 Pseudocode & Flow Charts

"Pseudocode Thinking" (**userpages.aug.com/frodo/pseudo.htm**) by David S. Linthicum and Larry Klien provides a brief overview of how pseudocode can help you plan a program. You'll find out how to use pseudocode to express program control structures at **jeffco.k12.co.us/dist_ed/c/c13.html**.

PC Magazine Online has a great roundup of flow-charting software at **www.zdnet.com/pcmag/features/flow/_open.htm**. You can download a trial version of SmartDraw from **www.smartdraw.com**, RFFlow from **www.rff.com**, or Micrographx FlowCharter from **www.micrografx.com/ENTERPRISE/flowcharter**. TheSmartDraw site also includes a variety of flow chart examples and a flow-charting tutorial.

Key to Flow Chart Symbols

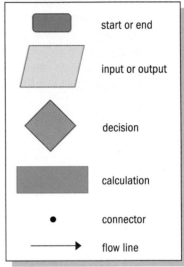

start or end

input or output

decision

calculation

connector

flow line

4 Programming Careers

For practical advice on how to prepare for a programming career, connect to Eugene Eric Kim's article, "Making Your Move: Programming as a Career" in the Fall 1997 issue of *Dr. Dobb's Journal* (**www.ddj.com/ddj/1997/1997.careers2/kim1.htm**). For an additional perspective, the same issue includes the article "Programming in the Real World" by Allen Holub (**www.ddj.com/ddj/1997/1997.careers2/holu.htm**). The Bureau of Labor Statistics provides a detailed description of programmers' working conditions, employment outlook, salaries, and educational requirements at **stats.bls.gov/oco/ocos110.htm**. You can find up-to-date job listings for programmers at any career Web site, such as The Monster Board (**www.monster.com**), The Canadian Hi-Tech Career Centre (**www.hitechcareer.com**), or the Mercury News employment ads (**www.talentscout.com**). What does Bill Gates think is the key to becoming a successful programmer? You can find out in Susan Lammers' book, *Programmers at Work* (Microsoft Press, 1986), featuring Bill Gates and a cast of other luminaries from the early days of microcomputers. For a humorous look at programmers, connect to **www.datamation.com/PlugIn/humor/classics/pascal.html** and read Ed Post's essay, "Real programmers don't use Pascal."

5 GOTO

Dijkstra opened a can of worms when he submitted his famous letter, "Go To Statement Considered Harmful" to the *Communications of the ACM* in 1968. You can read the text of this letter on the Web at **www.acm.org/classics/oct95/**. Steve McConnell discusses the issue in his book, *Code Complete*. The Construx Web site carries an excerpt at **www.construx.com/stevemcc/ccgoto.htm**. The use of GOTO pops up in an *IEEE Software* article called "Keep It Simple" at **www.construx.com/stevemcc/bp06.htm**.

6 Technical Writing

To learn more about your prospects as a technical writer, connect to the Bureau of Labor statistics page about writers and editors (**stats.bls.gov/oco/ocos089.htm**). You can get some great tips from the Micro Search site article "How to Break into Technical Writing" at **www.microsearchsf.com/breakin.htm**. Several Web sites provide good resources for technical writers, such as links to articles about improving your writing, technical writing tutorials, classes on technical writing, and job listings. Three of the best sites include Internet Resources for Technical Communicators (**www.interlog.com/~ksoltys/techcomm.html**), the Writer's Block (**www.niva.com/writblok/index.htm**), and the Mining Company (**texhwriting.miningco.com/**). You'll find an excellent bibliography of technical books at **www.afit.af.mil/Schools/LD/repwrit.htm**. The professional organization for technical writers is Society for Technical Communication (STC) at **stc.org**. For a laugh, connect to the COREcomm site at **www.corecomm.com/worst.html** where you can see the results of the Worst-Technical-Writing-Sample-of-the-Month Contest. David A. McMurrey has produced an excellent online technical writing text that you can connect to at **www.io.com/~hcexres/tcm1603/acchtml/acctoc.html**.

7 OOP

Terry Montlick has written an excellent introduction to object-oriented technology called "What is Object-Oriented Software?" You'll find the article on the Web at **www.soft-design.com/softinfo/objects.html**.

> **Calculate Best Deal**

For a quick overview of object-oriented terminology, connect to the Taligent site's Object Glossary at **www.taligent.com/Technology/OTTerminology.html**. For a more in-depth overview, connect to Bob Hathaway's' Object-Orientation FAQ at **www.cyberdyne-object-sys.com/oofaq/**. A well-respected authority in this field is Grady Booch, and his book, *Object-oriented Analysis and Design with Applications* (Benjamin Cummings, 1993), which is already a classic. You can find out more about object-oriented diagrams at Philipp Schneider's Web page, **www.itr.ch/courses/case/BoochReference/**. Object-oriented programming is most successful when it is based on object-oriented analysis (OOA) and design (OOD). The Web article "Object-Oriented Methodologies" at **www.pencom.com/case/oo.html** compares the Booch, Coad-Yourdon, Rumbaugh, and Shlaer-Mellor methodologies. For in-depth information on this subject, browse through the online version of the book, *Object-Oriented System Development* by Champeaus, Lea, and Faure (Addison Wesley, 1993) at **gee.cs.oswego.edu/dl/oosdw3/**.

8 Visual Basic

Visual Basic is a Microsoft product, so the Web site at **www.microsoft.com/vbasic** is a good place to get technical information. According to many VB programmers, the most useful site is Carl & Gary's Visual Basic Home Page on the apexsc Web server. Carl & Gary's site includes links, articles, downloads, and a great introduction to VB programming called "Visual Basic; Getting Off To A Good Start" at **www.apexsc.com/vb/newbie1.html**. Another Web page specially targeted at beginning VB programmers is Gary Beene's Visual Basic World Beginner's Corner at **web2.airmail.net/gbeene/begin.html**. You can download a Visual Basic Self-Study Tutorial from TegoSoft Inc. at **www.tego.com/Items/LearnVisualBasicFast/LearnVBFast.htm**. You'll find another tutorial at the Visual Basic Palace (**home.computer.net/~mheller/hints.html**).

For news about the latest VB components and programming techniques, programmers like the Devx site at **www.windx.com** and the *Visual Basic Online Magazine* (**www.vbonline.com/vb-mag/**). The *Visual Basic Programmer's Journal* is the standard paper-based reference resource.

9 C++

C++ was created in 1980 by Dr. Bjarne Stroustrup of Bell Laboratories (**www.research.att.com/~bs/C++.html**). Two of the major C++ language vendors are Microsoft (**www.microsoft.com/visualc**) and Borland (**www.borland.com/borlandcpp/cppprod.html**). For an overview of C++, connect to Mikes C++ Programming page at **www.wtvl.net/mike/webjr/begcpp.htm** where you'll find some simple examples of C++ programs, a description of C++ command words, a list of good reference books, and links to other C++ Web sites. A more lengthy list of links can be found at **www.cl.ais.net/morph/c++/main.html**. The *Visual C++ Developer's Journal* (**www.vcdj.com**) is an excellent resource for C++ programming tips, code samples, and information on conferences. The Global Network Academy is a consortium of educational institutions that sponsors an online course called Introduction to Object-Oriented Programming Using C++. You can read about the course and register at **www.gnacademy.org**. C++ has many similarities to C.

10 Java, etc.

The place to begin learning about Java is to read Marshall Brain's "Introduction to Java" at **www.iftech.com/oltc/webdev/webdev6.stm**. You can find several online Java tutorials, including the Beginner's Java Tutorial at **www.rand.com/tlung/java**. Java was developed by Sun Microsystems and its "official" Java page at **java.sun.com** has links to FAQs, articles, tutorials, documentation, and programming tips. Despite all the hype about Java, some industry analysts remain skeptical about its usefulness. Can Java improve your life? Check out Mark Hurst's survey at **www.creativegood.com/help/c011.html**. JavaScript differs in several ways from Java, but is a useful Web development tool in its own right. Hotsyte, which bills itself as The JavaScript Resource (**www.serve.com/hotsyte**) has a good set of links to articles, downloads, and sample scripts, including a link to the JavaScript Guide offered by JavaScript's creator, Netscape.

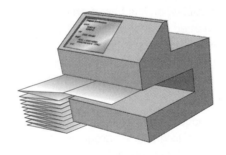

Review

1. Answer the questions listed under each of the section headings.

2. List each of the boldface terms used in this chapter, then use your own words to write a short definition of each term.

3. Describe how the job of a systems analyst differs from the job of a software engineer.

4. Is there a difference between an algorithm and a computer program? Why or why not?

5. Give an example of a sequence control structure, a selection control structure, and a repetition control structure.

6. Which lines in the program below contain branch or loop control structures?

```
INPUT "Employee Name:"; EmpName$
WHILE EmpName$ <> "EOF"
    INPUT "Hours Worked "; HoursWk
    INPUT "PayRate     "; PayRate
    GrossPay = HoursWk * PayRate
    IF GrossPay > 50 THEN
        Tax = GrossPay *.12
    ELSE
        Tax = 0
    END IF
    NetPay = GrossPay - Tax
    PRINT "Gross Pay "; GrossPay
    INPUT "Employee Name"; EmpName$
WEND
PRINT "Payroll complete."
END
```

7. Explain the difference between a syntax error and a logic error.

8. Explain the difference between program remarks and written documentation.

9. Fill in the following matrix to summarize the characteristics of today's popular programming languages. Most languages will have more than one characteristic.

	Procedural	Declarative	Low-level	High-level	Compiled	Interpreted	Object-oriented	Component	Event-driven	Scripting
BASIC										
Visual Basic										
COBOL										
FORTRAN										
Pascal										
C										
C++										
LISP/PROLOG										
SQL										
8086 assembly language										
Java/J++										
HTML										
JavaScript										

10. Use the New Perspectives CD to take a practice test or to review the key terms presented in this chapter.

Projects

1 What Information Do You Need? In this chapter you learned that problem solving requires information. List the known information required to solve the following problems:

a. Calculate the square footage of a rectangular room

b. Calculate the amount of gasoline required to drive your car from New York City to San Francisco

c. Calculate how much it costs to ship a box of books from Dallas, Texas to Portland, Oregon

d. Calculate how much it would cost to purchase new carpeting for your living room

e. Calculate your tuition for next semester

2 Assumptions and Known Information To grasp a problem, you must understand the assumptions on which the problem is based and the known information you can use to solve the problem. To practice identifying assumptions and known information, study the following problem. Think about the information you would need to solve the problem yourself. Identify the assumptions and known information.

Problem: Two tourists are planning a walking tour of a city. Starting at their hotel, they plan to visit a bookstore, a science museum, a Thai restaurant, and a craft market. A city map shows the location of each place. According to the legend on the map, one-half inch on the map is a one-mile walk. The tourists want to know how far they will walk on their tour.

3 Writing an Algorithm The algorithm is the key to writing an effective computer program. If you as the programmer understand the steps that efficiently carry out a task or solve a problem, you should be able to translate this algorithm into a workable computer program. To try your hand at writing an algorithm, use the problem statement in Project 2. Write an algorithm for determining the total distance the tourists will walk. Hint: Think about the steps you would take to solve this problem using the map, a calculator, and a ruler.

4 Find the Errors A friend has written a BASIC program to calculate the number of tanks of gas her car will require to go a specified number of miles. Unfortunately, the program doesn't work correctly. She shows you a printout of the program (see below) and asks for your help.

A syntax error and a logic error prevent the program from working correctly. Examine the program code carefully to locate the two errors; then write the corrected lines.

```
REM This program calculates the number of tanks of gas
REM required to drive my car a specified number of miles.
MilesPerGallon = 22.5
GallonsPerTank = 12
INPUT "Enter the number of miles to drive:", MilesToDrive
GallonsRequired is MilesToDrive / MilesPerGallon
TanksRequired = GallonsRequired / GallonsPerTank
PRINT "This trip will require:"
PRINT MilesPerGallon
PRINT "tanks of gas."
END
```

5 **Imagine You're a Computer** To understand a computer program or debug program code, computer programmers have a trick. They imagine that they are the computer executing the code. By following exactly what the computer should do at each step in a program, a programmer can discover how a program works or which instructions cause problems. Try a simple example. Imagine you are a computer instructed to execute the following BASIC program. Indicate the value of A and Y after you execute each instruction. At the beginning of the program, A and Y are each assigned a value of 0.

```
REM Sample program
A = 10
Y = A * 3
A = A * Y
END
```

6 **Documentation—Good or Bad?** Writing documentation is not an easy task. Many programs have hundreds of features. Organizing these features into a useful reference format and describing the features so that even a beginner can understand them requires good logical and writing skills. How good is the documentation for programs you use? Describe the documentation for a computer program that you have used. Discuss what you like or do not like about the documentation, and indicate how you think the documentation can be improved.

7  **Pick a Language—Any Language** Select a computer language. Use your library or Internet resources, such as **www.yahoo.com/ Computers/**, to research the language, then answer the following questions:

a. Is this a procedural or a declarative language?

b. Is this a high-level or a low-level language?

c. Is this a compiled language or an interpreted language?

d. Is this an object-oriented language?

e. Is this an event-driven language?

f. When was the language developed?

g. For what purpose was the language developed?

h. Who developed the language?

i. Is the language typically used on micro, mini, or mainframe computers?

8 **Batting Averages** A baseball player's batting average is calculated by dividing the number of times the player hit the ball by the number of times the player was at bat, minus the number of times the player "walked," as in the formula, Hits / (TimesAtBat − Walks). Write the specifications for a program that calculates a baseball player's batting average. Be sure to include the assumptions, known information, formula for calculation, and output description. Also, create a flowchart to express the algorithm.

9 **Grading Computer Literacy Exams**
Assume your school has a computer literacy exam that students must pass before they can graduate. Scores on the exams can be between 0 and 100. A student must score at least 70 to pass the test. Marsha Murray in the testing office has a list of students and scores for the exam given in December. Write the specification for a program that would allow Marsha to input student names and scores, analyze each score to see if the student passed, and print out a list of student names, scores, and "Passed" or "Failed." Also write pseudocode to express the algorithm.

10 **The Card Shark** Assume you are talking to a friend on the phone. You know your friend has three cards and they are all in the same suit. For example, your friend might have the two of clubs, the five of clubs, and the eight of clubs. Further, assume that the cards are shuffled so they are in no particular order. You need to tell your friend how to sort the cards so the lowest numbered card is first and the highest numbered card is last. However, you cannot see the cards and your friend cannot communicate with you except to say OK. You need to give your friend general instructions, such as "Take the first two cards and compare the numbers on them." Write out the instructions, or algorithm, for sorting the three cards.

11  **Computing Careers** What are the job prospects for computer programmers? Looking at employment ads is one way to find out. To research the employment opportunities in a large city of your choice, look in the classified ad section of a large city newspaper or check out Web sites, such as those listed in InfoWeb 4.

Write a summary of your research by answering the following questions:

a. Where did you look for information?

b. How many computer programmer jobs were available?

c. What was the average salary offered?

d. What were the educational requirements for entry-level positions?

e. What programming languages seem to be in greatest demand?

Visual Programming Lab

In the Visual Programming Lab, you use an event-driven, object-oriented programming environment to create simple programs. This Lab provides a "taste" of what it would be like to program in a visual language such as Visual Basic.

1. Click the Steps button to learn how to create a graphical user interface containing buttons, labels, and text boxes. As you work through the Steps, answer all of the Quick Check questions. After you complete the Steps, you will see a Quick Check Summary Report of your answers. Follow the directions on the screen to print this report.

2. In Explore, create a program to calculate the total cost of carpeting a room. Test your program, then print it showing the cost of $12.99/sq. yd. carpeting for a 10 x 14 foot room.

Assume that the room is rectangular. The known information is the length and width of the room, and the price of a square yard of carpet. You must calculate:

- the square feet of carpet needed (length * width of room)
- the square yards of carpet needed (square feet/9)
- total price of carpet (Price per square yard * the square yards needed)

Your user interface should look like the following screen:

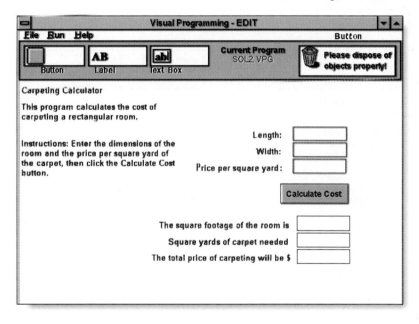

3 Suppose you like to shop from catalogs. Your favorite catalog is having a sale—selected merchandise is discounted 10%, 20%, 30%, or 40%. You want to know how much you'll save if you buy some of the merchandise you want. In Explore, create a program to calculate savings. Test your program, then print it showing the savings for a $863 item at 30% discount.

Assume that the items you purchase will be discounted and that there is no additional charge for shipping. The known information is the original price of the item and its discount—10%, 20%, 30% or 40%. Calculate how much you will save. (For example, for a 10% discount, multiply the original cost by .1.) Your user interface should look like the following screen:

4 In your recording studio, studio musicians are paid by the hour, but your sound technicians are salaried. You started to make a program to calculate weekly paychecks, but it doesn't seem to work.

Your assumption is that some employees are salaried and some are hourly. You know the salaries for salaried employees. You know the hourly wage and the hours worked each pay period by the hourly employees. You want to calculate the weekly pay for salaried employees (Wages / 52) and the weekly pay for hourly employees (Wages * Hours).

In Explore, open the program PAY.VPG and test it. Enter 32240 in the Wages box, then click the Salaried button. The output should be 620. Next enter 8 in the Wages box and 40 in the Hours box. Click the Hourly button. The output should be 320. Find what's wrong with this program and correct it. Print your solution.

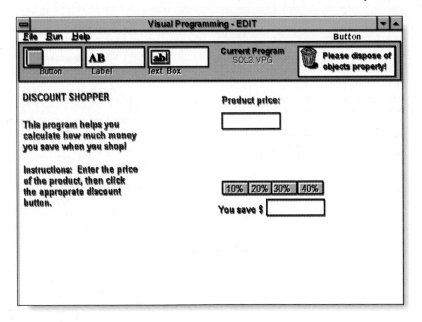

QuickCheck
Answers

Chapter 1

A

1. Processing (process, process data)
2. Data
3. Central
4. Memory (RAM)
5. Storage

B

1. Keyboard, monitor
2. Microcomputer (PC, personal computer)
3. Terminal
4. Mainframe
5. Compatible
6. Network

C

1. Prompt
2. Wizards
3. Enter (the Enter key)
4. Syntax
5. Submenu
6. Graphical user interfaces (GUIs)
7. Cursor, insertion point
8. Ctrl (Control)
9. Windows

Chapter 2

A

1. False (F)
2. False (F)
3. Data
4. Program
5. Software
6. Shareware
7. License (software license)
8. System, application

B

1. Multitasking
2. UNIX (VMS, MVS)
3. Micro (personal, microcomputer)
4. UNIX
5. Utility
6. Device driver (driver)
7. Programming language (computer programming language)

C

1. Suite (office suite)
2. Desktop publishing (DTP)
3. Vector (3-D)
4. False (F)
5. Web browser (browser)
6. Vertical

D

1. True (T)
2. False (F)
3. Hypermedia
4. MMX

Chapter 3

A

1. Document production
2. True (T)
3. Word wrap
4. False (F)
5. Template (document template), wizard (document wizard)
6. Electronic
7. Concordance
8. HTML

B

1. Column, row
2. References (addresses)
3. Functions
4. True (T)
5. True(T)
6. False (F)
7. What-if

C

1. Database
2. Structured, free-form
3. Access (find, locate)
4. True (T)
5. Query by example (QBE)
6. Query language
7. True (T)

Chapter 4

A

1. Data, information
2. Dat (.dat)
3. Exe (.exe)
4. Logical
5. Root
6. Source (batch)

B

1. Bytes (megabytes, MB, gigabytes, GB), milliseconds (ms, ms.)
2. Magnetic, optical
3. Tracks, sectors
4. Random, sequential
5. QIC
6. Hard disk (hard disk drive)
7. FAT (file allocation table)
8. False (F)

Chapter 5

A

1. Integrate circuit (IC)
2. Bit
3. Byte
4. ASCII
5. Binary
6. Bus (data bus)

B

1. Memory (primary storage)
2. Volatile
3. Megabytes (MB, bytes)
4. Capacitors
5. Nanoseconds (ns, ns.)
6. Virtual
7. ROM (read-only memory)
8. CMOS

C

1. Microprocessor
2. ALU (arithmetic-logic unit)
3. Control unit
4. Operand
5. Megahertz (MHz)
6. System clock

D

1. Expansion bus
2. Expansion card (controller card, expansion board)
3. Slot, port
4. USB (universal serial bus)

Chapter 6

A

1. Pentium
2. True (T)
3. EIDE
4. False (F)
5. LCD (liquid crystal)
6. One megabyte (1 MB)
7. PCMCIA
8. Color ink-jet

B

1. Vaporware
2. True (T)
3. Competitive
4. Tiers
5. False (F)
6. VAR (value-added reseller)

C

1. False (F)
2. Information systems (IS)
3. Northeast
4. Experience
5. Organizations
6. Job fairs (conferences)

Chapter 7

A

1. Server (file server)
2. Account (user account)
3. Mapped
4. True (T)
5. False (F)
6. Captured

B

1. Network interface card (NIC)
2. Non-dedicated
3. File server
4. True (T)
5. Host

C

1. Network operating
2. False (F)
3. Network license
4. Groupware
5. Workflow (document routing)

Chapter 8

A

1. Cyberspace
2. Internet
3. Terabytes
4. False (F)
5. TCP/IP (transport control protocol/Internet protocol)
6. URL (Web site)

B

1. Home
2. Streaming media
3. Plug-in (viewer)
4. False (F)
5. True (T)
6. True (T)

C

1. Links
2. False (F)
3. Body
4. False (F)
5. Web authoring
6. True (T)
7. Navigational
8. True (T)

Chapter 9

A

1. Operator
2. False (F)
3. Uninterruptible power supply (UPS)
4. Surge strip (surge suppressor, surge protector)
5. False (F)
6. False (F)
7. Backup (up-to-date backup)

B

1. Virus (computer virus)
2. Macro
3. Trojan horse
4. Worm
5. Virus
6. E-mail attachments
7. Signature
8. Data

C

1. Risk management
2. Policy
3. True (T)
4. Rights (user rights)
5. Trapdoor (back door)
6. Cookie
7. Downtime
8. Positive

Chapter 10

A

1. Information theory
2. Four (4)
3. Binary
4. ASCII
5. Unicode
6. Localization

B

1. Bitmap
2. Eight (8)
3. Dithering
4. Vector
5. False (F)
6. False (F)

C

1. Waveform, MIDI
2. Sampling
3. False (F)
4. False (F)
5. True (T)

D

1. Data compression (compression)
2. Volume
3. File compression

4. Adaptive pattern substitution

5. Lossy

6. True (T)

Chapter 11

A

1. Noise

2. Bandwidth

3. Full-duplex

4. Protocols

5. Even

6. True (T)

B

1. False (F)

2. Coaxial (Coax)

3. Electrical (electric), light (light waves)

4. Single-mode

5. True (T)

6. Microwave

C

1. Hub (concentrator, MAU)

2. Standards

3. Software

4. Protocols

5. True (T)

6. False (F)

7. Token

Chapter 12

A

1. Information

2. Mission

3. True (T)

4. Threats

5. Automation

6. TQM (total quality management)

7. Rightsize (downsize)

B

1. CEO (Executive management, senior management)

2. Goods

3. Strategic

4. Tactical

5. Unstructured

6. Internal, external

C

1. Office automation

2. Transaction

3. MIS (management Information)

4. Exception

5. DSS (decision support)

6. Expert

7. Expert system shell

8. Neural network

Chapter 13

A

1. SDLC (system development life cycle)

2. Systems analysts

3. Problem statement

4. CASE

5. System requirements (success factors)

6. Prototype

B

1. Design

2. Application development tool

3. RFP (request for proposal)

4. RFQ (request for quotation)

5. Application specifications

C

1. Programming (software engineering)
2. Knowledge engineering
3. Unit
4. Integration
5. Test area
6. System

D

1. Procedure manual
2. Conversion software
3. System conversion
4. Direct
5. Parallel
6. Phased
7. Pilot
8. Acceptance

E

1. Maintenance
2. Eighty (80)
3. Bugs (software errors, fixing bugs)
4. Cost effective
5. SDLC (systems development life cycle)

Chapter 14

A

1. Variable-length
2. Character (string)
3. Numeric
4. Type, occurrence
5. Flat
6. True (T)

B

1. Data model
2. Cardinality
3. One

4. Hierarchical
5. False (F)
6. Relational
7. True (T)

C

1. Custom
2. Data independence
3. Object-oriented
4. Database (Database management, DBMS)
5. Client/server
6. False (F)

D

1. Field format
2. Range check
3. Data redundancy
4. Case sensitive
5. Update (change, modify, edit)
6. Warehouse
7. Index
8. Query by example (QBE)

Chapter 15

A

1. Programmer (software engineer)
2. False (F)
3. Problem statement
4. Algorithm
5. Pseudocode
6. Flow chart

B

1. Coding
2. Sequence
3. Decision (branch)
4. Repetition control (repetition, loop)

C

1. Testing
2. Syntax
3. Run-time (logic)
4. Logic
5. Documentation
6. Remarks
7. Program manual, user reference (reference manual)

D

1. Procedural
2. Declarative
3. Low-level
4. Source
5. Interpreter
6. Object-oriented
7. Components
8. Event

Glossary/Index

Bootable floppy disk A disk containing the operating system files necessary to activate the computer, 5-31

Border A box around text or graphics—usually around a title, heading, or table, 3-11

BPR (business process redesign [re-engineering]), 12-5, 12-28

branches, 15-15

Bricklin, Dan, 3-28

Bureau of Labor Statistics, 6-37

Bus The component of a microcomputer motherboard that transports data between other components on the board, 5-4; in network terminology, a series of nodes connected by cable that is run directly from one node to the next, 5-4, 5-8, 5-14, 11-27–30

Business An organization that seeks profit by providing goods and/or services, 12-2

business magazines, 12-27

Business process redesign (BPR) The process of making radical changes to existing business practices in order to achieve improvement in performance (also called business process re-engineering), 12-5, 12-28

Business software Computer programs that help organizations to efficiently accomplish routine professional and clerical tasks, 2-29

business terminology, 12-27

Business Week magazine, 6-38

businesses, 12-2

Button An area of the screen containing a three-dimensional image (usually square or rectangular) that can be pressed with the mouse pointer to activate a function, 1-21

buying computers. *See* computer purchases

Byte An eight-bit unit of information, usually representing one character (a letter, punctuation mark, space, or numeral), 4-14, 5-5

Byte magazine, 6-23, 6-36

C

C A compiled procedural language that provides both high-level commands and low-level access to hardware, 15-30

C++ An object-oriented version of C, 15-31, 15-36

cable modems, 11-23, 11-37

cable television, 11-22–23

cable(s), 5-2, 5-26–27. *See also* communications links
    networks, 7-12

Cache Special high-speed memory that gives the CPU more rapid access to data (also called RAM cache or cache memory), 5-20
    level 2, 6-4

Cache memory *See* Cache, 5-20

calculations, spreadsheet software, 3-20–21

calculators, spreadsheets versus, 3-18

Capacitor Electronic circuit component that stores an electrical charge; in binary code, a charged capacitor represents an "on" bit, and a discharged one represents an "off" bit, 5-9

Caps Lock key Key that capitalizes all the letters the user types, when it is engaged, 1-24, 1-25

Capturing In communications terminology, the process of storing received input in a file for later use, 7-9

capturing printer ports, 7-9

card catalogs, online, 3-46

Cardinality A number describing the relationship (one-to-one, one-to-many, or many-to-many) that exists between two record types (for example, in a data diagram), 14-9

careers. *See* computer industry careers

Carrier sense multiple access with collision detection (CSMA/CD) A method used by Ethernet networks to deal with collisions, 11-28

cartridge tape storage, 4-25

CASE (computer-aided software engineering) tool Software that is used to summarize system requirements, diagram current and proposed information systems, schedule development tasks, prepare documentation, and develop computer programs, 13-8

Case sensitivity A condition in which uppercase letters are not equivalent to their lowercase counterparts, 14-25

CASE tools, 13-7, 13-30

Category 6 cable A category of cable that includes coaxial cable, 11-11

cc: option An option that allows the user to send a copy of an e-mail message to someone other than the primary recipient, 7-23

CD-R Compact discs on which the user can write data (acronym for compact disc-recordable), 4-27

CD-ROM A high-capacity, optical storage medium (acronym for compact disc read-only memory), 1-10, 4-26

CD-ROM disks, 1-10, 4-16, 4-26–27
    access times and transfer rates, 4-35
    capacity, 4-33
    information and reference software, 2-24

CD-ROM drive A storage device that uses laser technology to read data from a CD-ROM, 1-10, 4-26, 6-6
    expansion port, 5-27

Cell In spreadsheet terminology, the intersection of a column and a row, 3-19; in cellular communications, a limited geographical area surrounding a cellular phone tower, 11-20

cell addresses, worksheets, 3-19

Cell reference A letter/number combination that indicates the position of a cell in a spreadsheet, 3-20
    absolute, 3-23

cell(s), worksheets, 3-19

cellular phone service, 11-20–21